# DAEDALUS AND THESPIS

THE MACMILLAN COMPANY
NEW YORK · BOSTON · CHICAGO · DALLAS
ATLANTA · SAN FRANCISCO

MACMILLAN & CO., Limited
LONDON · BOMBAY · CALCUTTA
MELBOURNE

THE MACMILLAN CO. OF CANADA, Ltd.
TORONTO

THE ACROPOLIS
From the "Prison of Socrates"

Entrance    Propylaea    Nike Temple    Odeum of Regilla    Parthenon    Stoa of Eumenes    Asclepieum    Theatre

# DAEDALUS AND THESPIS

*The Contributions of the Ancient Dramatic
Poets to Our Knowledge of the Arts
and Crafts of Greece*

By

WALTER MILLER
UNIVERSITY OF MISSOURI

VOLUME I

ARCHITECTURE AND TOPOGRAPHY

New York
THE MACMILLAN COMPANY
1929

# PREFACE

The making of this volume has been a long labor of love. The impulse to the study of Greek art as it is presented in the Greek drama came from reading Euripides's Ion at Delphi in my first student days in Greece. The description of the temple-sculptures that Euripides in this tragedy gives suggested the possible wealth of such contributions to our knowledge of the arts and crafts of Greece that might be found in the rest of our *corpus dramaticorum*. To cull out the passages bearing upon the subject, it has been my joy, amid all the distractions of a college teacher and executive, to read and reread again and again all the ancient tragedy and comedy we have, including the fragments, to classify and organize the material, and make the combinations that have resulted from the study.

The question of a title for this work has not been easy to decide. In the *Proceedings of the American Philological Association* it has twice been called *The Contributions of the Ancient Dramatic Poets to our Knowledge of the Arts and Crafts of Greece*. This title is descriptive but too cumbersome; so I have decided to send forth the first volume under the caption of *Daedalus and Thespis*—Daedalus, the first artist and craftsman, and Thespis, the first dramatist of Hellas.

As Volume I has to do with Architecture and Topography, so Volume II will deal with the Sculpture, Volume III, with the Painting and Ceramics of Greece, as pictured to us by the dramatic poets. It is planned to include in the third volume complete Indexes—1) of all the passages cited from the ancient authors; 2) of all the artists named; 3) of the important subjects discussed. The first Index will also clear up any possible misunderstanding of the abbreviations of authors or titles quoted in the text. Most of them are the regularly accepted abbreviations and will cause no difficulty. "N.," for example, after a tragic fragment means Nauck's edition; "K." means Kock's *Fragmenta Comicorum*; "D.," Dindorf's *Poetae Scenici Graeci*.

I trust that the elevated figures will not be confusing, though they may have a triple significance: usually a small high 1 or 2 or 3 will refer to a footnote; but "R.³" will mean the third edition of Ribbeck's *Fragmenta*, Roscher *Myth. Lex.*, II² will mean the second half of the second volume of the *Mythologisches Lexikon*, and so forth.

In this "Greekless age," I have thought it best to translate all the citations from the Greek authors quoted in the text, rarely in the footnotes; I am assuming a better state of things for the Latin, and generally leave the Latin excerpts to my readers' understanding.

I want to take this opportunity to express to my old friend, Professor Wilhelm Dörpfeld, greatest of archaeologists in this field, my very hearty thanks for his kindness in reading my manuscript and for the suggestions he offered, and to my former pupil, Miss Florence Feaster, for her invaluable help in verifying the many references.

WALTER MILLER
*University of Missouri*

July 27, 1928

# CONTENTS

## VOL. I

# CONTENTS

# TABLE OF ILLUSTRATIONS

# DAEDALUS AND THESPIS

*The Contributions of the Ancient Dramatic Poets to Our*
*Knowledge of the Arts and Crafts of Greece*

## I. INTRODUCTION

The Greek dramatists, living in the era of the highest development of the arts of painting, sculpture, and architecture, might be expected to give us more of insight into those arts than we could reasonably hope to gain from poets of other days. Homer describes many works of Mycenaean art in elaborate detail—the decorations on the shield of Achilles (Il. XVIII 478 ff.), for example, and the baldric of Heracles (Od. XI 609–614), and Hesiod (Scut. Her. 139 ff.), the engravings on the shield of Heracles; Theocritus (I 32 sqq.) describes dramatically scenes carved upon a wooden bowl; Moschus (II 37 sqq.) copies in verse the figures on Europa's basket. "The Roman poets abound with similar descriptions: Vergil, besides the shield of Aeneas (Ae. VIII 625 sqq.) and the doors at Cumae on which were sculptured the death of Androgeos, the drawing of the lots for the victims of the Minotaur, and the story of Pasiphaë (Ae. VI 20 sqq.), describes the sculptures on the temple of Juno at Carthage (Ae. I 453–493) and a chlamys on which was embroidered the rape of Ganymede (Ae. V 250 sqq.); Ovid describes the carvings on the doors of the temple of the sun and on a cup given to Aeneas (Met. II 5, XIII 681 sqq.); Silius describes the shield of Hannibal (II 403 sqq.)." [1] Catullus (64) reproduces in picture words with great minuteness the story of Theseus and Ariadne embroidered on the coverlet of the Nuptial Couch of Peleus and Thetis.

The drama, with its application to the daily life of the people to whom it was presented, might well be expected to contribute to the history of the arts that played so extensive a rôle in their civilization, more by far than either epos or idyll; and it does.

The impulse to this investigation was given in my student days by the reading of Euripides's Ion. If Euripides could give so brilliant a description of the pediment sculptures of the fifth century temple at Delphi (Ion 190–218), why should not he and his great compeers in dramatic poetry have many another contribution to the history of the graphic, plastic, and architectural arts that had just reached their zenith within that generation?

It is only natural to look to the Greek drama for such descriptions and allusions. Aeschylus was living and working when Antenor carved his masterpieces in Athens, when Critius and Nesiotes were in their prime, when Polygnotus of Thasos was painting his great gallery pieces and decorating the walls of the public buildings of renascent Athens, when Phidias was embodying in metal and marble his stupendous conceptions of things divine, and when the Olympian Pericles was entering upon his unparalleled career. Sophocles, living through the administrations of Cimon, Themistocles, and Pericles, and through the Peloponnesian War, saw Athens rise from the ashes of the Persian devastation; saw the resurrection of the city and the growing and perfected glory of the Acropolis, and the beginnings of the new creations of the second bloom of Attic art. Euripides was even more the child of the fifth century; he was part of its joy and strife, its thought and aspirations; and he had besides the artist's instincts, if not the artist's training. Aristophanes outlived the last two only by a few years and must have gloried in the artistic glorification of his "enviable city."

It would seem, therefore, that Greek drama, which has so much of the modern spirit and of contemporary allusion, should be fairly filled with descriptions of works of art and allusions to the work of contemporary artists. For the dramatic poets of the Periclean Age have told us much about the religion, much about the culture, more about the politics and the history, and not a little about the institutions of their own age. The settings of their plays may be far more ancient than their own days; they may present before their audiences the scenes of the heroic age of Troy, or Thebes, or Mycenae, or Athens; but the sentiments they speak are the sentiments of that Athens which grew to greatness in the fifth century

[1] Ellis, *Com. on Cat.*, LXIV 50.

9

before our era.    A chance remark upon the lips of an Oedipus, a Prometheus, or a Heracles may reflect a ray of light upon some institution of historical Athens; when Danaus says (Ae. Sup. 746–747):

| | |
|---|---|
| πολλοὺς δέ γε εὑρήσουσιν ἐν μεσημβρίας | yet many shall they find whose muscled |
| θάλπει βραχίον' εὖ κατερρινημένους | arms have been trained in noontide heat |

he is voicing the contempt of the soldier-poet, who had fought at Marathon and Salamis, for the growing effeminacy of the Athenian youth of the fifth century, whose affectation was leading them to shrink from discipline and exposure that might spoil their complexions— "brought up not in the bright sun but in shady bowers, strangers to manly exercises and the sweat of toil."[1]    If Clytaemnestra (Ae. Ag. 312–314) can help us to understand even a little of the details of the Lampadephoria, or if the Paedagogus (Soph. El. 698–756) can give us so full and accurate a description of the chariot-race at the great games, why should not an Aeschylus or a Sophocles, who grew to greatness with a Phidias, an Alcamenes, an Agoracritus, a Polygnotus, a Callicrates, and an Ictinus, contribute in some verse to our knowledge of the architecture and the plastic and the graphic arts of their great contemporaries?    For the Athenians of their day gloried no less in the achievements of artistic Athens than of athletic or martial Athens.

If Sophocles may introduce upon the field of Troy so palpable an anachronism as the tale of Cresphontes and his lump of moistened clay, with which, as lot, he won the kingdom of Messenia (Aj. 1285–1286), or make the Salaminian at Troy long to round the promontory of Sunium and hail the sight of sacred Athens (Aj. 1218–1222), why should he not mention also with the feelings of one of Pericles's Table Round some of the glories that crowned that same Acropolis?    If Euripides (Ion 936 ff.) can so accurately describe the North slope of the Acropolis of Athens, the district called Macrae, with its grottos, its shrine of Pan, and the altars, why should he not have even more to say of the citadel itself?    Sometimes the tragic poets, though presenting scenes from the life and culture of the Mycenaean age, depict customs peculiarly Athenian: thus Electra (Ae. Cho. 96–99) says

| | |
|---|---|
| ἢ σῖγ' ἀτίμως, ὥσπερ οὖν ἀπώλετο | or dumb with ignominy, like that with which my father |
| πατήρ, τάδ' ἐκχέασα, γάποτον χύσιν, | died, shall I pour this out, a draught for earth to drink, and then |
| στείχω, καθάρμαθ' ὥς τις ἐκπέμψας πάλιν | shall I throw away the vessel and go back and look not after |
| δικοῦσα τεῦχος ἀστρόφοισιν ὄμμασιν; | me, as one who casts out pollution? |

When a house was cleansed and purified, after death or any other cause of uncleanness had left it defiled, the filth was gathered into an earthen vessel, carried to a place where three ways met; there the purifier flung the vessel behind him and hastened away without turning to look after it.    In A 314 the Greeks cast their lustral filth into the sea; in Theocritus XXIV 92–97, Alcmena's handmaid is to cast away beyond the boundaries the defilement of Hera's serpents, sent to slay the Infant Heracles:

| | |
|---|---|
| ῥιψάτω εὖ μάλα πᾶσαν ὑπὲρ ποταμοῖο φέροισα | let her take it all and cast it, every whit, from a rugged rock, |
| ῥωγάδος ἐκ πέτρας, ὑπερούριον· ἂψ δὲ νέεσθαι | across the river, beyond the bounds, and then come |
| ἄστρεπτος | back without a backward glance |

Sophocles describes in detail the ritual for appeasing the Eumenides with libations— forms which he had from his boyhood seen daily practiced on Colonus hill[2]—and the awful

---

[1] Plat. Phaedr. 239 c.
[2] O. C. 469–490:

| | |
|---|---|
| πρῶτον μὲν ἱρᾶς ἐξ ἀειρύτου χοὰς | . . . . . . |
| κρήνης ἔνεγκου, δι' ὁσίων χειρῶν θιγών. | ὕδατος, μελίσσης· μηδὲ προσφέρειν μέθυ. |
| . . . . . . | . . . . . . |
| κρατῆρές εἰσιν, ἀνδρὸς εὐχειρος τέχνη, | τρὶς ἐννέ' αὐτῇ κλῶνας ἐξ ἀμφοῖν χεροῖν |
| ὧν κρᾶτ' ἔρεψον καὶ λαβὰς ἀμφιστόμους. | τιθεὶς ἐλάας τάσδ' ἐπεύχεσθαι λιτάς. |
| . . . . . . | . . . . . . |
| οἰὸς νεαλοῦς νεοκόπῳ μαλλῷ βαλών. | . . . . . . ἐξ εὐμενῶν |
| . . . . . . | στέρνων δέχεσθαι τὸν ἱκέτην σωτήριον |
| χοὰς χέασθαι στάντα πρὸς πρώτην ἕω. | αὐτοῦ σύ τ' αὐτὸς κεἴ τις ἄλλος ἀντὶ σοῦ, |
| . . . . . . | ἄπυστα φωνῶν μηδὲ μηκύνων βοήν. |
| τρισσάς γε πηγάς (sc. χέου)· τὸν τελευταῖον δὲ χοῦν | ἔπειτ' ἀφέρπειν ἄστροφος. |

entrance to their "shrine where none may tread"; why should we not have some mention also of the plastic decorations of that shrine?

So, too, Euripides may have Athena herself give details about the ordinances of the feast of Tauropolia (I. T. 1435 ff.) with the laying of the sword to the throat of a human victim and the drawing of human blood in commemoration of the unfulfilled sacrifice of Orestes in the Taurian land. Why should he not tell us also of the temple or its artistic decoration as it was? Perhaps he does; we shall see.

We find a similar relation in the attitude of the poets to current politics. The Suppliants of Euripides, more, perhaps, than any other tragedy that has come down to us, was written for the definite purpose of influencing the politics of the day. In its whole spirit it is a picture of Periclean Athens. Theseus, the prudent statesman and brilliant general, who has built his state into a perfect democracy and yet so dominates it by the strength of his own personality that the people simply carry out his policies and are swayed by him as if he were their king, is but an heroic picture of the Olympian Pericles. This hero is a lover of peace; but he is ready to stake the very existence of his state in the defense of the principles of honor and liberty and the rights of humanity.

The treaty which Theseus, at the dictation of Athena, makes with Adrastus is more than an echo of that treaty which Alcibiades closed with the Argives whereby Athens was saved from invasion by the Spartan armies (Eur. Sup. 1183–1195).

The Peloponnesian War was a war of principles—democratic *versus* autocratic. And in the Suppliants these principles are victorious in debate (ll. 399–462) and on the field of battle (ll. 634–730).

If Euripides may give us such a picture of the Peloponnesian War as he does in the Suppliants, if he can even delineate the contemporary Athenian tactics and battle-order (ll. 650–694), if, for the public performance of the Hippolytus which came shortly after the death of Pericles, the poet could even alter the closing chorus, already composed, so as to pay tribute to the peerless statesman,[1] why may we not expect from him many a suggestion of artistic Athens—a description of a statue, a temple, a public building with its plastic ornament? And our expectations will not be unfulfilled.

In like manner the Choephori of Aeschylus has much to do with the politics of 458 B. C., when an alliance with Argos was the favorite political program of the conservative party in Athens. Aeschylus's advocacy of the measure is not even veiled (Eum. 289–291) (*Orestes loquitur*):

χτήσεται δ᾽ ἄνευ δορὸς
αὐτόν τε καὶ γῆν καὶ τὸν ᾽Αργεῖον λεών,
πιστὸν δικαίως ἐς τὸ πᾶν τε σύμμαχον

and without the help of spear she shall win
both myself and my land and my Argive folk,
an ally faithful and loyal for evermore

Apollo puts his sanction upon the alliance (ll. 669–673) and again Orestes, as type and symbol of the Argive people, speaks (762–774):

ἐγὼ δὲ χώρᾳ τῇδε καὶ τῷ σῷ στρατῷ
τὸ λοιπὸν εἰς ἅπαντα πλειστήρη χρόνον
ὀρκωμοτήσας νῦν ἄπειμι πρὸς δόμους,

μήτοι τιν ἄνδρα δεῦρο πρυμνήτην χθονός,
ἐλθόντ᾽ ἐποίσειν εὖ κεκασμένον δόρυ.
αὐτοὶ γὰρ ἡμεῖς ὄντες ἐν τάφοις τότε

τοῖς τἀμὰ παρβαίνουσι νῦν ὀρκώματα
ἀμηχάνοισι πράξομεν δυσπραξίαις,

and now will I go back home, now that I
have pledged my vows to this land and
to thy hosts, henceforth unto all the fulness of
time, that
no chieftain of my land shall ever
come and bring the strong array of spears.
For we ourselves, though we then be in our
graves,
will toward those who shall transgress
our present vows so deal with woes inextricable,
giving

[1] (Eur. Hip. 1459–1466):
ΘΗ. ὦ κλείν᾽ ᾽Αθηνῶν Πελοπίας θ᾽ ὁρίσματα,
οἵου στερήσεσθ᾽ ἀνδρός. ὦ τλήμων ἐγώ.
. . . . . . . . . . . .
ΧΟ. κοινὸν τόδ᾽ ἄχος πᾶσι πολίταις
ἦλθεν ἀέλπτως.
πολλῶν δακρύων ἔσται πίτυλος·
τῶν γὰρ μεγάλων ἀξιοπενθεῖς
ψῆμαι μᾶλλον κατέχουσιν.

THE. Oh glorious confines of Athens and Pelopia,
of what a man ye are to be bereft! Woe is me!

CHO. Unanticipated hath this sorrow come
in common to all our citizens.
There will be the dropping of many tears;
for a great man's fame, that calleth
for sorrow, binds more strongly our hearts.

| ὁδοὺς ἀθύμους καὶ παρόρνιθας πόρους | them marches of despair and ways of evil augury, |
| τιθέντες, ὡς αὐτοῖσι μεταμέλῃ πόνος· | that they may repent them of their pains; |
| ὀρθουμένων δέ, καὶ πόλιν τὴν Παλλάδος | but if all be well and if they continue to honor this city |
| τιμῶσιν ἀεὶ τήνδε συμμάχῳ δόρι, | of Pallas, our spear-ally, then we to them |
| αὐτοῖσιν ἡμεῖς ἐσμεν εὐμενέστεροι | are more devoted still |

Aeschylus also openly advocates certain much needed reforms in the procedures of the law courts of Athens. In case of criminal prosecution, the prosecutor's first move was to tender to the accused an oath that he was not guilty. The defendant might or might not consent to bind himself by such an oath. If he refused to plead "not guilty" under oath, the trial ended there, and a judgment of "guilty" was without further ceremony entered against him. On the other hand, if under oath he pleaded "not guilty," he was acquitted of the charge on which he was being prosecuted but was liable straightway to a prosecution for perjury. Aeschylus makes Orestes refuse to do either (Eum. 429):

| ἀλλ' ὅρκον οὐ δέξαιτ' ἄν, οὐ δοῦναι *θέλοι | but he would take no oath nor challenge us to swear |

and declares that such oaths are no fair method of procedure in trial (Eum. 432):

| ὅρκοις τὰ μὴ δίκαια μὴ νικᾶν λέγω | I say that injustice must not prevail by oaths |

The old method was a bulwark to the success of unscrupulousness; it was illogical, as well as cumbrous and unjust. Aristotle (Rhet. I 15) also assails it on the score of its illogical basis.

Territorial expansion also finds in him a strong advocate; and into Athena's own mouth he puts the claim of Athens to the promontory of Sigeum, as hers by right of concession at the capture of Troy (Eum. 397-402):

| πρόσωθεν ἐξήκουσα κληδόνος βοὴν | from afar did I hear the sound of thy cry, |
| ἀπὸ Σκαμάνδρου, γῆν καταφθατουμένη, | from Scamander, as I made haste thither to claim the land |
| ἣν δῆτ' Ἀχαιῶν ἄκτορές τε καὶ πρόμοι, | which, as is known, the leaders and chiefs of the Achaeans |
| τῶν αἰχμαλώτων χρημάτων λάχος μέγα, | apportioned me as choice portion of the spoils |
| ἔνειμαν αὐτόπρεμνον εἰς τὸ πᾶν ἐμοί, | —land and all therein—forever— |
| ἐξαίρετον δώρημα Θησέως τόκοις | a special gift for Theseus's children |

In the same way facts of history are presented, not only in Aristophanes, who is one of our chief sources (when used with discretion and insight) for the history of the Peloponnesian War, but also in the tragic poets. Aristophanes names, in one way and another, almost every man prominent in any capacity in his day—Thucydides, Sophocles, Euripides, Gorgias, Socrates, Chaerephon, Antiphon (the orator), Cleon, Cleonymus, Alcibiades, Theorus, Leagoras, Phayllus (the Pythionices), Lamachus, Theramenes, Nicias, Laches, Phrynichus, Androcles, Hyperbolus, Pericles, Simonides, Cratinus, Carcinus, Pisander, Eucrates, Diagoras, Clisthenes, Cleophon, Meletus, Callias, Thrasybulus, Dionysius, Prodicus; why should we not hope to find in his up-to-date verse some mention also of Phidias, Ictinus, the elder Praxiteles, Cephisodotus?

If Aristophanes may allude at length to the battle of Salamis (Vesp. 1078 sqq.) and name the great soldiers and statesmen of earlier generations and his own, why not some mention of the glorified Acropolis and the great artist souls that had created the visible splendor of the Athens of his day?

If Sophocles may allude, with patent disapproval, to Pericles's policy of centralization of government; if he may refer to contemporary literature, as he does to Herodotus's story of Hippias's dream (O. T. 981–982 = Hdt. VI 107) and to the story of Zalmoxis (El. 62–64 = Hdt. IV 95), if he can work into a tragedy (Ant. 909–912) material that he found in the story of Intaphernes (Hdt. III 119) and (O. C. 337 ff.) a description given by Herodotus (II 35); why should he not equally bring into his artistic verse the works of his great contemporaries in sculpture and painting and architecture? To be sure, the similarity between the first named passages has seemed to some a satisfactory ground for declaring them spu-

But the birds seem not to have taken kindly to the suggestion of baked bricks, and their walls are built of sun-dried bricks upon a substructure of stone and concrete construction. The method of constructing a wall of sun-dried bricks upon a base of concrete or stone is brought out with considerable detail in the Birds of Aristophanes (838–842):

| | |
|---|---|
| καὶ τοῖσι τειχίζουσι παραδιακόνει, | and tend the master-masons; |
| χάλικας παραφόρει, πηλὸν ἀποδὺς ὄργασον, | carry bricks to them; pull off your coat and mix mud; |
| λεκάνην ἀνένεγκε, κατάπεσ' ἀπὸ τῆς κλίμακος, | carry up the hod; tumble down the ladder; |
| φύλακας κατάστησαι, τὸ πῦρ ἔγκρυπτ' ἀεί, | station your watchers; keep the fire banked up; |
| κωδωνοφορῶν περίτρεχε, καὶ κάθευδ' ἐκεῖ | run around and ring the bell; take your nap there |

Here we have a suggestion of the rising wall of Cloud-cuckoo-town and the hod-carrier's duties in the construction: he mixes the "mud" (the *locus classicus* for the modern mason's colloquial word for mortar); he shoulders his hod (literally, his *pot*) filled with pieces of stone or with mortar for the concrete portion of the wall, and with sun-dried bricks or with mud for the succeeding courses of the wall of bricks; with his heavy hod he mounts the ladder—and creates a diversion for the master-masons by tumbling off; he is also a sort of head-overseer directing the sentries and keeping the watch-fires banked by day and running around and ringing the watchman's bell when on duty himself; staying right on the job even during his resting hours.

The hod-carrier, or "mud-carrier," is mentioned again in Aristophanes's Birds (1134, quoted below) and again in the Ecclesiazusae—in the latter passage with the interesting bit of information that a hod-carrier's wage at the beginning of the fourth century was three obols, the same as the ecclesiast's (Ar. Ec. 309–310):

| | |
|---|---|
| νυνὶ δὲ τριώβολον ζητοῦσι λαβεῖν ὅταν | and now they are striving to get their three obols whenever |
| πράττωσί τι κοινὸν ὥσπερ πηλοφοροῦντες | they perform any public service, same as hod-carriers |

And when the wall is finished, concrete and brick, a messenger pronounces it a wonder of masons' skill though built by birds (Ar. Av. 1133–1162):

| | |
|---|---|
| ὄρνιθες, οὐδεὶς ἄλλος, οὐκ Αἰγύπτιος πλινθοφόρος,[1] οὐ λιθουργός, οὐ τέκτων παρῆν. | Birds—none else—no Aegyptian brick-carrier,[1] no stone mason, no carpenter was there. |
| . . . . | . . . . |
| ἐκ μέν γε Λιβύης ἧκον ὡς τρισμύριαι γέρανοι, θεμελίους καταπεπωκυῖαι λίθους. | From Libya there had come thirty thousand cranes carrying in their crops stones for the foundation.[2] |
| τούτους δ' ἐτύκιζον αἱ κρέκες τοῖς ῥύγχεσιν. | These the crexes picked into shape with their beaks. |
| ἕτεροι δ' ἐπλινθούργουν πελαργοὶ μύριοι· ὕδωρ δ' ἐφόρουν κάτωθεν ἐς τὸν ἀέρα οἱ χαραδριοὶ καὶ τἄλλα ποτάμι' ὄρνεα. ΠΕ. ἐπηλοφόρουν δ' αὐτοῖσι τίνες; ΑΓ. ἐρωδιοὶ λεκάναισι. ΠΕ. τὸν δὲ πηλὸν ἐνεβάλλοντο πῶς; ΑΓ. τοῦτ', ὦγαθ', ἐξηύρητο καὶ σοφώτατα· | In addition, ten thousand storks moulded bricks; and water was fetched up into the sky by the curlews and the other water-fowl. PE. And who carried the "mud" for them? MES. Herons, in hods. PE. And how did they load the "mud"? MES. This, good Sir, was managed by a most clever invention: |
| οἱ χῆνες ὑποτύπτοντες ὥσπερ ταῖς ἄμαις ἐς τὰς λεκάνας ἐνέβαλον αὐτὸν τοῖν ποδοῖν. | the geese dipped down and with their feet for shovels loaded it into the hods. |
| . . . | . . . |
| καὶ νὴ Δί' αἱ νῆτταί γε περιεζωσμέναι ἐπλινθοφόρουν· ἄνω δὲ τὸν ὑπαγωγέα | And the ducks, by Zeus, put on overalls and carried up the bricks; and the swallows flew up with the |

[1] Diphilus wrote a comedy with the title Πλινθοφόρος "Brick-carrier" of which only two lines are preserved (Frag. 65 K.).

[2] An ancient nature-faker story tells that when cranes start to migrate across the sea, they swallow stones. They carry these in their crops to serve as ballast, to keep themselves from being blown by the storms into the skies; or, when the birds rise so high that they can no longer distinguish between land and sea, they may drop a stone to see (or hear) whether it strikes on terra firma or on water. According to results observed from this experiment, the cranes know whether they may alight or must fly on. Aristophanes means to suggest that on such unsubstantial stones the foundations of Cloud-cuckoo-town are laid.

ἐπέτοντ' ἔχουσαι κατόπιν, ὥσπερ παιδία,
καὶ πηλὸν ἐν τοῖς στόμασιν αἱ χελιδόνες.
ΠΕ.... τί δαί; τὰ ξύλινα τοῦ τείχους τίνες
ἀπειργάσαντ'; ΑΓ. ὄρνιθες ἦσαν τέκτονες
σοφώτατοι πελεκᾶντες, οἳ τοῖς ῥύγχεσιν

ἀπεπελέκησαν τὰς πύλας· ἦν δ' ὁ κτύπος

αὐτῶν πελεκώντων ὥσπερ ἐν ναυπηγίῳ.
καὶ νῦν ἅπαντ' ἐκεῖνα πεπύλωται πύλαις,
καὶ βεβαλάνωται καὶ φυλάττεται κύκλῳ,
ἐφοδεύεται, κωδωνοφορεῖται, πανταχῇ

φυλακαὶ καθεστήκασι καὶ φρυκτωρίαι
ἐν τοῖσι πύργοις.

> trowel behind them, like apprentices, and
> carried the "mud" in their bills.
> PE. . . . And say—who did the wood work of
> the wall?  MES. The carpenters were birds—
> wood-peckers—most skilful artizans: with their beaks
> they pecked out the gates; and there arose the noise
> of their pecking, like that in a shipyard.
> And now the whole plant is equipped with gates
> and bars and bolts and is under guard all round;
> the rounds are made; the watch-bell rings; everywhere
> the sentries are posted, and beacons are
> in place upon the towers.

The picture is rich in varied details: mixing "mud"; loading hods; carrying bricks with efficiency far surpassing that of the glory days of Egypt; laying bricks and stone and mortar, while the courses of the wall rose; hods, shovels, trowels, pick-chisels; carpenters with adzes—walls, towers, gates, bars and bolts, watchfires—the fortress and all the arts and crafts for its building are brought before us in the picture.

House walls were constructed in a very similar manner: a foundation of stone or concrete and walls of sun-dried bricks.  And with construction of that sort it was perfectly easy to drive pegs into the walls of a house, as Philocleon did in order to elude the watchers and escape from his forced confinement in his home (Ar. Vesp. 129–130):

ὁ δ' ὡσπερεὶ κολοιὸς αὐτῷ παττάλους
ἐνέκρουεν εἰς τὸν τοῖχον, εἶτ' ἐξήλλετο

> but he drove him pegs into the wall
> and then hopped down, like a jackdaw

The sun-dried bricks were not so hard but that the old gentleman could hammer wooden pegs into the wall with ease and without making noise sufficient to awaken the sleepy slaves on guard.

Roofs were made of burned tile from a very early day.  We have abundant remains of such tiles from the oldest treasuries of Olympia.  The use of burned bricks for the facing of walls, so common in Roman times, seems to have been unknown in the days of classical Greece.  Sun-dried bricks were used in house-walls; burned tiles were common upon the roofs.  We have the combination in Aristophanes (Nub. 1126–1127):

ἢν δὲ πλινθεύοντ' ἴδωμεν, ὕσομεν καὶ τοῦ
                                τέγους
τὸν κέραμον αὐτοῦ χαλάζαις στρογγύλαις
                                ξυντρίψομεν

> and if we see him making bricks, we shall rain;
> and the tiles
> of his roof we shall smash with hail-stones round

The soft, freshly molded bricks are to be dissolved by the rain; the tiles are to be shattered by the big hailstones.

The ordinary Athenian residence with its tiled roof, so prevalent in Greece unto this day, is referred to once more in Aristophanes (Vesp. 203–206):

ΣΩ. πόθεν ποτ' ἐμπέπτωκέ μοι τὸ βώλιον;

ΞΑ. ἴσως ἄνωθεν μῦς ἐξέβαλέ σοί ποθεν.

ΣΩ. μῦς; οὐ μὰ Δί', ἀλλ' ὑποδυόμενός τις
                                οὑτοσὶ
ὑπὸ τῶν κεραμίδων ἡλιαστὴς ὀροφίας

> SO. Where did that clod of dirt come from that fell on me?
> XA. Maybe a mouse knocked it down on you from somewhere up there.
> SO. A mouse?  No, by Zeus; but some
> mouse of a heliast is sneaking about under the tiles

So convenient a place was found in the space up under the roof, between the rafters and the tiles, for mice and lizards and snakes, that ὀροφίας became the natural epithet to distinguish between a common or domestic mouse and a field mouse, between a house-snake and a field-snake.

So characteristic of the roof were the burned tiles that κέραμος came to be used, early and late, for the *roof* itself (Ar. Κώκ., Frag. 349 K.):[1]

| | |
|---|---|
| κοφίνους δὲ λίθων ἐκέλευες<br>ἱμᾶν ἡμᾶς ἐπὶ τὸν κέραμον | and thou didst order us to pull up<br>baskets of stones upon the "tile" |

The flat roof was supported by beams extending from wall to wall. Because of the nature of such roof-construction, each room might be said to have its own roof; and for that reason the plural (στέγαι) is often used of the roof of one house.[2] These beams are the chief support of the roof; in such pregnant sense Strepsiades speaks of the beams of Socrates's house at the end of the Clouds (Ar. Nub. 1496):

| | |
|---|---|
| διαλεπτογοῦμαι τοῖς δοκοῖς τῆς οἰκίας | I am chopping logic with the beams of your house |

Such flat-roofed dwelling-houses were universal in the heroic age, the general thing in classical times. Only the more pretentious residences of the classical period were constructed with gabled roofs, with sloping rafters covered with burned tiles. Aristophanes, in the Birds, refers to such houses as an innovation (1109–1110):

| | |
|---|---|
| ὥσπερ ἐν ἱεροῖς οἰκήσετε·<br>τὰς γὰρ ὑμῶν οἰκίας ἐρέψομεν πρὸς ἀετόν | as if in temples you shall live;<br>for we will put gabled roofs upon your houses |

In the development of the gable construction the new-style roof was simply superimposed upon the old flat roof. Upon and across the heavier cross-beams of the flat roof and resting upon the house-walls, rafters of wood ran up at the proper pitch to the ridge-pole (Pl. Aul. 357–358):

C. Sunt asseres?
S. Sunt pol. C. Sunt igitur ligna

A less common, technical word for rafter we find in a fragment of Aristophanes's Babylonians (Frag. 72 K.):

| | |
|---|---|
| πόσους ἔχει στρωτῆρας ἀνδρὼν οὑτοσί; | how many rafters has this men's part of the<br>house here? |

Harpocration defines the word στρωτήρ with exactness:

| | |
|---|---|
| στρωτήρ·... τὰ ἐπάνω τῶν δουροδόκων<br>τιθέμενα στρωτῆρας ἔλεγον, ὥς φησι Δίδυμος | rafter: the timbers laid upon the joists they<br>used to call "rafters," as Didymus says |

We find the word still further defined (Bekk. Anecd. 302, 5):

| | |
|---|---|
| στρωτῆρές εἰσι τὰ μικρὰ δοκίδια<br>εἰς ὀροφὰς πεποιημένα· οἱ δέ<br>φασι πλέγματά τινα ἀπὸ ῥάβδων<br>εἰς ὀρόφωσιν πεποιημένα[3], οἱ<br>δὲ σανίδας πάλιν εἰς ὀροφὴν<br>ἐπιτηδείους | rafters are the small beams<br>made for roofs; some people<br>call them a kind of lattice-work<br>made of rods for roofing[3]; some,<br>again, call them sheeting ad-<br>apted to roofing |

All these terms are familiar in modern building—beams (joists), rafters, sheeting, cross-laid work; they need no further elucidation.

Upon the cross-beams of the flat-topped house was laid the wicker work to carry the clay of the concrete roof; upon the sloping rafters of the gabled house was laid the sheeting of wood, and upon the sheeting came the burned tiles, concave gutter-tiles covered by the convex tiles—tegulae and imbrices (Pl. Mos. 108–109):

tempestas venit
confringit tegulas imbricesque

(Pl. Mil. 504):

quod meas confregisti imbrices et tegulas

---

[1] So Pherecr. Πέρσ., Frag. 130, 6 K.; cf. also Pollux VII 162: καὶ αὐτὸ τὸ τέγος οὐ μόνον οἱ νῦν κέραμον ὀνομάζουσιν, ἀλλὰ καὶ Ἀριστοφάνης ἂν ἐοίκοι καλεῖν εἰπὼν ἐν Κωκάλῳ... Of course the usual words for "roof," ὀροφή, τέγος, and στέγη (στέγαι) are not infrequently used; for example, Eur. Med. 1143; 1164; Or. 1127; 1448; Ar. Nub. 173; Ach. 262; Lys. 389; 395; Αἰολ., Frag. 11 K.

[2] For example, Ae. Ag. 518; Diph. Παράσιτος, Frag. 61, 2 K.

[3] Photius, *s. v.* στρωτήρ, gives the same explanation in almost identical words.

The meaning of the Latin words is perfectly clear. In the light of them, Aristophanes's fragment also becomes perfectly clear (Βαβ., Frag. 73 K.):

| | |
|---|---|
| ὡς εὖ καλυμματίοις τὸν οἶκον ἤρεφε | how well he covered his house with roof-tiles |

Photius, citing Aristophanes, explains καλυμμάτια[1] as φατνώματα. We thus get a picture of a flat roof laid with square or oblong tiles with slightly raised borders—the kind of tile with which we are perfectly familiar in Greece both ancient and modern.

From such a roof, given a slight slant in the desired direction, the rain water was carried down in rain pipes and thrown away from the foundations, as is done to-day. In only one extant passage of the Greek drama do we find a reference to such down-spouts (Ar. Vesp. 126):

| | |
|---|---|
| ὁ δ' ἐξεδίδρασκε διά τε τῶν ὑδρορροῶν | and he would manage to escape down the rain-pipes |

Philocleon, locked up in his house, would go up on the roof and climb down the rain pipes to the street,[2] and thus making his escape from the house be off to the court-rooms.

What the rain pipes were made of we are not told. The same word (ὑδρορροαί) is used for the water-mains of the city water-works and for the sewers. We may perhaps from this fact safely conjecture that they were made of flanged tiles of clay.

A tiled roof of a gabled house or a house with an impluvium was not meant for people to walk upon. In the latter passage just cited from Plautus's Miles Gloriosus (505) Sceledrus had run over the tiled roof after a pet monkey and broken the tiling; in the former the wind had blown the tiles off the roof; the same thing happens also in Plautus's Rudens (78):

quoius deturbavit ventus tectum et tegulas

(87):

omnis de tecto deturbavit tegulas[3]

These passages from the Latin poet call to mind the dwellings of the later period. But the primitive roofs in Hellas were of packed clay or reed thatched. Such roofs of solidly packed clay, with a good strong railing or parapet wall about them, were characteristic of fifth and early fourth century Athens. The dwelling house of the later period might have either the new-fashioned gabled roofs or the flat, clay-packed roof of the older style.[4]

But the primitive roofs in Hellas were of packed clay or reed thatched. An echo of that we find as late as Plautus (Rud. 96; 100–102; 122–123):

SC. Si sapiam quod me mactat concinnem lutum.

. . . . . . . . . . . . . . . . . . . . . . . .

DAE.  Luto usust multo, multam terram confode.<br>villam integundam intellego totam mihi;<br>nam nunc perlucet ea quam cribrum crebrius.

. . . . . . . . . . . . . . . . . . . . . . . .

SC.  Quin tu in paludem is exsicasque harundinem<br>qui pertegemus villam, dum sudumst

These proposed repairs have to do with a country house. But the primitive Doric temple was provided with just such a roof, which in course of time developed into the structure with the beautiful marble tiles.

But the time was, as the poets realized, when roofed houses did not exist for man at all (Moschion, Inc. Frag. 6, 6–8, N.):

| | |
|---|---|
| οὐδέπω γὰρ ἦν | for not yet was there |
| οὔτε στεγήρης οἶκος οὔτε λαΐνοις | either roofèd house or spacious city |
| εὐρεῖα πύργοις ὠχυρωμένη πόλις | fortified with towers of stone |

---

[1] The correction of Fritzsche; the MSS. have καλύμματα.

[2] Such down-spouts were common enough in the fifth century. In the fourth the construction of rain pipes discharging on the street was prohibited (Arist. Const. Ath. 50, 2): τὰς ὁδοὺς κωλύουσι κατοικοδομεῖν καὶ ὀχετοὺς μετεώρους εἰς τὴν ὁδὸν ἔκρουν ἔχομ [ένους] ποιεῖν...

[3] For other instances of similar usage see Pl. Rud. 153; Mil., Arg. I 8; 156; 173; 178; 273; 285; 309; Calceolus, Frag. I; Ter. Eun. 588; Phor. 707.

[4] Cp. pp. 226 ff.

There are also many allusions to structural technique in stone. Palaces and temples, as we shall see, are built of stone. The floor is of stone (Aristias, Inc. Frag. 6 N.):

μυχαῖσι δ' ὠρέχθει τὸ λάϊνον πέδον | with cries resounded the floor of stone

We cannot venture even a guess at the nature of the building that was furnished with this particular floor of stone.

Doorposts are of stone, even in private houses (Ar. Ach. 449 [but the passage is manifestly a paratragoedia, parodying probably Euripides[1]]):

ἄπελθε λαΐνων σταθμῶν | depart from my doorposts of stone

In the fifth century the temples of the gods were normally built of costly stone and embellished with precious metals (Ar. Av. 612–614):

καὶ πρῶτα μὲν οὐχὶ νεὼς ἡμᾶς | and first of all, we must not build
οἰκοδομεῖν δεῖ λιθίνους αὐτοῖς | for them temples of marble nor
οὐδὲ θυρῶσαι χρυσαῖσι θύραις | furnish them with doors of gold

We shall presently study the poet's description of historic temples and find them built, even thus, of marble and decked with gold in magnificence scarcely imaginable. The Chorus of Birds speaks of doors of gold—that is, probably, doors inlaid with gold. The Hellenized Roman poet has even a gilded threshold (Inc. [Seneca?] H. O. 612–614):

> tenet auratum limen Erinys
> et quom magnae patuere fores
> intrant fraudes cautique doli

The most diverse parts of architectural structure find mention—foundations, steps, colonnades, floors, triglyphs, metopes, cornice, frieze, pediments, roof, acroteria. Some of these architectural elements are barely named; some are described in minute detail. Aeschylus has a most interesting reference to the Lesbian cyma (Θαλ., Frag. 78 N.):

ἀλλ' <εἴ'> ὁ μέν τις Λέσβιον φατνώματι | so come, let some one work out a Lesbian cyma
κῦμ' ἐν τριγώνοις ἐκπεραινέτω ῥυθμοῖς | in triangular rhythm about the coffering

In these two lines we have in words what we have in the ceiling of the colonnade of the Parthenon we know. The ceiling of the colonnade is coffered; about the edges of each lacunar is a Lesbian cyma, with its regular sequence of triangular leaf-like ornament. The Parthenon is not named; the Periclean Parthenon was as yet not even planned. We cannot guess what the context was in the Thalamopoei from which the fragment is preserved. It was the second tragedy in the trilogy of which the Suppliants was the first. The name suggests that it had to do, in part, with the building and adornment of the bridal chambers of the fifty daughters of Danaus. If that is correct, the Lesbian cyma, an apparent anachronism, is transported directly from some fifth century temple to the palace of the Danaids at Argos.

Columns are often mentioned, and all the component parts of a column—base, shaft, and capital. Only once do we find the style of the construction of the shaft specified as built up of drums or monolithic (Mimus [Dec. Laberius] 38–39 R.[2]):

> cum provincias
> dispoliavit, columnas monolitas, labella e balneis

So usual were columns in all sorts of ancient buildings that the absence of them might call for comment (Inc. Inc. Frag. 575 N.):

ἄστυλος οἶκος | a columnless house

The building material of the great temples and other monumental buildings of the classical period receives but the barest allusion. Poros, the local native limestone, is mentioned once by Aristophanes (Ταγ., Frag. 510 K.):

λίθους πωρίνους | poros stone

[1] Cf. Nauck, Fragmenta, 'Ἀδέσποτα 41, p. 847.

And the peerless Parian marble is mentioned once—whether as building material, however, or as material for statues, or both, is not clear (Alex. Ἀρχίλ., Frag. 22 K.):

| | |
|---|---|
| ὦ τὴν εὐτυχῆ ναίων Πάρον, ὄλβιε πρέσβυ, | fortunate old man, to live in happy Paros, |
| ἢ κάλλιστα φέρει χώρα δύο τῶν ἁπασῶν, | the land that produces the two finest things of all, |
| κόσμον μὲν μακάρεσσι λίθον, θνητοῖς δὲ | marble for an adornment for the blessed ones |
| πλακοῦντας | and pancakes for mortals |

There is never the slightest allusion to Pentelic or Hymettian marble, of which the most of the splendid buildings and sculptures of Athens were wrought.

Before turning to the specific buildings that appear in the poets' plays, let us glance for a moment in passing at the tools of the builder's trade that are mentioned in the plays. We find them in considerable variety.

## 2. Tools

The most common of all the tools in the armarium of carpenter or smith is the hammer. It seems to be named but rarely in the extant tragedy (Ae. P. V. 54–65):

| | |
|---|---|
| Η. καὶ δὴ πρόχειρα ψάλια δέρχεσθαι πάρα. | HE. The chains thou mayst see at hand. |
| Κ. βαλών νιν ἀμφὶ χερσίν, ἐγκρατεῖ σθένει | CR. Throw them about his arms; strike with all |
| ῥαιστῆρι θεῖνε, πασσάλευε πρὸς πέτραις. | thy might with the hammer, nail him to the rocks. |
| . . . . . . | . . . . . . |
| Κ. ἄρασσε μᾶλλον, σφίγγε, μηδαμῆ χάλα. | CR. Smite harder; tighten; leave nothing loose. |
| . . . . . . | . . . . . . |
| Κ. καὶ τήνδε νῦν πόρπασον ἀσφαλῶς | CR. Now rivet this other fast |
| Κ. ἀδαμαντίνου νῦν σφηνὸς αὐθάδη γνάθον | CR. Now drive with all thy strength the stubborn jaw of |
| στέρνων διαμπὰξ πασσάλευ' ἐρρωμένως | the adamantine spike straight through his breast |

A different word for "hammer" (τυπάς) is used by Sophocles in a fragment of an unidentified play (Inc. Frag. 760 N.):

| | |
|---|---|
| βᾶτ' εἰς ὁδὸν δὴ πᾶς ὁ χειρῶναξ λεώς, | go into the street, all ye artizan folk |
| οἳ τὴν Διὸς γοργῶπιν Ἐργάνην στατοῖς | who worship before the flashing-eyed Ergane, the daugher of Zeus, |
| λίκνοισι προστρέπεσθε <καὶ> παρ' ἄκμονι | with winnowing-fans set up and with heavy |
| τυπάδι βαρείᾳ | hammer by the anvil |

And still another word for "hammer" (κέστρα) we find used by Sophocles in a fragment of the Aegeus (19 N.):

| | |
|---|---|
| κέστρα σιδηρᾷ πλευρὰ καὶ κατὰ ῥάχιν | with an iron hammer to nail securely along |
| ἡλοῆσαι πλεῖον | the sides and the ridge |

We have other varieties of hammers mentioned in the comedy (Crat. Κλεοβ., Frag. 87 K.):

| | |
|---|---|
| ἔστιν ἄκμων καὶ σφύρα νεανίᾳ εὔτριχι πώλῳ | a sleek young colt has an anvil and a hammer |

What the answer to this riddle is we cannot guess.
(Pl. Ep. 524–525):

malleum
sapientiorem vidi excusso manubrio

(Pl. Men. 403–404):

saepe excussam malleo
quasi suppellex pellionis, palus palo proxumust

Here are hammers, with heads and handles, of various weights, used for driving nails or huge spikes into adamantine rocks or Titanic flesh, for driving pegs into furniture or hulls of ships, for forging upon an anvil, and for riveting chains of Hephaestus's own forging.

Human chains, with rivets and rings, forged for slaves, may be easily broken (Pl. Men. 84–86):

> nam se ex catenis eximunt aliquo modo:
> tum compediti aut anum lima praeterunt
> aut lapide excutiunt clavom

Another of the carpenter's most characteristic tools is his rule or square. We find it Euripides's Hippolytus (468–469):

| | |
|---|---|
| οὐδὲ στέγην γάρ, ἧς κατηρεφεῖς δόμοι, | neither could the rule make absolutely true the roof |
| κανὼν ¹ ἀκριβώσει' ἄν | with which the chambers are covered o'er |

Even the stone-mason works with plummet and straight-edge. The gods, Phoebus and Poseidon, when they rear the towers of windy Ilium, make use of the tools of the trade (Eur. Tro. 4–6):

| | |
|---|---|
| ἐξ οὗ γὰρ ἀμφὶ τήνδε Τρωικὴν χθόνα Φοῖβός τε κἀγὼ λαΐνους πύργους πέριξ ὀρθοῖσιν ἔθεμεν κανόσιν | ever since about this land of Troy Phoebus and I the towers of stone did set with straight-edge and with plummet |

The walls of Priam's Troy, in contradistinction to the Cyclopean masonry of Tiryns and Mycenae and Athens, were built of stones carefully cut and prepared and laid with the accuracy of ashlar masonry. The nature of the walls of City VI at Troy, which we may see to-day, seems to have been well known to the tragic poets of Athens and ascribed to the handiwork of gods (Eur. Tro. 813):

| | |
|---|---|
| κανόνων δὲ τυκίσματα Φοίβου | and the plummet-true masonry of Phoebus |

"Rules" and "squares" may be applied to literature and also to morals (Ar. Ran. 956):

| | |
|---|---|
| λεπτῶν τε κανόνων εἰσβολὰς ἐπῶν τε γωνιασμούς | [ I taught people] to introduce subtle rules and apply squares to verses |

But the mason's straight-edge and the carpenter's rule even more naturally suggest to the tragic poet ethical and moral standards (e. g. Eur. Εὐρ., Frag. 376 N.):

| | |
|---|---|
| οὐκ οἶδ' ὅτῳ χρὴ κανόνι τὰς βροτῶν τύχας ὀρθῶς σταθμήσαντ' εἰδέναι τὸ δραστέον | by measuring human fortunes correctly with some rule or other one should discover what one must do |

(Eur. El. 52–53):

| | |
|---|---|
| γνώμης πονηροῖς κανόσιν ἀναμετρούμενος τὸ σῶφρον | measuring chastity by his own soul's vicious rules |

(Eur. Hec. 602):

| | |
|---|---|
| οἶδεν τό γ' αἰσχρόν, κανόνι τοῦ καλοῦ μαθών | he knows the base, too, learning by honor's rule |

(Eur. Βελ., Frag. 303, 3–5 N.):

| | |
|---|---|
| οὐ γὰρ οὐδένος ἐκφὺς χρόνος δικαίους ἐπάγων κανόνας δείκνυσιν ἀνθρώπων κακότητας ἐμοί | for Time that owns no lineage applies the rules of justice and reveals to me men's wrong-doings |

In these latter citations the word κανών has its primary significance of the craftsman's tool; but in all of them, except the first three, it is used in the figurative, moral sense.

The "canon" may sometimes be a measuring line of much larger unit than the carpenter's rule. Aristophanes brings upon his scene in the Birds Meton (992–1020) the famous astronomer of the fifth century in Athens, the originator of the Metonic cycle—two hundred and thirty-five revolutions of the moon to nineteen of the sun, the numbers of which still persist, under the name of The Golden Numbers, in the Tables prefixed to the Book of

---

¹ The MSS. all read καλῶς. It was corrected to κανών by Musgrave, and the emendation is now generally accepted. In Theod. Inc. Frag. 6 N., the κανόνες are "bars"—the upright bars and the cross bar of the letter H.

Common Prayer. He carries with him various astronomic and geographic apparatus, among the rest of his paraphernalia some "canons of the air." He comes to Cloud-cuckoo-town to get a job as chief engineer, to lay out the new city on the most practical and beautiful plan; he will apply his "canon of the air," set his compasses, square the circle, locate the market-place—the forum—in the center, and have all the main streets radiate from this center in straight lines in every direction—the very prototype of Washington (Ar. Av. 997–1009):

| | |
|---|---|
| ΜΕ.           ὅστις εἴμ' ἐγώ; Μέτων, | ΜΕ. Who I am? Meton, |
| ὃν οἶδεν Ἑλλὰς χὠ Κολωνός. ΠΕ. εἰπέ μοι | whom all Hellas knows—and Colonus. PE. Tell me, |
| ταυτὶ δέ σοι τί ἔστι; ΜΕ. κανόνες ἀέρος. | what is this truck? ME. Air canons. |
| αὐτίκα γὰρ ἀήρ ἐστι τὴν ἰδέαν ὅλος | Why, you know, the atmosphere has the general |
| κατὰ πνιγέα μάλιστα. προσθεὶς οὖν ἐγὼ | form of a Dutch oven. Well then, I will |
| τὸν κανόν' ἄνωθεν τουτονὶ τὸν καμπύλον, | apply this curved measuring line from above, |
| ἐνθεὶς διαβήτην—μανθάνεις; ΠΕ. οὐ μανθάνω. | setting here the point of the compasses— understand? PE. No, I don't. |
| ΜΕ. ὀρθῷ μετρήσω κανόνι προστιθείς, ἵνα | ME. I will apply a straight measuring line and measure it off, so that |
| ὁ κύκλος γένηταί σοι τετράγωνος κἂν μέσῳ | the circle shall be squared and at the center shall be |
| ἀγορά, φέρουσαι δ' ὦσιν εἰς αὐτὴν ὁδοὶ | the forum, and there shall be straight streets |
| ὀρθαὶ πρὸς αὐτὸ τὸ μέσον, ὥσπερ δ' ἀστέρος, | running right into the middle of it, and like the rays |
| αὐτοῦ κυκλοτεροῦς ὄντος, ὀρθαὶ πανταχῆ | of the luminary, which is itself a perfect circle, running off |
| ἀκτῖνες ἀπολάμπωσιν | in straight lines in every direction |

The engineer from Athens, with its narrow, crooked streets, thought he had found in this newly prospected town the opportunity of an age to plot it out artistically and conveniently. Incidentally we have the civil engineer's measuring line introduced and another instrument of the worker in the realm of mathematics—the compasses (see below pp. 37–38).

The plumb-line or chalk-line for securing a straight edge we find mentioned in its literal sense in a fragment of Sophocles (Κηδ., Frag. 307 N.):[1]

| | |
|---|---|
| τοῖς μὲν λόγοις τοῖς σοῖσιν οὐ τεκμαίρομαι | by thy words I do not reach a conclusion any |
| οὐ μᾶλλον ἢ λευκῷ λίθῳ λευκὴ στάθμη | more than one is guided by a white chalk-line upon white marble |

The comparison is so clear that we can fairly see the chalk-line, snapped against a column, for example, to get the line for the fluting; but as white chalk would be unsatisfactory upon white marble, leaving no visible mark, the stone-cutters used vermilion upon their plumb-line, and of it we have seen traces even in our day upon unfinished buildings of antiquity. Euripides also makes mention of the red chalk-line in the building of the walls of Mycenae (H. F. 944–945):

| | |
|---|---|
| τὰ Κυκλώπων βάθρα | the Cyclopes' rising walls, |
| φοίνικι κανόνι καὶ τύκοις ἡρμοσμένα | fitted with the red chalk-line and mason's picks |

The connection here makes it clear that the red chalk-line or rule was drawn across the face of an ashlar block to reveal possible unevennesses on the surface of the stone; and where the chalk marks showed, the stone-cutter must chip further with his pick-chisel and secure a perfect facing.

The craftsman's procedure is further suggested in Sophocles's Oenomaus (Frag. 433, 3–5 N.):

| | |
|---|---|
| ἐξοπτᾷ δ' ἐμὲ, | he [Pelops] setteth me [Hippodamia] on fire, |
| ἴσον μετρῶν ὀφθαλμόν, ὥστε τέκτονος | measuring with a correcting eye, as, when the builder |
| παρὰ στάθμην ἰόντος ὀρθοῦται κανών | has recourse to his chalk-string, the line is corrected |

---

[1] So also in Homer; ρ 341.

In these three lines we have the builder, the chalk-line, and the rule.  And even the line drawn by the rule is corrected by the chalk-line.

In Euripides's Ion (1512–1514) the chalk-line marks the razor-edge of a crisis and passing it on either side, like missing the edge of the flutings of a Doric column, would bring disaster:

| | |
|---|---|
| ὦ μεταβαλοῦσα μυρίους ἤδη βροτῶν | oh Fortune, thou that ere now hast wrought changes with countless |
| καὶ δυστυχῆσαι καὖθις αὖ πρᾶξαι καλῶς, Τύχη, παρ' οἵαν ἤλθομεν στάθμην βίου | mortals, from weal to woe and from woe to weal again, to what a chalk-line of life did we come! |

στάθμη is similarly used in Aeschylus's Agamemnon (1045):

| | |
|---|---|
| ὠμοί τε δούλοις πάντα καὶ παρὰ στάθμην | and harsh are we to slaves in all things and beyond measure |

Still another tool from the stone-cutter's kit is the pick-chisel used for fast execution in working down a piece of stone.  We find it in the passage just quoted (p. 36) from Euripides (H. F. 945) and again in the same tragedy, ll. 1096–1097:

| | |
|---|---|
| πρὸς ἡμιθραύστῳ λαΐνῳ τυκίσματι ἧμαι | I sit here bound to this hewn stone now cleft in twain |

The finished product of the stone-cutter's work with the pick-chisel is found again in the well smoothed masonry of Homeric Troy (Eur. Tro. 813):

| | |
|---|---|
| κανόνων δὲ τυκίσματα Φοίβου | and the plummet-true masonry of Phoebus |

The same imagery is presented in the adjective εὔτυχος "well chiseled"   (Ae. Sup. 959):

| | |
|---|---|
| ἔνθ' ἔστιν ὑμῖν εὐτύχους ναίειν δόμους | there it is yours to dwell in houses well chiseled |

In this line the word is used in its literal sense; in the two following, it is used figuratively (Ae. Sup. 972–973):

| | |
|---|---|
| πᾶς τις ἐπειπεῖν ψόγον ἀλλοθρόοις εὔτοχος | everybody is well prepared to utter reproaches against foreigners |

(ibid. 994):

| | |
|---|---|
| πᾶς δ' ἐν μετοίκῳ γλῶσσαν εὔτυχον φέρει | everyone hath a tongue ready against the alien |

In Euripides's Mad Heracles (943–946) we find a considerable collection of the stone-worker's tools—some for constructing, some for demolishing walls of stone.  Heracles, in his madness, thinks he is starting off on an expedition to capture Mycenae, destroy the castle, and slay his hated master:

| | |
|---|---|
| πρὸς τὰς Μυκήνας εἶμι· λάζυσθαι χρεὼν μοχλοὺς δικέλλας θ', ὡς τὰ Κυκλώπων βάθρα | to Mycenae I go!  Crowbars and pickaxes must I take along to shatter with the curved steel the |
| φοίνικι κανόνι καὶ τύκοις ἡρμοσμένα στρεπτῷ σιδήρῳ συντριαινώσω πόλιν | city, its Cyclopes' walls fitted with the red chalk-line and mason's picks |

The crowbars and pickaxes are for tearing down the blocks of masonry; the chalk-line and the pick-chisels have been discussed in the foregoing pages.

The brick-mason, however, whether he was working with sun-dried or with kiln-burned bricks, must have a trowel (ὑπαγωγεύς), which Suidas explains as an iron tool, shaped like a winnowing-fan and used by plasterers for spreading mortar and also by brick-layers in laying their bricks in straight courses.  The word occurs but twice (Hermip. 'Ιαμβ., Frag. 69 K.; Ar. Av. 1149 (see above, p. 29).

Another tool of the craftsman mentioned by the poets is the compass for drawing a circle (Eur. Θησ., Frag. 382, 3–4 N.):

| | |
|---|---|
| κύκλος τις ὡς τόρνοισιν ἐκμετρούμενος, | a circle accurately drawn as with a pair of compasses, |
| οὗτος δ' ἔχει σημεῖον ἐν μέσῳ σαφές | and this has in its center a distinct mark |

A herdsman, one who does not know his letters, is describing an inscription that he had found, the first letter of which is the initial letter of the name of Theseus. The main body of Θ as executed in the inscription is a perfect circle drawn as with a pair of compasses.

The method of working with the compass is made a little clearer in a much misunderstood passage in Euripides's Bacchae (1066–1067):

| | |
|---|---|
| κυκλοῦτο δ' ὥστε τόξον ἢ κυρτὸς τροχός, | and it was arched as a bow or as a rounded wheel, |
| τόρνῳ γραφόμενος περιφοράν, ἕλκει δρόμον | when its periphery is being marked out with the compasses, traces its circle |

τόρνῳ here is often explained as a lathe for cutting out a chariot wheel. But it is not a turning lathe in these lines any more than it is a turning-lathe in the fragment just quoted. One does not use a lathe for turning out the circle of the letter Θ. The tool is obviously a compass. It may be a good mechanical tool with two arms and a joint connecting them, one arm provided with a point for a pivot and the other with a piece of chalk or crayon to draw the circle; or it may be an implement improvised from a string with a peg at one end and a piece of chalk or crayon at the other. But in either case we have a compass, and the explanation of τόρνος as a turning-lathe goes wide of the mark.

The circle described by a pair of compasses is also mentioned (Eur. H. F. 977–978):

| | |
|---|---|
| ὁ δ' ἐξελίσσων παῖδα κίονος κύκλῳ | but he, chasing the lad about the column |
| τόρνευμα δεινὸν ποδός... | in hideous circling course . . . |

τόρνευμα is again the line drawn by the compass or by the chalk, at the end of the string held fast by a peg, or otherwise, as a center.[1]

But there are also passages in the dramatic poets in which τόρνος may be taken as a turning-lathe. It is such a mechanism, beyond a doubt, in a fragment of Aeschylus ('Hδ., Frag. 57, 2–4 N.):

| | |
|---|---|
| ὁ μὲν ἐν χερσὶν | but he, holding in his |
| βόμβυκας ἔχων, τόρνου κάματον, | hands the flutes, the work of the lathe, |
| δακτυλόδικτον πίμπλησι μέλος | executes a melody thrown from the fingers |

The turning-lathe, on which pipes were turned out, differed in no essential from the simple foot-lathe of our own days.

The more technical word for compasses we find in Aristophanes's Clouds (177–178):

| | |
|---|---|
| κατὰ τῆς τραπέζης καταπάσας λεπτὴν τέφραν, | he sprinkled some fine ashes on the table, |
| κάμψας ὀβελίσκον, εἶτα διαβήτην λαβὼν | bent a skewer, took that as a pair of compasses and |

The word διαβήτης, a thing with "spreading-legs," aptly fits the instrument. Socrates has improvised a pair of compasses from a skewer lying near the altar in the palaestra; and this he uses to measure off in the ashes the distance between the footprints of the hopping flea.

A more scientific pair of compasses is that of the astronomer-engineer, Meton, in the passage quoted above (p. 36) from the Birds of Aristophanes, which that famous man of science proposes to use in drafting his plans for the new city of Cloud-cuckoo-town (Ar. Av. 1001–1003):

| | |
|---|---|
| προσθεὶς οὖν ἐγὼ | well then, I will |
| τὸν κανόν' ἄνωθεν τουτονὶ τὸν καμπύλον, | apply this curved measuring line from above, |
| ἐνθεὶς διαβήτην | setting here the point of the compasses |

The ancient mathematician's compasses or dividers, whether τορνός or διαβήτης, were apparently very like those we use in modern times.

The bow-drill is a familiar tool in the woodworker's shop, not only from the days of Homer,[2] but from ages before Homer, as we see it upon the walls of tombs of the Fourth

---

[1] Sandys, on Eur. Bacch. 1066, cites a number of passages from other Greek authors in which τόρνος and other words from the same root are used: Hdt. IV 36; Plat. Phil. 51C, 56B, Critias 113D, Tim. 33B; Arist. de Mundo 391b 22; Theognis 805; Dionys. Perieg. 157.

[2] ι 384 sqq.

Dynasty in Egypt.[1] Euripides may have had the Homeric passage clearly in mind as he wrote, but he himself also was no more stranger to the bow-drill in his own time than is the locksmith of to-day (Eur. Cy. 460–463):[2]

| | |
|---|---|
| ναυπηγίαν δ' ὡσεί τις ἁρμόζων ἀνὴρ<br>διπλοῖν χαλινοῖν τρύπανον κωπηλατεῖ, | and as a man working at shipbuilding drives<br>backwards and forwards with two thongs his<br>   drill, |
| οὕτω κυκλώσω δαλὸν ἐν φαεσφόρῳ<br>Κύκλωπος ὄψει καὶ συναυανῶ κόρας | so will I twirl the stake in the Cyclops's<br>eye of light and singe up his eyeball |

The bow-drill was an indispensable everyday tool in the kit of the worker in wood and metal and probably also in stone. The method of working it is clearly suggested in the passage just quoted. By the two thongs he does not, of course, mean two different straps or ropes, but Odysseus is speaking of the two ends of the same driving appliance. The process is brought out again in the same play, as Odysseus directs one and another of his companions in the act of boring out the Cyclops's eye (661):

| | |
|---|---|
| τόρνευ᾽, ἕλκε | twist; pull |

Very common tools in the crafts of all ages are the pincers and the vise (καρκίνος). The first meaning of the word is "crab." Doubtless from the claws of the beast and the pinching power in them, καρκίνος came to mean also a pair of pincers or tongs, or even a vise. In the latter sense it seems to be used, like the Latin *forceps*, in Euripides's Cyclops (608–610):

| | |
|---|---|
| λήψεται τὸν τράχηλον<br>ἐντόνως ὁ καρκίνος<br>τοῦ ξένων δαιτυμόνος | like a vise one will lay firm<br>hold upon the throat of<br>the brute that feeds on strangers |

Odysseus and his companions are just about to execute their vengeance upon Polyphemus; the chorus indulges in a lively anticipation of the operation. They see in fancy the glowing brand hidden in the ashes, and the Cyclops in his drunken stupor caught round the neck with a vise-like grip by one of Odysseus's men and held fast while the stake is plunged into his eye. It is the same situation as that in which, as Acheloüs describes himself, Heracles caught and held fast the river-god (Ov. Met. IX 78):

| | |
|---|---|
| angebar ceu guttura forcipe pressus | my mind was shut off as if my throat were held<br>   fast in a vise |

The frequent rendering of καρκίνος or *forceps* in these passages by "tongs" prompts the question as to who in the world would ever think of using tongs to throttle a person, or how it could be done.

The carpenter's saw and adze we might expect to find often in the comedy; but there they do not occur at all. The only place in which we do find them in the drama is in a fragment of Sophocles, and even in this we find nothing but the words (Inc. Frag. 729 N.):

| | |
|---|---|
| οὐ σκέπαρνος οὐδὲ πρίονος<br>πληγαί | not an adze nor strokes<br>of saw |

Certain technical processes also occasionally come in for mention in the poets. We have already seen the employment of steel implements in shaping the woodwork of temples, and of pegs and dowels for joining pieces of wood together, and the use of glue for fastening tight the joints. The shipwright followed the same mechanical technique, of course, even as the builder of wooden ships does unto this day (Ae. Sup. 843–846):

| | |
|---|---|
| εἴθ᾽ ἀνὰ...<br>ἁλμήεντα πόρον | would that upon the . . .<br>briny deep thou hadst |
| . . . . . . . .<br>γομφοδέτῳ τε δορὶ διώλου | . . . . . . .<br>perished with thy peg-fastened bark |

[1] The tomb of Ti, e. g., at Memphis (Sakkara).
[2] The ἀχάλκευτα τρύπανα of Soph. Φιν., Frag. 642 N., are explained by Hes. as "kindling wood."

And in the same manner the cartwright accomplishes much of the work of his trade by means of pegs and glue (Ar. Eq. 461–464):

ΠΑ. ταυτὶ μὰ τὴν Δήμητρά μ' οὐκ ἐλάνθανεν
τεκταινόμενα τὰ πράγματ', ἀλλ' ἠπιστάμην
γομφούμεν' αὐτὰ πάντα καὶ κολλώμενα.

PA. By Demeter, I failed not to see that such schemes were building, but I did realize that all those things were being pegged and glued together.

ΧΟ. οἴμοι, σὺ δ' οὐδὲν ἐξ ἀμαξουργοῦ λέγεις;

CHO. Dear me! Can't *you* say something from the cartwright's trade?

But the sausage-seller takes his metaphor from the blacksmith instead (*ibid.* 468–470):

καὶ ταῦτ' ἐφ' οἶσίν ἐστι συμφυσώμενα

and I know on what anvil these schemes are forged:

ἐγῷδ'· ἐπὶ γὰρ τοῖς δεδομένοις χαλκεύεται.
ΧΟ. εὖ γε, εὖ γε, χάλκευ' ἀντὶ τῶν κολλωμένων

they are welded on the prisoners.
CHO. Good! good! weld instead of glue!

The carpenter sometimes finds it necessary to splice out a piece of his material with wooden dowels. Such an instance we have in a fragment of Euripides's Erechtheus (Frag. 360, 11–13 N.):

ὅστις δ' ἀπ' ἄλλης πόλεως οἰκήσῃ πόλιν
ἁρμὸς πονηρὸς ὥσπερ ἐν ξύλῳ παγείς,
λόγῳ πολίτης ἐστί, τοῖς δ' ἔργοισιν οὔ

if a man moves from one city to dwell in another, he is like a weak splice made in a piece of lumber —in word he is a citizen but not in deed

The maker of metal tools must forge and temper them. An allusion to the process of forging we find in Aeschylus's Septem (206–208):

ἱππικῶν τ' ἀγρύπνων
πηδαλίων διὰ στόματα
πυριγενετᾶν χαλινῶν

and the sleepless guiding-gear
in the horses' mouths, the
fire-born bridles

The bits are born of fire—heated in the forge, hammered out, heated again and hammered again, until they are ready for the tempering.

A further allusion to the tempering of steel is found in Sophocles's Ajax (650-652):

κἀγὼ γάρ, ὃς τὰ δείν' ἐκαρτέρουν τότε,
βαφῇ σίδηρος ὥς ἐθηλύνθην στόμα
πρὸς τῆσδε τῆς γυναικός

for I, too, who once was so fearfully hard,
like iron tempered by the plunge, have now had
my tongue unmanned by this woman's words

The red-hot iron is plunged into the cold water to give it temper—a process known even in the Homeric age (ι 392).

The highly tempered steel of the ancient Greeks was, apparently, as sensitive and fragile as is the finest cutlery of to-day (Soph. Ant. 474–476):

τὸν ἐγκρατέστατον
σίδηρον ὀπτὸν ἐκ πυρὸς περισκελῆ
θραυσθέντα καὶ ῥαγέντα πλεῖστ' ἂν ἐπίδοις

the hardest
steel, heated to high temper in the fire,
thou mayst most often see snapped and shivered

The old Greeks knew how to temper bronze as well as steel. An instance of the tempering of bronze we have in Aeschylus's Agamemnon (611–612):

οὐκ οἶδα τέρψιν οὐδ' ἐπίψογον φάτιν
ἄλλου πρὸς ἀνδρὸς μᾶλλον ἢ χαλκοῦ βαφάς

nor know I more of dalliance or rumor of shame
from other man than—how to plunge the bronze

with, of course, the hideous double meaning of 1) plunging the bronze into the bath to temper it and 2) plunging the bronze into the heart of her husband. The tempering of bronze is now a lost art, but a part of the process was very like the simple way of putting temper into steel.

The forging was performed on an anvil. The great artificer uses a heavy anvil in forging the armor for Achilles (Σ 476); Pseudolus, in Plautus's play, will forge tricks on an anvil of cunning (Ps. 614):

haec mihi incus est: procudam ego hinc hodie multos dolos

We have often wondered how the contractors for the buildings upon the Acropolis and other such places with steep approaches got their building material up. The heavier pieces were drawn up over devices like the ways of a shipyard, up an inclined railway as it were, with windlasses; the less heavy material was hoisted directly from the first slopes of the Acropolis to the summit with derrick and pulley. While the work was still progressing on the Erechtheum, the various members of Lysistrate's band of women in possession of the Acropolis attempt to desert and go home: one of them sneaks out through Pan's grotto; another uses one subterfuge, and another another; one desperate dame slips down with the help of a windlass—presumably one of the derricks for hoisting building material up the precipitous north side of the Acropolis, crowned with its Themistoclean or Cimonian wall (Ar. Lys. 722):

τὴν δ' ἐκ τροχιλίας αὖ κατειλυσπωμένην | another slipping down with the help of a windlass

This hoisting machine, with its pulley-wheels and windlass turned by hand, could not have been very different from its modern counterpart.

## IV. TEMPLES

Many temples are definitely named in the dramas. Some, like the temple of Apollo at Delphi, the Artemisium in Tauria, and the Aphrodisium in Cyrene, occupy the center of the scene throughout the Ion, the Iphigenia Taurica, and the Rudens respectively. It is to be expected that they should also figure in the development of the plot. Many other temples play a more or less prominent part in the action of many ancient plays. Let us take them up in the order of their importance.

### 1. The Temple of Athena

*The* temple of Athena is, of course, the great temple in the centre of Athena-worship, the Parthenon upon the Acropolis of Athens. Contemporary authors, strange to say, have practically nothing to tell of it. In the nineteen extant plays of Euripides the artist-poet does not name it; he makes direct mention of it only once, in a fragment of the Erechtheus. Apparently, the Parthenon spoke for itself in tones so sublime that words of praise or appreciation could only detract from its transcendent perfection.

The only passage in all extant Greek drama in which the name Parthenon occurs is an unidentified comic fragment ('Αδέσπ., 340 K.):

| | |
|---|---|
| δέσποιν' ἁπασῶν πότνι', 'Αθηναίων πόλι, | mistress of the world, august city of Athens, |
| ὡς παγκαλόν σου φαίνεται τὸ νεώριον, | how perfectly beautiful seems thy arsenal, |
| ὡς καλὸς ὁ Παρθενών, καλὸς δ' ὁ Πειραιεύς. | how beautiful the Parthenon, and how beautiful the Piraeus! |
| ἄλση δὲ τίς πω τοιάδ' ἔσχ' ἄλλη πόλις; | What other city ever had such parks? |
| καὶ τοὐρανοῦ γ', ὥς φασιν, ἐστὶν ἐν καλῷ | It stands, as they say, in the beauty of heaven! |

The Parthenon was "beautiful" in the eyes of this unknown comic poet; but the ship-yards and docks and slips of the harbors about Munychia receive a more enthusiastic epithet! With this single exception, we find in the dramatic poets only allusions, more or less remote, to the one perfect thing that man's hand has created since the world began. One such distant allusion we have in a fragment of Euripides's Erechtheus (Frag. 369 N.):

| | |
|---|---|
| κείσθω δόρυ μοι μίτον ἀμφιπλέκειν ἀράχναις, | let my spear be laid away for spiders to spin their webs about it, |
| μετὰ δ' ἡσυχίας πολιῷ γήρᾳ συνοικοίην· | and may I dwell in silvered old age in peace. |
| ἀείδοιμι δὲ στεφάνοις κάρα πολιὸν στεφανώσας | May it be mine to sing, crowned with a garland twined about my hoary head, |
| Θρηίκιον πέλταν πρὸς 'Αθάνας | when that I have hung up a Thracian targe upon |
| περικίοσιν ἀγκρεμάσας θαλάμοις | Athena's pillar-girdled chambers, |
| δέλτων τ' ἀναπτύσσοιμι γῆρυν | and to unroll the message of the books |
| ἂν σοφοὶ κλέονται | which wise men bring to fame |

Athena's "pillar-girdled chambers" in a melic portion of the Erechtheus cannot very well be anything other than the Parthenon. But Euripides's words tell us nothing about it except that it was surrounded by a colonnade; that it contained more than one room; that it had, even in Euripides's day, captured shields riveted upon its architrave. Would that we had the entire tragedy! A play under that title should be particularly fruitful for our present studies.

Another allusion, slightly more definite, is found in Euripides's Phoenissae (1372–1373):

| | |
|---|---|
| Παλλάδος χρυσάσπιδος | he turned his eyes toward the house of |
| βλέψας πρὸς οἶκον ηὔξατο | Pallas of the golden shield and prayed |

The "Pallas of the golden shield" can well be none other than Phidias's gold and ivory indweller of the Parthenon; and her "dwelling" must be the Parthenon itself. But again Euripides refuses to give us any information about it.

THE PARTHENON

It is, of course, probable that in the Phoenissae Euripides would have us think of Eteocles turning to face the temple of Athena at Thebes, not at Athens. But his words must make every reader, as they must have made every spectator in the Athenian theatre, think of the temple upon the Acropolis in Athens.

The scene of Plautus's Bacchides is laid in Athens. We might have expected Plautus's Greek original of this comedy to have given us much valuable information about his city and its temples and Plautus to have followed him. But all such hopes prove vain. There is one reference to the temple of Minerva—doubtless the Parthenon—but it tells us only that the building was at that particular time open and that Bacchis had gone to see it (ll. 900–901):

> illa autem in arcem abivit aedem visere
> Minervae. nunc apertast. i, vise estne ibi.

Aristophanes twice refers to the opisthodome of the Parthenon, which, as we know abundantly from other sources, was the chief treasury of Athens as the head of the powerful maritime empire known as the Delian Confederation (Lys. 173–174):

| | |
|---|---|
| οὐχ ἇς πόδας κ' ἔχωντι ταὶ τριήρεις<br>καὶ τὠργύριον τὤβυσσον ᾇ πὰρ τᾷ σιῷ | nay; not so long as the galleys have tackle<br>and there is the inexhaustible supply of funds at the goddess's |

At the outbreak of the Peloponnesian War there were, among many other treasures in the Opisthodome, the "Parthenon" proper, six thousand talents of silver, of which one thousand talents were specially set apart for some critical emergency. Throughout nearly twenty years of the exhausting war that fund remained untouched; it was only in the archonship of Callias (412–411), in which year the Lysistrata was produced, that the Athenians were compelled to draw upon this special fund. And it is to that "inexhaustible" supply of funds in the opisthodome of the Parthenon that Lampito, the speaker of these lines, alludes.[1] Before the war was concluded, however, the treasury of the Parthenon was exhausted. And it was only after the war was well over, and Athens turned to the pursuits of peace, that prosperity came again, and the coffers of the state began once more to fill. Then the little Plutus under the fostering care of Irene grew and prospered, and by and by Plutus is established again in his old shrine in Athena's opisthodome. This is the direct allusion in Aristophanes's Plutus (1191–1193):

| | |
|---|---|
| ἱδρυσόμεσθ' αὐτίκα μάλ', ἀλλὰ περίμενε,<br>τὸν Πλοῦτον, οὕπερ πρότερον ἦν ἱδρυμένος,<br>τὸν ὀπισθόδομον ἀεὶ φυλάττων τῆς θεοῦ | nay, wait; we'll consecrate Plutus right<br>away, where aforetime he was consecrated,<br>forever keeping the goddess's opisthodome |

The allusion is perfectly clear: the opisthodome is the "Parthenon," in the technical use of that name; it was the treasury of Athens and, as such, the most appropriate place imaginable for the sanctuary of the god of wealth; there he had been installed as presiding divinity long ago; from it he had been removed by the terrible war; and there he is, with the return of peace and prosperity, to be reinstalled; the State Treasury is his peculiar sanctuary.[2]

In still another passage Aristophanes makes less direct allusion to the Opisthodome as the depository of this special fund. He locates it upon the Acropolis; it must be the fund deposited in the State Treasury of the Opisthodome for safe-keeping, though he does not name the building. The pacifist, suffragette politicians of the Lysistrata have seized the Acropolis and when called upon for an explanation of their extraordinary conduct they justify themselves by assigning as their motive in seizing and holding the citadel the following (Ar. Lys. 488–489; 491–496):

| | |
|---|---|
| ΛΥ. ἵνα τἀργύριον σῶν παρέχοιμεν καὶ<br>    μὴ πολεμοῖτε δι' αὐτό.<br>ΠΡ. διὰ τἀργύριον πολεμοῦμεν γάρ; ΛΥ....<br>. . . . . . . . . . . . .<br>...οἱ δ' οὖν τοῦδ' οὕνεκα δρώντων<br>ὅ τι βούλονται· τὸ γὰρ ἀργύριον τοῦτ' οὐκέτι<br>        καθέλωσιν. | LY. That we may keep the funds safe and that you may not go to war for them.<br>PR. What! we go to war for the funds! LY. . . .<br>. . . . . . . .<br>. . . And for all that, let them do just what they please; for they'll never get their hands on the funds. |

---

[1] Cf. also Ar. Lys. 624–626.
[2] This same passage is further discussed Vol. II, Chap. IV 2 d.

ΠΡ. ἀλλὰ τί δράσεις; ΛΥ.... ἡμεῖς ταμιευ-
                  σομεν αὐτό.
ΠΡ. ὑμεῖς ταμιεύσετε τἀργύριον; ΛΥ. τί
        δὲ δεινὸν τοῦτο νομίζεις;
  οὐ καὶ τἄνδον χρήματα πάντως ἡμεῖς
          ταμιεύομεν ὑμῖν;
ΠΡ. ἀλλ' οὐ ταὐτόν. ΛΥ. πῶς οὐ ταὐτόν;
ΠΡ. πολεμητέον ἔστ' ἀπὸ τούτου.

PR. But what will you do? LY. We'll be the stewards of them.
PR. You the stewards of the funds! LY. What do you find strange about that?
Is it not we that all the time are stewards of your moneys at home?
PR. But that is not the same thing. LY. Of course it is the same thing. PR. But we have to use these funds for prosecuting the war!

The whole point of the passage turns on the special fund set aside for emergency—primarily, of course, a war emergency. The war party, after the disasters in Sicily and Euboea, faces a crisis to meet which the funds in the Opisthodome are indispensable. The suffragette wing of the peace party takes possession of the Acropolis and all that is contained within the enclosing walls, in order to force the issue and bring about an immediate peace. With the Acropolis securely held, the sinews of war are in their hands to "administer" (ταμιεύειν) in the interests of peace.

An allusion to the Periclean Parthenon may be seen also in a fragment from the Thalamopoei of Aeschylus (Frag. 78 N.), discussed on page 33. The description contained in those two lines fits exactly the lacunaria of the ceiling of the colonnade of the Parthenon and is complete save for the gilded star in the depths of the lacunar.

## 2. The Hecatompedon

The Periclean Parthenon could not well be introduced into tragedy save by way of indirect allusion. But the pre-Persian temple of Athena, "the Old Temple," may play an active part in the settings of a play dealing with times long gone by. And such a part it does play in the Eumenides. The central scene of the Eumenides is the Old Temple of Athena upon the Acropolis,[1] a very ancient building containing the sanctuary of Athena and Erechtheus at the east, the treasury of the city, that of Athena, and that of the other gods at the west—a simple Doric *templum in antis*, until Pisistratus provided it with a peripteral colonnade and other adornments. With a shifting of scenery this old "Hecatompedon," as it was called, takes the place of the Delphic temple in the first part of the play. To it Orestes, in flight before the avengers of blood, comes and falls a suppliant at Athena's ancient statue (see also Vol. II, Chap. II 4) (Ae. Eum. 235; 242–243):

ἄνασσ' Ἀθάνα...
πρόσειμι δῶμα καὶ βρέτας τὸ σόν, θεά,

αὐτοῦ φυλάσσων ἀναμενῶ τέλος δίκης

sovereign Athena . . .
to thy dwelling and to thine image, goddess, I come.
Here watching will I await the outcome of the trial

The "image" is the all-holy figure of wood that fell from heaven; its place was in the old temple; it was a place of refuge for the persecuted and the guilty; temple and image are represented on the scene. The scenic temple door is open; the image stands by the goddess's altar—not the great altar before the temple but the ἑστία, the hearth, the inner altar of the temple (Ae. Eum. 439–440):

εἴπερ πεποιθὼς τῇ δίκῃ βρέτας τόδε
ἧσαι φυλάσσων ἑστίας ἀμῆς πέλας

if trusting in the justice of thy cause thou sittest here
keeping close to that image hard by my hearth

And further on in the same play the "hearth" of the goddess is definitely located in her "halls" (Ae. Eum. 669):

καὶ τόνδ' ἔπεμψα σῶν δόμων ἐφέστιον

and him have I sent to take his place at the hearth of thy halls

---

[1] For a discussion of the pre-Persian Athena Temple, its history and vicissitudes, see author's "Hist. of the Acrop.," A. J. A. 1893, pp. 499–503; 510; 512–513; 523–528.

THE OLD TEMPLE OF ATHENA
(From the roof of the Parthenon)

THE ARCHITRAVE, FRIEZE, AND CORNICE

of the Old Temple of Athena, built into the North Wall of the Acropolis

The plural form (δόμων) is used as if in the conscious intention to bring out the plurality of rooms in the old temple,[1] as the King does in Aeschylus's Suppliants (365–366):

| | |
|---|---|
| κάθησθε δωμάτων ἐφέστιοι ἐμῶν | ye sit at the hearth of my halls |

But the plural form here may have reference to more than one temple of Athena upon the Acropolis, as the plural ναῶν "shrines" almost certainly does in Euripides's Ion (495–498):

| | |
|---|---|
| ἵνα χοροὺς στείβουσι ποδοῖν Ἀγραύλου κόρα τρίγονοι στάδια χλοερὰ πρὸ Παλλάδος ναῶν | where the maidens three to Agraulus born tread with their feet the dance o'er the grassy lawns before Pallas's shrines |

There were many shrines of Pallas upon the Acropolis in the fifth century: the old Athena temple, the sanctuary of Athena in the Erechtheum, the Parthenon, the Athena Ergane, Athena Hygiea, Athena Nike, and perhaps more.

This old seat of Athena worship is older than Homer. In the old days of Mycenaean culture, Athena had a shrine within the palace gates of the feudal prince. Such must be the meaning of Homer's words where Athena, after accompanying Odysseus to the house of Alcinous, left him at the doors (η 80–81):

| | |
|---|---|
| ἵκετο δ' ἐς Μαραθῶνα καὶ εὐρυάγυιαν Ἀθήνην, δῦνε δ' Ἐρεχθῆος πυκινὸν δόμον | and came to Marathon and wide-wayed Athens and entered the goodly house of Erechtheus |

The "goodly house of Erechtheus" is that old Mycenaean Erechtheid palace—the great complex, like the palace of Tiryns, occupying in that age the greater part of the Acropolis. Athena came to Athens and entered the goodly house of Erechtheus for no other possible reason than that she had a sanctuary located within the gates of that palace and forming a part of it. Aeschylus, too, harking back to Homer, identifies the temple of Athena with the house of Erechtheus (Eum. 854–856):

| | |
|---|---|
| καὶ σὺ τιμίαν ἕδραν ἔχουσα πρὸς δόμοις Ἐρεχθέως τεύξει κτλ. | and thou [the Eumenides] shalt occupy a seat of honor before the halls of Erechtheus and receive etc. |

That is, ye shall be *my* next-door neighbors; for the house of Erechtheus implies the shrine of Athena; for the house is not that of Erechtheus alone but of Athena as well.[2] And Aeschylus does not fail to identify the δόμοι (Eum. 473–474):

| | |
|---|---|
| κατηρτυκὼς ἐμοῖς ἱκέτης προσῆλθες καθαρὸς ἀβλαβὴς δόμοις | with all due rites performed, thou hast come a suppliant pure and guiltless to my halls |

The halls of Erechtheus and the halls of Athena are in the same great complex of buildings, and the halls of Athena are to Aeschylus, as the only thing he knew surviving from that hoary age, the chambers (four, not counting the vestibules) of the old temple of Athena that he had seen with all the glories bestowed upon it by the tyrants, in the smoke and ruin wrought by the Persian, and in its restoration after Salamis—the great shrine of the Polias at the time of the production of the trilogy (458 B. C.). The likeness of it in the theatre—with its stately Pisistratic colonnade removed and with other marks of the havoc created by the savages from the east visible upon it—must have deeply stirred the hearts of the Athenians in the theatre, as they listened to the story so wondrously told of their most time-honored traditions.

## 3. THE TEMPLE OF APOLLO AT DELPHI

### a. *Exterior*

By far the most hopeful group of citations are those that describe or allude to the Pythian temple of Apollo at "earth's central shrine."[3] Euripides saw in all its glory of Parian marble

---

[1] The phrasing is almost identical with that of vss. 577–578 (καὶ δόμων ἐφέστιος | ἐμῶν), where Apollo speaks of his own hearth and halls, the great temple of Delphi with its various rooms. See also p. 68.
[2] Cp. also B 546–549 and the discussion in A. J. A. VIII, pp. 477 ff.
[3] Soph. O. T. 480–481.

and rich plastic decoration the splendid temple finished, if not entirely built, by the Alcmaeonidae in the last quarter of the sixth century B. C.  The few details that he gives us are the more valuable, because that temple was destroyed by an earthquake in the early part of the fourth century (probably in 373).  Pausanias's description, accordingly, and the remnants recovered by the French in their excavations at Delphi set before us the new temple, rebuilt after that disaster and rededicated about 330.  Many inscriptions containing building accounts connected with the restoration have been found and fix the dates beyond a peradventure.  Little is left of the sixth century temple except the foundation walls in part, some blocks of Parian marble from the façade of the building of the Alcmaeonidae built by the restorers into the foundation walls at the west end, and a few pieces of archaic sculpture from the pediments.  Pausanias gives[1] a sketch of the history of the temple from the earliest mythical times to his own—except for the destruction and the rebuilding or rebuildings of the fourth century and later.  How that escaped him I do not know; but the oversight got him into no end of trouble, for he thought that he had before him the temple built by the Alcmaeonids, with the plastic decorations of the sixth century, and tried to fit the fourth century B. C. or first century A. D. reality into his sixth century theory.  But there are few temples of antiquity in regard to which we are so well informed as we are in regard to this Alcmaeonid temple at Delphi.  Through Herodotus especially we are told its date, architect, contractors, builders, material, cost, and so forth.

After the fire of 548–7 B. C.,[2] "the Amphictyons contracted to have a new temple built for three hundred talents, of which the people of Delphi were to contribute one fourth.  To defray the rest of the cost emissaries went the round of the cities soliciting subscriptions."[3] The contract (or at least the contract for the completion of the temple[4]) was undertaken by the noble Athenian family of the Alcmaeonidae, then in exile and eager to secure their restoration to Athens together with the downfall of the tyrants, the sons of Pisistratus, by whom they had been banished.  Hence, to propitiate the god, or rather the priestly officials who worked the oracle, not to mention the Spartans and Amphictyons, they rebuilt the temple in more splendid style than had been stipulated in the contract, by constructing the façade of Parian marble instead of common stone.  This they were able to do out of the wealth they had inherited from a long line of distinguished ancestors.  Such is the account which Herodotus gives[5] of this transaction.  Other writers, however, place the action of the Alcmaeonids in a much less favorable light.  They tell us that, far from expending their private fortune in rebuilding the temple, the Alcmaeonids as a last resort undertook the contract for the purpose of providing themselves with funds to be used in their machinations against the sons of Pisistratus[6]; Pausanias[7] and Strabo[8] do not refer to the Alcmaeonids at all in this connection, simply stating that the temple of their day was built by the Amphictyons.  To this Pausanias adds that the expenses were defrayed out of the sacred treasures and that the architect was Spintharus of Corinth.

That the temple was built, and in a style of some magnificence, by the Alcmaeonids is plainly stated by Pindar in an ode[9] of which the date has been a good deal discussed.  Pomtow[10] rightly concludes that the Pythian victory of the Alcmaeonid Megacles which the ode commemorates was won in 487–6 B. C.  The temple must have been completed many years earlier, probably before 510 B. C., the date of the banishment of Hippias and the restoration of the democracy and the return of the Alcmaeonidae.

In the early part of the fourth century B. C. (371 *ca.*), the temple seems to have been destroyed by earthquake, and its reconstruction apparently was still proceeding in the

---

[1] X 5, 9–13.
[2] Jerome (in Eusebius, Chron. II p. 97, ed. Schöne) gives the date as Ol. 57[4] (= 549–8 B.C.); Paus. X 5,13 says Ol. 58[1] (= 548–7); Eusebius, Chron. II p. 96, ed. Schöne, Armenian version, assigns the date of the fire to Ol. 58[2] (= 547–6).
[3] Hdt. II 180.
[4] Homolle, B. C. H. XXVI (1892) pp. 611–621.
[5] V 62.
[6] Arist., Const. of Ath., 19; Philoch., cited by a scholiast on Pind., Pyth. VII 9; scholiast on Dem. Or. XXI 561.
[7] X 5,13.
[8] IX p. 421.
[9] Pyth. VII 10 sqq.
[10] *Rh. Mus.*, N. F. LI (1896), pp. 577–588.

THE TEMPLE OF APOLLO AND THE PHAEDRIADES
DELPHI

second half of that century (352–1–328–7).[1] The later history of the temple does not interest us here; to the plastic decorations we shall return later.

The old temple, as it stood, was a great Doric peripteros with six columns each on front and back and (probably) fifteen on each long side (the corner columns being counted twice, of course); inside, the roof was supported by two rows of Ionic columns. The earthquake seems to have destroyed the front of the temple down to the foundations; the back of the temple was destroyed, foundations and all. We have, therefore, only partial foundations of that old temple, fragments of the Parian marble façade, drums and capitals of poros columns, pieces of architrave of Parian marble and of poros triglyphs, cornice, sima, roof-tiles of marble, fragments of the pediment groups. Hence anything that Euripides might add would be most highly welcome.

And what does he contribute? Little, except for the pediments, although the temple plays so very large a part in the Ion and has an important place also in the Andromache. By far the greater number of the passages in the two plays say nothing more than that there was a temple of Phoebus Apollo at Delphi.[2] For example, in the Ion (5–7) the poet makes Hermes, as speaker of the prolog, locate the scene of the play as Delphi, the site of the oracular seat of Apollo, the mid-navel of the world:

| | |
|---|---|
| ἥκω δὲ Δελφῶν τήνδε γῆν, ἵν' ὀμφαλὸν | and I am come to this land of Delphi, where at the mid- |
| μέσον καθίζων Φοῖβος ὑμνῳδεῖ βροτοῖς | navel Phoebus hath his seat and chanteth unto mortals |
| τά τ' ὄντα καὶ μέλλοντα θεσπίζων ἀεὶ | forever revealing the things that are and are to be |

And when Ion enters, he also conveys the same information (ll.137–140):

| | |
|---|---|
| τὸν βόσκοντα γὰρ εὐλογῶ, | for I extol him that feedeth me |
| τὸ δ' ὠφέλιμον ἐμοὶ πατέρος | and the name of "father" I give |
| ὄνομα λέγω | to the sustaining hand of |
| Φοίβου τοῦ κατὰ ναὸν | Phoebus whose temple[3] this is |

Iphigenia Taurica 1272–1273:

| | |
|---|---|
| Πυθίων δόμων χθονίαν ἀφε-<br>λεῖν θεᾶς μῆνιν | to take away from the Pythian halls[3]<br>the goddess's wrath of hell |

Pseudo-Seneca, H. O. 93–94:

| | |
|---|---|
| Cirrhaea Paean templa et aetheriam domum<br>serpente caeso meruit | Paean slew the dragon and won for himself the<br>Cirrhaean temple and a home in heaven |

Aeschylus informs us that it was on the slopes of Mt. Parnassus (Eum. 11):

| | |
|---|---|
| ἐς τήνδε γαῖαν ἦλθε Παρνησοῦ θ' ἕδρας | unto this land he came and to Parnassus's seat |

There are many such passages,[4] but no purpose could be served by quoting more.

As to its location we are told that it was in the centre of the earth (Eur. I. T. 1258) (in a Choral Ode to Apollo):

| | |
|---|---|
| μέσον γᾶς ἔχων μέλαθρον | having earth's centre as thy dwelling place |

that it was close by the Castalian fountain (*ibid.* 1257–1258):

| | |
|---|---|
| Κασταλίας ῥεέθρων γείτων | neighbor to the streams of Castalia |

[1] See Frazer, *Paus.*, V pp. 328 ff.

[2] Inc. Inc. Frag. 262 N.: Πυθίων ἀνακτόρων. So, too, Soph. O. T. 70–71:
Κρέοντ'... ἐς τὰ Πυθικὰ
ἔπεμψα Φοίβου δώμαθ', ὡς πύθοιθ' κτλ.

[3] The temple is referred to under various names: 1)ναός: Eur. Ion 39; 79; 140; 219; 316; 420; 786; 795; 2)ναοί: Eur. Ion 97; 111; 115; 314; 555; 684; 1366; 1384; 3)ἱερόν: Eur. Ion 1190; 4)ἱερά: Eur. Ion 1331; 5)οἶκος: Eur. Ion 458; 513; 6) δῶμα: Eur. Ion 315; 514; 7) δώματα: Eur. Ion 370; 8) δόμος: Eur. Ion 45; 224; 1275; 9) δόμοι: Eur. Ion 34; 48; 129; 226; 249; 424; 510; 514; 535; 822; 1275; 1455; 1547; Eur. I. T. 1272; Sup. 1197; 10) μέλαθρον: Eur. I. T. 1258; 11) μέλαθρα: Eur. Ph. 205; Ion 738; 1373; 12)ἀνάκτορα: Eur. Ion 55; 1224; 13) μαντεῖον: Eur. Ion 42; 69; 130; 1122; Eur. Andr. 926; 14) μαντεῖα: Eur. Ion 66; 739; Ph. 284; 15) χρηστήρια: Eur. Ion 33; 299; 409; 727; 974; 1611; Ae. Sep. 747; 16) θυμέλη: Eur. Ion 114.

[4] E. g., Ae. Cho. 953–954; and many also from the comedy: e. g., Crat. Jr. Inc. Frag. 12, 2–3 K.; Men. Ἑαυτ. Τιμ., Frag. 147 K.; Inc. Inc. Frag. 460; 700 K.

The Castalian spring plays a more important role in the Ion of Euripides. In this play the oracular temple of Apollo is the centre of the scene; at the presentation of the Ion in the theatre at Athens, the fountain of Castalia was probably represented on one of the movable panels of the proscenium. All pilgrims to the temple of Loxias had first to perform their ablutions, with the prescribed lustral rites, before they might enter the sacred enclosure (Eur. Ion 95–97):

| | |
|---|---|
| τὰς Κασταλίας ἀργυροειδεῖς | go ye to Castalia's silvery, swirling springs |
| βαίνετε δίνας, καθαραῖς δὲ δρόσοις | and cleanse you with its purifying dews |
| φαιδρυνάμενοι στείχετε ναούς | before ye pass to the shrines |

In the same way the Phoenician maidens, sent from the East to serve Apollo in his temple at Delphi, must perform their lustral rites and purify themselves at the Castalian fount before they may enter the sacred place (Eur. Ph. 222–225):

| | |
|---|---|
| ἔτι δὲ Κασταλίας ὕδωρ | and Castalia's water still |
| περιμένει με κόμας ἐμᾶς | awaiteth me, to bedew the |
| δεῦσαι παρθένιον χλιδὰν | maiden glory of my hair[1] |
| Φοιβείαισι λατρείαις | for Phoebus's service |

And from the same purifying waters the neophyte Ion draws the water for cleansing the holy place itself (Eur. Ion 145–148):

| | |
|---|---|
| χρυσέων δ' ἐκ τευχέων ῥίψω | and from golden vessels I sprinkle |
| γαίας παγάν, | earth's fount |
| ἂν ἀποχεύονται | which the swirling springs |
| Κασταλίας δῖναι | of Castalia pour forth |

In Euripides's Ion (458–464)

| | |
|---|---|
| μόλε Πύθιον οἶκον | come to the Pythian halls, |
| πταμένα πρὸς ἀγυιάς, | winging thy way to the streets, |
| Φοιβήιος ἔνθα γᾶς | where Phoebus's hearth by the |
| μεσόμφαλος ἑστία | earth's mid-navel, fulfils |
| παρὰ χορευομένῳ τρίποδι | the oracles by the tripod round |
| μαντεύματα κραίνει | which the choruses move |

it is a place with streets by earth's mid-navel;[2] and the following passage states explicitly that the shrine was in "the city" (Eur. Andr. 1085–1091):

| | |
|---|---|
| ἐπεὶ τὸ κλεινὸν ἤλθομεν Φοίβου πέδον, | when we came to Phoebus's far-famed land, |
| τρεῖς μὲν φαεννὰς ἡλίου διεξόδους | three radiant courses of the sun we gave |
| θέᾳ διδόντες ὄμματ' ἐξεπίμπλαμεν. | to gazing at the sights and filled our eyes. |
| καὶ τοῦθ' ὕποπτον ἦν ἄρ'· εἰς δὲ συστάσεις | This bred suspicion; and the people dwelling |
| κύκλους τ' ἐχώρει λαὸς οἰκήτωρ θεοῦ. | in God's holy place drew off into knots and |
| Ἀγαμέμνονος δὲ παῖς διαστείχων πόλιν | groups of men. But Agamemnon's son passing up and down the city |
| εἰς οὓς ἑκάστῳ δυσμενεῖς ηὔδα λόγους | whispered into each man's ear words to fill his heart with hate |

The name of "the city" is not given in this passage; but the context makes it clear that Delphi is meant. Neither have we any hint as to its size; but we are told that the inhabitants and all the country round belonged to the god. The "fame," of course, came from the great temple and the oracle. In another passage in the Andromache (1263) the name of "the city" is given as Delphi:

| | |
|---|---|
| ἀλλ' ἕρπε Δελφῶν ἐς θεόδμητον πόλιν | but make thy way to the city of Delphi built of God |

Again it is a "city," and this time with the epithet that the Attic poets loved to bestow upon Athens, "built of God."

---

[1] Apollo himself sets the example of lustral cleansing and laves his divine locks in the pure dew of Castalia (Hor. Car. III 4, 60–64).

[2] Similarly, Ae. Sep. 745–747: Ἀπόλλωνος....
....τρὶς εἰπόντος ἐν μεσομφάλοις Πυθικοῖς χρηστηρίοις

THE FOUNTAIN OF CASTALIA

Euripides also testifies to the location of Apollo's temple at the "city of Delphi" (Ion 665):

| | |
|---|---|
| μέλλων Δελφίδ' ἐκλιπεῖν πόλιν | on the eve of quitting the city of Delphi |

In the days of Pausanias Delphi was still a "city" (X 9, 1):

| | |
|---|---|
| Δελφοῖς δὲ ἡ πόλις ἄναντες διὰ | the city of the Delphians presents a |
| πάσης παρέχεται σχῆμα· κατὰ | situation on a steep slope throughout; |
| τὰ αὐτὰ δὲ τῇ πόλει τῇ ἄλλη | the same is true not only of the rest of the city |
| καὶ ὁ ἱερὸς περίβολος τοῦ 'Απόλλωνος | but also of the sacred enclosure of Apollo |

We have thus abundant evidence that Delphi was a "city," and not merely, as Olympia was, a great religious centre, an aggregation of temples, shrines, altars, votive offerings, and so forth. It has been estimated from the records of the manumission of slaves inscribed on the retaining wall of the temple terrace that in the second century B. C. Delphi was a city of about ten thousand people. The same thought is suggested also in Euripides's Andromache 1063; 1065 (Chorus to Peleus):

| | |
|---|---|
| καὶ σοῦ γε παιδὸς παιδὶ πορσύνων μόρον | yea; and thy son's son's death he is compassing |
| . . . . . . . . . . . | |
| ἁγνοῖς ἐν ἱεροῖς Λοξίου Δελφῶν μέτα | with Delphians in Loxias's holy sanctuary |

The general topography suggested in the passage from Pausanias quoted above receives an addition from Euripides's Andromache (998 and 1144–1145):

| | |
|---|---|
| τελουμένων δὲ Δελφὶς εἴσεται πέτρα | and when these plans are being put into execution, the Delphian rock will know of it |
| . . . . . . . . . . . | |
| κραυγὴ δ' ἐν εὐφήμοισι δύσφημος δόμοις | and an unhallowed cry within the hallowed halls echoed |
| πέτραισιν ἀντέκλαγξ' | back from the rocks |

The allusion is most obviously to the Phaedriades, the twin "shining rocks" that tower above Delphi and add so much to the tremendous impressiveness of the place. In the Ion Euripides speaks in the same indefinite way of the "Pythian rock," meaning probably the western cliff which rises directly over the temenos (550):

| | |
|---|---|
| Πυθίαν δ' ἦλθες πέτραν πρίν; | and hast thou e'er come to the Pythian rock before? |

He is much more definite when he makes the Chorus say (714–715):

| | |
|---|---|
| ἰὼ δειράδες Παρνασοῦ πέτρας | ye ridges of Parnassus's rock, |
| ἔχουσαι σκόπελον οὐράνιόν θ' ἕδραν | with look-out point and seat in the skies |

With those lines one can fairly see the sharp edge of the Shining Rocks cutting the clear blue sky high above earth's central shrine. And in the winter months and even into early spring, those ridges are fringed with snow (Eur. Ph. 205–207):

| | |
|---|---|
| Φοίβου γὰρ δούλα μελάθρων, | for a bondmaid under Phoebus's roof, |
| ἵν' ὑπὸ δειράσι νιφοβόλοις | where, beneath the snow-sprent ridges |
| Παρνασοῦ κατενάσθη | of Parnassus, he hath ta'en his abode |

Those Phaedriades may shine with a wonderful glory. They may also frown with a gloom that was terrible; for criminals might be cast down from those sheer heights. With that sort of execution Ion threatens Creusa for her attempted murder of the boy (Eur. Ion 1266–1268):

| | |
|---|---|
| ἵν' αὐτῆς τοὺς ἀκηράτους πλόκους | that those smooth tresses of her hair may |
| κόμης καταξήνωσι Παρνησοῦ πλάκες, | be combed by the faces of Parnassus, from |
| ὅθεν πετραῖον ἅλμα δισκηθήσεται | which she shall be hurled like a discus down-plunged from the rock |

Sophocles also has an allusion to the Shining Rocks, when he speaks of the "rock oracular of Delphi," as the Phaedriades are so characteristic a feature of the landscape of Delphi and so dominate it, that the "rock of Delphi" may mean "Delphi" (O. T. 463–464):

| | |
|---|---|
| τίς ὅντιν' ἀ θεσπιέπεια Δελφὶς εἶπε πέτρα | who is it that the rock oracular of Delphi meant? |

The two great cliffs come together like colossal jaws; and that feature of the topography is pictured in Aeschylus's Choephori (806–807):

| | |
|---|---|
| τὸ δὲ καλῶς κτίμενον ὦ μέγα ναίων<br>στόμιον | oh thou that dwellest in the mighty fair-<br>built cavern's mouth |

The "cavern's mouth" is not "*a cave, a vault*, as if it were the entrance of the lower world," as Liddell and Scott interpret, nor yet "the Delphic oracular cave," as Sidgwick explains, in the holy of holies of the temple, but the great cavern of the Shining Rocks, as in the lines of Sophocles. And Aeschylus has the same thought once more, expressed in a slightly different form (Cho. 953–954):

| | |
|---|---|
| ὁ Λοξίας ὁ Παρνασίας<br>μέγαν ἔχων μυχὸν χθονός | Loxias who holds the mighty cavern<br>of the land of Parnassus |

There is no mention in the poets of anything touching the sacred enclosure, as such, except the temple proper and its belongings. Everything at Delphi is sacred. But there is at least a suggestion of the gate, or gates, of the τέμενος. At either side of the main entrance gate at the southeast corner of the sacred enclosure at Delphi are left evidences of the vessels containing the holy water for the symbolical purification of the pilgrims as they entered after the previous lustrations at the fountain of Castalia. Further evidence of the vessels and the holy water we have in Euripides's Ion (434–436):

| | |
|---|---|
| ἀλλὰ χρυσέαις<br>πρόχοισιν ἐλθὼν εἰς ἀπορραντήρια<br>δρόσον καθήσω | but I will go and with golden<br>pitchers place water-dews in the<br>vessels for sprinkling with the holy water |

That these were not at the temple-doors but at some distance away from the shrine itself is clear from the situation: Xuthus has entered the temple; Creusa is busy with her prayers at the altar; Ion makes his exit; the chorus sings a long ode; Ion re-enters and questions the chorus (ll.512–513):

| | |
|---|---|
| ἐκλέλοιπ' ἤδη τὸν ἱερὸν τρίποδα καὶ χρηστήριον<br>Ξοῦθος, ἢ μίμνει κατ' οἶκον | hath Xuthus left by now the holy tripod<br>and the shrine oracular or bideth he within the<br>building? |

If he had been filling fonts at the temple door, he would have been in a better position than the chorus to know whether or not Xuthus was still within. But he had gone first to the spring of Cassotis or Castalia to fill his pitchers and then to the gates to leave the water and has now returned.

So also at Athens, Pyrrhus's boy with the vessel for the sprinkling stood immediately inside the Propylaea by the southern column of the east portico for the service of those who were just entering the Acropolis proper.

As we have so many passages in which the temple at Delphi is casually mentioned without giving us any information about it, so we have as many more[1] in which mere mention is made of the oracle. For example, Euripides's Andromache 926:

| | |
|---|---|
| Φοίβου λιπὼν μαντεῖον | leaving the oracle of Phoebus |

We have, then, the location of Delphi at the centre of the earth, above the Cirrhaean plain, beneath the Shining Rocks, beside the fountain of Castalia; we have it as a place renowned, so holy that it was "built of God" himself; and we have there as the centre of interest the famous oracular temple of Apollo.

Details about the temple come in welcome profusion. Almost every architectural detail is observed and mentioned in one connection or another. From the messenger's report of the assassination of Neoptolemus at the hands of Orestes and his Delphian fellow-conspirators (Eur. Andr. 1097–1099)

| | |
|---|---|
| ἀρχαί τ' ἐπληροῦντ' εἰς τὰ βουλευτήρια<br>ἰδίᾳ θ' ὅσοι θεοῦ χρημάτων ἐφέστασαν | and the magistrates thronged into the council-<br>halls and, on their part, those who had charge of<br>the treasures |
| φρουρὰν ἐτάξαντ' ἐν περιστύλοις δόμοις | of the god posted guards in the building's colon-<br>nades |

[1] Ae. Cho.; Eum.; Soph. O. T.; El.; *passim*.

we learn that the building had a peristyle; but what the order was, what the number of columns, what it looked like—these questions it was not his to answer. We receive here also, by the way, the assurance which we shall find again and again that the temple contained the treasures of the god.

Such epithets as περίστυλος, περικίων, ἀμφικίων ("girdled with pillars") would naturally tend, with the fifth century poets, to become standing epithets of temples; and they do: for example,

Eur. I. T. 406–407: περικίονας ναούς    }    "pillared temples," and
Soph. Ant. 285–286: ἀμφικίονας ναούς    }    "pillared temples."

Above the columns should come the entablature—architrave, taenia, triglyphon, cornice, gable, raking cornice, roof. Here, again, Euripides does not fail us (Ion, 156) (to the birds that come flying toward the temple and are likely to defile the coping):

αὐδῶ μὴ χρίμπτειν θριγκοῖς   |   I warn you not to touch the cornices

This certainly means both the cornice below the gable and the raking cornice above,[1] while the following passage surely refers only to the latter (Ion 171–173):

τίς ὅδ' ὀρνίθων καινὸς προσέβα;   |   what new bird is this that has now arrived?
μῶν ὑπὸ θριγκοὺς εὐναίας   |   To build, I ween, under the cornices a
καρφηρὰς θήσων τέκνοις;   |   nest of straw for his young?

Statues standing in the open were provided with means of protection against defilement by birds; to protect the temple and insure its purity was part of the duty of the young neophyte (Ion 106–108):

πτηνῶν τ' ἀγέλας,   |   and the flocks of birds,
αἳ βλάπτουσιν σέμν' ἀναθήματα,   |   which injure the holy offerings,
τόξοισιν ἐμοῖς φυγάδας θήσομεν   |   I shall put to flight with my bow and arrows

And so here Ion speaks his warning and draws his bow (177—178):

ὡς ἀναθήματα μὴ βλάπτηται   |   that the offerings and Phoebus's
ναοὶ θ' οἱ Φοίβου   |   temple may suffer no harm

We shall have occasion to revert again to the care which the ancients took to save their statues out in the open from such defilement.

Above the gable and the raking cornice comes the roof. This, too, is not unnamed by Euripides (Ion 89–90):

σμύρνης ἀνύδρου καπνὸς εἰς ὀρόφους   |   and the smoke of frankincense, brought from the desert land,
Φοίβου πέτεται   |   flies up to Phoebus's roof

Finally, we have the acroteria crowning the roof at the corners of the gable—songstresses of gold, whose praises were chanted by Pindar in an ode in honor of the temple:

τὰ ἐς τὰς ᾠδοὺς τὰς χρυσᾶς, ἃ δὴ Πίνδαρος ᾖσεν ἐπ' ἐκείνῳ τῷ ναῷ (Pausanias X 5,12) (Pind., Frag. 53 Schroeder):

χρύσεαι δ' ἐξύπερθ' αἰετοῦ   |   and above the pediment sang
ἄειδον κηληδόνες   |   charmers of gold

These golden "charmers" (Pindar) or "songstresses" (Pausanias) that formed the acroteria of the temple must have been either Sirens, which would seem the more probable, or Sphinxes, which are so richly represented among the surviving sculptures of Delphi. The decision in favor of Sirens is rendered almost certain by a passage in Philostratus (Apoll. Ty. VI 11, 14):

ὅδ', οἶμαι, μικρὰ ταῦτα   |   he [the god], I presume, thought
ἡγούμενος καὶ τῆς ἑαυτοῦ   |   these buildings small and incom-
σοφίας ἥττω· καὶ ἄλλου ἐδε-   |   mensurate with his wisdom, and so he demanded
ήθη νεὼ <καὶ ἄλλου καὶ>   |   another temple and another and

---

[1] As the upper cornice, θριγκός came to be used figuratively for the extreme limit. See pp. 205ff.

μεγάλων ἤδη καὶ ἑκατομπέδων—

ἑνὸς δ' αὐτῶν καὶ χρυσᾶς ὥγγας
ἀνάψαι λέγεται Σειρήνων
τιν' ἐπεχούσας πειθώ

finally even great hundred-foot temples; and upon one
of these, it is said, he had set up high
Sirens of gold, with their magic influence,
endowed with strange persuasive power

The whole passage in Philostratus has reference to the earlier period in the artistic development of Delphi; of all the things he names there, the Iliupersis of Polygnotus in the Lesche of the Cnidians is the latest. It is, therefore, irresistible to connect these "Sirens" of Philostratus with the "songstresses" of Pausanias and Pindar; and, besides, the Sirens are more naturally singers than the Sphinxes would be[1]; and certainly the epithet of κηληδών is better applicable to a Siren than to a Sphinx.

Carl Robert[2] assigns to the acroteria the Heracles and Bellerophon groups described by Euripides (Ion 190–204), and the gigantomachia (Ion 206–219) to the metopes. Kinkel[3] assigns everything except the διδύμων προσώπων φῶς to metopes. To this problem we must presently return. Suffice it to say for the present that the battle with the Hydra and with the Chimaera might be compositions adaptable to acroteria decoration, but the acroteria are, through Pindar's verses, already preempted for the Sirens; for Pindar, of course, has before his vision the pre-Macedonian temple, not the temple Pausanias is describing. And it lies very close to the surface to conjecture that the chief reason why Pausanias refuses to believe "the story about 'the golden singers'" is that he did not see them; and he failed to see them because in his day they were not there! They had disappeared with the destruction of the Alcmaeonid temple, and the relation of the fourth century temple to it was not clear to Pausanias. Through Pausanias and Pindar, therefore, we have the acroteria fixed as "singers of gold"—Sphinxes or, far more probably, Sirens. And the representations of the Heracles-Hydra and Bellerophon-Chimaera stories will have to remain in their old places in the pediments, or upon the metopes.

We need not, for all this, reject the hypothesis often advanced that the archaic Nike in the Apollo room of the Museum at Delphi (a flying Nike of the Archermus or Delian Nike type but freer and further developed, as is to be expected from its late date) may well have been an acroterium of this temple. Our Sirens, the singers, occupy positions above the lower angles of the gable; the Nike may well have been poised on her pinions above the upper angle.

Then, within the triangle of the gable, comes the pediment group, the subject of Euripides's brilliant and detailed description of the sculptures, the most important section of all in our discussion. Although it properly belongs to the volume on Sculpture, these sculptures are so essentially a part of the temple that we may fairly anticipate their treatment in that connection and see them in their place in the temple pediment.

The chorus of Creusa's handmaids enters. They are filled with wonder and admiration at the splendid temple built by their fellow-townsmen, the Alcmaeonids. With characteristic, though pardonable provincialism so few years after the dedication of the Parthenon and the so-called "Theseum" and with the Erechtheum even then in course of construction, they had, like every other Athenian,[4] thought Athens the only place in the world where wonders of art were created. But here at Delphi, they find, is something at least comparable with the glories of the Athenian Acropolis, although by the very suggestion the Athenian audience was spurred to set off the splendor of the marble Parthenon and its Phidian sculptures to the disadvantage of the marble-fronted poros temple at Delphi and its archaic sixth century sculptures (Eur. Ion 184–186):

οὐκ ἐν ταῖς ζαθέαις 'Αθά-
ναις εὐκίονες ἦσαν αὐ-
λαὶ θεῶν μόνον

not in Athens alone, the city all divine,
were courts of gods with stately
colonnades

---

[1] And yet we may compare Soph. O. T. 36: σκληρᾶς ἀοιδοῦ; 130: ποικιλῳδὸς Σφίγξ; 391: ῥαψῳδὸς κύων; etc.

[2] Die Iliupersis des Polygnot, p. 36, note 23.

[3] Eur. u. die Bildende Kunst, p. 25.

[4] In like spirit the chorus of Clouds (Ar. Nub. 300–306) proposes to go to the bright land of Pallas, where there are high-roofed temples and statues to gladden eye and heart:

ἔλθωμεν λιπαρὰν χθόνα Παλλάδος...
.......οὗ............
ναοί θ' ὑψερεφεῖς καὶ ἀγάλματα

They look up at the splendid temple and see—apparently at one glance—the *two* façades of the temple! The one they actually see; the other, they assume, is in every spectator's memory (Ion 187–189):

| | |
|---|---|
| ἀλλὰ καὶ παρὰ Λοξία | but at the sanctuary of Loxias also, |
| τῷ Λατοῦς διδυμῶν προσώ- | Leto's son, there is the fair-browed |
| πων καλλιβλέφαρον φῶς | light of twin fronts |

This citation is of much importance and has usually been overlooked in the discussions of the location to be assigned to the sculptures: διδυμῶν προσώπων καλλιβλέφαρον φῶς cannot well refer to anything but gables. The "light of the forehead with its beauteous brows" is surely a pediment with sculptures overhung by the cornice above.

Then, with upward glance, one division of the chorus calls attention to the first scene represented among the sculptures (Ion 190–200):

| | |
|---|---|
| ἰδοὺ τάνδ', ἄθρησον, | Look here! see; the son of |
| Λερναῖον ὕδραν ἐναίρει | Zeus with scimitar of gold is |
| χρυσέαις ἅρπαις ὁ Διὸς παῖς. | slaying the hydra of Lerna. |
| | |
| ἀθρῶ. καὶ πέλας ἄλλος αὐ- | I see. And by him is an- |
| τοῦ πανὸν πυρίφλεκτον αἴ- | other, lifting a blazing torch |
| ρει τις· ἆρ' ὃς ἐμαῖσι μυ- | of fire; is it he whose story is |
| θεύεται παρὰ πήναις | told at my web, the |
| ἀσπιστὰς Ἰόλαος, ὃς | bucklered warrior Iolaus, who |
| κοινοὺς αἱρόμενος πόνους | bears a share in the labors of |
| Δίῳ παιδὶ συναντλεῖ; | Zeus's son and with him endured to the end? |

In excited haste another division of the chorus, taking up another portion of the scene, runs on (Ion 201–204):

| | |
|---|---|
| καὶ μὰν τόνδ' ἄθρησον | and lo! look here—a man |
| πτεροῦντος ἔφεδρον ἵππου· | mounted upon a winged horse! |
| τὰν πῦρ πνέουσαν ἐναίρει | He is slaying the fire-breathing, |
| τρισώματον ἀλκάν | triple-bodied monster! |

And still another and another division, with eyes running swiftly from one sculptured group to another, continues (Ion 205–219):

| | |
|---|---|
| παντᾷ τοι βλέφαρον διώ- | yea; I turn mine eyes in every direc- |
| κω· σκέψαι κλόνον ἐν τείχε- | tion. Mark there on the marble |
| σι λαΐνοισι Γιγάντων | walls the giants' rout! . . . |
| . . . . . . . . | |
| λεύσσεις οὖν ἐπ' Ἐγκελάδῳ | Beholdest thou, then, her who is brandishing over Enceladus |
| γοργωπὸν πάλλουσαν ἴτυν; | the circle of her Gorgon-shield? |
| λεύσσω Παλλάδ', ἐμὰν θεόν. | Pallas, mine own goddess, I behold. |
| . . . . . . . . | . . . . . . |
| τί γάρ, κεραυνὸν | and mark! the mighty thunderbolt, |
| ἀμφίπυρον ὄβριμον ἐν Διὸς | with double point of flame, in Zeus's |
| ἐκηβόλοισι χερσίν; | far-hurling hands! |
| . . . . . . | . . . . . |
| ὁρῶ τὸν δάϊον | I see; his foeman |
| Μίμαντα πυρὶ καταιθαλοῖ. | Mimas it is consuming with fire. |
| . . . . . . | |
| καὶ Βρόμιος ἄλλον ἀπολέμοισι | and Bromius, the Bacchian god, with |
| κισσίνοισι βάκτροις | unwarlike, ivy-wreathed wand |
| ἐναίρει Γᾶς τέκνων ὁ Βακχεύς | is slaying another son of Gaea there |

These are the scenes: 1) Heracles slaying the Hydra, with Iolaus standing by with torch in hand to help. 2) Bellerophon, mounted upon Pegasus, slaying the fire-breathing Chimaera. 3) The Gigantomachia: Athena brandishing her shield over the fallen Enceladus; Zeus, with a thunderbolt in his hand, above the lightning-blasted body of Mimas; Dionysus, smiting with his thyrsus the unnamed Rhoetus.[1] The vivid description of the representations seems to declare that the chorus sees them with the physical eye. Does the audience see

---

[1] We can confidently supply the name from Hor. Car. II 19, 23; Apollod. I 6, 22 says "Eurytus."

them, too? Are the scenes there in the theatre—represented on the front of the proscenium on the πίνακες, on the metopes, or on a temporary pediment? Or did the dramatic artists of fifth century Athens leave much to the imagination of the spectators? And did the vivid word-painting of the chorus and their eyes turned eagerly toward the temple in the centre of the proscenium recall to Pythian pilgrims, and to those who had heard from them, the plastic wonders of Apollo's fane? Or, finally, is Euripides giving us here not a description of the Delphic reality at all but only an imaginary, a fake description of three of the most hackneyed themes of vase-decorators, painters, and sculptors from the earliest to the latest days of Greek art production?

Before the excavations of Delphi, so magnificently carried out by the French government under the able direction of M. Théophile Homolle, each of these views suggested had its partisans and opponents. Now, there can be no serious question as to the correctness of the affirmative answer to at least our second group of questions: the dramatic artists of Athens did leave everything they possibly could leave to the imagination of the audience; there was in all probability no plastic representation of the Delphic sculptures in the Athenian theatre; Euripides is describing real sculptures that he and hundreds of his audience had seen at earth's central shrine. Any arguments to the contrary that may have seemed valid before 1894–5 are now shattered by the fragments found in the excavations. The Athena with a great aegis held on her left arm as a shield before her breast, and, over-thrown before her but still defending himself, the Enceladus from our gable are still to be seen in the Museum at Delphi. The group is strongly suggestive of the Athena-Enceladus group from the Pisistratic pediment of the Hecatompedon in Athens. Fragments of two quadrigas or bigas are there; one of them may have belonged to Athena; the other, to some other god. The existence of a fragment of a tiger or a panther, if such it be, substantiates the presence of the Dionysus of the poet's description of this western gable. It is quite conceivable that the fragment of a man in a long tunic and the skin of an animal over that should be identified as Dionysus himself. In point of workmanship and style, in the conventional treatment of the draperies and the nude, in the severity tempered by an effort after elegance characteristic of the ripening archaism, the fragments are the indisputable work of the closing decades of the sixth century. Their style, their date, their dimensions, the place where they were found, the material of which they are made—every possible circumstance goes to prove beyond a reasonable doubt that the Gigantomachia which we have in Euripides's chorus and in the fragments was the subject of the west pediment.

In the east pediment we should then find the Heracles-Hydra-Iolaus group in one wing near the centre, the Bellerophon-Chimaera group balancing it on the other side. Of these two groups not a fragment has yet been found or identified. It is, however, entirely possible that the fine figure of a young man, of more than human stature, standing in almost front view, with head turned slightly to the right and right arm extended also in that direction, may have stood somewhat to the right of the centre and may be Iolaus with the blazing torch in the extended right hand. We have his torso fairly well preserved; the head is sadly fractured; both arms and both legs (save the upper part of the left thigh) are gone. There is not enough left for a positive identification of the figure. M. Homolle[1] thinks he may be Hermes and places him in the left wing in charge of the biga there. Then we have on the left wing toward the corner on either side fragments of a biga driven straight out *en face* from the background; one of these chariots may be that of Heracles himself, as in the poros pediment in Athens and on many a blackfigured vase. Further on, on the right, in the northern corner of the gable, is a lion killing a fawn; in the left (southern) corner, balancing this group, a lion dragging down a bull and tearing his flesh. Between the groups of animals and the biga groups, and filling the space there, belong also the three female figures of the type of the best pre-Persian ladies of the Acropolis of Athens, in the south wing, and three youths balancing them in the north wing. The fragments of all these are sufficiently numerous for a satisfactory reconstruction.[2]

Some critics object to the number of different motives in such a gable. But the variety of subjects, with those scenes of Euripides and the fragments we have, offers no argument of any weight against the reconstruction I have given. Such multiplication of subjects—

[1] B. C. H. XXV (1901) pp. 457–515; especially pp. 491–492.

[2] See F. Courby, B. C. H. XXXVIII (1914) pp. 327–350, who combines the two bigas into one quadriga and puts it in the centre of the pediment, and leaves the corners quite empty.

animal combats, peaceful human beings, adventures of heroes, all in one and the same pediment—in the archaic period need prove no stumbling-block to us since the discovery of the pediments of the Treasuries of Cyrene and Byzantium at Olympia, and the frieze of Assos, and the poros pediments on the Acropolis of Athens; and I am convinced that we must hold to the strict interpretation of the διδύμων προσώπων (twin brows). It would be strange, indeed, even without the express mention of the διδύμων προσώπων, for Euripides to select for his enthusiastic description of the temple sculptures the poros pediment on the back of the temple and pass by in silence the more magnificent marble groups of the front. Furthermore, this distribution is borne out artistically by the division between strophe and antistrophe: the description of the Hydra-Chimaera pediment takes up strophe and antistrophe α'; then, with the turn to strophe β', the chorus is ready for the other front, each group filling completely one strophe and antistrophe. There is no real awkwardness in the chorus's describing both gables. The imagination of the audience would easily run, with the swing of the chorus to the new strophe, from the square in front of the temple on to the stairway ascending from the west front of the temple to the theatre and the way to the stadium, up which every visitor to the games must have passed. And besides we are reasonably certain, from the circumstances and place of the discovery of the fragments remaining, that the gigantomachia occupied the western gable. The centre of the gable was filled, of course, by the Zeus-Mimas group, now wholly lost.

Instead of ascribing the Heracles and Bellerophon groups to the east pediment, M. Homolle has assigned them to the metopes underneath the gigantomachia on the west façade and suggested for the east front the familiar scene of the contest between Apollo and Heracles, when the latter attempted to carry the sacred tripod away from Delphi, with Athena intervening to settle the dispute. This contest is the scene still preserved at Delphi on the pediment of the Treasury of Siphnos (Cnidus), while the frieze of that same Treasury is wondrously decorated with scenes from the gigantomachia. But the presence of a similar contest in the east pediment of the temple is only the merest hypothesis on the part of M. Homolle; and it does not at all follow from the fact that the north frieze of the Siphnian Treasury has the gigantomachia, the subject of the west pediment of the temple, that the east front of the temple must have had the subject of the gable of the Treasury, the stealing of the tripod. For the east pediment the marble fragments found fail to help us out to the extent that we desire. Euripides describes but a few figures among the many that he knew; the fragments unearthed include but a few figures among the many that were; and, with one questionable exception, the extant fragments unfortunately fail to coincide with the description. We have in Euripides the Heracles-Iolaus-Hydra group, and the Bellerophon-Chimaera group. These, as we have seen, must either be the two central groups, with no figure directly under the angle of the gable, or they must stand on either side of a single central figure; the marble fragments in Delphi give us the next groups —the *biga*, with the attendant women, and the lion seizing and rending its prey, on either wing of the pediment; the figures occupying the corners of the gable are wholly wanting both in the extant sculptures and in the description. In the centre we may, perhaps, place a figure of Athena, who is sometimes present in works of art representing Bellerophon and the Chimaera, and who is a very present divinity at the labors of Heracles.

The gable thus reconstructed is not subject to the criticism, so often passed upon it,[1] of being monotonous and stiff in comparison with the group of the west gable, like the east pediment of the temple of Zeus at Olympia in comparison with its western front. Our east gable is, in its variety of contrasts between figures in violent action and figures in dignified and quiet repose, more like the east pediment of the Parthenon and the west pediment of Olympia: in the centre a quiet figure commanding the situation like the Apollo of the west pediment of Olympia, the peaceful arbiter of the struggle on either hand; to the right and left, respectively, of that central figure, the violent action of the Heracles-Hydra and of the Bellerophon-Chimaera groups; following these, on either side, the quietly standing chariots and horses with their attendant women; again in sharp contrast to these quiet, peaceful groups, the furious attack of the lions upon the deer and the bull; and in the corners we should have, as on the Parthenon and the temple at Olympia, quietly resting local divinities— perhaps the nymph of Castalia and the nymph of Cassotis.

[1] Homolle, B. C. H. XX, p. 652; XXV, l. c. ; Frazer, *Paus.*, V, p. 633.

The scenes described by Euripides *could* easily be distributed and fitted into metope composition:—the gigantomachia *could* be broken up into many groups, as on the metopes of the Parthenon; Bellerophon and the Chimaera *could* be brought into admirable grouping for a metope; Heracles slaying the Hydra would work as well upon a metope at Delphi as it does upon one at Olympia, while Iolaus with the torch might possibly be coming to his aid upon an adjacent metope. But we have no scintilla of evidence, either literary or monumental, that the temple at Delphi had sculptured metopes at all (the one block that seemed to M. Homolle[1] to look like a metope and to have the dimensions of a metope from this temple has no visible decoration); and the happy coincidence between the description and the few, shattered, but very precious fragments of the Alcmaeonid gable groups makes all arguing superfluous. Euripides is describing with the hasty sketch of the artist poet the real sculptures of the pediments of the Alcmaeonid temple—not metopes, as has been held by Overbeck,[2] Ulrichs, Stuart, Karl Ottfried Müller, Welcker, Kinkel,[3] and others; nor acroteria, as suggested by Robert,[4] nor an invented scene out of his own imagination and the familiar stock in trade of the artists of his day; (indeed, as Welcker[5] long ago pointed out, Euripides would hardly have hazarded such a venture in the presence of hundreds or thousands who had been at Delphi and seen the great temple and its sculptures;) nor paintings, as Musgrave,[6] Tyrwhitt, and others; nor tapestries; nor sculptures or paintings adorning the Stoa of the Athenians down below the retaining wall of the temple precinct, far away and out of sight from the point where the chorus turn to ask Ion if they may enter the shrine itself.

All the figures of these gables found in the excavations—both the poros and the marble—show vivid traces of bright coloring. This is no place to enter into a discussion of the use of colors on Greek sculptures; but it is interesting to note that Euripides makes special mention of painted statues in gable-groups (Hypsipyle, Frag. 764 N.):

| | |
|---|---|
| ἰδού, πρὸς αἰθέρ' ἐξαμίλλησαι κόρας | look! turn thine eyes toward heaven |
| γραπτούς<τ' ἐν αἰετ>οῖσι πρόσβλεψον τύπους | and see the painted sculptures in the gables |

Before the excavations on the Athenian Acropolis in 1886, this would have been written down as a fairy story and the painted sculptures relegated to the land of fable. But now we know how well the literary sources and the proofs produced by the spade corroborate each other.

Let us note, too, the realistic touch with which some of the details of the art are brought out: how true to the realities of Greek art is the golden (that is, gilded bronze) sword of Heracles (l. 192), the Gorgon-head device of Athena's shield (l. 210), the ivy-wreathed thyrsus of Dionysus (l. 218).

The Ion was produced between 416 and 412 B. C., forty years before the destruction of the sixth century temple; it is, therefore, our most helpful literary document for the temple as rebuilt by the Alcmaeonids.

A very difficult question in connection with these pediment groups which we have thus established is the question of authorship. Pausanias names, as the sculptors of his gable figures, Praxias and Androsthenes (X 19, 4):

| | |
|---|---|
| τὰ δὲ ἐν τοῖς ἀετοῖς· | There are the following representations in the gables: |
| ἔστιν ῞Αρτεμις καὶ Λητὼ καὶ | Artemis and Leto and |
| ᾽Απόλλων καὶ Μοῦσαι, δύσις τε | Apollo and the Muses, and the setting |
| ῾Ηλίου, καὶ Διόνυσός τε καὶ | Sun; Dionysus and |
| αἱ γυναῖκες αἱ Θυιάδες. τὰ | the Thyad women. The |
| μὲν δὲ πρῶτα αὐτῶν ᾽Αθηναῖ- | former group was made |
| ος Πραξίας μαθητὴς Καλά- | by Praxias of Athens, a |
| μιδός ἐστιν ἐργασάμενος· | pupil of Calamis; but as the |

[1] Homolle, *B. C. H.* XX, p. 648.
[2] Overbeck, *Gesch. d. gr. Pl.* 1⁴, pp. 385; 557.
[3] Kinkel, *Eur. u. die bildende Kunst*, p. 25.
[4] Robert, *Iliupersis des Polygnot*, p. 36.
[5] Welcker, *Alte Denkm.*, I p. 175, quoted by Homolle, *B. C. H.* XXVI (1902) p. 589.
[6] Musgrave, *Eur. Ion, ad loc.*

χρόνου δὲ ὡς ὁ ναὸς ἐποιεῖ-
το ἐγγινομένου Πραξίαν μὲν
ἔμελλεν ἀπάξειν τὸ χρεών,
τὰ δὲ ὑπολιπόμενα τοῦ ἐν
τοῖς ἀετοῖς κόσμου ἐποίησεν
Ἀνδροσθένης, γένος μὲν
καὶ οὗτος Ἀθηναῖος, μαθη-
τὴς δὲ Εὐκάδμου.

time, during which the temple was building,
dragged on, fate was destined
to carry Praxias off,
and the portion of the decoration of the pediment remaining unfinished was executed
by Androsthenes, also of Athens, but a
pupil of Eucadmus.

Pausanias evidently means to ascribe the pediments which he actually saw to Praxias and Androsthenes. Could he have confused artists and pediments and ascribed to the sculptors of the sixth century pediment the works of the fourth century, even as many historians of art have thought (including Welcker, Karl Ottfried Müller, Letronne, Brunn,[1] Overbeck[2])? Did Praxias and Androsthenes execute the sculptures of the fourth, or those of the sixth century temple?

Praxias, says Pausanias, was the pupil of Calamis. Accepting that, we get approximately the following chronology: inasmuch as Calamis belongs to the first half of the fifth century, and as his productive activity, however long his life, cannot have covered more than the period between 500 and 440 B. C., it needs no argument to decide that his pupils could have had nothing to do with the temple built by the Alcmaeonids between 537 and 510 or with the fragments we have left from the pediments of that sixth century temple. We may at once dismiss such a Praxias, the pupil of that Calamis, from our discussion of Euripides's gable.

Neither may the question be fairly raised as to whether the gable decoration may not have been added many years after the dedication of the temple. We know practically for certain from Pindar's Seventh Pythian that the sculptures were in their place in 487-6, the date of that ode, and that it was the Alcmaeonidae "that had made Apollo's house a wonder to behold";[3] it stands to reason also, on a priori grounds, that the Alcmaeonidae, bent on winning the good will of the hierarchy of Delphi, should not have left off the crowning beauty of the temple when Athens, Selinus, Ephesus, and other cities at that time had temples so splendidly adorned with sculptures[4]; and the fragments of the gable groups, belonging so unmistakably to the art of the closing years of the sixth century, substantiate fully these conclusions.

On the other hand, if Calamis was working at his art even during the extraordinarily long career of Olympiads 70-80, a pupil of his would naturally belong to a period extending from 465 to 420 B. C.; or, if that pupil was the disciple of the master's old age, beginning work with the octogenarian Calamis and living to be an octogenarian himself, he could not have had anything to do with the reconstruction of a temple destroyed in 370. We know from the official records of the building accounts of the Erechtheum in Athens that "Praxias of Melite," a deme of Attica, was the sculptor of one of the groups[5] of the frieze in 409. This Praxias may well have been a pupil of Calamis's old age, but he could not possibly have been both a pupil of Calamis and the artist of a gable group for a temple that was not completed till after the battle of Chaeronea (338).

Still another Praxias of Athens, the son of Lysimachus, of the Deme of Ancyle, is known to us.[6] His activity as an artist was at its height in the middle of the fourth century; we have an inscription[6] from a dedication of a work of his that must be dated between 370 and 360, and another executed between 366 and 338 (probably between 360 and 350); he is in all probability the Praxias to whom Pausanias meant to ascribe the sculptures of the pediment of the fourth century temple at Delphi. He did not survive to see the completion of the temple, but he is far removed from the possibility of discipleship to Calamis, unless

---

[1] Brunn, *K. G. I*[2], p. 174.
[2] Overbeck, *Gesch. d. Gr. Pl. I*[4], pp. 278, 385, 557.
[3] Pindar, *Pyth. VII*, 10–12: οἳ τεὸν γε δόμον
Πύθωνι δίᾳ
θαητὸν ἔτευξαν.
[4] Cf. Homolle, *B. C. H.* XXVI (1902), p. 593.
[5] "The horse and the man behind striking it."
[6] Loewy, *Inschr. Gr. Bildh.* 127, S. XXII; cf. E. Reisch, *Jahreshefte des arch. Insts.* I, IX (1906), p. 204.

we accept (with Reisch[1]) a younger Calamis as master of the Praxias famous in Athens and Delphi in the fourth century. Not even the slightest fragment of Pausanias's gable group has been found that might by the quality or the style of its workmanship contribute to fixing the date of those sculptures. The gable figures have disappeared as completely as the pediment groups from the so-called Theseum in Athens—probably carried off to Rome in imperial times.

The efforts to find a suitable emendation for the name of Calamis—Callimachus, who made the famous bronze lamp for the Erechtheum,[2] or Calliades[3]—must be pronounced futile.

Androsthenes we do not otherwise know; his master Eucadmus is not named anywhere except in this passage of Pausanias.

Georg Karo[4] has attempted to remove our Euripidean sculptures from the temple of Apollo altogether; he finds in them no pediments at all. The "fair-browed light of twin fronts" to him is not a pair of pediments, east and west, but literally the faces of the two fair-browed Caryatids of the Siphnian treasure house. The gigantomachia is not that upon the temple, but the well preserved north frieze of the treasury of Siphnos; there we have Athena and Enceladus, Zeus and Mimas, Dionysus and Rhoetus. But the first and last we have also, at least in part, from the temple pediment; and it would be strange, indeed, if the chorus, standing in front of the temple that was the glory of Panhellenic Greece at earth's central shrine, should sing such strains in praise of the private treasury of a little island like Siphnos; if they were going to sing about a treasury building at Delphi, Euripides would have chosen the splendid Treasury of Athens herself for the theme of their song. There could be only some minor suggestion of either treasury in the scenic decorations, while the temple was certainly the centre of the scene. Furthermore, the sculptures of the Siphnian treasure house are complete, and there is no Heracles-Hydra group there, nor Bellerophon-Chimaera—neither on the north side nor on any side nor in the gables. Karo has not made a case, in spite of his confident assumption (p. 217) that "cette explication est trop satisfaisante dans sa simplicité pour n'être pas généralement accueillie." It would be exceedingly interesting if we could find in literature a clear reference to those caryatids, astounding prototypes of the maidens of the Erechtheum. But the Siphnians' treasure house, away down the steep slope of the sacred enclosure, against the southeast temenos wall, is too far removed from the centre of interest to make the suggestion that the description in the Ion refers to its sculptures plausible or even possible.

We now have our temple reconstructed for us with the help of Euripides—steps, colonnade, cornice, sculptured pediments, raking cornice, roof, and acroteria.

The outer splendor of the temple consisted not only in its beautiful façade of Parian marble and its pediment groups of sculptured marble, and, possibly, sculptured metopes, but also in rich adornment of dazzling gold. We know further from Pausanias[5] and Pliny[6] that in the vestibule of the later fourth century temple were inlaid in letters of gold the famous sayings of the seven sages: Γνῶθι σεαυτόν, Μηδὲν ἄγαν, Ἐγγύη πάρα δ᾽ ἄτη. There were others but these are the only ones that have come down to us. The last of the three is given to us, as quoted, by Plato[7] and vouched for also by the younger Cratinus (Inc. Frag. 12, 2–3 K.):

| | |
|---|---|
| οὔπω τότ᾽ ἐν Δελφοῖσιν ἦν τὰ γράμματα<br>τὴν ἐγγύην ἄτην λέγοντ᾽; | weren't the letters at Delphi yet, at that time,<br>declaring that "Going security spells ruin"? |

The maxims were inlaid in the stone of the temple by order of the Amphictyonic Council; but the exact location in the fore-temple is not clear. Pausanias says simply ἐν τῷ προνάῳ "in the pronaos." Macrobius says they were engraved "on the front of the temple"[8] "on

[1] Emil Reisch, *Jahresb. des Arch. Insts.*, I. IX (1906), pp. 199–268, brings many bits of evidence together to establish the identity of a younger Calamis, active 390–360, with Scopas, Praxiteles, and other famous sculptors of the fourth century.
[2] Homolle, *B. C. H.* XXVI (1902), pp. 635 ff.
[3] Frazer, *l. c.*
[4] *B. C. H.* XXXIII, pp. 212–219.
[5] X 24, 1.
[6] *N. H.* VII 119.
[7] *Char.* 165 a.
[8] *Som. Scip.* I 9, 2.

the door-post of the temple."[1]   According to Diodorus[2] and Varro,[3] they were "on a column."
Pausanias's statement is surely correct for the temple of his day; the natural place for them
would be on the face of the pillars of the antae of the pronaos; and there we may safely
locate them in the Alcmaeonid temple in the fifth century.

We know also[4] that upon the architrave of the later temple that took the place of this
one the Athenians (in 340–339) hung up golden shields, with an inscription upon them
setting forth the offensive boast that the shields had been taken by the Athenians from
the Medes and Thebans when Thebes fought with the barbarians against the Greeks.   The
shields were still hanging there down to the time of Pausanias who mentions shields of gold
upon the architrave,[5] the dedication of the Athenians from the battle of Marathon.   Pausanias is wrong, however, in the latter detail, and Aeschines is right: the shields commemo-
rated the battle of Plataea, not Marathon—there were no Thebans at Marathon.   But the
shields were there, and they were shields of glittering gold.   And one of the four famous
hymns found at Delphi, the Paean to Dionysus, dating from 338 (*ca.*), when this new temple
was still in course of construction, "indulges in a beatific vision of the time when a happy
generation shall behold the temple of Phoebus all glittering with gold, eternal and undefiled."[6]

Gold leaf was evidently used lavishly upon the decoration of the exterior of temples, as
in our own country upon capitol domes and Congressional Libraries.   A Roman tragic
poet whom we cannot identify, apparently echoing a Greek original, brings before us the
same picture of lofty splendor in buildings (roofs) flashing with gold [Inc. Inc. Fab. (CXLIII)
242 (Ribbeck³)]:

micant nitore tecta sublimi aurea.

As the most magnificent statues were constructed of gold and ivory, so also both gold and
ivory were lavished upon the most splendid temples and palaces (Enn. Fab. 169):
o Priami domu' . . . caelatis lacuatis, auro, ebore instructam regifice
(Cic. Paradox. I 3, 13): marmoreis tectis, ebore et auro fulgentibus.

In like manner the Greek poets themselves love to dwell upon the wealth of gold that
adorned the temples of their gods.   Zeus's temple has quantities of gold (Eur. Hip. 68–69):

| | |
|---|---|
| ναίεις εὐπατέρειαν αὐλάν, | thou dwellest at the court of thy great father, |
| Ζανὸς πολύχρυσον οἶκον | in the house of Zeus bedight with gold |

The earthly habitation of the god must correspond with the heavenly home in its glory-
sheen of infinite wealth; the halls of Olympus were all of gold (Eur. Ion 459–460):

| | |
|---|---|
| Ὀλύμπου χρυσέων θαλάμων | from Olympus's chambers of gold |
| πταμένα | winging thy way |

And one plank in the platform of Cloud-cuckoo-town's proposed declaration of independence
of the gods is that there will no more be need of building temples of marble with doors of
gold (Ar. Av. 612–614):

| | |
|---|---|
| καὶ πρῶτα μὲν οὐχὶ νεὼς ἡμᾶς | and first of all we need not |
| οἰκοδομεῖν δεῖ λιθίνους αὐτοῖς | build them temples of marble |
| οὐδὲ θυρῶσαι χρυσαῖσι θύραις | nor furnish these with doors of gold |

(Bacchyl. 27, 8):

| | |
|---|---|
| χρυσῷ δ' ἐλέφαντί τε μαρμαίροισιν οἶκοι | halls gleam with gold and ivory |

We are indebted to Euripides for the assurance that the brilliant decoration in gold
was not wanting in the old temple built by the wealthy Alcmaeonids in the opulent days
of Greece (Ion 156–157) (to the birds):

| | |
|---|---|
| αὐδῶ μὴ χρίμπτειν θριγκοῖς | I warn you not to come anigh the cornices |
| μηδ' εἰς χρυσήρεις οἴκους | nor to approach the halls bedight with gold |

[1] Macrob.  Sat. I 6, 6.
[2] Frag. IX  9, 1 (Dind.).
[3] Sat. Men. 56, 6 (Oehler).
[4] Aeschines, *contra Ctes.* 115 sqq.
[5] X 19, 4.
[6] Fraser, *l. c.*; cp. Henri Weil, *B. C. H.* XIX (1895), p. 396.

This means surely decorations of gold on the outside of the temple, not on the inside. That this is true is proved beyond a peradventure by Euripides's Iphigenia Taurica 126–131:

| | |
|---|---|
| ὦ παῖ τᾶς Λατοῦς | oh daughter of Leto, |
| . . . . . . . . . . . . | |
| πρὸς σὰν αὐλάν, εὐστύλων | to thy courts, to the cornices bedecked with |
| ναῶν χρυσήρεις θριγχούς, | gold upon thy fair-pillared temple |
| πόδα παρθένον... | my maiden foot . . . |
| . . . . . . . . . πέμπω | . . . I guide |

The gilded cornices can be nowhere save upon the entablature of the temple. There gold leaf or gilding is used for more splendid decorative effect in place of the more usual paint. The same fact is further substantiated by another passage in Euripides (El. 713–714):

| | |
|---|---|
| θυμέλαι δ' ἐπίτναντο | and the shrines, gold-wrought, |
| χρυσήλατοι | were filled to overflowing. |

This may mean that the walls of the shrine were encrusted with gold decoration, as above, or inlaid with gold decorative pattern, or adorned with articles of gold ornamentation. But at any rate, it is the outside of the θυμέλαι that are gold-laid—and certainly not "pavements," as Mr. Way interprets—and the shrines are thronged with worshipers or with religious choruses.

But there is another cornice (θριγχός) somewhere about the Delphic temple of Apollo. In the unraveling of the knot, as the plot becomes too thick toward the end of the Ion, the Pythian priestess comes out of the temple with Ion's long-hidden cradle in her arms and says (Ion 1320–1321):

| | |
|---|---|
| τρίποδα γὰρ χρηστήριον | for I have left the tripod oracular |
| λιποῦσα θριγχοῦ τοῦδ' ὑπερβάλλω πόδα | and above this cornice I set my foot[1] |

Obviously this is not the cornice of the entablature of the temple. But a cornice does not necessarily have to be located upon the superstructure of a building. The oldest θριγχός we know, the θριγχὸς κυάνοιο of Odyssey VII 87, like its counterpart in reality from Tiryns, was not high on the outside of the palace but comparatively low—a wainscoting—on the inside of one of the rooms. But the natural use for a cornice is as an ornamental finish to an upper edge. And so it is in this place: the great altar of the Chians at Delphi, at which Creusa has taken refuge and away from which Ion is trying to terrify her with his words of wrath, stands beside the Sacred Way before the temple. It was not separated from it by any "fence" or "wall," as Liddell and Scott interpret, citing this passage, and as Mr. Way translates; no "temple-fence" was there or could have been there. But the temple platform stood, and still stands, higher than the Sacred Way, and most naturally the coping of the edge of the platform between it and the altar was finished off with a cornice of some kind, and above this the priestess would naturally set her foot when she stops to address Ion who must be thought of as standing near the Sacred Way and close to the great altar.

The only other passage cited by Liddell and Scott to support the meaning of "fence" or "wall" is Aristophanes's Thesmophoriazusae 58–62:

> ΘΕ. τίς ἀγροιώτας πελάθει θριγχοῖς;
> ΜΝ. ὃς ἕτοιμος σοῦ τοῦ τε ποιητοῦ
>     τοῦ καλλιεποῦς κατὰ τοῦ θριγχοῦ
>     ξυγγογγύλας καὶ ξυστρέψας
>     τουτὶ τὸ πέος χοανεῦσαι

The whole dialog runs to the coarsest obscenity; and this passage at arms between Mnesilochus and the servant is the limit. Neither the plural θριγχοῖς (l. 58) nor the singular θριγχοῦ (l. 60) has anything to do with any sort of "fence" or "wall"; but that both are used *sensu obscoeno* is obvious from the context.

With all this magnificence of size and beauty, of marble sculpture and gold, it is no wonder that the splendor of Apollo's temple made a powerful impression upon the visitor, so that Euripides could sing its glories and compare it with the adornment of his own city (Ion 184 sqq., quoted on p. 52). And again (Ion 232–235):

---

[1] Reading πόδα with Badham and most edd.; the mss. have ποδί; Hartung, πέδον.

XO. ἃ δ' ἐκτὸς ὄμμα τέρψει.

CHO. 13. But on what is here without mine eyes shall feast.

ΙΩΝ. πάντα θεᾶσθ', ὅτι καὶ θέμις, ὄμμασι.

ION. Look with your eyes on all that it is right for you to see.

XO. μεθεῖσαν δεσπόται
με θεοῦ γύαλα τάδ' ἐσιδεῖν

CHO. 14. My masters have given me leave to look upon these halls of God

It is a universal joy to behold the wondrous temple; any other sentiment than one of joy arouses surprise (Eur. Ion 241–246) (Ion to Creusa):

ἔα·

Ah!

ἀλλ' ἐξέπληξάς μ', ὄμμα συγκλήσασα σὸν

thou fillest me with astonishment—closing thine eyes

δακρύοις θ' ὑγράνασ' εὐγενῆ παρηίδα,
ὡς εἶδες ἀγνὰ Λοξίου χρηστήρια.

and bedewing thy noble cheek with tears
at sight of Loxias's holy oracles.

. . . . . . . .

. . . . . .

οὗ πάντες ἄλλοι γύαλα λεύσσοντες θεοῦ
χαίρουσιν, ἐνταῦθ' ὄμμα σὸν δακρυρροεῖ

Where all others rejoice at beholding
God's holy place, thine eyes brim with tears

Euripides gives expression to a similar appreciation of the beauty of the place again (Andr. 1085–1087) (the Messenger to Peleus):

ἐπεὶ τὸ κλεινὸν ἤλθομεν Φοίβου πέδον
τρεῖς μὲν φαεννὰς ἡλίου διεξόδους
θέᾳ διδόντες ὄμματ' ἐξεπίμπλαμεν

when unto Phoebus's famed land we came,
three radiant courses of the sun we
devoted to the sights and sated our eyes with gazing

It required three days even then to get a fair view of Delphi's attractions.

After thus viewing the outside of the temple with the poet's help, let us pass with him into the shrine. But before we may cross the threshold (Ion 220–221), we must gain the right to do so:

θέμις γυάλων ὑπερ-
βῆναι λευκῷ ποδὶ βηλόν;

is it lawful with bared feet to
pass the threshold of the shrine?

Even marble temples, we see, have thresholds. There was a stone threshold there even in the primitive temple of Homer's days. It is mentioned once in both Iliad and Odyssey (I 404–405):

οὐδ' ὅσα λάινος οὐδὸς ἀφήτορος ἐντὸς ἐέργει

nor even all that the stone threshold of the archer,

Φοίβου 'Απόλλωνος, Πυθοῖ ἔνι πετρηέσσῃ

Phoebus Apollo, contains within, at rocky Pytho

In this passage from the Iliad the "stone threshold" is used figuratively for the temple itself. In the Odyssey, however, the "stone threshold" is used in its literal sense (θ 79–81):

ὣς γάρ οἱ χρείων μυθήσατο Φοῖβος 'Απόλλων

for thus Phoebus Apollo had spoken in an oracle to him

Πυθοῖ ἐν ἡγαθέῃ, ὅθ' ὑπέρβη λάινον οὐδὸν

at goodly Pytho, what time he crossed the threshold of stone

χρησόμενος

to inquire of the oracle

The threshold at Delphi the worshipers are not suffered to pass, without first having paid their sacrifice at the altar before the doors (Ion 226–229) (Ion to Chorus):

εἰ μὲν ἐθύσατε πέλανον πρὸ δόμων

if ye have offered before the temple your gift of sacrifice

καί τι πυθέσθαι χρήζετε Φοίβου,
πάριτ' εἰς θυμέλας, ἐπὶ δ' ἀσφάκτοις

and wish to make some inquiry of Phoebus,
pass into the sanctuary, but pass not into the holy

μήλοισι δόμων μὴ πάριτ' εἰς μυχὸν

place without sacrifice of victims first

The same altar is mentioned again in the Andromache (1100–1102):

ἡμεῖς δὲ μῆλα...
λαβόντες ἧμεν, ἐσχάραις τ' ἐφέσταμεν,
ξὺν προξένοισι μάντεσί τε Πυθικοῖς

but we took sheep . . .
and went and took our place beside the altars
with our public-hosts and Pythian seers

This is the great altar of burnt sacrifice beside the Sacred Way, before the temple's doors— the "altar of the Chians," as we know it from the excavations. Here great public sacrifices were performed (Eur. Ion 419–420):

| χρηστήριον πέπτωκε τοῖς ἐπήλυσι | a victim has fallen before the temple |
| κοινὸν πρὸ ναοῦ | for all the pilgrims in common |

And not only did this altar receive sacrifices of victims slain but upon it were placed also bloodless offerings (Eur. Ion 422–423):

| σὺ δ' ἀμφὶ βωμούς, ὦ γύναι, δαφνηφόρους | and, wife, do thou take the sacred branches and |
| λαβοῦσα κλῶνας... εὔχου | place them at the laurel-covered altars and pray |

By this Xuthus means the great altar outside the temple; for he straightway goes into the temple, and Ion, outside, observes his mother's execution of her husband's bidding.

To this altar, later on, that same mother, when convicted of an attempt to murder the god's priest and son and condemned to die for her premeditated crime, flies for refuge. Creusa enters the scene in hopeless flight; the chorus directs her (1255–1256):

| ΧΟ. ποῖ δ' ἂν ἄλλοσ' ἢ 'πὶ βωμόν; | CHO. Whither else than to the altar? |
| ΚΡ. καὶ τί μοι πλέον τόδε; | CR. Pray what avail were this to me? |
| ΧΟ. ἱκέτιν οὐ θέμις φονεύειν | CHO. A suppliant it is not lawful to slay |

And Ion in his fury swears to her that (1275–1276)

| οὔτε βωμὸς οὔτ' Ἀπόλλωνος δόμος | neither Apollo's altar nor house |
| σώσει σ' | shall save thee |

That this is the altar of burnt sacrifice is a matter of course; but we are not left to mere assumption in the matter. A few lines further on the poet makes the chorus use the word that leaves no doubt; the coryphaeus directs Creusa (1258):

| ἵζε νῦν πυρᾶς ἔπι | take now thy seat upon the fire-altar |

Earlier in the play we have been shown by Ion that the great altar is an altar for sacrifice of sheep (Ion 376–377):

| προβωμίοις | by sacrifice of sheep |
| σφαγαῖσι μήλων | before the altars |

The sacrifices at the altar were one of the sources of the young Ion's sustenance (Eur. Ion 323):

| βωμοὶ μ' ἔφερβον | the altars fed me |

(*ibid.* 52):

| νέος μὲν οὖν ἂν ἀμφὶ βωμίους τροφάς | so the youngster, about the altars that sustained him |

The implication of the burnt sacrifice is clear in all these passages; but in line 1280 it is again simply "the altar":

| βωμὸν ἔπτηξεν θεοῦ | at the god's altar she crouched |
| ὡς οὐ δίκην δώσουσα τῶν εἰργασμένων | as though she should not pay the penalty of her crimes |

Ion orders her with threats to leave her place of refuge (1306):

| ἔκλειπε βωμὸν καὶ θεηλάτους ἕδρας | leave the altar and seats built for the gods |

and 1401 Creusa says, as she recognizes the swaddling-bands of her own lost babe:

| λείψω δὲ βωμὸν τόνδε, κεἰ θανεῖν με χρή | I will leave this altar,[1] even though I must die for it |

and once more, by implication, the Chian altar is βωμός (Ion 1314):

| τοὺς μὲν γὰρ ἀδίκους βωμὸν οὐχ ἵζειν ἐχρῆν | the unrighteous ought not to have a seat (of safety) at an altar |

[1] cf. l. 1403, quoted below, p. 63.

Only in general terms do the poets give us even a vague hint as to the form of the altar. In keeping with marble altars that we know and with the pictures of altars on painted vases, the poets' descriptions have the altar proper constructed upon a base of a step or steps. Such a step is called by the same name as the step or steps that form the topmost courses of the foundation of a temple (e.g. Eur. H. F. 984–985):

| | |
|---|---|
| ἄλλῳ δ' ἐπεῖχε τόξ', ὃς ἀμφὶ βωμίαν | and at another he aimed his bow, who at the altar- |
| ἔπτηξε κρηπῖδα ὡς λεληθέναι δοκῶν | step cowered, hoping there to be unseen |

(Soph. Tr. 993):

| | |
|---|---|
| ὦ Κηναία κρηπὶς βωμῶν | oh step of altars Cenaean |

Beside this altar, or about it, were statues of the ξόανον type. Euripides calls them ξόανα (Ion 1402–1403):

| | |
|---|---|
| θεομανὴς γὰρ ἤλατο | for impelled by God she had leapt |
| βωμοῦ λιποῦσα ξόανα | away from the ξόανα of the altar |

By these ξόανα the sacred, heaven-fallen image cannot be meant; the plural form tells us that there were several images. It is quite possible that these, set up out of doors about the great altar of the god, were marble copies of the holy thing preserved within the temple; or perhaps they are other very ancient and very sacred statues that had their places hard by the great altar of Apollo.

We pass up the temple steps; even these Euripides names (Ion 38–39):

| | |
|---|---|
| τὸν παῖδα κρηπίδων ἔπι | upon this temple's steps the |
| τίθημι ναοῦ τοῦδ' | babe I lay |

Similarly (Ion 510–511):

| | |
|---|---|
| πρόσπολοι γυναῖκες, αἱ τῶν δ' ἀμφὶ κρηπῖδας δόμων | ye ladies-in-waiting, who at the steps of these incense- |
| θυοδόκων φρούρημ' ἔχουσαι δεσπότην φυλάσσετε | receiving halls keep watch, awaiting your lord's coming |

The κρηπῖδες are the great steps of the crepidoma, or the steps by which worshipers ascended from the temple platform to the colonnade.

We have a strange expression for threshold in Euripides's Ion 514:

| | |
|---|---|
| ἐν δόμοις ἔστ', ὦ ξέν'· οὔπω δῶμ' ὑπερβαίνει τόδε | he is within the halls, stranger; not yet doth he step across the threshold yonder |

The threshold, this time, is called the "building," the temple; but the meaning is clear: Xuthus is within the shrine oracular; he is not yet passing the threshold of the door; and the door is closed, for in the next instant comes the noise of the opening doors to let him pass out (Ion 515–516):

| | |
|---|---|
| ὡς δ' ἐπ'ἐξόδοισιν ὄντος τῶν δ' ἀκούομεν πυλῶν δοῦπον | the creaking of yonder doors we hear— evidence that he is at the exits |

In Andromache (1111–1113) κρηπίς is used figuratively[1] for the enclosure of the building itself; the Messenger is speaking here of Apollo's temple at Delphi:

| | |
|---|---|
| ἔρχεται δ' ἀνακτόρων κρηπῖδος ἐντός, ὡς πάρος χρηστηρίων | he passed within the enclosure of the lordly halls to make his prayer to Phoebus, before the oracles were given, |
| εὔξαιτο Φοίβῳ, τυγχάνει δ' ἐν ἐμπύροις | and was in the act of sacrificing at the altar of burnt offering |

[1] By a simpler and more natural metaphor κρηπίς is used in the sense of foundation (Eur. H. F. 1261–1262):

| | |
|---|---|
| ὅταν δὲ κρηπὶς μὴ καταβληθῇ γένους | and when the foundation of a race is not laid |
| ὀρθῶς, ἀνάγκη δυστυχεῖν τοὺς ἐκγόνους | in rectitude, the later generations must needs have illfortune |

So in Ae. Pers. 814–815:

| | |
|---|---|
| χοὐδέπω κακῶν | and not yet is the foundation |
| κρηπὶς ὕπεστιν | of our misfortunes laid |

The steps of temples belonged to the foundation rather than to the building proper.

Gaining the vestibule (the πρόδομος), we pause upon the pavement before the doors (Ion 103–106) (Ion sings):

| | |
|---|---|
| πτόρθοισι δάφνης | with branches of laurel |
| στέφεσίν θ' ἱεροῖς ἐσόδους Φοίβου | and with consecrated broom we shall cleanse |
| καθαρὰς θήσομεν, ὑγραῖς τε πέδον | Phoebus's portals and the pavement |
| ῥανίσιν νοτερόν | wet with drops from the stream |

These words have to do with the space before and about the portal. The doors themselves were two great valves of bronze, swung on hinges of bronze[1] and rolling open upon wheels of bronze, as we see the traces upon the floor of the Parthenon and other temples. As such doors were swung open, they necessarily made considerable noise. That is clear from the words of Virgil.[1] It is also clear from Euripides's Ion 515–516:

| | |
|---|---|
| ὡς δ' ἐπ' ἐξόδοισιν ὄντος τῶνδ' ἀκούομεν πυλῶν | but he is now at the exit; for we hear the grating sound of |
| δοῦπον, ἐξιόντα τ' ἤδη δεσπότην ὁρᾶν πάρα | yonder doors; and there, thou mayst see our lord coming forth |

The great doors rolled back with the noise of creaking bronze. That the doors were spacious and the entrance wide goes without saying; all Greek temples were built on that plan, for through the open doors in the translucent air of Hellas came all the light needed for even a vast interior. The doorway of the temple of Zeus at Olympia was nearly five metres wide by ten metres high; that of the Parthenon in Athens, nearly as spacious. The temple at Delphi must have had doors of about the same proportions. Accordingly, when Euripides speaks of the "narrow exit" of the sanctuary (Andr. 1140–1143)

| | |
|---|---|
| οἱ δ' ὅπως πελειάδες | but they, like doves that |
| ἱέρακ' ἰδοῦσαι πρὸς φυγὴν ἐνώτισαν. | have caught sight of a hawk, turned their backs in flight. |
| πολλοὶ δ' ἔπιπτον μιγάδες ἔκ τε τραυμάτων | And in the mêlée many fell by wounds |
| αὐτοὶ θ' ὑφ' αὑτῶν στενοπόρους κατ' ἐξόδους | and many crushed by their own comrades in the narrow exit |

he is speaking of a door not in and of itself narrow, but too narrow to accommodate the panic rout of the mob composing the Delphian ambush.

Here the doors afford an "exit" from within; from the other point of view they would, of course, be the "entrance," as in the prolog to the Ion (34):

| | |
|---|---|
| καὶ θὲς πρὸς αὐταῖς εἰσόδοις δόμων ἐμῶν | and place him at the very entrance to my halls |

The great doors themselves are called sometimes πύλαι "gates," and sometimes πυλώματα "gateways" (Eur. Ion 1613):

| | |
|---|---|
| προσεννέπω πύλας | I bid his gates farewell |

The great bronze doors must have been splendid in their own beauty, and upon them was reflected in addition the plastic splendor of the "twin brows," the sculptured pediments (Eur. Ion 1611):

| | |
|---|---|
| αἵδε εὐωποὶ πύλαι | and these fair-faced gates |

The bronze gates, with their sunken panels, perhaps engraved, would, even on the high places of Parnassus and within the sacred enclosure of Delphi, gather dust and dirt, as do Ghiberti's "Gates of Paradise" in Florence; and it was a part of young Ion's office to keep them bright and clean (Eur. Ion 79–80):

| | |
|---|---|
| ὡς πρὸ ναοῦ λαμπρὰ θῇ πυλώματα δάφνης κλάδοισι | to make the gates before the temple bright with boughs of bay |

The doors were provided with great handles, in the form of rings,[2] like knockers; by these rings the doors might be pulled open from the outside; and to them Creusa clings as she bids farewell to the temple of the father of her child (Eur. Ion 1612–1613):

| | |
|---|---|
| νῦν δὲ καὶ ῥόπτρων χέρας ἡδέως ἐκκρηνάμεσθα καὶ προσεννέπω πύλαις | and now with joy to the handles we cling and I bid his gates farewell |

[1] As described in Virg., Aen. I 449: foribus cardo stridebat aënis

[2] Cf. Ar. Amph., Frag. 39 K.: ῥόπτρον, which Harpocration explains as τὸν τῆς θύρας κρίκον; and Bekker aptly cites Xen. Hel. VI 4, 36: ἐπισπάσασα τὴν θύραν εἴχετο τοῦ ῥόπτρου.

These rings, which served also as knockers, are the handles of the doors of a great temple. Private doors also had their "knobs," which may also have served as knockers (Pl. As. 426):

iussin in splendorem dari bullas has foribus nostris

But the usual method[1] of knocking at a door in ancient times was with the foot; and frequently such "knocking" was very violent (Ar. Ran. 38-39):

| | |
|---|---|
| τίς τὴν θύραν ἐπάταξεν; ὡς κενταυρικῶς | who banged at the door?  How like a Centaur |
| ἐνήλαθ' ὅστις | he jumped at it, whoever it was |

It seemed to Heracles that the "knocking" came from at least a pair of horse's heels rather than from a human hand.  With similar violence the Merchant's servant in Plautus's Asinaria (384–391) assails the doors of Demaenetus:

LI.   quis nostras sic frangit fores? . . . .

. . . . . . . . . . . .

. . . . nolo ego fores conservas
meas a te verberarier . . . . . . . .
ME. pol hau periclum est cardines ecfringantur

. . . . . . . . . . .

LI.   . . . . extemplo ianitorem
clamat, procul si quem videt ire ad se calcitronem

### b. *Interior*

Crossing the threshold we stand upon the floor of the cella, the real abode of the god (Eur. Ion 576):

| | |
|---|---|
| ἐκλιπὼν θεοῦ δάπεδ' | leave the god's floors |

The plural is used either of the various chambers or recesses of the cella or of the various component parts of the pavement.  And it was a part of young Ion's duty to keep the floors also spotless (Eur. Ion 120–122):

| | |
|---|---|
| ἱερὰν φόβαν | the holy sprays |
| ᾇ σαίρω δάπεδον θεοῦ | with which I daily sweep God's floor |
| παναμέριος ἅμ' ἁλίου | at the hour when the sun's swift |
| πτέρυγι θοᾷ | pinions come, rendering my |
| λατρεύων τὸ καθ' ἡμαρ | service day by day |

In the back part of the cella stood the temple statue of Apollo.  Even in the days of Euripides the cultus statue in the Delphian temple was the time-honored ξόανον—the wooden image, ages old, or a stone image made in the likeness of one of wood to replace the wooden one when it decayed.  Stone copies of this, as we have seen,[2] may have stood by the great altar before the temple.

To the ξόανα, of which the poets have much to say, we shall return in the volume on Sculpture for a full discussion of these early images and the allusions of the dramatic poets to them.  At this point there is, however, one passage that calls for attention (Ae. Cho. 1059–1060):

| | |
|---|---|
| Λοξίου δὲ προσθιγὼν | and touching Loxias, he will |
| ἐλεύθερόν σε τῶνδε πημάτων κτίσει | make thee free from these woes |

Such is the reading of the manuscripts, and it is retained by many editors.  If the reading is correct—and that is possible, harsh as the construction may be—the Chorus says in effect: "Go, throw thy arms about the statue of Loxias, and he will make thee free."  But Loxias is not a cultus name.[3]  Loxias is the god of oracles; this is the only name of the god

---

[1] There were various methods of knocking for admittance.  Aristophanes makes even the god Dionysus ask how "the natives" in Hades do their knocking (Ran. 460–461), and Xanthias answers that his master should not hesitate to do it with a vim worthy of Heracles at least (462–463).

[2] See p. 63.

[3] In one passage Loxias has at first sight some apparent claim to being a cultus name (Ae. Eum. 60–61):

τῶνδε δεσπότῃ δόμων
αὐτῷ μελέσθω Λοξίᾳ μεγασθενεῖ

But even here he is strictly the god of prophecy, the indweller of the oracular temple.

that is never attached as by-name to any other name of the god of light; Phoebus Apollo, Delian Apollo, all sorts of Apollos, but never Loxias Apollo. As the oracular god, Loxias apparently never had a statue; at least none has come down to us, nor any record of his ever having had one; Loxias is unknown in art, except upon one vase, on which he is engaged in the contest with Heracles for the possession of the Delphic tripod.[1] Here, too, he is the god of prophecy. If he never had a statue, then Orestes could not have touched it. Accordingly, it is better to adopt, with most editors, the reading of Auratus Λοξίας for Λοξίου. The syntax is better; the sense is vastly better: "The touch of Loxias will set thee free."

Aristophanes contributes one detail to our conception of the appearance of this statue of Apollo at Delphi: the god is represented with his bow and quiver (Ar. Eq. 1270–1271):

| | |
|---|---|
| καὶ γὰρ οὗτος, ὦ φίλ' Ἄπολλον, ἀεὶ πεινῇ, θαλεροῖς δακρύοις σᾶς ἁπτόμενος φαρέτρας Πυθῶνι δία μὴ κακῶς πένεσθαι | for this fellow, beloved Apollo, is always hungry and with copious tears touches thy quiver at goodly Pytho, that he may not be so miserably poor |

The god of the oracular temple is the archer-god, the god of light, to whom the bow and arrows and quiver are an essential attribute.[2] Did this famous cultus image have also somewhere in its composition a hawk, the darting attendant of the far-darter? As the Zeus at Olympia had his eagle perched upon his sceptre; as the Hera of the Argive Heraeum had her peacock by her side; as the Athena of the Parthenon had her owl upon her helmet; did the Apollo at Delphi also have his peculiar bird, the hawk, perched upon some part of the figure? Compare Ar. Av. 514–516:

| | |
|---|---|
| ὁ Ζεὺς γὰρ ὁ νῦν βασιλεύων ἀετὸν ὄρνιν ἕστηκεν ἔχων ἐπὶ τῆς κεφαλῆς, βασιλεὺς ὤν· ἡ δ' αὖ θυγάτηρ γλαῦχ', ὁ δ' Ἀπόλλων ὥσπερ θεράπων ἱέρακα | for Zeus, who is now king, stands with the eagle bird upon his head, for he is king; his daughter has an owl, and Apollo, his attendant, a hawk |

Leaving the statue of the god, then, let us consider first the altar or altars of the god. The great altar for burnt sacrifice is the one that we have already seen before the temple. But here inside the temple also, directly before the ἕδος, the cultus image, is an altar with fire upon it (Eur. Andr. 1111–1113) (the Messenger, recounting to Peleus the death of Neoptolemus at Delphi):

| | |
|---|---|
| ἔρχεται δ' ἀνακτόρων κρηπίδος ἐντός, ὡς πάρος χρηστηρίων εὔξαιτο Φοίβῳ, τυγχάνει δ' ἐν ἐμπύροις | he passed within the enclosure of the lordly halls to make his prayer to Phoebus, before the oracles were given, and was in the act of sacrificing at the altar of burnt offering |

This blazing altar, we are generally told, is not for offerings of blood but of incense. Incense was burned in Grecian temples universally. The temple at Delphi has "incense-receiving" as a standing *epitheton ornans;* Euripides uses it in at least four passages referring directly to this temple (Ion 89–90):

| | |
|---|---|
| σμύρνης ἀνύδρου καπνὸς εἰς ὀρόφους Φοίβου πέτεται | and the smoke of frankincense brought from the desert land flies up to Phoebus's roof |

and (Andr. 1156–1157) (again the Messenger, telling Peleus of the death of Neoptolemus at Delphi):

| | |
|---|---|
| νεκρὸν δὲ δή νιν κείμενον βωμοῦ πέλας ἐξέβαλον ἐκτὸς θυοδόκων ἀνακτόρων | and him, then, lying dead beside the altar they cast forth from the incense-receiving shrine |

A similar phrase occurs again (Eur. Ion 510–511):

| | |
|---|---|
| πρόσπολοι γυναῖκες, αἳ τῶνδ' ἀμφὶ κρηπίδας δόμων θυοδόκων φρούρημ' ἔχουσαι δεσπότην φυλάσσετε | ye ladies-in-waiting, who at the steps of these incense-receiving halls keep watch, awaiting your lord's coming |

[1] Roscher, *Myth. Lex.* II², Sp. 2145.
[2] So essential an attribute of Apollo's is the quiver, that εὐφαρέτρης came to be used as an *epitheton ornans* of the god (Soph. Tr. 208–209): τὸν εὐφαρέτραν Ἀπόλλω

and again (Ion 1549–1550):

| τίς οἴκων θυοδόκων ὑπερτελὴς | who of the gods is it that above the incense-receiving fane |
| ἀντήλιον πρόσωπον ἐκφαίνει θεῶν; | shows a face that fronts the sun? |

But when Neoptolemus stands before the temple image in act of sacrificing at the blazing altar in Andromache 1113, it is not incense that he is about to offer there. It was not only at the great altar in front of the temple, against the Sacred Way, that burnt offerings of beasts were made. The altar in the cella also received gifts of victims slain. Euripides makes that clear in the Andromache (1111–1157) [the Messenger has told how Neoptolemus passed within the temple, was set upon by the Delphians there, snatched down votive weapons from the pillars, and leapt upon the altar for a position of advantage, and fought from there (l. 1123)]:

| ἔστη ἐπὶ βωμοῦ | he took his stand upon the altar |

and then later:

| βωμοῦ κενώσας δεξίμηλον ἐσχάραν | he abandoned the altar's hearth that sheep receives |
| . . . . . . . | |
| χωρεῖ πρὸς αὐτούς | . . . and moved upon them |

The epithet δεξίμηλον applied to the altar inside the temple can mean only one thing: this altar, too, was an altar of burnt sacrifice of flesh and blood of sheep and goats.

So, too, the temple of Thetis in Phthia receives sacrifice of sheep (Andr. 129–130) (Chorus to Andromache):

| λεῖπε δεξίμηλον | leave the halls that sheep receive |
| δόμον τᾶς ποντίας θεοῦ | of the goddess of the sea |

while in the Phoenissae (632), when Polynices bids farewell to the

| δεξίμηλ' ἀγάλματα | images of gods that sheep receive |

he is addressing the statues before the temple represented in the proscenium; and he singles out one, Apollo Agyieus, for a special farewell.

To these stage figures, which of course had their counterpart in the relations of actual life, we must later return in our volume on Sculpture.

We observe that sometimes Euripides calls this altar βωμός "altar" (Ion 1403) and sometimes ἐσχάρα "hearth" (Andr. 1138). Sophocles uses the two words as if they meant something quite different (Ant. 1016–1017):

| βωμοὶ γὰρ ἡμῖν ἐσχάραι τε παντελεῖς | for we see our altars and hearths, one and all, |
| πλήρεις ὑπ' οἰωνῶν τε καὶ κυνῶν βορᾶς | tainted with the food of dogs and birds of prey |

Both the "altars" and the "hearths" are holy things. Just what the difference in meaning may be is not clear;[1] but the "hearth" is something more intimate, belonging to the home of the divinity. ἐσχάρα may, therefore, be used as a close synonym for βωμός; and so we find it in Euripides's Phoenissae (284):

| μαντεῖα σεμνὰ Λοξίου τ' ἐπ' ἐσχάρας | to Loxias's revered oracles and hearths |

(Eur. Πλεισθ., Frag. 628 N.):

| μηλοσφαγεῖ τε δαιμόνων ἐπ' ἐσχάραις | and slaughters sheep at hearths of gods |

The plural "hearths" includes the many altars within the sacred enclosure of Delphi. But somewhere at Delphi was Apollo's famous hearth with its undying fire. Such a hearth would be holy as an altar and might be used as an altar of sacrifice. Sometimes, too, the

---

[1] The distinction made by Steph. Byz. (p. 198, 8) will not always hold in the drama. He says: Βωμοί— καὶ βωμὸς ὁ τόπος τῶν θυσιῶν, ὁ πρὸς τὴν ἐσχάραν διάφορος· ὁ μὲν γὰρ οἰκοδομητός, ἡ δὲ σκαπτή. Sophocles couples the two words once more (Αἰχ., Frag. 35 N.):

καὶ βωμιαῖον ἐσχάρας λαβών

The mere word ἐσχάρα of Soph. Χρύσ., Frag. 662 N., though we are assured that it means "altar" affords no further help.

poets speak of Apollo's sanctuary as ἑστία, "hearth." There is no distinction between the synonymous ἐσχάρα and ἑστία that I can discover further than that the former is always a poetic word, the latter, a homely name used in prose and poetry alike. Let us examine the passages in the dramatic poets in which the two words occur and see if they furnish light. In the passage already quoted from the Ion, ἐσχάρα "hearth" is undoubtedly the same thing as βωμός and is the altar in the cella of the temple. In the same tragedy we read in the invocation to Athena (ll. 457–464):

| | |
|---|---|
| ὦ πότνια Νίκα | oh victory-queen, |
| μόλε Πύθιον οἶκον | come to the Pythian dwelling, |
| Ὀλύμπου χρυσέων θαλάμων | winging thy way from Olympus's golden |
| πταμένα πρὸς ἀγυιάς, | halls to the streets, |
| Φοιβήιος ἔνθα γᾶς | where Phoebus's hearth |
| μεσσόμφαλος ἑστία | at earth's mid-navel, |
| παρὰ χορευομένῳ τρίποδι | by the tripod where choruses move, |
| μαντεύματα κραίνει | fulfilling its oracles |

Here the ἑστία, "hearth," is "by the tripod," which was certainly in the adytum, the holy of holies of the temple; and it has for its modifier μεσσόμφαλος, and the omphalus was certainly in the cella. We may fairly infer, then, that the ἑστία here is identical with the ἐσχάρα and the βωμός of the later passages in the Ion.

In Sophocles's Oedipus Tyrannus (964–965) ἑστία seems to have an even more mystic association and to belong in the very holy of holies itself:

| | |
|---|---|
| τί δῆτ' ἄν, ὦ γύναι, σκοποῖτό τις | why then, pray, my queen, should anyone have regard |
| τὴν Πυθόμαντιν ἑστίαν | for Pytho's oracular hearth? |

Here ἑστία is clearly used of the source of the oracle, which was from within the holy of holies, beyond the cella proper, where none might enter.

It is used in exactly the same way also in Sophocles's Oedipus Coloneus (413):

| | |
|---|---|
| ἀνδρῶν θεωρῶν Δελφικῆς ἀφ' ἑστίας | from men on sacred mission to the Delphic hearth |

These men had been sent to Delphi to get an oracle and they had brought the god's message "from the Delphic hearth," the holy of holies where the oracles were uttered.

Aeschylus is still more exact, in one passage, locating the hearth unequivocally in the innermost shrine (Eum. 166–170):

| | |
|---|---|
| πάρεστι γᾶς ὀμφαλὸν προσδρακεῖν αἱμάτων | one may behold earth's navel that hath taken |
| βλοσυρὸν *ἀρόμενον ἄγος ἔχειν | upon it a fell pollution of blood. |
| ἐφεστίῳ δὲ *μάντις ὢν μιάσματι | And, though a seer, thou hast fouled thy innermost |
| μυχὸν ἔχρανας | shrine with guilt that stains thy hearth |

Orestes has taken refuge at the omphalus; he has penetrated into the innermost shrine where the omphalus stood; the pollution of his presence has stained the hearth that symbolized the true indwelling of the god. In the same tragedy he sat a suppliant at "the hearth of Apollo's halls" (Ae. Eum. 577–578):

| | |
|---|---|
| ἱκέτης ὅδ' ἀνήρ, καὶ δόμων ἐφέστιος | this man is my suppliant and (sat) |
| ἐμῶν | at the hearth of my halls |

A suppliant at the hearth of the halls could have been nowhere save in the heart of the home—the innermost sanctuary of the temple. And into the innermost sanctuary the Furies had followed him, for Apollo orders them to get out of the adytum, the place of the oracle itself (Ae. Eum. 179–180):

| | |
|---|---|
| ἔξω, κελεύω, τῶνδε δωμάτων τάχος | out, I bid you; leave with all speed these |
| χωρεῖτ', ἀπαλλάσσεσθε μαντικῶν μυχῶν | halls; depart from the shrine oracular |

He emphasizes the situation again (ll. 194–195):

| | |
|---|---|
| οὐ χρηστηρίοις | and not to rub off their foul |
| ἐν τοῖσδε †πλησίοισι τρίβεσθαι μύσος | pollution in these places of oracle hard by |

In other passages the meaning of ἑστία is not so clearly defined (Eur. Andr. 1066–1068):

| | |
|---|---|
| οὐκ ὅσον τάχος | will not some one with all speed |
| χωρήσεταί τις Πυθικὴν πρὸς ἑστίαν | depart to the Pythian hearth |
| καὶ τἀνθάδ' ὄντα τοῖς ἐκεῖ λέξει φίλοις | and tell our friends there of the situation here |

Here the "Pythian hearth" is nothing more or less than Delphi, and Peleus selects for the place of his messenger's meeting with the friends there "the hearth," perhaps the hearth of the Prytaneum, where strangers of note found public entertainment.

Aeschylus (Eum. 282–283) seems to be again a little more definitely topographical in his allusion:

| | |
|---|---|
| ποταίνιον γὰρ ὂν πρὸς ἑστίᾳ θεοῦ | for when it [the stain of mother's blood] was fresh, |
| Φοίβου καθαρμοῖς ἠλάθη χοιροκτόνοις | it was washed away at God's hearth by Phoebus's cleansing with the blood of swine[1] |

Purification from bloodguiltiness by a mere human agency could be performed at the purifier's hearth. So here this may be Apollo's hearth in the Prytaneum, or it may be his altar in the temple. The preceding passages make the latter interpretation more probable. The probabilities in favor of the altar in the temple are made almost certainty by the vase-painters.[2] The oxybaphon from Armento in Apulia,[3] now in the Louvre, may almost be taken as an illustration made for the scene to which Orestes alludes: Orestes sits upon the upper step of the basis that supports the filleted omphalus; he holds his naked sword in his lifted right hand and with his left braces himself against a possible attack from the Furies, while he looks uneasily in the direction of his enemies. Apollo, wrapped in splendid robes and holding a laurel branch in his left hand,[4] stands behind Orestes upon the upper step of the omphalus base and swings over the matricide's head a little pig. That is the "cleansing with the blood of swine," to which Orestes has referred. The vase-painter, however, did not rest content with that, but for additional dramatic interest he introduced also a suggestion from the first scene of the Eumenides: before Orestes are the Furies inside the temple; they have slept while Apollo has been performing the rites of purification. Enter the ghost of Clytaemnestra rousing them from their sleep to renewed action and pointing toward the son that has shed his mother's blood. Two Furies still snore (Ae. Eum. 53; 117–129); one is awakening, stretching her arms and opening her eyes, suggesting the pursuit and persecution that are presently to begin anew. Behind Apollo stands, like him in untroubled divinity, his huntress sister Artemis.

The vase-painter has included in his illustration of the Eumenides many of the poet's details: the "snoring" Furies (Ae. Eum. 53; 117–129); the "man abhorred of god" (l. 40), inside the temple (l. 35), sword in hand (ll. 42–43); the "omphalus" (l. 40); the "approach to the inner sanctuary" (l. 39) from which the Pythia has suddenly come forth; the "ghost of Clytaemnestra" (ll. 94–139); the "pig with blood of cleansing" (l. 283); "Phoebus performing the cleansing rites" (ll. 282–283). (For the location of the omphalus see pp. 71 ff.)

The point that I wish to make is this: the picture is an illustration of the Aeschylean scene (or scenes); the picture represents the interior of the Delphic temple, for the omphalus was certainly not in the Prytaneum; the vase-painter was working while Aeschylus yet lived and knew not only the poet but also the "hearth"; the scene of the cleansing is, therefore, inside the temple; the ἑστία, the hearth, therefore, was in the cella of Apollo's temple.

[1] Cf. Ae. Frag. Inc. 327 N.: πρὶν ἂν σταλαγμοῖς αἵματος χοιροκτόνου
αὐτός σε χράνῃ Ζεὺς καταστάξας χεροῖν.
Cf. also Ae. Eum. 450.

[2] For the material see Overbeck, *Heroengal.* Taf. 29, and pp. 700–720; Roscher, *Myth. Lex., s. v.* Orestes, III¹ Sp. 983–984.

[3] Reproduced, Baum. *Denkm., s. v.* Orestes II, p. 1117, Fig. 1314; Roscher, *l. c.*; Overbeck, *l. c.*; *Mon. Inst.* IV 48.

[4] Ar. (Plut. 212–213) gives just this picture of Apollo, the giver of prophecy:

| | |
|---|---|
| ἔχω τιν' ἀγαθὴν ἐλπίδ' ἐξ ὧν εἶπέ μοι | I have right high hopes, in view of what Phoebus |
| ὁ Φοῖβος αὐτὸς Πυθικὴν σείσας δάφνην | himself told me, waving the Pythian laurel |

In the Choephori, on the other hand, we have a passage in which, apart from the later scene just cited from the Eumenides, ἑστία might be, and often is, interpreted as the holy hearth of the Prytaneum (Ae. Cho. 1035–1039):

| | |
|---|---|
| ξὺν τῷδε θαλλῷ καὶ στέφει προσίξομαι | with this filleted [olive] branch will I go to the |
| μεσόμφαλόν θ' ἵδρυμα, Λοξίου πέδον, | foundation at earth's navel, the place of Loxias, |
| πυρός τε φέγγος ἄφθιτον κεκλημένον, | and to the blazing fire called undying, |
| φεύγων τόδ' αἷμα κοινόν· οὐδ' ἐφ' ἑστίαν | to escape this stain of kindred blood; for |
| ἄλλην τραπέσθαι Λοξίας ἐφίετο | Loxias bade me turn to no other hearth |

It is to the Prytaneum that we should naturally look first for the "undying" fire. Frazer[1] seems to argue for the Prytaneum as "the Common Hearth, where distinguished strangers and benefactors of the city were entertained, and a perpetual fire, tended by widows and fed only with pine-wood, burned upon it." Such a hearth there was at Delphi, with its fire that was never allowed to die out—just as in the Prytaneum at Athens[2] and at Olympia.[3] And if it ever did chance to go out, it had to be lighted from the rays of the sun by means of burning-glasses! "There may very well have been two perpetual fires at Delphi," Mr. Frazer concedes, "one in the Prytaneum and one in the temple, just as at Athens there was one in the Prytaneum and another—the ever burning lamp—in the Erechtheum." But Plutarch[4] tells us that when the temple was burned by the Medians in the Mithridatic War, this undying fire was extinguished. Plutarch obviously is speaking of the undying fire on the hearth in the temple. Pausanias no less clearly places the ἑστία in the cella of the temple. And so Aeschylus, associating the "hearth" (ἑστία) with the "foundation at earth's navel" (μεσόμφαλον ἵδρυμα), is in all probability thinking of the hearth in the temple; for the omphalus, let us bear in mind, was certainly in the cella of the temple; still μεσόμφαλον ἵδρυμα may, of course, mean nothing more definite than the temenos of Delphi generally.

To resume, then, ἑστία ("hearth") may be used in any one of three ways: 1) The hearth of Apollo's temple, an altar with undying fire;[5] 2) the "common hearth" of Delphi, in the Prytaneum, with its undying fire; 3) Delphi, the sacred enclosure generally.

ἐσχάρα, as we have seen, may also be used 1) for the hearth of Apollo's temple, an altar at which burnt sacrifice might be made (Eur. Andr. 1138, quoted above); 2) Delphi, the sacred enclosure generally. Compare Euripides's Suppliants 1197–1204 (Athena, *dea ex machina*, to Theseus):

| | |
|---|---|
| ἔστιν τρίπους σοι χαλκόπους εἴσω δόμων, | thou hast within thy halls a tripod with feet of bronze; |
| ὃν Ἰλίου ποτ' ἐξαναστήσας βάθρα σπουδὴν ἐπ' ἄλλην Ἡρακλῆς ὁρμώμενος στῆσαί σ' ἐφίετο Πυθικὴν πρὸς ἐσχάραν. | when Heracles had overturned Troy's foundation and was hastening on to another task, he commissioned thee to set this up at the Pythian hearth. |
| ἐν τῷδε λαιμοὺς τρεῖς τριῶν μήλων τεμὼν ἔγγραψον ὅρκους τρίποδος ἐν κοίλῳ κύτει, κἄπειτα σῴζειν θεῷ δὸς ᾧ Δελφῶν μέλει, | Over it cut three throats of three sheep and grave upon the tripod's belly the oaths and then give it to the god whose care is Delphi to guard, |
| μνημεῖά θ' ὅρκων μαρτύρημά θ' Ἑλλάδι | to be to Hellas a memorial and witness of oaths |

That is, most obviously, Theseus is to set up within the sacred enclosure at Delphi as an offering a tripod of bronze—suggesting very naturally Gelon's three bronze tripods, whose bases still stand by the northeast corner of the temple. For it goes without saying that this is not the tripod of the adytum. The same general sense is conveyed also in Euripides's Andromache 1239–1242 (Thetis, *dea ex machina*, to Peleus):

| | |
|---|---|
| τὸν μὲν θανόντα τόνδ' Ἀχιλλέως γόνον θάψον πορεύσας Πυθικὴν πρὸς ἐσχάραν, Δελφοῖς ὄνειδος, ὡς ἀπαγγείλῃ τάφος | as for Achilles's son who lies here dead, fare thou to the Pythian hearth and bury him— a reproach to the Delphians, that his sepulchre may proclaim |
| φόνον βίαιον τῆς Ὀρεστείας χερός | his murder by the violence of Orestes's hand |

---

[1] *Paus.* IV, p. 441 and V, p. 351.
[2] Cf. Arist. Pol. 1322 b 28; C. I. A. II, Nos. 467, 470, 471, 605.
[3] Cf. Paus. V 15, 9.
[4] Plut. de EI apud Delphos; *id.* Numa 9.
[5] ἑστία is often used of the altar of burnt sacrifice; e. g. Ae. Sep. 275;

| | |
|---|---|
| μήλοισιν αἱμάσσοντας ἑστίας θεῶν | staining with blood of sheep the hearths of gods |

MARBLE OMPHALUS
In the Museum at Delphi

Here, too, ἐσχάρα is not literally Apollo's hearth. Neoptolemus's body had long since been cast forth from the temple and the altar which his blood had defiled (ll. 1156–1157):

| | |
|---|---|
| νεκρὸν δὲ δή νιν κείμενον βωμοῦ πέλας | and him, then, lying dead beside the altar, |
| ἐξέβαλον ἐκτὸς θυοδόκων ἀνακτόρων | they cast forth from the lordly halls with incense filled |

The hearth here, therefore, as in the last citation, must be used of Delphi generally and does not refer to any hearth or altar, as such. So far as I have been able to find, ἐσχάρα is never used in extant dramatic literature of the hearth with the never-dying fire in the Prytaneum.

Conspicuous in the cella of the Delphian temple was the omphalus, the "navel" of the earth, marking the earth's central point. The story, as told by Strabo[1], runs that the question arose as to where the centre of the earth's surface was, and that Zeus, to solve the problem, sent out two eagles simultaneously to fly at the same speed, one from the western and one from the eastern limit of the world. The two eagles came together at Delphi, and that was the centre of the world—γᾶς ὀμφαλός "earth's navel" (Ae. Eum. 166); τὰ μεσόμφαλα γᾶς μαντεῖα "the oracles spoken at earth's central shrine" (Soph. O. T. 480–481[2]). We have almost the same turn of expression in Euripides (Ion 461–464):

| | |
|---|---|
| Φοιβήιος ἔνθα γᾶς | where Phoebus's hearth at |
| μεσόμφαλος ἑστία | earth's central shrine by |
| παρὰ χορευομένῳ τρίποδι | the tripod where choruses move |
| μαντεύματα κραίνει | fulfils its oracles |

and a similar use of ὄμφαλος we find again in Aeschylus's Septem (745–747):

| | |
|---|---|
| Ἀπόλλωνος... | though Apollo thrice spake the word at his |
| ...τρὶς εἰπόντος ἐν μεσομφάλοις Πυθικοῖς | Pythian oracles at earth's central |
| χρηστηρίοις | shrine |

The same idea, expressed in slightly different form, occurs in Euripides's Ion (913–914):

| | |
|---|---|
| πρὸς χρυσέους θάκους καὶ | to his golden throne and |
| γαίας μεσσήρεις ἕδρας | earth's midmost seat |

The same thought, an elaboration of Sophocles's words, occurs in an unknown Latin tragic poet (Ribbeck.[3], Frag. Trag. Lat., Inc. Inc. Fab. 19–20):

> O sancte Apollo, qui umbilicum certum terrarum optines,
> unde superstitiosa primum saeva evasit vox foras

"O hallowed Apollo, who hast in thy keeping the sure navel of the earth, from whence the voice of prophecy, unkind at first, came forth." The Latin poet speaks with Greek sentiments and repeats the idea of the navel as associated with the prophetic shrine of Apollo.

And there in Delphi, to mark the spot where the two eagles came together, was set up the egg-shaped stone with the two eagles in gold beside it. The precise location of the omphalus is not given by the poets, but they leave no doubt that it was inside the temple. The chorus in Euripides's Ion, standing in front of the temple at Delphi, ask if they may go inside. Ion says "No"; but prompted by a natural curiosity to know about what was inside of the temple, they ask again (223–224):

| | |
|---|---|
| ἆρ' ὄντως μέσον ὀμφαλὸν | does Phoebus's house really contain |
| γᾶς Φοίβου κατέχει δόμος; | the navel, the centre of the earth? |

and Ion replies (225):

| | |
|---|---|
| στέμμασί γ' ἐνδυτόν, ἀμφὶ δε γοργόνες | yea; twined with fillets, and the gorgons at its side |

There can be no doubt as to Euripides's words: the omphalus was inside the temple. In the Medea (667–668) ὀμφαλός is used almost synonymously with χρηστήριον, the oracle itself:

| | |
|---|---|
| ΑΙ. Φοίβου παλαιὸν ἐκλιπὼν χρηστήριον. | AE. Leaving Phoebus's ancient oracle. |
| ΜΗ. τί δ' ὀμφαλὸν γῆς θεσπιῳδὸν ἐστάλης; | ME. On what mission sent to earth's prophetic navel? |

[1] Strabo, IX p. 419.
[2] Cf. Pind. Pyth. IV 73–74: μάντευμα...
παρ' μέσον ὀμφαλὸν εὐδένδροιο ῥηθὲν ματέρος

The chamber of the temple that served for the real indwelling of the god was of course the holy of holies, and there was Apollo's "mid-navel seat" from which he pronounced his oracles (Eur. Or. 591–592):

| | |
|---|---|
| Ἀπόλλων ὃς μεσομφάλους ἕδρας | Apollo dwelling in his mid-navel seat |
| ναίων βρότοισι στόμα νέμει σαφέστατον | opens to mortals lips in clearest revelation |

And again, in a passage in which Phoebus himself is represented as uttering the oracles with his own lips, the omphalus, rather than the oracular tripod, is the seat from which the god reveals the things that are and the things that are to be (Eur. Ion 5–7):

| | |
|---|---|
| ἥκω δὲ Δελφῶν τήνδε γῆν, ἵν' ὀμφαλὸν | and I am come to this land of Delphi, where, sitting |
| μέσον καθίζων Φοῖβος ὑμνῳδεῖ βροτοῖς | at the mid-navel, Phoebus chants to mortals, forever revealing unto them the things that are and are to be |
| τά τ' ὄντα καὶ μέλλοντα θεσπίζων ἀεί | |

When Phoebus himself utters oracles, he certainly must have his place in the holy of holies, and that is here represented by the "mid-navel."

While such passages are not decisive, in themselves, they still do lend support to the more definite testimony already cited and to the evidence contained also in the following verses that the navel was inside the temple (Eur. Ion 460–464):

| | |
|---|---|
| πταμένα πρὸς ἀγυιάς, | winging thy way to the streets, where |
| Φοιβήιος ἔνθα γᾶς | Phoebus's hearth by the earth's |
| μεσσόμφαλος ἑστία | mid-navel, beside the tripod |
| παρὰ χορευομένῳ τρίποδι | where the choruses move, ful- |
| μαντεύματα κραίνει | fils the oracles |

The omphalus is by the inner hearth; it is beside the tripod of the oracular shrine; it is "dressed," covered with fillets; and on either side of it is a "fierce" or "grim" creature of some sort. Euripides's γοργόνες are not the three Gorgons, Euryale, Theino, and Medusa. They may be any sort of creature with "grim," "fierce" eyes. And the common story, as told by the ancients, from Pindar (Pyth. IV 4–6):

| | |
|---|---|
| ἔνθα ποτὲ χρυσέων Διὸς αἰετῶν πάρεδρος | where once the priestess that hath her seat beside |
| οὐκ ἀποδάμου Ἀπόλλωνος τυχόντος ἱέρεια | the golden eagles of Zeus gave them an oracle |
| χρῆσεν | —and Apollo chanced not to be away— |

to the scholiasts (on Eur. Or. 331, for example):

| | |
|---|---|
| ἀνακεῖσθαί τε χρυσοῦς ἀετούς φασι | and there were set up golden eagles, they say, |
| τῶν μυθευομένων ἀετῶν ὑπομνήματα | in memory of the eagles of the story |

is that they were eagles and that they were made of gold; and eagles we have beside it in a few representations of the omphalus in works of Greek art: for example, a coin of Cyzicus (reproduced in the *Numismatic Chronicle*, 1887, Pl. I 23); the exquisitely beautiful Apollo-Artemis relief in the Museum of Sparta (reproduced on the opposite page); an imperial bronze coin of Megara with the eagles on top of the omphalus (reproduced Imhoof-Blümner and Gardner, *Numism. Com. on Paus.*, pl. A ix; cp. Strabo, quoted p. 71).

To Aeschylus it is quite as clear that the omphalus was inside the temple. The Pythian prophetess, who speaks the prolog in the Eumenides, staggers terrified from out the temple of Apollo and says (Eum. 39–41):

| | |
|---|---|
| ἐγὼ μὲν ἕρπω πρὸς πολυστεφῆ μυχόν· | I was moving toward the inner sanctuary garland-twined |
| ὁρῶ δ' ἐπ' ὀμφαλῷ μὲν ἄνδρα θεομυσῆ | and I saw at the navel a man abhorred of God |
| ἕδραν ἔχοντα προστρόπαιον | holding a seat of supplication |

There was Orestes in the cella of the temple bedecked with many garlands, like the altar in front of the temple,[1] kneeling or crouching on the steps of the basis that bore the filleted omphalus. And there, defiling the omphalus, he still is in lines 166–170 in the innermost sanctuary, by the sacred hearth:

[1] Cp. Eur. Ion 422 and p. 62.

APOLLO AND ARTEMIS
BY THE OMPHALUS, WITH THE TWO EAGLES, AT DELPHI
Relief in the Musuem of Sparta

πάρεστι γᾶς ὀμφαλὸν προσδρακεῖν αἱμάτων
βλοσυρὸν ἀρόμενον ἄγος ἔχειν.
    ἐφεστίῳ δὲ μάντις ὢν μιάσματι

μυχὸν ἔχρανας

| | |
|---|---|
| | one may behold earth's navel that hath taken upon it a fell pollution of blood. |
| | And, though a seer, thou hast fouled thy innermost |
| | shrine with guilt that stains thy hearth |

The guilt of Orestes's defilement of the omphalus is heightened by its well known, un-approachable sanctity (Soph. O. T. 897–898):

οὐκ ἔτι τὸν ἄθικτον εἶμι γᾶς ἐπ'
ὀμφαλὸν σέβων | never again will I go on reverent pilgrimage
to earth's navel inviolable

The oft-recurring epithet μεσόμφαλος ("mid-navel") is not without significance. When Orestes takes up his laurel branch with fillets and says he will go as a suppliant to Apollo to beg salvation from the avengers of his mother's blood, he puts his determination into the significant words (Ae. Cho. 1035–1036):

ξὺν τῷδε θαλλῷ καὶ στέφει προσίξομαι
μεσόμφαλον ἵδρυμα, Λοξίου πέδον | with this filleted branch will I go to the
mid-navel shrine, the home of Loxias

The home where Loxias dwelt was the oracular temple; the mid-navel shrine is the shrine that contained the omphalus. The μεσόμφαλος ἑστία of Euripides's Ion 462 is also suggestive (see pp. 69–71; 72) and lends force to the location of the omphalus in the cella of the temple. And when the epithet is attached to χρηστήριον or μυχοί the evidence seems conclusive (Ae. Sep. 746–747):

ἐν μεσομφάλοις Πυθικοῖς χρηστηρίοις. | at the Pythian oracles at earth's central shrine

(Eur. Or. 329–331):

τρίποδος ἄπο φάτιν, ἂν ὁ Φοῖβος
 
ἔλαχεν ἔλαχε, δεξάμενος ἀνὰ δάπεδον
 
ἵνα μεσόμφαλοι λέγονται μυχοί | receiving from the tripod the commission that Phoebus
uttered—uttered, as thou stoodest upon the floor,
where, they say, is the mid-navel holy of holies

Orestes, the chorus says, stood upon the floor of Phoebus's temple, in hearing distance of the awful tripod itself from which the voice of Phoebus came, and there were the penetralia —the inner chambers of the cella containing the omphalus. In like manner when Euripides applies the epithet to γύαλα Φοίβου, the very use of γύαλα (strictly, the "treasure vaults" of the temple[1]) implies that the omphalus is in the holy place (Ph. 237–238):

παρὰ μεσόμφαλα γύαλα Φοί-
βου Δίρκαν προλιποῦσα | leaving Dirce for Phoebus's
mid-navel holy place

This fact receives some additional strength from a much mutilated fragment of Sophocles, in which, however, the restoration of γυάλων naturally suggests itself ('Oδ. 'Aχ., Frag. 422 N.):

νῦν δ' οὔτε μ' ἐκ Δωδῶνος οὔτε Πυθικῶν
γυ<άλων> τις ἂν πείσειεν | and now one could not persuade me with a word
from either Dodona or the Pythian holy of holies

It was from the innermost holy place that the responses of the oracle came.

The above interpretation of μεσόμφαλος ἑστία should, perhaps, not be pressed too far. It is, of course, the "central hearth" and, as such, is the most holy place. Aeschylus uses the phrase of the central hearth, the altar of Zeus Herceius, the god of the household enclosure, the penetralia of the family (Ag. 1056–1057):

τὰ μὲν γὰρ ἑστίας μεσομφάλου
ἕστηκεν ἤδη μῆλα πρὸς σφαγὰς πυρός | the victims stand even now by the central
hearth, ready for the fiery sacrifice

But here, too, the μεσόμφαλος ἑστία is the holiest spot about the palace of the king of men. The region about the altar was most sacred; the "hearth" is the altar—an altar of burnt sacrifice—and it is the mid-navel of the home. And so it was in Apollo's home at Delphi.

In the poets, then, the omphalus is in the cella of the temple and is not visible from out of doors; it is covered with a network of fillets; it is flanked by the two eagles of gold.

---

[1] γύαλα may, of course, by synecdoche, be put for the whole temple; so, for example, Eur. Ion 234.

These data are corroborated by many other witnesses. Strabo (IX 6, p. 419 ff.), after telling the story of the two eagles, goes on:

| | |
|---|---|
| δείκνυται δὲ καὶ ὀμφαλός τις ἐν τῷ ναῷ | and there is exhibited also in the temple a |
| τεταινισμένος καὶ ἐπ' αὐτῷ | certain navel, decked with fillets and upon it |
| αἱ δύο εἰκόνες τοῦ μύθου | the two figures of the story |

The vase-paintings inspired by Aeschylus (like the Armento oxybaphon described on page 69 and the magnificent composition reproduced from Baumeister, on the opposite page) illustrate just what has been described: a block (of marble), shaped like an egg with the larger end cut off square to afford it a surface on which it may stand, and covered with a network of woolen fillets tied in oval bunches. On some vase-paintings[1] the fillets look like ordinary ribbons thrown over it.[2]

The golden eagles were still in place down to the closing years of the fifth century B. C., for they appear in the Attic relief in Sparta (p. 72). And an omphalus was still inside the temple at the time of the restoration in the fourth century; for an official account of that restoration defines the façade of the cella as "the façade in front of the omphalus."[3] The front wall of the temple is here located by the position of the omphalus within the cella. Another (or a portion of the same) inscription mentions "work about the omphalus."

But Pausanias, who follows a strictly topographical order in his description, describes the omphalus as he comes to it among the votive offerings outside and in front of the temple; all he says is (X 16, 3):

| | |
|---|---|
| τὸν δὲ ὑπὸ Δελφῶν καλούμενον | as for the omphalus, as it is called by |
| ὀμφαλόν, λίθου πεποιημένον λευκοῦ, | the Delphians, it is made of white marble, and |
| τοῦτο εἶναι ἐν μέσῳ γῆς πάσης αὐτοί τε | the Delphians themselves say that it is in the centre |
| λέγουσιν οἱ Δελφοί, καὶ ἐν ᾠδῇ τινι | of the whole earth, and Pindar too in an ode of his |
| Πίνδαρος ὁμολογοῦντά σφισιν ἐποίησε | has written verses in agreement with what they say |

That is all; the omphalus is outside the temple, and there are no eagles mentioned. The eagles were of gold, as we saw. We are expressly told (by the Scholiast on Pindar, Pyth. IV 6) that they were carried off by the Phocians in the Phocian War and melted down and minted into coin. They were evidently saved from the ruins of the temple that Pindar and the tragic poets knew—the Alcmaeonid temple—when it was destroyed in 373. And the omphalus may have been moved out of the temple when Nero committed his infinite plundering of the shrine. At all events, a marble omphalus decorated with fillets was found by the French excavators in just the place where, from Pausanias's description, we should have expected to find it—near the Altar of the Chians.

But Strabo, in the passage quoted above (p. 74), states that the omphalus was inside the temple and that the eagles were "upon it" (ἐπ' αὐτῷ). We need not reject his statement and force upon him honorary membership in the Ananias Club as Mr. Frazer[4] does, just because his story is not exactly like Pausanias's. It is still entirely possible that there was in Strabo's day an omphalus *inside* the temple, with eagles *on it* (for the engraver of the Megarian coin from the days of Geta must have known such an omphalus with eagles on it, renewed in this form at some restoration after 371), and there may have been another omphalus outside the temple, without any eagles, and we are not surprised to find at Delphi to-day *two* omphali discovered in the excavations, one with fillets and one without. There may have been a dozen, or dozens, of them at Delphi in the olden days. Both Pausanias and Strabo, therefore, may be telling the truth, if not the whole truth and nothing but the truth. Strabo has no occasion to mention any omphalus outside the temple, and Pausanias mentions hardly anything inside the temple. Having said all that he cared to say about the outside, he passes over the one inside, when he reaches that point a little later on in his description, along with the many, many other objects that must have been there and that he does not deign to mention.

[1] E. g., Baum. *Denkm.* II p. 1110, Fig. 1307.
[2] The omphalus is represented not only on coins and vase-paintings, but it occurs often also in sculptures. For a partial list see Müller, *Hdb. d. Archaeol.*, § 362, 5, p. 546; Frazer, *Paus.* V pp. 315 ff.
[3] ἁ πρόστασις ἁ πρὸ τοῦ ὀμφαλοῦ; see Homolle, *Comptes Rendus de l'Ac. des Inscr.* XXIII (1895), p. 335.
[4] *Paus.* V p. 315.

ORESTES AT DELPHI

Vase-painting in the Louvre

So we return to our poets. They and the vase-paintings inspired by them tell us really all that we know or can know of the Delphian omphalus—a truncated oval of white marble two to four feet high, covered with a net-work of fillets, flanked by two eagles of gold; and the marble remains corroborate all that they say.

Poulsen quotes[1] the ancient heresies that according to some the omphalus marked the grave of the dragon, according to others the grave of Dionysus.[2] "In reality," Poulsen continues, "the Omphalos was a primitive stone fetish prior to Apollo, which was taken over by him. It was not the only stone in the cella of the temple; here was also shown the stone that Rhea gave to Kronos in place of the child (Zeus) she had borne, which Kronos disgorged later. The stone of Kronos was anointed daily, and at each festival was draped with unwrought wool.[3] This testifies that the stone was a primitive image, and it is natural to conceive these two remarkable stone fetishes as the couple who originally ruled Delphi —Poseidon and Ge—whom the new religion had to take over, explain, and work into its cult, just as Mohammed was compelled to recognize the old fetish of Mecca, the famous black stone, and make it the stone of Abraham. Even the Jews had difficulty in overcoming fetishism: according to Genesis, chapter xxviii, Jacob raised a stone where he had had his dream, poured oil over it, and called the spot Beth-el (God's House)."

Besides the temple statue and the altar and the omphalus, the cella contained rich votive offerings. Here were the famous ἀναθήματα of Croesus and Gyges; here were the many rich gifts of Greeks and barbarians, who had trusted in the oracle infallible. The wealth of the Delphian sanctuary was proverbial. Pausanias says (I 9, 3):

| | |
|---|---|
| ὡς μηδὲ ὑπόμνημα ληφθῆναι Θηβαίοις | so that to the Thebans is not left |
| τῆς ποτὲ εὐδαιμονίας προελθούσης | a vestige of their one-time prosperity, |
| ἐς τοσοῦτον ὡς ὑπερβαλέσθαι πλούτῳ | which had grown so great that they surpassed |
| τοὺς Ἑλλήνων πολυχρημάτους, τό τε ἱερόν | in wealth the sanctuary at Delphi and |
| τὸ ἐν Δελφοῖς καὶ Ὀρχομενίους | Orchomenus, the two richest places of Hellas |

The tragic poets, too, half a millennium before Pausanias, sing of the treasures of gold, the wealth of the god of Pytho (Soph. O. T. 151–153):

| | |
|---|---|
| τίς ποτε τᾶς πολυχρύσου | what, pray, means thy coming from |
| Πυθῶνος ἀγλαὰς ἔβας | Pytho rich in gold to glorious |
| Θήβας; | Thebes? |

And so Euripides also alludes to the immense wealth of gold accumulated from the gifts of worshipers at Apollo's shrine oracular (I. T. 1274–1275):

| | |
|---|---|
| γέλασε δ' ὅτι τέκος ἄφαρ ἔβα | and he [Zeus] smiled that his son had quickly come |
| πολύχρυσα θέλων λατρεύματα σχεῖν | willing to gain the worship that brought in wealth of gold |

Even in the days of Homer the wealth of the temple at Delphi was proverbial. When Achilles tells the tale of the riches that he would not accept to be reconciled to Agamemnon, naming the countless treasures of Egyptian Thebes, the wealth of Priam before the sons of the Achaeans came, and other rich gifts outnumbering the sands and the particles of dust, he caps the climax with (I 403–404):

| | |
|---|---|
| οὐδ' ὅσα λάϊνος οὐδὸς ἀφήτορος ἐντὸς ἐέργει, | nor all the treasure that the stone threshhold of the archer, |
| Φοίβου Ἀπόλλωνος, Πυθοῖ ἔνι πετρηέσσῃ | Phoebus Apollo, encloses at rocky Pytho |

and Pindar puts into the mouth of Medea, long before the time of the Trojan war (though, of course, the adjective is the standing epithet of the poet's own days) the significant phrase (Pyth. IV 53–55):

| | |
|---|---|
| τὸν μὲν πολυχρύσῳ ποτ' ἐν δώματι | and him one day Phoebus in his dwelling |
| Φοῖβος ἀναμνάσει θέμισσιν | rich in gold will admonish with oracles, |
| Πύθιον ναὸν καταβάντα | when that he is come to the Pythian temple |

---

[1] Frederik Poulsen, *Delphi*, Transl. Richards, p. 19.
[2] Tatian, Adv. Graecos VIII 25.
[3] Paus. X 24, 6. In the Theogony (468 ff.) Hesiod states that the stone vomited by Kronos was set up at Delphi.

The Delphians, under authority delegated to them by the Amphictyonic Council, had all the responsibility for the conduct of the Pythian games and the administration of the temple and its oracle. They appointed also the steward who kept the treasures of the temple (Eur. Ion 54–55):

| Δελφοί σφ' ἔθεντο χρυσοφύλακα τοῦ θεοῦ | the Delphians made him keeper of the god's gold |
| ταμίαν τε πάντων πιστὸν | and steward faithful of all |

States and princes and private individuals in all periods of classical antiquity showered gifts upon the god of prophecy. Their cupidity also was frequently aroused to rob him— from the days of the Trojan heroes to the days of Sulla and Nero. Neoptolemus is said to have gone to Delphi and to have robbed the temple, either to get revenge on Apollo for the death of his father (Eur. Andr. 50–53):

| ἀπὼν | away in the land of Delphi, |
| Δελφῶν κατ' αἶαν, ἔνθα Λοξίᾳ δίκην | to atone to Loxias for the mad fit in |
| δίδωσι μανίας, ᾗ ποτ' ἐς Πυθὼ μολὼν | which he went to Pytho once and |
| ᾔτησε Φοῖβον πατρὸς οὗ κτείνει δίκην | demanded of Phoebus redress for having slain his sire |

or to provide himself with needed funds (*ibid.* 1092–1095) (Orestes's alleged speech to the Delphians to stir them up to kill Neoptolemus):

| ὁρᾶτε τοῦτον, ὃς διαστείχει θεοῦ | see ye yon fellow, prowling about the shrines |
| χρυσοῦ γέμοντα γύαλα, θησαυροὺς βροτῶν, | of God teeming with gold, treasures by mortals |
| τὸ δεύτερον παρόντ' ἐφ' οἷσι καὶ πάρος | here bestowed? He is here a second time on the same errand |
| δεῦρ' ἦλθε Φοίβου ναὸν ἐκπέρσαι θέλων; | on which he came before, aiming to plunder Phoebus's shrine. |

The γύαλα[1] are the inner parts, the safe-deposit vaults of the temple; the θησαυροὺς βροτῶν are treasures presented here by all the world, the coveted prey of the sacrilegious needy. Euripides had often heard his elders tell of the attempted raid of Xerxes on the temple treasures,[2] and he knew from having seen with his own eyes the vast wealth of gold and silver offerings there. He alludes to it again in the Iphigenia in Tauris (1252):

| μαντείων δ' ἐπέβας ζαχρύσων | thou didst enter upon the oracles rich in precious gold |

The safe-deposit vaults, however, were not sufficient to protect the treasures, and their safe-keeping demanded a special guard of policemen (Eur. Andr. 1098–1099):

| ὅσοι θεοῦ χρημάτων ἐφέστασαν | and they who were charged with the keeping of the god's |
| φρουρὰν ἐτάξαντ' ἐν περιστύλοις δόμοις | treasure-hoard set guards along the pillared halls |

and in times when the treasury was thus threatened, it was the duty of these guards to be present, armed for its protection.

Among votive offerings in the cella proper were also weapons. Pausanias does not mention anything of the sort. But in Euripides we are told (Andr. 1121–1123):

| ἐξέλκει δέ, καὶ παραστάδος | he drew his sword and, pulling down |
| κρεμαστὰ τεύχη πασσάλων καθαρπάσας | weapons hanging by pegs upon the pillar, |
| ἔστη 'πὶ βωμοῦ | he took his stand upon the altar |

The "parastade" ought to be in the vestibule. It means an *anta*, and, strictly speaking, an anta must be outside the walls in the vestibule or portico. The word is used in that sense where it occurs elsewhere in Euripides. We shall find it again in the Iphigenia Taurica (1159) (Iphigenia to Thoas, who catches her in the act of bringing the statue from the shrine):

[1] Cf. Eur. Ph. 237–238 (quoted on p. 73) and Ion 245 (quoted on p. 61) where γύαλα is loosely used for Delphi generally. In the Ion (220–221)

| θέμις γυάλων ὑπερ- | is it lawful with bared feet to pass |
| βῆναι λευκῷ ποδὶ βηλὸν | the threshold of the shrine |

γύαλα is used figuratively for the interior of the temple, even as Parthenon, the treasury of the temple, came in time to be used for the whole building.

[2] Hdt. VIII 35–39.

ἔχ' αὐτοῦ πόδα σὸν ἐν παραστάσιν | stay thy foot right there in the pillared vestibule

He must not enter the temple; she stops him in the vestibule. In this case it is the vestibule of a temple. In Euripides's Phoenissae (415) it is the vestibule of a king's palace:

Ἀδράστου δ' ἦλθον ἐς παραστάδας | and I came to Adrastus's vestibule

In both these instances the παραστάς is an anta. But in the passage in the Andromache, Neoptolemus is in the temple; the whole scene of his assassination is there. As he starts back to defend himself against his enemies and gain a position of advantage, he leaps upon the altar; when he was slain, his body lay beside the altar and was cast out of the building. The παραστάς must, therefore, be inside. We may render παραστάς by "pillar." It may be that Euripides is thinking of attached pillars like those of the Heraeum at Olympia or like those of the temple of Apollo at Bassae. It is entirely possible that the Alcmaeonid temple had such attached pillars in the cella. If so, παραστάς would be just the word for such a pillar. I am inclined to think that Euripides chooses his word advisedly and that the interior colonnade of the Delphic temple had attached columns. At all events, his vision is of a pillar with defensive armor—helmet and shield—hanging against it, within a man's reach. Here again we have a striking corroboration of Euripides's decoration of the temple at Delphi in a vase-painting made under the influence of Aeschylus. At the top of the painting described on page 69, above and between the pig and the sleeping Erinyes, hangs a votive shield within Apollo's temple. Euripides was describing what his audience knew and what the vase-painter felt to be a natural element in his composition.

But even better corroboration of Euripides's picture with the votive weapons in the sanctuary proper we have in Herodotus VIII 37:

ἐπεὶ δὲ ἀγχοῦ τε ἦσαν οἱ βάρβαροι | and when the barbarians advanced and were near
ἐπιόντες καὶ ἀπώρεον τὸ ἱερόν, ἐν | by, in sight of the sanctuary, at that
τούτῳ ὁ προφήτης, τῷ οὔνομα ἦν | moment the prophet, whose name was
Ἀκήρατος, ὁρᾷ πρὸ τοῦ νηοῦ ὅπλα | Aceratus, saw placed ready in front of the temple weapons

προκείμενα ἔσωθεν ἐκ τοῦ μεγάρου | that had been brought out from inside
ἐξενηνειγμένα ἱρά, τῶν οὐκ ὅσιον | the cella—consecrated weapons which it was not lawful

ἦν ἅπτεσθαι ἀνθρώπων οὐδενί | for any man to touch

The weapons were dedications to the god; some were of gold, like the shield of Croesus consecrated to Athena of the Outer Precincts at Delphi;[1] some may have been the consecrated spoils of enemies. At any rate Herodotus was familiar with the weapons in the holy place and Euripides also was familiar with them and he knew as well as Herodotus that it was not lawful for any man to touch them. But his whole scene in the Andromache is a scene of sacrilege and desecration. For us, the essential thing at present is the fact that in both Euripides and Herodotus the weapons belong inside the cella proper.

From the front hall of the cella a door led into the adytum. Of the holy of holies of the Delphian temple we know very little, whether from poets or prose-writers or excavations or all together. As Pausanias says (X 24, 5):

ἐς δὲ τοῦ ναοῦ τὸ ἐσωτάτω | and into the innermost part of the temple
παρίασί τε ἐς αὐτὸ ὀλίγοι | few enter in; and there is set up
καὶ χρυσοῦν Ἀπόλλωνος ἕτερον | there another statue of Apollo, of gold
ἄγαλμα ἀνάκειται

In other words, even in the late days of Delphic influence few people saw the inside of the holy place, and the temple authorities did not make any exception of the compiler of the popular guidebook. The poets of the earlier day had no better access to it than had Pausanias. They knew only what Plutarch (de Pythiae Oraculis) knew—that in, or under, the holy place was the source of prophecy and that the prophetess had her seat there upon a tripod most holy and acted as the mouthpiece of the god (Eur. Ion 91–93):

Θάσσει δὲ γυνὴ τρίποδα ζάθεον | upon a tripod most holy a Delphian
Δελφὶς ἀείδουσ' Ἕλλησι βοάς, | maiden hath her seat, chanting to the Hel-
ἃς ἂν Ἀπόλλων κελαδήσῃ | lenes voices that Apollo uttereth

[1] Hdt. I 92; cp. pp. 84–85.

There Earth herself had once presided, and after her her daughter Themis took her seat at the famous oracle; then Phoebe; then Apollo;[1] his priestess usually spoke for him.

The keeping of the tripod is in her care; it is her natural place; when she leaves it, her doing so seems to call for explanation (Eur. Ion 1320–1323):

| | |
|---|---|
| τρίποδα γὰρ χρηστήριον<br>λιποῦσα θριγκοῦ τοῦδ' ὑπερβάλλω πόδα<br>Φοίβου προφῆτις, τρίποδος ἀρχαῖον νόμον<br><br>σώζουσα, πασῶν Δελφίδων ἐξαίρετος | for I have left the tripod oracular and<br>above this cornice I set my foot,<br>the prophetess of Phoebus, who observe the<br>    tripod's ancient<br>use—I, the elect of all the maids of Delphi |

The tripod here receives its epithet as "the oracular"; its function is ancient; the Pythia, a chosen maid of Delphi, is in charge.

Inquirers of the oracle had some sort of immediate access to the oracular seat, though they might not enter the adytum itself. So much is clear from such passages as Euripides's Ion 512–513:

| | |
|---|---|
| ἐκλέλοιπ' ἤδη τὸν ἱερὸν τρίποδα καὶ<br>                                χρηστήριον<br>Ξοῦθος, ἢ μίμνει κατ' οἶκον ἱστορῶν ἀπαιδίαν; | has Xuthus by this time left the holy tripod and<br>    the oracle,<br>or bides he in the building inquiring of his<br>    childlessness? |

The chorus assumes that Xuthus was in the presence of the tripod and the priestess; he is certainly within the temple; he is certainly inquiring of the oracle; and when he comes out, he is "leaving the tripod and the oracle."

So immediate, moreover, might that access to the holy of holies be, that Euripides makes Xuthus say, as he comes forth from the temple a few moments later (Eur. Ion 662):

| | |
|---|---|
| ἀδύτων ἐξιόντι μοι | as I came forth from the holy of holies |

It is noteworthy that he uses the plural ἀδύτων, not ἀδύτου, as if there were various parts of the holy of holies; into the very presence of the god he had not gone. The language is probably accurate, as it also is in Aristophanes's Knights (1015–1016):

| | |
|---|---|
| λογίων ὁδόν, ἥν σοι 'Απόλλων<br>ἴαχεν ἐξ ἀδύτοιο διὰ τριπόδων ἐριτίμων | the tenor of the deliverances which Apollo<br>uttered from the holy of holies through the<br>    precious tripods |

Here the singular ἀδύτοιο refers to that innermost chamber conceived as the dwelling-place of the god himself. And in the loosest possible sense Euripides again uses the plural form, when he makes Creusa, who has taken refuge at the great altar of the Chians and whom Ion is threatening with death even there, say (Eur. Ion 1309):

| | |
|---|---|
| ἣν γ' ἐντὸς ἀδύτων τῶν δέ με σφάξαι θέλῃς | yea—if thou wilt slay me inside this holy of holies |

The location of the tripod is given a little more definitely in a choral ode in the Ion—a prayer addressed to Athena (457–464):

| | |
|---|---|
| ὦ πότνια Νίκα<br>μόλε Πύθιον οἶκον,<br>'Ολύμπου χρυσέων θαλάμων<br>πταμένα πρὸς ἀγυιάς,<br>Φοιβήιος ἔνθα γᾶς<br>μεσσόμφαλος ἑστία<br>παρὰ χορευομένῳ τρίποδι<br>μαντεύματα κραίνει | oh victory-queen,<br>come to the Pythian dwelling,<br>winging thy way from Olympus's<br>golden halls to the streets<br>where Phoebus's hearth at<br>earth's mid-navel, by the<br>tripod where choruses move,<br>fulfils its oracles |

No new fact is added about the tripod, except that about it choruses move. This does not mean that the choruses entered the holy of holies, but that the choruses performed their evolutions in the larger, eastern, hall of the cella or, perhaps, before the temple itself.

Sometimes, too, the god of prophecy does not avail himself of the Pythia as his mouthpiece, but himself takes his seat upon the tripod and pronounces the truth to his worshipers (Eur. I. T. 1252–1258):

[1] Ae. Eum. 1–8; P. V. 209–210; Eur. I. T. 1242–1269.

| | |
|---|---|
| μαν-<br>τείων δ' ἐπέβας ξαθέων,<br>τρίποδί τ' ἐν χρυσέῳ<br>θάσσεις, ἐν ἀψευδεῖ θρόνῳ<br>μαντείας βροτοῖς<br>θεσφάτων νέμων<br>ἀδύτων ὕπο, Κασταλίας ῥεέθρων<br>γείτων, μέσον γᾶς ἔχων μέλαθρον | thou didst<br>enter upon the oracle most holy<br>and hast thy seat upon the tripod of gold,<br>from the depths of the holy of holies<br>upon a throne that knows not lies<br>dispensing prophecies to mortal men—<br>neighbor to the streams of Castalia,<br>dwelling in halls at earth's centre |

Apollo speaks as if it were his custom to take his place in person upon the oracular seat and speak with his own voice the word that he received from his father (Ae. Eum. 616; 618):

| | |
|---|---|
| οὐπώποτ' εἶπον μαντικοῖσιν ἐν θρόνοις<br>. . .<br>ὃ μὴ κελεύσαι Ζεύς | never did I utter upon thrones oracular<br>. . .<br>aught that Zeus did not command |

The source of prophecy is Zeus[1]; Apollo is but his mouthpiece; the tripod is his throne (or "thrones"). And in the Ion of Euripides the "thrones" on which the god of the oracle sat are "seats of gold" (913–914):

| | |
|---|---|
| πρὸς χρυσέους θάκους καὶ<br>γαίας μεσσήρεις ἕδρας | to his golden thrones and<br>earth's midmost seat |

Various passages from the drama leave no doubt that the tripod is Apollo's own peculiar seat at Delphi (Eur. Or. 955–956):

| | |
|---|---|
| οὐδ' ὁ Πύθιος<br>τρίποδα καθίζων Φοῖβος | nor the Pythian<br>Phoebus throned upon his tripod |

(Eur. Ion 366):

| | |
|---|---|
| εἴπερ καθίζει τρίποδα κοινὸν Ἑλλάδος | because he is throned upon the tripod national of Greece |

The tripod is, therefore, the "throne" on which Zeus seated Apollo when he placed him in charge of the oracle (Ae. Eum. 17–18):

| | |
|---|---|
| τέχνης δέ νιν Ζεὺς ἔνθεον κτίσας φρένα<br>ἵζει τέταρτον τόνδε μάντιν ἐν θρόνοις | and him Zeus stablished, his mind with skill inspired,<br>the fourth and present prophet on the throne |

And it is still a throne (or "thrones") when the Pythia takes her seat upon it to speak as God inspires her utterance (Ae. Eum. 29; 33):

| | |
|---|---|
| ἔπειτα μάντις εἰς θρόνους καθιζάνω .<br>μαντεύομαι γὰρ ὡς ἂν ἡγῆται θεός | then I take my seat as prophetess upon the "thrones."<br>For I speak prophecy as God directs |

The "thrones" on which the Furies sat, as they lay in wait for Orestes in the temple at Delphi, belonged to the temple furniture of the outer cella (Ae. Eum. 46–47):

| | |
|---|---|
| θαυμαστὸς λόχος<br>εὕδει γυναικῶν ἐν θρόνοισιν ἥμενος | a marvelous troop<br>of women is sitting asleep on thrones |

or they may have been the plinths of the attached columns or the slightly raised floor between the colonnade and the cella walls.

Again, it is Apollo's self that gives Orestes his fateful oracle, and again the tripod from which Phoebus speaks is a tripod of gold (Eur. I. T. 976–977):

| | |
|---|---|
| ἐντεῦθεν αὐδὴν τρίποδος ἐκ χρυσοῦ λακὼν<br>Φοῖβός μ' ἔπεμψε δεῦρο | then Phoebus from the golden tripod uttered<br>a voice and sent me hither |

The god speaks to men with his own lips (Eur. I. T. 1084–1085):

| | |
|---|---|
| ἢ τὸ Λοξίου<br>οὐκέτι βροτοῖσι διά σ' ἐτήτυμον στόμα | else must the lips of Loxias lose their<br>truth in the eyes of men, through thee |

[1] Aeschylus in a fragment declares no less unequivocally that it is Zeus himself that inspires the oracles of Loxias ('Ιερ. Frag. 86 N.):

ταῦτα γὰρ πατὴρ
Ζεὺς ἐγκαθίει Λοξίᾳ θεσπίσματα

The same thought is contained, by implication at least, in Euripides's Electra 977–980:

| | |
|---|---|
| ΟΡ. ἐγὼ δὲ μητρὶ τοῦ φόνου δώσω δίκας. | OR. And I shall to my mother pay the penalty for her death. |
| ΗΛ. τῷ δ', ἣν πατρῴαν διαμεθῇς τιμωρίαν. | EL. And to *him*, if thou set aside the vengeance for our sire. |
| ΟΡ. ἆρ' αὖτ' ἀλάστωρ εἶπ' ἀπεικασθεὶς θεῷ. | OR. Perchance those words were uttered by a fiend in likeness of the god? |
| ΗΛ. ἱερὸν καθίζων τρίποδ'; ἐγὼ μὲν οὐ δοκῶ. | EL. Seated on the holy tripod? I trow not. |

As the oracle was given to Orestes by Apollo in person, it was the god himself, Electra implies, who sat upon the tripod and from it delivered his commission to Orestes; no other could occupy that holy seat (Ae. Eum. 797):

| | |
|---|---|
| αὐτός θ' ὁ χρήσας αὐτὸς ἦν ὁ μαρτυρῶν | and he himself who gave the oracle was himself my witness |

There is more than an implication in Euripides's Orestes (329–331):

| | |
|---|---|
| τρίποδος ἄπο φάτιν, ἃν ὁ Φοῖβος | receiving from the tripod the commission which Phoebus |
| ἔλακεν ἔλακε, δεξάμενος ἀνὰ δάπεδον ἵνα μεσόμφαλοι λέγονται μυχοί | uttered—uttered, as thou stoodst upon the floor where, they say, is the mid-navel holy of holies |

Orestes stood within the holy place which contained also the omphalus; he received the oracle from the tripod; Phoebus uttered it; there is no implication that he spoke by the voice of his priestess. The natural inference is that Phoebus, seated upon the tripod himself, delivered the oracle to Orestes. And Aristophanes, in a line that has a very tragic sound, has Loxias speaking his own oracle from the tripod (Plut. 8–10):

| | |
|---|---|
| τῷ δὲ Λοξίᾳ, ὃς θεσπιῳδεῖ τρίποδος ἐκ χρυσηλάτου μέμψιν δικαίαν μέμφομαι ταύτην | and with Loxias, who pronounces his prophecies from the tripod of gold, I have this just fault to find |

It is Apollo who occupies the tripod, we see again; and the further contribution is made that the tripod was of gold or, possibly, overlaid with gold.

Apollo (Loxias) might deliver his oracles from the tripod with his own lips, as we have just seen;[1] the Pythia might take his place and speak for him, as not a few witnesses testify. Still other ministers might serve as his mouthpiece and deliver his prophecies; they sat, not upon the all-holy tripod, but near it (Eur. Ion 413–416):

| | |
|---|---|
| ΞΟΥ.    τίς προφητεύει θεοῦ; ΙΩΝ. ἡμεῖς τά γ' ἔξω, τῶν ἔσω δ' ἄλλοις μέλει, | XU. Who is the god's mouthpiece? ION. We, of things without; others are in charge of things within, |
| οἳ πλησίον θάσσουσι τρίποδος, ὦ ξένε, Δελφῶν ἀριστῆς, οὓς ἐκλήρωσεν πάλος | who have their seat near the tripod, stranger— chiefest of the Delphians, upon whom the lot has fallen |

Sophocles in one passage seems to imply that still other ministers might be the mouthpiece of the infallible god, whose inerrancy through a human medium may become questionable (O. T. 711–712):

| | |
|---|---|
| χρησμὸς γὰρ ἦλθε Λαΐῳ ποτ', οὐκ ἐρῶ Φοίβου γ' ἀπ' αὐτοῦ, τῶν δ' ὑπηρετῶν ἄπο | an oracle came to Laius once, I will not say from Phoebus himself, but from his ministers |

In "ministers" we may have a plural of generality, or it may be that during unusually busy times the oracles were spoken in the holy of holies and delivered outside to the inquirers by certain mediators.

There were probably many tripods at Delphi. There may have been many in the great temple itself. We know of at least two: 1) There was the primaeval tripod, the all-holy one of gold, that Themis herself was supposed to have occupied and that Loxias inherited (Eur. Or. 162–164):

[1] Cf. also Soph. O. T. 786–793; 853–854; El. 32–35; Eur. Or. 28–30; 76; 162–164; 191–193; 285–286; 416; 591–592; Ph. 958; 1598–1599; El. 1245; 1266–1267; 1302; Ion 681–682; 690–691; Ar. Eq. 1081; Ran. 1184–1185; Pl. Men. 840–841; 848–850; 855–856; 858; 862; 868–869; 871.

UNDERGROUND PASSAGE TO ORACLE
AT DELPHI

| | |
|---|---|
| ἄδικος ἄδικα τότ' ἄρ' ἔλακεν ἔλακεν, | unrighteous was he who then uttered, uttered then, unrighteous words, |
| ἀπόφονον ὅτ' ἐπὶ τρίποδι Θέμιδος ἄρ' ἐδίκασε φόνον ὁ Λοξίας ἐμᾶς ματέρος | when upon Themis's tripod Loxias decreed the unnatural murder of my mother |

2) We know also of a tripod of bronze in the holy place, the gift of Heracles by the hand of Theseus, engraved with that ancient treaty of alliance between Argos and Athens sealed by the hands of Adrastus and the prince of Athens (Eur. Sup. 1197–1204):

| | |
|---|---|
| ἔστιν τρίπους σοι χαλκόπους εἴσω δόμων, δὸν 'Ιλίου ποτ' ἐξαναστήσας βάθρα | thou hast a bronze-footed tripod in thy halls, which Heracles once upon a time, when he had overturned Ilium to her foundations |
| σπουδὴν ἐπ' ἄλλην 'Ηρακλῆς ὁρμώμενος στῆσαί σ' ἐφεῖτο Πυθικὴν πρὸς ἐσχάραν. | and was hastening to another task, bade thee set up at the Pythian hearth. |
| ἐν τῷδε λαιμοὺς τρεῖς τριῶν μήλων τεμὼν | Over this do thou cut the three throats of three sheep |
| ἔγραψον ὅρκους τρίποδος ἐν κοίλῳ κύτει, | and engrave the oaths upon the tripod's hollow bowl, |
| κἄπειτα σώζειν θεῷ δὸς ᾧ Δελφῶν μέλει, | and then dedicate it to the god to keep who cares for Delphi, |
| μνημεῖα θ' ὅρκων μαρτύρημά θ' 'Ελλάδι | for Greece a monument and witness of her oaths |

The whole region of the holy tripod was hung with wreaths of laurel and bay[1] (Eur. Ion 1310):

| | |
|---|---|
| τίς ἡδονή σοι θεοῦ θανεῖν ἐν στέμμασι | what pleasure hast thou in dying amid the garlands of the god |

(Ar. Pl. 39):

| | |
|---|---|
| τί δῆτα Φοῖβος ἔλακεν ἐκ τῶν στεμμάτων | what, pray, did Phoebus utter from among the garlands?[2] |

This is another line of tragic ring. And again it is Phoebus himself that utters the prophecy from among the garlands. Lucretius caught the same inspiration, with the Pythia in Apollo's place (de R. N. I 739):

Pythia, quae tripode e Phoebi lauroque profatur

"the Pythia, who speaks prophecy from the tripod and laurel of Phoebus."

Apollo seated upon a tripod is a very common conception in art; we find it on vases, on coins, in sculpture. One of the most familiar is the Apollo sailing across the seas seated upon a winged tripod.[3]

In the passages just quoted the poets contribute two things for which we had not before any voucher from the classical period: 1) that the tripod was of gold; 2) that the source of the oracles was from a lower chamber in the adytum; and here the holy of holies is called ἀδύτων. Plutarch's statement, quoted above from *de Pythiae Oraculis*, thus receives valuable support. The statement of Frazer[4] is probably correct that "the inner shrine which the Greeks call ἄδυτον was generally if not always subterranean." The ἄδυτον of the oracular temple at Corinth, excavated in the last few years by the American School, is certainly underground. A long, low passage, through which a man must have crept, communicates with an opening under the floor upon which the questioner stood in the presence of his god, and the oracle spoken through a megaphone beneath his feet resounded with mysterious awe about him. At Delphi there appears to be a similar arrangement. At the south side of the temple, on the terrace some ten or twelve feet below the peristyle, there is a covered stairway descending six or eight feet and connecting with a low canal through which a

---

[1] There were garlands also at the door (Eur. Ion 79–80):
ὡς πρὸ ναοῦ λαμπρὰ θῇ πυλώματα<br>δάφνης κλάδοισιν
(ibid. 104–105): στέφεσίν θ' ἱεροῖς εἰσόδους Φοίβου<br>καθαρὰς θήσομεν

[2] Cf. also Ar. Plutus 213; Virg. Aen. III 90–91 (of the Delian sanctuary):
tremere omnia visa repente<br>liminaque laurusque dei

[3] See the Vatican hydria, reproduced in Baum. *Denkm.*, *s. v.* Apollo, I p. 102, Fig. 108.

[4] *Paus.*, V p. 353.

man may creep deep under the floor of the colonnade. Perhaps it continued on under the floor of the adytum itself. On the French plan this mysterious structure is labeled "Fontaine." But a fountain it surely is not. When the temple terrace was there, covering up the foundation walls of the temple, this stairway was covered pretty thoroughly, too. If this is not the underground passage-way leading to the underground adytum, we do not know where it was.

And in what region of this westernmost division of the temple the golden tripod was set we shall probably never know. But somewhere in this holy of holies the mystic tripod stood. Lying upon the ruined floor at Delphi to-day is a block of marble, with the three points where the feet of the tripod rested and with channels cut into it, through which the mystic waters of Cassotis were led to help in some way in the prophetic spell.[1] But just where this block originally belonged, just how the oracles were delivered, no one knows. The excavations have thrown not a ray of light upon this most interesting question; the excavators cleared away every morsel of débris, every bit of dirt from the adytum; but no sign of the famous cleft from which issued the miraculous vapor was found; nothing was unearthed to help our scanty information from the literary sources.

The investigations of the French excavators[2] have thrown some light upon the location of the holy of holies in the Hellenistic temple: the Adytum was a small square room built in on the south side of the cella, interrupting the southern row of interior columns. This room, though small in size (15 square metres), was one of the biggest things in all Hellenism; for there the destinies of individuals, of states, and of empires were pronounced; and the utterances of the god through his oracle were infallible. There, too, are some remains of the stone benches on which sat those who came to consult the oracle; there are traces also of the stairway leading down into the vault in which the holy tripod stood and under which flowed the prophetic spring water. The Alcmaeonid temple, in all probability, had an identical arrangement.

### c. *Immediate Surroundings*

The steep incline of that part of the slope of Parnassus enclosed by the temenos walls of Delphi, necessitating the many gates for the convenience of pilgrims and visitors, is one of the conspicuous features of the place to the modern visitor, especially if he first comes to Delphi after having visited Olympia. From the main entrance the Sacred Way must wind, like an inverted S up the steep ascent to the temple. The ancient visitor appreciated the toilsome climb no less than we do (Eur. Ion 739–740):

| | |
|---|---|
| αἰπεινά τοι μαντεῖα· τοῦ γήρως δέ μοι | steep is the path to the oracle; be thou |
| συνεκπονοῦσα κῶλον ἰατρὸς γενοῦ | physician to mine old age and help my legs |

Near the temple, whether inside or outside the sacred enclosure we cannot be sure, was the manse, the home of the Pythian priestess and the other ministers of Apollo's shrine. At Olympia the building commonly identified as the Theocoleum, the manse, is just outside the temenos wall and as near to the temple of Zeus as it could be located. At the Tauric Artemisium, on the other hand, as we shall see,[3] the tragic poet represents the dwelling of Iphigenia and her colleagues as inside the temenos. The conception of the temple manse is much clearer in the Iphigenia in Tauris than it is in the Ion. We may be fairly certain that there was a theocoleum at Delphi, as there was at Olympia, but we cannot feel quite sure that that is the building to which Euripides refers (Ion 54–56):

| | |
|---|---|
| Δελφοί σφ' ἔθεντο χρυσοφύλακα τοῦ θεοῦ | the Delphians made him keeper of the god's treasures |
| ταμίαν τε πάντων πιστόν, ἐν δ' ἀνακτόροις | and faithful steward of everything, and in the palace |
| θεοῦ καταζῇ | of the god he lives |

[1] This arrangement of the tripod mounted upon a marble base may be echoed upon the famous vase from Ruvo, representing the murder of Neoptolemus at Delphi. Behind the altar to which Neoptolemus has fled to defend himself and beside which the filleted omphalus is conspicuous stands a great tripod upon a marble base. (Reproduced, Baum., *Denkm.* II p. 1009, Fig. 1215; *Annali*, XL (1868), Plate E; Roscher, *Myth. Lex.*, *s. v.* Neoptolemus, III Sp. 175.)

[2] Especially Courbet, *Fouilles de Delphes*, II.

[3] Pp. 109–110; 114.

TRIPOD BASE
TEMPLE OF APOLLO AT DELPHI

The "palace" may be the manse; it probably is; but it might be the temple itself. For Ion himself declares that he lodges anywhere within the god's demesnes (314–315):

| | |
|---|---|
| ΚΡ. ναοῖσι δ' οἰκεῖς τοισίδ' ἢ κατὰ στέγας; | CR. Dwellest thou in the temple here or in a house? |
| ΙΩΝ. ἅπαν θεοῦ μοι δῶμ', ἵν' ἂν λάβῃ μ' ὕπνος | ION. All God's dwelling-place is mine, wherever sleep o'ertakes me |

Creusa's question suggests the two-fold possibility: either the temple itself might be a lodging house for the neophyte; or a separate manse might be his dwelling. Ion's answer is evasive; the manse might be his proper home, but he does not confine himself to any one roof.

An artistic feature of landscape gardening about the temple of Apollo we have from Euripides and Euripides alone (Ion 112–124):

| | |
|---|---|
| ἄγ' ὦ νεοθαλὲς ὦ | come for our service, thou fresh and blooming |
| καλλίστας προπόλευμα δάφνας | spray of fairest laurel |
| ἃ τὰν Φοίβου θυμέλαν | that sweepest Phoebus's |
| σαίρεις, ὑπὸ ναοῖς | fane; come from the gardens |
| κήπων ἐξ ἀθανάτων, | immortal beside the shrine, |
| †ἵνα δρόσοι τέγγουσ' ἱεραί, | where holy rills, pouring forth |
| τὰν ἀέναον παγὰν | their ever-flowing fount, bedew |
| ἐκπροεῖσαι, | the holy sprays of myrtle |
| μυρσίνας ἱερὰν φόβαν | with which I daily sweep |
| ᾇ σαίρω δάπεδον θεοῦ | God's floor at the hour when |
| παναμέριος ἄμ' ἁλίου | the sun's swift pinions |
| πτέρυγι θοᾷ | come, rendering my service |
| λατρεύων τὸ κατ' ἦμαρ | day by day |

ὑπὸ ναοῖς obviously means that the myrtle groves were almost under the eaves of the temple; the "holy rills" are, of course, the waters of Cassotis led down from the spring above to the secret places of the temple. And along this stream grew the sacred laurels that furnished the branches for the sacred service that it was Ion's duty daily to perform.[1]

The closeness to the oracular spot is emphasized again by Euripides (I. T. 1245–1248):

| | |
|---|---|
| ὅθι ποικιλόνωτος οἰνωπὸς δράκων | where the scaly dragon, with blood-red eyes, |
| σκιερᾷ κατάχαλκος εὐφύλλῳ δάφνᾳ, | gleaming in mail of bronze, earth's giant |
| γᾶς πελώριον τέρας, ἄμφεπεν εὖ | monster, lurked safely in the laurel's thick |
| μαντεῖον κλεινὸν χθόνιον | shade about the famed oracular spot |

The laurel grove must have been up in the vicinity of the Cassotis spring; for to it Hermes, at the end of the prolog, retires to watch the issue of the plot of the play (Eur. Ion 76–77):

| | |
|---|---|
| ἀλλ' εἰς δαφνώδη γύαλα βήσομαι τάδε, | now to yonder laurel dell will I retire, |
| τὸ κρανθὲν ὡς ἂν ἐκμάθω παιδὸς πέρι | that I may learn what is predestined for the lad |

With these words Hermes passes through one of the side entrance-doors of the proscenium adjoining which, we may presume, was a panel containing a picture of the Cassotis spring and its encircling laurel grove.

The same laurels are mentioned by Euripides again (Andr. 1114–1115) (the ambush set by the Delphians for the murder of Neoptolemus):

| | |
|---|---|
| τῷ δὲ ξιφήρης ἄρ' ὑφειστήκει λόχος | and for him, there, sword in hand the ambush lay in wait |
| δάφνῃ πυκασθείς | concealed behind the laurels |

The clumps of laurel must, therefore, have been close to the temple and they must have extended near to the entrance to the temple.

Similarly at Olympia, we know, the sacred wild olive tree from which the victors' crowns were cut stood close to the temple of Zeus, but back of it (Paus. V 15, 3):

| | |
|---|---|
| κατὰ δὲ τὸν ὀπισθόδομον | directly back of the opisthodome |
| μάλιστά ἐστιν ἐν δεξιᾷ | there is growing on the right |
| πεφυκὼς κότινος·... καὶ τοῖς | a wild olive tree; . . . and it is the |
| νικῶσι τὰ 'Ολύμπια καθέστηκεν | custom for the victors in the Olympic |
| ἀπ' αὐτῆς δίδοσθαι | games to be given their crowns |
| τοὺς στεφάνους | made from it. |

[1] Besides this passage cp. also Eur. Ion 103; 144–145.

Pindar, however, has Heracles design the planting of the sacred olive trees at the end of the hippodrome (Ol. III 33–34):

| | |
|---|---|
| τῶν νιν γλυκὺς ἵμερος ἔσχεν δωδεκάγναμπτον | and sweet desire thereof gat hold on him |
| περὶ τέρμα δρόμου | to plant them at the end of the steeds' course |
| ἵππων φυτεῦσαι | twelve times turned |

But the direct testimony of Pausanias and the traditions of the Altis through all times locate the famous olive trees inside the temenos walls.

So, too, at Corinth, the sacred pines from which the victors in the Isthmian games received their crowns were within the sacred enclosure and close to the walls of Poseidon's temple (Paus. II 1, 7):

| | |
|---|---|
| ἐλθόντι δὲ ἐς τοῦ θεοῦ τὸ ἱερὸν | when you have passed into the sanctuary of the god, |
| τοῦτο μὲν ἀθλητῶν νικησάντων | on one side stand the statues of athletes |
| τὰ ᾽Ισθμια ἐστήκασιν εἰκόνες, | who have been victorious in the Isthmian games; |
| τοῦτο δὲ πιτύων δένδρα ἐστὶ | on the other side are pine-trees |
| πεφυτευμένα ἐπὶ στοίχου | planted in a row |

In all these sacred enclosures the tree of famous local sanctity is part of the landscape beautiful.

It is to Euripides that we are indebted for the assurance that there was a "Council Hall" at Delphi. The Buleuterium at Olympia is well vouched for in the literary sources, and its identification among the extant buildings is certain. For the Council Hall at Delphi this is all we have (Eur. Andr. 1097):

| | |
|---|---|
| ἀρχαί τ᾽ ἐπληροῦντ᾽ εἴς τε βουλευτήρια | and the magistrates thronged into the Council Halls[1] |

Among the ruins the name Buleuterium has been attached tentatively to the large temple-shaped structure next above the Treasury of the Athenians—between it and the Sibyl's rock—abutting on the Sacred Way. This building, in comparison with the Buleuterium at Olympia, seems disproportionately small for the business the magistrates at Delphi must have had to superintend.

Euripides makes Thetis, appearing as *dea ex machina*, give orders for the erection of the tomb of Neoptolemus at Delphi (Andr. 1239–1242):

| | |
|---|---|
| τὸν μὲν θανόντα τόνδ᾽ ᾽Αχιλλέως γόνον | as for Achilles's son who lies here dead, |
| θάψον πορεύσας Πυθικὴν πρὸς ἐσχάραν, | fare thou to the Pythian hearth and bury him— |
| Δελφοῖς ὄνειδος, ὡς παραγγέλλῃ τάφος | a reproach to the Delphians, that his sepulchre may proclaim |
| φόνον βίαιον τῆς ᾽Ορεστείας χερός | his murder by the violence of Orestes's hand |

The passage tells us nothing that we do not know from Strabo IX p. 421; the scholium on Pindar, Nemea VII 62; Heliodorus II 34–III 6; and from the fragmentary remains of the tomb itself which we may still see just to the northeast of the great temple. But it does help us in our conviction of the correctness of the statements of these late authors.[2]

### 4. The Temple of Athena Pronaia at Delphi

A second temple at Delphi is mentioned by Aeschylus—the temple of "Athena of the Outer Precincts," ᾽Αθηνᾶ Προναία (Ae. Eum. 21):

| | |
|---|---|
| Παλλὰς Προναία δ᾽ ἐν λόγοις πρεσβεύεται | and Pallas of the Outer Precincts is praised and honored |

The words are spoken by the Pythia in the prolog, in which she lists the deities worshiped and revered at Delphi. This "Athena of the Outer Precincts" is the goddess of the temple

---

[1] The text is obviously corrupt; the second τε of the line has nothing to connect. It may be that a line has fallen out after 1097 and that some other group thronged into the Council Hall. [See Kinkel, *Eur. u. die bild. Kunst*, note 33.] But even a correct reconstruction of the passage would help us no further.

[2] For the literature and the elaborate ceremonies connected with the Thessalian rites associated with this monument, see Frazer, *Paus.* V pp. 353–354.

found by the excavators just east of the Gymnasium, the westernmost of the group of five buildings at the eastern approach to the city of Delphi. Pausanias names it as the fourth in a group of *temples* at the entrance to the city (X 8, 6):

| | |
|---|---|
| εἰσελθόντι δὲ ἐς τὴν πόλιν εἰσὶν | upon entering the city one finds |
| ἐφεξῆς ναοί... ὁ τέταρτος δὲ ᾿Αθηνᾶς | temples in close succession . . . the fourth |
| χαλεῖται Προνοίας | is that of Forethought Athena, as she is called |

The surname ("Forethought") is wrong in Pausanias, but it is an old error which we find in Demosthenes,[1] Aeschines,[2] Aristides,[3] and other classical authors. Προνοίας seems to be a corruption for Προναίας—an easy one. It is at least clear that Pausanias's Athena Pronoia is identical with Herodotus's Athena Pronaia (VIII 37):

| | |
|---|---|
| οἱ δὲ βάρβαροι ἐπειδὴ ἐγίγνοντο ἐπειγόμενοι | and when, as they pushed on, the barbarians reached |
| κατὰ τὸ ἱρὸν τῆς Προνηίης ᾿Αθηναίης, | the neighborhood of the sanctuary of Athena of the |
| ἐπιγίγνεταί σφι τέρεα ἔτι μείζονα | Outer Precincts, there came upon them wonders still greater . . . |

The Persian raiders were in sight of the temple of Apollo but were still some distance away. This corresponds perfectly with Pausanias's description, but Pausanias, we must note, did not include the *Tholos* in his list of temples; hence the discrepancy between "fourth" and the remains actually existing today. The same Athena Pronaia is named in two other passages in Herodotus (VIII 39[4] and I 92[5]) and in one of the two famous Delphian hymns to Apollo recovered in the excavations and now in the museum at Delphi. Both Photius and Harpocration also have her name correctly written. Προναία is not a cult name; it is due only to the accident of topography, even as Scopas's Athena and Phidias's Hermes at the entrance of the temple of Apollo Ismenius at Thebes were called "Foretemplars" (and here Pausanias IX 10, 2 has the word correctly Πρόναοι), because they stood in the forecourt or outer precinct of the temple.

### 5. The Sanctuary of Bacchus at Delphi

The high places of Parnassus in the vicinity of Delphi were famous for Bacchic revels in celebration of the wine-god's rites.[6] And somewhere, not far from Apollo's temple, there was a Baccheum, a sanctuary and altar of Dionysus. Euripides speaks of the place as the "two rocks"; perhaps the twin heights of the Phaedriades were sacred to Dionysus (Eur. Ion 1125–1127):

| | |
|---|---|
| Ξοῦθος μὲν ᾤχετ᾿ ἔνθα πῦρ πεδᾷ θεοῦ | Xuthus went to the place where leaps God's |
| βαχχεῖον, ὡς σφαγαῖσι Διονύσου πέτρας | Bacchic fire, to wet with blood of sacrifice |
| δεύσειε δισσάς | Dionysus's twin rocks |

[1] *Or. XXV* p. 780.
[2] *In Ctes.* 108, 110, 111, 121.
[3] *In Minerv.*
[4] In the sacred enclosure of the temple of ᾿Αθηναίη Προνηίη were preserved the rocks that rolled down upon the barbarians and frightened them away. Many such rocks are still to be seen there.
[5] In the temple of ᾿Αθηναίη Προνηίη was a great shield of gold, the dedication of Croesus.
[6] Cf. Eur. Ion 550 ff; Eur. I. T. 1243–1248:

    τὰν βαχχεύουσαν Διονύσῳ
    Παρνάσιον κορυφάν,
    ὅθι ποικιλόνωτος οἰνωπὸς δράκων

    . . . . . . . . ἄμφεπε
    μαντεῖον χθόνιον.

Cf. also Eur. Hyps. Frag. 752 N. (= Ar. Ran. 1211–1213):
    Διόνυσος, ὃς θύρσοισι καὶ νεβρῶν δοραῖς
    καθαπτὸς ἐν πεύκαισι Παρνασὸν κάτα
    πηδᾷ χορεύων παρθένοις σὺν Δελφίσιν.
Cf. also Eur. Bac. 306–308; Ph. 226–228; Soph. Ant. 1126–1130.

## 6. Dodona and Other Oracles

In the preceding pages we have brought together many allusions to the oracle at Delphi. Many other famous oracles there were in Hellas—Dodona, Didyma, Claros, Patara, Delos, Abae, Lebadea, Corinth, Olympia, Thymbra, and others. Some of them—Didyma, Claros, Patara, and Delos, for example—are not so much as mentioned in the dramatic poets.

### a. *Olympia*

Olympia, in spite of all the glory of its great national games, in spite of all the splendor of its temples and sculptures, and in spite of its fame as the great centre of united Hellas, is but rarely alluded to, and then only in the most casual way. Aristophanes mentions Olympia, Pylae [Thermopylae], and Pytho as the three great centres that stood for the national unity of the Hellenic world (Lys. 1129–1131):

| | |
|---|---|
| οἱ μιᾶς ἐκ χέρνιβος βωμοὺς περιρραίνοντες, ὥσπερ ξυγγενεῖς, Ὀλυμπίασιν, ἐν Πύλαις, Πυθοῖ | you, who, as brethren of one kindred race, from the selfsame lustral bowl sprinkle the altars at Olympia, Pylae, Pytho |

There were, as the excavations have suggested, many altars at Olympia and at Delphi; the Amphictyonic Council succeeded in creating about Thermopylae also a sentiment of Hellenic national unity. The altar, *par excellence*, at Olympia was, of course, the great altar of Olympian Zeus. The oracle at Olympia was on Cronion Hill; but it is not of the oracle that Lysistrate is thinking, but of the altar of the great national god of all Hellenes.[1] So, too, Orestes, in the Electra of Euripides, is made to declare that he and his companions are going to Olympia to do sacrifice to the national god (781–782):

| | |
|---|---|
| πρὸς δ' Ἀλφειὸν θύσοντες ἐρχόμεσθ' Ὀλυμπίῳ Διί | to the Alpheus we go, to sacrifice to Olympian Zeus |

In a very few passages allusion is made to the games at Olympia (Ar. Pl. 583–586; 592):

| | |
|---|---|
| πῶς ἂν ποιῶν τὸν Ὀλυμπικὸν ἀγῶνα, ἵνα τοὺς Ἕλληνας ἅπαντας ἀεὶ δι' ἔτους πέμπτου ξυναγείρει, ἀνεκήρυττεν τῶν ἀσκητῶν τοὺς νικῶντας στεφανώσας κοτίνῳ στεφάνῳ [2]....... | how came it that when he was establishing the Olympic games to which he gathers every four years all the Hellenes, he crowned with only a wreath of wild olive[2] the contestants whom he proclaimed victors |
| Ζεύς... κοτίνῳ στεφάνῳ [2] στεφανώσας | · · · · · · Zeus . . . crown you with a crown of wild olive[2] |

And once in Plautus, Olympia and Nemea are named together as the chiefest of the world's great national games (Cas. 759–762):

> nec pol ego Nemeae credo neque ego Olympiae
> neque usquam ludos tam festivos fieri
> quam hic intus fiunt ludi ludificabiles
> seni nostro et nostro Olympioni vilico

In the Greek passage it is the national spirit of the Olympic festival that is foremost in the poet's thought, and the simplicity of the crown of wild olive as the reward of victory; in the Latin passage, the great games of Nemea and Olympia are called into requisition to serve as a foil to the still greater game that is to be the undoing of the old man and Olympio.

In the Wasps[3] Aristophanes goes into details about a boxing contest at Olympia, but without adding anything to our knowledge of either the place or the games; and in as unenlightening a way Plautus, following his Greek model, alludes to the foot-race at Olympia (Stichus 306–307):

> simulque [ad] cursuram meditabor [me] ad ludos Olympios.
> sed spatium hoc occidit: brevest curriculo . . .

[1] Cf. Ar. Pl. 583–584, quoted below.
[2] Euripides also has an allusion to the crown: El. 862–863; and Timocles to the prizes: Δραχ., Frag. 8, 16–17 K.
[3] 1382–1387.

SITE OF DODONA

It is the oracle at Olympia to which Sophocles refers in Oedipus the King (897–900):

| | |
|---|---|
| οὐκ ἔτι τὸν ἄθικτον εἶμι γᾶς ἐπ’ ὀμφαλὸν<br>    σέβων | no more shall I go on reverent pilgrimage to<br>    earth's navel inviolate |
| οὐδ’ ἐς τὸν ῎Αβαισι ναὸν | nor to the temple at Abae |
| οὐδὲ τὰν ᾿Ολυμπίαν | nor to Olympia |

It is noteworthy that Sophocles in this passage mentions Olympia without, apparently, a thought of the magnificent temple of Zeus, with its wonderful sculptures, or of the time-honored Heraeum of transcendent historical interest, or the forest of statues that had grown up in the sacred precinct, but only as the seat of the primaeval oracle, second only to Dodona's in historical interest but of only ordinary religious interest in fifth century Greece. It is named third in the list by the chorus of Theban elders.

### b. *Abae*

In the second place of honor, next after Delphi, the poet mentions Abae as the seat of an oracle. He even names in this instance the temple. For at Abae, far away in the rugged hill country of northern Phocis, Apollo had an oracular temple dating from the ages before the Dorian invasion. The temple with its oracle stood outside the town of Abae. It was partially destroyed by the army of Xerxes; it was, we may assume, repaired after the barbarians were driven back to Asia; it was completely destroyed by the Thebans in the Phocian War and left in ruins as a monument to the hatred of the enemies who had thus vented their fury upon things so sacred. But in the time of Sophocles, we are expressly told by Herodotus, though the temple had been destroyed and its treasures and votive offerings plundered and carried off, the oracle at Abae still functioned (VIII 33):[1]

| | |
|---|---|
| κατὰ μὲν ἔκαυσαν... ῎Αβας, ἔνθα | they burned . . . Abae to the ground; here |
| ἱρὸν ᾿Απόλλωνος πλούσιον, | there was a rich temple of Apollo, filled |
| θησαυροῖσί τε καὶ ἀναθήμασι πολλοῖσι | with treasures and votive offerings |
| κατεσκευασμένον· ἦν δὲ καὶ | in large quantity. There was also |
| τότε καὶ νῦν ἐστὶ χρηστήριον | at that time and still is an oracle |
| αὐτόθι· καὶ τοῦτο τὸ ἱρὸν | there. They plundered even this temple |
| συλήσαντες ἐνέπρησαν | and set fire to it |

The spade has as yet revealed nothing of the temple or the oracle; the poet contributes nothing to our knowledge of either temple or oracle.

### c. *Dodona*

Inferior in classical times to the oracle of Delphi alone and in pre-homeric times outranking all others was the famous oracle of Zeus at Dodona; and yet it is mentioned but very few times in extant Greek drama. Aristophanes puts Delphi, Dodona, and Ammon together as the most important sources of oracular information (Av. 716):

| | |
|---|---|
| ἐσμὲν δ’ ὑμῖν ῎Αμμων,[2] Δελφοί, Δωδώνη,<br>    Φοῖβος ᾿Απόλλων | we [birds] are your Ammon,[2] Delphi, Dodona,<br>    Phoebus Apollo |

Aeschylus locates Dodona in the mountains (Sup. 258):

| | |
|---|---|
| ὄρη τε Δωδωναῖα | and the mountains of Dodona |

Sophocles puts Dodona and Delphi together as the two sources from which would come utterances of infallible truth (᾿Οδ. ᾿Αχ., Frag. 422 N.):

| | |
|---|---|
| νῦν δ’ οὔτε μ’ ἐκ Δωδῶνος οὔτε Πυθικῶν | and now no one could bring me conviction from |
| γυ<άλων> τις ἂν πείσειεν | either Dodona or the Pythian holy of holies |

[1] See also the account in Paus. X 35, 1–3.

[2] Ammon may be thrown in by the bird-chorus as an antiquarian suggestion of the story of the two black doves that flew from Aegyptian Thebes, one to Libya and one to Dodona, where, speaking with human voice, they ordered the founding of the oracles of Zeus. See p. 89.

Similarly Inachus sends to Pytho and Dodona on the all-important matter touching his daughter Io (Ae. P. V. 658–659):

| | |
|---|---|
| ὁ δ' ἔς τε Πυθὼ κἀπὶ Δωδώνης πυκνοὺς | and he would send frequent inquirers |
| θεοπρόπους ἴαλλεν | both to Pytho and Dodona-ward[1] |

Sophocles, without mentioning the name, makes Heracles tell us something of the oracle (Tr. 1164–1171):

| | |
|---|---|
| φανῶ δ' ἐγὼ τούτοισι συμβαίνοντ' ἴσα | and I will reveal recent oracles coinciding with and |
| μαντεῖα καινά, τοῖς πάλαι συνήγορα, | confirming those ancient ones, and in accord with them; |
| ἃ τῶν ὀρείων καὶ χαμαικοιτῶν ἐγὼ | to get them I went into the grove of the Selli, |
| Σελλῶν ἐσελθὼν ἄλσος εἰσεγραψάμην | men of the hills who sleep upon the bare ground, and wrote |
| πρὸς τῆς πατρῴας καὶ πολυγλώσσου δρυός, | down the words dictated by my father's oak of many tongues |
| ἥ μοι χρόνῳ τῷ ζῶντι καὶ παρόντι νῦν | which declared to me that in this living present |
| ἔφασκε μόχθων τῶν ἐφεστηκότων ἐμοὶ | moment release should be provided from the toils imposed on me |
| λύσιν τελεῖσθαι | imposed on me |

In this long passage Sophocles tells us nothing about any building at Dodona. But in a fragment of his Odysseus Acanthoplex we have (Frag. 417 N.) "Zeus dwelling at Dodona" (Δωδῶνι ναίων Ζεύς), which clearly implies a temple as the house in which the god dwells. That there was a temple there, with colonnades and manse and sacred offerings in great quantity, seems clear from Polybius IV 67, where he describes the destruction of the city by the Aetolians and says:

| | |
|---|---|
| παραγενόμενος δὲ πρὸς τὸ | and when he came to the sanctuary |
| περὶ Δωδώνην ἱερὸν τάς τε | at Dodona, he set fire |
| στοὰς ἐνέπρησε καὶ πολλὰ | to the colonnades and demolished |
| τῶν ἀναθημάτων διέφθειρε, | many of the votive offerings |
| κατέσκαψε δὲ καὶ τὴν ἱερὰν | and tore down also the sacred |
| οἰκίαν | building |

This is borne out also by Pausanias (I 17, 5):

| | |
|---|---|
| καὶ ἄλλα θέας ἄξια, ἱερόν τε Διὸς | and other things worth a visit—the sanctuary of Zeus |
| ἐν Δωδώνῃ καὶ ἱερὰ τοῦ θεοῦ φηγός | at Dodona and the sacred oak of the god |

By "sanctuary" Pausanias cannot mean merely the sacred enclosure, for the sacred oak was inside that, and the "sanctuary" also should, therefore, be inside the temenos. Various buildings inside the temenos came to light in the excavations of Karapanos;[2] but none of them could be identified with certainty, though the sacred building containing the multitude of Zeus statuettes found in the excavation may have been the temple of Zeus. This building had been converted into a Christian church and may possibly be the "temple" that Wordsworth saw with fourteen columns or fragments of columns still standing when he visited Dodona in 1832.

But while Sophocles tells us nothing about the temple building, he does give us a bit of interesting information about the oracle—the oak of Zeus with its many whispering tongues. He gives us also an interesting glimpse of that curious priesthood of primitive Hellas, the most ancient of the race, preserving many of the prehistoric customs of the Hellenic wave of migration as it spread from the original Indo-European home into the peninsula that we know as Greece. They still preserve the primitive form of the national name; for Σελλός is nought but a very ancient form of the name that later became Ἕλλην;

[1] It was to that same oracle of Dodona and its oak with lofty foliage that Odysseus represents himself as having gone to learn the will of Zeus as to his return (τ 296–298):

τὸν δ' ἐς Δωδώνην φάτο βήμεναι, ὄφρα θεοῖο
ἐκ δρυὸς ὑψικόμοιο Διὸς βουλὴν ἐπακοῦσαι,
ὅππως νοστήσειε φίλην ἐς πατρίδα γαῖαν.

[2] *Dodon et ses Ruines.*

DODONA—ITS OAKS AND ITS THEATRE

they are mountain folk, for Dodona lies in a valley 1600 feet above the sea and is surrounded by mountains, chief among which is Mount Tmarus, with the cult of Zeus Tmarius upon its peak.  The Selli are a race of ascetics; they sleep upon the ground (and, in Homer,[1] go with unwashed feet), a custom surviving from days of barbarism but so ancient that it had become a mark of great sanctity.[1]  These curious ascetes, "monks" we might call them, had become a college of priests even before Homer's day (Π 235) and interpreted from the rustling of the leaves of the world-oak[2] the messages from Zeus to men.  Heracles, upon receiving the words from his father by the lips of these reverend fathers, wrote them down for safe-keeping upon his tablets (εἰσεγραψάμην, Soph. Tr. 1167).

According to another passage in the Trachiniae, a speech of Dejanira, the interpretation of the divine messages spoken by Zeus through the rustling leaves of the sacred oak was given, not by these monkish Selli but by a college of priestesses called Peleads (171–172):

| | |
|---|---|
| ὡς τὴν παλαιὰν φηγὸν αὐδῆσαί ποτε <br> Δωδῶνι δισσῶν[3] ἐκ Πελειάδων ἔφη | as, he said, the ancient oak at Dodona <br> had once declared by the mouth of Peleads twain[3] |

Sophocles once more refers to "the priestesses of Dodona, the chanters of oracles" ('Οδ. 'Αχ., Frag. 418 N.: τὰς θεσπιῳδοὺς ἱερέας Δωδωνίδας).  But history knows but little of them.  Herodotus (II 55–57) has a fantastic story about the two black doves that flew from Egyptian Thebes, one to Libya and one to Dodona, and, speaking with human voice, ordained the founding of the "Zeus oracle" in either place.  These doves, he explains aetiologically as two women, who were called Peleads ("dove-children") because they spoke with a foreign tongue that none could understand.  It may be that Sophocles is again[4] adopting one of the stories of his story-telling friend.[5]  At all events, the priestesses could have been at most only a subordinate and a temporary institution.  And their task as interpreters of the oracles of Zeus from the cooing of the doves about the shrine of Dodona seems to rest solely upon a popular etymology of their title.[6]

It is the ancient oak with its many tongues that is the generally recognized medium for the revelations of the will of Zeus at Dodona.  And, with one exception, it is always a single tree[7]—like the world-oak of the Norse legend.  But in Prometheus's prophecy to Io, Aeschylus seems to know of a plurality of speaking oaks at the place of the oracle (P. V. 830–834):

| | |
|---|---|
| τὴν αἰπύνωτόν τ' ἀμφὶ Δωδώνην, ἵνα <br><br> μαντεῖα θᾶκός τ' ἐστὶ Θεσπρωτοῦ Διός, <br> τέρας τ' ἄπιστον, αἱ προσήγοροι δρύες, <br> ἀφ' ὧν σὺ λαμπρὰς κοὐδὲν ἀνικητηρίως <br> προσηγορήθης | and to the region of Dodona with its ridges steep, where <br> are the oracles and seat of Thesprotian Zeus <br> and the portent incredible, the talking oaks, <br> by which, in language clear and riddle-free <br> thou wast addressed . . . |

Besides the talking oak and the more or less problematical doves, there seems to have been at some time, apparently in the fourth century, still a third medium through which

[1] Cf. Π 233—235: Ζεῦ ἄνα, Δωδωναῖε, Πελασγικέ, τηλόθι ναίων, <br> Δωδώνης μεδέων δυσχειμέρου· ἀμφὶ δὲ Σελλοὶ <br> σοὶ ναίουσ' ὑποφῆται ἀνιπτόποδες χαμαιεῦναι.

[2] Cf. also ξ 327–328 = τ 296–297.

[3] Schol. ad loc.: Εὐριπίδης τρεῖς γεγονέναι φησὶν αὐτάς, οἱ δὲ δύο.

[4] See p. 12.

[5] Pausanias may also be harking back to Herodotus when he speaks of the oracular doves (VII 21, 2): αἱ πέλειαι καὶ τὰ ἐκ τῆς δρυὸς μαντεύματα μετέχειν μάλιστα ἐφαίνετο ἀληθείας; and (X 12, 10): αἱ Πέλειαι παρὰ Δωδωναίοις ἐμαντεύσαντο μὲν ἐκ θεοῦ καὶ αὐταί.  In the latter passage surely, and perhaps also in the former, Pausanias's "Doves" are priestesses.  Cf. also Strabo and his "three doves" VII Frag. 1.

[6] The fragment of Hesiod ('Ηοῖαι, Frag. LXXX [149] Flach) should not be warped into evidence for the existence of a dove-oracle in early times, as is done by Mr. Evelyn-White in the Hesiod of the Loeb Classical Library (Frag. 97).  The lines read naturally:

ἔνθα δὲ Δωδώνη τις ἐπ' ἐσχατιῇ πεπόλισται. <br> τὴν δὲ Ζεὺς ἐφίλησε, καὶ ὃν χρηστήριον εἶναι, <br> τίμιον ἀνθρώποις· ναῖον δ' ἐν πυθμένι φηγοῦ.

And Hesiod does not say and should not be made to say that "the doves lived in the hollow of an oak," but he does seem to say that they (the priests) abode by the foot of the oak.  Cf. also Frag. CXCII (224).

The simple explanation of the origin of the dove story seems to be contained in the remark of the Scholiast A to Π 234: Ἑλλοῦ τοῦ δρυτόμου ᾧ φασι τὴν περιστερὰν πρώτην καταδεῖξαι τὸ μαντεῖον.

[7] ξ 328, τ 296; Hes. 'Ηοι., Frag. LXXX (149); Soph. Tr. 171, 1165; Pl. Phaedr. 275 B; Paus. I 17, 5; VII 21, 2; 23, 5; Luc. Amor. 31; etc.; etc.

the god of Dodona manifested his will to those who sought his oracle. This was the famous χαλκεῖον, the cauldron of bronze, sonorous and vibrant as a bell. From the combined testimony of Demon, Callimachus, Polemon, Strabo, and others, the bronze vessel was suspended in the sanctuary; near it was a bronze boy, the gift of Corcyra, holding in his hand a whip. The whip had three lashes; at the end of each was an astragal; as the wind swung the lashes, the astragals would strike the bronze cauldron, and the priests would interpret the oracle of Zeus from the manner and number of the vibrations. But this dedication of the Corcyraeans was not there from the first. Before it came, the seeker after an oracle passing by the bronze would touch it and set it ringing. And again through the manner and number of the vibrations the god would manifest his will by the mouth of his chosen interpreters. That bronze vessel might even ring all day. Such is the interesting contribution to the nature of the oracle and to the sonorous vibrating qualities of some of the bronze ware of antiquity that we have in a fragment of Menander ('Aρρ., Frag. 66, 3–6 K.):

| | |
|---|---|
| τὸ Δωδωναῖον ἄν τις χαλκίον | the bronze vessel of Dodona, they say, |
| ὃ λέγουσιν ἠχεῖν, ἣν παράψηθ’ ὁ παριών, | rings all day long, if the passer-by touches |
| τὴν ἡμέραν ὅλην, καταπαύσαι θᾶττον ἢ | it; but one could sooner quiet that than |
| ταύτην λαλοῦσαν · νύκτα γὰρ προσλαμβάνει | this woman's chatter, for she keeps it up all night as well |

It is not a recognition of more than one sort of oracle nor a corroboration of Aeschylus's plurality of oaks, when Euripides makes Orestes, explaining his sudden arrival in Phthia, say (Andr. 885–886):

| | |
|---|---|
| ἔρχομαι δὲ πρὸς Διὸς μαντεῖα Δωδωναῖ’ | and I am on my way to Zeus's oracle (s) at Dodona |

μαντεῖα, though plural in form, is often used of a single oracular seat.[1]

Again Dodona is mentioned as a place of refuge. When Creon hears that Thebes may be saved from the Seven only by the sacrifice of his own son, he proposes that the young Menoeceus shall flee for protection to that famous shrine (Eur. Ph. 982):

| | |
|---|---|
| ΚΡ. Θεσπρωτὸν οὖδας. ΜΕ. σεμνὰ Δωδώνης βάθρα; | CR. To the Thesprotian land. ME. To Dodona's hallowed seat? |

It is a hallowed place and it is in Thesprotia. More of it we are not told, except that the divinity of the place will be his companion. βάθρα is strongly suggestive of a temple building, but may be no more than an altar. There all the oppressed and heavy-laden might find a blessing from on high (Soph., 'Οδ. 'Αχ., Frag. 423 N.):[2]

| | |
|---|---|
| καὶ τὸν ἐν Δωδῶνι πᾶσι[3] δαίμον’ εὐλογούμενον | and the deity at Dodona who hath a blessing for everyone |

### d. *Lebadea*

Still another famous oracle of Greece was that of Trophonius at Lebadea. Very little is known of it from any source. Our chief source of information is Pausanias.[4] But though he himself consulted the oracle and studied the topography of Lebadea so carefully, he leaves us strangely in the dark, and excavations have not thrown much light upon the problems involved. Pausanias clearly says, beyond the possibility of misunderstanding, that the oracle is "above the grove on the mountain."[5] And yet Ulrichs,[6] finding near the church of the Panagia down on the river-bank close to the cave some granite columns and other architectural fragments and two inscriptions having to do with Trophonius, claims that region for the temple and the cave for the place of the oracle. And there by the cave are numerous cuttings in the face of the rock suggesting votive tablets or the accounts

---

[1] Cf. Eur. Ion 66.
[2] No light can be gained from the corrupt and unintelligible fragment of Cratinus ('Aρχῖλ., Frag. 5 K.):
　　　　Δωδωναίῳ κυνὶ βωλοκόπῳ, τίτθη, γεράνῳ προσέοικας.
[3] Adopting Nauck's suggestion for the MS. παῦσον
[4] IX 39, 1–40, 1.
[5] IX 39, 9: ἔστι δὲ τὸ μαντεῖον ὑπὲρ τὸ ἄλσος ἐπὶ τοῦ ὄρους.
[6] *Reisen u. Forschungen*, I p. 167.

CAVE OF THE TROPHONIUS ORACLE

With cuttings for votive tablets in the Hercyna Gorge at Lebadea

that Pausanias says every one who consulted the oracle must leave behind—all that he saw and heard, graven on a tablet.[1] Schmidt champions the chapel of St. Anna and St. Constantine on the eastern slope of the castle-hill as the site of the temple, while the place of the oracle was on the very summit of the hill. The latter view is more likely to be correct.

In the extant dramatic literature Euripides's Ion is the only tragedy that mentions Trophonius or his oracle. Xuthus had gone to consult the Boeotian prophet on his child-lessness before he sought the oracle of Delphi. Three times it is mentioned, and each time with a peculiar turn of speech (Ion 300):

| σηχοῖς δ᾽ ἐνστρέφει Τροφωνίου | he is "taking a turn" at the "enclosures" of Trophonius |

(393–394):

| τὰς Τροφωνίου<br>λιπόντα θαλάμας | he has left the<br>"chambers" of Trophonius |

(405):

| τί θέσπισμ᾽ ἐχ Τροφωνίου φέρεις | what oracle bringest thou "out of" Trophonius |

Whatever the relation between the temple and the place of the oracle, the plural forms "enclosures," "chambers," confirm Pausanias's account of temple and place of oracle and house of Good Demon and Good Fortune as at least separate apartments connected with the Lebadean oracle.

Aristophanes, on the other hand, makes it perfectly clear that the "house of Tro-phonius" is a dark, awesome, subterranean place, with all the horrors that Plutarch (Mor. 592 e) and Athenaeus (XIV 614 a) associate with it (Nub. 505–508[2]):

| ΣΩ. οὐ μὴ λαλήσεις, ἀλλ᾽ ἀχολουθήσεις ἐμοὶ<br>ἀνύσας τι δευρὶ θᾶττον. ΣΤΡ. ἐς τὼ χεῖρέ νυν<br>δός μοι μελιτοῦτταν πρότερον· ὡς δέδοιχ᾽ ἐγὼ<br>εἴσω χαταβαίνων ὥσπερ εἰς Τροφωνίου | SOC. You mustn't say a word, but follow me<br>quickly this way—quick! STR. Put a honey-<br>cake in my hands first; for I'm scared<br>of going down in as into the house of Trophonius |

The horrors were apparently moral as well as physical, and to combat the excesses prevalent there in the fifth and fourth centuries no less than four of the comic poets wrote plays entitled Trophonius (Alex. Frag. 236–238 K.; Cephisod. Frag. 3–6 K.; Crat. Frag. 218–227 K.; Men. Frag. 462–465 K.). If we only had these comedies complete, instead of the few scanty fragments that have been preserved, we might be in a position to understand more of this interesting oracle which stood so high in the esteem of Socrates's contemporaries.

### e. Bacis

Herodotus four times mentions Bacis, the Boeotian giver of oracles. Bacis, as an oracle, belongs in the same category with Orpheus, Musaeus, and Melampus, prophets, mouth-pieces of God, who uttered inspired truth. Even in the time of Aristotle doubts were expressed as to whether Bacis, Orpheus, Musaeus, and the rest of their class ever existed.[3] Indeed, it would seem that these names are only apellativa, standing for the type of prophecy they represented.[4] This is especially true of Bacis. But Herodotus looked upon him as a very real personality inspired to utter unerring truth,[5] and with the people of his time such prophecies were very popular. To Herodotus Bacis meant the Boeotian prophet; but there are at least three Bacides to be distinguished: 1) the Boeotian, from the village of Eleon; 2) the Arcadian, from Caphyae; 3) the Athenian. Pisistratus claimed connection with him and added Bacis as a surname to his own.

[1] IX 39, 14.
[2] The Scholiast on the passage calls Trophonius a λιθοξόος ἄριστος, ὃς χατεσχεύασεν ἱερὸν ἐν Λεβαδείᾳ... ὑπὸ γῆν. It was the same Trophonius who was architect of the great temple of Apollo at Delphi.
[3] Arist. Probl. XXX 1, p. 954a 36; Plato, Theages 124 D.
[4] See Rohde, *Psyche*, pp. 349–357.
[5] VIII 20; 77; 96; IX 43. Pausanias also, even in his late day, seems to hold to the infallibility of Bacis's inspiration (from the Nymphs, IV 27, 4; X 12, 11); IX 17, 5; X 14, 6; X 32, 8; 9; 11.

It is the Boeotian, the oldest and most famous of the Bacides, whose prophecies Aristophanes quotes and to whom the comic poet often alludes.[1]  But as there seems to have been no temple or permanent oracular seat for his oracles but only a collection or collections of his prophecies, the problems of the Bacis oracle do not concern us.

## 7. OTHER SANCTUARIES OF APOLLO

### a. *At Delos*

Only inferior in importance and fame to the seat of Apollo worship on Mount Parnassus was the temple of the god of light, with the oracle and the games, on the island of Delos. From early times Delian, like Pythian and Lycian and Thymbraean, is a standing epithet of Apollo[2] (Eur. Rh. 224–225):

| | |
|---|---|
| Θυμβραῖε καὶ Δήλιε καὶ Λυκίας | Apollo, Thymbraean and Delian and |
| ναὸν ἐμβατεύων Ἄπολλον | haunting the temple of Lycia |

(Ar. Ran. 659):

| | |
|---|---|
| Ἄπολλον, ὅς που Δῆλον ἢ Πυθῶν' ἔχεις, | Apollo! Lord!—of Delos and of Pytho |

Delos was the very centre of the Ionian world; there was the sanctuary and oracle of the god common to Panionia; there was held the great fifth-year festival that bound all Ionians together in Ionic unity; it was for many years the capital of united Ionia; it was for centuries the clearing-house for the commerce of the eastern Mediterranean; and yet it calls for scarcely a comment at the hands of the dramatic poets, early or late.  There is no reference to the temples of Apollo or Artemis or Leto in the sacred enclosure; no allusion to the treasure-houses or the business houses; no praise of the great horned altar, one of the seven wonders of the world.  The things that seem most to have interested the dramatic poets are some of the prominent, natural features of the topography of the island—Mount Cynthus, the Sacred Lake, the Sacred Palm, under which Leto gave birth to Apollo and Artemis, the laurels and the olives (Eur. I. T. 1097–1105):

| | |
|---|---|
| ποθοῦσ' Ἄρτεμιν ὀλβίαν | longing for Artemis the blessed |
| ἃ παρὰ Κύνθιον ὄχθον οἰκεῖ | who dwells by the Cynthian height |
| φοίνικά θ' ἁβροκόμαν, | and the feathery palm, |
| δάφναν τ' εὐέρνεα καὶ | and the laurel with its strong branches and the |
| γλαυκᾶς θαλλὸν ἱρὸν ἐλαίας, | sacred boughs of the grey-green olive— |
| Λατοῦς ὠδῖνα φίλαν, | Leto's loved travail— |
| λίμναν θ' εἱλίσσουσαν ὕδωρ | and the circular lake with |
| κύκλιον | its rippling water |

(Eur. Ion 919–922):

| | |
|---|---|
| μισεῖ σ' ἁ Δᾶλος καὶ δάφνας | thou art hated of Delos and the laurel- |
| ἔρνεα φοίνικα παρ' ἁβροκόμαν, | shoots by the feathery palm, |
| ἔνθα λοχεύματα σέμν' ἐλοχεύσατο | where Leto travailed in |
| Λατώ | travail holy |

These two passages suggest a few of the many interesting things that the visitor may see to-day on the little island of Delos—Cynthus, commanding a view of all the Cyclades, the almost perfect circle of the Sacred Lake, slight remnants of the palm of bronze that early took the place of Leto's growing palm, the glades of under-brush of laurel and wild olive.

In other places Cynthus is referred to as "a hogback" (Ae. Eum. 9):

| | |
|---|---|
| λιπὼν δὲ λίμναν Δηλίαν τε χοιράδα | leaving the lake and the rock of Delos |

(Eur. Tro. 89):

| | |
|---|---|
| Δήλιοί τε χοιράδες | and the Delian rocks |

[1] Ar. Eq. 123–124; 1002–1003; Av. 961–963; 967–968; 970; 971–973; 975; 976–978; 982–985; 987–988; Pax 1070–1072.

[2] Cp. the Homeric Hymn to the "Delian Apollo"; Pind. Pyth. I 74.

Rheneia.
Sacred Harbor

DELOS FROM THE SUMMIT OF CYNTHUS

Temenos

Sacred Lake

Myconos

These epithets suggest the island as a low-lying reef; in another passage of the Iphigenia in Tauris Euripides pictures Delos as a rocky ridge (1239–1240):

| | |
|---|---|
| φέρε δ' ἴνιν <br> ἀπὸ δειράδος εἰναλίας | and she brought her child <br> from the sea-girt rock |

while Aristophanes magnifies Cynthus, a hill whose single peak rises but three hundred seventy feet above the sea, into a rock with towering horns (Nub. 596–597):

| | |
|---|---|
| Δήλιε, Κυνθίαν ἔχων <br> ὑψικέρατα πέτραν | God of Delos, who dwellest on the <br> Cynthian rock with its towering horns |

So much about the island. Nothing at all about the temple or the oracle.

Menander quotes the proverb ('Εαυτ. Τιμ., Frag. 147 K.):

| | |
|---|---|
| ταὐτά σοι καὶ Πύθια <br> καὶ Δήλια | that's your Pythia <br> and Delia |

that is, "you've done your utmost, and it's all over with." Pythia and Delia here refer to the festivals.

### b. *In Attica*

There were at least seven well-known sanctuaries of Apollo in Attica: 1) the cave sanctuary of Apollo in the north cliff of the Acropolis, which will be discussed in connection with the cave of Pan (pp. 182 ff.); 2) the most familiar of all, the Lyceum, just outside the northeast gate of the city; 3) next in fame to the Lyceum, the Pythium in the pass of Aegaleus on the Sacred Way to Eleusis; 4) the temple at Prasiae; 5) the shrine of Apollo at Oenoe; 6) a sanctuary of Apollo Pythius; and 7) of Apollo Delphinius not far from the temple of Olympian Zeus, just outside the city walls.[1] We find no reference to any one of the last four in the dramatic poets; the first three do find casual mention.

### α. *The Lyceum in Athens*

The Lyceum was one of the oldest sanctuaries in the lower city of Athens; it was there when the Amazons invaded Attica.[2] Its name is derived from the epithet of Apollo as Λύκειος, which originally had nothing to do with *wolf*[3] but is derived from the same root as *lux, lucis*, and English *light*. The Lyceum was, therefore, the sanctuary of Apollo, the god of light.[4] Of the temple proper we know nothing from any source. But connected with it was the famous gymnasium, the Lyceum, in which stood the beautiful statue of the god described by Lucian[5] in an attitude of rest after the exertions of the palaestra, leaning with his left arm resting upon a pillar, his left hand holding his bow, and his right arm bent over his head.

The gymnasium was added to the Lyceum, according to Theopompus, by Pisistratus; according to Philochorus, it was founded during the administration of Pericles; other authorities ascribe its foundation to the orator Lycurgus.[6] The last account can refer only to a restoration or extension of the grounds. For we know from Plato[7] that the Lyceum was one of Socrates's favorite places for heart to heart talks with young men. And even in the days of Aristophanes the Lyceum afforded an extensive parade-ground for military training (Ar. Pax 355–357):

| | |
|---|---|
| καὶ γὰρ ἱκανὸν χρόνον ἀπολλύμεθα καὶ <br> κατατετρίμμεθα πλανώμενοι <br> ἐς Λύκειον κἀκ Λυκείου ξὺν δορὶ ξὺν ἀσπίδι | for long enough have we been worn to death and <br> frazzles with marching back and forth, <br> to the Lyceum and from the Lyceum, with spear <br> and shield |

Here is where the citizen soldiers of Athens got their final training before they were sent to the field of war.

[1] Paus. I 19, 1.

[2] Plut. Thes. XXVII 4.

[3] All the wolf stories connected with Apollo are aetiological myths, originating in an epoch when √ luc had long since disappeared from the Greek of daily use and when obscure names needed explanation.

[4] Cf. Soph. El. 645: Λύκει' ἄναξ, and *ibid.* 655 and 1379: ὦ Λύκει' Ἄπολλον.

[5] Anach. 7. It was evidently the Apollo-type represented by the beautiful Apollino of the Uffizzi in Florence; reproduced in Baum., *Denkm.* I p. 100, Fig. 105.

[6] So Paus. I 29, 16; Plut. Vit. X Or., pp. 841c, 852c.

[7] Euthyd. 271 A; Euthyphro 2 A; Lysis 203 A.

From the days of Socrates to the days of Aristotle, and after, the porticos of the Lyceum were a famous place for the lectures of the teachers of philosophy. Alexis classes the Lyceum with the Academy and the porch of the Odeum as a typical lecture-hall for the sophists ('Ασωτοδ., Frag. 25, 1–3 K.)[1]:

| | |
|---|---|
| τί ταῦτα ληρεῖς, φληναφῶν ἄνω κάτω | what do you mean by this nonsense—yapping up and down |
| Λύκειον, 'Ακαδημίαν, 'Ωιδείου πύλας, λήρους σοφιστῶν; οὐδὲ ἕν τούτων καλόν. | the Lyceum, the Academy, the Odeum porches— sophists' nonsense? Not one of these things is right! |

It is only the gymnasium of the Lyceum that the poets mention, and they tell us nothing beyond the fact that the big open space of the gymnasium was used as a parade-ground for the army, and the stoas as lecture-halls for the philosophers.

### β. The Pythia

Besides the Lyceum, at the northeast corner of the city, there was a Pythium not far from the temple of Olympian Zeus, another at Oenoe, and a third on the Sacred Way to Eleusis. Of the first Pausanias says only (I 19, 1):

| | |
|---|---|
| Μετὰ δὲ τὸν ναὸν τοῦ Διὸς τοῦ 'Ολυμπίου πλησίον ἄγαλμά ἐστιν 'Απόλλωνος Πυθίου. ἔστι δὲ καὶ ἄλλο ἱερὸν 'Απόλλωνος ἐπίκλησιν Δελφινίου | A little way beyond the temple of the Olympian Zeus is a statue of the Pythian Apollo. And there is also another sanctuary of Apollo surnamed the Delphinian |

While Pausanias does not explicitly say that there was anything more than a statue of the Pythian Apollo, the words ἔστι δὲ καὶ ἄλλο ἱερὸν 'Απόλλωνος very plainly imply that there was a Pythium as well as a Delphinium. Besides we know from Thucydides[2] that there was a Pythium at Athens, and the historian mentions it in immediate connection with the temple of Olympian Zeus. We even have the original inscription[3] from an altar erected in this Pythium by Pisistratus, the son of Hippias and grandson of the great Pisistratus, so that we know that this sanctuary dates back into fairly remote antiquity.

From the description of Pausanias, the words of Thucydides, hints from other Greek authors,[4] and from the place where the fragment of Pisistratus's altar and inscribed bases supporting tripods won by choruses in the Thargelia and dedicated[5] to the Pythian Apollo were found, we may locate this Pythium with probable accuracy a little distance to the southwest of the Olympieum, close beside the Ilissus.[6]

It may be the indweller of the Pythium or of the Lyceum whom Chrysalus salutes on his return from Ephesus (Plaut. Bacch. 172–173):

> saluto te, vicine Apollo, qui aedibus
> propinquos nostris accolis, veneroque te

but it is much more likely a statue of Apollo of the Ways before the house of Bacchis (see Vol. II, Chap. viii).

A second well known Pythium of Athens is the one situated beside the Sacred Way in the saddle between the two heights of Aegaleus, about four and a half miles from the Dipylum Gate of Athens, upon the site of which now stands the decaying convent of Daphne. Pausanias mentions it on his way from Athens to Eleusis (I 37, 6):

| | |
|---|---|
| ἔστι δὲ ἱερὸν.. καὶ 'Αθηνᾶς τε καὶ 'Απόλλωνος· 'Απόλλωνι δὲ ἐποι- ήθη μόνῳ τὸ ἐξ ἀρχῆς | then there is a sanctuary to Athena and Apollo conjointly; originally it was erected to Apollo alone |

[1] So also Antiph. Κλεοφ., Frag. 122, 2–3 K.: ἀκολουθεῖν ἔρις ἐν τῷ Λυκείῳ μετὰ σοφιστῶν
Ephip. Ναυαγ., Frag. 14, 1–2 K.; Epicr. Inc. Frag. 11, 9–11 K.
[2] Thuc. II 15, 4.
[3] C. I. A. I 422; cf. Thuc. VI 54, 7: Μνῆμα τόδ' ἧς ἀρχῆς Πεισίστρατος Ἱππίου υἱὸς θῆκεν 'Απόλλωνος Πυθίου ἐν τεμένει.
[4] E. g. Suidas, Photius, Hesychius, s. v. Πύθιον; Plato, Gorgias, 472 A.
[5] C. I. A. II 1236, 1237, 1251 = Dittenb., Sylloge 411–413; cf. also C. I. A. II 1154, 1176; III 247.
[6] On the Pythium at Athens, see Curtius, Das Pythion in Athen, Hermes XII (1877) pp. 492–499 (= Ges. Abh. I pp. 451–458); Frazer, Paus. II pp. 189–190; Harrison, Mon. and Myth., pp. 203–207.

It is probably this Pythium to which a company is bidden go out, without torches, in the Ποτάμιοι of Strattis (Frag. 37 K.):

| | |
|---|---|
| ὑμεῖς τε πάντες ἔξιτ' ἐπὶ τὸ Πύθιον<br>ὅσοι πάρεστε, μὴ λαβόντες λαμπάδας<br><br>μηδ' ἄλλο μηδὲν ἐχόμενον Φιλυλλίου | all of you that are here, go on out in the<br>direction of the Pythium, and take no torches<br>with you<br>nor anything else that has to do with Philyllius |

The people addressed are to go *out;* they are not to take *torches;* they are to proceed toward the Pythium. There is in these words a triple suggestion of the sacred procession to Eleusis: the procession passed out of the city by the Sacred Way; it was a torchlight procession; it followed the Sacred Way which led directly past the Pythium in the Aegaleus pass. We cannot even conjecture what the context was; we do not know when this company was to "go out"; it may have been out of the house where the command is given; we do not know why they were to take no *torches.* The discovery of the context might shift the allusion to the Pythium near the temple of Olympian Zeus, and so Kock, following Hemsterhuys, interprets the passage.

### c. *In the Peloponnesus*

### α. *The Argive Lyceum*

The Peloponnesus seems to have shown a larger preference for Apollo as the god of light. Phigalia had a temple in his honor; Sicyon also had one but had early allowed her temple to Apollo Lycius to fall into decay[1]; but at Argos the most famous building of the city was the Lyceum, the temple of the "wolf-slaying" god. Pausanias gives no description of the temple building but he dwells at some length[2] upon the sculptures it contained—a new cultus statue by Attalus of Athens; Danaus's throne; an athlete carrying a bull on his shoulders by Biton; wooden images of Aphrodite and Hermes, the one ascribed to Epeus, who built the Trojan horse with the aid of Athena, the other (the Aphrodite) an offering made by Hypermnestra, the daughter of Danaus; a statue of Ladas [Myron's?], the famous long-distance runner; a Hermes in the act of manufacturing the first lyre from a tortoise shell. The original temple, with the original statue, was ascribed to Danaus himself as founder.

The temple, of which no vestige has as yet been discovered, would seem to have stood near the agora, at the base of the Larissa hill. Sophocles, with a fine human touch, has the old paedagogus conduct Orestes home after his long years of exile, and the old man points out to the youthful prince, as they enter, the most famous features of the landscape that lay spread before the gates of the home from which he had been rescued and sent away to prepare for his deed of vengeance (Soph. El. 4–8):

| | |
|---|---|
| τὸ γὰρ παλαιὸν Ἄργος οὑπόθεις τόδε,<br><br>τῆς οἰστροπλῆγος ἄλσος Ἰνάχου κόρης·<br><br>αὕτη δ', Ὀρέστα, τοῦ λυκοκτόνου θεοῦ<br>ἀγορὰ Λύκειος· οὑξ ἀριστερᾶς δ' ὅδε<br>Ἥρας ὁ κλεινὸς ναὸς | yonder is the ancient plain of Argos which thou<br>hast longed to see,<br>the solemn haunt of the vexed wanderer, the<br>daughter of Inachus;<br>over there, Orestes, the Lycean agora of the wolf-<br>slaying[3] god; and here, upon our left, is<br>Hera's famous temple[4] |

For all the fame of this most conspicuous building of the city of Argos, neither periegete nor historian nor poet gives us the slightest information about it.

[1] Paus. II 9, 7.
[2] Paus. II 19, 3–8.
[3] The poet seems to accept the popular etymology of Λύκειος as derived from λύκος. So does Aeschylus (Sept. 145–146):

| | |
|---|---|
| καὶ σύ, Λύκει' ἄναξ, λύκειος γενοῦ<br>στρατῷ δαΐῳ | and thou, Lycean Lord (Lord of Light), be wolf-like<br>to the host of foes |

Cf. Soph. O. T. 203; 919. See also p. 93 ft. n. 3.
[4] See p. 101.

## β. *The Apollo of Amyclae*

A few miles south of Sparta was once the town of Amyclae, the site of the original settle-ment of the Dorians in the Eurotas Valley.[1]  It was a place of peculiar sanctity, and a Sacred Way connected it with Sparta; for here each summer was held a festival in honor of Hyacinthus, the son of Amyclas and the favorite of Apollo.  Over the lamented Hya-cinthus's tomb stood the archaic, colossal statue of Apollo, and about this venerated figure Bathycles of Magnesia constructed his marvelous throne embellished with sculptures in gold.[2]  The statue and the throne are described by Pausanias and not otherwise men-tioned in ancient literature.  The silence of the dramatic poets, therefore, need occasion no surprise.  The only hints at the sanctuary of Apollo at Amyclae are made by the Laconian Woman in the Lysistrate of Aristophanes (1299):

κλέωα τὸν Ἀμύκλαις [Ἀπόλλω] σιόν　　　　| I sing the praise of Apollo, the god at Amyclae

and likewise with strong Laconian accent, by some one in Epilycus (Κωρ., Frag. 3 K.):

ποττὰν κοπίδ', οἰῶ, σῶμαι·　　　　　| to the festival, methinks, I must haste;
ἐν Ἀμύκλαισι παρ' Ἀπέλλω　　　　| at Apollo's shrine at Amyclae
βάραχες πολλοὶ χᾶρτοι　　　　　　| one will find many cakes and loaves
καὶ δωμός τοι μάλα ἡδύς　　　　　| and soup most delicious

This song is apparently sung as the chorus moves off to the three-day festival held each year at Amyclae in memory of Hyacinthus, with its splendid procession, its sacrifices and feasting and gifts.[3]

## d. *On the Island of Leucas*

On the southwest point of the island of Leucas, standing high above the blue Ionian Sea upon a precipitous rock, the most conspicuous object that one sees as one sails from Corcyra to the Gulf of Corinth, is a modern lighthouse.  It is built upon the site of an ancient temenos of Apollo, from which Sappho, in her hopeless love for Phaon, is fabled to have cast herself into the sea.[4]  Here, too, during the festival of Leucadian Apollo, a criminal was made, as a sort of scapegoat to bear away the sins of the people, to leap into the sea. But he was not killed; care was taken to lighten his fall, and boats were in waiting below to pick him up and convey him beyond the confines of the country, for in being made the scapegoat he became sacred to the god.[5]  It is quite possible that it is to this rite that a fragment of Menander's Lady from Leucas (313 K.) refers:

εὐφημείσθω　　　　　　　　　| let there be auspicious silence
τέμενος πέρι Λευκάδος ἀκτῆς　　| about the shrine of the Leucadian promontory

Of the temple itself, which Aeneas is said to have founded,[6] scanty remains have been discovered in recent years.

## 8. TEMPLES OF ZEUS

One might naturally expect that the supreme deity of the Greek Pantheon might claim most frequent mention in any class of literature that has to do with the religion of the people and that his great temples—such as that at Olympia or Athens or Nemea—should be often the object of the poets' praise.  But not a word do we find in the drama, early or late, about the great temple at Olympia, and very little about any other temple of Zeus.

[1] Pind. Pyth. I 125.
[2] For a discussion of the throne see Paus. III 18, 9; Overbeck, *Gesch. d. gr. Plastik*, I⁴, pp. 67 ff.
[3] Ath. (IV 139 d-f) gives a full account of the festival.  It is referred to also by Ar. or Philyl.  (Πόλ., Frag. 16 K.) and Crat.  (Πλ., Frag. 164 K.).
[4] Cf. Men. Λευκ., Frag. 312 K.
[5] Cf. Paus. X 32, 6.
[6] Cf. Serv. ad Virg. Aen. III 279.

SITE OF APOLLO'S TEMPLE ON THE LEUCADIAN CLIFFS

OLYMPIA

Echo Hall      Nero's Arch      Buleuterium      Metroum      Zeus Temple      Leonidaeum

### a. At Olympia

The only occurrence of the name Olympieum is an extremely doubtful one quoted by Photius in an unidentified fragment of Aristophanes (Frag. 832 K.):

| | |
|---|---|
| τὸ ἱερὸν 'Ολυμπίειον [MS. 'Ολύμπιον] πεντασυλλάβως ὡς 'Ασκληπίειον [MS. 'Ασκληπιεῖον]. 'Αριστοφάνης | the hallowed Olympieum— in five syllables, like Asclepieum. Aristophanes |

But whether it is an Olympieum or an Asclepieum that Photius found in Aristophanes he does not make clear. And if it is 'Ολυμπίειον that he is quoting from the comic poet, we are at a loss to conjecture what possible Olympieum Aristophanes was talking about. It may have been one in Athens; it may have been the famous one in Olympia; it may have been any other conceivable temple of Zeus in the Hellenic world. We gain absolutely nothing from the fragment. And we gain as little from another allusion to "the temple of Zeus" in Aristophanes's Clouds (401):

| | |
|---|---|
| ἀλλὰ τὸν αὑτοῦ γε νεὼν βάλλει καὶ Σούνιον | but he strikes his own temple and Sunium |

Socrates is persuading Strepsiades that it is not perjurers that are the special object of the lightnings of Zeus, but that the god's bolts are just as likely to strike his own temple as anything else. What temple of Zeus has Aristophanes in mind? To "his own temple" he adds at once very specifically "Sunium the headland of Athens." But "his own temple" may be any one of a multitude of Zeus temples. Probably some Olympieum in Attica had recently been struck by lightning, an event that made an impression upon the popular mind; it may have been the sanctuary by the Ilissus; we do not know.

### b. On the Cenaean Promontory

One temple of Zeus owes its fame largely, if not entirely, to the tragic poets. On the extreme northwestern promontory of Euboea, overlooking the Malaic Gulf, stood from remotest antiquity the temple of Cenaean Zeus, so called from the name of the promontory itself. Here it was that Heracles made sacrifice to his father after the capture of Oechalia.[1] It naturally plays an important rôle, therefore, in such plays as the Trachiniae of Sophocles. Sophocles describes the locality briefly (Tr. 752–756):

| | |
|---|---|
| ἀκτή τις ἀμφίκλυστος Εὐβοίας ἄκρον Κήναιον ἔστιν, ἔνθα πατρῴῳ Διὶ βωμοὺς ὁρίζει τεμενίαν τε φυλλάδα | there is a sea-washed headland of Euboea, the promontory of Cenaeum, where to his father Zeus he marks off the bounds of altars and enclosure rich in shade, |
| . . . . . . . . | . . . . . . |
| μέλλοντι δ' αὐτῷ πολυθύτους τεύχειν σφαγὰς | and as he was about to do sacrifice of many victims |

There, upon the Cenaean promontory, stood the temple of Zeus in the days of Heracles, as in the days of Sophocles. It was important enough to need a plurality of altars, apparently, though the plural form βωμούς need not necessarily mean more than *altaria*, one altar. It is certainly singular in the lyric passage in which Heracles tries to give expression to his agony (Soph. Tr. 993–995):

| | |
|---|---|
| ὦ Κηναία κρηπὶς βωμῶν, ἱερῶν οἵαν οἵων ἐπί μοι | oh step of altar Cenaean, what sacrifice of mine and with what a recompense |
| μελεῷ χάριν ἠνύσω, ὦ Ζεῦ. | hast thou requited me to my woe, oh Zeus! |

Almost the same thought as that expressed in lines 752–754 had been brought out in lines 237–238:

| | |
|---|---|
| ἀκτή τις ἔστ' Εὐβοιίς, ἔνθ' ὁρίζεται βωμοὺς τέλη τ' ἔγκαρπα Κηναίῳ Διὶ | there is a headland of Euboea; there he marks off altars and dues of fruits in honor of Cenaean Zeus |

[1] Cf. the full account given in Ov. Met. IX 134–272.

The location, with an allusion to the sharp bend in the Euripus about the northwest corner of Euboea and to the tragic death of Lichas, is further defined in a fragment of Aeschylus's Glaucus of the Sea (Frag. 30 N.):

| | |
|---|---|
| Εὐβοΐδα καμπὴν ἀμφὶ Κηναίου Διὸς | the bend above Euboea at the headland of |
| ἀκτήν, κατ' αὐτὸν τύμβον ἀθλίου Λίχα | Cenaean Zeus, hard by the unhappy Lichas's tomb |

Seneca (?) also alludes to the antiquity of the temple of Cenaean Zeus and its lofty site; the author of the Oetaean Hercules is, of course, but echoing a Greek original (H. O. 786–787):

> hic rupe celsa nulla quam nubes ferit
> annosa fulgent templa Cenaei Iovis

The poets' contributions, though all we have, do not contribute much: the existence of a temple to Zeus on the Cenaean promontory; its high antiquity; its altars and its grove. That is all. Of its shape, size, style, plastic decorations—the things of real interest—we know nothing.

### c. *At Marathon*

No other literary source, save Euripides alone, knows aught of a temple of Zeus at Marathon. In the Heraclidae the centre of the scene is occupied by the temple of Zeus with the great altar of the Olympian before it. As the play opens, Iolaus and the children of Heracles are sitting as suppliants at the altar steps (Eur. Heracl. 32–33):

| | |
|---|---|
| Μαραθῶνα καὶ σύγκληρον ἐλθόντες χθόνα | we have come to Marathon and the confederate land |
| ἱκέται καθεζόμεσθα βώμιοι θεῶν | and sit as suppliants at the altars of the gods |

The scene is Marathon; the suppliants sit at "the altars of the gods." Not yet is it specified that the altar is consecrated to Zeus nor that it is connected with a shrine. The temple, with its altar, is named a few lines further on (41–44):

| | |
|---|---|
| ἡ δ' αὖ τὸ θῆλυ παιδὸς 'Αλκμήνη γένος | but she, Alcmene, inside the temple yonder holds |
| ἔσωθε ναοῦ τοῦδ' ὑπηγκαλισμένη | the daughters of her son in her embrace and |
| σώζει· νέας γὰρ παρθένους αἰδούμεθα | saves them; for we hesitate to bring young maidens |
| ὄχλῳ πελάζειν κἀπιβωμιοστατεῖν | into the presence of a crowd and have them stand at public altars |

The ναός might be anything from the simplest sanctuary to the most magnificent peripteral temple. We have not as yet any conception of the temple's form. It is simply ναός once more (Heracl. 657):

| | |
|---|---|
| σὺ πρόσθε ναοῦ τοῦδ' ὅπως βαίης πέλας | that thou mightest draw near before this temple |

Alcmena, to whom this line is addressed, had been inside the temple building[1] (584):

| | |
|---|---|
| τήν τ' ἔσω γραῖαν δόμων | and the aged woman inside the halls |

The temple now is called δόμοι "halls"; the plural implies at least a pronaos and a cella, with perhaps also an opisthodome. Even before Alcmena's entrance, Macaria had come out of the temple building.[2] Inside the temple were hanging upon pegs, as at the temple of Delphi, spoils of arms taken in wars (Heracl. 695–699):

| | |
|---|---|
| ἔστ' ἐν δόμοισιν ἔνδον αἰχμάλωθ' ὅπλα | there are within yonder halls arms taken |
| τοῖσδ', οἷσι χρησόμεσθα... | in war; these will we use . . . |
| . . . . . . | . . . . . . |
| ἀλλ' εἴσιθ' εἴσω κἀπὸ πασσάλων ἑλὼν | go in, then, and from the pegs take down |
| ἔνεγχ' ὁπλίτην κόσμον ὡς τάχιστά μοι | and bring me with all speed a hoplite's panoply |

[1] She is called forth by Iolaus (643): ἔξελθ'.

[2] 474–475: θράσος μοι μηδὲν ἐξόδοις ἐμαῖς
προσθῆτε....

479: ἐξῆλθον.

Only once more does the poet refer to the temple proper, and this time as a "roof" (Eur. Heracl. 646):

| | |
|---|---|
| τί χρῆμ' ἀϋτῆς πᾶν τόδ' ἐπλήσθη στέγος; | what means the cry that has filled all this roof? |

We gain then, for the temple of Zeus at Marathon, a building with several apartments under one roof. Whether it had a colonnade all about it or was a simple temple *in antis*, we are not told and have as yet no means of discovering. Whether it was Doric or Ionic we cannot tell.

Before it was, as we have seen, the great altar of Zeus at which Iolaus and the sons of Heracles sat as suppliants. And it is in connection with the altar that Euripides informs us that the sanctuary is holy unto Zeus (Heracl. 238–239):

| | |
|---|---|
| τὸ μὲν μέγιστον Ζεὺς ἐφ' οὗ σὺ βώμιος θακεῖς...[1] | and the chiefest [influence] is Zeus, at whose altar thou art sitting . . .[1] |

At the time of my first visit to the plain of Marathon, in 1886, I was wandering through the fields to the south of the Soros and came unexpectedly upon the foundations of a large marble building about twenty-five by twelve paces (weary ones), with fragments of sculpture lying half buried in the ground about it. The guide-books contain no mention of any ruins in that part of the plain. Excavations conducted there might reveal something of importance—perhaps the very temple that we have been discussing. Perhaps also those foundations might belong to the monument of Miltiades or to the trophy of Zeus which was built of white marble[2] and must have stood not far from that locality. There is another building about five hundred yards to the north of the Soros,[3] which may, upon excavation, prove to be one or the other of these two important buildings. The Marathonian plain is as yet comparatively virgin soil for the excavator's spade; it was fairly covered with monuments of one sort and another, and the only thing that has been investigated is the tomb of the immortal one hundred ninety-two Athenians who fell on that great day in August, 490 B. C.

The trophy was one of the most precious monuments in the eyes of the patriotic Athenian; Themistocles declared that the thought of the trophy of Miltiades would not let him sleep;[4] and Aristophanes makes repeated reference to it as the very proudest symbol of Athenian liberties (Eq. 1334):

| | |
|---|---|
| τῆς γὰρ πόλεως ἄξια πράττεις καὶ τοῦ 'ν Μαραθῶνι τροπαίου | you are doing things befitting the state and in keeping with the trophy at Marathon |

and in almost the same words (Vesp. 711):

| | |
|---|---|
| ἄξια τῆς γῆς ἀπολαύοντες καὶ τοῦ Μαραθῶνι τροπαίου | enjoying things befitting the land and in keeping with the trophy at Marathon |

and again (Lys. 285):[5]

| | |
|---|---|
| μὴ νῦν ἔτ' ἐν τῇ τετραπόλει[6] τοὐμὸν τροπαῖον εἴη | may my trophy no longer stand in the Four-city[6] district |

And even Euripides, in the same spirit, sets a famous trophy there as a monument erected by no one less an Athenian than Hyllus himself and Iolaus (Heracl. 936–937):

| | |
|---|---|
| βρέτας Διὸς τροπαίου καλλίνικον ἵστασαν | and they erected unto Zeus that gives the trophy a post of glorious victory |

[1] The altar is frequently alluded to, sometimes as βωμός: 33; 61; 73; 79; 123; 196; 238; 244; 249; 344; sometimes as ἐσχάρα ("hearth"): 121; 127; 341; sometimes as ἕδρα ("seat"): 55; 260; 631.

[2] Paus. I 32, 5: πεποίηται δὲ καὶ τρόπαιον λίθου λευκοῦ.

[3] Leake, *Topogr. of Ath.*, II 101.

[4] Plut. Them. III 3.

[5] Cf. also Ar. 'Ολκ., Frag. 413 K.:
καὶ κολλύραν τοῖσι περῶσιν διὰ τοὐν Μαραθῶνι τροπαῖον.

[6] See p. 122.

## d. *At Argos*

Under the surname of Clarius "the allotter" Zeus was worshiped in the highlands of Arcadia above Tegea, as we learn from Pausanias (VIII 53, 9).[1] The same Zeus would seem from Aeschylus's Suppliants to have had a shrine in Argos (359–360):

| | |
|---|---|
| ἴδοιτο δῆτ᾽ | may then Themis, child of |
| ἄνατον φυγὰν ἱκεσία Θέμις | Zeus the Allotter, look |
| Διὸς Κλαρίου | upon our refuge innocent |

Pausanias explains the surname of the Allotter as having been derived from the casting of lots for the sons of Arcas—most probably at the time of the allotment of the lands among them when they settled in central Peloponnesus. A similar allotment may be safely assumed for the original colonists in the Argolid, and Zeus Clarius would naturally find a place in the worship of their descendants. In connection with the worship of this particular Zeus in Arcadia we have no information of any temple or statue or anything else beyond the altar mentioned by Pausanias. For the sanctuary at Argos Aeschylus tells us even less; the chorus of Danaids only appeals to Themis as the embodiment of sacred Law, the child of Zeus Clarius, to lend her sanctifying power to their position as suppliants.

## e. *At Nemea*

In the lovely little valley between Cleonae and Phlius still stand in isolated beauty three graceful Doric columns of the once famous temple of Nemean Zeus. Most of the other thirty-one columns of this peripteral temple lie about the cella, drum against drum, just as they were left by the successive earthquakes that overthrew them. The columns of the peristyle are thirty-four feet high (about as high as the columns of the Parthenon) and five and a quarter feet in diameter at the base (considerably more slender than the columns of the Parthenon). There is no evidence from ancient times in regard to the time of the erection of the temple; we have no hint as to its architect or builder. The slender proportions of the columns indicate a date not far from the close of the fifth century B. C. Pausanias[2] marks the temple with his asterisk (θέας ἄξιος) and says of it only that, when he visited it, the roof had fallen in, and the temple statue was gone. He adds that there was a grove of cypress trees about the temple and the building occupied the spot where Opheltes (Archemorus) was left by his nurse and slain by the dragon. It was in commemoration of this event that the Argive Seven instituted the Nemean games.

These scant words of Pausanias and the remains of temple and theatre give us practically all that we know of Nemea. If we only had the whole of Euripides's Hypsipyle, some further information might be obtained from it, comparable with the knowledge of Delphi and its buildings that we gain from the Ion. The fragments of the Hypsipyle recovered in Egypt and published in the Oxyrhynchus Papyri tell us a little but nothing strikingly new (Frag. 1, IV 20–21):

| | |
|---|---|
| ἄσμενος δ᾽ εἶδον δόμους | with joy did I behold yon temple |
| τούσδ᾽ ἐν Διὸς λειμῶνι Νεμεάδος χθονός | in Zeus's meadow in the land of Nemea |

(*ibid.* line 28):

| | |
|---|---|
| κληδοῦχός ἐστι τοὐπιχωρίου Διός | he keeps the keys of Zeus, the guardian of the land |

(*ibid.* lines 10 and 14):

| | |
|---|---|
| ὦ Ζεῦ Νεμέας τῆσδ᾽ ἄλσος ἔχων | oh Zeus, dwelling in the grove of Nemea yonder |
| . . . . . . | . . . . . . |
| στείχοντας ἐρῆμον ἀν᾽ ἄλσος | moving through the lonely grove |

---

[1] τὸ δὲ τὸ χωρίον τὸ ὑψηλόν, ἐφ᾽ οὗ οἱ βωμοὶ Τεγεάταις εἰσὶν οἱ πολλοί, καλεῖται μὲν Διὸς Κλαρίου· δῆλα δὴ ὡς ἐγένετο ἡ ἐπίκλησις τῷ θεῷ τοῦ κλήρου τῶν παίδων ἕνεκα τῶν Ἀρκάδος.

[2] II 15, 2

TEMPLE OF ZEUS AT NEMEA

(Frag. 1, II 29–30):

δεῦρ' ὅτ' ἂν λειμῶνα Νέμειον
ἀπάγει

| when hither along Nemea's meadow
| he leads

(Frag. 60, II 108):

Νεμέας κατ' ἄλσος

| through Nemea's grove

In all the lines here cited we find only the land of Nemea, the (cypress) grove, the meadow of Zeus, the temple with its (doors and) lock and key; and in the passage from the Casina of Plautus cited above[1] we have a reference to the games. While the dramatic poets afford no really new light, we do find in them some gratifying confirmation of what we know apart from them.

### f. On Mount Athos

Of an actual temple on the towering height of Athos we have no definite knowledge. But the mountain-top belonged to Zeus (Ae. Ag. 284–285):

μέγαν δὲ πανὸν ἐκ νήσου τρίτον
'Αθῷον αἶπος Ζηνὸς ἐξεδέξατο

| and from the isle, the height of Athos, dear to
| Zeus, received the third great torch of flame

(Soph. Θάμ., Frag. 216 N.):

Θρῆσσαν σκοπιὰν Ζηνὸς 'Αθώου

| the Thracian height of Athoan Zeus

The mountain belonged to Zeus; Hesychius (I p. 66), commenting on the fragment from Sophocles, mentions a statue of Zeus upon Mount Athos. We may be sure that there was there a temple of the supreme god of Greece, and its site may well be occupied now by one of the churches on the "Holy Mountain."

### g. On Mount Ida

From Homeric days on, there was a famous shrine of Zeus on the top of Mount Ida. It was, of course, the dwelling-place of the supreme god of the land of Troy,[2] reigning in a place from which he could survey the whole land with one glance of his eye.[3] He was addressed in prayer by the Achaean heroes and naturally adopted by the later Greek world. Homer tells us that there was a priest at this sanctuary,[4] and Aeschylus supplies the altar (Νι., Frag. 162, 1–3 N.):

οἱ θεῶν ἀγχίσποροι
οἱ Ζηνὸς ἐγγύς, ὧν κατ' 'Ιδαῖον πάγον
Διὸς πατρῴου βωμός ἐστ' ἐν αἰθέρι

|      the gods' close kin,
| those near to Zeus, who have in the regions of Ida
| an altar to ancestral Zeus in the heights

And there on the heights Schliemann found both throne and altar of Zeus—the former a colossal cube of slate, and on an adjacent peak what appeared to be the remains of an ancient altar.

### 9. THE ARGIVE HERAEUM—AND OTHER TEMPLES OF HERA

#### a. The Argive Heraeum

Scarcely less famous than the temple of Apollo at Delphi or of Zeus at Olympia was the temple of Hera in the Argive land. There the suitors of Helen had met and sworn to defend the honor of the queen of the king of men. There, when she was wronged by Prince Paris, they were marshalled by the king of men to avenge the wrong. It was the centre

---

[1] P. 86.
[2] Γ 276 = Γ 320, Η 202, Ω 308:

Ζεῦ πάτερ, "Ιδηθεν μεδέων, κύδιστε, μέγιστε

[3] Ω 290–291:      κελαινέφει Κρονίωνι

'Ιδαίῳ, ὅς τε Τροίην κατὰ πᾶσαν ὁρᾶται

[4] Π 604–605:      ὃς Διὸς ἱρεὺς

'Ιδαίου τέτυκτο

of Hera worship on the mainland of Europe.  It would be only natural to find it occupying a large place in Greek tragedy—especially in the many tragedies that have come down to us dealing with the royal house of Mycenae.  And yet Sophocles, alluding to it once, gives it but the briefest mention (El. 7–8):

| | |
|---|---|
| οὖξ ἀριστερᾶς δ' ὅδε<br>Ἥρας ὁ κλεινὸς ναὸς | and yonder on our left<br>Hera's famous temple |

This casual mention comes at the very opening of the play, where the old paedagogus gives the returning Orestes a hasty introduction to the outstanding topographical features of his native land.  The bare mention of the Heraeum was enough for Orestes; but we could wish that the paedagogus had said more.

Aeschylus, with the scene of four of his seven extant tragedies laid in Argolis, and two others having much to do with Argos, might be expected to be a little more generous with his information about the Heraeum.  But he, too, is disappointing; in two lines only does he refer to it, and they tell us nothing except that there was a temple in the Argive land and that Io was once the priestess (Sup. 291–292):

| | |
|---|---|
| κληδοῦχον Ἥρας φασὶ δωμάτων ποτὲ<br>Ἰὼ γενέσθαι τῇδ' ἐν Ἀργείᾳ χθονί | they say that once upon a time Io was warder<br>of Hera's halls here in the Argive land |

Euripides, with four extant tragedies dealing with the tragic house of Pelops, is still more disappointing.  He has in all but four possible allusions to the Heraeum (Rh. 376):

| | |
|---|---|
| Ἀργείας ποτ' ἐν Ἥρας δαπέδοις χορεύσει | [no one] will ever dance on Argive Hera's floors |

The chorus refers to the celebration of Hera's great festival held every four years with the choral dances performed, probably, on the great platform between the temple and the telesterium, excavated by our American School.  To such a celebration the maidens at the beginning of Euripides's Electra must go in festal procession (173–174):

| | |
|---|---|
| πᾶσαι παρ' Ἥ-<br>ραν μέλλουσι παρθενικαὶ στείχειν | and unto Hera all the<br>maidens are to pass |

The great Heraeum, as already observed, served all the surrounding towns.  It is not strange, therefore, that the poets sometimes assign the temple and its altars definitely to Mycenae or to Argos (Eur. H. F. 416–417):

| | |
|---|---|
| τὰ κλεινὰ δ' Ἑλλὰς ἔλαβε βαρβάρου κόρας<br>λάφυρα, καὶ σώζεται Μυκήναις | Hellas received the barbarian maiden's famous<br>spoils, and the trophy is still preserved at My-<br>cenae |

The chorus locates the temple at Mycenae, instead of seven miles away;[1] for in the heroic times Mycenae was the chief city of the Argive Heptapolis that together controlled the temple.  The temple itself is not even named.  Even the indirect allusion to it is made only to locate the famous girdle of Hippolyte which Heracles brought home and dedicated in the temple of Hera.  It is mentioned, accordingly, not as the famous sanctuary but as a museum.  And, as a matter of fact, at the time of the presentation of the Hercules Furens neither temple nor girdle was there: the temple had been burned to the ground in 423 and with it had been destroyed all the ancient relics that it had ......

b.

Of the great Argive Heraeum ....... poets.  But Euripides, in his love ...... antiquarian lore and his fondness for making learned explanations of local cults and ...... monies, seems to go out of his way to pay his respects to the temple of Hera Acraea on the rocky headland over against Corinth and Sicyon and about equally distant from either.  Of this temple Livy says simply (XXXII 23): Promuntorium est adversus Sicyonem Iunonis, quam vocant Acraeam, in altum excurrens; traiectus inde Corinthum, septem milia ferme passuum.

[1] Euripides seems to make a similar assignment of her altar again (El. 674):

$$\text{Ἥρα τε, βωμῶν ἢ Μυκηναίων κρατεῖς.}$$

[2] See pp. 101–102.

SITE OF THE TEMPLE OF HERA ACRAEA

The sanctuary, according to Livy, was on the promontory that juts out into the northeast corner of the Gulf of Corinth, about seven miles northwest of the city of Corinth. There rites were performed each year in expiation of the murder of Medea's children. According to Euripides himself Medea, to wreak vengeance upon the unfaithful Jason, slew her two children with her own hand. According to the scholiast on Euripides's Medea 273, it was the women of Corinth that, unwilling to be ruled by a foreign woman and a witch, laid a plot against Medea and her eight children. The children, four boys and four girls, fled, when attacked, to the sanctuary of Hera Acraea for refuge. But even Hera's temple did not protect them, for the Corinthians slew them all upon the goddess's very altar. Then a pestilence fell upon the city. To be saved, the Corinthians were bidden by the oracle to expiate the pollution. To fulfil the conditions of the oracle, the Corinthians each year assigned seven boys and seven girls from the noblest families of the city to spend the year in the sanctuary and by their service to appease the anger of the murdered children and of the goddess.

There are various stories in regard to the murder of Medea's children, but nearly all are agreed that they were buried in the sanctuary of Hera Acraea. That is most explicitly declared by Euripides (Med. 1378–1381):

| | |
|---|---|
| οὐ δῆτ', ἐπεὶ σφᾶς τῇδ' ἐγὼ θάψω χερί, | Never! for them will I bury with this hand of mine, |
| φέρουσ' ἐς Ἥρας τέμενος Ἀκραίας θεοῦ, | bearing them to the sanctuary of Hera, the goddess of the Headland, |
| ὡς μή τις αὐτοὺς πολεμίων καθυβρίσῃ τύμβους ἀνασπῶν | that no foeman may do offense to them by tearing open their tombs |

The modern chapel of St. Nicholas probably occupies the site of the old temple of Hera. It is generally accepted that it was there that Medea's children were buried. But the scholiast on the passage quoted from Euripides (Med. 1378–1381) says they were buried "upon the acropolis"; and the acropolis, in this connection, must be the Acrocorinthus. Diodorus (IV 55) points in the same direction. Apparently there was on a spur of the Acrocorinthus in the direction of Sicyon a temple of Hera Bunaea, and βουναία led to a natural confusion with ἀκραία. And Pausanias also follows what seems to have been a common tradition that Medea's children's tomb was in the city (II 3, 6):

| | |
|---|---|
| καὶ ὀλίγον ἀπωτέρω κρήνη καλουμένη Γλαύκης·..... ὑπὲρ ταύτην πεποίηται κρήνην καὶ τὸ καλούμενον Ὠιδεῖον. παρὰ δὲ αὐτὸ μνῆμά ἐστι τοῖς Μηδείας παισίν... καταλωσθῆναι δὲ ὑπὸ Κορινθίων λέγονται τῶν δώρων ἕνεκα... | and a little further on is the Spring of Glauce, as it is called . . . Beyond this spring is constructed also the so-called Odeum. And beside it is a monument to Medea's children . . . And it is said that they were stoned to death by the Corinthians on account of the gifts . . . |

According to this, there must have stood alongside the main street of Corinth leading in the direction of Sicyon a monument to Medea's children. Pausanias does not say that their tomb was there; but the monument rather implies the tomb. If so, then we have a contradictory tradition. At all events, so much seems clear: in addition to the Heraeum on the Acraean promontory, with which the atonement for the murder of Medea's children was associated, there was also in the city of Corinth another temple of Hera, with which the sacrifice of children was originally connected. In place of the human sacrifices came later the celebration of a year of mourning, which selected children of noble families of Corinth spent, with shorn hair, black dress, and other marks of mourning, in the temple. This celebration came also in time to be connected with the murder of Medea's children, and their city monument belonged to the temple precinct of Hera.[1]

### c. The Heraeum and Other Temples at Plataea

The especial protectress of Plataea and the chief divinity of the town was Hera. And for her worship the Plataeans had erected a temple that called for a star in Pausanias's guidebook (IX 2, 7):

---

[1] Cf. Curtius, *Peloponnes* II p. 533.   Karl Ottfried Müller, *Orchomenos u. d. Minyer*[2] p. 264 ff.

Πλαταιεῦσι δὲ ναός ἐστιν Ἥρας
θέας ἄξιος μεγέθει τε καὶ ἐς τῶν
ἀγαλμάτων τὸν κόσμον....
τὴν δὲ Ἥραν Τελείαν καλοῦσι,
πεποίηται δὲ ὀρθὸν μεγέθει
ἄγαλμα μέγα· λίθου δὲ ἀμφό-
τερα τοῦ Πεντελησίου, Πραξιτέλους δέ ἐστιν ἔργα

the Plataeans have a temple of Hera, worth
looking at—both for its magnitude and for
the plastic decoration . . .
They call their Hera Teleia,
and there is a colossal standing
image of her . . . Both works
are of Pentelic marble, and both from
the hand of Praxiteles

It is in all probability this temple that was discovered in 1891 by the American School in Athens.[1] Nothing but the merest foundations are left. But they reveal a fifth century, possibly sixth century, Doric hexastyle temple of considerable magnitude—49.9 by 16.7 metres, with two treasury chambers in the opisthodome—located in the most prominent part of the town, upon a terrace included in the later city[2] but out in front of the fifth century city.[3]

Nothing of the plastic decorations was found, even though the temples were spared when jealous, spiteful Thebes in 374–373 so thoroughly destroyed the heroic little city of devoted patriots.

Besides the temple of Hera, Pausanias mentions also temples of Athena Aria and Demeter at Plataea (IX 4, 1 and 3):

Πλαταιεῦσι δὲ Ἀθηνᾶς ἐπίκλησιν Ἀρείας ἐστὶν ἱερόν· ᾠκοδομήθη δὲ ἀπὸ λαφύ-
ρων ἃ τῆς μάχης σφίσιν Ἀθηναῖοι τῆς
Μαραθῶνι ἀπένειμαν.[4] τὸ μὲν δὴ ἄγαλμα ξόανόν ἐστιν ἐπίχρυσον, πρόσωπον
δέ οἱ καὶ χεῖρες ἄκραι καὶ πόδες λίθου
τοῦ Πεντελησίου εἰσί. μέγεθος μὲν οὐ πολὺ δή τι ἀποδεῖ τῆς ἐν Ἀκροπόλει χαλκῆς
ἣν καὶ αὐτὴν Ἀθηναῖοι τοῦ Μαραθῶνι
ἀπαρχὴν ἀγῶνος ἀνέθηκαν· Φει-
δίας δὲ καὶ Πλαταιεῦσιν ἦν ὁ τῆς
Ἀθηνᾶς τὸ ἄγαλμα ποιήσας...
ἔστι δὲ καὶ Δήμητρος ἐπίκλησιν
Ἐλευσινίας ἱερὸν ἐν Πλαταιαῖς....

Plataea has a sanctuary of Athena, surnamed
Aria; it was erected from the share of the spoils
that the Athenians awarded to them from the
battle of Marathon.[4] As for the statue, it
is a wooden image overlaid with gold; its face
and the hands and feet are of Pentelic
marble; in size it falls not very far
short of the bronze Athena on the Acropolis
and this also the Athenians erected out of the
tithes of the conflict at Marathon. And it was
Phidias who made the statue of Athena
for Plataea also . . .
And there is at Plataea a sanctuary of
Demeter also, surnamed the Eleusinian . . .

Although Pausanias states so unequivocally that the temple of Demeter Eleusinia was *in* Plataea, the evidence of Herodotus,[5] supported also by Plutarch,[6] is convincing that this temple stood at some distance to the north of the city. Plutarch supplies us also with a sanctuary of Artemis Euclea, which, as it received the bones of the famous long-distance runner, Euchidas, was probably also outside the city.

It may be that it is to these three or four temples, or to two of them and a stoa between, that Posidippus refers in a fragment of which little can be made out (Inc. Frag. 29 K.):

ναοὶ δύ' εἰσὶ καὶ στοά, καὶ τοὔνομα,

καὶ τὸ βαλανεῖον, καὶ τὸ Σαράβου κλέος,
τὸ πολὺ μὲν ἀκτή, τοῖς δ' Ἐλευθερίοις πόλις

temples twain there are and a portico, and the
name,
and the bath-house, and Sarabus's fame—
mostly a beach, but at the Eleutheria a city

The festival of the Eleutheria, with such throngs of celebrants as to make a city out of what was normally but a village, points unmistakably to Plataea; but the seashore or waterfront is out of place; the reading ἀκτή is, therefore, strongly suspected; Sarabus, though famous (or infamous) in the time of Posidippus, is wholly unknown to us, and his name

[1] See Report by Henry S. Washington, *A. J. A.* VII (1891) pp. 390–405.
[2] Paus. IX 2, 7.
[3] See Hdt. IX 52.
[4] The value of the Plataeans' share in the spoils was 80 talents; but according to Plutarch (Arist. XX 3) it was not from the battle of Marathon but from the battle of Plataea that the funds were secured for the rebuilding of the temple of Athena: ἐξεῖλον ὀγδοήκοντα τάλαντα τοῖς Πλαταιεῦσιν, ἀφ' ὧν τὸ τῆς Ἀθηνᾶς ἀνῳκοδόμησαν ἱερὸν καὶ τὸ ἕδος ἔστησαν καὶ γραφαῖς τὸν νεὼν διεκόσμησαν, αἳ μέχρι νῦν ἀκμάζουσαι διαμένουσιν...
[5] IX 57: τὸ δὲ ἀπελθὸν ὅσον τε δέκα στάδια ἀνέμεινε τὸν Ἀμομφαρέτου λόχον, περὶ ποταμὸν Μαλόεντα ἱδρυμένον Ἀργιόπιόν τε χῶρον καλεόμενον, τῇ καὶ Δήμητρος Ἐλευσινίης ἱρὸν ἧσται. Cf. also ch. 62 and ch. 65.
[6] Aristides XI 3 [the oracle of Delphi speaks]: καὶ τὸν κίνδυνον ἐν γῇ ἰδίᾳ ποιουμένους ἐν τῷ πεδίῳ τᾶς Δάματρος τᾶς Ἐλευσινίας καὶ τᾶς Κόρας.... 5: τὸ δὲ τῆς Ἐλευσινίας Δήμητρος πεδίον.... 6: τῶν Ὑσιῶν πλησίον ὑπὸ τὸν Κιθαιρῶνα ναός ἐστιν ἀρχαῖος πάνυ Δήμητρος Ἐλευσινίας καὶ Κόρης προσαγορευόμενος.

affords no help; neither does "the name," though the poet couples it significantly with the two temples, the stoa, and the baths. The application to the three temples of which we have some knowledge at Plataea is only helpless conjecture.

### 10. The Tauric Artemisium

We turn now from several of the most familiar scenes, from some of the most frequented temples of the ancient world and some best known to an Athenian audience, to one that Euripides had probably never seen, one that only the fewest, if any, of his audience had ever seen, one perhaps that nobody had ever seen, one, it may be, that had to be constructed by the imagination of the spectators out of the words of the poet with the meagre assistance of the stage properties introduced for the occasion—the temple of Artemis in the Taurian land.

There are many passages in the Iphigenia Taurica that mention the temple without giving any information about it, except to attest its existence. No purpose could be served by quoting more than one or two, e. g. (1024):

τί δ', εἴ με ναῷ τῷδε κρύψειας λάθρα;[1] | but what if thou secretly conceal me in the temple here?[1]

(34):

ναοῖσι δ' ἐν τοῖσδ' ἱερίαν τίθησί με[2] | and establishes me as priestess in these shrines[2]

(1027):

εἴσ' ἔνδον ἱεροῦ φύλακες | inside the sanctuary are guards

(1079):

σὸν ἔργον ἤδη καὶ σὸν εἰσβαίνειν δόμους[3] | thy part and thine it is to pass into the building[3]

(1307):

τίς ἀμφὶ δῶμα θεᾶς ὅδ' ἵστησιν βοήν; | who is this raising a clamor at the goddess's house?

(1153):

ποῦ 'σθ' ἡ πυλωρὸς τῶνδε δωμάτων;[4] | where is the warder of these apartments?[4]

(41):

ἔσωθεν τῶνδ' ἀνακτόρων θεᾶς [5] | within the goddess's lordly halls[5]

(1216):

ἄγνισον πυρσῷ μέλαθρον[6] | purify with fumigation her roof[6]

One time the edifice is a ναός "a temple," or ναοί "shrines," another it is a ἱερόν "a sanctuary," a third it is δόμοι "buildings," a fourth it is δῶμα "a house," a fifth it is δώματα "apartments," a sixth it is ἀνάκτορα "royal halls," and a seventh it is μέλαθρον "roof"; and, an eighth time, we have δόμοι and οἶκος in succeeding lines (1309–1310):

ψευδῶς λέγουσαί μ' αἵδ' ἀπήλαυνον δόμων, | these women spoke me false that thou wert gone and tried to

ὡς ἐκτὸς εἴης· σὺ δὲ κατ' οἶκον ἦσθ' ἄρα | drive me from the building; but thou, it seems, wast in the house

Reference here is to the temple from which Thoas has just come forth. But whatever the appellation, we are told no more than that it is a building, a temple, the dwelling-place of a goddess, which the spectators in the theatre have in some form before their eyes.

[1] Cp. 196; 404; 470; 1215; 1227; 1294.
[2] Cp. 138; 460.
[3] Cp. 1040; 1309. Cf. also Ae. Ἱερ., Frag. 87 N.
[4] Cp. 748; 1222.
[5] Cp. 66; 636.
[6] Cp. 69.

We obtain the further information that this temple was across the sea from Argos (I. T. 69–70):

| | |
|---|---|
| Πυλάδη, δοκεῖ σοι μέλαθρα ταῦτ' εἶναι θεᾶς, | dost deem, Pylades, that this is the goddess's roof, |
| ἔνθ' Ἀργόθεν ναῦν ποντίαν ἐστείλαμεν; | for which we sailed our ship across the sea from Argos? |

that it stood upon the seashore (l. 1196):

| | |
|---|---|
| οὔκουν πρὸς αὐτὸν ναὸν ἐκπίπτει κλύδων; | does not the surf break at the very temple's foot? |

It was of the Doric order (l. 113):

| | |
|---|---|
| ὅρα δέ γ' εἴσω τριγλύφων | ay; but look between the triglyphs |

and at first sight it seems to have had a peristyle—a colonnade running quite about it (I. T. 403–405):

| | |
|---|---|
| ἔνθα κούρᾳ | where to honor Zeus's daughter |
| Δίᾳ τέγγει | blood of mortals staineth |
| βωμοὺς καὶ περικίονας ναοὺς αἷμα βρότειον | her altars and pillared shrines |

We have here again the same epithet that was applied to the temple at Delphi.[1] This time, moreover, we know from the passage cited just before (l. 113) that the columns were Doric columns. We may be perfectly sure, however, that the poet did not in this case think of a colonnade running clear around his temple; he may have been, and probably was, influenced by the possibilities of his stage-settings. At all events, as we shall see later, he certainly had in mind not a Doric peripteros this time, but a Doric *templum in antis*—a temple with two columns between two pilasters, forming a portico. This porch with its antae comes in for special mention by Euripides, making it clear that both in the temple as he conceived it and upon the proscenium in his stage-setting the *templum in antis* was present (1159) (Iphigenia to Thoas who threatens to rush into the temple):

| | |
|---|---|
| ἄναξ, ἔχ' αὐτοῦ πόδα σὸν ἐν παραστάσιν | Sire, stay thy foot right there at the pillars |

The vestibule is before us, between the parastades, and, granting the parastades, the two columns also *must* be there.

The epithet περικίνοας, which comes in later (405), can be interpreted only in the sense of an *epitheton ornans*, as we saw above (p. 51), not as a peristyle. But even with our columns reduced in number to two, Euripides praises the beauty of them (126–130):

| | |
|---|---|
| ὦ παῖ τᾶς Λατοῦς, | oh daughter of Leto, |
| πρὸς σὰν αὐλάν, εὐστύλων | to thy courts, to the gold adorned cornices |
| ναῶν χρυσήρεις θριγχούς, | of thy fair-pillared shrine, |
| πόδα παρθένιον... | I guide my maiden |
| . . . . . . . . . . . . . πέμπω | foot . . . |

This passage recalls once more the richly decorated entablature that we saw at Delphi, the walls of gold, the cornices overlaid with gold instead of common paint.[2] By the cornices we must again understand both the horizontal cornice above the triglyphon and the raking cornice above the gables.

Upon the pillars rested the architrave, of course, though in this case there is no mention of it, and above the architrave came the triglyph frieze (113):

| | |
|---|---|
| ὅρα δέ γ' εἴσω τριγλύφων | ay; but look between the triglyphs |

which was cited a moment ago and to which we must return for a fuller discussion presently.

No sculptures upon the temple anywhere are mentioned—neither metopes, nor pediments, nor acroteria; and it may be safely assumed that the Tauric temple had none; it was too ancient and too barbaric.

---

[1] Cp. p. 51.

[2] For the various passages in which we find this application of gold or gilding in the decoration of the architectural members of a temple see pp. 58–60.

Entering the vestibule, our *porticus in antis* that we have just seen, we stand before the great double doors (I. T. 1307–1308):

| | |
|---|---|
| τίς ἀμφὶ δῶμα θεᾶς ὅδ' ἵστησιν βοήν, | who is this that raises an outcry at the goddess's house |
| πύλας ἀράξας...; | and bangs at the doors? |

They are solid doors of well-doweled timbers (I. T. 1286–1287):

| | |
|---|---|
| καλεῖτ', ἀποπτύξαντες εὐγόμφους πύλας, | fling back the well-doweled doors and call |
| ἔξω μελάθρων τῶνδε κοίρανον χθονός | the country's king from out these lordly halls |

With εὐγόμφους πύλας we get a picture of great doors of heavy oak, with heavy cross-beams, mortised and doweled firmly to the upright pieces. Euripides means to adhere to the simplicity of an early day, before the introduction of the great bronze temple doors with which his Athenian audience were more familiar.

The doors are closed and they may be locked and bolted and barred. The temple had various guards and overseers (I. T. 1284):

| | |
|---|---|
| ὦ ναοφύλακες βώμιοί τ' ἐπιστάται | ye temple-guards and altar-ministers |

and keepers of the doors (I. T. 1227–1229):

| | |
|---|---|
| εἴ τις ἢ ναῶν πυλωρὸς χεῖρας ἁγνεύει θεοῖς | if any one of you is a gate-keeper whose hands are consecrate to holy services, |
| φεύγετ', ἐξίστασθε | away! give place |

Of such Iphigenia was obviously the chief; for Thoas, upon entering to find out if the sacrifice has been accomplished, asks (1153–1154):

| | |
|---|---|
| ποῦ 'σθ' ἡ πυλωρὸς τῶνδε δωμάτων γυνὴ Ἑλληνίς; | where is the Grecian lady, the door-keeper of these halls? |

She was *the* gate-keeper, *par excellence*. And she, too, had charge of the key to the temple doors (130–131):

| | |
|---|---|
| ὁσίας ὅσιον πόδα παρθένιον χληδούχου δούλα πέμπω | a holy warder's slave, I guide my holy virgin foot |

And in various works of art,[1] Iphigenia is characterized by the possession of the great key in her hand.

In like manner, Cassandra had charge of the keys of Apollo's temple at Troy and when her fate is announced to Hecabe, the aged queen bids her priestess-daughter fling the keys away (Eur. Tro. 256–257):

| | |
|---|---|
| ῥῖπτε, τέκνον, ζαθέους χλῆδας | fling, my child, fling away the all-holy keys |

In like manner also Io, before her conquest of the heart of the loud-thundering husband of Hera, had been warder of the Argive Heraeum and had kept the keys of Hera's shrine (Ae. Sup. 291–292):

| | |
|---|---|
| χληδοῦχον Ἥρας φασὶ δωμάτων ποτὲ Ἰὼ γενέσθαι τῇδ' ἐν Ἀργείᾳ χθονί | they say that once upon a time Io was warder of Hera's halls here in this Argive land |

It was, accordingly, customary in the ancient times to provide the sanctuaries with locks and for the chief priest or priestess to have charge of the keys.[2]

[1] E. g., upon a splendid Apulian amphora, published *Arch. Ztg.* 1849, Taf. 12; Baum., *Denkm.* I p. 757, Fig. 808; Roscher, *Myth. Lex. s. v.* Iphigenia, II¹, Sp. 301–302.

[2] We find Iphigenia again as χληδοῦχος to the temple of Artemis in Brauron later on (Eur. I. T. 1462–1463): σὲ δ' ἀμφὶ σεμνὰς Ἰφιγένεια, κλίμακας
Βραυρωνίας δεῖ τῇδε κληδουχεῖν θεᾷ
And we find the same provision at the temple of Asclepius at Epidaurus (Pl. Cur. 203–204):
sonitum et crepitum claustrorum audio,
aeditumum aperire fanum
And it was not otherwise in the primitive days of Rome, as we see from a fragment of a Fabula Atellana of Lucius Pomponius Bononiensis (Aeditumus, 2–3 R²):
qui postquam tibi adpareo atque aeditumor in templo tuo,
nec mortalis nec mortalium ullum in terra miseriust
And thus, too, Eros is χληδοῦχος to the chambers of golden Aphrodite (Eur. Hip. 538–541):
Ἔρωτα δὲ τὸν τύραννον ἀνδρῶν,
τὸν τᾶς Ἀφροδίτας
φιλτάτων θαλάμων
κληδοῦχον, οὐ σεβίζομεν

The key at one and the same turn shot back the lock and lifted the bolts; the bolts are expressly mentioned (Eur. I. T. 99):

| | |
|---|---|
| χαλκότευκτα κλῆθρα λύσαντες μοχλοῖς | the bronze-forged bolts springing with our crowbars |

They could thus, with the application of sufficient force, be sprung from the outside; Orestes and Pylades propose to use crowbars to force the temple doors; Oedipus, in the frenzy of his discovered guilt, leaps against the bolted doors of the queen's apartment and forces the bolts from the sockets in threshold and lintel (Soph. O. T. 1261–1262):

| | |
|---|---|
| πύλαις διπλαῖς ἐνήλατ'· ἐκ δὲ πυθμένων | he leapt against the double doors; and from their sockets |
| ἔκλινε κοῖλα κλῆθρα | he forced the bolts and left them hollow |

These are the doors and bolts of the Labdacid palace, but the device was the same as in the temple.[1] Such locks could, of course, be sprung or unsprung from the inside, without the aid of force or keys (Soph. O. T. 1287):

| | |
|---|---|
| βοᾷ ἀνοίγειν κλῆθρα | he calls to throw back the bolts |

(*ibid.* 1294–1295):

| | |
|---|---|
| κλῆθρα γὰρ πυλῶν τάδε<br>διοίγεται | for the bolts of the doors yonder<br>are being thrown back |

In like manner the temple doors may be readily unlocked from the inside (Eur. I. T. 1304):

| | |
|---|---|
| ὠή, χαλᾶτε κλῆθρα, τοῖς ἔνδον λέγω | what ho! within there, throw back the bolts |

The doors open, and we find within sometimes a temple-guard (Eur. I. T. 1027):

| | |
|---|---|
| εἶσ' ἔνδον φύλακες, οὓς οὐ λήσομεν | there are guards within, whose eyes we shall not escape |

Here, within the shrine, the priestess performed her offices (Eur. I. T. 34):

| | |
|---|---|
| ναοῖσι δ' ἐν τοῖσδ' ἱερίαν τίθησί με | and in her temple here she set me as her priestess |

(*ibid.* 748):

| | |
|---|---|
| Ἄρτεμιν, ἐν ᾗσπερ δώμασιν τιμὰς ἔχω | Artemis, in whose halls I hold mine office |

In the back part of the cella stood the cultus image of the Taurian Artemis (Eur. I. T. 1040):

| | |
|---|---|
| ἐν δόμοισι βρέτας | within the halls, the image |

There are many allusions to this ancient idol; but the discussion of them must be reserved for the volume on Sculpture.

In front of the image was an altar. And in Tauria again, as at Delphi, we have two altars of sacrifice—the one within the temple and the other without. Here before the awful image, as well as at the altar before the temple, the still more awful human sacrifice took place. Iphigenia (Eur. I. T. 725–726) bids the guards "go in" (into the temple) and make things ready for the sacrifice of Orestes and Pylades:

| | |
|---|---|
| ἀπέλθεθ' ὑμεῖς καὶ παρευτρεπίζετε | depart ye; go and make ready all |
| τἄνδον μολόντες τοῖς ἐφεστῶσι σφαγῇ | within for those whose office is the sacrifice |

Her "within" means in the holy of holies; and there in the presence of the Zeus-fallen image the hideous sacrifice of human beings and the actual burning of their flesh upon the altar might take place (Eur. I. T. 1154–1155):

| | |
|---|---|
| ἤδη τῶν ξένων κατήρξατο, | has she already begun the consecration of the strangers, |
| ἀδύτοις τ' ἐν ἁγνοῖς σῶμα δάπτονται πυρί; | and are their bodies blazing in the fire within the holy of holies? |

---

[1] For the fuller discussion of doors and their fastenings, see pp. 207 ff.

The plurality of the altars is brought out by Euripides himself (I. T. 85–86) (Orestes in prayer to Apollo):

σὺ δ' εἶπας ἐλθεῖν Ταυρικῆς μ' ὅρους χθονός, | and thou badst me come to the Taurian coasts
ἔνθ' Ἄρτεμις σὺ σύγγονος βωμοὺς ἔχει | where thy sister Artemis hath her altars

The chorus also speaks of the "altars,"[1] in the plural, at which perforce they must serve (Eur. I. T. 1115–1116):

παῖδ' Ἀγαμεμνονίαν λατρεύω βωμοὺς | I serve Agamemnon's daughter and altars
θ' Ἑλληνοθύτας | at which Greeks are sacrificed

It required, too, a considerable force of men to superintend the keeping of altars and temple (I. T. 1284):

ὦ ναοφύλακες βώμιοί τ' ἐπιστάται | ye temple-guards and altar-ministers

Iphigenia addresses them again at verse 638 as "attendants":

φυλάσσετ' αὐτούς, πρόσπολοι | keep them, attendants

and refers to them in 725–726 (quoted above) and in 468.

In front of the temple (and so represented also upon the scene) conspicuous stood the great altar—this, too, an altar of human sacrifice. In the opening scene it comes prominently to the attention: Pylades enters followed by Orestes, who questions his friend about the temple first and then the altar (72–75):

OP. καὶ βωμός, Ἕλλην οὗ καταστάζει φόνος; | OR. And an altar on which Grecian blood trickles down?

ΠΥ. ἐξ αἱμάτων γοῦν ξάνθ' ἔχει θριγκώματα. | PY. Ay; and it has cornices discolored with stains of blood.

OP. θριγκοῖς δ' ὑπ' αὐτοῖς σκῦλ' ὁρᾷς ἠρτημένα; | OR. And under the cornices are fastened spoils of men?

ΠΥ. τῶν κατθανόντων γ' ἀκροθίνια ξένων | PY. Ay; trophies of strangers who have been slain

There we have our great altar—rising upon a basis, of course, and crowned with a projecting cornice, perhaps a Doric triglyphon about the top of the square (or oblong) block, as in the case of the great altar discovered by Dörpfeld at Corcyra; and about the cornice were the skulls of Greeks who there had met their doom, as we see them fastened up in the Iphigenia-Orestes sarcophagus relief in Munich.[2]

But temple and altar are not the only buildings in this sacred enclosure; for we have the whole temenos of Artemis here to reconstruct as far as we can with the poet's help.

First, and above all, we must locate, in close proximity to the temple, the dwelling of the priestess—the manse, as it were, of the Taurian sanctuary. It is a part of the consecrated property (I. T. 65–66):

εἶμι εἴσω δόμων | I will go into my apartments
ἐν οἷσι ναίω τῶνδ' ἀνακτόρων θεᾶς | in which I dwell within the lordly halls of the goddess here

The apartments of the priestess and her colleags in Tauris correspond to the Theocoleum at Olympia. But here the priestess's dwelling is inside the temenos; at Olympia the priests' home is just outside the Altis walls. Without specifying—for there is no need to specify, for, as a matter of course it is not the shrine from which she fetches her treasured letter but her private apartments within the temple-close—Iphigenia again alludes to her home as (a part of) the goddess's lordly halls (Eur. I. T. 636–637):

ἀλλ' εἶμι δέλτον τ' ἐκ θεᾶς ἀνακτόρων | but I will go and fetch the letter
οἴσω | from the goddess's lordly halls

And when she again enters with the letter, Orestes remarks to Pylades (1. 724):

γυνὴ γὰρ ἥδε δωμάτων ἔξω περᾷ | for here comes the lady out from the halls

This, too, must necessarily mean from the theocoleum.

[1] So, too, the messenger (Eur. I. T. 1320):
ὃν τοῖσδε βωμοῖς θεὰ καθωσιώσατο | whose consecration at these altars the goddess received
Cp. also line 383.

[2] Reproduced in Baum., *Denkm.* I p. 758, Fig. 809.

It is not Iphigenia alone, therefore, that has her apartments within the temenos.  Her assistants, who actually perform the bloody sacrifice,[1] dwell there too (ll. 623–624):

| | |
|---|---|
| ΟΡ. ὁ δὲ σφαγεὺς τίς; . . . . | OR. And the slayer—who? . . . |
| ΙΦ. εἴσω δόμων τῶνδ' εἰσὶν οἷς μέλει τάδε | IPH. Within the dwellings here are the men whose task this is |

These are men, even though their office is within the doors of the temple of a female divinity.  The same meaning is contained also in lines 40–41:

| | |
|---|---|
| κατάρχομαι μέν, σφάγια δ' ἄλλοισιν μέλει | I consecrate the victim; the unspeakable sacrifice |
| ἄρρητ' ἔσωθεν τῶνδ' ἀνακτόρων θεᾶς | is for other hands—within these lordly halls of the goddess |

The ναοφύλακες βώμιοί τ' ἐπιστάται "temple-guards and altar-ministers" of line 1284 may or may not have had their abodes within the temenos enclosure.  No hint is given.  But it is probable that they dwelt near by but outside somewhere, like the king.  For the palace of Thoas is not suggested in the stage-properties.  His palace is so far away that the chorus may avail themselves of the distance from the temple to it as a ruse to keep the king out of the way until the escape of the fugitives is assured (l. 1301):

| | |
|---|---|
| οὐκ εἶ κρατούντων πρὸς πύλας ὅσον τάχος | away with all speed to the masters' gates |

The palace is at some distance removed from the temple, and the messenger will not venture to make the trip to it without assurance that he will be sure to find the king there.

With this we have gained a general view of the temple on the shore of the Tauric land.  With his words and with the stage-properties the poet has brought before his audience a sacred enclosure, with the manse—the dwelling-place of Iphigenia and her assistants; with a great altar, crowned with a (Doric?) cornice and decorated with the skulls and bones of Hellenic victims; with a Doric *templum in antis*, crowned with a triglyph frieze, and not only no sculptured metopes but no metope blocks at all—the metopes were open, as we shall soon see.

Various difficulties in the restoration of the temple to our imagination have been suggested.  They will be cleared up, I think, by a careful analysis of the opening scene (Eur. I. T. 67–122).  The proscenium presents the sacred enclosure of Taurica with the temple and its appurtenances.  It is early morning—probably just after dawn.  No one is yet astir to interfere with the observations of the two spies.  Orestes and Pylades enter furtively, Pylades leading the way.  Orestes follows cautiously behind him and puts to him questions prompted by what he has heard about the place; Pylades, being ahead—that is beyond the corner of the parascenium—is able to confirm by what he sees the marks by which the place is identified as the bourn of their quest.  When that fact has become clear to the two friends, they proceed to lay plans for securing the sacred image and getting away with it:

| | |
|---|---|
| ΟΡ. ὅρα, φυλάσσου μή τις ἐν στίβῳ βροτῶν. | OR. Look—be on thy guard lest some one be on our path. |
| ΠΥ. ὁρῶ, σκοποῦμαι δ' ὄμμα πανταχοῦ στρέφων. | PY. I am looking; and I am watching, with an eye turned in every direction. |
| ΟΡ. Πυλάδη, δοκεῖ σοι μέλαθρα ταῦτ' εἶναι θεᾶς; | OR. Pylades, dost thou deem this to be the goddess's roof?[2] |
| ΠΥ. ἔμοιγ', Ὀρέστα· σοὶ δὲ συνδοκεῖν χρεών. | PY. Ay, Orestes; and thou must needs so deem with me. |
| ΟΡ. καὶ βωμός, Ἕλλην οὗ καταστάζει φόνος; | OR. And the altar, down which is dripping Grecian blood? |
| ΠΥ. ἐξ αἱμάτων γοῦν ξάνθ' ἔχει θριγκώματα. | PY. Ay; and it has cornices discolored with stains of blood. |
| ΟΡ. θριγκοῖς δ' ὑπ' αὐτοῖς σκῦλ' ὁρᾷς ἠρτημένα; | OR. And seest thou the spoils of men fastened under the cornices? |

[1] Cp. ll. 617–622.  In ll. 444–446 and 775–776 Iphigenia's responsibility in the sacrifice makes her seem to be the actual slayer of the victims, but this office on her part is only apparent.

[2] I would omit l. 70:

| | |
|---|---|
| ἔνθ' Ἀργόθεν ναῦν ποντίαν ἐστείλαμεν | whither we steered our ship across the sea from Argos |

as spoiling the stichomythy and adding nothing that we need to know.

ΠΥ. τῶν κατθανόντων γ' ἀκροθίνια ξένων.

ΟΡ. ἀλλ' ἐγκυκλοῦντ' ὀφθαλμὸν εὖ σκοπεῖν χρεών—

ὦ Φοῖβε, ποῖ μ' αὖ τήνδ' ἐς ἄρκυν ἤγαγες

χρήσας, ἐπειδὴ πατρὸς αἷμ' ἐτισάμην

μητέρα κατακτάς; διαδοχαῖς δ' Ἐρινύων

ἠλαυνόμεσθα φυγάδες, ἔξεδροι χθονός,
δρόμους τε πολλοὺς ἐξέπλησα καμπίμους

PY. Yea; the trophies of strangers who have been slain.

OR. Well, we must keep our eyes wide open and be well upon our guard.[1]

Oh Phoebus! why hast thou again with thine oracle brought

me into this snare, when I have slain my

mother and avenged my sire? And with relays of Furies

we were driven to exile, outcast from our land,

and many doubling stretches have I raced to the end

Then follows a recital of the oracle that brought him here—to get the image and take it home to Attica—and he turns again to his companion (94 ff.):

σὲ δ' ἱστορῶ,
Πυλάδη, σὺ γάρ μοι τοῦδε συλλήπτωρ πόνου,
τί δρῶμεν; ἀμφίβληστρα γὰρ τοίχων ὁρᾷς

ὑψηλά· πότερα κλιμάκων[2] προσαμβάσεις

ἐκβησόμεσθα; πῶς ἂν οὖν λάθοιμεν[3] ἄν;
ἢ χαλκότευκτα κλῇθρα λύσαντες μοχλοῖς;

ὧν οὐδὲν ἴσμεν. ἢν δ' ἀνοίγοντες πύλας

ληφθῶμεν εἰσβάσεις τε μηχανώμενοι,
θανούμεθ'. ἀλλὰ πρὶν θανεῖν, νεὼς ἔπι

φεύγωμεν, ἧπερ δεῦρ' ἐναυστολήσαμεν.
ΠΥ. φεύγειν μὲν οὐκ ἀνεκτὸν οὐδ' εἰώθαμεν,

τὸν τοῦ θεοῦ τε χρησμὸν οὐ κακιστέον·

ναοῦ δ' ἀπαλλαχθέντε κρύψωμεν δέμας

κατ' ἄντρ' ἃ πόντος νοτίδι διακλύζει μέλας,

νεὼς ἄπωθεν, μή τις εἰσιδὼν σκάφος

βασιλεῦσιν εἴπῃ κᾆτα ληφθῶμεν βίᾳ.

ὅταν δὲ νυκτὸς ὄμμα λυγαίας μόλῃ,
τολμητέον τοι ξεστὸν ἐκ ναοῦ λαβεῖν

ἄγαλμα   πάσας προσφέροντε μηχανάς.

ὅρα δὲ γ' εἴσω τριγλύφων ὅποι κενὸν

δέμας καθεῖναι. τοὺς πόνους γὰρ ἀγαθοὶ
τολμῶσι, δειλοὶ δ' εἰσὶν οὐδὲν οὐδαμοῦ.
οὔτοι μακρὸν μὲν ἤλθομεν κώπῃ πόρον,

ἐκ τερμάτων δὲ νόστον ἀροῦμεν πάλιν.
ΟΡ. ἀλλ' εὖ γὰρ εἶπας, πειστέον· χωρεῖν χρεών

thee I ask,
Pylades, for thou art the partner of my labors,

what shall we do? for the engirdling walls, thou seest,

are high. Shall we mount to our goal by the ladder's[2]

rungs? How then should we fail to be seen?[3]

Or shall we force with our crowbars the bronze-forged bolts?

Of all this we nothing know. And if we are caught opening

the gates and devising a means of getting in,

we are dead men. Nay; before we die, let us flee back to

our ship with which we hither made our voyage.

PY. Flee? That is unthinkable, nor is that our wont;

and the god's oracle must not be brought to shame.

Let us withdraw from the temple and hide ourselves

in caves which the black sea oversprinkles with its spray,

far from our ship, lest some one catch sight of her hull

and report it to the royal house, and we then be taken by force.

But when the eye of dusky night is come,

then, I tell thee, we must make the venture to take the polished image

from the shrine, bringing all possible contrivances to bear.

Only look between the triglyphs, where there is an empty

space to let ourselves down. The brave risk toils; cowards are nothing anywhere.

Surely, we have not come this long journey with the oar

only to take up our return again at the very goal!

OR. I object no more; for thou hast spoken well; I must obey.

[1] This line is assigned by Reiske and some other editors to Pylades; but again the stichomythy is spoiled and the dramatic force greatly weakened by such assignment. I have not hesitated, with the authority of the manuscripts, to restore it to Orestes, who with the words lifts his eyes in prayer and cries "Oh Phoebus etc."

[2] κλιμάκων; δωμάτων MSS. and most editors.

[3] λάθοιμεν Sallier and many editors; μάθοιμεν MSS.

ὅποι χθονὸς κρύψαντε λήσομεν δέμας.

οὐ γὰρ τὸ τοῦδέ γ᾽ αἴτιον γενήσεται
πεσεῖν ἄχρηστον θέσφατον· τολμητέον·

μόχθος γὰρ οὐδεὶς τοῖς νεοῖς σκῆψιν φέρει.

| |
|---|
| We must needs withdraw to a spot where we may hide and remain unseen. |
| For it shall not be this man's fault, if the oracle falls unfulfilled. The venture must be made; |
| for there is no toil that brings to young men an excuse for avoiding it. |

In this much vexed passage, so unsatisfactory in the light that has thus far been cast upon it, our problem in attempting to interpret it is a three-fold one: 1) we must come to a clear understanding of the situation:—What did Orestes and Pylades and the audience in the theatre in Athens actually see before them, in reality helped out by imagination, while the two friends were laying their plans for effecting an entrance to the temple and securing the image of the goddess? 2) the text must give the clew to the understanding of that situation; and 3) the text, emended if necessary, must be interpreted in the light of the possibilities of the situation.

1) We can set down at the outset, as agreed upon by all and taken for granted throughout the play, that the temple of Artemis must have occupied the centre of the proscenium —with its steps, its door and the altar before it, its columns, its architrave, and its triglyph frieze, in full sight of actors and audience.

Orestes and Pylades come stealthily in (ll. 67–68); the first words, uttered as they reach the inner end of the parados passage, are words of caution lest they be observed; the third line of their excited conversation is devoted to the temple, which is at once identified as the shrine of the Taurian Artemis, and the altar discolored with the blood of human victims. So much is clear: the temple was there in plain sight; the altar of sacrifice was in just as plain sight to the two friends as they came stealing in.

When so much has been recognized, Orestes bids Pylades "watch" (so the manuscripts, l. 76), while he "prays." At one side of the entrance to the temple, we can safely assume, stood a statue of Apollo; on the other, a statue of Artemis. To Apollo, represented there in his statue, Orestes addresses his prayer, while Pylades continues his careful reconnoitering for fear that some one may be near and they be surprised. They are by this time fairly upon the scene; they feel reasonably well assured that they are not observed. Accordingly, they are ready to continue their reconnaissance. And then their trouble (and ours) begins. Orestes, calling Pylades's attention, remarks that the ἀμφίβληστρα τοίχων (which I have rendered "engirdling walls") are high. Now, what are the ἀμφίβληστρα τοίχων? ἀμφίβληστρον is "anything thrown round";[1] "a fishing-net";[2] "a fetter." It is used of walls only here. At first sight, it seems as if the words ought to refer to the enclosure walls of the temenos. But the temple was in sight; even the temple altar was in sight; and both would have had to be within the temenos walls; and if these walls were so high, then neither altar nor temple would be plainly seen or seen at all. Accordingly, granting readily that the temple stood within a temenos enclosure, the "stage-settings" must have assumed that Orestes and Pylades were inside its gates and standing immediately by the temple; and the ἀμφίβληστρα τοίχων must then be the walls of the cella and not the walls of the temenos.

In another passage from Euripides we have, not indeed ἀμφίβληστρα but ἀμφιβλήματα used in a similar sense (Hel. 68–70):

---

[1] Euripides twice uses the word in its literal sense (Τήλ., Frag. 697 N.; Hel. 1079):

τάδ᾽ ἀμφίβληστρα σώματος ῥάκη | these rags thrown round my body

Aeschylus twice uses ἀμφίβληστρον of the "net" in which Clytaemenestra entangled Agamemnon for her deed of murder (Ag. 1382–1383):

ἄπειρον ἀμφίβληστρον, ὥσπερ ἰχθύων, περιστιχίζω | a net, as if for fishes, with not an outlet, I cast

(Cho. 492–494):

ΗΛ. μέμνησο δ᾽ ἀμφίβληστρον ὡς ἐκαίνισας — | EL. Remember in what strange mantle thou wast snared—

ΟΡ. πέδαις δ᾽ ἀχαλκεύτοισι θηρευθείς, πάτερ— | OR. In fetters not forged of bronze, father, thou wast entrapped—

ΗΛ. αἰσχρῶς τε βουλευτοῖσιν ἐν καλύμμασιν— | EL. In a veil so shamefully devised.

Sophocles uses the word of the poisoned robe sent to Heracles by Dejanira (Tr. 1051–1052):

Ἐρινύων | the Erinyes'

ὑφαντὸν ἀμφίβληστρον, ᾧ διόλλυμαι | woven net in which I perish

[2] Antiph. Πρόβ., Frag. 194, 1 K.; Men. Ἀλ., Frag. 27 K.

τίς τῶνδ' ἐρυμνῶν δωμάτων ἔχει κράτος;
Πλούτου γὰρ οἶκος ἄξιος προσεικάσαι
βασίλειά τ' ἀμφιβλήματ' εὔθριγχοί θ' ἕδραι

who hath the lordship of these castle halls?
Why, one might fitly guess it were Plutus's
palace and royal enclosures and abodes with
cornice fair

Like ἀμφίβληστρον, ἀμφίβλημα is "anything thrown around," a garment,[1] armor.[2] Like ἀμφίβληστρον in the Iphigenia Taurica, ἀμφίβλημα might here also be the walls of the fortification about the old palace of Proteus on the Isle of Pharos. But again Teucer, who has just appeared upon the scene and caught sight of Helen at the tomb of Proteus, is directly in front of the palace; the palace opens immediately upon the scene; Teucer may even look into the ante-rooms and see the εὔθριγχοι ἕδραι ("abodes with cornice fair"), as he might have done at Tiryns. We note, too, that the βασίλεια ἀμφιβλήματα ("royal enclosures") are named between οἶκος and εὔθριγχοι ἕδραι. Accordingly, we should interpret the βασίλεια ἀμφιβλήματα as the walls of the palace proper. The tomb of Proteus is *outside*, of course, and is made a part of the proscenium properties.

We have seen, moreover, that we have in the Iphigenia Taurica to do with the façade of a simple Doric *templum in antis*, not a peripteros; for Orestes and Pylades were not so mad as to suggest climbing up and through a metope of a peripteros to get into the building. If any one climbs up a column of a peripteral temple and lets himself down through a metope-opening between two triglyphs, he finds himself not in the temple proper, that is, in the cella, but in the open colonnade at practically the same spot from which he started to climb. Orestes and Pylades in such a procedure would after their effort have been just as far along toward securing an entrance to the temple as they were before they made their hazardous climb! All about this templum in antis ran a triglyph frieze, as in the Treasury of Sicyon at Olympia. It is between two of the side triglyphs that they propose to climb by means of a ladder set against the encircling walls.

This, moreover, is not the only passage in Euripides where the triglyph-frieze with open metopes is made to serve as a means of passage from scene to interior or from interior to scene. In that wild scene in the Orestes in which Orestes and Pylades within the palace have attempted the murder of Helen and seized Hermione as a hostage, one of Helen's Phrygian slaves in terror bursts upon the scene. But how? The Phrygian tells (Or. 1369-1372):

Ἀργεῖον ξίφος ἐκ θανάτου πέφευγα
βαρβάροις εὐμάρισιν,
κεδρωτὰ παστάδων ὑπὲρ τέραμνα
Δωρικάς τε τριγλύφους

from death by Argive sword I have fled,
with barbaric slippers on my feet,
over the cedar beams of the chamber
and through the Doric triglyphs

The "beams" seem to be the architrave; on this the triglyphs rest. The Phrygian in his panic-terror, unable to pass the door, had climbed up behind the proscenium, crawled through the open metope between two triglyphs, and tumbled down upon the scene before the astonished chorus. A terror-stricken barbarian might well do that for the amusement of the dignified Hellenic spectators, even in a highly tragic scene.[3] In the Orestes the Phrygian gets out of the palace by climbing up through an open metope; in the Iphigenia Taurica Orestes and Pylades propose to get into the temple by way of the triglyph frieze and the open metope.

To return to the opening scene of the Iphigenia Taurica. Having remarked that the walls are high, Orestes next asks Pylades something about the manner of their getting into the temple. Here is the real *crux* of the situation. The manuscripts read with unanimity:— πότερα δωμάτων προσαμβάσεις ἐκβησόμεθα, which is a curious way of expressing what seems

[1] Eur. Hel. 423.
[2] Eur. Phoen. 779.
[3] The lines that immediately precede the entrance of the Phrygian,

ἀλλὰ κτυπεῖ γὰρ κλῆθρα βασιλικῶν δόμων·
σιγήσατ'· ἔξω γάρ τις ἐκβαίνει Φρυγῶν,
οὗ πευσόμεσθα τὰν δόμοις ὅπως ἔχει

but hush! for there is the clank of the bolts of the royal palace: some one of the Phrygians is coming out, and from him we shall learn how matters within the palace stand

are rightly suspected. The chorus could not tell from the clank of the bolts that it is a Phrygian rather than Orestes or Pylades or some one else that is unfastening the door; and besides, the confusion of the slave and his words tell that he has come over the architrave and has dropped from the triglyphon to the scene—no neck-breaking performance, for the entire height of the proscenium columns is at most nine or ten feet. The lines were apparently added by a scholastic who held that there could be no exception to the rule that each new entrance should be properly announced.

to mean in plain Anglo-Saxon: "Shall we go up the steps into the building," for ἐκβησόμεθα here has to do with going *in*, not *out*, and ἐκ- must imply the "success" of their going. But what conceivable sense is there in his remarking: "The walls of the temple are high" and following it up immediately with the question: "Shall we walk up the front steps and go in at the front door?" We need hardly stop for a moment over Klotz's theory that the δωμάτων προσαμβάσεις may be the steps of the dwelling of Iphigenia, into which Orestes might enter and from which he might pass by a side entrance into the temple. No such side entrance from a manse into a Greek temple ever existed, so far as we know. Iphigenia's remark that she was going

| | |
|---|---|
| εἴσω δόμων | into my apartments |
| ἐν οἷσι ναίω τῶνδ' ἀνακτόρων θεᾶς | in which I dwell within the lordly halls of the goddess here |

does not imply more than that her dwelling was inside the temenos. Another question, however, may be raised: did Orestes and Pylades come only to reconnoitre in the early morning and to lay their plans for a night raid, when the sun had set? And did Orestes, therefore, raise all possible questions at this point, without any intention of carrying out anything before nightfall:—"The walls are high; shall we scale them? Or shall we go up the steps into the temple, if it be open, or force the locks, if it be not open? Which of these plans shall we adopt for our line of action to-night?" The theory of a mere reconnaissance in the early morning seems untenable in view of the panic that seizes him at the end of his speech (I. T. 102–103):

| | |
|---|---|
| ἀλλὰ πρὶν θανεῖν, νεώς ἔπι | nay; before we die, let us flee back to our ship |
| φεύγωμεν, ἧπερ δεῦρ' ἐναυστολήσαμεν | on which we hither made our voyage |

The plan they did adopt—for a return by night to effect their purpose—was the result of a compromise wisely suggested by Pylades to save his friend from the utter defeat of the purpose for which they had come. We must, therefore, take Orestes's present proposals as proposals for immediate action.

To return, then: "The enclosing walls are high; shall we go up the steps and into the temple?" And then comes an uncertain reading; L and P both have πῶς[1] οὖν λάθοιμεν ἄν (?); an inferior reading, adopted by many modern editors, is πῶς ἄρ' οὖν μάθοιμεν ἄν[2].

Let us look first at the reading of P and L: πῶς ἄν οὖν λάθοιμεν ἄν ("how should or could we escape notice?").—In doing what? Going up the steps? That makes good sense so far; but, again, what has "going up the steps" to do with the height of the walls? When Pylades takes up Orestes's suggestions, he says:

| | |
|---|---|
| τολμητέον τοι ξεστὸν ἐκ ναοῦ λαβεῖν | we must, I tell thee, make the venture to take the polished image |
| ἄγαλμα πάσας προσφέροντε μηχανάς | from the shrine, bringing all possible contrivances to bear |

and then he calls attention to the open spaces between the triglyphs, through which they could let themselves down into the temple. He takes it for granted, as Orestes does in verse 96, that the doors are locked (as they are) and that it would be less easy to force them than to go through the metopes. Pylades, accordingly, adopts the suggestion to scale the walls. But the walls were high. How get up over them? By a ladder, naturally; they had one at the ship, of course—the ship's gangway. That also gives an additional reason for their return to the ship and the postponement of action till nightfall. That same necessity for a ladder prompted Kirchhoff to correct δωμάτων in line 97 to κλιμάκων; his conjecture, furthermore, is well based upon that same familiar collocation of words found in Aeschylus's Septem (466–467):

| | |
|---|---|
| ἀνὴρ δ' ὁπλίτης κλίμακος προσαμβάσεις | and a hoplite-man mounts by the ladder's |
| στείχει πρὸς ἐχθρῶν πύργον | rungs against a foeman's tower |

---

[1] P has ἄν added by a later hand.
[2] This is obviously a confusion of ΟΥΝΛΑΘ-, where the *N* and Λ coming close together could easily be mistaken for *M*.

Similarly in Euripides's Phoenissae (488–489):

| | |
|---|---|
| καὶ μήτε πορθεῖν πατρίδα μήτε προσφέρειν | and neither to lay waste my native land nor bring against |
| πύργοισι πηκτῶν κλιμάκων προσαμβάσεις | her towers the firm-set ladders with their rungs |

and once more *ibid.* (1173–1174) (of the mad insolence of Capaneus):

| | |
|---|---|
| μακραύχενος γὰρ κλίμακος προσαμβάσεις[1] | for grasping the rungs of a long-necked |
| ἔχων ἐχώρει | ladder, on he came |

and finally, Euripides's Bacchae (1212–1215) (Agave, with the severed head of Pentheus):

| | |
|---|---|
| αἱρέσθω λαβὼν | let him get a firm-set ladder with its |
| πηκτῶν πρὸς οἴκους κλιμάκων προσαμβάσεις | rungs and raise it against the palace-walls |
| ὡς πασσαλεύσῃ κρᾶτα τριγλύφοις τόδε | that he may nail to the triglyphs this |
| λέοντος ὃν πάρειμι θηράσασ' ἐγώ | lion's head with which as spoil I come from the chase |

and this time again, observe, in order to reach a triglyphon![2]

We may note in passing that Agave's plan to nail the lion's head to the triglyphs is not altogether the fruit of a maddened brain; there is, indeed, a peculiar propriety in wishing to decorate the entablature of the building with a lion's head: the cyma of classical Greek temples (for example, the Parthenon and the temple of Zeus at Olympia) was finished off with lion's heads. And Vitruvius (III 5, 15) specifies that design as an architectural law: in cymis capita leonina sunt scalpenda.

Thus we get complete sense for our passage: "The enclosing walls, thou seest, are high; shall we climb up with ladders? How, then, should we fail of being seen? Or, [shall we get in] by forcing with crowbars the bronze-forged bolts, of which we nothing know?" But again we face a difficulty in ὧν οὐδὲν ἴσμεν. If the reading be right, which many editors doubt, what is it "of which they nothing know"? Is it the bolts? What difference does it make to one who can handle a "jimmy," whether he know in advance that the bolts are high or low, thick or thin? It is unnecessary to refute the idea that with ὧν οὐδὲν ἴσμεν Orestes is explaining to Pylades that they are not professional burglars and do not understand housebreaking! No; the jimmy will do its perfect work, when applied with force. Besides, from the position of the keyhole he could easily have located the bolts; for there was a keyhole, and Iphigenia, as we have already seen, is κληδοῦχος (131), "the keeper of the key." Or is it the crowbars "of which we nothing know"? What sense is there in saying that? Or is it (cutting out verse 99 with Dindorf, or changing ἤ to μὴ with Paley, and reading μάθοιμεν in 98[3]) "how might we learn that of which we nothing know?" None of these alternatives is entirely satisfactory. For that reason editors have flown to conjecture upon conjecture, some of them clever and some of them absurd.[4] The text at this point seems to me to be in perfect order, save that we should close our question with the word μοχλοῖς, and let ὧν οὐδὲν ἴσμεν stand as a sentence complete in itself. "Shall we climb up ladders? How should we fail of being seen? Or shall we get in by forcing the bronze-forged bolts with crowbars? Of these things we nothing know"; that is, "we do not know

---

[1] In the same way προσβάσεις is used of the possibility of scaling a tower (Eur. Ph. 181–182):

προσβάσεις τεκμαίρεται
πύργων ἄνω τε καὶ κάτω τείχη μετρῶν.

But in Eur. Ph. 744 τειχέων προσαμβάσεις, without any mention of the ladder, means "the scaling of the walls."

[2] Cp. Eur. Bacch. 1238–1240:

φέρω δ' ἐν ὠλέναισιν, ὡς ὁρᾷς, τάδε
λαβοῦσα τἀριστεῖα, τοῖσι πρὸς δόμοις
ὡς ἀγκρεμασθῇ.

The spoils of the hunt are here to be hung up upon the palace's front.

[3] Other conjectures are: Badham:—ὧδ' οὐδὸν ἔσιμεν. But the epic οὐδὸς is not used in Attic dialog. Accordingly, this conjecture is modified by Weil:—ἂν' οὖδας ἔσιμεν "we enter over the threshold." Köchly:—ὧδ' ἱερὸν ἔσιμεν. Wecklein:—ὧδ' ἄδυτον ἔσιμεν.

[4] Bates's ἀλλ' for the second ἂν gives a sense anything but "logical." Not only is there no sequence of thought but no thought at all.

which plan to follow; for," he goes on, "if we are caught opening the doors or [he says "and"] effecting an entrance [going through the metope with a ladder], we are dead men."[1]

The ladder and the metope opening are the route adopted for the night assault upon the temple statue. And once more we review our temple—a Doric *templum in antis*, with architrave, triglyphs, open metopes, gilded cornice, roof; and all devoid of plastic decoration.

Long after the foregoing discussion was written,[2] Professor Washburn's article on "Iphigenia Taurica 113 as a Document in the History of Architecture" appeared in the American Journal of Archaeology XXII (1918) pages 434–437, in which he rejects the meaning of "between the triglyphs" for εἴσω τριγλύφων and proposes to translate the phrase "within" or "beyond" or "behind the triglyphs." That is, "behind the frieze is an opening in the ceiling of the vestibule; by means of this opening one can make his way to the attic and let himself down into the cella." In support of this view Dr. Washburn cites the method of the entrance of the Phrygian in the passage from the Orestes discussed above and Pausanias V 20, 5. But the context in the Orestes makes it perfectly clear that the Phrygian was not up in the attic of the palace, but, failing in his panic haste to get out through the barred and locked and bolted doors,[3] climbed up and over the triglyph frieze. And Pausanias, in the passage cited, says anything but that the dead hoplite in the attic climbed up into it through an opening in the ceiling of the peristyle of the Heraeum: he had been fighting upon the roof of the building and there had been wounded; he must have got into the attic from the roof—not from below. Neither have we any intimation as to how Orestes and Pylades would have got down from the attic into the cella!

Professor Washburn maintains that "Euripides was no archaeologist, deliberately reproducing on the stage a type of Greek construction which was in his day two or more centuries out of date." But, as we have seen and as we shall see still more clearly as we proceed, Euripides was very much of an archaeologist; and not only he but all his audience may have been perfectly familiar with temples, already very ancient in their day, which conservative reverence for antiquity had not permitted to be modernized. Furthermore, "openings" very close akin to metope openings were not only not two or more centuries out of date in Euripides's day but very familiar indeed. And through them men might escape from a building, even as the Phrygian did. Aristophanes is not archaizing when he makes old Philocleon climb out of his confinement through ὀπαί or down the rain-spout (Ar. Vesp. 126–128):

| | |
|---|---|
| ὁ δ' ἐξεδίδρασκε διά τε τῶν ὑδροροῶν | but he would make his escape by way of the rain-pipes |
| καὶ τῶν ὀπῶν· ἡμεῖς δ' ὅσ' ἦν τετρημένα ἐνεβύσαμεν ῥακίοισι | and the openings; but we stuffed up with rags every opening there was |

ὀπαί is so like μετόπαι that one is tempted to see in Philocleon's house in the comic proscenium a triglyph frieze with open metopes. Liddell and Scott cite the passage and explain it as a hole in the roof for an outlet for the smoke. But, in the first place, the word is plural and we should have to think of an Homeric clere-story over the hearth—which is not likely; and besides, the "hole in the roof" would not fit at all in verses 317–319:

| | |
|---|---|
| φίλοι, τήκομαι μὲν πάλαι διὰ τῆς ὀπῆς ὑμῶν ὑπακούων | friends, I have this long time been fretting to death at hearing you only through the opening |

and line 352:

| | |
|---|---|
| πάντα πέφρακται κοὐκ ἔστιν ὀπῆς οὐδ εἰ σέρφῳ διαδῦναι | every chink is stuffed up and there isn't an opening that even a midge could get through |

[1] Some editors have found difficulty with verse 113 also: ὅρα δέ γ' εἴσω τριγλύφων ὅποι κενόν (with its variant ὥρα δέ γ' εἴσω). Blomfield, reads ὅρα δὲ γεῖσα; Elmsley, ὥρα δὲ γείσων τριγλύφων ὅπου; Madvig, πείρα δέ γ' εἴσω; Wecklein, Δωρικὰ δὲ γεῖσα τριγλύφων ὀπὴν κενοῖ; and again (1888) ὅρα δὲ γείσων τριγλύφων τύπους κενούς; Köchly, ῥᾷστον δέ γ' εἴσω; Paley, ὅρα δέ γ' εἴσω, τριγλύφων ὅπου κενόν; Weil, ὅρα δ' ἔνεστι, τριγλύφων ὅπου κενόν, δέμας καθεῖναι; and many more. None of these changes is necessary, and all fail to help in any way. Nothing is gained by any one of them. Pylades is not discovering a new way of getting in but selecting that one which seems to him the better of the two plans proposed by Orestes.

[2] It was read before the Philological Club of the University of Missouri in 1915.

[3] Cf. ll. 1366–1367: ἀλλὰ κτυπεῖ γὰρ κλῆθρα βασιλικῶν δόμων,
σιγήσατ'· ἔξω γάρ τις ἐκβαίνει....
See page 113, foot-note 1, where the passage is quoted in full.

Locked up under careful watch, poor old Philocleon sits behind his barred door and hears through a metope hole, or something very like it, his fellow-heliasts talking in the street before his house. Until that method of escape was cut off he would climb up on the inside and crawl through one of those openings, or mount to the roof and slide down the rain-spout. And he prays to be turned into smoke, so that he may get through to them.[1]

All this is in direct support of our interpretation of the passage in the Orestes and the situation in the Iphigenia Taurica. The passage in the Iphigenia Taurica and that from the Bacchae (1212–1215) cited above[2] are alone adequate proof of the presence of a Doric entablature upon the proscenium in the theatre. But as final proof, we may cite the scene from Euripides's Orestes quoted above[3] in which Helen's Phrygian slave behind the proscenium climbs up over the architrave and between two triglyphs and tumbles down outside the palace before the feet of the chorus in the presence of the spectators.

Very ancient temples with triglyph frieze and open metopes were, no doubt, still standing in many places in Greece in the fifth century and were familiar to Euripides and his contemporaries. The open metopes in palaces and temples were an easy ingress for robbers, like Orestes and Pylades in the Iphigenia Taurica; architects and builders, therefore, soon filled them up with rectangular plates, and these in time invited graphic and plastic decoration.

## 11. ARTEMISIA IN ATTICA

### a. *The Temple of the Brauronian Artemis at Brauron*

Closely connected in religious and literary tradition with the temple in the Taurian land and its cultus and ritual was the worship of Artemis at Brauron, a town near the eastern coast of Attica, not far from Prasiae and Halae Araphenides.

Of the temple itself we know nothing; not a certain vestige of it is left; we do not even know its site; I have tramped all over the hills in the vicinity of where it must have been searching for a trace of it, as others have done, and failed to discover any sign of it; the Greek authors have nothing, beyond a mere mention, to say of it. The only object of real interest there was the Zeus-fallen, wooden image of Artemis, brought, as the story has it, by Iphigenia and Orestes from Taurica. Euripides makes the transfer of the statue from the Taurian land to Attica the substance of the Iphigenia Taurica, the service that finally frees Orestes from the pursuit of the avengers of blood (I. T. 85–92):

| | |
|---|---|
| σὺ δ' εἶπας ἐλθεῖν Ταυρικῆς μ' ὅρους χθονός, | thou bad'st me come to the coasts of the Taurian land, |
| ἔνθ' Ἄρτεμίς σοι σύγγονος βωμοὺς ἔχοι, | where thy sister Artemis hath her altars, |
| λαβεῖν τ' ἄγαλμα θεᾶς, ὅ φασιν ἐνθάδε | and get the goddess's statue which they say fell |
| εἰς τούσδε ναοὺς οὐρανοῦ πεσεῖν ἄπο· | down from heaven into this temple here; |
| λαβόντα δ' ἢ τέχναισιν ἢ τύχῃ τινί, | and, having got it by craft or by some happy chance, |
| κίνδυνον ἐκπλήσαντ', Ἀθηναίων χθονὶ | all danger past, to give it to the land |
| δοῦναι· τὸ δ' ἐνθένδ' οὐδὲν ἐρρήθη πέρα· | of Athens. Naught more than this was said. |
| καὶ ταῦτα δράσαντ' ἀμπνοὰς ἕξειν πόνων | And this done, I should have respite from my woes |

And again, Orestes explains to Iphigenia his quest in the Tauric land (I. T. 977–986):

| | |
|---|---|
| Φοῖβός μ' ἔπεμψε δεῦρο, διοπετὲς λαβεῖν | Phoebus sent me hither to get the statue fallen |
| ἄγαλμ' Ἀθηνῶν τ' ἐγκαθιδρῦσαι χθονί. | from Zeus and set it up in Athens' land. |
| ἀλλ' ἥνπερ ἡμῖν ὥρισεν σωτηρίαν, | Now, help me to the safety which he hath |
| σύμπραξον· ἢν γὰρ θεᾶς κατάσχωμεν βρέτας, | ordained; for if we get possession of the goddess's image |
| μανιῶν τε λήξω καὶ σὲ πολυκώπῳ σκάφει | and I have surcease of my madness, thee also shall I speed away in our ship |

---

[1] Ar. Vesp. 323–324: ἀλλ' ὦ Ζεῦ, Ζεῦ, μέγα βροντήσας
　　　　　　　ἤ με ποίησον καπνὸν ἐξαίφνης, κτλ.

[2] P. 115.

[3] P. 113.

στείλας Μυκήναις ἐγκαταστήσω πάλιν.
ἀλλ', ὦ φιληθεῖσ', ὦ κασίγνητον κάρα,
σῶσον πατρῷον οἶκον, ἔκσωσον δ' ἐμέ·
ὡς τἄμ' ὄλωλε πάντα καὶ τὰ Πελοπιδῶν,

οὐράνιον εἰ μὴ ληψόμεσθα θεᾶς βρέτας

of many oars and restore thee again to Mycenae.
But, oh belovèd sister mine,
save our father's house; deliver me;
for all my fortunes—all the house of Pelops's line
    —are ruined quite,
unless we gain possession of the goddess's image

The same thought is repeated a third time by Athena, as *dea ex machina*, speaking for her people (I. T. 1438–1442):

πεπρωμένος γὰρ θεσφάτοισι Λοξίου
δεῦρ' ἦλθ' Ὀρέστης, τόν τ' Ἐρινύων χόλον
φεύγων ἀδελφῆς τ' Ἄργος εἰσπέμψων δέμας
ἄγαλμά θ' ἱερὸν εἰς ἐμὴν ἄξων χθόνα,
τῶν νῦν παρόντων πημάτων ἀναψυχάς

for foreordained by Loxias's oracles is
Orestes come, in flight from the Erinyes'
wrath, to bring to Argos his fair sister
and convey the holy image to my land
and thus gain respite from his present woes

And Thoas, accepting her decree, dismisses the children of Agamemnon and bids farewell to the precious statue (I. T. 1480–1481):

ἴτωσαν εἰς σὴν σὺν θεᾶς ἀγάλματι
γαῖαν, καθιδρύσαιντό τ' εὐτυχῶς βρέτας

let them go with the goddess's statue to thy
land and with fair fortune install the image there

As for the statue itself, sometimes it is an ἄγαλμα, sometimes a βρέτας[1], sometimes a ξόανον (1359)—that is, "a thing of joy," or "a graven image," or "a wooden figure." Euripides uses the former two words apparently without the slightest distinction (Eur. I. T. 1038; 1040[2]):

τί δῆτα μᾶλλον θεᾶς ἄγαλμ' ἁλίσκεται;

yet how is the goddess's statue aught the more
    secured?

ἔτ' ἐν δόμοισι βρέτας

Still stands the image in the shrine

ξόανον is more definite and specific (Eur. I. T. 1359). It stood upon a pedestal of stone (Eur. I. T. 996–997):

δέδοικα καὶ τύραννον, ἡνίκ' ἂν κενὰς
κρηπῖδας εὕρῃ λαΐνας ἀγάλματος

I fear the king, too, when he shall find
the stone pedestal void of its statue

The pedestal is κρηπῖδες (997) or βάθρα (1157; 1201) or ἕδρα (1165). The figure was small enough to be easily carried, even in a woman's arms (Eur. I. T. 1000):

ἄγαλμά τ' οἴσεις

thou [Orestes[3]] shalt bear the statue

(1044):

ΟΡ. οὐ δ' ἢ τις ἄλλος ἐν χεροῖν οἴσει βρέτας;

ΙΦ. ἐγώ

OR. Wilt thou [Iphigenia] bring the image in
    thine arms, or shall some one else?
IPH. I will

(1157–1158):

τί τόδε μεταίρεις ἐξ ἀκινήτων βάθρων,
......... θεᾶς ἄγαλμ' ἐν ὠλέναις;

why bearest thou in thine arms from its inviolable
base the statue of the goddess?

(1176):

ἢ τῶνδ' ἕκατι δῆτ' ἄγαλμ' ἔξω φέρεις;

and on their account thou dost bear the image
    forth?

The image was most ancient;[4] it was most reverend;[5] it was small;[6] it was graven;[7] it was made of wood;[8] it was polished;[9] it had fallen from heaven into the temple in the land

[1] In addition to the passages cited above, cp. also Eur. I. T. 980; 986; 1044; 1179; 1199; 1481.
[2] Cp. also Eur. I. T. 1291–1292; 1315–1316.
[3] Cp. also Eur. I. T. 1477–1478.
[4] Paus. I 23, 7 (quoted on p. 119 below); 33, 1 (quoted on p. 119 below).
[5] σεμνόν: Eur. I. T.  1291–1292; 1315–1316; 1489 (quoted on page 124 below); ἱερόν: 1441; none might touch it, save the priestess alone: θιγεῖν γὰρ ὁσιόν ἐστ' ἐμοὶ μόνῃ (Eur. I. T. 1045).
[6] Eur. I. T. 1000 (quoted above); 1044 (quoted above); 1157–1158 (quoted above); 1176 (quoted above); 1477–1478; Paus. III 16, 10.
[7] Eur. I. T. 986; 1044; 1179; 1199; 1481; 1489 (quoted on p. 124 below).
[8] ξόανον: Eur. I. T. 1359; Paus. I 23, 7 (quoted on p. 119 below); 33, 1 (quoted on p. 119 below); III 16, 7–11 (quoted on pp. 119–120 below).
[9] Eur. I. T. 111–112: ξεστὸν ἐκ ναοῦ λαβεῖν  ἄγαλμα

of the Taurians;[1] it was brought to Attica by Orestes in fulfilment of the divine command.[2] In works of art in which the image is represented, especially the long series of sarcophagi, it is a small statue of the Artemis type, corresponding to the description in the text of Euripides.

Euripides was not the only tragic poet to sing the praises of the shrine at Brauron. We have in Diphilus ('Eλ., Frag. 30, 1-3K.) the passage from some tragic poet (Inc. Inc. Frag. 145 N.):

ὦ τόνδ' ἐποπτεύουσα καὶ κεκτημένη
Βραυρῶνος ἱεροῦ θεοφιλέστατον τόπον
Λητοῦς Διός τε τοξόδαμνε παρθένε

oh thou that dwellest in and watchest over sacred Brauron, a spot best loved of God, thou archer maiden-daughter of Leto and Zeus

Pausanias has but little more to add. As he passes from the Propylaea into the inner Acropolis he remarks (I 23, 7):

καὶ 'Αρτέμιδος ἱερόν ἐστι Βραυρωνίας,

Πραξιτέλους μὲν τέχνη τὸ ἄγαλμα, τῇ θεῷ δέ ἐστιν ἀπὸ Βραυρῶνος δή- μου τὸ ὄνομα. καὶ τὸ ἀρχαῖον ξόανόν ἐστιν ἐν Βραυρῶνι, ῎Αρτεμις, ὡς λέγουσιν, ἡ Ταυρική

there is also a sanctuary of the Brauronian Artemis; the statue is the work of Praxiteles, and the goddess has her name from the deme of Brauron; and at Brauron is the ancient wooden image—the Tauric Artemis, they say

In this passage Pausanias repeats the tradition set forth by Euripides in the lines quoted above, namely that the sanctuary at Brauron contained the wooden image of Artemis, brought, according to popular belief, from Tauria to Attica. He himself, however, does not accept the local tradition; his ὡς λέγουσιν betrays his skepticism. In I 33, 1 he frankly declares his disbelief in the Attic tradition:

Μαραθῶνος δὲ ἀπέχει τῇ μὲν Βραυ- ρών, ἔνθα 'Ιφιγένειαν τὴν 'Αγαμέμνονος ἐκ Ταύρων φεύγουσαν, τὸ ἄγαλμα ἀγομένην τὸ 'Αρτέμιδος ἀποβῆναι λέγουσι, καταλιποῦσαν δὲ τὸ ἄγαλμα ταύτῃ καὶ ἐς 'Αθήνας καὶ ὕστερον ἐς ῎Αργος ἀφικέσθαι. ξόανον μὲν δὴ καὶ αὐτόθι ἐστὶν 'Αρτέμιδος ἀρχαῖ- ον· τὸ δὲ ἐκ τῶν βαρβάρων οἵτινες κατὰ γνώμην ἔχουσι τὴν ἐμὴν ἐν ἑτέρῳ λόγῳ δηλώσω.

Some distance from Marathon in one direction is Brauron, where, they say, Iphigenia, the daughter of Agamemnon, disembarked with the statue of Artemis when she made her escape from Tauria. Here she deposited the statue and made her way to Athens and later on to Argos. Now, there is, to be sure, an ancient wooden image of Artemis here also; but who, in my opinion, are the real possessors of the statue that came from the barbarian lands, I will explain in another connection

In III 16, 7-11 he presents his arguments for the sanctuary of Artemis Orthia in Sparta as the custodian of the true image from Taurica:

Τὸ δὲ χωρίον τὸ ἐπονομαζόμενον Λιμναῖον 'Ορθίας ἱερόν ἐστιν 'Αρτέμιδος. τὸ ξόανον δὲ ἐκεῖνο εἶναι λέγουσιν ὅ ποτε 'Ορέστης καὶ 'Ιφιγένεια ἐκ τῆς Ταυρικῆς ἐκκλέπτουσιν· ἐς δὲ τὴν σφετέραν Λακεδαιμόνιοι κομισθῆναί φασιν 'Ορέστου καὶ ἐνταῦθα βασιλεύοντος. Καί μοι εἰκότα λέγειν μᾶλλόν τι δοκοῦσιν ἢ 'Αθηναῖοι. ποίῳ γὰρ δὴ λόγῳ κατέλιπεν ἂν ἐν Βραυρῶνι 'Ιφιγένεια τὸ ἄγαλμα; ἢ πῶς,

The place called Limnaeum is a sanctuary of Artemis Orthia. The wooden image, moreover, is, they say, the famous statue that Orestes and Iphigenia once stole from the Taurian land; and the Lacedaemonians maintain that it was brought to their country because Orestes was king there also. And this story seems to me rather more plausible than the one the Athenians tell. For on what possible grounds would Iphigenia have left the statue in Brauron? Or how

[1] Eur. I. T. 87-88 (quoted on p. 117 above); 977; 986 (quoted on p. 118 above); I. T. 1384-1385: τό τ' οὐρανοῦ πέσημα, τῆς Διὸς κόρης ἄγαλμα

[2] Eur. I. T. 87-91 (quoted on p. 117 above); 977-978 (quoted on p. 118 above); 1000 (quoted on p. 118 above); 1013-1014 (quoted on p. 123 below); 1086-1088 (quoted on page 124 below); 1448-1457 (quoted on pp. 121-122 below).

ἡνίκα Ἀθηναῖοι τὴν χώραν ἐκλιπεῖν
παρεσκευάζοντο, οὐκ ἐσέθεντο καὶ
τοῦτο ἐς τὰς ναῦς; καίτοι διαμε-
μένηκεν ἔτι καὶ νῦν τηλικοῦτο ὄνομα
τῇ Ταυρικῇ θεῷ, ὥστε ἀμφισβητοῦσι μὲν Καππαδόκαι οἱ τὸν Εὔξει-
νον οἰκοῦντες τὸ ἄγαλμα εἶναι
παρὰ σφίσιν, ἀμφισβητοῦσι δὲ καὶ
Λυδῶν οἷς ἐστιν Ἀρτέμιδος ἱερὸν
Ἀναιίτιδος. Ἀθηναίοις δὲ ἄρα παρώφθη

γενόμενον λάφυρον τῷ Μήδῳ·[1] τὸ γὰρ

ἐκ Βραυρῶνος ἐκομίσθη τε ἐς Σοῦσα,
καὶ ὕστερον Σελεύκου δόντος Σύροι
Λαοδικεῖς ἐφ᾽ ἡμῶν ἔχουσι.

Μαρτύρια δέ μοι καὶ τάδε τὴν
ἐν Λακεδαίμονι Ὀρθίαν τὸ ἐκ
τῶν βαρβάρων εἶναι ξόανον·

τοῦτο μὲν γὰρ Ἀστράβακος
καὶ Ἀλώπεχος οἱ Ἴρβου τοῦ
Ἀμφισθένους τοῦ Ἄγιδος τὸ ἄγαλμα εὑρόντες αὐτίκα παρεφρόνησαν·
τοῦτο δὲ οἱ Λιμνᾶται Σπαρτιατῶν
καὶ Κυνοσυρεῖς καὶ ἐκ Μεσόας
τε καὶ Πιτάνης θύοντες τῇ Ἀρτέ-
μιδι εἰς διαφοράν, ἀπὸ δὲ αὐτῆς
καὶ ἐς φόνους προήχθησαν,
ἀποθανόντων δὲ ἐπὶ τῷ βωμῷ
πολλῶν νόσος ἔφθειρε τοὺς
λοιπούς. καὶ σφισιν ἐπὶ τούτῳ
γίνεται λόγιον αἵματι ἀνθρώπων
τὸν βωμὸν αἱμάσσειν· θυομέ-
νου δὲ ὄντινα ὁ κλῆρος ἐπε-
λάμβανε, Λυκοῦργος μετέβαλεν
ἐς τὰς ἐπὶ τοῖς ἐφήβοις μάστι-
γας, ἐμπίπλαταί τε οὕτως ἀνθρώπων αἵμασι ὁ βωμός· ἡ
δὲ ἱέρεια τὸ ξόανον ἔχουσά σφισιν ἐφέστηκε. τὸ δέ ἐστιν ἄλλως μὲν κοῦφον ὑπὸ σμικρό-
τητος, ἢν δὲ οἱ μαστιγοῦντές
ποτε ὑποφειδόμενοι παίωσι
κατὰ ἐφήβου κάλλος ἢ ἀξί-
ωμα, τότε ἤδη τῇ γυναικὶ
τὸ ξόανον γίνεται βαρὺ καὶ
οὐκέτι εὔφορον· ἡ δὲ ἐν αἰτίᾳ
τοὺς μαστιγοῦντας ποιεῖται καὶ
πιέζεσθαι δι᾽ αὐτούς φησιν.
οὕτω δὲ τῷ ἀγάλματι ἀπὸ τῶν ἐν
τῇ Ταυρικῇ θυσιῶν ἐμμεμένη-
κεν ἀνθρώπων αἵματι ἥδεσθαι

did the Athenians, when they were preparing to abandon their country, fail to take this
also on board their ships? And yet, even
to this day, the name of the Tauric
goddess commands such reverence that
the Cappadocians on the Euxine
claim that the statue is in their
possession, and the same claim is made by those
Lydians who have the sanctuary of Artemis
Anaeitis. But the Athenians, be it remarked,
    carelessly allowed
it to be taken as spoils of war by the Mede[1]; for
    the
statue at Brauron was carried away to Susa,
and afterward, by the gift of Seleucus, the Syrians
at Laodicea received it and they have possession
of it in our day.

Moreover, I can produce as proofs
that the Orthia in Lacedaemon is that
wooden image from the barbarian land the fol-
    lowing:
(1) Astrabacus and Alopecus,
the sons of Irbus, the son of
Amphisthenes, the son of Agis,
upon finding the image, at once went mad.
(2) The Limnatae of Sparta and the
Cynosurians and the people of Mesoa
and Pitane were sacrificing to Artemis, fell
into a dispute, and from that they
were led on to bloodshed;
and when many had been slain at
the altar, sickness wasted the
rest. And in consequence of this it was ordained
that they should wet the altar
with human blood. As the man upon
whom the lot fell was sacrificed,
Lycurgus changed the custom to that
of scourging the boys,
and so the altar reeks
with human blood; and the
priestess stands over them with the
wooden image in her arms. It is, moreover, naturally light, for it is small;
but if ever those who do the scourging
lay on the blows with sparing hand because a boy is handsome or high-
born, then the wooden image becomes
heavy in the woman's hands and no longer
easy for her to hold, and she lays the
blame on the scourgers and says it is
they that lay the load on her. And so
the joy in human blood has continued
in the statue from the days of its human
sacrifice in the Tauric land.

From this we learn that not only Attica, but Sparta and Argos and Cappadocia (Comana[2])
and Lydia and Syria (Laodicea[3]) as well—all claimed to be the possessors of the true image

---

[1] Cf. also VIII 46, 3.

[2] Strabo XII 535; Dio Cassius XXXVI 11.

[3] "According to Porphyry (de Abstin. II 56) a virgin was formerly sacrificed every year to Athena at
Laodicea; but a deer was afterward substituted. This Athena was probably the goddess whom Pausanias
calls Artemis. It is likely that she was neither Artemis nor Athena, but the native Syrian goddess Astarte.
Cp. W. Robertson Smith, *Religion of the Semites*[2], pp. 466 *sq.* Still Seleucus may perfectly well have identi-
fied her with Artemis and presented to the city the old Greek image of Artemis which had once stood at
Brauron." (Frazer, *Paus.* III pp. 340 f.)

from the Taurian shrine.[1]  The "proofs" that Pausanias offers for the case of Sparta are astounding, even for him.  If there were no better arguments current in the days of Euripides, we may well believe that the case for Athens, as he presents it in the Iphigenia Taurica, permitted no shadow of a doubt; for it is obvious that the patriotic purpose in Euripides's tragedy was to establish the claim of Attica to the possession of the true image once the care of Iphigenia in the Tauric land.

"Carl Robert[2] thinks that the legend of the bringing of the image from the Crimea to Brauron was an invention of Euripides, and that the popularity which this fiction obtained through the medium of the poet's verses induced various towns, which possessed ancient images of Artemis, to set up claims to the possession of the genuine image of the Tauric Artemis.  The story that the ancient image at Brauron was carried off by Xerxes (Paus. III 16, 8; VIII 46, 3) is treated by Professor Robert as another fiction devised to support the claims of Laodicea to the possession of the true image.  He thinks that if the image at Brauron had really been carried off by Xerxes, Euripides must have alluded to its capture in his play and must have put into the mouth of Athena a promise that the image would one day be restored.  The argument is scarcely convincing, though Professor Robert regards it as conclusive."[3]

So, too, the cultus statue of Artemis Tauropolos was a very ancient one.  It was still in its place in the days of Euripides.  The tale of its rape[4] belongs to after days, when it was necessary to explain the existence of several images whose votaries vindicated for them severally the title to being the original one brought from Tauris and to reconcile the several claims.

In spite of the evidence of Pausanias, the claims of Athens seem to have been most generally accepted.  To the sources already quoted we might add also the two following: Apollodorus, Epit. 6, 27:

| | |
|---|---|
| τὸ ἐν Ταύροις ξόανον... κομισθὲν εἰς Ἀθήνας νῦν λέγεται τὸ τῆς Ταυροπόλου | the wooden statue in Tauria . . . brought to Athens is now called that of the Tauropolos |

Servius ad Virg. Aen. III 331:

Orestes . . . accepto responso, sublato Dianae simulacro sororem reduxit in Atticam, ubi in honorem conservati numinis Tauropolin appelavit.

### b.  *Artemis Tauropolos in Halae*

The cultus of Artemis Tauropolos at Halae has often been confused with that of the Tauric Artemis at Brauron.  But the Brauronian temple was in the Deme of Philaïdae at Brauron, the Tauropolian in Halae Araphenides.  They were, nevertheless, so closely related both in nature and in location, that they became subject to endless confusion, and it is altogether impossible to disentangle the snarls.  Both are called "Brauronian"; both received the epithet "Tauropolos"; and both, by a natural process of etymologizing,[5] are identified with the Tauric virgin.  Thus also both are brought into connection with the story in accordance with which the cultus image was brought by Orestes and Iphigenia from the Tauric land to Attica.  Athena herself, speaking as *dea ex machina* at the end of the Iphigenia Taurica, hopelessly confounds the two (1448–1457):

| | |
|---|---|
| χώρει λαβὼν ἄγαλμα σύγγονόν τε σήν. | take thou the statue and thy kinswoman and go thy way. |
| ὅταν δ' Ἀθήνας τὰς θεοδμήτους μόλῃς, χῶρός τις ἔστιν Ἀτθίδος πρὸς ἐσχάτοις ὅροισι, γείτων δειράδος Καρυστίας, | And when thou comest to Athens built of God, a place there is upon the Attic marches hard by Carystus's ridge, a |

[1] No less than twenty localities claimed possession of the true image: Attica, Sparta, Argos, Cappadocian Comana, Pontic Comana, Castabala (Cataonia), Mt. Amanus, Lydia, Patmos, Sminthe, Rhodes, Laodicea, Oreste (Adrianople), Argos Oresticum, Oreste (Euboea), Rhegium, Caulonia, Tyndaris, Aricia.  For the literature see Roscher, *Myth. Lex.* III[1], Sp. 998–1001; IV[1] Sp. 137–143.

[2] *Arch. Märchen*, pp. 144–150; cf. also Robert, *A. Z.* XXXIII (1876), p. 134.

[3] Frazer, *Paus.* II p. 284.

[4] Paus. III 16, 7 ff.

[5] Cf. Phot. *s. v.* Ταυροπόλον = Suid. *s. v.* Ταυροπόλον and Ταυροπόλα; Schol. Soph. Aj. 172; Apollodorus (Schol. Ar. Lys. 447).

ἱερός, ᾿Αλάς νιν οὑμὸς ὀνομάζει λεώς·
ἐνταῦθα τεύξας ναὸν ἵδρυσαι βρέτας,
ἐπώνυμον γῆς Ταυρικῆς πόνων τε σῶν
....᾿Αρτεμιν δέ νιν βροτοὶ
τὸ λοιπὸν ὑμνήσουσι Ταυροπόλον θεάν

holy spot—my people call it Halae;
there build a shrine and set the image up,
named for the Taurian land and for thy toils
. . . and men for all time to come shall
sing the praises of the goddess as Artemis Tauropolos

Here we have Halae and the Tauropolos; only five lines further on it is Brauron and Brauronia (1462–1463):

σὲ δ' ἀμφὶ σεμνάς, ᾿Ιφιγένεια, κλίμακας
Βραυρωνίας δεῖ τῇδε κληδουχεῖν θεᾷ

thou, Iphigenia, by Brauron's holy stairs
must be warden to this goddess

It was the close geographical connection and the association of Iphigenia, that is, Artemis Iphigenia, and her cult in Brauron with Iphigenia, the Tauric maiden, that led to the complete identification between the Artemis of Brauron and the Artemis Tauropolos of Halae, as we find it in Attica. And so, too, all the famous shrines of the Tauropolos came naturally to claim possession of the Tauric statue.

The claim of possessing the Tauric image in Comana of Cappadocia prompted the invention of the story that Orestes and Iphigenia on their flight from Tauria came to Cataonia, established there the worship of the Tauropolos, and built two temples—one to Artemis and one to Iphigenia—and that Comana received its name from Iphigenia's offering to the goddess her long hair (κόμη)[1].

Strabo, for one, keeps the Tauropolos and the Brauronian sanctuaries clearly distinguished (VIII 399 *in.*):

εἶτα Πρασιὰ Στειριὰ Βραυρών,
ὅπου τὸ τῆς Βραυρωνίας ἱερόν,
['Αλαὶ 'Αραφη] νίδες, ὅπου τὸ τῆς
Ταυροπόλου, Μυρρινοῦς Προβά-
λινθος Μαραθών, ὅπου Μιλτιάδης....

then come Prasia, Stiria, and Brauron,
where the sanctuary of the Brauronian is;
Halae Araphenides, where we find that
of the Tauropolos; Myrrhinus, Proba-
linthus, and Marathon,[2] where Miltiades . . .

The topographical order of Strabo's list leaves no possible doubt of the relative location of Brauron, with its Brauronian sanctuary, and Halae Araphenides, with its Tauropolos. The former lies south of Halae Araphenides, and the latter is the next town to the north on the way to Marathon.

Servius seems to know the divinity whose worship Orestes established in Attica and whose statue he brought from the Tauric temple only as Tauropolis. But he is also perfectly sure that the only original and true image from Tauria was in the temple of Diana at Aricia.[3]

The worship of Artemis Tauropolos at Halae was directed toward her as a goddess presiding over animal breeding (Eur. I. T. 1456–1457):

᾿Αρτεμιν δέ νιν βροτοὶ
τὸ λοιπὸν ὑμνήσουσι Ταυροπόλον θεάν

and men in future days shall sing her praise
as Artemis, the Goddess of the Kine

The Ταυροπόλος, the protectress of kine, would naturally have filled an important place in the regard of the people among whom the Vapheio cups, the Tirynthian and Cnossian bulls, and all that these and other such works of art suggest were popular.

Her worship, moreover, had much in it that was reminiscent of the primaeval rites of human sacrifice so indissolubly connected with the Tauric Artemis; Athena further prescribes (Eur. I. T. 1458–1461):

νόμον τε θὲς τόνδ'· ὅταν ἑορτάζῃ λεώς,

τῆς σῆς σφαγῆς ἄποιν' ἐπισχέτω ξίφος

δέρῃ πρὸς ἀνδρὸς αἷμά τ' ἐξανιέτω,
ὁσίας ἕκατι, θεά θ' ὅπως τιμὰς ἔχῃ

enact this law: whenever the folk shall keep the
festival,
in atonement for thy slaying they shall set a
sword
to a man's throat and spill blood for the
sake of hallowing and for the goddess's honor's
sake

---

[1] Strabo XII 535; cp. Dio Cass. XXXVI 11; Et. Magn. 526, 22.
[2] Cf. Eur. Heracl. 80–81:     τετράπτολιν
                    ξύνοικον ἦλθες λαόν
[3] Ad Virg. Aen. III 331, quoted on p. 121, *q. v.*

And the change to purer forms of worship is suggested in Iphigenia's prayer (I. T. 1231):

καθαρὸν οἰκήσεις δόμον | in a home of purity thou shalt dwell

The Brauronian festival was famous. Closely connected with it is the story of the rape of the Attic women by Etrurians or Pelasgians from Lemnos during the celebration of the festival on one occasion.[1] In the consequent confusion, the famous old cultus statue brought from the Taurian land was carried away.[2]

### c. *The Sanctuary of Artemis Colaenis at Myrrhinus*

At Myrrhinus, just a few miles south of Brauron, in eastern Attica, was still another seat of Artemis worship. Colaenus, a son of Hermes, in obedience to an oracle, had founded a temple to Artemis there, and from him she received her surname Colaenis. The worship of Colaenis at Myrrhinus must have been very ancient, for Colaenus, according to the tradition, lived before Cecrops.[3]

The modern town of Merenda, built on the site of the ancient Myrrhinus, is now in ruins; but a number of inscriptions found there attest the importance of Artemis Colaenis.[4]

So revered was this Artemis that her cult extended to Amarynthus, the modern Ἀμαροῦσι, the most considerable village between Athens and Cephisia. And, like the Brauronian Artemis, the Colaenis worship was brought from the country into Athens,[5] and in the Dionysiac theatre is still to be seen the seat reserved for her priest. Where her city temple stood we do not know; but it is probably the city and not the country goddess to whom the comic poets allude (Metag. Αὖρ., Frag. 1 K.):

τί σοι (6) Κολαινὶς Ἄρτεμις; | what have you to do with Artemis Colaenis?
ἱερεὺς γὰρ ὢν τετύχηκα τῆς Κολαινίδος | Why, I happen to be Colaenis's priest!

(Ar. Av. 871–872):

καὶ Ἀρτέμιδι Ἀκαλανθίδι — | and Artemis Thistle-finch—
ΠΕΙ. οὐκέτι Κολαινὶς ἀλλ' Ἀκαλανθὶς | PI. No longer Colaenis but Acalanthis
Ἄρτεμις | Artemis

There is no visible point in the lines from the Birds, except the none too successful play upon the words A-calanthis and Colaenis.

### d. *The Sanctuary of Brauronian Artemis on the Acropolis*

From Brauron the worship of Artemis Brauronia was carried on to Athens. The sanctuary adjoining the Propylaea on the southeast, supposed to have been established upon the Acropolis by the Pisistratidae,[7] contained a very ancient statue, together with a new one by the hand of Praxiteles. The ancient figure was an idol of stone in a sitting posture;[8] the new one by Praxiteles was of gold and ivory, or possibly of bronze.[9] Neither one, therefore, can have anything to do with the idol brought by Orestes and Iphigenia from Tauria, although in one passage Euripides makes Orestes say that Athens itself was the destination ordained for the Tauric statue (I. T. 1013–1014):

πῶς ἂν Λοξίας ἐθέσπισε | how had Loxias's oracle bidden
κομίσαι μ' ἄγαλμα θεᾶς πόλισμα Παλλάδος | me convey the statue to Pallas's town?

---

[1] Hdt. IV 145; VI 138; Philoch. Frag. 6 (Schol. on Hm. A 594); Plut. Quaest. Graec. 21; Zenob. III 85.
[2] Plut. Virt. Mulier. 8; K. O. Müller, *Orchomenos* 305 ff.; Busolt, *Griech. Gesch.* I 185; Studniczka, *Kyrene* 45 ff., 51, 145.
[3] Paus. I 31, 4–6.
[4] C. I. A. II 575: ἱερὸν Ἀρτέμιδος Κολαινίδος. Cf. also C. I. A. III 360; *Ath. Mitt.* XII (1887) pp. 277 (No. 149), 288 (No. 150), 282 (No. 180).
[5] C. I. A. III 216.
[6] Adopting Kock's correction for the MS. τίς ἡ.
[7] Wilamowitz, *Aus Kydathen*, 128, 47. Robert, *Archaeol. Märchen*, 150; cf. Paus. I 23, 7; C. I. A. II 728; Hitzig-Blümner, *Paus.* I 260.
[8] See references in Jahn-Michaelis, *Paus. Arx. Ath.*², pp. 48–49.
[9] See discussion in Frazer, *Paus.* II, pp. 284–285; Jessen in Pauly-Wissowa, *s. v. Brauronia*, III Sp. 824–825.

The Athenian audience, at hearing these words, would naturally have thought of both Brauron and its city counterpart upon the Acropolis, for πόλισμα Παλλάδος must mean Athens. In 1086–1088 the words name explicitly the very city of Athens itself:

| | |
|---|---|
| ἀλλ' εὐμενὴς ἔκβηθι βαρβάρου χθονὸς | but graciously come forth from a barbarian land |
| εἰς τὰς 'Αθήνας· καὶ γὰρ ἐνθάδ' οὐ πρέπει | to Athens; yea, it is not meet for thee here |
| ναίειν, παρόν σοι πόλιν ἔχειν εὐδαίμονα | to dwell, when it is thine to have a city blest |

But, even with the mention of Athens, the hearer would still think of Brauron; for to the Athenian Athens meant also Attica. Thus, too, Athena clearly speaks as *dea ex machina* (I. T. 1441):

| | |
|---|---|
| ἄγαλμά θ' ἱερὸν εἰς ἐμὴν ἄξων χθόνα | and bring the holy statue to my land |

signifying Attica, not Athens. And yet only a few lines further on she bids the winds waft Orestes specifically to Athens (I. T. 1487–1489):

| | |
|---|---|
| ἴτ', ὦ πνοαί, ναυσθλοῦσθε τὸν 'Αγαμέμνονος | come, ye breezes, waft Agamemnon's |
| παῖδ' εἰς 'Αθήνας· συμπορεύσομαι δ' ἐγώ, | son to Athens; and I will journey with him |
| σώζουσ' ἀδελφῆς τῆς ἐμῆς σεμνὸν βρέτας | and keep my sister's revered image safe |

But the great majority of the passages point to Attica only generally, or to Brauron specifically. In all cases Brauron is primarily intended, though, of course, neither the poet nor his audience could or should forget that there was a very important sanctuary of the Brauronian Artemis upon the Athenian Acropolis.

### e. *Other Artemisia in Athens*

Besides the sanctuary of the Brauronian Artemis upon the Acropolis, Pausanias names only one other temple of Artemis in the city (I 19, 6):[1]

| | |
|---|---|
| διαβᾶσι δὲ τὸν Εἰλισσὸν χωρίον "Αγραι | after crossing the Ilissus one finds a place called |
| καλούμενον καὶ ναὸς 'Αγροτέρας | Agrae and a temple of Huntress Artemis. |
| 'Αρτέμιδος. ἐνταῦθα "Αρτεμιν πρῶτον | Here, they say, was the first place that |
| θηροῦσαι λέγουσιν ἐλθοῦσαν ἐκ | Artemis hunted after she came from |
| Δήλου· καὶ τὸ ἄγαλμα διὰ τοῦτο ἔχει τόξον | Delos; and for this reason her statue has a bow |

As this sanctuary lay across the Ilissus and north of the Stadium, upon a slight elevation where, until recently at least, there was a considerable mass of architectural fragments about the church of "Αγιος Πέτρος Σταυρωμένος, it may well be the Artemisium included in the exhausting wild-goose chase on which Syrus sends old Demea in the Adelphi of Terence (582–583): ubi ad Dianae veneris,

    ito ad dextram

The topography is not clear in Terence; it may or may not have been clearer in Menander, from whom Terence drew his material for the Adelphi. But Menandrian the scene certainly is, and if we are right in assuming that Menander worked into his play an Artemisium in the body-breaking chase of Demea, nothing would be more fitting than the shrine of the Huntress famous for the yearly sacrifice of five hundred goats in recognition of her help at Marathon. The, to us, unhappy feature of the Syrus-Demea episode is the poet's failure to say anything about the temple beyond its mere existence in an out of the way corner of Athens.

### 12. AN ARTEMISIUM AT ARGOS

Aeschylus seems to have known a temple of Artemis at Argos, of which we have no information from any other source, unless it be the temple of Artemis-Pitho, mentioned by Pausanias, between the theatre and the market-place.[2] But even if we may make proper allowance for the anachronism and identify the temple of which the chorus speaks with

---

[1] Pausanias mentions other Artemisia in Attica: at Munychia (I 1, 4), between the city gate and the Academy (I 29, 2), at Salamis (I 36, 1), and at Eleusis (I 38, 6), but only the two named above in the city of Athens.

[2] II 21, 1: κατελθοῦσι δὲ ἐντεῦθεν καὶ τραπεῖσιν αὖθις ἐπὶ τὴν ἀγορὰν ἔστι...τὸ δὲ τῆς 'Αρτέμιδος ἱερὸν ἐπίκλησιν Πειθοῦς, 'Υπερμνήστρα καὶ τοῦτο ἀνέθηκε, νικήσασα τῇ δίκῃ τὸν πατέρα, ἣν τοῦ Λυγκέως ἕνεκα ἔφυγε.

THE TEMPLE
OF THE
"GREAT DIANA OF THE EPHESIANS"

the temple dedicated a little later by Hypermnestra herself, that primitive structure must have given way long since to Aeschylus's temple adorned with sculptured pediments (Sup. 144–145):

| | |
|---|---|
| ἀγνά μ' ἐπιδέτω Διὸς κόρα | and may Zeus's daughter pure, who dwells in temple walls |
| ἔχουσα σέμν' ἐνώπι' ἀσφαλέστατα [1] | revered and most secure look upon me |

Neither poet nor periegete has anything to tell us of this Artemisium, save only its existence and its high antiquity.

### 13. The Artemisia of Ephesus

#### a. *The Fourth Century Temple*

The temple of "the Great Diana of the Ephesians," built in the latter half of the fourth century, was one of the seven wonders of the ancient world. The poets of the later days might have been expected to contribute something to our scanty knowledge of it. The great temple itself is not so much as alluded to by any extant Greek comic poet. Menander does name Ephesus and a sacrifice to Ephesian Artemis but the fragment contains no mention of the temple or its decorations (Men. Κιθ., lines 93–95 L. C. L.):

| | |
|---|---|
| εἰς τὴν Ἔφεσον ἔπεσον... | arrived at Ephesus I fell in with . . . |
| τῆς Ἀρτέμιδος ἦν τῆς Ἐφεσίας γὰρ τότε | For at that time there was an offering made by |
| δειπνοφορία τις παρθένων ἐλευθερίων | free-born maidens to Artemis of the Ephesians |

Plautus lays the scene of the Miles Gloriosus at Ephesus, but not once does any one in that long play suggest that there is in the city the architectural wonder of the world. In the Two Bacchises, however, Plautus does barely mention Diana of the Ephesians and her temple, but he tells us nothing about either (Bac. 306–307; 312–313):

> nos apud Theotimum omne aurum deposivimus
> qui illic sacerdos est Dianae Ephesiae
>
> . . .
>
> quin in eapse aede Dianae conditumst;
> ibidem publicitus servant.

#### b. *The Sixth Century Temple*

We have in Aristophanes the only extant allusion to the scarcely less famous predecessor of the temple that Paul the Apostle and John the Evangelist knew at Ephesus, the Ionic temple built by Chersiphron in the days of Croesus with the first *columnae celatae*, of which a few fragments only remain (Ar. Nub. 599–600):

| | |
|---|---|
| ἥ τ' Ἐφέσου μάχαιρα πάγχρυσον ἔχεις | and thou, blessed one, who dwellest in the all-golden house of |
| οἶκον, ἐν ᾧ κόραι σε Λυδῶν μεγάλως σέβουσιν | Ephesus, wherein Lydian maidens deeply reverence thee |

The old temple at Ephesus was, according to this hymn of praise of the Cloud-chorus, "all-golden"; that is, it was, like the temple of Apollo at Delphi, richly adorned with gold; its walls were inlaid with decorations of gold, and other architectural units overlaid with gold leaf. We know that enormous sums were lavished in its construction and that Croesus's fabulous wealth was levied upon for its embellishment. So very rich was its decoration that Aristophanes in a lyric passage, a hymn to Apollo and Artemis, might speak of it as "a dwelling all of gold." This is a real contribution, though not at all definite, to our knowledge of the great masterpiece of Chersiphron.

[1] The MSS. read ἀσφαλὲς (D) or ἀσφαλέστατα (cett.); various editors adopt Hermann's conjecture and read Ἄρτεμις, who clearly is meant.

Autocrates, another poet of the Old Comedy, has, in the only fragment we have of him (Τυμπ., Frag. 1 K.), an allusion probably to the same festival as that referred to in the fragment of Menander just cited in connection with the fourth century temple:

| | |
|---|---|
| οἷα παίζουσιν φίλαι | as sport the dear |
| παρθένοι Λυδῶν κόραι, | maiden-daughters of the Lydians, |
| κοῦφα πηδῶσαι κόμαν, | letting their hair fly loose |
| κἀνακρούουσαι χεροῖν, | and clapping their hands |
| ’Εφεσίαν παρ’ ’Άρτεμιν | before Artemis of the Ephesians |
| καλλίσταν, καὶ τοῖν ἰσχίοιν | most fair, and moving |
| τὸ μὲν κάτω τὸ δ’ αὖ | their legs in the dance— |
| εἰς ἄνω ἐξαίρουσαι, | one up and one down— |
| οἷα κίγλος ἄλλεται | as the ousel hops |

## 14. Dionysium ἐν Λίμναις—Enneacrunus

There were in Athens not less than three temples of Dionysus: two of them stood within the sacred precinct of which the great Dionysiac theatre was a part, the sanctuary of Dionysus Eleuthereus. One of these two was a very old temple built under Pisistratus; it contained the famous old wooden image of the god, brought, with his worship, from Eleutherae.[1] The other temple near the theatre was a new sanctuary built to take the place of the old one; but, as usually happened in such cases, so in this instance also the superior sanctity of and deeper reverence for the ancient caused the old building to continue on beside the one that should have completely succeeded it. In the new temple stood the gold and ivory Dionysus from the hand of Alcamenes.

The third temple of Dionysus was the far older temple of the Lenaeum, known as Διόνυσος ἐν Λίμναις—"Dionysus of the Marshes." Aristophanes sings its praises in the choruses of the Frogs (211–219):

| | |
|---|---|
| λιμναῖα κρηνῶν τέκνα, | marshy children of the founts, let us |
| ξύναυλον ὑμνῶν βοὰν | sound forth to the accompaniment of the flute the tune of |
| φθεγξώμεθ’ εὔγηρυν ἐμὰν ἀοιδάν, | our lays, my melodious song, |
| κοὰξ κοάξ, | coáx, coáx, |
| ἣν ἀμφὶ Νυσήιον | which we are wont to sing at |
| Διὸς Διώνυσον ἐν | Limnae in honor of Dionysus, |
| Λίμναις ἰαχήσαμεν, | the child of Zeus from Nysa, |
| ἡνίχ’ ὁ κραιπαλόκωμος | when, tipsy from the feast |
| τοῖς ἱεροῖσι χύτροισι | of the hallowed jars, the throng |
| χωρεῖ κατ’ ἐμὸν τέμενος λαῶν ὄχλος | of people moves along my demesnes |

A suggestion of the nature of that temenos the chorus gives (ll. 231–233; 243–244):

| | |
|---|---|
| προσεπιτέρπεται δ’ ὁ φορμικτὰς ’Απόλλων | and the harper Apollo is also delighted with me |
| ἕνεκα δόνακος, ὃν ὑπολύριον | because of the reed, which I nurture in the |
| ἔνυδρον ἐν λίμναις τρέφω | water in the marshes for the service of his lyre |
| . . . . . . . | . . . . . . . |
| ἡλάμεσθα διὰ κυπείρου | we hopped through galingale |
| καὶ φλέω | and rushes |

This was the temple that was known *par excellence* as *the Dionysium*. This is probably the popular resort, with its annual revels and its tipsy crowd, to which Lysistrate makes her bitter reference at the beginning of the play that bears her name (Ar. Lys. 1–3):

| | |
|---|---|
| ’Αλλ’ εἴ τις ἐς Βακχεῖον αὐτὰς ἐκάλεσεν, | Well! if anyone had called them to the Baccheum, |
| ἢ ’ς Πανός, ἢ ’πὶ Κωλιάδ’, ἢ ’ς Γενετυλλίδος, | or to the sanctuary of Pan or of Genetyllis or to Colias, |
| οὐδ’ ἂν διελθεῖν ἦν ἂν ὑπὸ τῶν τυμπάνων | you couldn't have made your way through for the timbrels |

[1] Paus. I 2, 5; 20, 3.

MOSQUE OF SELIM AT EPHESUS
(What became of the Artemisium)

The great festival of the Anthesteria-Choes-Chytri lasted through three days, the 11th to the 13th of Anthesterion. On the first day came the celebration of the πιθοιγία, "the opening of the wine casks," in which all alike, old and young, high and low, took part. The second day was the day of Choes, "wine cups," with the grand carouse with unmixed wine; in the evening the tipsy crowd of revelers brought their jars to the temple of Dionysus ἐν Λίμναις. On the third day, the crowd, still with aching heads, moved in sacred procession from the old Agora along the Panathenaic festal street, to the Dionysium, where offerings were made to the chthonic deities, and so on past the Lenaeum to the sanctuary of Ge Olympia.

The sanctuary of Dionysus ἐν Λίμναις was one of the most ancient and most revered in Athens. But where did it stand? On all the older maps and plans of Athens (before 1890) the Limnae are located in the depression to the south of the modern tramway below the theatre. Miss Harrison, in the *Mythology and Monuments of Athens*[1] (published in 1890), boldly transplants the Marshes to the low ground on either side of the Eridanus between the Colonus Agoraeus and the Dipylum gate. She is followed by Pickard[2] who argues strongly for that location. Dörpfeld himself seems to have been the originator of the new theory.[3] But the spade sits in judgment on most matters archaeological; and Dörpfeld's excavations (1891–1895) in the old quarters of Athens between the Areopagus and the Pnyx have relegated both sites, both the one below the theatre and the one out toward the Dipylum, to the resting place of exploded theories. Dörpfeld found the actual temple of Dionysus ἐν Λίμναις and cleared up the whole precinct in which the temple stood.[4] It proved to be even more ancient than one would have thought; for parts of the walls of the temenos enclosure go back to the second millennium before our era.

The τέμενος ἐν Λίμναις, included within the fairly well preserved ancient polygonal περίβολος walls, occupied the triangular space at the foot of the western slope of the Acropolis hill, in the corner where Pnyx and Areopagus come closest together; its three sides measure respectively about forty-five by thirty by twenty-five metres. Just above the Dionysium was the famous Enneacrunus, the public fountain from which all Athens in the early days drew its water supply. In spite of the drainage system for carrying off the surplus water, the angle between the two hills, with its rocky spur, must have caught and held enough of the waste water to keep it always wet. And yet, in the course of time the level of the ground was raised, as it is along all busy streets, and by the beginning of the Roman period, the hollow was filled up, the buildings were elevated to meet the new level, and the place was no longer marshy, though the name Limnae was always retained.[5]

Dörpfeld found in the immediate neighborhood not only the great fountain of Athens, with the watermains and reservoirs that supplemented it, but some seventy wells besides. Doubtless the rocky spur connecting the Areopagus and Pnyx caught all the waste water and provided the necessary marsh for the growing of the reeds and for the breeding place of frogs.[6] The name Λίμναι was, therefore, appropriate enough.

[1] See the plan facing p. 5.

[2] John Pickard, *Dionysus ἐν Λίμναις, Papers of the Am. School*, 1891, pp. 130 ff.

[3] Pickard, *l. c.*, p. 131; Dörpfeld, *Die Ausgrabungen am Westabhange der Akropolis* II, *Ath. Mitt.* XX (1895) p. 182.

[4] The reports of the results of the excavations are given by Dörpfeld, *Funde, Ath. Mitt.* XVI (1891), pp. 443 ff.; Dörpfeld, *Funde, Ath. Mitt.* XVII (1892), pp. 90 ff.; Dörpfeld, *Die Ausgrabungen an der Enneakrunos, Ath. Mitt.* XVII (1892), pp. 439 ff.; Körte, *Bezirk eines Heilgottes, Ath. Mitt.* XVIII (1893), pp. 231 ff.; Dörpfeld, *Die Ausgrabungen an der Enneakrunos, Ath. Mitt.* XIX (1894), pp. 143 ff.; Wide, *Inschrift der Iobakchen, ibid.*, pp. 248 ff.; Dörpfeld, *Die Ausgrabungen am Westabhange der Akropolis* I, *ibid.*, pp. 498 ff.; Dörpfeld, *Die Ausgrabungen am Westabhange der Akropolis* II, *Ath. Mitt.* XX (1895), pp. 161 ff.; Schrader, *Die Ausgrabungen am Westabhange der Akropolis* III, *Ath. Mitt.* XXI (1896), pp. 265 ff.; Körte, *Die Ausgrabungen am Westabhange der Akropolis* IV, *ibid.*, pp. 287 ff.; Dörpfeld, *Das alte Athen vor Theseus, Rh. Mus.* LI (1896), pp. 127 ff.; von Prott, *Enneakrunos, Lenaion u. Διονύσιον ἐν Λίμναις, Ath. Mitt.* XXIII (1898), pp. 205 ff.; Watzinger, *Die Ausgrabungen am Westabhange der Akropolis* V, *Ath. Mitt.* XXVI (1901), pp. 305 ff.; Wachsmuth (rejecting Dörpfeld's results), *Ber. d. kgl. Sächs. Ges., Phil.-Hist. Cl.* XXXIX (1897), pp. 382 ff.; Frazer (also rejecting Dörpfeld's results), *Paus.* II, pp. 112–118; Frickenhaus (seeing in the remains the Heracleum in Melite), *Ath. Mitt.* XXXVI (1911), pp. 113 ff.; Judeich, *Topographie v. Athen* (Iwan Müller's Hdb. III 2, pp. 177 ff.; cf. also Dörpfeld, Ἐφ. Ἀρχ. 1894, pp. 1 ff.; *Berl. Philol. Wochenschr.* 1896, pp. 123 ff. Dörpfeld (answering Frickenhaus), *Ath. Mitt.* XLVI (1921), pp. 81 ff.

[5] Strabo VIII 5 (C 363): καὶ τὸ τοῦ Διονύσου ἱερὸν ἐν Λίμναις ἐφ' ὑγροῦ βεβηκὸς ἐτύγχανε, νῦν δ' ἐπὶ ξηροῦ τὴν ἵδρυσιν ἔχει. Cf. Bölte, *Ath. Mitt.* XXXIV (1909) pp. 388 ff.; Dörpfeld, *Ath. Mitt.* XLVI (1921) pp. 82–83.

[6] In order to prevent the flooding of the ground in that quarter even now, with Enneacrunus dried up and gone, the excavators had to fill up the lower end of their diggings to a height of over three feet.

We are indebted to a poet of the Old Comedy for the comment that the Enneacrunus was a locality abounding in water (Polyzelus Δημοτ., Frag. 2 K.):

| | |
|---|---|
| ἴξει πρὸς Ἐννεάκρουνον, εὔυδρον τόπον | you will come to Enneacrunus, a locality abounding in water |

The line is preserved in the Etymologicum Magnum (343, 42) which also adds

| | |
|---|---|
| Ἐννεάκρουνος, κρήνη Ἀθήνησιν παρὰ τὸν Ἰλισσόν, ἣ πρότερον Καλλιρρόη ἔσχεν. ἀφ' ἧς λουτρὰ ταῖς γαμουμέναις μετίασι | Enneacrunus: a spring at Athens beside the Ilissus; it used to be Callirrhoe. From it they fetch water for brides' baths |

There undoubtedly was a Callirrhoe—"a fair flowing fountain"—by the Ilissus; but there was also another at the foot of the Pynx. The Etymologicum Magnum has confused the two. It was not the Callirrhoe by the Ilissus, but the Callirrhoe at the base of the Pnyx, directly opposite the Propylaea, close by the westernmost gate of the pre-Persian city and the temple of Dionysus ἐν Λίμναις, that Pisistratus amplified and beautified into the famous Enneacrunus with its nine spouts. One of the springs, excavated and enlarged into caves along the right hand side of the boulevard as one ascends toward the Acropolis, may be the original Callirrhoe. Directly below the Assembly Hall on the Pynx a number of springs issued in the olden days. As the city grew in population, and the need of a more generous water supply increased, the city authorities (the tyrants) bored deeper into the veins and conducted the water through galleries cut through the live rock to the half dozen big rock-cut basins beside the highway. But even these numerous springs and tappings of the rock soon proved inadequate, and Pisistratus constructed a great aqueduct (still largely preserved), led through vast rock-cut and stone-built galleries, from the sources of the upper Ilissus to what was then the centre of the city about half way between the old Agora and the Acropolis gates. Much even of the sixth century piping is still preserved in these various tunnels.

Just below these reservoirs, at the end of the great aqueduct, he constructed his splendid fountainhead, a commodious spring-house with nine spouts pouring out a never-failing supply of excellent water.[1] From the nine spouts the fountain got its name Enneacrunus, but the older name Callirrhoe was never forgotten.

And there Dörpfeld has found sufficient remains of the old plant to establish beyond a reasonable doubt the exact location of the Enneacrunus. There we see the canals and water-mains, the reservoirs and, before the rock-wall of the Pynx, the scanty but indubitable remains of the fountain-house approached through a great open square 20 x 40 metres opening through an entryway ten metres wide from the street leading from the Agora to the Acropolis. Literary sources and archaeological discoveries are in complete harmony, save for the rare instances of late authorship (the Etymologicum Magnum is the earliest), in which the double meaning of Callirrhoe has led to confusion. The name Enneacrunus was transferred to the spring by the Ilissus after, in late Roman times, the old nine-spouted fountain-house was destroyed and the site built up with Roman buildings and the water piped off to the Roman market-place and the old associations with the name Enneacrunus forgotten. Thucydides locates the Enneacrunus near the Acropolis gates; and here Pausanias also finds it on his way from the Agora to the Acropolis (I 14, 1):

| | |
|---|---|
| πλησίον δέ ἔστι κρήνη, καλοῦσι δὲ αὐτὴν Ἐννεάκρουνον, οὕτω κοσμηθεῖσαν ὑπὸ Πεισιστράτου· φρέατα μὲν γὰρ καὶ διὰ πάσης τῆς πόλεώς ἔστι, πηγὴ δὲ αὕτη μόνη | near this [the Odeum by the Agora] is a spring; they call it the Enneacrunus; it was thus fitted out by Pisistratus. There are wells all over the city, but this is the only fountain |

Even as reconstructed, with the Pnyx springs concentrated in the one great fountain, Enneacrunus was in fact not the only spring in the city; there was the spring in the Asclepieum and another in the cave above the theatre, and there was the Clepsydra spring; the Callirrhoe spring at the Ilissus was not inside the pre-Persian nor even the Themistoclean

---

[1] εὔυδρον in the fragment of Polyzelus may mean "with good water" as well as "abounding in water." At any rate, the water of the Enneacrunus was excellent water.

city. There were also public hydrants in the city in Pausanias's day.[1] But the Enneacrunus *was the only* copious spring and *the only* public spring in the city.

A fragment from the Pytine of Cratinus may throw some light upon the question, though the poet's words, without any context to guide, may be open to a variety of interpretations (Frag. 186 K.):

| | |
|---|---|
| ἄναξ ᾽Απολλον, τῶν ἐπῶν τῶν ῥευμάτων. | oh Lord Apollo, what floods of words! |
| χαναχοῦσι πηγαί, δωδεκάκρουνον τὸ στόμα, | The fountains plash; his mouth is a fountain with twelve jets; |
| ᾽Ιλισσὸς ἐν φάρυγγι· τί ἂν εἴποιμ' ἔτι; | an Ilissus in his throat. What can I say more? |
| εἰ μὴ γὰρ ἐπιβύσει τις αὐτοῦ τὸ στόμα, | If some one does not shut off his mouth, |
| ἅπαντα ταῦτα κατακλύσει ποιήμασιν | he will deluge all this with his poetry |

The poet puts into the mouth of one of his characters a criticism of himself. The substance of it is that Cratinus talks too much—pours out floods of words. The "fountain with twelve jets" is obviously a play upon Pisistratus's "fountain with nine spouts"; Cratinus pours out a more voluminous flood than the Enneacrunus! The mention of the Ilissus in this connection is made to give aid and comfort to the supporters of the Ilissus–Callirrhoe theory of the Enneacrunus. But on the contrary; the Ilissus does not flow into the Callirrhoe; whereas the Ilissus (the upper Ilissus) does flow into Enneacrunus; and so the metaphor continues consistent. Again, no one could possibly "shut off" the mouth of Callirrhoe; and failure to shut it off would not deluge anything. But Enneacrunus could be shut off, and if not regulated it might deluge the whole region of the Marshes and doubtless often did! For that very reason they were the "Marshes." At Callirrhoe one fountain might "plash"; at Enneacrunus nine fountains plashed continuously.

A discussion of all the arguments adduced in the literature cited in the foot-note to page 127 would lead too far afield. Suffice it to say that Pausanias (with his orderly, systematic, topographical description), and Thucydides (rightly understood), and all the great weight of literary evidence, and the strikingly corroborative excavations convince me thoroughly that the Enneacrunus of our poets is the great fountain-house built by the tyrants about two hundred yards from the citadel gates at the foot of the Acropolis and the Pnyx hills. All possible claims for the Callirrhoe spring by the Ilissus as the Enneacrunus of Pisistratus must have vanished with the investigations and excavations of the Greek Archaeological Society at that place in 1893. Not a trace of any fountain-house or of any artificial changes about the spring could be discovered; the verdict pronounced by Skias[2] was that there never could have been a fountain-house or artificial transformation of the place.[3]

To return to the Lenaeum: the sacred enclosure contains the remains of buildings that in age range all the way from the sixth century B. C. to the second or third century A. D. The later buildings were erected after the early Greek buildings had long since fallen in ruin and become buried beneath more than two metres of accumulated débris. The early Greek structures include 1) a small temple of Bacchus in the southern angle of the triangle facing the probable entrance to the enclosure; 2) a large wine-press[4] in the north-west angle; and 3) a large, square altar in the centre of the temenos.

Not the least interesting feature of the sanctuary of "Dionysus in the Marshes" is the wine-press. It was the more sacred to Dionysus, because it was apparently the first public wine-press of the city.[5] The press-room proper, an irregular quadrangle of about 4.70 x 2.80 metres, has a concrete floor sloping sharply (0.25 metres) from every side to the south-east corner. At that point the grape-juice, as the grapes were trodden, flowed out through a round hole in the wall into the vat below in one of the lower rooms of the plant.

[1] Lyc. Leocr., 112; Thuc. VII 92, 2; Pollux VIII 113; C. I. A. III 196; cf. Judeich, *Topogr. v. Ath.*, Iwan Müller, *Hdb.* III 2, p. 186.

[2] Σκιᾶς, Πρακτικά 1893; ᾽Εφημερὶς ᾽Αρχαιολογική 1893.

[3] See also pp. 259 ff.

[4] Dionysus ἐν Λίμναις and Dionysus Ληναῖος are, in Athens, of course, identical. The Dionysium Lenaeum is the same as the Dionysium ἐν Λίμναις. The designation ἐν Λίμναις is due to the marshy nature of the location below the great nine-mouthed spring; the epithet Ληναῖος is correctly explained by the Scholiast to Ar. Ach. 201: διὰ τὸ πρῶτον ἐν τούτῳ τῷ τόπῳ ληνὸν τεθῆναι. The name clung because the wine-press was always there, and the festival was known as ὁ ἐπὶ Ληναίῳ ἀγών.

[5] See foot-note 4, above.

The Dionysium in the Marshes was not simply a sacred enclosure with a sacred old wine-press; it included a temple. The Scholiast to Aristophanes's Frogs (216) states categorically:

Λίμνη· τόπος ἱερὸς Διονύσου ἐν ᾧ
καὶ οἶκος καὶ νεὼς τοῦ θεοῦ. Καλ-
λίμαχος ἐν ῾Εκάλῃ· "Λιμναίῳ δὲ
χοροστάδας ἦγον ἑορτάς."

*Limne:* a place sacred to Dionysus, in which there is both a house and a temple of the god. Callimachus in the Hecale says: "And in honor of the Limnaean they celebrated festivals with choral dances."

The "house" may be the building with the wine-press; the "festival with choral dances" is the Festival of the Chytri mentioned in the text of Aristophanes; the temple is the structure in the southern corner of the precinct. It was a plain little building consisting only of cella and pronaos and without any colonnade; its foundations measure only 5.40 x 3.96 metres, including the pronaos. They are very ancient—older even than the times of Pisistratus.[1] The wine-press, the inscriptions (however late), the century-long connection with Bacchic rites prove that the temenos belonged to Dionysus. The location of it—between the Acropolis gate and the older market-place and close by the central fountain of the city— and its great antiquity bespeak the importance of the sanctuary. It is the centre of the scene celebrated in the chorus of the Frogs. The reality revealed to us by Dörpfeld's excavations is in perfect harmony with the testimony of the classical writers. Thucydides, though long misunderstood, now leads us naturally to this spot (II 15, 3–4):

τὸ δὲ πρὸ τούτου[2] ἡ ἀκρόπολις
[ἡ] νῦν οὖσα πόλις ἦν καὶ τὸ
ὑπ' αὐτὴν πρὸς νότον μάλιστα
τετραμμένον. τεκμήριον δέ·
τὰ γὰρ ἱερὰ ἐν αὐτῇ τῇ
ἀκροπόλει * * καὶ ἄλλων θεῶν
ἐστι, καὶ τὰ ἔξω πρὸς τοῦτο τὸ
μέρος τῆς πόλεως μᾶλλον ἵδρυται
τό τε τοῦ Διὸς ᾿Ολυμπίου καὶ τὸ
Πύθιον καὶ τὸ τῆς Γῆς καὶ τὸ τοῦ

before his[2] time what is now the Acropolis, with the quarters adjoining it toward the south mostly, was the city. Here is proof of the fact: the sanctuaries of * * and the rest of the gods are upon the Acropolis it- self; those that are outside were built well up toward this part of the city— the shrine of Olympian Zeus and the Pythium and the shrine of Mother Earth and that of

ἐν Λίμναις Διονύσου, ᾧ τὰ ἀρ-
χαιότερα Διονύσια τῇ δωδε-
κάτῃ ποιεῖται ἐν μηνὶ
᾿Ανθεστηριῶνι.... ἵδρυται
δὲ καὶ ἄλλα ἱερὰ ταύτῃ
ἀρχαῖα. καὶ τῇ κρήνῃ τῇ
νῦν μὲν τῶν τυράννων οὕτω
σκευασάντων ᾿Εννεακρούνῳ
καλουμένῃ, τὸ δὲ πάλαι
φανερῶν τῶν πηγῶν οὐσῶν
Καλλιρρόῃ ὠνομασμένῃ[3] ἐκείνῃ[4]
τε ἐγγὺς οὔσῃ τὰ πλείστου
ἄξια ἐχρῶντο, καὶ νῦν ἔτι
ἀπὸ τοῦ ἀρχαίου πρό τε γα-
μικῶν καὶ ἐς ἄλλα τῶν
ἱερῶν νομίζεται τῷ ὕδατι
χρῆσθαι

Dionysus in the Marshes, in whose honor the most ancient Dionysia are celebrated on the twelfth of the month of Anthesterion . . . and there are also other ancient sanctuaries built in this quarter. And the fountain now called Enneacrunus (for the tyrants remodeled it with "Nine Spouts" and gave it this name, whereas in the olden times it was called Callirrhoe[3], and its springs were uncovered) was used by them on all great occasions because it was near their abode;[4] and from antiquity even to this day, it is still customary to use the water for marriage rites and other religious ceremonies

[1] The style of early polygonal masonry, the absence of even a single step in the crepidoma, the quantities of potsherds found there with decorations in the geometric style—all point to the early sixth century B. C. or even to the seventh.

[2] Theseus's.

[3] Black-figured vases from the time of Pisistratus represent his new Enneacrunus with women drawing water from it but call it KALIPOE (or KALIPEKPENE). The new name had not yet become general when the vases were painted. See *Ath. Mitt.* XIII (1888), pp. 227–228; one of them is published by Gerhard, *Auserl. Vas.* IV 307, reproduced in Harrison and Verrall, *Mon. and Myth.*, p. 91.

[4] I prefer to retain the MS. reading ἐκείνῃ (= Acropolis) instead of the almost universally adopted emendation ἐκείνοι (= the people of those olden times); the meaning is not essentially different.

The location assigned to the Dionysium ἐν Λίμναις and to the Enneacrunus is (now that we have both before our eyes!) perfectly clear. And the Scholiast on this passage, with more accuracy than he has ever before been given credit for, says

Λίμναι· τόπος ἐν τῇ ἀκροπόλει τῶν Ἀθηνῶν | *Limnae:* a place on the Acropolis of Athens

The sanctuary now identified as the Dionysium in the Marshes is at the base of the western slope of the Acropolis hill; ἐν τῇ Ἀκροπόλει should, of course, naturally, though it does not necessarily, mean *upon the summit of the Acropolis*. And, allowing for some looseness of expression on the Scholiast's part, his statement is fairly correct: the four sanctuaries of which Thucydides speaks, including the Dionysus ἐν Λίμναις, must all have stood in close proximity to the great gate of the Pelargicum, which was essentially a part of the early πόλις, that is, of the Acropolis. The city fountain of the Πόλις was just before the gate; the Dionysium was close by the fountain. And there they stand in Dörpfeld's excavations. Up above them, nearer to the upper Acropolis, stood, in the topographical order named by Thucydides, the sanctuary of Gaea (beside that of Demeter Chloe),[1] the Pythium (the cave of Apollo Pythius),[2] and the Olympieum.[3]

Pausanias does not mention the temple of Dionysus ἐν Λίμναις—for the very good reason that it was buried under six feet of earth and débris and built over with the new guild-hall of the Iobacchi. Above the ruins of the archaic Lenaeum the votaries of Bacchus in Roman days had built a new but much smaller wine-press and a very large hall for the meetings of the Society of the Iobacchi. A long inscription (162 lines) preserved on a drum of one of the interior columns gives us in full the constitution and by-laws of this Bacchic fraternity.[4] The hall with its adjacent rooms[5] covered the greater part of the old temenos and extended even beyond it to the east. The official name of this new building, we learn from the inscription, was The Baccheum. This plant was altogether too modern to attract the attention of the antiquarian Pausanias for a moment. The fraternity, however, may well have been an ancient organization. The Iobacchean festival is named in a law inscribed on a pillar in the precinct of Dionysus ἐν Λίμναις in letters that time had almost effaced as early as the days of Demosthenes (?) (Apollodorus).[6] The Iobacchean festival would seem to have been connected with the Lenaean contests and the feast of the Chytri. From a fragment of Aristophanes's Old Age I would conjecture that the Iobacchi contributed to the fun of the celebration with a masquerade and that their masks and other paraphernalia were kept in their guild-hall (Ar. Γῆρ., Frag. 131 K.):

A. τίς ἂν φράσειε ποῦ 'στι τὸ Διονύσιον; | A. Who can tell me where the Dionysium is?
B. ὅπου τὰ μορμολυκεῖα προσκρεμάννυται; | B. Where the boo-boos are hung up?

The "boo-boos" are the masks in all their ugliness;[7] and between festivals they would be stored in the Iobacchic guild-house adjoining the temple of their god.[8] It may be the same Dionysium[9] to which Aristophanes refers in another fragment (Γηρυτ., Frag. 161 K.):

ἦσαν εὐθὺ τοῦ Διονυσίου | they went straight for the Dionysium

---

[1] Discussed on pp. 144 ff.

[2] Discussed on pp. 182 ff.

[3] Not yet excavated, but doubtless to be found just to the east of the Pythium and not far from the Anaceum, the shrine of the sons of Zeus. Strabo also (p. 404) refers to an Olympieum and a Pythium from which the "Pythiasts" watched looking toward Harma (near Phyle) for the divine signals of lightning; their observatory was "the hearth of Zeus of the Lightnings" ἐν τῷ τείνει [a portion of the ruined Pelargicum?] μεταξὺ τοῦ Πυθίου καὶ τοῦ Ὀλυμπίου. This Olympieum and this Pythium are not to be confused with the well known sanctuaries by those names consecrated by the house of Pisistratus near the Ilissus, south-east of the Acropolis; for that quarter was far from the gates of the old πόλις; those Pisistratic shrines lay outside of even the fifth century city walls, and Harma was not in sight from there. In harmony with Thucydides's testimony, Hesychius (ἐπὶ Ληναίῳ) and Isaeus (VIII 35) and others state explicitly that τὸ ἐν Λίμναις or τὸ Ληναῖον was ἐν ἄστει.

[4] Published and discussed by Wide, *Inschrift der Iobakchen, Ath. Mitt.* XIX (1894), pp. 248 ff.

[5] One of these rooms, the north-eastern, is proved by inscriptions to have been a sanctuary of Artemis Curotrophos.

[6] Dem. in Neaeram, LIX 103: ΟΡΚΟΣ ΓΕΡΑΙΡΩΝ· Ἁγιστεύω καὶ εἰμὶ καθαρὰ καὶ ἁγνὴ ἀπὸ τῶν ἄλλων τῶν οὐ καθαρευόντων καὶ ἀπ' ἀνδρὸς συνουσίας, καὶ τὰ θεοίνια καὶ τὰ ἰοβάκχεια γεραρῷ τῷ Διονύσῳ κατὰ τὰ πάτρια καὶ ἐν τοῖς καθήκουσι χρόνοις.

[7] μορμολυκεῖον... ἔστι προσωπεῖον ἐπίφοβον (*Et. Mag.* 590, 52); Schol. Ar. Pax 474: τὰ προσωπεῖα τὰ αἰσχρὰ μορμολυκεῖα, καὶ τὰ τραγικὰ καὶ τὰ κωμικά. Cf. also Ar. Ἀμφ., Frag. 31 K.: ἀφ' οὗ κωμῳδικὸν μορμολυκεῖον ἔγνων that is, "ever since I have been a comic playwright."

[8] Dionysus himself is sometimes called Ἰόβακχος (Hesych. *s. v.*; Planud. IV 289; Archil., Hephaest. 94; and others).

[9] Isaeus is more exact when he refers to this temple (VIII 35): τὸ ἐν Λίμναις Διονύσιον.

The extant walls show that the temple, in the southern corner of the precinct, was shut off from the rest of the temenos by a wall at the rear of the temple building. In this wall there was a doorway. The temple itself was probably accessible at stated hours or on stated days. The precinct behind the temple was open only once a year—at the festival of the Chytri—on the twelfth day of Anthesterion. This, we learn from the Oration against Neaera, ascribed doubtfully to Demosthenes (Or. LIX). The orator in describing the symbolic marriage of the wife of the King Archon of Athens to the god Dionysus[1] cites the law prescribing the qualifications of the "queen" and says of it (§ 100):

| | |
|---|---|
| καὶ τοῦτον τὸν νόμον γράψαντες | and this law they inscribed upon a slab |
| ἐν στήλῃ λιθίνῃ ἔστησαν ἐν τῷ ἱερῷ | of marble and set it up in the sanctuary |
| τοῦ Διονύσου παρὰ τὸν βωμὸν ἐν | of Dionysus against the altar in the |
| Λίμναις (καὶ αὕτη ἡ στήλη ἔτι καὶ | Marshes (and this slab is standing there |
| νῦν ἔστηκεν, ἀμυδροῖς γράμμασιν | even unto this day; though the Attic letters are |
| Ἀττικοῖς δηλοῦσα τὰ γεγραμμένα), | much effaced, the writing can still be read); |
| μαρτυρίαν ποιούμενος ὁ δῆμος | thus the people render testimony |
| ὑπὲρ τῆς αὐτοῦ εὐσεβείας πρὸς | to their piety toward |
| τὸν θεὸν καὶ παρακαταθήκην καταλείπων | the god and leave a sacred |
| τοῖς ἐπιγιγνομένοις ὅτι | trust to their posterity, that |
| ............... | . . . . . . |
| καὶ διὰ ταῦτα ἐν τῷ ἀρχαιοτάτῳ | and for this reason they set it up in the |
| ἱεροῦ τοῦ Διονύσου καὶ ἁγιωτάτῳ | most ancient and most hallowed shrine of |
| ἐν Λίμναις ἔστησαν, ἵνα μὴ | Dionysus in the Marshes, that not |
| πολλοὶ εἰδῶσι τὰ γεγραμμένα· | many might know what is written; |
| ἅπαξ γὰρ τοῦ ἐνιαυτοῦ ἑκάστου | for only once each year is the place |
| ἀνοίγεται, τῇ δωδεκάτῃ τοῦ | opened—namely, on the twelfth day of |
| Ἀνθεστηριῶνος μηνός. | the month of Anthesterion. |

The orator confirms various facts that we had already established: the sanctuary of Dionysus in the Marshes was (one of) the most ancient and most hallowed shrines of Athens; in it was an altar. We have seen both temple and altar within the sacred precinct. He adds that there was a law inscribed upon a marble slab and set up against the altar. And wonder of wonders! there upon the edge of the altar-base in Athens is the unmistakable double cutting for just such a pair of slabs as must have been used for the erection of the inscribed law.

The orator adds also that the inscription could be seen by the general public (οἱ πολλοί) but once a year—on the twelfth of Anthesterion; that is, at the Feast of the Chytri, the Iobacchea, the Anthesteria. And there is the wall separating the temple proper from the rest of the temenos, and in the wall a door that could be opened on such especial occasions for the people and daily for the priestess and her fourteen attendants in the performance of their regular temple duties.

Comic poet, historian, orator, archaeological exploration all unite in clearing up a most interesting but long vexing problem, the sanctuary of Dionysus ἐν Λίμναις.

## 15. THE CABIRIUM IN LEMNOS

But for the unkindness of Fate that has robbed us of all but a very small portion of the world's one-time wealth of Greek tragedy, we might know much more of the Cabiri and their most celebrated sanctuaries than we do. Sophocles wrote a play entitled *The Lemnian Women*, dealing with that episode in the story of the Argonauts of which the scene is laid in Lemnos. Unhappily, there are but a scant half dozen lines of it preserved, and they tell us nothing to help us here. From the Cabiri of Aeschylus we have even less. From the title we may infer that the chorus may have been composed of Cabiri, and the comment of Athenaeus may, perhaps, imply that the Cabiri were intimate members of the Bacchic circle (Ath. X 428 F):

[1] This ceremony took place in the Bucolium near the Prytaneum, which was near the market-place and close by the Dionysium ἐν Λίμναις. Cf. Arist. Const. of Ath. 3.

ALTAR OF DIONYSUS IN THE MARSHES

τὸν Αἰσχύλον ἐγὼ φαίην ἂν τοῦτο
διαμαρτάνειν· πρῶτος γὰρ ἐκεῖνος,
καὶ οὐχ ὡς ἔνιοί φασιν Εὐριπίδης,
προσήγαγε τὴν τῶν μεθυόντων ὄψιν
εἰς τραγῳδίαν. ἐν γὰρ τοῖς Καβείροις
εἰσάγει τοὺς περὶ Ἰάσωνα μεθύοντας

it was Aeschylus, I should say, that was guilty
of this fault; for he, and not Euripides,
as some say, was the first to
introduce into tragedy the spectacle of
drunken men. For in the Cabiri he
brings on Jason and his companions drunk.

In one of the two pitiful fragments left to us (96 N.[1]) "pitchers for neither wine nor water
are to be left to the wealthy halls." But not a ray of light is thrown by the fragments of
either Aeschylus or Sophocles upon the shrine of the Cabiri or the nature of the gods themselves.

What the Cabiri were is another of the mysteries never betrayed by any of the countless
initiates, but guarded so well, that we are as completely in the dark as were the profanest
of the *volgus profanum* in antiquity. Many modern scholars—Karl Ottfried Müller, Welcker,
Lobeck, and others—have set forth various theories only to be demolished by some one else.
Even Goethe gave them more than a passing glance in his classical Walpurgisnacht (the
Sirens sing):

> Was denken sie zu vollführen
> Im Reiche der hohen Kabiren?
> Sind Götter wundersam eigen,
> Die sich immerfort selbst erzeugen,
> Und niemals wissen was sie sind.

Neither did any one else! but for all that, they are brought in (Nereids and Tritons sing):

> Wir bringen die Kabiren
> Ein friedlich Fest zu führen;
> Denn wo sie heilig walten,
> Neptun wird freundlich schalten.

And when they pass, Homunculus, with a thrust at the philologists, remarks:

> Die Ungestalten seh' ich an
> Als irdenschlechte Töpfe,
> Nun stossen sich die Weisen dran
> Und brechen harte Köpfe.

And many "hard heads" have been broken in the attempt to get behind the curtain. Clear
at least it is that the Cabiri are not Greek. They are Phoenician; the name is obviously
derived from the root כָּבַר, "mighty." They are, therefore, called μεγάλοι θεοί or ἰσχυροὶ
θεοί or δυνατοὶ θεοί. The earliest trace we have of them is on the island of Lemnos, but they
are altogether un-Greek. As Phoenician deities, they must have been imported even here;
but Strabo, quoting Acusilaus of Argos and Pherecydes of Leros,[2] makes them out to be
the grandsons of Hephaestus and Cabiro. They are, according to these authorities, three
in number, though the numerous inscriptions and at least one vase-painting from the Theban
Cabirium know of only one Cabirus and his son.[3] Wherever we find them in the Greek
world, they become, as often happens upon the importation of foreign gods, subordinated
in some way to the chief deity of the land. As in Lemnos they were subordinated to son-
ship to Hephaestus, so in Samothrace they were brought into association with Hermes;
and at Thebes they fell naturally into the train of Dionysus.[4] Nonnus goes so far as to

---

[1] μήτε κρωσσοὺς
μήτε οἰνηροὺς μήθ' ὑδρηλοὺς
λιπεῖν ἀφνεοῖσι δόμοισιν

which may also mean: "and pitchers neither of water nor of wine shall fail the wealthy halls." And from this
fragment Lobeck, Aglaophamus, pp. 1207 ff., sees in the Cabiri friendly spirits that promise rich crops of
fruits and grain for the coming harvest; to him, then, they are not Bacchic deities but favoring, protecting
spirits of the island of Lemnos.

[2] Strabo X p. 472, 21.

[3] The Schol. Ap. Rh. Argon. A 917 may have reference to the Κάβειρος and the Παῖς: οἱ δὲ δύο εἶναι τοὺς
Καβείρους φασὶ πρότερον, πρεσβύτερον μὲν Δία, νεώτερον δὲ Διόνυσον. Both Acusilaus and Pherecydes know of three
Cabiri and three Cabirid nymphs. The sailor's prayer, on the other hand, (Anthol. Pal. VI 245) knows only
one Cabirus, like the god of the Boeotian sanctuary. One Cabirus appears also in the late stage of the
mysteries in which they reappear in Thessalonica; upon coins of this city the Cabirus is a youthful Hephaestus.

[4] On one of the most striking vase-paintings from the sanctuary near Thebes a figure inscribed ΚΑΒΙΡΟΣ
is a perfect Dionysus type and would with absolute assurance be called Dionysus, were it not for the name
inscribed above him. Many of the vases from this temple are decorated with Satyrs, Maenads, Sileni, ivy
and grape ornaments—all sorts of people and things that belong characteristically to the Bacchic circle.

name two Cabiri, Alcon and Eurymedon of Lemnos,[1] sons of Hephaestus and Cabiro, and have them accompany Dionysus on his expedition to India.[2]

The worship of Cabirus or the Cabiri was, as we have seen, deeply mystical; it was probably closely akin to the mysteries of Eleusis; for in Attica it was completely absorbed in the Eleusinian cult. It is doubtful whether Aeschylus or Sophocles would or could have given us any satisfying information about this mysterious religious phenomenon, if their tragedies dealing somewhat with it were preserved. Sophocles's Philoctetes, with its scene laid in Lemnos, certainly does not help us at all; but Accius's Philoctetes would serve us better, for the one considerable fragment we possess gives us nearly all we know of the Lemnian Cabiri worship (Acc. [Phil. II] 525–536 R.[3] ):

> Lemnia praesto
> litora rara, et celsa Cabirum
> delubra tenes, mysteria quae
> pristina castis concepta sacris
>
>    * * *
>
> Volcania < iam > templa sub ipsis
> collibus, in quos delatus locos
> dicitur alto ab limine caeli
>
>    * * *
>
> Nemus expirante vapore vides,
> unde ignis cluet mortalibus clam
> divisus: eum dictus Prometheus
> clepsisse dolo poenasque Iovi
> fato expendisse supremo

Would we had the Greek tragedy that the Roman poet made the basis of his Latin play! But even from the few fragments of Accius's drama we learn that the Cabirium of Lemnos stood upon a lofty height above the seashore; that it was not far from the great temple of Hephaestus at the foot of the hills upon which he struck when he was hurled down from heaven; during the nine days of the celebration of the Cabiric mysteries all fires were extinguished upon the island and at the end rekindled with new fire brought over from the Cabirium in Delos.[3]

From Lemnos the Cabiri cult seems to have passed on to Samothrace, which became the chief centre of their worship in Hellenistic and Roman times.[4] It was closely bound up with the worship of Demeter here, and in that association it may easily have come to Attica and so on to Boeotia.

The Cabirian mysteries seem to have been connected with the greater mysteries of Eleusis. This is obvious from the association of Cabirus with Dionysus, on the one hand, and with Demeter and Cora, on the other. The Cabirus of Thebes is closely related to Dionysus; while only a little way from the Boeotian Cabirium, above the main highway from Thebes to Onchestus, stood a sacred grove of Demeter Cabiria[5] and Cora. And in the pediment group of the Samothracian Cabirium Demeter was represented seeking for her lost child.[6] At all events the worship of the Cabiri is closely associated in Greece with the worship of the chthonic deities; as at Eleusis the central feature of the mysteries was the future life of man, so in the worship of the Cabiri the problem seems to have been the question of the origin of man.[7]

The mysteries of the Cabiri and their nature lay buried for more than a millennium at the Cabirium in Samothrace, at the Cabirium near Thebes, and at the Cabirium in Lemnos. They were buried too deep for even the archaeologist's spade to bring them to the light.

---

[1] Mnaseas of Patara (Schol. Ap. Rh. Argon. A 917) (cf. Et. Mag. 482, 27) names Axiocersus (= Hades) and Casmilus (= Hermes) as two of the Cabiri, Axiocersa (= Persephone) and Axieros (= Demeter) as two of the Cabirid nymphs.

[2] Dionysiaca XIV 17 ff.; XXIV 93 ff.; XXVII 120 ff., 327 ff.; in XIX 113 he assigns them to Samothrace instead of Lemnos.

[3] Cf. Philostr. Heroic. 740.

[4] Even in the fifth century, the mysteries of Samothrace were famous; cf. Ar. Pax 277–278.

[5] Paus. IX 25, 5: σταδίους δὲ αὐτόθεν [from the Neïstan Gate] πέντε προελθόντι καὶ εἴκοσι Δήμητρος Καβειρίας καὶ Κόρης ἐστὶν ἄλσος· ἐσελθεῖν δὲ τοῖς τελεσθεῖσιν ἔστι. This was probably the place of the Cabiric mysteries and not the temple five stadia to the west. The latter was of secondary importance.

[6] Conze, *Unters. auf Samothr.* I Taf. 42 (p. 26).

[7] This seems also to be the meaning of the πρωτόλαος of the vase-painting from the Cabirium of Thebes.

The excavations at Samothrace were very disappointing; the excavations conducted by the German Archaeological Institute at the Cabirium about four miles west of Thebes brought to light a curious temple, a vast number of fragments of vases and votive offerings, and many inscriptions. The temple underwent several rebuildings. Of the earliest temple, dating from the sixth or fifth century, only a scanty remnant of a polygonal apse is left. The next rebuilding dates from Macedonian times. In it we have a Greek temple, altogether unique in Greek architecture: it is an Ionic prostylos tetra-stylos, with a pronaos, a vestibule, a cella, and an opisthodomos. From the portico one passed through a spacious portal down one step into a large fore-cella, and from this by a second wide door down another step into a still larger inner cella where stood (or, more probably, reclined) the cultus statue. The opisthodome, as in the Parthenon, was not accessible from the cella; it was entered by a door on either side of the temple.

In Roman times the temple was again rebuilt. The soft stone introduced into the foundations of the Macedonian building may even then have begun to crumble—it crumbles easily in one's hands to-day—and the Roman architect simply cased in the old foundations with the new. At the same time he also eliminated the fore-cella and made of the two older rooms a new cella nearly twice as large as the old. Otherwise the old plan is kept.

The opisthodome contains a double sacrificial pit, the two chambers separated by a common wall. Into these (at least, into the southern compartment, which was found full of thigh bones) was thrown the flesh of beasts. In spite of the lid that covered both halves of the pit, the stench from the decaying meat must have been frightful, but it rose into the free air of heaven; for, as the weaker walls about this room show, the opisthodome probably never had a roof. The same sort of sacrificial pit is found also at the Cabirium of Samothrace and seems to have been a characteristic feature of Cabiric worship.[1]

Besides the four great centres of Cabiri worship—Delos, Lemnos, Samothrace, Boeotia —of which we know a little, there were more or less famous Cabiria also in Imbros, Thasos, Troas, Teos, Ephesus, Syros, Cythnos, Miletus, Macedon, and other places. But as none of them are mentioned in the dramatic poets, save Lemnos and Samothrace alone, and as none of the others shed any real light upon the problem in hand, we may pass them by.[2]

### 16. Sanctuaries of Demeter and Cora

The worship of Demeter was wide-spread throughout the entire Greek world. She had shrines in almost every quarter. In Attica alone we find eight or nine temples in her honor, four or five in Athens,[3] and four near by.[4] Mother Earth is not only the giver of food and clothing and shelter; she is also the upholder of the state, the giver of laws and all that makes for higher civilization among men. In this latter activity she was revered as Demeter Thesmophoros; she and Cora are known and addressed as the two Thesmophoro;[5] and the temples to this specific Demeter and Cora are called Thesmophorea; and in her honor, and her daughter's, the great festival of the women, the Thesmophoria, was celebrated annually on the eleventh to the thirteenth[6] of Pyanepsion.

#### a. *The Thesmophoreum in Athens*

For nearly all that we know of the Thesmophoreum in Athens we are indebted to Aristophanes. Two passages from the Thesmophoriazusae give us practically all the

---

[1] For Pausanias's full account of the Boeotian Cabiri and the little that he knew of their mystic cult see his Descr. Graec. IX 25, 2–26, 1. According to Pausanias the Cabiri were the only inhabitants of Boeotia, and to them Demeter revealed herself and her mysteries.

[2] The principal recent literature is: Lobeck, *Aglaophamus;* Conze, *Unters. auf Samothrake;* Judeich (topography), Dörpfeld (architecture), Winnefeld (vases), Wolters (terracottas), and Szanto (inscriptions), *Das Kabirenheiligtum bei Theben, Ath. Mitt.* XIII (1888) and XV (1890); Kern, *die Böotischen Kabiren, Hermes* XXV (1890); Bloch, in Roscher, *Myth. Lex., s. v. Megaloi Theoi,* II Sp. 2522 ff.; Preller-Robert, *Griech. Myth.;* Rubensohn, *Mysterienheiligtümer.*

[3] Paus. I 2, 4; 13, 8; 14, 1; 22, 3; the Eleusinium of I 14, 3 is almost certainly not identical with the temple of Demeter mentioned in § 1, and its name suggests Demeter and Cora.

[4] Paus. I 1, 4; 31, 1 (*bis*); 37, 2.

[5] Θεσμοφόρω, Ar. Thes. 282; 297.

[6] From Ar. Thes. 80 it would seem, however, that the celebration lasted five days: ἐπεὶ τρίτη 'στι Θεσμοφορίων ἡ μέση. He probably includes the days of purification and preparation.

information we have; the play represents the women in council at the celebration of their great festival. The signal for their gathering is raised at the Thesmophoreum (Ar. Thes. 277–278):

| | |
|---|---|
| τὸ τῆς ἐκκλησίας<br>σημεῖον ἐν τῷ Θεσμοφορείῳ φαίνεται | we can see the signal for the<br>assembly at the Thesmophoreum |

The signal that Euripides saw would seem to have been the blazing torches on the hilltop by the temple (Ar. Thes. 280–281):

| | |
|---|---|
| θᾶσαι καομένων τῶν λαμπάδων<br>ὅσον τὸ χρῆμ' ἀνέρχεθ' ὑπὸ τῆς λιγνύος | look what a glare goes up from the<br>murky flame as the torches blaze |

The hilltop upon or near which the temple stood was the Pnyx. This also we learn from Aristophanes (Thes. 655–658):

| | |
|---|---|
| ἡμᾶς τοίνυν μετὰ τοῦτ' ἤδη τὰς λαμπάδας ἀψα-<br>μένας χρὴ | after this, therefore, we must light our torches at<br>once and |
| ξυζωσαμένας εὖ κἀνδρείως τῶν θ' ἱματίων<br>ἀποδύσας | gird up well our loins and manfully, throw off<br>our wraps, |
| ζητεῖν εἴ που κάλλος ἀνὴρ ἀνελήλυθε καὶ<br>περιθρέξαι | and see if haply another man has come up here,<br>and explore |
| τὴν Πύκνα πᾶσαν καὶ τὰς σκηνὰς καὶ τὰς<br>διόδους διαθρῆσαι | the entire Pnyx, and search the booths and pas-<br>sage-ways |

The women seem to have taken complete possession not only of the temple precincts but of the entire Pnyx hill for their celebration and to have camped out there in booths for the duration of the festival; and as the crowds were great, one booth or tent had to accommodate more than one woman (Ar. Thes. 624):

| | |
|---|---|
| καὶ τίς σοὐστὶ συσκηνήτρια; | and who is your tent-mate? |

But the important thing for our present problem is that the temple was upon the Pnyx. It was high up upon the hilltop, too. Aristophanes seems to imply as much in ἀνελήλυθε (l. 657)[1] "has come up"; but the Scholiast on line 585 states the fact explicitly:

| | |
|---|---|
| ἐν ὑψηλῷ γὰρ κεῖται τὸ Θεσμοφόριον | for the Thesmophoreum is high up |

Only once more in the play does the name Thesmophoreum occur (880):

| | |
|---|---|
| Θεσμοφόρειον τουτογί | this here is the Thesmophoreum |

And once he alludes to it as the "sanctuary" (1045–1046):

| | |
|---|---|
| ἐς τόδ' ἀνέπεμψεν<br>ἱερόν | he sent me up to this<br>sanctuary |

by which the poet means the sacred enclosure about the temple where the women celebrated the festival of the Thesmophoria. Once also in high tragic tone Aristophanes makes Euripides repeat a line from the Helena (68) and call the temple "castle-halls" (Thes. 871):

| | |
|---|---|
| τίς τῶνδ' ἐρυμνῶν δωμάτων ἔχει κράτος; | who wields the power in these castle-halls? |

The massive retaining walls of the Pnyx hill, suggestive of the huge Mycenaean masonry of the earlier days, would justify Aristophanes's Euripides-Menelaus in talking about the "castle-halls." Doubtless one of the panels in the proscenium contained a picture of that great wall which excites our wonder to this day.

Pausanias mentions the temple but gives us no information beyond its mere existence in that general locality. After mentioning the Odeum (at the base of the Areopagus and near the older Agora) and the Enneacrunus, he goes on to say (I 14, 1):

| | |
|---|---|
| ναοὶ δὲ ὑπὲρ τὴν κρήνην ὁ<br>μὲν Δήμητρος πεποίηται<br>καὶ Κόρης, ἐν δὲ τῷ Τριπτολέμου<br>κείμενόν ἐστιν ἄγαλμα | above the spring stand temples,<br>the one to Demeter<br>and Cora; in the other, to Trip-<br>tolemus, is set a statue |

[1] Cf. also lines 585; 623; 893.

THE TEMPLE OF THE MYSTERIES AT ELEUSIS

"Above the Enneacrunus" obviously means up upon the Pnyx hill. There, somewhere upon the upper reaches of the Pnyx, the two temples must have stood. Dörpfeld searched and excavated diligently but could find not the slightest trace of either temple. There are many cuttings in the rock of the hill but traces of only one building, utterly ruined, that could possibly be our temple of the Thesmophoros: upon the rock-cut terrace, artificially leveled off, immediately above the Assembly Hall of the Pnyx and directly southeast of the Bema, are cuttings in the rocky surface that may have served as the footings for a temple. Lolling[1] long ago claimed the site for the sanctuary of Heracles Alexikakos in Melite; Judeich[2] admits the possibility of such identification. But it exactly fits all the data we possess in regard to the Thesmophoreum: it is on the Hill of the Pnyx, close by the Assembly Hall; it is high up upon the hill; it is in an elevated and open spot from which the blazing torches could easily be seen from every direction; there is plenty of space on and about this terrace for the encampment of the women celebrating the festival of the Thesmophoria. It is, therefore, at least possible that this is the long sought site of the Thesmophoreum, and that this ruined sanctuary, with its altar, is what we have left of a temple of Demeter and Cora Thesmophoro.

### b. *Sanctuary of Demeter and Cora at Eleusis*

One spot in Attica, holy beyond all others, was Eleusis with its sacred mysteries, its altars, and its temples. It would be reasonable to expect that the tragic poets of Athens would lend us here considerable aid. But we are doomed to disappointment; there is but little, even in the way of allusion, however remote, in the surviving dramas.

A plurality of temples of Demeter at Eleusis seems to be mentioned by Euripides (Sup. 1–2):

| | |
|---|---|
| Δήμητερ ἑστιοῦχ' Ἐλευσῖνος χθονὸς | Demeter, that keepest the hearth of our Eleusis land, |
| τῆσδ', οἵ τε ναοὺς ἔχετε πρόσπολοι θεᾶς | and ye attendants of the goddess who her temples keep |

The various "temples" may mean the different parts of the great complex that we know as the Telesterium, or Euripides's plural form may include with the sanctuary of Demeter and Cora also the familiar temple of Artemis Propylaea, so-called, the Sanctuary of Dionysus, the sanctuary of Pluto, and other lesser shrines connected with the worship of the chthonic deities at Eleusis. The former alternative is the more probable one. In line 88 Demeter's sanctuary is called ἀνάκτορα "royal palace"—plural because of its various apartments:

| | |
|---|---|
| τῶνδ' ἀνακτόρων ἄπο ἠχοῦς ἰούσης | as from these royal rooms the sound rang out |

It is the common sanctuary, moreover, of Demeter and Persephone; Cora has her share in the temple, or temples (Eur. Sup. 271) (the Chorus to Aethra):

| | |
|---|---|
| βᾶθι, τάλαιν', ἱερῶν δαπέδων ἄπο Περσεφονείας | come, poor suppliant, from Persephone's holy floors |

The "temples" and the "royal rooms" include the temple proper and the Telesterium, the great "hall of initiation" built by Ictinus, the architect of the Parthenon and of the temple of Apollo at Bassae. Even the ruins of the later masterpiece of the great architect at Eleusis are most imposing—a huge quadrangle 178 x 170 feet, with its forty-two columns that once supported an upper story, and Philon's magnificent portico overlooking the town and the bay and the island of Salamis beyond. Strabo says[3] that it was big enough to accommodate "the whole theatre crowd," and Sophocles says practically the same thing (Ant. 1120–1121):

| | |
|---|---|
| παγχοίνοις Ἐλευσινίας Δηοῦς ἐν κόλποις | in the all-receiving vales of Eleusinian Deo |

[1] *Topogr. v. Ath.* p. 334.
[2] *Topogr. v. Ath.* p. 353.
[3] IX 1, 12 (p. 395): ὁ μυστικὸς σηκός.... ὄχλον θεάτρου δέξασθαι δυνάμενος.

We may infer from Plutarch's account that the upper story contained the sanctuary proper of Demeter and Cora and we may be sure that the lower story was the hall of initiation, the μυστοδόχος δόμος of Aristophanes's Clouds (302–309):

| | |
|---|---|
| οὗ σέβας ἀρρήτων ἱερῶν, ἵνα | where reverence is paid to sacred mysteries; where |
| μυστοδόχος δόμος | the hall that receives the initiated |
| ἐν τελεταῖς ἁγίαις ἀναδείκνυται, | is thrown wide open at the holy rites; |
| οὐρανίοις τε θεοῖς δωρήματα, | and where there are gifts for the gods of heaven |
| ναοὶ θ' ὑψερεφεῖς καὶ ἀγάλματα, | and high-roofed temples and statues |
| καὶ πρόσοδοι μακάρων ἱερώτατοι, | and most holy processions of the blest |
| εὐστέφανοί τε θεῶν θυσίαι θαλίαι τε | and sacrifices to the gods and festivals with goodly garlands |

Ictinus's splendid temple was new when Aristophanes brought out the Clouds; its praises were probably on every tongue; but that is all the contemporary poet may venture to say about it—festivals, processions, high-roofed temples, sculptures (and these may apply just as well to Athens itself), and the hall that receives the initiated, and the sacred mysteries.

Plutarch's account of the building is as follows (Per. XIII 3–4):

| | |
|---|---|
| τὸ δ' ἐν Ἐλευσῖνι τελεστήριον | and the Telesterium at Eleusis |
| ἤρξατο μὲν Κόροιβος οἰκοδο- | Coroebus began to build, |
| μεῖν, καὶ τοὺς ἐπ' ἐδάφους κί- | and he put in place the columns |
| ονας ἔθηκεν οὗτος καὶ τοῖς ἐπι- | on the ground floor and joined their |
| στυλίοις ἐπέζευξεν· ἀποθα- | capitals with architraves. |
| νόντος δὲ τούτου Μεταγένης | And when he died, Metagenes |
| ὁ Ξυπέτιος τὸ διάζωμα καὶ | of Xypete erected, above, the frieze |
| τοὺς ἄνω κίονας ἐπέστησε· | and the columns of the upper story. |
| τὸ δ' ὀπαῖον ἐπὶ τοῦ ἀνα- | And Xenocles of Cholargus |
| κτόρου Ξενοκλῆς ὁ Χο- | crowned the palace |
| λαργεὺς ἐκορύφωσε | with the roof |

Plutarch's words make it clear that whereas Ictinus was the designer of the whole, the architects who carried out his plans in the actual erection of the building were successively Coroebus (who completed the lower story with its massive pillars and columns), Metagenes (who erected the upper story, the temple proper, with its peristyle and interior columns), and Xenocles (who executed Ictinus's plans of the very difficult roof).[1]

The centre of the scene in the Suppliants is the great temple of Eleusis; before it is the great altar[2]—also common to Demeter and Persephone (ll. 33–34):

| | |
|---|---|
| μένω πρὸς ἁγναῖς ἐσχάραις δυοῖν θεαῖν; | I hold my place at the holy hearths of the goddesses twain, |
| Κόρης τε καὶ Δήμητρος | —Demeter's and Cora's |

About it are Aethra and the Argive widows as suppliants, while at its doors sits Adrastus overwhelmed with sorrow (104):

| | |
|---|---|
| τίς δ' ὁ στενάζων οἰκτρὸν ἐν πύλαις ὅδε; | who is that making piteous lament at the gates? |

Though the temple, so familiar to every Athenian, was the centre of this sanctuary, Euripides tells us very little about it. True to the evidence of the scanty remains of the Eleusinian temple, he does indicate that it was built into and against a cliff that rose above it (Sup. 980–989):

[1] Strabo and Vitruvius both name Ictinus alone as architect of the Telesterium. The three named by Plutarch probably stand in the same relation to Ictinus in the erection of this building as Callicrates in the building of the Parthenon.

[2] In verse 1, Demeter's altar is ἑστία; in 33 and 290 it is ἐσχάραι; in 65 it is θυμέλαι; in 93 it is βωμός: μητέρα γεραιὰν βωμίαν ἐφημένην [ὁρῶ]; see the discussion of these words, pp. 66–71. Here also there is no real difference in the meaning of the various words: βωμός is the common, every-day prose word for "altar"; θυμέλη is the poetic word for "the place of sacrifice" (θύω), the "altar." ἑστία and ἐσχάρα mean primarily "hearth," the former being the common, prose word; the latter, more poetical. All four may be, and are throughout the Suppliants of Euripides, used of an altar of burnt sacrifice. The plural forms are probably all (like altaria) plurals of the component parts.

The excavations at Elsusis brought to light no altar at all.

καὶ μὴν θαλάμας τάσδ' ἐσορῶ δὴ
Καπανέως ἤδη τύμβον θ' ἱερὸν

......

τί ποτ' αἰθερίαν ἔστηκε πέτραν

ἢ τῶνδε δόμων ὑπερακρίζει,
τήνδ' ἐμβαίνουσα κέλευθον;

|  |  |
|---|---|
|  | and lo! now I look upon yon cells and |
|  | the hallowed pyre of Capaneus |
|  | . . . . . . . |
|  | What meaneth the stand she hath taken upon the |
|  | towering rock |
|  | that overhangs this building, and why |
|  | hath she trodden this path? |

Evadne has climbed up above the proscenium building and to the astonished chorus and spectators she appears upon the cliff above the temple.[1]  Upon the entrance of her father, Iphis, she thus describes her position herself, poised upon the cliff above the temple (Eur. Sup. 1045–1047):

ἤδ' ἐγὼ πέτρας ἔπι
ὄρνις τις ὡσεὶ Καπανέως ὑπὲρ πυρᾶς
δύστηνον αἰώρημα κουφίζω, πάτερ

|  |  |
|---|---|
|  | here, father, upon the cliff, aloft, in my |
|  | woe, I am lightly perched, like a bird, |
|  | above the pyre of Capaneus |

The temples, we are further told, were in a sacred enclosure (Eur. Sup. 29–30):

ἐκ δόμων ἐλθοῦσ' ἐμῶν
πρὸς τόνδε σηκόν

|  |  |
|---|---|
|  | from my home I have come |
|  | to this sacred enclosure |

But we are not told whether the enclosure was large or small, whether it contained anything besides the shrines of Demeter and Cora, or how it was located.  Aethra is the speaker of the prolog; she has come from her home to Eleusis; her home is, of course, in Athens; but the manner of her words suggests but a step.  So little seriously does Euripides sometimes interest himself in the question of topography.

Hippolytus, son of Theseus, comes over from Troezen to Athens, at the time of the festival, to be initiated into the Eleusinian mysteries (Eur. Hip. 24–27):

ἐλθόντα γάρ νιν Πιτθέως ποτ' ἐκ δόμων

σεμνῶν ἐς ὄψιν καὶ τέλη μυστηρίων
Πανδίονος γῆν, πατρὸς εὐγενὴς δάμαρ
ἰδοῦσα Φαίδρα...

|  |  |
|---|---|
|  | for Phaedra, his father's high-born queen, saw |
|  | him when once he came |
|  | from Pittheus's halls to Pandion's |
|  | land to witness the awful mys- |
|  | teries and to be initiated in them . . . |

The lines contain nothing but a commonplace, familiar to every Athenian.  Even less is included in another passage of Euripides, mentioning the mysteries (Sup. 173):

πρεσβεύματ' οὐ Δήμητρος εἰς μυστήρια  |  no missions to Demeter's mysteries

(*ibid.* 470[2]):

λύσαντα σεμνὰ στεμμάτων μυστήρια  |  free from wreaths the sacred mysteries

Sophocles adds a little to the praise of the mysteries; the chorus in the Oedipus at Colonus yearn for the scenes they loved at Pytho or Eleusis with its secret rites (O. C. 1048–1052):

ἢ πρὸς Πυθίαις
ἢ λαμπάσιν ἀκταῖς,
οὖ πότνιαι σεμνὰ τιθηνοῦνται τέλη
θνατοῖσιν, ὧν καὶ χρυσέα

κλὴς ἐπὶ γλώσσᾳ βέβηκε προσπόλων
                                    Εὐμολπιδῶν

|  |  |
|---|---|
|  | either at the Pythian shrines |
|  | or at the torch-lit strand |
|  | where the awful goddesses cherish dread rites |
|  | for mortals, even for those upon whose lips the |
|  | golden |
|  | key of the ministering Eumolpids is set |

Here is allusion to the torch-light procession that moved at the sacred season from Athens over the Sacred Way to Eleusis; to the mysteries with their unfathomable secrets; perhaps the golden key of the Eumolpids played an actual part in the symbolic sealing of the secrets.

Few things were too high and holy for Aristophanes's irreverent mockery.  The rollicking fun and boisterous horse-play of the Frogs gives way to lofty strains of reverence and deep religious feeling almost immediately with the entrance of the Chorus of the Mystae.  And in the very first couplet in the ἀγών "the contest" between Euripides and Aeschylus, Aeschylus,

---

[1] For a full discussion of the stage-setting of this scene see pp. 306 ff.
[2] Cf. Soph. Inc. Frag. 736 N.:
            σεμνὰ τῆς σῆς παρθένου μυστήρια.

himself born at Eleusis[1] and an initiate in the mysteries, utters a prayer that in the contest before him he may prove himself worthy of Demeter's sacred mysteries (Ar. Ran. 886–887):

| | |
|---|---|
| Δήμητερ ἡ θρέψασα τὴν ἐμὴν φρένα, | Demeter, thou that didst nurture my soul, |
| εἶναί με τῶν σῶν ἄξιον μυστηρίων | grant that I prove worthy of thy mysteries |

## 17. SANCTUARIES OF THE EUMENIDES

### (WITH DEMETER EUCHLOUS AND DEMETER CHLOE)

### a. *The Areopagus Shrine*

The great cave, facing toward the northeast, just below the summit of Ares's Hill in Athens, and much ruined by an earthquake which shook down a great mass of overhanging rock in modern times, has always been accepted unanimously as the "Cave of the Furies." Euripides locates the site accurately (El. 1270–1272):

| | |
|---|---|
| δειναὶ μὲν οὖν θεαὶ τῷδ' ἄχει πεπληγμέναι | and the Dread Goddesses, stricken with grief at this |
| πάγον παρ' αὐτὸν χάσμα δύσονται χθονός, | shall pass into a cleft of the earth by the Hill itself, |
| σεμνὸν βροτοῖσιν εὐσεβὲς χρηστήριον | an awful place of oracle revered by men |

The trial is to take place upon the Hill of Ares; the Erinyes are to pass directly from the tribunal into the chasm right there in the hill (Eur. I. T. 969):

| | |
|---|---|
| ψῆφον παρ' αὐτὴν ἱερὸν ὡρίσαντ' ἔχειν | they consented to have a shrine right at the voting place |

Athenian tradition has this locality assigned to the "Dread Goddesses" as a habitation by Athena herself at the time of the trial of Orestes for the murder of his mother.[2] The appeasing of the wrath of these "children of Night"[3] against Athena and her people on account of the verdict in favor of the matricide, with the transformation of the Erinyes, the implacable pursuers, the avengers of blood, into the Eumenides, the kindly hearted ones, forms an essential part of the dénouement of the Eumenides of Aeschylus. It is Pallas herself, the divine embodiment of Cecrops's folk, that bestows upon her land the eternal blessing[4] of the favor of the dread goddesses who turn men's hearts, through fear, to righteousness (Ae. Eum. 926–928):

| | |
|---|---|
| τάδ' ἐγὼ προφρόνως τοῖσδε πολίταις | this is what I do in care for my citizens, |
| πράσσω, μεγάλας καὶ δυσαρέστους | housing in my city here these powers |
| δαίμονας αὐτοῦ κατανασσαμένη | mighty and hard to be appeased |

As "children of Night" and as "Curses, as they were called in their home beneath the earth,"[5] the most natural place for their sanctuary would be a subterranean one. And to such a dwelling Athena assigns them (Ae. Eum. 1022–1023):

| | |
|---|---|
| πέμψω δὲ φέγγει λαμπάδων σελασφόρων | and with the light of blazing torches will I escort |
| εἰς τοὺς ἔνερθε καὶ κάτω χθονὸς τόπους | you to your place down there beneath the earth |

And before the one-time Furies, now the beneficent powers, Athena moves, accompanied by torchbearers, to the cave just set apart to be the abode of the "Awful Deities" (ll. 1003–1007):

---

[1] Schol. Ar. Ran. 886: Ἐλευσίνιος τὸν δῆμον ἦν ὁ Αἰσχύλος.

[2] Cf. Ae. Eum. *passim* (cited in the following pages); Dinarchus I 87; Schol. Thuc. I 26, 11; Schol. Luc. III p. 68 (Jacobitz); Schol. Eur. Or. 1560; Paus. I 28, 6; VII 25, 2.

[3] Ae. Eum. 1033–1034.

[4] Their sanctuary at Colonus, with its "bronze-footed threshold," is the very stay and bulwark of the city's safety, ἔρεισμ' Ἀθηνῶν (Soph. O. C. 57–58).

[5] Ae. Eum. 416–417: ἡμεῖς γὰρ ἐσμεν Νυκτὸς αἰανῆς τέκνα·
Ἀραὶ δ' ἐν οἴκοις γῆς ὕπαι κεκλήμεθα.

THE CAVE OF THE EUMENIDES
ON THE AREOPAGUS

προτέραν δ' ἐμὲ χρὴ
στείχειν θαλάμους ἀποδείξουσαν
πρὸς φῶς ἱερὸν τῶνδε προπομπῶν.
ἴτε, καὶ σφαγίων τῶνδ' ὑπὸ σεμνῶν
κατὰ γῆς σύμεναι

and on before you I must
move to show you your chambers
by the holy light of our escorts' torches.
Come; and attended by these awful rites
speed you beneath the earth

The great Areopagus cave, it would seem from this, was divided into various apartments—one, perhaps, for each of the "Dread Goddesses." And there their escorts leave them at the end of the play (ll. 1032; 1036):

βᾶτε δόμῳ, μεγάλαι φιλότιμοι
..........
γᾶς ὑπὸ κεύθεσιν ὠγυγίοισιν

pass to your home, ye mighty and jealous powers,
.............
down into the ancient caverns of the earth

Again the plural (κεύθεσιν)—suggestive of the different apartments of the famous cave.

The only hint at the equipment of the cave is contained in Athena's first proposal to keep these divinities as sojourners[1] in her land (Ae. Eum. 804–807):

ὑμῖν πανδίκως ὑπίσχομαι
ἕδρας τε καὶ κευθμῶνας ἐνδίκου χθονὸς

λιπαροθρόνοισιν ἡμένας ἐπ' ἐσχάραις
ἕξειν ὑπ' ἀστῶν τῶνδε τιμαλφουμένας

and I faithfully promise you that ye shall
have seats of power and grottos in this righteous
  land,
sitting on shining thrones by your hearths
and honored by my citizens

In or at the cave there were "hearths," that is, altars for burnt sacrifice;[2] and by these "hearths" were thrones—radiant thrones—for the several deities henceforth honored by the people of Athens.

Besides the hearths and thrones, we know from other sources, there were statues there—one to each of the three Erinyes.[3] Two of them were by Scopas, the other by Calamis. In keeping with the Attic euphemism that refused to call these awful divinities Furies or Erinyes but named them "Dread Goddesses" or "Kindly-hearted Ones," these statues, Pausanias assures us, had nothing terrible in their aspect.

They are to have a share with Athena in the land of Attica, blessing, blessed, and honored;[4] they are to dwell with Pallas herself;[5] their seat is to be an honored one before the very shrine of Athena in the goodly palace of Erechtheus (Ae. Eum. 854–855):[6]

καὶ σὺ τιμίαν
ἕδραν ἔχουσα πρὸς δόμοις Ἐρεχθέως

and thou shalt have a seat
of honor before the palace of Erechtheus

and their situation is to be one free from every touch of ill.[7] And yet these "daughters of Night and Darkness,"[8] whose natural abiding place was beneath the earth, at first rebel against the indignity of being relegated, with all their ancient wisdom and all the power and prestige that went with their position in the older theogony, to a cave in the rocks for a temple (Ae. Eum. 837–839):

ἐμὲ παθεῖν τάδε, φεῦ,
ἐμὲ παλαίφρονα, κατά τε γᾶς οἰκεῖν,

φεῦ, ἀτίετον μύσος

for me to come to this—out upon it!—
for me, of ancient wisdom, to dwell beneath the
  earth—
out upon it!—in dishonor and loathing

and they feel so keenly on the subject of that cave with its sunless and cheerless approach that they repeat the same song after Athena's next attempt to appease them (ll. 870–872).

[1] Cp. ll. 1018–1020: μετοικίαν δ' ἐμὴν
  εὐσεβοῦντες οὔτι μέμ-
  ψεσθε συμφορὰς βίου.

[2] These altars are vouched for also by Thuc. I 126, 7; Plut. Thes. 12; Paus. VII 25, 2: ἐς τὸν Ἄρειον πάγον καὶ ἐπὶ τῶν θεῶν, αἳ Σεμναὶ καλοῦνται, τοὺς βωμούς. Dinarch. c. Dem. 47: φράζεο δ' Ἄρειόν τε πάγον βωμούς τε θυώδεις Εὐμενίδων. The service was in charge of the descendants of Hesychus who also had a cult near by (cf. Schol. Soph. O. C. 489).

[3] Paus. I 28, 6; Clem. Alex. Προτρ. IV 47; Schol. Aesch. I 188.

[4] Ae. Eum. 868–869; 890.

[5] *ibid.* 916–917; 833.

[6] Cp. also ll. 868; 891.

[7] Ae. Eum. 892–893.

[8] Soph. O. C. 40.

But at last the dreadful Gorgons,[1] the hounds of wrath,[2] monsters[3] hated and abhorred of gods and men,[4] appeased and satisfied take up their abode as honored deities of the land, defending the people of Attica against every sort of ill.[5]   It also came to be a place of refuge for those oppressed and in danger.   The Athenian galley in the passage from Aristophanes's *Knights* (1311–1312 cited below, p. 171) couples the sanctuary of the Dread Goddesses with that of Theseus as a place of safety:

| | |
|---|---|
| ἐς τὸ Θησεῖον πλεούσας ἢ 'πὶ τῶν σεμνῶν θεῶν | sailing to the Theseum or to the protection of the Dread Goddesses |

The two were located not far apart; and there is perhaps a special point in the galley's taking refuge by the shrine of the Eumenides, the temenos of which must have extended out some distance before the cave; for in that immediate vicinity the sacred galley of the Panathenaic processions must have rested, while its peplus-sail was taken down and the procession moved on up into the Acropolis to the temple of the Polias.

### b. *The Colonus Shrine*

Scarcely less famous than the Cave of the Furies on the Areopagus was the sanctuary of the same Dread Goddesses at the suburban hill known as Colonus Hippius.   The latter owes its fame in large measure, if not wholly, to Sophocles and the glory he sheds about the hallowed place in the Oedipus at Colonus.   And yet, although Sophocles frequently manifests his deep affection for the home of his childhood and makes it the scene of his latest and longest extant tragedy, he tells us surprisingly little about Colonus save for the charm of its natural beauty.   And the little that he does tell is likely to lead to confusion rather than to clearness, unless scrutinized with careful criticism, because the poet for the sake of his drama has woven into the Oedipus at Colonus events that happened at Thebes and events that took place at Athens.

Pausanias, "after careful investigation," discovers that Oedipus did not die in Attica at all, but at Thebes, and rejects the historicity of the whole plot of the Oedipus at Colonus (I 28, 6–7):

| | |
|---|---|
| Πλησίον δὲ ἱερὸν θεῶν ἐστιν ἃς καλοῦσιν Ἀθηναῖοι Σεμνάς... ἐνταῦθα θύουσι μὲν ὅσοις ἐν Ἀρείῳ πάγῳ τὴν αἰτίαν ἐξεγένετο ἀπολύσασθαι... ἔστι δὲ καὶ ἐντὸς τοῦ περιβόλου μνῆμα Οἰδίποδος. πολυπραγμονῶν δὲ εὕρισκον τὰ ὀστᾶ ἐκ Θηβῶν κομισθέντα· τὰ γὰρ ἐς τὸν θάνατον Σοφοκλεῖ πεποιημένα τὸν Οἰδίποδος Ὅμηρος οὐκ εἴα μοι δόξαι πιστά, ὃς ἔφη Μηκιστέα τελευτήσαντος Οἰδίποδος ἐπιτάφιον ἐλθόντα εἰς Θήβας ἀγωνίσασθαι. | Near by is a sanctuary of goddesses whom the Athenians call "the Dread Ones" . . . Here they offer sacrifice who have been successful in securing acquittal at the Areopagus . . . And there is also, inside the enclosure, the tomb of Oedipus. Upon investigation, however, I found that his bones were brought here from Thebes; for all that Sophocles has written about the death of Oedipus is, I think, rendered incredible by Homer, who says that Mecisteus upon the death of Oedipus went to Thebes to take part in the funeral games |

According to the universally accepted tradition, the tomb of Oedipus possessed the occult power of miracuously preserving in safety the state in which his bones rested.   The location of the grave was a profound secret known originally, according to Sophocles and in keeping with common tradition, only to Theseus and passed on by him to his successor and so on, for all time, to Athens' chief magistrate alone.   But the secret seems to have become an open one—not in the time of Sophocles, for he certainly locates it, as he had received the story from of old, at the shrine of the Eumenides at Colonus instead of by the one on the Areopagus, but certainly by the beginning of our era.   For not only does Pausanias locate the tomb without hesitation inside the sacred enclosure of the Awful Goddesses on Mars

[1] Ae. Eum. 48.
[2] Ae. Cho. 1054.
[3] Ae. Eum. 644.
[4] Ae. Eum. 73; 644.
[5] See note 4, p. 140.   For the manner of worship at this shrine see Frazer, *Paus.* Vol. II pp. 365–366.

COLONUS—ACROPOLIS

Hill, but Valerius Maximus, a century and a half earlier, knows of the presence of the grave and an altar in the saddle between the Acropolis and the Areopagus (V 3, Ext. 3): Oedipodis ossa caede patris nuptiis matris contaminata inter ipsum Arium pagum divini atque humani certaminis venerabile domicilium et excelsam praesidis Minervae arcem honore arae decorata ut ossa sacrosancti herois colis [sc. the city of Athens].

But in spite of the fact that Oedipus died and was buried at Thebes and that his bones later were conveyed to Athens and, later still, interred in a consecrated spot in the saddle between the Acropolis and the Areopagus, Euripides and Sophocles make Colonus Hippius the scene of his passing, and a mysterious spot in the grove of the Eumenides at Colonus the place of his unknown tomb  (Eur. Ph. 1705–1707):

| | |
|---|---|
| OI. ἐν ταῖς ᾿Αθήναις κατθανεῖν μ᾿ ἀλώμενον. | OE. That I must wander away and die at Athens. |
| AN. ποῦ; τίς σε πύργος ᾿Ατθίδος προσδέξεται; | AN. Where?  What Attic castle will receive thee? |
| OI. ἱερὸς Κολωνός, δώμαθ᾿ ἱππίου θεοῦ. | OE. Hallowed Colonus, home of the god of steeds. |

(Soph. O. C. 16–17):

| | |
|---|---|
| χῶρος δ᾿ ὅδ᾿ ἱερός, ὡς σαφ᾿ εἰκάσαι, βρύων | the spot here is a consecrated one, as one may clearly infer; for it abounds |
| δάφνης, ἐλαίας, ἀμπέλου | with laurel, olive, vines |

It is called directly a "grove" in lines 97–98:

| | |
|---|---|
| οὐκ ἔσθ᾿ ὅπως οὐ πιστὸν ἐξ ὑμῶν πτερὸν | now I am sure that on this journey some faithful |
| ἐξήγαγ᾿ εἰς τόδ᾿ ἄλσος. | omen from you must have led me to this grove |

and lines 126–127:

| | |
|---|---|
| ἄστιβες ἄλσος ἐς | into the grove, where none may tread, |
| τῶνδ᾿ ἀ̣ αἱμακετᾶν θεᾶν | of the maidens against whom none may strive |

and again at line 505:

| | |
|---|---|
| τοὐκεῖθεν ἄλσους, ὦ ξένη, τοῦδ᾿ | beyond the grove here, stranger |

All about the shrine at Colonus were the great groves of olive and laurel and grape-vines, "the covert of green glades, where the nightingale, a constant guest, trills her clear notes."[1] And along one side of the grove ran the main highway from Athens to Thebes (Soph. O. C. 113–114):

| | |
|---|---|
| καὶ σύ μ᾿ ἐξ ὁδοῦ πόδα | and do thou direct my steps from the |
| κρύψον κατ᾿ ἄλσος | road into the protection of the grove |

And approaching Athens from Thebes, this is the first resting-place that Oedipus and Antigone think to have found (*ibid.* 84–85):

| | |
|---|---|
| ὦ πότνιαι δεινῶπες, εὖτε νῦν ἕδρας | oh queens of awful aspect, now that I have bent |
| πρώτων ἐφ᾿ ἡμῶν τῆσδε γῆς ἔκαμψ᾿ ἐγώ | my steps to your abodes first in this land |

(*ibid.* 466–467):

| | |
|---|---|
| τῶνδε δαιμόνων ἐφ᾿ ἃς | to these deities, to whom |
| τὸ πρῶτον ἵκου καὶ κατέστειψας πέδον | at the first thou hast come and profaned their soil |

Pausanias and Valerius Maximus both are clear as to the location of the tomb of the Theban hero in the saddle between the Acropolis hill and the Areopagus.  But that does not necessarily mean that the location of the tomb of Oedipus at Colonus Hippius was not universally accepted in the days of Sophocles.  If it was indeed the talisman that it is represented to be; if it was the bulwark of Athens against any invading foe; if its occult power could so readily pass to the nation that possessed the hero's bones; then it must have been a very precarious policy for Athens to leave those bones outside the city walls, where they would fall at once into the power of the first successful invaders.[2]  So it stands to reason that the tomb should have been moved—certainly not later than the calamitous invasion of the Spartans in the Peloponnesian War.  Sophocles is not confusing his topography; he

[1] Soph. O. C. 670 ff.

[2] According to Dinarchus (I 9) it was the business of the Council of the Areopagus to "guard the secret graves [Oedipus's was apparently not the only one of its kind] on which the safety of the State depends."

is perfectly sure that the unseen tomb on the possession of which the safety of the Athens he loved depended was at Colonus. The proximity of the heroum of Pirithous and Theseus does not argue any confusion on the poet's part; there were two sites of the striking of the covenant between these bosom friends of early Athens, just as there were two sites of the worship of the Eumenides—one on the Areopagus and one at Colonus, and each with a cavernous opening descending down to Hades—and just as there were various seats of worship of other divinities. So with the sites of the covenant between Theseus and Pirithous, one was in the city proper, on the north side of the Acropolis, on the way from the Acropolis gates to the temple of Olympian Zeus;[1] and the other was at Colonus Hippius. For the latter we are not left to the evidence of Sophocles alone, but his testimony is abundantly confirmed by Pausanias himself.[2]

If the location of the grave of Oedipus at Colonus was a successfully guarded state secret down to the time of the Peloponnesian War, and if the bones of the blind old king were moved about that time, then Sophocles was betraying no state secret in making that tomb the centre of his tragedy and was using a motive that must have appealed powerfully to his contemporaries. He patriotically does not hint at the new location, if, indeed, he was cognizant of it.[3]

The whole region was one of continuous sanctuaries—the Academy,[4] a Prometheum, a sanctuary of Theseus and Pirithous,[5] a Posideum, a monument and heroum of the knightly Colonus, a shrine of Demeter Euchlous, and, chief of all, the sanctuary of the Eumenides (Soph. O. C. 54–56):

| | |
|---|---|
| χῶρος μὲν ἱερὸς πᾶς ὅδ' ἔστ'· ἔχει δέ νιν<br>σεμνὸς Ποσειδῶν· ἐν δ' ὁ πυρφόρος θεὸς<br>Τιτὰν Προμηθεύς | all this region is holy ground: dread Poseidon owns it; and in it the fire-bringing god, the Titan Prometheus, has a place |

(*ibid.* 58–65):

| | |
|---|---|
| ΞΕ.       οἱ δὲ πλησίοι γύαι<br>τόνδ' ἱππότην Κολωνὸν εὔχονται σφίσιν<br>ἀρχηγὸν εἶναι, καὶ φέρουσι τοὔνομα<br>τὸ τοῦδε κοινὸν πάντες ὠνομασμένοι.<br>τοιαῦτά σοι ταῦτ' ἐστίν, ὦ ξέν', οὐ λόγοις<br><br>τιμώμεν', ἀλλὰ τῇ ξυνουσίᾳ πλέον.<br>ΟΙ. ἦ γάρ τινες ναίουσι τούσδε τοὺς τόπους;<br><br>ΞΕ. καὶ κάρτα, τοῦδε τοῦ θεοῦ γ' ἐπώνυμοι | ST.      and the fields hereabout claim yonder knight Colonus as their primal lord, and all the people bear his name in common for their own.<br>Such, thou mayst know, stranger, are these haunts, not famed<br>in story but more so in the life that loves them.<br>OE. What! does any one actually dwell in such a locality?<br>ST. Ay; they who bear the name of yonder god |

Here we have the general environment of the shrine of the Venerable Ones at Colonus: a great grove of varied trees and bushes and vines, in which there are sanctuaries of Poseidon, Prometheus,[6] and Colonus. In the last passage quoted above, Colonus is not only hero eponymous of the district but he is unequivocally called a god; and the repetition of the deictic pronoun (τόνδ', τοῦδε) seems to leave no doubt that there was a statue of the knightly

---

[1] Paus. I 18, 4–6.

[2] Paus. I 30, 4.

[3] Aristides (XLVI, Vol. II p. 230 ed. Dind.: θαρρούντως ἂν ἔχοις λέγειν ὑποχθονίους τινὰς φύλακας καὶ σωτῆρας τῶν Ἑλλήνων, ἀλεξικάκους καὶ πάντα ἀγαθούς· καὶ ῥυεσθαί γε τὴν χώραν οὐ χεῖρον ἢ τὸν ἐν Κολωνῷ κείμενον Οἰδίπουν) and the Scholiast on Eur. Phoen. 1707 add the strength of their testimony to the existence of the grave of Oedipus at Colonus.

There is still another tradition about the resting place of the blind wanderer. It is given by the Scholiast on Soph. O. C. 91: εἰσί γ' οἵ φασι τὸ μνῆμα τοῦ Οἰδίποδος ἐν ἱερῷ Δήμητρος εἶναι ἐν Ἐτεωνῷ μεταγαγόντων αὐτὸν ἐκ Κεοῦ τινος ἀσήμου χωρίου καθάπερ ἱστορεῖν φησιν Ἀρίζηλον Λυσίμαχος ὁ Ἀλεξανδρεὺς ἐν τῷ ιγ' τῶν Θηβαϊκῶν γράφων οὕτως· Οἰδίπου δὲ τελευτήσαντος καὶ τῶν φίλων ἐν Θήβαις θάπτειν αὐτὸν διανοουμένων ἐκώλυον οἱ Θηβαῖοι διὰ τὰς προγεγενημένας συμφορὰς ὡς ὄντος ἀσεβοῦς· οἱ δὲ κομίσαντες αὐτὸν εἴς τινα τόπον τῆς Βοιωτίας καλούμενον Κεὸν ἔθαψαν αὐτόν· γινομένων δὲ τοῖς ἐν τῇ κώμῃ κατοικοῦσιν ἀτυχημάτων τινῶν οἰηθέντες αἰτίαν εἶναι τὴν Οἰδίπου ταφὴν ἐκέλευσαν τοὺς φίλους ἀναιρεῖν αὐτὸν ἐκ τῆς χώρας· οἱ δὲ ἀπορούμενοι τοῖς συμβαίνουσιν ἀνελόντες ἐκόμισαν εἰς Ἐτεωνόν· βουλόμενοι δὲ λάθρα τὴν ταφὴν ποιήσασθαι καταθάπτουσι νυκτὸς ἐν ἱερῷ Δήμητρος ἀγνοήσαντες τὸν τόπον· καταφανοῦς δὲ γενομένου πέμψαντες οἱ τὸν Ἐτεωνὸν κατοικοῦντες τὸν θεὸν ἐπηρώτων τί ποιῶσιν· ὁ δὲ θεὸς εἶπεν μὴ κινεῖν τὸν ἱκέτην τῆς θεοῦ διόπερ αὐτοῦ τέθαπται· τὸ δὲ ἱερὸν Οἰδιπόδειον κληθῆναι.

[4] In the midst of the olive groves near Colonus was the suburban gymnasium with its shrine and altar to the hero Academus. The dramatic poets testify to the exuberant shade of its groves (Eup. Ἀστρ. Frag. 32 K.): ἐν εὐσκίοις δρόμοισιν Ἀκαδήμου θεοῦ.

[5] Paus. I 30, 4.

[6] The Sanctuary of Prometheus must be the one that we know from Schol. Soph. O. C. 57 was established in the Academy itself. This fixes, perhaps, the western limits of this complex of sanctuaries.

Colonus there and that it was reproduced in the theatre at the presentation of the Oedipus at Colonus.

The hill probably received its epithet "Hippius" from Poseidon Hippius or from the Knight Colonus, and then "Colonus Hippius" became a fixed name to distinguish this hill from the "Market Hill," Κολωνὸς Ἀγοραῖος. As Poseidon also has a rightful claim on the place, and as Poseidon is the creator of the horse and patron of horsemen, Colonus hill became the "Hill of the Knights" Κολωνὸς τῶν ἱππέων (Pherecr. Πετ., Frag. 134 K.):

| | |
|---|---|
| οὗτος, πόθεν ἦλθες; Β. εἰς Κολωνὸν ἱέμην, | say, you, where did you come from? B. To Colonus I was sent— |
| οὐ τὸν ἀγοραῖον, ἀλλὰ τῶν ἱππέων | not the market hill, but the hill of the knights |

Pausanias (I 30, 4) is constrained at this turn in his periegesis to follow the tradition of Sophocles and to confirm the setting of the place:

| | |
|---|---|
| δείκνυται δὲ καὶ χῶρος καλούμενος | and they point out also a locality called |
| Κολωνὸς ἵππιος, ἔνθα τῆς Ἀττικῆς | Colonus Hippius, the first point in Attica |
| πρῶτον ἐλθεῖν λέγουσιν Οἰδίποδα | to which, they say, Oedipus came; |
| διάφορα μὲν καὶ ταῦτα τῇ Ὁμήρου | this also is different from the account in |
| ποιήσει, λέγουσι δ' οὖν. καὶ βωμὸς | Homer; but, at any rate, that is what they say. |
| Ποσειδῶνος Ἱππίου καὶ Ἀθηνᾶς | There is also an altar to Poseidon Hippius and |
| Ἱππίας, ἡρῷον δὲ Πειρίθου καὶ | Athena Hippia, and an heroum to Pirithous and |
| Θησέως, Οἰδίποδός τε καὶ Ἀδράστου. | Theseus, another to Oedipus and Adrastus. |
| τὸ δὲ ἄλσος τοῦ Ποσειδῶνος καὶ | The grove of Poseidon and the temple were |
| τὸν ναὸν ἐνέπρησεν Ἀντίγονος | burned by Antigonus (263 B. C.) |

Nearly six centuries after Sophocles Pausanias still finds, out before the north suburbs of Athens in the district of Colonus Hippius, a grove of Poseidon with an altar and the ruins of a temple once shared between Athena and her rival for the possession of the land, a shrine to the heroes Theseus and Pirithous, and another to Oedipus and Adrastus. The Prometheum may have disappeared or Pausanias may have chosen to ignore it, even as he ignores the shrine of the Eumenides.

Not far away—indeed, upon the very next hillock, adjoining Colonus on the north—was the shrine of Demeter Euchlous. It was situated close at hand, perhaps upon the spot now occupied by the little church of the Panagia Eléousa; and surely the surname is not accidental; for Eléousa is not the "Mary of Mercy" [Ἐλέουσα], but the "Virgin of the Olive Groves" [Ἐλαίουσα], that is, the logical successor of the Demeter "all clad in green" (Soph. O. C. 1598–1602):

| | |
|---|---|
| παῖδας ἀνώγει ῥυτῶν | he bade the maidens fetch from somewhere |
| ὑδάτων ἐνεγκεῖν λουτρὰ καὶ χοὰς ποθεν· | running water for ablutions and for libations; |
| τὼ δ' Εὐχλόου Δήμητρος ἐς προσόψιον | and they twain went to the hill of Demeter Euchlous, |
| πάγον μολοῦσα τάσδ' ἐπιστολὰς πατρὶ | full in view, and in brief space of time |
| ταχεῖ πόρευσαν ξὺν χρόνῳ | fulfilled their father's bidding |

By the church of the Panagia there is said to have been a spring. And with these lines of Sophocles we have another, otherwise unknown sanctuary of Athens located with a fair degree of certainty upon the little, olive-covered hillock immediately adjoining Colonus hill upon the north—"in plain sight" and so near that water could be brought from its spring in a very "brief space of time" indeed.

There was another shrine of "Demeter Clad in Green"[1] close by the Eumenides shrine on the Areopagus. The Scholiast on the last quoted lines of the Oedipus at Colonus remarks:

| | |
|---|---|
| Εὐχλόου Δήμητρος ἱερόν | there is a sanctuary of Demeter |
| ἔστι πρὸς τῇ Ἀκροπόλει | Euchlous toward the Acropolis |

and then he quotes Eupolis (Μαρικᾶς, Frag. 183 K.):

| | |
|---|---|
| ἀλλ' εὐθὺ πόλεως εἶμι· θῦσαι γάρ με δεῖ | well, I am going straight for the city; for I must offer |
| κριὸν Χλόῃ Δήμητρι | a ram to Demeter Chloe |

---

[1] ἐκ τῆς τῶν κήπων χλοῆς (Schol. Soph. O. C. 1671).

At first sight Eupolis's words seem to say that the temple of Demeter Chloe was on the Acropolis; for "the city" is here used in its long familiar sense of the old city, the Acropolis.[1] But the words do not necessarily mean that the Demeter temple was upon the upper Acropolis; the speaker says only that he means to go in that immediate direction. The Scholiast corrects the natural error by explaining that the shrine is "at" (or "near" or "by," not necessarily *on*) the Acropolis, but he commits another error by calling this Demeter "Demeter Euchlous" instead of "Chloe," the epithet used by Eupolis.

Aristophanes also helps us to locate the shrine of Demeter Chloe on the path that led from the lower city up to the entrance to the Acropolis. Lysistrate, watching from the battlements of the citadel, sees a man whirled up the slopes of the Acropolis under the spell of Aphrodite and gives the cry of alarm; one of her women asks excitedly where the villain is; Lysistrate locates him as he climbs up past the temple of Demeter Chloe (Ar. Lys. 835):

| | |
|---|---|
| ΓΥ. ποῦ δ' ἐστὶν ὅστις ἐστί; ΛΥ. παρὰ τὸ τῆς Χλόης | WO. Where is he, whoever he is? LY. By the temple of Chloe |

Cinesias (for he it is) is hurrying up to the Acropolis to find Myrrhine; he is discovered as he reaches the saddle between the Acropolis and the Areopagus, and there was the temple of "the goddess of the green,"[2] near enough for Myrrhine within the Acropolis gates to recognize her husband. Both Aristophanes and Eupolis call her Chloe, not Euchlous.

We may locate the site of this Demeter temple a little more accurately still with the help of Pausanias.[3] As he comes up from the southern approach to the Acropolis, he mentions, between the Phaedra-Hippolytus temple of Aphrodite and the entrance to the Acropolis (the Porte Beulé) only the Aphrodite Pandemus and "a sanctuary of Gaea, the Nurturer of the Young, and of Demeter Chloe" (Δήμητρος ἱερὸν Χλόης). The temple of the Pandemus, by general acceptation, stood not far from the southwest approach to the Porte Beulé; the temple of Demeter Chloe was also slightly southwest of the Beulé gate but nearer to it than the Pandemus temple. Pausanias's location of the temple near the southwest approach to the entrance of the Acropolis is surprisingly substantiated by a fragment of Ennius (Medea 243–244, R.[3]):

> asta atque Athenas anticum, opulentum oppidum
> contempla et templum Cereris ad laevam aspice.

The persons of the drama in this scene enter before a picture of the Acropolis painted on the scenes behind them; they face the audience; their left is the spectators' right; the speaker of the lines gives directions in accordance with his own standpoint, just as, in the opening lines of Sophocles's Electra, the old Paedagogus, pointing out to Orestes the striking features of the Argive topography, points to the Heraeum on the left;[4] it was on their left as they faced an audience sitting before the castle walls of Mycenae. Accordingly, in the Medea of Ennius, the temple of Demeter stood to the right of the Acropolis gate. Curtius[5] cites a number of inscriptions from the sanctuary of Demeter Chloe found in this vicinity, south or southwest of the present entrance to the Acropolis and close to it: one of them[6] "records that a certain Isidotus, in obedience to a dream, had dedicated an image" of Ge Curotrophus to Demeter Chloe and Cora;[7] a second inscription,[8] found in the same place,

---

[1] See pp. 253 ff.
[2] The Scholiast on this passage explains carefully that "the goddess of the green" is Demeter who had a sanctuary "on the Acropolis."
[3] I 22, 3.
[4] Soph. El. 7–8: οὐξ ἀριστερᾶς ὅδε
"Ηρας ὁ κλεινὸς ναός.
[5] *Stadtgesch v. Ath.*, S. XXV. Michaelis, Arx. Ath.[2] p. 41, cites all the material.
[6] Cf. also Δελτίον Ἀρχαιολ. 1889, p. 130.
[7] According to Pausanias's words, ἔστι δὲ καὶ Γῆς Κουροτρόφου καὶ Δήμητρος ἱερὸν Χλόης, it might seem that Ge and Demeter occupied a common shrine; but the inscriptions, in which we find listed, among other things, a priestess of Demeter Chloe alone and a boundary of the τέμενος of Γῆ Κουροτρόφος alone, make the separation of the two shrines imperative.
[8] Δελτίον Ἀρχαιολ. 1889, p. 130; B. C. H. XIII (1889) pp. 167 ff.

contains a dedication by a priestess named Nicobule to Demeter Chloe; a third,[1] an oracle in metrical form, mentions the sanctuary of Demeter Chloe and Cora as situated near the Acropolis (παρ' ἄκρας πόλεως); it was found in 1889 to the southwest of the Nike pyrgos; still a further inscription[2] records another dedication to Demeter Chloe.

After this little excursion from Demeter Euchlous near Colonus Hippius to Demeter Chloe near the entrance to the Acropolis, let us return once more to Colonus. The Scholiast on Sophocles falls into the easy confusion of the two similar by-names, for both have to do with the fresh greenery of the growing crops.[3] But the poet himself is guilty of no such confusion of cults. He speaks of "the hill of Demeter Euchlous"; and that can mean only the hillock near Colonus Hippius; there was no hill between the Areopagus and the Acropolis for Demeter to own.

In the clear conviction, then, that Sophocles is dealing with the topography about Colonus Hill, we return to that scene with its grove and its shrines as already described. In the midst of that setting was the Colonus sanctuary of "the Dread Goddesses, who watch over and protect the folk"[4] of Cecrops's land. Whatever shrine there was, it was in a sacred enclosure (τέμενος) of considerable extent (Soph. O. C. 135–137):

| | |
|---|---|
| ὃν ἐγὼ λεύσσων περὶ πᾶν οὔπω | though I peer about all the sacred |
| δύναμαι τέμενος | enclosure, I cannot yet discover |
| γνῶναι ποῦ μοί ποτε ναίει | where in the world my man bideth |

It was the sacred seat of the Eumenides, we are expressly told (Soph. O. C. 41–43):

| | |
|---|---|
| ΟΙ. τίνων τὸ σεμνὸν ὄνομ' ἂν εὐξαίμην κλύων; | OE. Whose the awful name that I might hear and invoke? |
| ΞΕ. τὰς πάνθ' ὁρώσας Εὐμενίδας ὅ γ' ἐνθάδ' ἂν εἴποι λεώς νιν· ἄλλα δ' ἀλλαχοῦ καλά | ST. The all-seeing Eumenides. Thus the people here might call them; different customs are honored in different places |

Only in this passage and in line 486 of this play are the goddesses of the place called "Eumenides." In line 40 (quoted below) they are called "daughters of Earth and Darkness" (Γῆς τε καὶ Σκότου κόραι); in line 127 they are the "maidens against whom none may strive" (τῶνδ' ἀμαιμακετᾶν κορᾶν); in line 84 they are "queens of awful aspect" (πότνιαι δεινῶπες); but usually they are simply δαίμονες,[5] "deities," θεαί or θεοί,[6] "goddesses," to whom the epithet "awful," "venerable" (σεμναί) may be attached.[7] But in any case, it is perfectly clear from the passages quoted that it is a sanctuary of the Eumenides that Sophocles is bringing before us and that that sanctuary was situated at Colonus beyond the northern gate of Athens. The fact that Sophocles tells us—yea, *can* tell us—so little of what was inside the sacred enclosure is due to the sacrosanctity of the place, so awful that no man might set foot inside the dreadful place and live. Oedipus, blind but guided by fate, had stumbled into it accompanied by his faithful Antigone. The inhabitants threaten him with death for his transgression; and he never did come forth. Not merely might no one set

[1] Δελτίον 'Αρχαιολ. 1889, p. 113; Ath. Mitt. XVIII (1893), pp. 192–198. Her by-name in this inscription, not earlier than the second century A. D., is spelled ΧΛΟΙΗ. The whole inscription reads:

Φοῖβος 'Αθηναίοις Δελφοὺς ναίων τάδε [εἶπεν]·
Ἔστιν σοι παρ' ἄκρας πόλεως παρὰ............
οὗ λαὸς σύμπας κλῄζει γλαυκώ[πιδ' 'Αθήνην]
Δήμητρος Χλόης ἱερὸν Κού[ρης τε μαχαίρας],
οὗ πρῶτον στάχυς ηὐξῆ[θη ζειῶν ἱεράων]
ἃς πρότεροι πατ[έρες...........................
ἀδρύσαντο......................................
............................................... ἀπαρχάς
............... δρ............................
........................... δ]ρεπτά

Phoebus reminds the Athenians that they have a temple of Demeter Chloe and that they are still owing to her and her Daughter blest the tithes of the harvest.

[2] C. I. A. III No. 191; cf. C. I. A. II Nos. 349, 375, 722.

[3] Schol. Soph. O. C. 1600: Εὐχλόου Δήμητρος ἱερόν ἐστι πρὸς τῇ 'Ακροπόλει... οὕτω δὲ τιμᾶται ἐκ τῆς τῶν κήπων χλοῆς· θύουσι δὲ αὐτῇ Θαργηλιῶνος ἕκτη [about the 20th of May]. Cornutus 28: περὶ τὸ ἔαρ τῇ Χλόῃ Δήμητρι θύουσι μετὰ παιδιᾶς καὶ χαρᾶς, ἰδόντες χλοάζοντα καὶ ἀφθονίας αὐτοῖς ἐλπίδα ὑποδεικνύντα.

[4] Soph. O. C. 458–459.

[5] E. g. ll. 466, 864, 1391.

[6] ll. 38, 458, 1010.

[7] As in ll. 89–90, 458; cp. l. 41.

foot within the place, but so overpoweringly awful was it that men passed by without even a sidelong glance, without a word, without a sound (Soph. O. C. 123–133):

| | |
|---|---|
| πλανάτας, πλανάτας τις ὁ πρέσβυς, οὐδ' | some wanderer, some wanderer the old man must be and not |
| ἔγχωρος· προσέβα γὰρ οὐκ | a native; for otherwise he would never have approached |
| ἄν ποτ' ἀστεβὲς ἄλσος ἐς | the grove, where none may tread, |
| τῶνδ' ἀμαιμακετᾶν κορᾶν, | of the maidens here against whom none may strive, |
| ἇς τρέμομεν λέγειν, | whose name we tremble to speak; |
| καὶ παραμειβόμεσθ' ἀδέρκτως, | and we pass by their shrine with averted eyes, |
| ἀφώνως, ἀλόγως τὸ τᾶς | moving our lips without sound or word |
| εὐφάμου στόμα φροντίδος | in silent devotion |
| ἱέντες | |

The inviolability of the sacred spot is brought out more than once in Sophocles's play. The first Colonian to discover Oedipus's intrusion dares not go in to fetch him out but does venture to stand near by and order him out (O. C. 36–40):

| | |
|---|---|
| ΞΕ.　　　　ἐκ τῆσδ' ἕδρας | ST.　　　　Come away from yon |
| ἔξελθ', ἔχεις γὰρ χῶρον οὐχ ἁγνὸν πατεῖν. | seat; for thou art in a place not lawful to tread. |
| ΟΙ. τίς δ' ἔσθ' ὁ χῶρος; τοῦ θεῶν νομίζεται; | OE. What is the place? To whom of the gods is it consecrate? |
| ΞΕ. ἄθικτος οὐδ' οἰκητός, αἱ γὰρ ἔμφοβοι | ST. A place inviolable, where none may bide; for the fearful |
| θεαί σφ' ἔχουσι, Γῆς τε καὶ Σκότου κόραι | goddesses own it, the daughters of Earth and Darkness |

and again (ll. 156–158):

| | |
|---|---|
| ἵνα τῷδ' ἐν ἀ- | that thou mayst not blindly |
| φθέγκτῳ μὴ προσπέσῃς νάπει | intrude upon that grassy dell, where |
| ποιάεντι | no voice may be uttered |

and (167–169):

| | |
|---|---|
| ἀβάτων ἀποβάς, | step out from where none may step, |
| ἵνα πᾶσι νόμος | and speak where it is lawful |
| φώνει | for all to speak |

In spite of the awful unapproachableness of this shrine, Sophocles, growing up in its immediate neighborhood and grown familiar with its awe-inspiring sanctity from childhood, had sloughed off the ordinary terror of the place. He may, like the very modern boy we may assume him to have been, have ventured, in youthful, dare-devil abandon or on a boyish "dare," to enter the fearsome place and see what it was like. He may even have gone as far as the writer did one summer day, bribing the mistress of the house with the green shutters at the southeast foot of the hill and entering through her cellar over a "sheer threshold" and penetrating with a dim, smoking candle into an uncomfortable rift in the rock for some distance below the light of day. And when that venturesome, devil-may-care lad of 2300 years ago reached the age of ninety, he put into his wonderful verse some of the impressions of the things he saw on that hair-raising expedition of years long gone by. There was not much to see, it is safe to assume. But here are the things he tells us about.

At the very entrance to the sacred enclosure of the Eumenides, amid the thickets of laurel, olive, and vine in which the feathered choirs of nightingales made music, was a seat of native rock, whereon the blind, old Oedipus, entering the inviolable demesnes, was seated by Antigone (Soph. O. C. 19; 21):

| | |
|---|---|
| οὗ κῶλα κάμψον τοῦδ' ἐπ' ἀξέστου πέτρου | here bend thy knees and rest upon this native rock |
| . . . . . . . | . . . . . . |
| κάθιζέ νύν με· | now let me sit |

But the Chorus will not suffer him to remain there upon that unhewn rock; they insist upon his moving to another seat of native rock—a dramatic device, probably, for a better grouping, now that the chorus is present—and from this new place no one, the Chorus assures him, will ask him to yield (Soph. O. C. 192–193; 195–196):

| αὐτοῦ· μηκέτι τοῦδ' ἀντιπέτρου βήματος ἔξω πόδα κλίνῃς | right there; move not thy foot beyond that rocky ledge |
|---|---|
| . . . . . λέχριός γ' ἐπ' ἄκρου λᾶος βραχὺς ὀκλάσας | . . . . . . move a bit sidewise and sit low upon the edge of yonder stone |

(*ibid.* 176–177):

| οὔ τοι μήποτέ σ' ἐκ τῶνδ' ἑδράνων, ὦ γέρον, ἄκοντά τις ἄξει | no fear, old man, that any one will ever drive thee from yonder seat |
|---|---|

The Chorus stands upon the highway and directs Antigone and Oedipus to the natural seats of native stone upon which they may now take their place but which Antigone has difficulty in distinguishing from the rest of the stony outcroppings of Colonus Hill. And yet, in spite of this assurance given, the Chorus does, when it learns who and what the stranger is, attempt to drive him from the hallowed spot (Soph. O. C. 233–234):

| σὺ δὲ τῶνδ' ἑδράνων πάλιν ἔκτοπος | but away with thee! Get thee from that seat! Avaunt! |
|---|---|
| αὖθις ἄφορμος ἐμᾶς χθονὸς ἔκθορε | Get thee with all speed away from my land |

And again the plural is used, as if, in keeping with the actual geological condition of the Colonus hillock to-day, the place where Oedipus sat was a succession of ledges of stone, one above the other, whereas the first seat that Oedipus and Antigone had found is, with one exception, always simply ἕδρα "seat" (Soph. O. C. 36–37):

| ἐκ τῆσδ' ἕδρας ἔξελθ', ἔχεις γὰρ χῶρον οὐχ ἁγνὸν πατεῖν | come away from yon seat; for thou art in a place not lawful to tread |
|---|---|

But Oedipus at first refuses to stir (*ibid.* 45):

| οὐχ ἕδρας γῆς τῆσδ' ἂν ἐξέλθοιμ' | I should be loath to leave the seat I have taken in this land |
|---|---|

With a double meaning in lines 89–90:

| ὅπου θεῶν σεμνῶν ἕδραν λάβοιμι καὶ ξενόστασιν | where I should find a haven and a place of rest with awful Goddesses |
|---|---|

It is at once the "seat of the Awful Goddesses" and a "place of rest vouchsafed by Awful Goddesses."

The passage in which Oedipus's first resting-place is called by another name than ἕδρα is a striking one (ll. 100–101):

| κἀπὶ σεμνὸν ἐζόμην βάθρον τόδ' ἀσκέπαρνον | and took my place upon this awful seat unshapen by man's hand |
|---|---|

The epithet σεμνὸν "awful" is at once suggestive of the Σεμναί, the "Awful Goddesses" of the place; while the word βάθρον which we have rendered with "seat" really means "that on which one steps," or "a step," and is suggestive of the gradually rising successive ledges of rock of which the hill is composed. It is "unshapen" because of the primeval sanctity of the place, where man may not enter—much less employ pickaxe or chisel. The gradually rising series of steps is emphasized again (ll. 263–264):

| οἵτινες βάθρων ἐκ τῶνδέ μ' ἐξάραντες εἶτ' ἐλαύνετε | [ye,] who made me rise from yonder seats and now would drive me forth |
|---|---|

But there is another "step" (βάθρον) or flight of "steps" in connection with the Eumenides shrine at Colonus, much more awful than the open, sunlit ledges of the hill. These are the steps that go down into the regions of gloom in the depths of the cave, the deepest recess of the abode of the Furies (Soph. O. C. 1661–1662):

| τὸ νερτέρων εὔνουν διαστὰν γῆς ἀλύπητον βάθρον | the step that leads to the region of the dead beneath the Earth, where there is no more pain, opening kindly to receive him |
|---|---|

The approach to this "step" had already been anticipated almost at the beginning of the play, where the Colonian stranger informs Oedipus of the nature of the spot in which he has chosen to rest (O. C. 56–58):

| | |
|---|---|
| ὃν δ' ἐπιστείβεις τόπον<br>χθονὸς καλεῖται τῆσδε χαλκόπους ὁδός,<br>ἔρεισμ' Ἀθηνῶν | and the spot whereon thou treadest<br>is called the bronze-foot threshold of this land,<br>the stay of Athens |

The "bronze-foot threshold" was probably the beginning of the mysterious stairway that descended to the under-world. In the latter part of the play the "bronze-foot threshold" is more clearly defined (O. C. 1590–1591):

| | |
|---|---|
| ἐπεὶ δ' ἀφῖκτο τὸν καταρράκτην ὁδὸν<br>χαλκοῖς βάθροισι γῆθεν ἐρριζωμένον | and when he came to the sheer threshold,<br>with treads of bronze firmly let into the earth |

Here the threshold was sheer. The entrance to the subterranean passage drops sheer to-day down into the cellar of the house referred to above. It may once have been fitted with a plate of bronze. Then came the steps—reinforced with metal, to withstand the wear of the χαλκόπους Ἐρινύς "the bronze-footed Erinys, with the tramp of many feet and arms in many hands."[1] Here the natural stone steps must have been more or less "shapen by man's hand," and the metal plates let into the rock-steps—"rooted in the earth," as a literal translation would make it, immovable.

Professor Jebb, by what seems an arbitrary addition to the Scholiast's quotation from Istrus of Cyrene,[2] makes of the "bronze-foot threshold" the whole district about Colonus Hill. But παρὰ τὸν χαλκοῦν might mean "past the bronze statue" or "the bronze man" or any one of a score of other possible bronze things quite as well as "the Brazen Threshold." And, besides, the use of "Bronze Threshold" for a whole region would be passing strange. The fact is we do not know what Istrus meant by ἀπὸ τούτου; and we do not know what he meant by παρὰ τὸν χαλκοῦν προσαγορευόμενον.

The only furnishings of the sanctuary of the Erinyes at Colonus, as far as we are told, were various craters or mixing-bowls. In the grove itself, above ground, there was at the very entrance a lustral bowl where gifts of water and honey were made (Soph. O. C. 158–160):

| | |
|---|---|
| κάθυδρος οὗ<br>κρατὴρ μειλιχίων ποτῶν<br>ῥεύματι συντρέχει | where the bowl of water<br>blends with the stream of honied<br>offerings |

Further on in the same play this same lustral bowl, apparently, is only one of several lustral bowls in the grove of the Eumenides. They may have been stone or they may have been earthenware; in any case, they were artistically fashioned. They were there to function in rites for appeasing the wrath of the Awful Ones, and Oedipus is bidden to crown these mixing-bowls with flocks of wool preparatory to pouring a libation by way of atonement for his transgression in entering the holy place (Soph. O. C. 472–473):

| | |
|---|---|
| κρατῆρές εἰσιν, ἀνδρὸς εὔχειρος τέχνη,<br><br>ὧν κρᾶτ' ἔρεψον καὶ λαβὰς ἀμφιστόμους | there are bowls, the art of some man's clever<br>  hands;<br>crown their tops and handles at either brim |

A few lines later these "mixing-bowls" are called κρωσσοί "jars" (477):

| | |
|---|---|
| ἦ τοῖσδε κρωσσοῖς οἷς λέγεις | with those jars, pray, thou tellest of?[3] |

Very different is the sacred bowl that is introduced toward the end of the play. This is down at the very jumping-off place into the infernal passage to the realms of darkness, the abode proper of the Erinyes. It is the stone vessel that is said to have received the blood of the sacrifice that confirmed the league of Theseus and Pirithous (Soph. O. C. 1592–1597):

[1] Soph. El. 489–491.
[2] Schol. Soph. O. C. 1059: ἀπὸ δὲ τούτου ἕως Κολωνοῦ παρὰ τὸν χαλκοῦν προσαγορευόμενον· ὅθεν πρὸς τὸν Κηφισὸν ἕως τῆς μυστικῆς εἰσόδου εἰς Ἐλευσῖνα,
[3] Then follow the long details of the libation rites that the ex-king is to perform. For the discussion of the bowls themselves see the chapter on Pottery, Volume III, Chap. XIII.

| | |
|---|---|
| ἔστη κελεύθων ἐν πολυσχίστων μιᾷ, | he stopped at one of the many-branching paths |
| κοίλου πέλας κρατῆρος, οὖ τὰ Θησέως | near to the hollow bowl in which the compacts of Theseus and Pirithous |
| Πειρίθου τε κεῖται πίστ' ἀεὶ ξυνθήματα· | are placed away to be kept forevermore. |
| ἀφ' οὖ μέσος στὰς τοῦ τε Θορικίου πέτρου | There he stopped between the Thorician stone |
| κοίλης τ' ἀχέρδου κἀπὸ λαΐνου τάφου | and the hollow wild-pear tree and on the tomb of stone |
| καθέζετ' | he sate him down |

The whole place is one of unfathomable mystery.  By the "many-branching paths" we must necessarily understand various, intersecting paths that ran through the grove and led finally to the "sheer threshold" where one plunged down into the realms of Tartarus. At one corner of such intersecting paths stood the "hollow bowl," preserving, like the ephah of the sacred manna in the temple at Jerusalem, the blood of the covenant between Theseus and Pirithous; for it was at this spot, according to Attic tradition, that the two friends bound themselves by their compact of fidelity, as they entered upon their supreme adventure of going down together to the realm of Pluto to fetch away the queen of the underworld.  The expression κοίλου κρατῆρος "the hollow bowl" suggests naturally that this bowl was either a natural formation in the rock of the cave or a bowl hollowed out of the live rock of the cave.  The heroum of Theseus and Pirithous, to which Pausanias also refers,[1] would have been above ground.

At another corner made by the many-branching paths was the "stone from Thoricus." What this stone was also lies behind an impenetrable veil of mystery.  Thoricus in the Deme of Acamantis, near Sunium, we know;[2] its limestone formations we know; but what the mysterious "Thoricus stone" was doing at the entrance of the cave of the Erinyes at Colonus we do not know.  Professor Campbell suggests that it may have been a piece of Laurian silver ore.  We would do better not to attempt to lift the veil.  Let it be as mysterious as Sophocles meant it to be.

At a third corner of the cross-ways of the grove was the "hollow wild-pear tree."  It may have been significant to Sophocles and to his audience.  If it was, that significance is lost to us.  We cannot so much as hazard a guess as to its history or its meaning.

At the fourth corner was the "tomb of stone."  Whose tomb?  How did it happen to be there in the grove of the Eumenides?

With all this awful mystery, the awfulness of Hecate's three ways is outdone.


### c. *The Shrine of* Ἀρά

One of the most abstract of Greek deities, more like a Latin god than anything else we know, was the personification of a Curse.  She is, thus personified, closely associated with the chthonic divinities.  When Electra reaches the height of her passion in the review of her wrongs and her consuming thirst for vengeance upon the wrong-doers, she includes the "royal Curse" in her wild appeal (Soph. El. 110–112):

| | |
|---|---|
| ὦ δῶμ' Ἀΐδου καὶ Περσεφόνης, | oh home of Hades and Persephone, |
| ὦ χθόνι' Ἑρμῆ καὶ πότνι' Ἀρά, | oh Hermes of the underworld and thou royal Curse, |
| σεμναί τε θεῶν παῖδες Ἐρινύες | and Erinyes, dread children of the gods |

Here the Curse is πότνια "royal," "sovereign," and works in conjunction with the Erinyes, the goddesses of vengeance.  In Aeschylus's Eumenides the Erinyes call themselves Ἀραί "Curses" (l. 417):

| | |
|---|---|
| Ἀραὶ δ' ἐν οἴκοις γῆς ὕπαι κεκλήμεθα | Curses are we called in our home beneath the earth |

[1] I 30, 4, quoted above, p. 145.
[2] See Miller & Cushing, *The Theatre of Thoricus, Papers of the American School of Classical Studies in Athens*, Volume III.

In the Seven against Thebes the poet again identifies Curse and Erinys, as if the Curse were the very personification of the imprecation uttered by dying lips that sets the Fury on her path of vengeance (Ae. Sep. 720–725):

| | |
|---|---|
| πέφρικα τὰν ὠλεσίοικον<br>θεόν, οὐ θεοῖς ὁμοίαν,<br>........<br>πατρὸς εὐκταίαν Ἐρινὺν<br>τελέσαι τὰς περιθύμους<br>κατάρας Οἰδίποδα βλαψίφρονος | I shudder at the thought of Erinys, the goddess<br>—yet not like the gods—the wrecker of<br><br>homes, fulfilling the passionate<br>curses invoked by the<br>maddened Oedipus |

In lines 69–70 the individual Curse and the Erinys are still more closely identified:[1]

| | |
|---|---|
| ὦ Ζεῦ τε καὶ Γῆ καὶ πολισσοῦχοι θεοί,<br>Ἀρά τ' Ἐρινὺς πατρὸς μεγασθενής | oh Zeus and Earth and city-saving gods,<br>and thou Curse, my father's Erinys of mighty<br>power |

while again, without using the name Erinys, at all, Aeschylus speaks of the Curses as shouting in triumph over the doom fulfilled upon the house of Oedipus (*ibid.* 953–955):

| | |
|---|---|
| τελευταῖαι δ' ἐπηλάλαξαν<br>Ἀραὶ τὸν ὀξὺν νόμον<br>τετραμμένου παντρόπῳ φυγᾷ γένους | and now at the end the Curses have<br>raised their shrill lay of triumph<br>over the utter rout of your family turned to defeat |

Quite similarly in the Choephori Aeschylus, after the Chorus has declared how "Slaughter calls upon Erinys, bringing for those slain of old woe on woe," has Electra say (ll. 405–406):

| | |
|---|---|
| πόποι δᾶ νερτέρων τυραννίδες <τ'>,<br>ἴδετε πολυκρατεῖς Ἀραὶ τεθυμένων | oh Earth and kingdoms of the powers below,<br>behold, ye mighty Curses of the slain |

As the Athenians set apart shrines and instituted cults for the Erinyes—Eumenides— so they also seem to have had a sanctuary for Ara, this sovereign Curse (Ar. Ὧραι, Frag. 575 K.):

| | |
|---|---|
| Ἀρᾶς ἱερόν | the sanctuary of Ara |

quoting which Hesychius remarks:

| | |
|---|---|
| ἱερὸν Ἀρᾶς Ἀθήνησιν.<br>[ἔνιοι δὲ τὴν βλάβην<br>λέγειν αὐτὸν ἐνόμισαν] | the sanctuary of Ara at Athens.<br>[but some have thought that<br>he means "injury"] |

What this sanctuary of Ara was; where it was situated in the city; what it was like; on not one of these questions are we from any source enlightened. It is quite possible that this temple possessed a cultus statue and that a statue of the goddess adorned the proscenium at the presentation of the Septem along with the statue of Zeus and the other gods to whom Eteocles makes his appeal (ll. 69 ff.).[2]

## 18. APHRODISIA

### a. *The Temple of Aphrodite Hippolytia in Athens*

The city of Athens contained several famous sanctuaries dedicated to the goddess of love: we know approximately the location of (1) Aphrodite of the Gardens; (2) Aphrodite Pandemus; (3) Aphrodite Urania. In addition to these three, from various sources we learn of an Aphrodisium ἐπὶ Ἱππολύτῳ. The founding of this temple is ascribed by Euripides to Phaedra, wife of Theseus (Hip. 30–33):

| | |
|---|---|
| πέτραν παρ' αὐτὴν Παλλάδος κατόψιον<br>γῆς τῆσδε[1] ναὸν Κύπριδος καθείσατο,<br>ἐρῶσ' ἔρωτ' ἔκδημον· Ἱππολύτῳ δ' ἔπι<br>τὸ λοιπὸν ὠνόμαζεν ἱδρῦσθαι θεάν | hard by Pallas's rock she built to Cypris, out<br>of love for a love abroad, a temple that looks<br>down upon this land;[3] and for all time to come<br>she gave the goddess a surname[4] in honor of<br>Hippolytus |

---

[1] See also Ae. Sep. 695–700; 832–833.
[2] For the discussion of this question see Vol. II, Chap. VIII.
[3] The scene is Troezen.
[4] Hippolytia, see below p. 153.

From these few words we learn that Athens had a temple of Aphrodite ἐπὶ Ἱππολύτῳ; that the temple is to be sought not upon the summit of the rock of Athena but on its slope; that its site affords a view across the Athenian plain and the Saronic gulf to Troezen; that it was built by Phaedra to win the goddess's favor in her guilty love for Hippolytus; that from him it received its name; and that the goddess herself received a surname from the hero. The same facts are confirmed by Diodorus Siculus who, however, seems to have Euripides's words clearly in mind when he writes (IV 62):

| | |
|---|---|
| μικρὸν δ' ὕστερον Ἱππολύτου ἐπανελθόντος εἰς τὰς Ἀθήνας πρὸς τὰ μυστήρια, Φαίδρα διὰ τὸ κάλλος ἐρασθεῖσα αὐτοῦ τότε μὲν ἀπελθόντος εἰς Τροιζῆνα ἱδρύσατο ἱερὸν Ἀφρο- δίτης παρὰ τὴν Ἀκρόπολιν, ὅθεν ἦν καθορᾶν τὴν Τροιζῆνα. | and a little later, when Hippolytus returned to Athens to take part in the mysteries, Phaedra, under the spell of his beauty, fell in love with him. And when he had gone back to Troezen, she founded a sanctuary to Aph- rodite upon the slope of the Acropolis in a spot where there was a view across to Troezen. |

The temple was to bear a name in memory of Hippolytus. And in time it came to be familiarly known to the Athenians as the Hippolyteum (Asclepiades, Schol. Od. XI 321):

| | |
|---|---|
| Φαίδρα.... σφοδρῶς ἐπ' αὐτῷ τηχομένη τὸ μὲν πρῶτον ἱερὸν Ἀφροδίτης ἐν Ἀθήναις ἱδρύσατο τὸ νῦν Ἱππολύτειον καλούμενον, εἰς Τροιζῆνα δὲ ὕστερον παραγομένη διενοεῖτο πείθειν τὸν νεανίσκον ὅπως αὐτῇ μιγείη | Phaedra . . . utterly pining away for him founded the first sanctuary to Aphrodite in Athens—the one now called the Hippolyteum; and afterwards she went over to Troezen with the purpose of persuading the young man to accept her love |

The Ἀφροδίτη ἐπὶ Ἱππολύτῳ was, according to this statement, the earliest Aphrodisium in Athens; and it had a long though not conspicuous history; the purpose of its founding also is made clear from this Homeric note, which also throws some light upon our passage in Euripides.

As the temple in the popular speech came to be called the Hippolyteum, so the goddess herself came to have the surname of Hippolytia, as we have inferred before and as we now have the fact stated categorically by a Scholiast on the passage in the Hippolytus of Euripides (l. 29):

| | |
|---|---|
| Ἀφροδίτης ἱερὸν ἱδρύσασθαι τὴν Φαίδραν | they say that Phaedra founded a sanctuary of Aphrodite; |
| φασίν· ἐκάλεσε δὲ Ἀφροδίτην ἐφ' Ἱππολύτῳ, ἣν καὶ Ἱππολυτείαν καλοῦσι | and she gave Aphrodite a name in honor of Hippolytus, and they call her also Hippolytia |

But Ἀφροδίτη ἐπὶ Ἱππολύτῳ is her official name; for so we find it in an official inscription (C. I. A. I 212).

A further confirmation, which also rests immediately upon the lines of Euripides, is found in the scholium to line 32:

| | |
|---|---|
| ἐν γὰρ τῇ Ἀκροπόλει ἱδρύσατο Ἀφροδίτης ναὸν ἐπὶ [κακῷ, for which read ] ἔρωτι Ἱππολύτου | for upon the Acropolis she founded a temple to Aphrodite for the sake of her love for Hippolytus |

This Scholiast is overconfident in his interpretation of Euripides and places the temple— wrongly—*upon* the Acropolis.

Another Scholiast on our Euripides passage is less sure as to the location of the temple and he writes:

| | |
|---|---|
| καὶ μὴ παρόντος ἐρῶσα τοῦ Ἱππολύτου, ὥστε καὶ ἐπ' αὐτῷ ἱδρύσασθαι τὸ ἱερὸν ἐπὶ πέτρας τινός | and though he was not present, she fell in love with Hippolytus, so that she also founded the sanctuary in his memory upon a certain rock |

This scholium is not remarkable for its depth of understanding: the writer misses altogether the meaning of ἐρῶσ' ἔρωτ' ἔκδημον, which he renders with μὴ παρόντος ἐρῶσα and has the temple built upon "a certain rock," as if undecided whether the πέτρα Παλλάδος was the Acropolis rock or Lycabettus or something else.

From the summit of the Acropolis Troezenian Methana stands out conspicuously in view across the Gulf. But from the slopes of the Acropolis hill there is but one short stretch from which the view toward Troezen is not cut off by the Hill of the Muses and the mountains of Aegina. That short stretch lies just west of the Dionysiac Theatre, between the Asclepieum and the Odeum of Herodes Atticus—rather nearer the Asclepieum. Take but a few steps down the hillside from here toward the theatre, and the heights of Troezene drop out of sight behind the ridge of the Hill of the Muses; move but a few steps toward the Odeum of Herodes Atticus, and the hills of Aegina intercept the view across the Gulf. And here Pausanias, on his way from the Asclepieum to the Acropolis, finds a monument to Hippolytus (I 22, 1):

| | |
|---|---|
| μετὰ δὲ τὸ ἱερὸν τοῦ Ἀσκληπιοῦ ταύτῃ πρὸς τὴν ἀκρόπολιν ἰοῦσιν Θέμιδος ναός ἐστι. κεχῶσθαι δὲ πρὸ αὐτοῦ μνῆμα Ἱππολύτῳ. | and next after the sanctuary of Asclepius, as you go by this route toward the Acropolis, is a temple of Themis. And before this is reared a monument to Hippolytus. |

With that he leaves his topography and makes an excursus to tell the circumstances of the young man's death, but he makes no mention of any sanctuary of Aphrodite here. This has led Curt Wachsmuth[1] to argue at length, though without being persuaded by his own reasoning, that the temple of Aphrodite ἐπὶ Ἱππολύτῳ was not on the slopes of the Acropolis at all but upon the southern slopes of Lycabettus. Lycabettus could very fittingly be called the "rock of Pallas." It was peculiarly her own; for she had gone to fetch it to Athens and there, overcome by the news of the unfaithfulness of the Dew-sisters, she had dropped it in her flight, to remain forever; and upon it she had a sanctuary of her own, the temple of Athena Glaucopis.

But the Athenians, after the Persian invasion, if not before, were wont fondly to call the Acropolis "the rock of Athena." Euripides himself varies the appellation: Παλλάδος ὄχθον "Pallas's hill" (Ion 12), Ἀθάνας σκόπελον "Athena's cliff" (Ion 1434, 1479). The later Greek writers who mention it all interpret Euripides's "rock of Pallas" as the Acropolis. And the only possible argument for another site is the *argumentum ex silentio* from Pausanias. It is indeed surprising that Pausanias should mention the monument of Hippolytus and even indulge in reflections about the young prince's death and yet fail to mention the Aphrodite Hippolytia, if the temple was there. But here he is brief; he passes the Aphrodite temple in silence; he mentions only with the name the temple of Themis and, with a little detail, the monument of Hippolytus; and then, without a word, he skips over everything till he reaches the Aphrodite Pandemus. For it is in the very next sentence after the Hippolytus episode that he passes to the Pandemus, whose sanctuary, we know, stood further toward the western slope of the Acropolis, on the edge of "the ancient agora," which lay between the citadel and the Pnyx. That has led some topographers, notably Leake[2] and Curtius,[3] to identify the Pandemus and the Hippolytia. The nature of the Pandemus and that of Phaedra's Aphrodite are identical;[4] but the Pandemus temple was a great state institution; while Phaedra's, in its origin at least, was a private chapel. Both date from very ancient times.

There may also be something in the apparent play upon the words in Euripides. The older temple to Aphrodite was founded by Theseus, the next one by his wife; the first was in honor of the goddess of Love *Pandemus*, the second in honor (or dishonor) of a love *ecdemus;* the first was to commemorate the great prince's splendid statesmanship in uniting the scattered people of Attica into one state (πανδημί) through the powers of Love and Persuasion (Aphrodite and Pitho), the second to secure a union between herself and the foreign object of her guilty affection (ἔρως ἔκδημος).

We conclude, therefore, from the evidence of the Scholiasts, of Diodorus, of Euripidean usage, and from the striking fact that the only spot on the slopes of the Acropolis from which a view of Troezene is possible is in the neighborhood of the monument of Hippolytus

[1] *Stadt Athen*, I pp. 375–379.
[2] *Topogr.*, I. p. 103, n. 8 (German ed.). This theory has found very little acceptance, Verrall's [*C. R.* XV (1901), p. 449] "general" to the contrary notwithstanding. Neither can ναόν in the Eur. passage mean "statue," as Verrall seems to translate it.
[3] *Attische Studien*, I p. 48.
[4] Paus. IX 16, 4.

THE SOUTH SLOPE OF THE ACROPOLIS
Asclepieum Aphrodisium (?) Odeum     Salamis
Prison of Socrates

by the Asclepieum, that here, just to the west of the sanctuary of the healing god who raised our hero from the dead, stood Euripides's temple of Aphrodite ἐπὶ Ἱππολύτῳ.[1]

The official designation of this temple is confirmed by an inscription, which, though badly mutilated, reads

| | |
|---|---|
| ['Αφροδ] ίτης ἐ | Aphrodite's temple in |
| [πἰ'Ἱππ] ολύτῳ | honor of Hippolytus |

We have other inscriptions naming Aphrodite Pandemus, which must, therefore, be the official name of the temple further west. Accordingly, there can be no question as to the approximate location of the two Aphrodite temples on the south and southwest slope of the Acropolis.

There is a fitness in the local associations, too, that is striking; here are, in a closely associated group, the temple to the goddess who caused the trouble, a barrow in memory of the unhappy victim, a temple of the goddess of justice who vindicated the young man's innocence, a sanctuary of the healing god who raised him from the dead. We find also a striking parallel in the same conjunction of shrines at Epidaurus: a sacred enclosure and temple to Hippolytus, a sanctuary of Aphrodite, and a shrine of Themis, all in immediate connection with the worship of Asclepius at the Hieron of Epidaurus. It looks as if the whole combination had been brought over together from the Argolid to Athens.

Unhappily, the excavations on the southern slope of the Acropolis have not solved the problems involved. Immediately adjoining the temple of Asclepius on the west are the foundations of a temple, built or rebuilt in Roman times, partly with material (Kara limestone) apparently taken from the older temple of Dionysus Eleuthereus built by Pisistratus down below the theatre. It stands, facing slightly south of east, a little too far to the west to answer Euripides's description. It may possibly be the temple of Themis. Immediately to the west of this are the foundations of another building, with two columns in antis, also rebuilt in Roman times. It may be a temple or a choragic monument or something else. On the spot where the temple of Aphrodite Hippolytia ought to be there are no remains whatever; and further west there are no foundations of anything except walls of fortification and a Mycenaean tomb, until we reach the Odeum of Herodes Atticus, for this region lay within the old Pelargicum, which the oracle declared should remain unoccupied.[2]

### b. *Aphrodite Pandemus*

A little farther on toward the west, as we have noted, was the temple of Aphrodite Pandemus, and in close conjunction with her was also the temple of Persuasion. We have in our dramatic poets no certain reference to the Pandemus, but we have one vague allusion to the temple of Pitho (Eur. Ant., Frag. 170 N.):

| | |
|---|---|
| οὐκ ἔστι Πειθοῦς ἱερὸν ἄλλο πλὴν λόγος, | there is no other temple to Pitho than persuasive words, |
| καὶ βωμὸς αὐτῆς ἔστι' ἐν ἀνθρώπου φύσει | and her altar is in the heart of man |

The lines are characteristic of the poet of rhetoric and the sophists' schools. Whatever the context may have been, no Athenian who heard the lines could have failed to think of the material altar and the material temple that overlooked his ancient Agora and reminded him of the persuasive power that had made for him a united Attica.

### c. *Other Aphrodisia*

Various other temples of Aphrodite find mention in the dramatic poets; but there is not the faintest light thrown upon them beyond the bare fact of their existence. Aristophanes names two sanctuaries of the goddess of love, otherwise unknown to us (Lys. 1–3):

[1] In the walls of the chapel of the Παναγία Σπηλαιώτισσα, built into the cave above the theatre, Ross found an inscription (C. I G. INo. 481) dealing with an Aphrodite. The evidence that he would adduce from this for the location of our temple is wholly fallacious; the stone with the inscription might have been brought from no one knows where and may refer to any one of the many Aphrodites that we know in Athens.

[2] See pp. 256 ff.

Ἀλλ' εἴ τις ἐς Βαχχεῖον αὐτὰς ἐκάλεσεν | Well—if any one had called them to the Bac-
cheum,

ἢ 'ς Πανός, ἢ 'πὶ Κωλιάδ', ἢ' ς Γενετυλλίδος, | or to the Paneum, or to Colias, or to the shrine of
Genetyllis,

οὐδ' ἂν διελθεῖν ἦν ἂν ὑπὸ τῶν τυμπάνων | it would not have been possible to get through for
the tambourines

Colias and Genetyllis seem to have been by-names of Aphrodite. Colias is obviously derived
from the cape to the southeast of Athens, where Aphrodite had a shrine and where, with
her, were worshiped the goddesses that preside over childbirth (Γενετυλλίδες θεαί).[1] The
sanctuary of Aphrodite on Cape Colias is mentioned also by Strabo,[2] Harpocration, and
Hesychius,[3] and the Scholiast on Aristophanes's Lysistrate 2 and Clouds 52, where both
Colias and Genetyllis are used as by-names of Aphrodite. "On some Athenian coins there
appears, beside the usual owl, a figure holding in its right hand three draped female figures.
Beulé[4] interpreted this device as the Colian Aphrodite with the Genetyllides. A terra cotta
group found in the south of Russia represents Aphrodite and Eros with a tiny draped female
figure standing by Eros. Stephani[5] interprets the small female figure as Genetyllis or
Ilithyia."[6]

Still another Attic temple of Aphrodite is alluded to by Aristophanes (Δράμ. ἢ Κέν.
Frag. 273 K.):

τὸ δὲ πορνεῖον Κύλλου πήρα | and the brothel, Cyllus's pouch

on which Photius makes the comment (p. 185, 21):

Κύλλου πήραν· ἡ Πήρα χωρίον πρὸς | Cyllus's pouch: the Pouch is a district on the
slopes

τῷ Ὑμηττῷ, ἐν ᾧ ἱερὸν Ἀφροδίτης, | of Hymettus, in which there is a shrine of Aphro-
dite

καὶ κρήνη, ἐξ ἧς αἱ πιοῦσαι εὐτοκοῦσι | and a spring; women who drink from it have easy
labor,

καὶ αἱ ἄγονοι γόνιμοι γίγνονται. Κρατῖνος
δὲ ἐν Μαλθακοῖς[7] καλιὰν αὐτήν φησιν | and the barren become fruitful. And Cratinus
in his Malthaci[7] calls it a "nest"

Hesychius adds:

ἔστι γὰρ χωρίον
Ἀθήνησιν ἐπηρεφὲς καὶ κρήνη | for it is a place at Athens
with an overhanging cliff and a spring

This wonder-working shrine of Aphrodite is mentioned only in this fragment of Aristophanes
and in the lexicographers commenting on the name. All we can infer from any or all of them
is that out in the glades among the first foothills of Hymettus near Athens was a sanctuary
of the goddess, with a spring of miraculous powers, a boon to women, resorted to especially
by prospective young mothers. For want of any definite data, therefore, we do not know
whether this sanctuary included a temple or was only a sacred enclosure about the spring,
with an altar for sacrifice; if we assume from Aristophanes's few words that there was a
temple, we cannot guess whether it was large or small, pillared or plain. There are a few
ancient fragments about the deserted old monastery of Καισαριανή; there is a fine spring
there much visited even unto this day by pregnant women; and it is quite probable that
the monastery occupies the site of the old Κύλλου πήρα.

The Latin poets bring in various temples of Venus. Plautus lays the scene of the Rudens
in Cyrene. This wealthy Greek colony must have had a rich temple of Aphrodite; it occupies

---

[1] Κωλιάδες and Γενετυλλίδες are not uncommon plural forms: Ar. Thes. 130; Luc. Am. 42; Alciphron III
11; Paus. I 1, 5: ἄκρα Κωλιάς... Κωλιάδες δέ ἐστιν ἐνταῦθα Ἀφροδίτης καὶ Γενετυλλίδες ὀνομαζόμεναι θεαί.

[2] IX p. 398.

[3] s. v. Κωλιάς.

[4] *Les Monnaies d'Athènes*, pp. 365 sq.

[5] *Compte Rendu pour l'année* 1873, pp. 10–16, Atlas I, No. 2; 1875, pp. 74 sq.; 1880, p. 117.

[6] Frazer, *Paus.*, II p. 36.

[7] Frag. 102 K.

the centre of the stage and it plays an extensive part in the development of the plot of Plautus's play. At almost the very beginning (ll. 59–61) we find

> leno . . . . . .
> ait sese Veneri velle votum solvere
> —id hic est Veneris fanum—

and        (94-95):

> nunc huc ad Veneris fanum venio visere,
> ubi rem divinam se facturum dixerat.

The temple is mentioned again and again;[1] but nowhere is there even the vaguest hint at the outward appearance of what may have been one of the most magnificent Doric creations of the fifth or fourth century. Plautus himself may never have seen Cyrene; the author of the Greek comedy on which he based the Rudens may never have seen Cyrene; and yet it is quite possible that both the Greek poet and the Roman were quite familiar with that thriving emporium in Africa. At all events, it is safe to assume that they knew much about it. The excavations, when interrupted by the Italo-Turkish War in 1911, had not yet brought to light any building that might have been a Greek temple; but they did yield one of the most beautiful statues of Aphrodite that we know—the Aphrodite of Cyrene now in the Museo delle Terme in Rome. It is altogether possible that this statue may have had to do with the temple so prominent in the Rudens.

Only a little less prominent than the Aphrodisium of Cyrene in the Rudens is the temple of Venus at Calydon in the Poenulus. Although the latter temple is not a part of the stage-setting as the former is, it still plays an important rôle in the solution of the plot and the recognition of the lost children at the festival of Aphrodite celebrated at the temple. The Latin poet tells us nothing of the temple except that it was there; that it was thronged on the great festival day of the goddess; that before it was an altar of sacrifice (Pl. Poen. 190–191):

> ego in aedem Veneris eo . . .
> Aphrodisia hodie sunt.

(*ibid.* 264–265):

> erus nos apud aedem Veneris mantat. AD. Maneat pol. mane.
> turba est nunc apud aram.[2]

(*ibid.* 1179–1181):

> haud sordere visust
> festus dies, Venus, nec tuom fanum:
> tantus ibi clientarum erat numerus,
> quae ad Calydoniam venerant Venerem.

(*ibid.* 318–320):

> Quia non iam dudum ante lucem ad aedem Veneris venimus,
> primae ut inferremus ignem ad aram. AD. Aha, non factost opus:
> quae habent nocturna ora, noctu sacruficatum ire occupant.[3]

An altar to Venus—not a temple altar, but a street altar—stands near the temple of Asclepius at Epidaurus, according to the stage-setting of the Curculio (Pl. Cur. 71):

> nunc ara Veneris haec est ante horunc fores.[4]

These temples that we have been considering are Greek temples in Greek cities. Occasionally the Roman comic poets introduce into their scenes bits of Roman topography, with temples that are distinctively Roman. Thus Plautus, in a kind of comic parabasis, has his Chorus ("the Company's Property Manager"[5]) talk about the Vicus Tuscus (Pl. Cur. 482) and the temple of Castor and Pollux (*ibid.* 481) and the shrine of Venus Cloacina (*ibid.* 471) and a variety of other familiar things about the Forum (*ibid.* 466–485).[6] Even

---

[1] ll. 128–130, 136, 253–261, 271, 283–285, 305, 308, 322, 329, 331, 334, 350, 386, 430, 432, 454, 559–560, 564, 570, 586, 613, 622, 643–644, 663, 670–673, 688, 688–690, 691, 695, 697, 698, 706, 723, 784, 822, 840, 846, 849, 865, 1048, 1065, 1286, 1332–1333, 1338. The altar is mentioned especially in ll. 707, 768, 1336.

[2] Cf. l. 1132.

[3] Cp. also ll. 190, 323, 333, 339, 821, 847, 1132, 1175.

[4] Cf. also ll. 72–74, 123, 196, etc. In Pl. Truc. 476 it is an altar to Juno Lucina.

[5] Nixon, *ad* Pl. Cur. 461–462.

[6] The Comitium (470; mentioned also in Poen. 807); a basilica (472); the Forum Piscarium (474); a canal (476); the Lacus Curtius (477); the Tabernae Veteres (480); the Velabrum (483); Leucadia Oppia (485).

in a dialog part of the same play, in a scene laid directly in front of the temple of Asclepius in Epidaurus, one of the speakers refers to the temple of Jupiter on the Capitoline (ll. 266–269). Of the same local Roman coloring is the fragment of a Fabula Atellana (of Lucius Pomponius Bunonius, 133 R.²):

> ad Veneris est profectus mane vetulus, votum ut solveret.

If we had more of the earlier Latin drama, we should have still more of Roman scenes and Roman topography and Roman temples. But our problem has to do with things Greek, and we need not dwell upon these Roman temples of Venus or Castor or any other god of Italy.

### 19. The Temple of Athena Chalcioecus at Sparta

Upon the acropolis of Sparta stood the famous sanctuary of "Athena of the House of Bronze." Pausanias gives all the details available to us (III 17, 2–3):

| | |
|---|---|
| Ἐνταῦθα Ἀθηνᾶς ἱερὸν πεποίηται, Πολιούχου καλουμένης καὶ Χαλκιοίκου τῆς αὐτῆς. τοῦ δὲ ἱεροῦ τῆς κατασκευῆς Τυνδάρεως, καθὰ λέγουσιν, ἤρξατο· ἀποθανόντος δὲ ἐκείνου δεύτερα οἱ παῖδες ἐξεργάσασθαι τὸ οἰκοδόμημα ἤθελον, ἀφορμὴ δέ σφισιν ἔμελλε τὰ ἐξ Ἀφιδνῶν ἔσεσθαι λάφυρα. προαπολιπόντων δὲ καὶ τούτων, Λακεδαιμόνιοι πολλοῖς ἔτεσιν ὕστερον τόν τε ναὸν ὁμοίως καὶ τὸ ἄγαλμα ἐποιήσαντο Ἀθηνᾶς χαλκοῦν. Γιτιάδας δὲ εἰργάσατο ἀνὴρ ἐπιχώριος.... ἐπείργασται δὲ τῷ χαλκῷ πολλὰ μὲν τῶν ἄθλων Ἡρακλέους, πολλὰ δὲ καὶ ὧν ἐθελοντὴς κατώρθωσε.... | On this spot is builded a sanctuary of Athena surnamed "The City-upholder" and likewise "Goddess of the House of Bronze." Tyndareos, as they say, began the construction of the sanctuary; after his death, his sons again proposed to complete the building, and they were to find the means for it in the spoils taken from Aphidnae. But as these funds were exhausted before the completion of the work, the Lacedaemonians many years later had both the temple and a statue of Athena made of bronze. Gitiadas, a native sculptor, executed the work; ... upon the bronze many of the labors of Heracles and many also of the exploits that he voluntarily performed are wrought ... |

In commenting on the passage just quoted, Mr. Frazer says "it is probable that the building was merely lined with bronze plates, like the so called Treasury of Atreus at Mycenae."[1] But the Treasury of Atreus was not "lined with bronze plates," as Frazer very correctly states at page 126. And there can be no doubt as to Pausanias's intention to state definitely that the temple was constructed of bronze. Pausanias himself sweeps away any possible skepticism as to the material of which the walls were constructed in a later passage (X 5, 11):

| | |
|---|---|
| τὰ δὲ ἐς τὸν τρίτον τῶν ναῶν², ὅτι ἐγένετο ἐκ χαλκοῦ, θαῦμα οὐδέν, εἴ γε Ἀκρίσιος μὲν θάλαμον χαλκοῦν τῇ θυγατρὶ ἐποιήσατο, Λακεδαιμονίοις δὲ Ἀθηνᾶς ἱερὸν Χαλκιοίκου καὶ ἐς ἡμᾶς ἔτι λείπεται.... οὕτω καὶ ναὸν τῷ Ἀπόλλωνι οὐκ ἂν ἀπό γε τοῦ εἰκότως εἴη γενέσθαι χαλκοῦν. | the fact that the third one of the temples² was made of bronze need occasion no surprise, for Acrisius had a chamber of bronze made for his daughter; and at Sparta a sanctuary of Athena of the House of Bronze is left even unto our day ... And in the same way, it is not at all unlikely that Apollo's temple was made of bronze. |

Livy also speaks of the temple as made of bronze (XXXV 36, 9): Aetoli circa Chalcioecon —Minervae aereum est templum—congregati caeduntur. The words *aereum est templum* do not easily admit of any other interpretation than that the temple was, in large part at least, constructed of bronze.

Mr. Frazer, in the same connection,[3] says "We must similarly interpret the statement

[1] Frazer, *Paus.*, III p. 345. So also Weissenborn on Livy XXXV 36, 9: Chalcioecus nennt Livius den Tempel, weil dessen Wände im inneren durch eherne Platten mit Reliefs in getriebener Arbeit geschmückt waren.

[2] The temples of Apollo at Delphi.

[3] III p. 345.

of Pausanias (VI 19, 2) that two chambers in the treasury of the Sicyonians at Olympia were made of bronze." Pausanias's words are:

ἐν δὲ τῷ θησαυρῷ καὶ θαλάμους
δύο ἐποίησε, τὸν μὲν Δώριον, τὸν
δὲ ἐργασίας τῶν Ἰώνων. χαλκοῦ μὲν
δὴ αὐτοὺς ἑώρων εἰργασμένους . . .

. . . . . . .

ἐπιγράμματα ἐπὶ τῷ ἐλάσσονι
ἐστι τῶν θαλάμων, ἐς μὲν τοῦ
χαλκοῦ τὸν σταθμόν, ὅτι πεντα-
κόσια εἴη τάλαντα, ἐς δὲ τοὺς
ἀναθέντας, Μύρωνα εἶναι καὶ
τὸν Σικυόνων δῆμον

and in the treasury he[1] had two chambers made, the one Doric and the other in the Ionic order. They were made of bronze, as I saw . . .

. . . . . . .

There are upon the smaller one of the chambers inscriptions, referring, the one to the weight of the bronze, stating that it was five hundred talents, and the other to the donors, stating that they were Myron and the Sicyonian people

Again Mr. Frazer has occasion to correct himself. For when he comes to his commentary[2] on this later passage, he has discovered the fact that these two chambers are not a part of the treasury building, for the Sicyonian treasury at Olympia did not have two chambers, and that the walls of the interior of the building were never covered, even partially, with bronze plates. And so he accepts the obvious conclusion that these "chambers" were "portable models." The smaller, Doric, "chamber" was dedicated by Myron; the larger, Ionic, one was probably considerably later. If the smaller one weighed approximately nineteen tons, we are curious as to what the weight of the larger one might have been and what its dimensions were. At all events, we are by the facts in the case justified in concluding that the Greeks did not hesitate to put an enormous quantity of bronze into the walls of a building, and a bronze sanctuary of Athena of the House of Bronze is entirely within the bounds of possibility and of probability.

The bronze sanctuary of Athena at Sparta acquired such fame that the Spartan goddess became known as the "Athena of the House of Bronze" or simply the "Goddess of the House of Bronze." Thucydides so refers to her (I 134, 1); and so does Polybius (IV 35, 2). The name necessarily carries with it an allusion to the temple. The poets also are familiar with the Goddess of the House of Bronze and with her temple. Euripides twice alludes to the shrine; unhappily he assumes that his hearers also are acquainted with it and tells us no more than the mere name (Hel. 227–228):

οὐδέ ποτ' ἔτι πάτρια μέλαθρα
καὶ τὰν Χαλκίοικον ὀλβιεῖς

nor ever shalt thou again gladden thy father's halls and her of the House of Bronze

(*ibid.* 244–246):

ὅς[4] με[3] χλοερὰ δρεπομέναν ἔσω πέπλων

ῥόδεα πέταλα, Χαλκίοικον ὡς Ἀθάναν
μόλοιμ', ἀναρπάσας δι' αἰθέρος

and as I[3] was gathering the fresh blossoms of the rose into my lap,
that I might go to Athena of the House of Bronze, he[4] caught me up through the air

Or it may be that Sparta was too far away from Athens and that Euripides, assuming that only the fewest of his audience had ever seen the "house of bronze," thought it unwise to mention any details. Furthermore the Athena of the House of Bronze was the Athena who stood as most formidable rival of their own Polias, and Athenians thought of her chiefly as the goddess who had failed to afford due protection to the hero of Plataea.

Aristophanes also alludes to the famous shrine; but again we have nothing but the name (Lys. 1299–1300):

κλέωα τὸν Ἀμύκλαις σιὸν
καὶ Χαλκίοικον ἄνασσαν

calling upon the god at Amyclae and the sovereign one of the House of Bronze

and (1318):

καὶ τὰν σιὰν δ' αὖ τὰν κρατίσταν Χαλκίοικον
ὕμνη

and sing, too, in her turn, the all-mighty Queen of the House of Bronze

[1] *Sc.* Myron, tyrant of Sicyon.
[2] IV pp. 58–59.
[3] Helen.
[4] Hermes.

Sometimes the poets merely allude to the House of Bronze; but the allusion is nevertheless unmistakable (e. g. Eur. Tro. 1110–1113):

| | |
|---|---|
| μηδὲ γαῖάν ποτ' ἔλθοι Λάκαιναν.... | ne'er may he[1] come to the Laconian |
| μηδὲ πόλιν Πιτάνας | land nor to Pitane's town |
| χαλκόπυλόν τε θεάν. | and the goddess of the Gates of Bronze |

and with a slightly more veiled allusion (Eur. Hel. 1465–1468):

| | |
|---|---|
| ἤ που χόρας ἂν ποταμοῦ[2] | perchance by the rolling river[2] thou[3] shalt |
| παρ' οἶδμα Λευκιππίδας ἢ πρὸ ναοῦ | find the daughters of Leucippus, |
| Παλλάδος ἂν λάβοις[3] | or before the shrine of Pallas |

In these few passages the dramatic poets add nothing to our previous knowledge of the House of Bronze upon the acropolis of Sparta. The excavations conducted there by the British School have now added somewhat more. The exact site is fixed just above the theatre. But the remains are so scanty that we are still just where Pausanias and Thucydides left us at the first: we know that the Spartans had a famous temple of Athena Chalcioecus and that the material of its construction was bronze. How large it was, how it appeared, what decoration it had without or within (save for the cultus statue of bronze)—these are questions for which no answer can yet be forthcoming.

Besides the temple proper, however, the temenos contained at least one small building. For it was to this sanctuary that Pausanias, traitor to Greece and one time hero of Plataea, fled for refuge when his acts of treason were uncovered. This little building had its own door and roof. The Spartan authorities, to escape the sacrilege of desecrating the sanctuary, blocked up the door and removed the roof and left Pausanias to starve to death.[4]

But it was into the temple itself that the ephors fled for refuge from the assassins in the Aetolian wars; and the reckless fury of their enemies refused to spare them at the very altar and sacred table of the goddess.[5]

## 20. POSEIDEA

The sea-god also had many temples and shrines and statues in his honor. These, too, have little light from the Attic poets. Euripides gives a list of temples of Poseidon, but he goes no further than only to name their sites (Cy. 290–296):

| | |
|---|---|
| οἳ τὸν σόν, ὦναξ, πατέρ' ἔχειν ναῶν ἕδρας | we, my lord, have saved thy father the sites |
| ἐρρυσάμεθα γῆς ἐν Ἑλλάδος μυχοῖς. | of temples that he holds in every corner of Hellas: |
| ἱερός τ' ἄθραυστος Ταινάρου μένει λιμήν, | Taenarum's holy haven remains unshattered |
| Μαλέας τ' ἄκροι χευθμῶνες, ἥ τε Σουνίου | and Malea's promontory-retreats, and divine |
| δίας 'Αθάνας σῶς ὑπάργυρος πέτρα, | Athena's silver-veined rock of Sunium is safe, |
| Γεραίστιοί τε καταφυγαί, τά θ' Ἑλλάδος | and the refuge of Geraestus, and we allowed not to |
| δυσφορά γ' ὀνείδη Φρυξὶν οὐκ ἐδώκαμεν | the Phrygians their unbearable reproaches against Greece |

Euripides here tells us only that upon the promontory of Taenarum Poseidon had a shrine, another on that of Malea, a third at Sunium, and a fourth upon the southernmost point of Euboea, the promontory of Geraestus. And Aristophanes (Ran. 664–665) sums them all up with

| | |
|---|---|
| Πόσειδον.. ὃς Αἰγαίου πρῶνας... μέδεις | Poseidon . . . who holdest sway over the Aegean headlands |

### a. *The Temple of Poseidon at Sunium*

In regard to only one of the four does he add a word of further interest: at Sunium Poseidon's temple has to do with the goddess Athena's silver-veined rock. The silver-veined

[1] Menelaus.
[2] Eurotas.
[3] Helen.
[4] See Thuc. I 134, 1–3; Diod. XI 45; Polyaen. VIII 51; Lyc., in Leocr. 128; Plut., Parol. 10. Cp. also Plut., Lyc. 5, Agis 11, Apophth. Lacon., Lyc., 11.
[5] Polybius IV 35, 2–4: κατὰ γάρ τινα θυσίαν πάτριον ἔδει τοὺς μὲν ἐν ταῖς ἡλικίαις μετὰ τῶν ὅπλων πομπεύειν ἐπὶ τὸν τῆς 'Αθηνᾶς τῆς Χαλκιοίκου νεών....καίτοι πᾶσι τοῖς καταφυγοῦσι τὴν ἀσφάλειαν παρεσκεύαζε τὸ ἱερόν, κἂν θανάτου τις ἦ κατακεκριμένος· τότε δὲ διὰ τὴν ὠμότητα τῶν τολμώντων εἰς τοῦτ' ἦλθε καταφρονήσεως ὥστε περὶ τὸν βωμὸν καὶ τὴν τράπεζαν τῆς θεοῦ κατασφαγῆναι τοὺς ἐφόρους ἅπαντας.

THE PROMONTORY OF SUNIUM

THE TEMPLE OF POSEIDON AT SUNIUM

rock **is,** of course, the mountain which runs from the silver mines above Laurium down to the promontory and on which the temple stands; and it all belongs to Athena whose temple stood about five hundred yards to the north of the Poseideum, the splendid fifth century Doric peripteral temple, of which eleven beautiful columns still stand above the sea upon "Tritonia's airy height."[1]

Aristophanes has three further allusions to Sunium and its temples, but they are only casual references; they tell us nothing further. The first (Eq. 551; 560)

| | |
|---|---|
| ἵππι' ἄναξ Πόσειδον . . . | oh Poseidon, lord of steeds, . . . |
| . . . Σουνιάρατε | . . . worshiped at Sunium |

only assures us again that Poseidon had a temple at Sunium. It is from other sources[2] that we learn to assign the temple with the standing columns at Sunium to Poseidon, the other to Athena. In the second passage (Ar. Nub. 401) Socrates explains to the guileless Strepsiades that it is not the wicked that Zeus smites with his lightnings, but his own temple and Sunium:

| | |
|---|---|
| ἀλλὰ τὸν αὑτοῦ γε νεὼν βάλλει καὶ Σούνιον | but his own temple he smites and Sunium, head- |
| ἄκρον 'Αθηνέων | land of Athens |

The third is a blasphemous parody on the prayer in the first passage (Ar. Av. 869):

| | |
|---|---|
| ὦ Σουνιέρακε,[3] χαῖρ' ἄναξ Πελαργικέ[4] | thou Hawk of Sunium, all hail, oh king of stork-land |

### b. *The Temple of Poseidon at Geraestus*

Of the temples of Poseidon on Cape Geraestus in Euboea and on Cape Malea in Laconia nothing in known from any source, except that there were such temples. Geraestus is coupled with Sunium as a seat of Poseidon worship again (Ar. Eq. 551; 560–561):

| | |
|---|---|
| ἵππι' ἄναξ Πόσειδον . . . | oh Poseidon, lord of steeds . . . |
| . . . Σουνιάρατε, | . . . worshipped at Sunium, |
| ὦ Γεραίστιε . . . | god of Geraestus . . . |

### c. *The Temple of Poseidon at Taenarum*

Besides the mention of the temple of the sea-god at Taenarum in the Cyclops (292)[5], there are two others that might be cited, although they say nothing beyond the fact that there was a temple of Poseidon there (Ar. Ach. 510–511):

| | |
|---|---|
| χαὐτοῖς ὁ Ποσειδῶν οὑπὶ Ταινάρῳ θεὸς | and may Poseidon, the god at Taenarum, cause |
| σείσας ἅπασιν ἐμβάλοι τὰς οἰκίας | the earth to quake and bring down their houses upon them all |

and that in connection with it there was a festival, with rites more than ordinarily wild (Hermip. Θεοί, Frag. 32 K.):

| | |
|---|---|
| καὶ σέ τι χρὴ παραταιναρίζειν | and you must be outdoing the Taenaria |

The following fragment does not name Taenarum specifically (Eup. Εἵλ., Frag. 140 K.):

| | |
|---|---|
| τέμενος Ποτειδᾶ ποντίῳ | a sacred enclosure of Poseidon of the sea |

But the passage is from the Helots; a Dorian is speaking; the Poseidon shrine cannot, therefore, well be any other than the one at Taenarum or, possibly, the one at Malea.

[1] For the topography of Sunium since the excavations of the Greek Archaeological Society in 1889, see Staes, Πρακτικά, 1890.
[2] Vitruvius IV 8, 4; and an inscription.
[3] With an unreproduceable pun upon Σουνιάρατε (cf. Eq. 560).
[4] With a triple play between Πελαργικόν, Πελασγικόν, and πέλαγος.
[5] Quoted above, p. 160.

### d. *The Temple of Poseidon at Cape Malea*

Upon Cape Malea there are two Christian chapels upon a small terrace leveled off upon the face of the bluff at the extremity of the cape. The Poseideum may have preceded them there, or it may have stood further back in the recesses of the Laconian Gulf. But over on the west shore of the gulf, "on the north side of the bay of Kisternes, close to the flat beach and about 40 paces east of the church of the Ἀσώματος, are the remains of the sanctuary of Poseidon. The foundations are 19.60 meters long by 16 meters broad. The walls are partly formed of the rock, which has been cut and smoothed; above these rock-walls are courses of regularly hewn stones. . . . Within this building there were found, in 1856, seventy bronze statues representing bulls and horses. These were evidently votive offerings and make it certain that the building was a temple of Poseidon."[1] . . . It was both sanctuary of the sea-god, an asylum for criminals,[2] and an oracle of the dead.[3] "Close to the west side of the building is a shallow grotto in the rock. It may have been through this grotto that Heracles was supposed to have brought up Cerberus. Pausanias does not indeed distinguish between the cave and the temple; but Strabo[4] says plainly that the cave was near the sanctuary. The neighboring church of the Ἀσώματος is composed wholly of ancient blocks."[5]

All sanctuaries of Poseidon were naturally built upon precipitous cliffs towering above the sea. Euripides counts it worth while to give us specific assurance of the fact (Cy. 318–319):

| | |
|---|---|
| ἄκρας δ᾽ ἐναλίας ἃς κάθ᾽ ἵδρυται πατὴρ<br>χαίρειν κελεύω | I bid the heights above the sea, on which my<br>father has his seats, go hang |

But we have *uterque Neptunus*—the sea-god who is sovereign of the placid mere as well as of the mighty billows that crash against the dizzy cliffs (Soph. Λαοκ., Frag. 342 N.):

| | |
|---|---|
| Πόσειδον, ὃς Αἰγαίου μέδεις<br>πρῶνας ἢ γλαυκᾶς μέδεις<br>εὐανέμου λίμνας ἐφ᾽ ὑψηλαῖς σπιλάδεσσι<br>στομάτων | oh Poseidon, who rulest over the headlands<br>of the Aegean, or the placid, blue mere,<br>upon the lofty crags of harbors' entrances |

### e. *The Temple of Poseidon at Colonus*

But there were sanctuaries of the sea-god in the plains and well back from the sea. Such a one was the temple of Poseidon Hippius who was worshipped at Colonus and whose surname gave the distinguishing epithet to that hill—Colonus Hippius. In literature it is known to us chiefly from Sophocles, the scene of whose Oedipus Coloneus is laid in the region thereto adjacent. Indeed, the whole region was sacred to Poseidon (Soph. O. C. 54–56):

| | |
|---|---|
| χῶρος μὲν ἱερὸς πᾶς ὅδ᾽ ἔστ᾽· ἔχει δέ νιν<br>σεμνὸς Ποσειδῶν· ἐν δ᾽ ὁ πυρφόρος θεὸς<br>Τιτὰν Προμηθεύς . . . | all this region is holy ground: dread Poseidon<br>owns it; and in it the fire-bringer god,<br>the Titan Prometheus . . . |

Sophocles tells us nothing of the temple; it does not appear upon his scene. But he does several times mention the altar. Before it Theseus is busied with sacrifice on the day on which the action of the Oedipus takes place (O. C. 888–889):

| | |
|---|---|
| βουθυτοῦντά μ᾽ ἀμφὶ βωμὸν ἔσχετ᾽ ἐναλίῳ θεῷ<br>τοῦδ᾽ ἐπιστάτῃ Κολωνοῦ | did ye stay me as I was offering a bullock at the<br>altar of the sea-god, the lord of Colonus here |

Six hundred lines later he is still occupied with the sacrifice (1492–1495):

| | |
|---|---|
| εἴτ᾽ ἄκρον ἐπὶ γύαλον<br>ἐναλίῳ Ποσειδαονίῳ θεῷ<br>βούθυτον ἑστίαν ἁγίζων, ἵκου | or if thou art performing an holy act<br>at the hearth of sacrifice in honor<br>of Poseidon the god of the sea, come |

---

[1] Frazer, *Paus.*, III p. 397.
[2] Thuc. I 128.
[3] Plut., de sera num. vind. 17.
[4] VIII p. 363.
[5] Frazer, *Paus.*, III p. 397.

CAPE MALEA

Sometimes the altar is βωμός; sometimes it is ἑστία "hearth"; sometimes it is plural (ll. 897–898):

| | |
|---|---|
| οὔκουν τις ὡς τάχιστα προσπόλων μολὼν<br>πρὸς τούσδε βωμούς | will not one of you attendants go with<br>all speed to yonder altars |

(ll. 1157–1159[1]):

| | |
|---|---|
| προσπεσόντα πως<br>βωμῷ καθῆσθαι τῷ Ποσειδῶνος, παρ' ᾧ<br>θύων ἔκυρον, ἡνίχ' ὡρμώμην ἐγώ | hath for some reason or other set himself a<br>suppliant at the altar of Poseidon, where I<br>was in the act of sacrificing and just as I came<br>away |

The altar (or altars) of this Poseideum was not far from the sanctuary of the Eumenides at Colonus, for Theseus is within easy call. The Poseideum seems, in fact, to have included the sanctuary of the Eumenides and various other deities. It also closely adjoined, or perhaps even included the Academy; for the shrine of Prometheus mentioned above stood in the grove of Academus,[2] and from the altar of Prometheus the race of the torch-bearers had its start. Inside the Academy Pausanias[3] found an altar to Prometheus, another to the Muses, another to Hermes, and still others to Athena and Heracles. The altar of Prometheus was not the exclusive property of that demigod but was dedicated to him in conjunction with the other great god of fire, Hephaestus, as we learn from the Scholiast on Sophocles's Oedipus at Colonus just cited. The Scholiast quotes from Apollodorus a description of an ancient block containing in relief figures of Prometheus and Hephaestus; Prometheus was represented as an elderly man with a staff (the ferrule of the story?) in his right hand; Hephaestus, younger; their common altar also is represented on the same relief.

The poets of the New Comedy know the Academy also as the home of philosophy and philology (Alexis, Ἀσωτοδ., Frag. 25, 1–3 K.):

| | |
|---|---|
| τί ταῦτα ληρεῖς, φληναφῶν ἄνω κάτω | what do you mean by this nonsense, chattering<br>in season and out of season about |
| Λύκειον, Ἀκαδήμειαν, Ὠιδείου πύλας,<br>λήρους σοφιστῶν; οὐδὲ ἓν τούτων καλόν | the Lyceum, the Academy, the Odeum doors, the<br>nonsense of the sophists? There's not one good<br>thing about them |

The hatred of sophists was at full tide, it would seem, in the days of Alexis. He takes a fling at their philological activities in his Knight (Ἱπ., Frag. 94 K.):

| | |
|---|---|
| τοῦτ' ἔστιν Ἀκαδήμεια, τοῦτο Ξενοκράτης;<br>πόλλ' ἀγαθὰ δοῖεν οἱ θεοὶ Δημητρίῳ<br>καὶ τοῖς νομοθέταις, διότι τοὺς τὰς τῶν λόγων,<br>ὥς φασι, δυνάμεις παραδιδόντας τοῖς νέοις<br>ἐς κόρακας ἔρρειν φασὶν ἐκ τῆς Ἀττικῆς | is that the Academy? that, Xenocrates?<br>May the gods bestow rich blessings on Demetrius<br>and the City Council for telling those who deliver<br>to the youth the true meanings of words, as they<br>say, to get out of Attica and go to the devil |

The god who presided over all this great complex of sanctuaries in northern Ceramicus is the Poseidon that rolls up the great billows of the sea and shakes the firm-fixed cliffs, the creator and tamer of the horse, the special lord of Colonus. It is particularly fitting that the knightly Theseus, son of Aegeus (who is so easily and naturally identified with Poseidon), should be diligent in his worship at this Poseidon sanctuary.

Sophocles, we have seen, makes no mention of any temple but only of hearth or altar or altars of Poseidon. Thucydides calls the holy place at Colonus simply a "sanctuary" (VIII 67, 2):

| | |
|---|---|
| ξυνέκλησαν τὴν ἐκκλησίαν ἐς<br>τὸν Κολωνὸν (ἔστι δὲ ἱερὸν Ποσειδῶνος<br>ἔξω πόλεως ἀπέχον<br>σταδίους μάλιστα δέκα) | they locked the assembly up at<br>Colonus (a sanctuary of Poseidon<br>outside the city and distant from it<br>just about ten furlongs) |

[1] Cp. ll. 1285–1286.

[2] Cf. Schol. Soph. O. C. 57: Τιτὰν Προμηθεύς] περὶ τοῦ τὸν Προμηθέα περὶ τὴν Ἀκαδήμειαν καὶ τὸν Κολωνὸν ἱδρῦσθαι Ἀπολλόδωρος [Frag. 32 Müller] γράφει οὕτω τῇ π[ερὶ θεῶν]· συντιμᾶται δὲ καὶ ἐν Ἀκαδημίᾳ τῇ Ἀθηνᾷ καθάπερ ὁ Ἥφαιστος. καὶ ἔστιν αὐτῷ παλαιὸν ἵδρυμα καὶ βωμὸς ἐν τῷ τεμένει τῆς θεοῦ. δείκνυται καὶ βάσις ἀρχαία κατὰ τὴν εἴσοδον, ἐν ᾗ τοῦ τε Προμηθέως ἐστὶ τύπος καὶ τοῦ Ἡφαίστου. πεποίηται δέ, ὡς καὶ Λυσιμάχης φησίν, ὁ μὲν Προμηθεὺς πρῶτος καὶ πρεσβύτερος ἐν δεξιᾷ σκῆπτρον ἔχων, ὁ δὲ Ἥφαιστος νέος καὶ δεύτερος· καὶ βωμὸς ἀμφοῖν κοινός ἐστιν ἐν τῇ βάσει ἀποτετυπωμένος.

[3] I 30, 2: ἐν Ἀκαδημίᾳ δέ ἐστι Προμηθέως βωμός, καὶ θέουσιν ἀπ' αὐτοῦ πρὸς τὴν πόλιν ἔχοντες καιομένας λαμπάδας... ἔστι δὲ Μουσῶν τε βωμός, καὶ ἕτερος Ἑρμοῦ, καὶ ἔνδον Ἀθηνᾶς, τὸν δὲ Ἡρακλέους ἐποίησαν. καὶ φυτὸν ἐστιν ἐλαίας.

Thucydides apparently has in mind a building, for the assembly was held behind locked doors. Either the ruse of holding the assembly away out there in the suburbs was a political *coup* to secure the attendance of a very small number of the citizens that could be locked up in the temple; or the locked gates were the gates of the temenos. But Pausanias explicitly mentions at the hillock of Colonus Hippius not only the altar to Poseidon but also the grove and the temple of Poseidon, adding that these had been burned by Antigonus.[1] In the time of Sophocles both grove and temple stood.

## 21. ASCLEPIEA

### a. *The Asclepieum on the South Slope of the Acropolis of Athens*

Ancient authors, in general, have nothing to say about the great sanctuary of Asclepius in Athens.[2] Pausanias passes it by, with barely a reference to the building (I 21, 4):

| | |
|---|---|
| τοῦ δὲ Ἀσκληπιοῦ τὸ ἱερὸν | and the sanctuary of Asclepius is |
| ἔς τε τὰ ἀγάλματά ἐστιν, ὁπόσα τοῦ | worth seeing, both for the various statues which have |
| θεοῦ πεποίηται καὶ τῶν παίδων, καὶ ἐς | been made of the god and his children and |
| τὰς γραφὰς θέας ἄξιον. ἔστι δὲ ἐν αὐτῷ | for the paintings. Then, there is in it a |
| κρήνη, παρ' ᾗ λέγουσι Ποσειδῶνος παῖδα . . . | spring, by which, they say, Poseidon's son . . . |

The excavator's spade[3] has given us what we really know of the sanctuary; it occupies the next terrace west of the Dionysiac theatre and consists of several parts: 1) the temple, of which nothing is left but the foundations, 10.50 x 6 M.; 2) the manse (?); and 3) the sanitarium, attached to the temple—a double colonnade 49.50 x 11 M. This last part of the sanctuary was built against and into the Acropolis rock, facing the south and sheltered from the north winds. From the inner colonnade one enters through an arched doorway into a grotto, or chamber, artificially enlarged, in which is the sacred spring, still flowing with pure water with a strong mineral taste and slightly brackish. The sanitarium was provided with rooms or wards and appears to have had an upper story.

This sanctuary of Asclepius plays an important part in the Plutus of Aristophanes; for it is at the sanitarium and at the hands of the healing god that the blind god of wealth recovers his sight. Chremylus determines to secure the admission of Plutus to the hospital (**Ar.** Pl. 411–412):

| | |
|---|---|
| κατακλίνειν αὐτὸν εἰς Ἀσκληπιοῦ κράτιστόν ἐστι | the best thing to do is to get a bed for him at the sanctuary of Asclepius |

and Chremylus proposes that he and his servant transfer their blind guest thither (*ibid.* 620–621):

| | |
|---|---|
| ἐγὼ δὲ καὶ σύ γ' ὡς τάχιστα τὸν θεὸν ἐγκατακλινοῦντ' ἄγωμεν εἰς Ἀσκληπιοῦ | let's you and me take the god at once to the sanctuary of Asclepius and get him a bed there |

And then the procedure of getting the poor, afflicted patient into a general ward in the hospital is described (*ibid.* 653–663):

| | |
|---|---|
| ΚΑ. ὡς γὰρ τάχιστ' ἀφικόμεθα πρὸς τὸν θεὸν ἄγοντες ἄνδρα τότε μὲν ἀθλιώτατον, νῦν δ' εἴ τιν' ἄλλον μακάριον κεὐδαίμονα, πρῶτον μὲν αὐτὸν ἐπὶ θάλατταν ἤγομεν, ἔπειτ' ἐλοῦμεν. ΓΥ. νὴ Δι' εὐδαίμων ἄρ' ἦν ἀνὴρ γέρων ψυχρᾷ θαλάττῃ λούμενος. ΚΑ. ἔπειτα πρὸς τὸ τέμενος ᾖμεν τοῦ θεοῦ. | CA. The moment we reached the god's abode, leading a man then most wretched but now the happiest and most blest of men, first of all we took him to the pool and gave him a bath. WO. What bliss, by Zeus!— for an old man to get a ducking in a cold pool! CA. Then we went on to the sacred enclosure of the god. |
| ἐπεὶ δὲ βωμῷ πόπανα καὶ προθύματα καθωσιώθη, πέλανος Ἡφαίστου φλογί, | And when our cakes and preliminary sacrifice had been laid upon the altar, goo for Hephaestus's flame, |
| κατεκλίναμεν τὸν Πλοῦτον, ὥσπερ εἰκὸς ἦν· ἡμῶν δ' ἕκαστος στιβάδα παρεκαττύετο | we got Plutus a proper bed there; and we drew together, each of us, a bed of straw |

---

[1] The whole passage, I 30, 4, is quoted in full on p. 145.

[2] The scanty material, mostly epigraphic, is collected by Curtius, *Stadtgesch. v. Athen*, p. XVII.

[3] The excavations were made by the Greek Archaeological Society 1876–1878. See the Πρακτικά for 1877. See illustration facing p. 154.

With these lines Aristophanes gives us several helpful hints. In the first place, there was at the outer precincts a "pool." θάλαττα in this passage is usually explained as "the sea." But they did not go down four or five miles to the sea in order to get from Chremylus's house to the Asclepieum; and Carion expressly states that they plunged Plutus into the water at the very moment of their reaching the god's abode, and in the next instant they entered the sacred enclosure. The temenos walls are still fairly well to be traced; in some of the unidentified walls just outside the walls of the precinct, near its south-east entrance, we must look for the remains of this pool; for the water that supplied the pool must have been conducted to it from the sacred spring in the grotto of the sanitarium proper. And the water in which they gave the new patient his bath of purification we are expressly told was cold —spring water.

Besides the pool, Aristophanes gives us assurance, though we scarcely need it, that there was a general altar for offerings before the temple. On this they laid their offerings of cakes and other things as a preliminary sacrifice. There has been some diversity of opinion as to the identification of the altar. But in front of the temple and squarely in the axis of it and almost directly in front of the spring is an oblong structure in which we may well see the foundations of the altar of burnt sacrifice, and the flames of Hephaestus were to devour the offerings left upon it by our trio.

After the bath and the offering of the sacrifices they make their arrangements for the cure at the hospital proper. The patient is given a proper bed—somewhere in the colonnade; the friends of the patient are admitted with him, but they must scrape together such beds of straw as they can manage to secure. That they are all in a general ward is made clear by Carion's further recital (ll. 742–744):

οἱ δὲ ἐγκατακείμενοι παρ' αὐτῷ πῶς δοκεῖς   |   and those who had their beds beside him—you can't believe

τὸν Πλοῦτον ἠσπάζοντο καὶ τὴν νύχθ' ὅλην   |   how they cheered for Plutus, and they stayed awake

ἐγρηγόρεσαν   |   doing it all night long

There was no careful separation of patients in those old health-establishments connected with the worship of Asclepius. All sorts of illnesses were being treated in this same general ward (Ar. Pl. 664–671):

ΓΥ. ἦσαν δέ τινες χἄλλοι δεόμενοι τοῦ θεοῦ;   |   WO. And were there also others there in need of the god's help?

ΚΑ. εἷς μέν γε Νεοκλείδης, ὅς ἐστι τυφλός   |   CA. Yes, one, Neoclides, who is blind.

. . . . . . .   |   . . . . . . .

ἕτεροί τε πολλοὶ παντοδαπὰ νοσήματα   |   And there were a lot more, with all sorts of
ἔχοντες· ὡς δὲ τοὺς λύχνους ἀποσβέσας   |   diseases. And when the god's attendant put out
ἡμῖν παρήγγειλ' ἐγκαθεύδειν τοῦ θεοῦ   |   the lights and told us to go to sleep,
ὁ πρόπολος, εἰπών, ἤν τις αἴσθηται ψόφου,   |   adding that if any one should hear a noise he
σιγᾶν, ἅπαντες κοσμίως κατεκείμεθα   |   should make no sound, we all turned duly in

The sanitarium had its lighting system, too, it seems, and at bedtime all lights were extinguished, and the patients were expected to go to sleep.

Of course, Aristophanes's object in all this recital is to make the whole performance at the Asclepieum as ridiculous as possible. Still, we may be sure, he is using the realities of the place and of the system as a basis for his fun. The pool is real; the sacred enclosure is real; the temple is real; the altar of burnt sacrifice is real; the sanitarium building and sick-ward and its appurtenances are real. Among those appurtenances of the colonnaded building were other altars for sacrifices that were not by fire and tables for gifts from grateful patients. These also are introduced by Aristophanes in Carion's recital (676–680):

ἔπειτ' ἀναβλέψας ὁρῶ τὸν ἱερέα   |   and then I glanced up and saw the priest
τοὺς φθοῖς ἁρπάζοντα καὶ τὰς ἰσχάδας   |   grabbing the pancakes and the figs off
ἀπὸ τῆς τραπέζης τῆς ἱερᾶς. μετὰ τοῦτο δὲ   |   from the table of consecration; and after that
περιῆλθε τοὺς βωμοὺς ἅπαντας ἐν κύκλῳ,   |   he went around about all the altars to see
εἴ που πόπανον εἴη τι καταλελειμμένον   |   if any cooky happened to have been left

As every Asclepieum had its corps of physicians, so, too, it had its pharmacy. The sanitarium of Athens also had its drug shop and the paraphernalia appertaining thereunto —pestles and mortars and pill-boxes and what not (Ar. Pl. 710–712):

ΚΑ. ἔπειτα παῖς αὐτῷ λίθινον θυείδιον

παρέθηκε καὶ δοίδυκα καὶ κιβώτιον.
ΓΥ. λίθινον; ΚΑ. μὰ Δι' οὐ δῆτ', οὐχί γε
          κιβώτιον

The mortar comes in again (ll. 718–720):

      ἔπειτα ἔφλα
ἐν τῇ θυίᾳ συμπαραμιγνύων ὀπὸν
καὶ σχῖνον

| |
CA. And then a helper set before him a little stone

mortar and pestle and a little box.
WO. Of stone? CA. Of course not, by Zeus—any way, not the pill-box

       and then he ground up
in the mortar a mixture of fig-tree-juice
and mastich

The pestle and mortar are very real, though the concoctions that the drug-shop puts up and the method of treatment that follows may be the veriest nonsense, to ridicule the whole medical profession.

At the western end of the colonnade of the sanitarium is a square platform, with a circular shaft 2.20 M. deep and 2.70 M. wide. It suggests the Tholos at Epidaurus. The original purpose of both is mysterious. Some people still hold to the view that these curious pits were the cage for the serpents of Asclepius. Whatever may have been the purpose of the Tholos at Epidaurus, the snakes of the Asclepieum of Athens certainly were not housed in this cistern or whatever else it may have been. They dwelt with the god in his temple. Aristophanes is not making fun, when the snakes are summoned from the temple and when they return with Asclepius to the temple (Pl. 732–734):

εἶθ' ὁ θεὸς ἐπόππυσεν.
ἐξῃξάτην οὖν δύο δράκοντ' ἐκ τοῦ νεὼ
ὑπερφυεῖς τὸ μέγεθος

      then the god gave a whistle.
And then two serpents—of enormous size—shot
out from the temple

And when their healing work was done (740–741)

      ὁ θεὸς δ' εὐθέως
ἠφάνισεν αὐτὸν οἵ τ' ὄφεις εἰς τὸν νεών

      the god in an instant
disappeared, and the snakes with him, into the temple

In the temple these serpents had their dwelling, even as the Erichthonius serpent dwelt inside the Erechtheum upon the Acropolis. They were supposed, as Carion tells the tale, to slip into the hospital and do their work; and lying there and hungering and thirsting for the porridge, he plays the part of one of them himself.[1]

An unnamed comic poet uses the "incubation" in a sanctuary of Asclepius as a symbol of recovery, or of resurrection, from spiritual blindness or spiritual death to the new insight and the new life that comes through the moral and intellectual regeneration by philosophical truth (Inc. Inc. Frag. 104, 6–11 K.):

τοιοῦτον ἦν τί μου πάλαι σκότος
περὶ τὴν διάνοιαν, ὡς ἔοικε, κείμενον,
ὃ πάντ' ἔκρυπτε ταῦτα κἠφάνιζέ μοι.

νῦν δ' ἐνθάδ' ἐλθών, ὥσπερ εἰς Ἀσκληπιοῦ

ἐγκατακλιθείς, ὡς ἴστε, μετ' ὀλίγον χρόνον
ἀναβεβίωκα· περιπατῶ, λαλῶ φρονῶν

such was the darkness that lay, in times
past, it seems, about my mind,
that hid all these things and kept them from my sight.

But now that I have come here, as if I had found a bed in the house of
Asclepius, after a little while, as you know,
I have come back to life; I walk; I speak intelligently

## b. *The Asclepieum of Epidaurus*

The cult of Asclepius at Athens,[2] like that of the healing god throughout Hellas and the Roman world, was an offshoot of the famous cult at his central sanctuary at Epidaurus.[3] The famous temple at the Hieron of Epidaurus, the ground-plan of which we now know fairly well[4] since the splendid work of excavation conducted there by Kavvadias and the

---

[1] Ar. Pl. 689–690. They open the eyes of Plutus, *ibid.* 735–738.
[2] Cp. C. I. A. II 1649.
[3] Cf. Paus. II 26, 8: τὰ γὰρ Ἀσκληπιεῖα εὑρίσκω τὰ ἐπιφανέστατα ἐξ Ἐπιδαύρου. τοῦτο μὲν γὰρ Ἀθηναῖοι τῆς τελετῆς λέγοντες Ἀσκληπιῷ μεταδοῦναι τὴν ἡμέραν ταύτην Ἐπιδαύρια ὀνομάζουσι, καὶ θεὸν ἀπ' ἐκείνου φασὶν Ἀσκληπιόν σφισι νομισθῆναι.... Ἀρχίας.... ἰαθεὶς ἐν τῇ Ἐπιδαυρίᾳ τὸν θεὸν ἐπηγάγετο ἐς Πέργαμον.... τὸ δ' ἐν Βαλάγραις ταῖς Κορηναίων, ἔστιν Ἀσκληπιὸς καλούμενος καὶ οὗτος κ. τ. λ.
[4] A Doric peripteros 24.35 x 13.04M., with 6 x 11 columns, built of poros covered with white marble stucco. It had doors of ivory.

THE SANCTUARY AND SANITARIUM OF EPIDAURUS

Lodging house, Temples, Stoas, Baths—Titthium, Arachnaeum

Greek Archaeological Society, is mentioned by the Greek dramatic poets apparently but twice, and it is even questionable whether it is actually the sanctuary of Epidaurus that is meant in those two passages. The original seat of Asclepius worship,[1] with the temple of the god, at the city of Epidaurus, occupies the centre of the stage in the Curculio of Plautus. It is reasonable to suppose that this is also the stage-setting of Plautus's Greek original. It stands to reason also that the city of Epidaurus should have had a temple of Asclepius, even without the testimony of Plautus and the new comedy from which he drew his plot and his scene, although the words of Pausanias in his disappointingly hasty mention of the sights of the town seem to imply that in the sacred enclosure of Asclepius at Epidaurus city there was no temple (II 29, 1):

| | |
|---|---|
| Αὐτὴ δὲ τῶν Ἐπιδαυρίων ἡ πόλις παρείχετο ἐς μνήμην τάδε ἀξιολογώτατα. τέμενος δή ἐστιν Ἀσκληπιοῦ, καὶ ἀγάλματα ὁ θεὸς αὐτὸς καὶ Ἠπιόνη... ταῦτά ἐστιν | The city of Epidaurus itself has to offer the following chief objects of interest: there is, of course, a sacred enclosure of Asclepius; there are statues of the god himself and of Epione . . . These are |
| ἐν ὑπαίθρῳ, λίθου Παρίου. ναοὶ δὲ ἐν τῇ | of Parian marble and stand under the open sky. There are temples |
| πόλει καὶ Διονύσου καὶ Ἀρτέμιδός ἐστιν ἄλλος | in the city—one to Dionysus and another to Artemis |

And yet, while Pausanias does not explicitly state that there was no temple in the sacred precinct of Asclepius, and while he does say that the statues of the god and his wife stood out in the open air, and while he omits from his hasty account of Epidaurus city and his very brief list of city temples any notice of a temple of the god of healing, we may still feel quite sure, both on the natural assumption that the Epidaurians could not have failed to have a temple to their own particular national divinity and on the evidence of Plautus, that Asclepius did have a temple there.

The comic poet tells us nothing about the temple save the fact of its existence and the "incubation" of patients in it (Cur. 14):

> hoc Aesculapi fanum est

(Cur. 61–62):

> aegrotus incubat
> in Aesculapi fano

The sick Cappadox resorts to the temple for prayer to the physician god (*ibid.* 527):

> volo hic in fano supplicare[2]

(*ibid.* 270–273):

> CO. pacem ab Aesculapio
> petas. . . . .
> CA. ibo atque orabo.

The great doors of the temple creak and groan as the sacristan unfastens the bolts and the valves turn on their great hinges and the wheel rolls round on the marble floor (*ibid.* 203–204)

> . . . sonitum et crepitum claustrorum audio,
> aeditumum aperire fanum

after his unavailing "incubation" and the leno, Cappadox, comes out with prayers unheard and ills unhealed[3] (*ibid.* 216–219):

> migrare certumst iam nunc e fano foras,
> quando Aesculapi ita sentio sententiam
> ut qui me nihili faciat nec salvom velit.
> valetudo decrescit, adcrescit labor.

The two passages in the Greek drama which may refer to the famous ἱερόν of Epidaurus are 1) Aristophanes's Wasps 122–123:

| | |
|---|---|
| διέπλευσεν εἰς Αἴγιναν· εἶτα ξυλλαβὼν νύκτωρ κατέκλινεν αὐτὸν εἰς Ἀσκληπιοῦ | he sailed across to Aegina; then at night he took him and put him to bed in Asclepius's temple |

[1] Asclepius was born at Epidaurus, and it was from this place that his worship became diffused throughout the world. Cf. Paus. II 26, 8: μαρτυρεῖ δέ μοι καὶ τόδε ἐν Ἐπιδαύρῳ τὸν θεὸν γενέσθαι· τὰ γὰρ Ἀσκληπιεῖα κτλ. See note 3, p. 166.

[2] Cf. ll. 532; 558.

[3] The *leno* makes his salutation with covered head (Pl. Cur. 389–390):

> operto capite Aesculapium
>     salutat.

The presence of the temple on the stage is referred to once more, line 699.

Philocleon was suffering from no ordinary malady; his case was desperate; it refused to respond even to the extraordinary measures that Bdelycleon had applied; his case must be submitted to the world's greatest specialists. Where were they? The Asclepieum in Athens had not yet gained a reputation—was perhaps not even yet built. So the son, says Aristophanes, sailed across to Aegina with his father. Why to Aegina? Was there an Asclepieum there? Or was Aegina only a first "station-stop" on the way to Epidaurus and its most famous Asclepieum? Xanthias's account moves very rapidly. But the action moves very rapidly, too; for bright and early next morning after the trip to Aegina or Epidaurus, there was Philocleon at the dicastery again! Aegina was only half as far away as the Epidaurus sanctuary; but it was almost as preposterous for the old man to escape from a temple at Aegina and get back to Athens as it was for him to make the journey by night from Epidaurus. Perhaps the comic element was all the more pronounced if Aristophanes meant his audience to think of Epidaurus rather than Aegina. We know of no Asclepieum at Aegina, though there may have been one; the desperate case of Philocleon called for the most skilful specialists;[1] even the Athenian sanitarium was not adequate; we would conclude, therefore, that this line from Aristophanes points to the Hieron of Epidaurus.

2) Euripides's Hippolytus 1209:

| | |
|---|---|
| ἔκρυπτε δ' Ἰσθμὸν καὶ πέτραν Ἀσκληπιοῦ | and hid from view the Isthmus and Asclepius's rock |

The wave surged up so high that the outstanding features of the landscape, the lofty summits of Sciron's Cliff, Geraneum, Acrocorinthus, and the rugged hills that stood between Epidaurus city and the Hieron of Asclepius, were hidden from the view of the witnesses of Hippolytus's death.

### c. Sanitarium in Piraeus

Not only in Epidaurus and in Athens were there sanitariums in connection with the temples of Asclepius. The harbor-town also had its hospital and temple to the god of healing. Crates, the poet of the Old Comedy, calls it a Paeonium "the place of healing" (Θηρ., Frag. 15, 2–5 K.):

| | |
|---|---|
| τὰ θερμὰ λουτρὰ πρῶτον ἄξω τοῖς ἐμοῖς | hot baths first of all I will bring in for my folks in an aque- |
| ἐπὶ κιόνων ὥσπερ διὰ τοῦ παιωνίου | duct on pillars, just as it is all through the sanitarium |
| ἐπὶ θαλάττης, ὥσθ' ἑκάστῳ ῥεύσεται | by the sea, so arranged that there will be running water in |
| εἰς τὴν πύελον. ἐρεῖ δὲ θ' ὕδωρ «ἀνέχετε» | each individual's bath-tub. And the water will say "Hold! enough" |

This up-to-date sanitarium with its hot and cold baths is by the sea. It is in all probability a part of the Asclepieum mentioned by the Scholiast on Aristophanes's Plutus (621):

| | |
|---|---|
| δύο γάρ εἰσιν (Ἀσκληπιοί), ὁ μὲν ἐν ἄστει, ὁ δὲ ἐν Πειραιεῖ | for there are two Asclepiuses, the one in the city, and the one in the Piraeus |

The location of this important Asclepieum has been determined by the excavations of the middle and later eighties, in which remains of the walls, a colossal statue of Asclepius, and a considerable number of inscriptions—votive reliefs and dedications to the god of healing and official records of the temple—were brought to light.[2] The building or buildings stood near the shore on the Zea side of the peninsula.

[1] Körte, *der Bezirk eines Heilgottes, Ath. Mitt.* XVIII (1893), p. 249, infers from this passage that there could have been no Asclepius worship in Athens when Aristophanes brought out the Wasps. As well infer from some one's going to consult the oracle at Delphi that there was no Apollo worship in Athens! The Asclepieum of Epidaurus was as much more famous and reliable than the Asclepieum in Athens as the temple of Apollo at Pytho was greater than all the Pythia in Athens. There may have been no Asclepieum in Athens until 420–419, but it is not proved by Philocleon's forced trip to Aegina or Epidaurus! With the help of a badly mutilated inscription, Körte comes to the conclusion that Asclepius came to Athens first in 420 B. C. But the inscription in question does not necessarily have to do with the first founding of an Asclepius cult in Athens, but only with that particular foundation with which the inscription deals. We know that there was more than one Asclepieum in Athens.

[2] Ἐφ. Ἀρχ. 1884; 1885; Δελτ. Ἀρχ. 1888; C. I. A. II 1504; 1651.

We may reasonably infer from the fragment from Crates that the baths were an important feature of this sanitarium. Indeed, "Baths" and "Sanitarium" had become synonymous before the end of the fifth century. When Dionysus complains that his kidneys are seriously affected by the constant buffetings from Aeschylus, he proposes to go to the "Baths" for relief (Ar. Ran. 1279–1280):

| | |
|---|---|
| ἐγὼ μὲν οὖν εἰς τὸ βαλανεῖον βούλομαι· | well, I'll to the "Baths"; |
| ὑπὸ τῶν κόπων γὰρ τὼ νεφρὼ βουβωνιῶ | for my kidneys are swollen from the blows |

The Serangeum, with its baths,[1] stood just below the temple of Asclepius and may have been an integral part of one and the same extensive institution.

It is interesting to note that in the period of the Old Comedy the Piraeus was equipped with a system of water-works,[2] probably constructed soon after the beginning of the Peloponnesian War and that, in the days before the Roman arch, the water-mains were carried in on pillars. The material comforts of the old Athenians were not so limited; and hot and cold baths, with plenty of water to be had by simply turning on a faucet, formed a part of the daily life of the comfortably well-to-do (Ar. Pl. 614–617):

| | |
|---|---|
| εὐωχεῖσθαι μετὰ τῶν παίδων | to have a good time with my children |
| τῆς τε γυναικός, καὶ λουσάμενος | and my wife, and coming after my bath |
| λιπαρὸς χωρῶν ἐκ βαλανείου | fresh and clean from the bath-house |

In this passage Blepsidemus is probably talking about the public baths in the city rather than a private bath in his own home. Such, of course, existed. The baths that played so large a part in the daily life of imperial Rome were not wholly wanting in fifth century Athens,[3] though there was no such mania for bathing as in the days of Trajan and Caracalla.[4] Amphis wrote a comedy entitled Βαλανεῖον "The Bath-house" (Frag. 7 K.), and the bath-house is not infrequently mentioned in the comedy.[5]

Those big bathing establishments like the one at the Serangeum had their various rooms for special bathing features like the great Roman baths. There was, for example, a *sudatorium*, with its vapor baths (Eup. Δῆμ., Frag. 128 K.):

| | |
|---|---|
| ὅτι; τὸ πυριατήριον | what! the sudatorium |

(Pl. St. 226-227):

> vel unctiones Graecas sudatorias
> vendo vel alias malacas, crapularias

The "Turkish" bath is at least as old as the fifth century B. C.; it is called "Greek" by the Roman poet; it is called "Laconian" by the Greeks.[6] The sudatorium was a vaulted room, shaped like a bee-hive,[7] and the heat for inducing the perspiration was artificial (Alex. Καύν., Frag. 101 K.):

| | |
|---|---|
| ἐν τῷ βαλανείῳ μήτε πῦρ ταῖς ἐσχάραις | when there is no fire in the fur- |
| ἐνόν | naces in the bath-house |

What Alexis calls a "hearth," "furnace," Aristophanes calls more directly (Inc. Frag. 720 K.)

| | |
|---|---|
| κάμινον βαλανείου | a bath-house furnace |

The furnace-room of the public baths was a fine warm place, and it proved very popular with the poor in cold weather.[7] The Good Man (now become rich) bids the Informer (now poor) in the Plutus (952–953)

| | |
|---|---|
| εἰς τὸ βαλανεῖον τρέχε· | to the bath-house run; |
| ἔπειτ' ἐκεῖ κορυφαῖος ἑστηκὼς θέρου | and there take your stand at the head of the line and warm yourself |

---

[1] See p. 192.

[2] The water had been piped into the great Arsenal before the production of Aristophanes's Acharnians (425 B. C.); for in that play Aristophanes (918–922) ridicules the fear entertained by some that an enemy might use the water-mains (ὑδρορρόη) to set fire to the arsenal. See p. 300.

[3] Even in Mycenaean times the bath was both a necessity (κ 363) and a luxury (θ 451). Witness also the facilities for bathing provided at the Mycenaean palaces we know.

[4] And yet in Menander's *Wrath* ('Οργ., Frag. 363 K.) we find an elderly gentleman boasting that he bathes five times a day!

[5] E.g., Ar. Nub. 837; 991; Eq. 1060. Cf. also Hermip. Inc. Frag. 76 K.

[6] Dio Cas. LIII 27; Strabo III 3, 6.

[7] Alciphr. Ep. I 23.

It sometimes was too warm a place; for Chremylus (Ar. Pl. 535) reproaches poverty with, among other things, having brought him nothing

πλὴν φῴδων ἐκ βαλανείου                     | but blisters from the bath-house

As in Homeric times the bath was always followed by the anointing with olive oil, so in classical times a special room and a special attendant were provided for that necessary operation (Alex. Καύν., Frag. 101, 2 K.):

κεκλεισμένον τε τἀλειπτήριον[1]                     | and the anointing-room[1] was locked

There were, as we learn from vase-paintings, separate bath-rooms for women in the public baths,[2] as in Roman times. The women's side of the house was equipped in the same fashion as the men's.

There were in the equipment of these great public baths in Greece rooms with tubs,[3] with swimming pools,[4] with big lavers and with showers.[5] Whether it is a tub or a shower in Anaxilas's Lyre-maker (Frag. 17 K.),

ἐν τοῖς βαλανείοις οὐ τίθεται λουτήρια

depends on whether we put a period or an interrogation point at the end. With the interrogation point, the line means: "don't they put bath-tubs in bath-rooms?" With the period, it says: "There are no tubs in the bath-rooms"—that is, we have to take the shower.

## 22. The Theseum in Athens

A very few passages from the comic poets make some reference to "The Theseum" in Athens. It is on all sides now agreed that that most perfectly preserved building from classical antiquity, the so-called "Theseum," is not *the* heroum of Theseus, built to receive the bones of the great hero when they were brought from Scyros to Athens by Cimon about 469 B. C. However luring the problem, it does not fall within the province of this study to discuss the so-called "Theseum"—what it is or to whom it was consecrated. The real Theseum, one of the most holy places of Athens, was not on the Ceramicus side of the Agora but "in the middle of the city,"[6] east of the market-place, north of the central part of the Acropolis, and near the first ascent to the main entrance to the citadel through the Propylaea.[7] How large the Theseum building was we do not know; not one of our sources says anything about the building or its dimensions. But the temenos, though in the heart of the ancient city, must have been quite extensive. A military unit of considerable strength could find quarters and bivouac within the limits of the precinct.[8] The Council of the Five Hundred sometimes held its meetings at the Theseum.[9] If the topography described in Aristotle's Constitution of Athens is correct—and we have every reason to rely implicitly upon such a witness as he—there was a Theseum in Athens at least half a century before Cimon brought the hero's bones home to the city; and that sanctuary stood near the Anaceum on the north slopes of the Acropolis hill. There may have been a new glorification of the old heroum when the relics of Theseus were deposited there.

One of the special features of this holy place was its function as an asylum for anyone whose life was threatened or in danger. It was, in an especial sense, a place of refuge for runaway slaves to whom the oppression of cruel masters had grown to be no longer endurable. There they might find safety and claim the right to be sold into other hands; and they might stay there under the hero's protection until such sale could be effected. To this fact Aristophanes makes occasional reference ('Ὧραι, Frag. 567 K.):

ἐμοὶ                                                                                          for me
κράτιστόν ἐστιν ἐς τὸ Θησεῖον δραμεῖν,          it is best to run to the Theseum
ἐκεῖ δ' ἕως ἄν πρᾶσιν εὕρωμεν μένειν          and to stay there until we find a sale

---

[1] Called by the Romans unctorium.
[2] The last argument is the vase published by Tischbein (IV 30) with the word ΔΗΜΟΣΙΑ written across the big washbowl. Cf. Ar. Pax. 1139; Varro, L. L. IX 68.
[3] See under λουτήρ, λουτήριον and πύελος in the Alphabetical List, Vol. III.
[4] As at Delphi, in the Gymnasium, for example.
[5] Vase-paintings; Gymnasium at Delphi.
[6] Plut. *Thes.* 36.
[7] Arist. ' Ἀθ. Πολ. 15.
[8] Thuc. VI 61, 2.
[9] C. I. A. II 481, 2 ff.; cf. also Photius and Et. Mag. *s.v.* Θησεῖον.

THE SO-CALLED "THESEUM"

Pollux, who quotes the lines, adds (VII 13):

ὃ δὲ οἱ νῦν φασι τοὺς οἰκέτας
πρᾶσιν αἰτεῖν ἔστιν εὑρεῖν
ἐν ταῖς Ἀριστοφάνους Ὥραις

and as to what modern people say—that servants
demand sale—we can find that
in Aristophanes's Seasons

And in the Knights of Aristophanes the Chorus imagines one of the Athenian war-galleys complaining of the cruelty proposed by Hyperbolus and declaring that she and her sisters of the navy will take refuge in the Theseum or at the sanctuary of the Eumenides, close by (Ar. Eq. 1311–1312):

ἢν δ' ἀρέσκῃ ταῦτ' Ἀθηναίοις, καθῆσθαί μοι
δοκεῖ
ἐς τὸ Θησεῖον πλεούσαις ἢ 'πὶ τῶν σεμνῶν θεῶν

and if the Athenians pass this bill, I propose that we
sail to the Theseum or to the Eumenides' shrine and there take our stand

The war fleet of Athens, rather than submit to a hazardous expedition against Carthage, will fly for refuge to the Theseum and demand that the ships be sold to a more merciful master.

The same custom crops out in a single word preserved in a fragment of Aristophanes's Polyidus (Frag. 458 and 459 K.): Θησειότριψ (according to the Etymologicum Magnum, "one who spends time at the Theseum") and Θησ<ει>ομύζειν ("to complain at the Theseum"). From the Slave-teacher of Pherecrates we have but one word θησέω (for Θησείῳ, most probably) (Frag. 49 K.); but from the mere title of the play, we can scarcely go wrong in our conjecture that the Theseum plays a part in it as a place of refuge for a frightened or oppressed slave or slaves.

All these comic passages deal with the Theseum only as an asylum for the oppressed. None of them help in the slightest degree toward locating the sanctuary in its topographical setting in Athens; for that we have to depend upon Aristotle,[1] Plutarch,[2] Pausanias,[3] and a series of inscriptions that originally were deposited in the temple.[4] Neither do they afford any suggestion as to the size or style or decoration of the building that formed the heroum or sanctuary proper; for that we are left on all hands entirely in the dark.[5]

## 23. HERACLEA IN ATTICA

With allusions to the worship of Heracles in Attica, by no means specific or clear, Euripides puts into the mouth of Theseus the following invitation to Heracles to make his home in Athens (H. F. 1322–1335):

Θήβας μὲν οὖν ἔκλειπε τοῦ νόμου χάριν,

ἕπου δ' ἅμ' ἡμῖν πρὸς πόλισμα Παλλάδος.
ἐκεῖ χέρας σὰς ἁγνίσας μιάσματος
δόμους τε δώσω χρημάτων τ' ἐμῶν μέρος.
ἃ δ' ἐκ πολιτῶν δῶρ' ἔχω σώσας κόρους
δὶς ἑπτά, ταῦρον Κνώσιον κατακτανών,

σοὶ ταῦτα δώσω. πανταχοῦ δέ μοι χθονὸς
τεμένη δέδασται· ταῦτ' ἐπωνομασμένα

σέθεν τὸ λοιπὸν ἐκ βροτῶν κεκλήσεται

ζῶντος· θανόντα δ', εὖτ' ἂν εἰς Ἅιδου μόλῃς,

θυσίαισι λαΐνοισί τ' ἐξογκώμασιν
τίμιον ἀνάξει πᾶσ' Ἀθηναίων πόλις.
καλὸς γὰρ ἀστοῖς στέφανος Ἑλλήνων ὕπο

ἄνδρ' ἐσθλὸν ὠφελοῦντας εὐκλείας τυχεῖν

well then, leave Thebes, under the law's constraint,
and come with us to Pallas's town.  There
will I cleanse thy hands from bloodguiltiness and
bestow a home on thee and half my wealth.
And the gifts I have from my citizens for having
saved twice seven children by the slaying of the Cnosian
bull, those will I present to thee.  And all
through the land estates have been assigned to me:
these shall henceforth be called by men by thy name
while thou livest; and when thou art gone to Hades' halls,
all the city of the Athenians will exalt thee in honor with sacrifices and with piles of stone.
For a glorious crown it is to win a good report from Greeks
by lending a helping hand to a noble man

[1] Ἀθ. Πολ. 15.
[2] Thes. 36.
[3] I 17, 2.
[4] C. I. A. I 210, 273; II 444, 445, 446, 448, 471.
[5] For a brief discussion of the various problems of the Theseum see Frazer, *Paus.*, Vol. II pp. 145–156, and V p. 489.

We find in Seneca's Mad Hercules a clear echo of this Atticizing of Heracles, where Theseus invites the Doric hero to his land which is accustomed to free even great gods from their guilty stains (Sen. H. F. 1341–1344):

THES.  Nostra te tellus manet

. . . . . .

illa te, Alcide, vocat,
facere innocentes terra quae superos solet

And Heracles accepts the invitation (*Eur. H. F.* 1351–1352):

| | |
|---|---|
| εἶμι δ' ἐς πόλιν | and to thy city I will go; |
| τὴν σήν, χάριν τε μυρίαν δώρων ἔχω | and for thy gifts ten thousand thanks! |

Here is confusion of things human and divine.  Theseus boasts of the bounteous gifts of the Athenians to him for his deeds of extraordinary service to his state.  The custom of thus rewarding public service in Greece is as old at least as Homer.  Phoenix tells the story of Meleager and the promise of "a great gift" on the part of the Aetolians—a splendid estate, plowlands and vineyards—if Meleager would come to their relief (I 524–599).  In the same way, the king of Lycia bestowed not only his daughter but half of all the honor of his kingdom upon Bellerophon for slaying the Chimaera and performing other deeds of prowess; and the people of Lycia set apart for him an estate preëminent above all others, a fair demesne of plowland and vineyard to possess it.[1]

We find the same custom still surviving in fifth century Athens: to Antidorus of Lemnos, who deserted from the Persian side to the Greek fleet at Artemisium, the Athenians gave for that service a plot of ground on the Island of Salamis.[2]

Accordingly, we see in the passage quoted from the Hercules Furens, in the first place, what was to Euripides's hearers the familiar method of rewarding excellent service.  The second element Euripides seems to take for granted in the minds of his audience—the community of heroa between Heracles and Theseus.  In the light of such a passage as this, we are the less surprised to find the deeds of Heracles and those of Theseus side by side in equal honor upon the metopes of the Athenian treasury at Delphi and upon those of the so-called "Theseum" in Athens.

Of a temple of Heracles in Attica, or a temple to Heracles and Theseus in common in Attica, we have no certain knowledge.  The famous Cynosarges was a sanctuary of Heracles,[3] but whether or not it contained a temple-building we do not know.  A sanctuary to Heracles is to be found in every province of Greece.  Pausanias almost always names it simply a ἱερόν;[4] at Olmones in Boeotia, however, it is a ναός;[5] and at Megalopolis it is a ναός (in ruins) and it was shared by Heracles and Hermes together;[6] at Erythrae, at Thebes, near the Electran gate, and the village of Tipha on the sea it is a Heracleum.[7]  Pausanias names seven sanctuaries in Boeotia alone; in Attica the Cynosarges is the only one he mentions.

The Cynosarges sanctuary of Heracles is only vaguely alluded to in the drama.  This precinct with its famous gymnasium stood in the small Deme of Diomeia,[8] approximately the ground now occupied by the palace gardens and the space extending eastward to the Ilissus.  From the name of the eponymous founder of the sanctuary, Diomus, we have also the name of the festival of Heracles, the Diomeia.  It was an occasion, like the Saturnalia in Rome, when the most unrestrained license prevailed, with endless fun and frolic organized by a company of burlesquers known as "The Sixty."  A suggestion of the jolly times enjoyed by lovers of fun we have in Dionysus's outcry in the flogging test (Ar. Ran. 649–651):

| | |
|---|---|
| ἰατταταῖ . . . | Oh dear! . . . |
| . . . ἐφρόντισα . . . . . . | . . . I was wondering . . . . . . |
| ὁπόθ' Ἡράκλεια τἀν Διομείοις γίγνεται | when the Heraclea in Diomeia was coming off |

[1] Z 192–195.  Cp. also the prospect of public donations for Aeneas in case he should succeed in slaying Achilles (Y 184–185); and the estate of Glaucus and Sarpedon (M 310–314).

[2] Hdt. VIII 11; Cf. Plut. Arist. 27.

[3] Paus. I 19, 3: Ἔστι δὲ Ἡρακλέους ἱερὸν καλούμενον Κυνόσαργες.

[4] E.g., I 19, 3; II 10, 1; III 15, 3; IV 23, 10; 30, 1; VI 21, 3; IX 26, 1; 32, 2.  The Ἡρακλέους ἱερὸν at Thespiae had its priestess (Paus. IX 27, 6) and in paragraph 7 it is called ναός.

[5] Paus. IX 24, 3.  So also seven stadia beyond Orchomenus, IX 38, 6.

[6] VIII 32, 3: Ἡρακλέους δὲ κοινὸς καὶ Ἑρμοῦ πρὸς τῷ σταδίῳ ναὸς μὲν οὐκέτι ἦν, μόνος δέ σφισι βωμὸς ἐλείπετο.

[7] Paus. VII 5, 5; IX 11, 4–7; 32, 4.

[8] Steph. Byz. and Harpocr., s. v. Κυνόσαργες; Athen. XIV p. 614 d; Schol. Ar. Ran. 651.

SITES OF TEMPLE AND ORACLE OF APOLLO ISMENIUS

And in the Acharnians (605) Dicaeopolis lists among the slackers and those who were having too good a time when they should have been in the army Διομεαλαζόνας "frolickers at the Diomeia."

Unquestionably there was a cultus of Heracles at the Cynosarges in Diomeia. And the "sacrifices" and the "piles of stones" for the honor of the translated Heracles, in the passage quoted from Euripides, point unmistakably to the worship of Heracles in Attica, and that, too, in many instances a worship combined with that of Theseus. But where we may locate these shrines is beyond the hazard of a guess. The words λάϊνα ἐξογκώματα ("piles of stone") would most naturally refer to a tomb of Heracles, but every spectator in the theatre and every reader later knew full well that Heracles was not buried in Attica.

With Theseus's proposal to transfer to Heracles estates that had been assigned to himself Euripides alludes directly to the familiar historical fact that in the earlier days there were many Thesea in Athens and Attica and that a goodly portion of these had been rededicated to Heracles.

### 24. Temples in Thebes

#### a. *Temple of Apollo Ismenius*

The most celebrated of the sanctuaries of Thebes was the temple of Ismenian Apollo. Pausanias approaches the city from Plataea and informs us that the gate by which one enters Thebes from that direction is the Electran Gate.[1] On the right of the gate, he says,[2] is a hill, sacred to Apollo; both the hill and the divinity bear the distinguishing name of Ismenius, for the river Ismenus flows hard by. In the outer precincts stand statues of Athena and Hermes by Scopas and Phidias respectively. Then comes the temple, of which Pausanias says nothing; but in it was a statue of Apollo carved of cedar-wood, of the same size and of the same appearance as the archaic bronze Apollo at Branchidae—both of them the work of Canachus. There, too, is the stone on which Manto, the daughter of Tiresias, used to sit[3]—for here also was a famous oracle. The oracle is attested by Pausanias (IV 32, 5):

| | |
|---|---|
| λέγεται μὲν οὖν καὶ τὰ [χρησ-<br>τήρια] παρὰ τοῦ 'Ισμηνίου | now, the oracles from the Ismenium<br>are still repeated |

and his evidence is corroborated by Sophocles (O. T. 21):

| | |
|---|---|
| ἐπ' 'Ισμηνοῦ τε μαντείᾳ σπόδῳ | and by the oracular embers of Ismenus |

and the Scholiast on the passage explains:

| | |
|---|---|
| καὶ γάρ ἐστι παρὰ τ ῷ 'Ισμηνῷ<br>'Απόλλωνος ἱερόν, διό φησι<br>μαντείᾳ σπόδῳ, τοῦτο<br>δὲ ἀντὶ τοῦ βωμῷ, ὅτι<br>διὰ τῶν ἐμπύρων ἐμαν-<br>τεύοντο οἱ ἱερεῖς | for, as we know, there is beside the Ismenus a<br>sanctuary of Apollo; it is for this<br>reason that he says "oracular embers";<br>by this he means "altar," for it was by<br>the burnt sacrifices that the<br>priests gave their prophecies |

The location we have, therefore, defined with fair accuracy: the temple stood upon a hill above the river Ismenus, to the right of the Electran Gate, as one approaches the city. And there it has been found within the last few years—not, as was generally accepted previously to Keramopoullos's excavations on the site in 1910, in the precincts of the modern church of St. Luke and the cemetery, but somewhat to the northwest, directly above the Ismenus stream. The site is established beyond dispute by two inscribed bronze vases, discovered in the ruins, dedications to the Ismenian Apollo and Athena of his Outer Precincts. The great Doric peripteros, the scanty ruins of which we now see—the huge[4] foundations and scattered fragments of the superstructure[5]—dates from the period of Thebes' greatest prosperity, the first half of the fourth century.[6]

[1] Paus. IX 8, 7; cp. pp. 264 ff.
[2] Paus. IX 10, 2.
[3] For the material on Manto's Seat see Κεραμόπουλλος, 'Αρχ. Λελτ. III (1917) p. 41 with footnote 1.
[4] The foundations of the stylobate measure 46.25 x 22.83 m., of the cella 21.60 x 9 m.
[5] Drums and capitals of columns, architrave blocks, triglyphs, geison, marble roof-tiles, etc.
[6] The date of the temple is established not only by the style of the architecture, but also by the epigraphical evidence of the guide-marks on one of the capitals.

This fourth century building was erected on the site of an older temple. Some stones of this older temple are built into the foundations of the later structure. The earlier temple was much smaller and built of native poros. At the beginning of the fourth century, this little poros temple was no longer in keeping with the rising power and glory of Thebes and it was pulled down to make way for a new and larger and more splendid temple. The scanty fragments of stone and of terra cotta tiling indicate a building of the late seventh or early sixth century. This is the temple of Ismenian Apollo that Herodotus[1] and the dramatic poets of Athens actually knew. But the temple that figures in the scenes of Sophocles and Aeschylus was far more ancient than even this. And there on the same site Keramopoullos found evidences of a Mycenaean temple of sun-dried bricks and wood, with terra cotta plates for the protection of the walls of sun-dried bricks. Some of the sun-dried bricks are disintegrated, some vitrified; the latter, together with quantities of charcoal and ashes, show that the temple, like all other buildings of the Mycenaean civilization, was destroyed by fire.

Out of the débris of this oldest temple came many fragments of objects of terra cotta, decorated, some in the geometric, others in proto-Corinthian style. These finds would indicate that the old Mycenaean temple of Apollo Ismenius was in use until about the end of the eighth or the earlier years of the seventh century.

The great altar of the temple of Ismenian Apollo must have lain, not in the axis of the temple, but, as the great altar of Zeus at Olympia and the great altar of Athena on the Acropolis of Athens lay to the left of the axes of their temples, so the altar of the "oracular embers" lay to the southeast, perhaps within the confines of the modern church of St. Luke. The Christian sanctuary may have taken the place of the "oracular embers," the great altar. The altar of Ismenian Apollo is identical with the altar of the oracular embers.[2] Two oracular shrines of the same god in the same city and within a stone's throw of each other would be most unlikely. "Of the Embers" must be a popular name originating from the nature of the altar and the manner of divination, and the oracular altar is the altar of the indweller of the Ismenian sanctuary.[3]

We can further confirm the location of the "oracular embers of Ismenus" with the help of Pausanias, who says (IX 11, 7):

| | |
|---|---|
| ὑπὲρ δὲ τὸν Σωφρονιστῆρα λίθον βωμός ἐστιν Ἀπόλλωνος ἐπίκλησιν Σποδίου | above the Chastener Stone is an altar of Apollo surnamed "of the embers" |

The Chastener Stone was the stone with which Athena had stayed Heracles in his murder-frenzy, when after the murder of his wife and children he was madly rushing on to take his father's life (Eur. H. F. 1002–1005):

| | |
|---|---|
| ἀλλ' ἦλθεν εἰκών, ὡς ὁρᾶν ἐφαίνετο | but there came a Shape, as it seemed to our eyes |
| Παλλὰς κραδαίνουσ' ἔγχος ἐπιλόφῳ κάρᾳ | —Pallas brandishing in her hand a spear above her crest— |
| χἄρριψε πέτρον στέρνον εἰς Ἡρακλέους, ὅς νιν φόνου μαργῶντος ἔσχε | and hurled against the breast of Heracles a stone which stayed him from his murder-frenzy |

This stone was preserved at the sanctuary of Heracles just outside the Electran Gate—probably where stands now the little church of St. Nicholas. Above this was the altar of Apollo surnamed "Apollo of the Embers." The similarity of the Ἀπόλλωνος Σποδίου of Pausanias is too close to the μαντεία σπόδῳ of Sophocles to be accidental; Apollo of the Embers must be the prophetic god that presided over the embers oracular. Pausanias adds (*l. c.*) that the altar consisted wholly of the ashes of the victims, like the great altar of Zeus at Olympia, and that the mantic art was exercised through sounds (ἀπὸ κληδόνων, *ominibus*). This is not out of harmony with the scholium quoted above. The victims, moreover, as we learn also from the testimony of Pausanias (IX 12, 1), were originally bulls, later, owing to an accidental precedent, work-oxen.

[1] I 52; VIII 134.
[2] Cf. Philoch., F. G. H. I 416, Frag. 197: διὰ τῶν ἐμπύρων ἐμαντεύοντο οἱ ἱερεῖς τοῦ Ἰσμηνίου Ἀπόλλωνος. Cp. also Schol. Soph. O. T. 19; Schol. Eur. Ph. 1255–1256.
[3] So also Holleaux, *Mélanges H. Weil*, 1898, pp. 193 ff.; otherwise, Κεραμόπουλλος, Ἀρχ. Δελτ. III (1917) pp. 331–333 footnote.

RUINS OF THE TEMPLE OF APOLLO ISMENIUS

(After Κεραμόπουλλος)

## b. *The Temple of Athena Onca*

Outside the southern gates of Thebes stood a temple to Athena Onca. It was a very ancient foundation dating back to Cadmus himself and the hour when the cow that led him from Delphi rested there. The surname Onca is Phoenician, according to the testimony of Pausanias,[1] Stephanus of Byzantium,[2] and various scholiasts,[3] though their testimony is sometimes seriously questioned. Pausanias, to be sure, speaks only of an altar and an image of Athena "Onga" and states explicitly that they stood out under the open sky (IX 12, 2):

| | |
|---|---|
| ἐνταῦθα ἔστι μὲν ἐν ὑπαίθρῳ βωμὸς | in this quarter there are under the open sky an altar |
| καὶ ἄγαλμα ['Αθηνᾶς]· ἀναθεῖναι δὲ αὐτὸ Κάδμον λέγουσι | and a statue (of Athena); and they say that Cadmus dedicated it |

But the Scholiast on Euripides's Phoenissae (1062) is equally explicit in regard to a sanctuary; over the sanctuary, he says, ran the following inscription:

| | |
|---|---|
| "Ογκας νηὸς ὅδ' ἐστὶν 'Αθήνης ὅν ποτε Κάδμος | this is the temple of Athena Onca which once upon a time Cadmus founded, |
| εἴσατο βοῦν θ' ἱέρευσεν, ὅτ' ἔκτισεν ἄστυ τὸ Θήβης | and he sacrificed a cow, when he built the city of Thebes |

Moreover, there must have been a covered sanctuary for the safe housing of the wooden image set up in her shrine by Cadmus himself;[4] for that we have the testimony of Polyaenus (II 3, 12):

| | |
|---|---|
| ἦν ἐν Θήβαις τὸ βρέτας τῆς 'Αθηνᾶς, τὸ μὲν δόρυ τῇ χειρὶ διειληφὸς τῇ δεξιᾷ . . . . . . ἐπεὶ δὲ καιρὸς ἦν ἐξόδου, τοὺς νεὼς ἅπαντας ἀνέῳξεν ὡς θύσων | there was in Thebes the image of Athena, grasping her spear in her right hand . . . . . . And when it was time to start, he opened all the temples, intending to sacrifice |

Aeschylus speaks of the goddess herself, rather than of her material possessions;[5] and he locates her, in two different passages, close to but outside of the city gates (Sep. 486–487; 501–502):

| | |
|---|---|
| τέταρτος ἄλλος, γείτονας πύλας ἔχων | the next, the fourth, having the gate that is neighbor to |
| "Ογκας 'Αθάνας, ξὺν βοῇ παρίσταται | Athena Onca, advances against it with his war-cry |
| πρῶτον μὲν "Ογκα Παλλάς, ἥδ' ἀγχίπτολις πύλαισι γείτων . . . . | first then, oh Pallas Onca, close neighbor to our city gates, out yonder . . . |

Aeschylus does not name the gate nor the direction. That it was on the south side of the city is clear from the description of Pausanias, who is passing around on the south side of the city from the Ismenus valley to the Dircaean valley. And following the method of exclusion in Aeschylus's account, we are reduced to a choice between two gates: it was not the Proetidian Gate, for Tydeus is stationed there (Sep. 377); it is not the Crenaean, for that had fallen to the lot of Parthenopaeus (527); it is not the Homoloidian, for Amphiaraus was there (570); it is not the Electran, for Capaneus was to lead the attack at that point

---

[1] IX 12, 2.

[2] *s. v.* 'Ογκαῖαι. Cf. also Hesych. *s. v.* "Ογκα 'Αθηνᾶ.

[3] On Pind. Ol. II 48; Ae. Sep. 163; 486: ἤτοι γείτονας τῶν ὧν εἶπεν ἄνωθεν. γείτονας οὖν πύλας τὰς τῆς 'Αθηνᾶς φησι τῆς 'Ογκαίας, ἀφ' ἧς καὶ αἱ πύλαι αὗται 'Ογκαῖαι ἐλέγοντο. ἄνωθεν γὰρ τῶν πυλῶν ἐκεῖσε ἡ 'Αθηνᾶ ἐγέγραπτο. σημείωσαι δὲ ὅτι ἐξ ἱστορίας τοιαύτης "Ογκα ἡ 'Αθηνᾶ Θηβαίοις ἐλέγετο. [Then follows the familiar story of Cadmus and the cow.] καὶ ἔθυσε τὴν βοῦν 'Αθηνᾷ, καὶ τῇ Αἰγυπτίων φωνῇ ταύτην ἐτίμησεν "Ογκαν ὀνομάσας. οὕτω γὰρ ἐν τῇ Αἰγύπτῳ καὶ τῇ Τύρῳ καὶ τῇ Φοινίκῃ καλεῖται ἡ 'Αθηνᾶ· ὅθεν οὕτως καὶ αἱ πύλαι ὠνομάσθησαν. Schol. Eur. Ph. 1062: δοκεῖ 'Αθηνᾶ συμπρᾶξαι τῷ Κάδμῳ κατὰ τῶν σπαρτῶν, διὸ καὶ ἱδρύσατο ταύτην, "Ογκαν προσαγορεύσας τῇ τῶν Φοινίκων διαλέκτῳ. Then follows the inscription (see above).

[4] Schol. Lycoph. 1225: εἰσὶ καὶ "Ογκαι κώμη Θηβῶν, οὗ καὶ Κάδμος 'Αθηνᾶς ἄγαλμα ἱδρύσατο. The "village" of Oncae seems to have been a suburb lying close under the Cadmea.

[5] The chorus addresses a prayer to her (Sep. 161–165): μάκαιρ' ἄνασσ' "Ογκα.

(423); it was not the Neïstan Gate, for that was the post of Eteoclus (460); Polynices had the "Seventh Gate" (631), unnamed; Hippomedon was assigned, therefore, to either the Hypsistan or the Ogygian Gate. Now another name for Athena Onca is Athena Ogygia. And Hesychius, *s.v.* Ὄγκας Ἀθηνᾶς, leaves no doubt that she was just outside the Ogygian Gate. Ogygian and Oncaean were, therefore, two names for the same gate in the Cadmean wall. The location of Athena Onca is fixed for us by Pausanias, who, approaching Thebes from the direction of Plataea and Potniae, locates the house of Amphitryon and Alcmena, the Heracleum and the tomb of Heracles's children, the Gymnasium, and the Apollo temple outside the Electran Gate, and then, before entering the acropolis, mentions the altar and statue of "Athena Onga."[1] Her shrine is on the south side of the city and close to the city walls.

Though Pausanias does not actually name any temple of Athena at all in his rather hasty description of Thebes, Sophocles was acquainted with at least two (O. T. 19–21):

| | |
|---|---|
| τὸ δ' ἄλλο φῦλον ἐξεστεμμένον | and yonder are other companies, with garlands crowned, |
| ἀγοραῖσι θακεῖ πρός τε Παλλάδος διπλοῖς | sitting in the market-places and by the temples twain |
| ναοῖς | of Pallas |

The one temple of Pallas we have just seen—that of Athena Onca. The other is the shrine of the Ismenian Athena.

### c. *The Temple of Athena Ismenia*

We owe our knowledge of the name and the identity of this temple to the Scholiast on the passage just quoted from the Oedipus Rex. He says:

| | |
|---|---|
| δύο ἱερὰ ἐν ταῖς Θήβαις ἵδρυται | two temples to Athena stand |
| τῇ Ἀθηνᾷ, τὸ μὲν Ὀγκαίας, | in Thebes—1) to Athena Oncaea, |
| τὸ δὲ Ἰσμηνίας | 2) to Athena Ismenia |

But neither the poet nor his ancient commentator gives us any hint as to either location or appearance of the second temple. Only the name "Ismenia" suggests that it stood on the eastern side of Thebes, on one of the hills above the Ismenus stream, just as the temple of Athena Cadmea, the name of which we know, must have stood upon the hill of Cadmea.[2] The shrine of the Ismenian Athena may be more accurately located by the presence of her statue in classical times at the entrance to the temple of Ismenian Apollo. On one side of the gate Pausanias mentions[3] a statue of Hermes (by Phidias); on the other side, a statue of Athena (by Scopas); they were called the Hermes and the Athena "of the outer precincts." The space in which these statutes stood might well be called "sanctuaries" of Athena and Hermes, though the epithet "of the outer precinct" usually implies a separate sanctuary, as at Delphi.[4]

Which one of these two temples it is toward which Eteocles turns to pray for victory over his brother in Euripides's Phoenissae (1372–1373)

| | |
|---|---|
| Παλλάδος χρυσάσπιδος | he turned his eyes toward golden- |
| βλέψας πρὸς οἶκον ηὔξατο | shielded Pallas's dwelling and prayed |

is uncertain; it may easily have been either one, or, in view of the "golden-shielded" Pallas, it may be that the poet is not thinking of either one, but of the temple in which stood the golden-shielded Pallas that every Athenian knew.[5] Polynices turns his eyes toward Argos when he prays (Eur. Ph. 1364); his brother may quite possibly, in an Athenian poet, pray toward Athens.

[1] Paus. IX 11, 1–12, 3.
[2] This temple of Athena Cadmea is probably the fourth century temple at which Plutarch represents Epaminondas and Gorgidas gathering with their friends at the time of the revolution led by Pelopidas against the oppressive occupation of Thebes by the Spartans, B. C. 379. (See Plut. de Gen. Soc. 33.)
[3] IX 10, 2.
[4] See pp. 84–85.
[5] See Vol. II, Chap. IV 2 c.

### d. *The Temple of Zeus*

Zeus must have been one of the chief divinities of Thebes. But again Pausanias fails us for any information about his worship there. Not a temple of Zeus does he mention in the brief glimpse of the Boeotian capital that he gives us. The poets, though so many of their scenes are laid in Thebes, help us quite as little—save that Sophocles does introduce as one of the persons of the Oedipus Rex the priest of Zeus. This does not necessarily imply a temple to Zeus, but the probabilities are all in favor of one. The priest identifies himself (Soph. O. T. 18):

ἱερῆς, ἐγὼ μὲν Ζηνός | priests—I, the priest of Zeus

And after the prolog he disappears, he or his temple never to be heard of again in the play.

### e. *The Anaceum*

Our inference that there was a temple of Zeus at Thebes seems the more certainly sound, as we are assured by Euripides that the Dioscuri, the sons of Zeus, had a temple there (Ph. 606):

καὶ θεῶν τῶν λευκοπώλων δώμαθ', οἳ | and the halls of the gods of the white steeds, who
στυγοῦσί σε | abhor thee

We have no information from any other source about such an Anaceum. But the Dioscuri are preëminently Dorian divinities and their worship extends from Thessaly to Sparta. The tragic poet may well have been within the bounds of reality in including the temple of Castor and Pollux among the sanctuaries threatened by the war of the Seven against Thebes. And from Roman times we have in the Museum at Thebes a dedicatory inscription to the Dioscuri in connection with Dionysus (Keramopoullos, Ἀρχ. Δελτ. III [1917], p. 368; Arch. Anz. 1911, p. 57):

Διοσκό]ροις καὶ Διονύσῳ . . . | to the Dioscuri and Dionysus . . .
Ῥοῦφος ἐκ τῶν [ἰδίων ἀ]νέθηκεν | Rufus from his own dedicated

Euripides's "gods of the white steeds" are certainly Castor and Pollux, the Dioscuri "sons of Zeus" κατ' ἐξοχήν. There were other sons of Zeus, especially at Thebes. And at the Boeotian capital was one particular pair of twin sons of Zeus to whom were given especial honors. "By the twain gods" (νεὶ τὼ Σιώ Ar. Ach. 905), meaning Amphion and Zethus, is as natural an oath on the lips of the Boeotian as the same words from a Spartan, meaning Castor and Pollux, or νὴ τὼ θεώ in the mouth of an Athenian woman, meaning Demeter and Persephone. But nowhere are Amphion and Zethus officially called Dioscuri; nowhere are they "gods of the white steeds." These epithets belong of right to Castor and Pollux. We have, therefore, an Anaceum at Thebes from Mycenaean days, as represented by the tragic poet, and continuing on as a seat of worship well into Roman times.

### f. *The Artemisium*

In the Market-Place of Thebes, near the Proetidian Gate, stood a temple of Artemis. Sophocles locates the Theban Artemisium directly in the Agora (O. T. 161):

Ἄρτεμιν, ἃ κυκλόεντ' ἀγορᾶς θρόνον | Artemis, who sits upon her glory-throne within
εὐκλέα θάσσει | our circled agora

The literal meaning of the phrase, "the well-famed, circular throne of the agora," seems to imply that the Agora was her throne and that the Agora of Thebes was a circular enclosed space. Pausanias[1] locates the market-place near the Proetidian Gate. From Xenophon's Hellenica[2] we gain the further information that the Agora was outside the Cadmea. On the basis of these data we may feel confident of the correctness of the location of the Agora just below the Cadmea to the northeast, to the left and below the road as one comes

[1] IX 16–17.
[2] V 2, 29; 4, 9.

into the modern city from the railway station. In classical times the Theban Agora was surrounded with colonnades, adorned with armor taken from the Athenians at the battle of Delium.

Though the epithet εὐκλέα grammatically modifies θρόνον, it is unmistakably suggestive of the surname of the Artemis Euclea, honored with at least an altar and a statue in every market-place in Boeotia and Locris.[1]  But here in Thebes she has, apparently within the limits of the Agora, a temple and a temenos of sufficient extent to provide a burial place for at least two famous heroines (Paus. IX 17, 1):

| | |
|---|---|
| πλησίον δὲ Ἀρτέμιδος ναός | and near by is a temple of Artemis |
| ἐστιν Εὐκλείας· Σκόπα δὲ | Euclea; the statue is a work |
| τὸ ἄγαλμα ἔργον. ταφῆναι δὲ | of Scopas.[2]  Inside the sanc- |
| ἐντὸς τοῦ ἱεροῦ θυγατέρας | tuary, they say, were buried |
| Ἀντιποίνου λέγουσιν | the daughters of Antipoenus |

Beyond its existence and location, its cultus statue and its churchyard, we learn nothing from either dramatists, historians, or guide-books.  Excavations have not as yet been undertaken in this part of the Theban city.

The reference to "Guardian Artemis" in Aeschylus's Seven against Thebes (448–450)

| | |
|---|---|
| αἴθων τέτακται λῆμα, Πολυφόντου βία, | a man of fiery spirit is assigned, the mighty Polyphontes, |
| φερέγγυον φρούρημα, προστατηρίας | a trusty bulwark by the grace of Guardian |
| Ἀρτέμιδος εὐνοίαισι σύν τ' ἄλλοις θεοῖς | Artemis and the other gods |

may allude to the presiding deity of this same shrine of Artemis; but it is much more probably only a figure of Artemis the Protectress as shield device upon the buckler of Polyphontes.

## g. *Temple of Ares*

The Theban nobles "of the dragon's brood" boasted their descent straight from the god of war himself.  It is, therefore, a matter of course that the worship of Ares should have stood in high favor with the Cadmeans.  There must have been, from the earliest times, a temple of Ares on the Theban citadel.  We have but one allusion to it in the extant drama (Ae. Sep. 478–479):

| | |
|---|---|
| ἢ καὶ δύ' ἄνδρε καὶ πόλισμ' ἐπ' ἀσπίδος | he shall overcome two heroes and a city [that on the |
| ἑλὼν λαφύροις δῶμα κοσμήσει πατρός | shield] and deck with spoils his father's house |

The warrior who is to win this victory is Megareus, King Creon's son, Ares's own offspring; and his "father's house" is not the palace of the king but the temple of his father-god; for men do not dedicate spoils of war at private residences but only at the shrines of gods.  As Megareus is the son of Ares, his "father's house" must be the temple of Ares.  It may well be that this Ares temple on the acropolis of Thebes was in close connection with the palace of the king, just as Athena's oldest temple in Athens was in close connection with "the goodly house of Erechtheus."[3]

## h. *Other Temples in Thebes*

As Pausanias passes from the temple of Heracles and the holy place of Athena Onca into the Cadmea, he comes to the house of Cadmus, in the heart of the old castle-hill,[4] and "not far away is 1) a temple of Ammon . . . and beyond the sanctuary of Ammon is 2) the so-called Place of Augury of Tiresias; and near it is 3) a sanctuary of Tyche . . . and 4) wooden images of Aphrodite [probably in a protecting shrine], and 5) the sanctuary of Demeter Thesmophoros, which they say was once the house of Cadmus and his descendants"; and 6) a temple of Dionysus.  In an earlier chapter he names the temple of Zeus Hypsistus.[5]

---

[1] Plut. Aristides XX 6: τὴν δὲ Εὔκλειαν οἱ μὲν πολλοὶ καὶ καλοῦσι καὶ νομίζουσιν Ἄρτεμιν . . . ἔχειν παρά τε Βοιωτοῖς καὶ Λοκροῖς τιμάς. βωμὸς γὰρ αὐτῇ καὶ ἄγαλμα κατὰ πᾶσαν ἀγορὰν ἵδρυται.

[2] For a full discussion of this Artemis see Urlichs, *Skopas' Leben u. Werke*, pp. 77 ff.

[3] See above, pp. 44 ff.

[4] Paus. IX 11, 7–16, 6.

[5] IX 8, 5.

Of these five temples the dramatic poets mention, or ever so vaguely refer to only three. The temple of Ammon—Zeus Ammon, of course—was there in Thebes before their day; Pindar sings the praise of "Ammon, lord of Olympus," [1] and it was the great lyric poet who dedicated at the Ammon shrine the temple statue, a work of the great Calamis. [2] When the worship of Ammon was introduced into Hellas, we do not know. It must have been right early; and in the days of Pindar the connection between the Egyptian and Hellenic cults was still close, for the great poet of Thebes also composed a hymn in honor of Ammon himself and sent it to the priests of Ammon in Libya. [2]

The Temple of Zeus Hypsistus is different from the Temple of Zeus Ammon; the former was inside the Cadmea, but close to the Hypsistan Gate on the south side of the city; the latter was nearer the centre of the acropolis. The chief temple of Zeus at Thebes was probably the temple of Zeus Hypsistus. [3]

Tiresias's place of observing the flight of birds, like the similar Roman institution on the Palatine, was not a building at all but a high-placed seat under the open sky in the loftiest part of the Cadmea affording the widest view (Soph. Ant. 999–1000):

| | |
|---|---|
| εἰς γὰρ παλαιὸν θᾶκον ὀρνιθόσκοπον | taking my place at the ancient seat of augury, |
| ἵζων, ἵν' ἦν μοι παντὸς οἰωνοῦ λιμήν | where I found the haven of every sort of bird |

Euripides mentions this holy place with a little more of detail (Bac. 347–350):

| | |
|---|---|
| ἐλθὼν δὲ θάκους τοῦδ' ἵν' οἰωνοσκοπεῖ | go to his seats, where he observes the birds, |
| μοχλοῖς τριαίνου κἀνάστρεψον ἔμπαλιν, | upheave it with crowbars and overturn it utterly, |
| ἄνω κάτω τὰ πάντα συγχέας ὁμοῦ, | turn everything in confusion upside down, |
| καὶ στέμματ' ἀνέμοις... μέθες | and fling his fillets to the winds |

From these two passages we gain some conception of "Tiresias's high place," with its seats that could be overturned with bars, and its fillets and "everything." It could not have been outside the Cadmea, for in such case Tiresias could not pass, as he does, from his seat of augury to the beleaguered palace of the king (Eur. Ph. 838–840[4]):

| | |
|---|---|
| κλήρους τέ μοι φύλασσε παρθένῳ χερί, | and guard, pray, in thy maiden hand the auguries |
| οὓς ἔλαβον οἰωνίσματ' ὀρνίθων μαθὼν | that I took, when I studied the omens of the birds |
| θάκοισιν ἐν ἱεροῖσιν, οὖ μαντεύομαι | at the holy seats where I gain prophecies |

The temple of Tyche, containing the statue of the goddess Fortune with the infant Plutus in her arms, the work of Xenophon of Athens, a co-worker with the elder Cephisodotus, whose Irene-Plutus group [5] was strikingly like the Tyche-Plutus, has, perhaps, a distant allusion in Sophocles's Oedipus the King (1080–1081):

| | |
|---|---|
| ἐγὼ δ' ἐμαυτὸν παῖδα τῆς Τύχης νέμων | but I regarding myself the child of Fortune |
| τῆς εὖ διδούσης | the beneficent |

The poets make no mention of any temple of Aphrodite or of Demeter. The Chorus of the Seven directs a part of their long, parados prayer to Cypris [6] and the closing chorus of Aeschylus's Suppliants acknowledges her part in the early history of Thebes. [7] In the same way, Demeter is invoked as "sovereign of all," and she and Persephone are called "founders" of the land. [8] The conclusion would naturally follow that, notwithstanding the silence of the dramatic poets in regard to buildings, these divinities also had their temples in Mycenaean and in classical times upon the Cadmean acropolis and close by the Mycenaean palace of Cadmus.

No temple of Dionysus is named by the dramatic poets, though Dionysus is frequently named and though he plays an important rôle in the Bacchae. But Thebes must from very early times have had a temple to this one of her greatest divinities. In classical times the

[1] Frag. 36: Ἄμμων Ὀλύμπου δέσποτα.
[2] Paus. IX 16, 1. Cf. also Pind. Pyth. 4, 16 and Schol. Pind. Pyth. 9, 89.
[3] See § d above, p. 177.
[4] Cf. also *ibid.* 956.
[5] See Vol. II, Chap. IV 2 d.
[6] Ae. Sep. 140.
[7] Ae. Sup. 1041.
[8] Eur. Ph. 681–689.

temple of Dionysus stood outside the Cadmea, in close proximity to the theatre.[1] The theatre, as a Dionysiac institution, was probably built within the precincts of Dionysus at Thebes, as it was at Athens. The location is obviously, from Pausanias's description, just below the northeast brow of the Cadmea, a little way from the Proetidian Gate, by which the periegete left the city to proceed to Chalcis.[1]

## 25. THE THETIDEUM IN PHTHIA

Another temple that plays an important rôle in Euripidean tragedy is the sanctuary of Thetis at Phthia. It is one of the principal features of the setting of the Andromache; with the palace of Neoptolemus, it was the chief thing represented upon the proscenium. The palace occupies the centre and the Thetideum occupies a position to the right or to the left of it. At the shrine Andromache, persecuted and threatened with death by Hermione and Menelaus, has taken refuge, and the close proximity of palace and temple is explained in the prolog, spoken by Andromache herself (16–20):

| | |
|---|---|
| Φθίας δὲ τῆσδε καὶ πόλεως Φαρσαλίας | here in the regions on the marches of Phthia and |
| ξύγχορτα ναίω πεδί’, ἵν’ ἡ θαλασσία | the Pharsalian city do I dwell, where Thetis of the sea, |
| Πηλεῖ ξυνῴκει χωρὶς ἀνθρώπων Θέτις | shunning the throngs of men, dwelt apart with Peleus; |
| φεύγουσ’ ὅμιλον· Θεσσαλὸς δέ νιν λεὼς | and the Thessalian folk call it "The |
| Θετίδειον αὐδᾷ θεᾶς χάριν νυμφευμάτων | Thetideum" from the goddess's espousals |

The location, as thus given, is indefinite: the palace and shrine are not in a city, but "apart from people"; they are on the border between Pharsalia and Phthiotis. They are probably not on the seashore; for in the closing scene Thetis directs Peleus to transfer his dwelling to the seaside to await his translation to the realms of her father Nereus (Eur. Andr. 1265–1266):

| | |
|---|---|
| ἐλθὼν παλαιᾶς χοιράδος κοῖλον μυχὸν | go and take up thine abode in the hollow retreat |
| Σηπιάδος ἵζου | of the ancient cliff of Sepias |

The Thetideum was, first of all, a sacred enclosure (Eur. Andr. 253):

| | |
|---|---|
| λείψεις τόδ’ ἁγνὸν τέμενος ἐναλίας θεοῦ | thou shalt leave this hallowed enclosure of the goddess of the sea |

But that it was also a building and that it was closely connected with the palace of Neoptolemus, formerly the palace of his grandfather Peleus, even as the shrine of Athena in Homeric days was closely connected with the Erechtheid palace on the Acropolis of Athens,[2] is proved by Andromache's further specifications (ibid. 42–46):

| | |
|---|---|
| δειματουμένη δ’ ἐγὼ | and I in fear have come and taken refuge |
| δόμων πάροικον Θέτιδος εἰς ἀνάκτορον | in Thetis's royal dwelling, adjoining the |
| θάσσω τόδ’ ἐλθοῦσ’, ἤν με κωλύσῃ θανεῖν· | palace here, if it will ward off my death; |
| Πηλεύς τε γάρ νιν ἔκγονοί τε Πηλέως | for Peleus and Peleus's children reverence it, |
| σέβουσιν, ἑρμήνευμα Νηρῇδος γάμων | the material evidence of the Nereid's marriage |

Still clearer proof that we are dealing with a hallowed building is given in the opening chorus (ll. 129–130):

| | |
|---|---|
| λεῖπε δεξίμηλον | leave the sea-goddess's house |
| δόμον τᾶς ποντίας θεοῦ | that sacrifice of sheep receiveth |

The shrine is a building (δόμος, l. 130; δῶμα, l. 161); it is a place of worship where sacrifices are offered to a deity. It is no mere sacred enclosure or mere indefinite locality, as Paley (on line 17) suggests, nor even a simple chapel, but a temple of some pretensions (l. 135):

| | |
|---|---|
| λεῖπε θεᾶς Νηρῇδος ἀγλαὸν ἕδραν | leave the Nereid goddess's glorious seat |

For that same reason the building is called ἀνάκτορον (l. 43, see above, and l. 117):

| | |
|---|---|
| Θέτιδος δάπεδον καὶ ἀνάκτορα θάσσεις | thou hast taken refuge upon the floor of Thetis's royal dwellings |

[1] Paus. IX 16, 6.
[2] Cf. B 546–549; η 80–81.

It was, therefore, as we see, no empty enclosure. We see further that it contained both temple and altar (Eur. Andr. 161–162):

| | |
|---|---|
| χοὐδέν σ' ὀνήσει δῶμα Νηρῇδος τόδε, | and nought will the Nereid's dwelling there avail thee, |
| οὐ βωμὸς οὐδὲ ναός, ἀλλὰ κατθανεῖ | neither altar nor temple, but thou shalt die the death |

The words δῶμα and ναός give it the dignity of a temple of some importance. The altar mentioned was inside the shrine. Andromache had taken refuge in the temple and thrown herself crouching, sitting, upon the altar-steps with one hand clasping the altar itself, and from there she speaks her part until line 411.

That the altar was inside the temple is most clearly brought out by Menelaus's words at line 380:

| | |
|---|---|
| ἐξανίστω τῶνδ' ἀνακτόρων θεᾶς | arise and leave the goddess's royal dwelling there |

It is implied also in the ἐξ- of ἐξαναστήσω in lines 262–263:

| | |
|---|---|
| ἀλλ' ἐγώ σ' ἕδρας ἐκ τῆσδ' ἑκοῦσαν ἐξαναστήσω | but I will make thee of thine own free will rise from thy seat and come forth |

A like implication is contained in Andromache's words as she leaves the shrine (ll. 411–412):

| | |
|---|---|
| ἰδοὺ προλείπω βωμὸν ἥδε χειρία σφάζειν | lo, I leave the altar and come forth; I put myself in thy hands to slay me |

and again in line 427:

| | |
|---|---|
| ἵν' ἁγνὸν βωμὸν ἐκλίποις θεᾶς | that thou mightest leave the goddess's holy altar and come forth |

That Andromache was sitting, not kneeling, at the altar is suggested by ἕδρας, "seat," brought out more clearly by θάσσω in lines 44 and 117 (see above), but left without a doubt by

| | |
|---|---|
| κάθησ' ἑδραία | sit thou on that seat (l. 266). |

That she was clasping the altar is clear from her own statement—an exaggeration which she purposely makes to strengthen her case with Peleus (ll. 565–567):

| | |
|---|---|
| καὶ νῦν βωμοῦ Θέτιδος . . . | and now they have dragged me away from . . . |
| . . . . . . . . | . . . . . . . . |
| ἄγουσ' ἀποσπάσαντες | Thetis's altar and are leading me away |

We have in this sanctuary an otherwise unknown temple to Thetis—a sacred enclosure, with a temple and its altar. It may be wholly the poet's creation; but that Phthia, with its traditions of Peleus and Thetis and the great Achilles, should have had a temple to the Nereid upon the Mycenaean site of Peleus's palace is not at all improbable. Our only regret is that the poet has given us no more details.

## 26. THE LYCAEUM IN ARCADIA

Castor as *deus ex machina* in the Electra of Euripides directs Orestes to Athens for his trial, after which he is to emigrate from Argos to Arcadia and there found a city near the Lycaean shrine. His words touching the latter command are (Eur. El. 1273–1275):

| | |
|---|---|
| σὺ δ' 'Αρκάδων χρὴ πόλιν ἐπ' 'Αλφειοῦ ῥοαῖς | but thou by Alpheus's streams shalt found a |
| οἰκεῖν Λυκαίου πλησίον σηκώματος· | city of Arcadians, hard by the Lycaean shrine; |
| ἐπώνυμος δὲ σοῦ πόλις κεκλήσεται | and the city shall be called by thy name |

The city that Euripides has in mind can be no other than Oresthasium, which was in reality founded by Orestheus, son of Lycaon; but the name of the town was later changed to Oresteum in the belief that it was founded by Orestes. The story of its founding by Orestes is borne out also by Pausanias, who, drawing probably from good sources, has

Orestes add a large part of Arcadia to his kingdom[1] and move his seat of power from Mycenae to Arcadia in obedience to a Delphic oracle;[2] Pausanias[3] also records the change of name from Oresthasium to Oresteum in honor of Agamemnon's son.

But our chief interest lies in the "Lycaean Shrine" of Euripides's lines. It is located by Alpheus's streams and it must stand in some relation to the Lycaean mountain in the southwest corner of Arcadia. It must, therefore, have been situated on the northeast or eastern foothills of Mount Lycaeus. And whose is the shrine? We find on Mount Lycaeus a sanctuary of Zeus,[4] a sanctuary of Pan[5] and of Apollo.[6] The most famous was that of Zeus, though it was at the sanctuary of Lycaean Pan that the Lycaean games were celebrated; on the topmost peak of the mountain was the altar of Lycaean Zeus with its mysterious rites.[7]

The "Lycaean shrine" seems, therefore, that of Zeus Lycaeus, as the most important shrine upon the mountain; the shrine of Lycaean Pan, however, is not far distant. Mount Lycaeus has two peaks, one but little lower than the other; in the saddle between the two are to be seen to-day considerable remains of the hippodrome[8] and other structures—perhaps the stadium and the temple of Pan. A scant half hour's climb brings one to the summit with its well-preserved altar of Zeus, covered even yet with an ancient layer of ashes and bones and potsherds. This is apparently the centre of the Λυκαίου σηκώματος of Euripides.

## 27. SANCTUARIES OF PAN

We have just alluded to a sanctuary of Pan upon Mount Lycaeus. The "Lycaean Sanctuary" of Euripides's Electra, 1273 ff., we have ascribed to Zeus Lycaeus. Pan had many altars, temples, and shrines in Arcadia,[9] Attica,[10] Corinth,[11] Elis,[12] Phocis,[13] and elsewhere.[14]

### a. *Pan's Grotto and the Northwest Slope of the Acropolis of Athens*

As we look up any one of the various streets in Athens converging from the stoas of the Agora toward the northwest approach to the Acropolis, one of the most conspicuous features of the rock is the series of caves in its northern face. As Pausanias descends from the upper citadel, he casts a glance "just below the Propylaea," toward "a spring of water, a sanctuary of Apollo in a cave, and [with a lacuna] a sanctuary of Pan."[15] The spring is, of course, the Clepsydra; the first cave, without any trace of cuttings for tablets or other votive offerings, seems never to have been consecrated to any deity; the next cave, considerably deeper than the first, its rear wall fairly covered with receptacles for inscriptions and votive offerings, is the cave of Apollo. Frazer, missing the obvious content of the lacuna in the text of Pausanias, has put Apollo and Pan in the same cave. Bursian and Beulé had fallen into the same error before him. We may readily admit that these two gods might dwell together in perfect harmony; but Euripides makes it quite clear that each divinity had his own separate grotto. The amour of Apollo and Creusa plays a very important part in the Ion. The scene of their union is frequently brought in; it is a grotto on the northern face of the Acropolis, and, granting that Apollo had such a grotto consecrated to him, that would *a priori* be the natural place for the love scene. And there can be no doubt that Apollo had a cave on the north-northwest face of the Acropolis; Pausanias distinctly says (I 28, 4):

| | |
|---|---|
| καὶ πλησίον [*sc.* τῆς πηγῆς] Ἀπόλλωνος ἱερὸν ἐν σπηλαίῳ | and hard by [*sc.* the Clepsydra spring] a sanctuary of Apollo in a cave |

[1] Paus. II 18, 5.
[2] Paus. VIII 5, 4.
[3] VIII 3, 2.
[4] Paus. VIII 38, 5.
[5] *Ibid.* § 4.
[6] *Ibid.* § 8.
[7] Paus. VIII 38, 7.
[8] Paus. VIII 38, 5.
[9] Paus. VIII 26, 2; 36, 7; 37, 2; 11; 38, 5; 11; 54, 4; 6.
[10] Paus. I 32, 7; 34, 3.
[11] Paus. II 24, 6.
[12] Paus. V 15, 9.
[13] Paus. X 32, 7.
[14] Paus. II 32, 6 (Corinth).
[15] Paus. I 28, 4.

THE ACROPOLIS
From below the Theseum

CAVES OF PAN AND APOLLO
NORTHWEST SLOPE OF THE ACROPOLIS

and a number of inscriptions found just below it testify to a dedication to "Apollo beneath the heights" (ΑΠΟΛΛΩΝΙ ΥΠΑΚΡΑΙΩΙ[1]). And here it was that Phoebus forced Creusa to his will,[2] and here at the cave-dwelling of the father of her child she deposited her new-born babe in its swaddling clothes (Eur. Ion. 10–13; 16–18):[3]

| | |
|---|---|
| παῖδ' Ἐρεχθέως Φοῖβος ἔζευξεν γάμοις | Phoebus by force united to himself in wedlock Erechtheus's |
| βίᾳ Κρέουσαν, ἔνθα προσβόρρους πέτρας | daughter, Creusa, where stand the northward-facing cliffs |
| Παλλάδος ὑπ' ὄχθῳ τῆς Ἀθηναίων χθονὸς Μακρὰς καλοῦσι . . . . | beneath the hill of Pallas in the Athenians' land; they call them Macrae . . . |
| . . . . . . . . | . . . . . . . . . |
| τεκοῦσ' ἐν οἴκοις παῖδ' ἀπήνεγκεν βρέφος | and when she gave birth to a child at the palace, Creusa bore the babe away |
| εἰς ταὐτὸν ἄντρον οὗπερ ηὐνάσθη θεῷ | to that same cave where she had couched with the god |
| Κρέουσα, κἀκτίθησιν ὡς θανούμενον | and exposed it there to die |

And there, at Apollo's request, Hermes rescued the babe, took him from the rocky cavern, and bore him away to Delphi to be reared in Phoebus's holy place (Eur. Ion 31):

| | |
|---|---|
| λαβὼν βρέφος νεογνὸν ἐκ κοίλης πέτρας | I took the babe, new born, from the cave in the rock and . . . |

The "northward-facing cliffs," we see from these opening lines of the Ion, were what the Athenians called "Macrae," "the Long Cliffs." The name applies to that whole portion of the north face of the Acropolis, including the Clepsydra spring and the caves of Apollo and Pan (Eur. Ion 283–286;[4] 936–938[5]); in line 1401 of the Ion, Euripides applies to it the illuminating epithet Μακρὰς πετρηρεφεῖς, "Macrae roofed with cliffs," and in line 494 Macrae is "filled with caverns," μυχώδεσι Μακραῖς. Both epithets are strikingly true to nature.

The scene of the union of Apollo and Creusa is fixed still more precisely in another passage from the Ion (936–938):

| | |
|---|---|
| ΚΡ. οἶσθα Κεκροπίας πέτρας, | CR. Knowest thou the Cecropian rocks, |
| πρόσβορρον ἄντρον, ἃς Μακρὰς κικλήσκομεν; | the northward-facing cave, that we call Macrae? |
| ΠΑΙ. οἶδ', ἔνθα Πανὸς ἄδυτα καὶ βωμὸς πέλας | PAE. Ay—and there nearby, the shrines and altars of Pan |

The "northward facing cave" where the babe was exposed is the cave of Apollo—albeit it faces north-northwest—not the cave of Pan; for the Paedagogus at once locates the cave of Apollo by its nearness to the "shrine [or shrines[6]] and altars of Pan." The latter, we may judge also from the far greater multiplicity of votive offerings, was much more familiar to the average Athenian than was Apollo's cave.[7] The point here to be emphasized is the separation of the two shrines—near each other, but not identical. Creusa has before named the sanctuary of Apollo as the scene of her ravishing (Eur. Ion 283–288):

| | |
|---|---|
| ΙΩΝ. Μακραὶ δὲ χῶρός ἐστ' ἐκεῖ κεκλημένος; | ION. And is there a place there called Macrae? |
| ΚΡ. τί δ' ἱστορεῖς τόδ'; ὥς μ' ἀνέμνησάς τινος. | CR. Why askest thou that? What memories thou hast awakened! |
| ΙΩΝ. τιμᾷ σφε Πύθιος ἀστραπαί τε Πύθιαι; | ION. Do the Pythian god and Pythian lightnings honor it? |

[1] E.g., C. I. A. III No. 91. There have been found no less than twenty-eight such inscriptions.
[2] Cf. also Eur. Ion 892–896; 899–901; 949.
[3] Cf. also 958.
[4] Quoted below.
[5] Cited below.
[6] The use of the plural will be discussed below, pp. 186–187.
[7] How popular the shrine of Pan was is suggested in the opening lines of Aristophanes's Lysistrate, where Lysistrate, impatiently walking up and down, complains that the women have not promptly responded to her call for the "strike," whereas if they had been called to the shrine of Bacchus or of Pan or Aphrodite the streets would be jammed with celebrants (Ar. Lys. 1–3):

Ἀλλ' εἴ τις ἐς Βακχεῖον αὐτὰς ἐκάλεσεν
ἢ 'ς Πανὸς ἢ 'πὶ Κωλιάδ' ἢ 'ς Γενετυλλίδος,
οὐδ' ἂν διελθεῖν ἦν ἂν ὑπὸ τῶν τυμπάνων.

| | |
|---|---|
| ΚΡ. τιμᾷ—τί τιμᾷ; μήποτ' ὤφελόν σφ' ἰδεῖν. | CR. Honor it? Honor it! Would I had never seen it! |
| ΙΩΝ. τί δέ; στυγεῖς σὺ τοῦ θεοῦ τὰ φίλτατα; | ION. What! Dost thou abhor what God loves best? |
| ΚΡ. οὐδέν· ξύνοιδ' ἄντροισιν αἰσχύνην τινά | CR. Not so. That cave and I know deed of shame |

The "Pythian lightnings" and the "Pythian" god of line 285 stamp this sanctuary beyond a doubt as a sanctuary of the Pythian Apollo. Euripides emphasizes with "honor" the high repute in which it stood, due in part at least to its high antiquity. And Apollo "loves it best" for that same reason. Its high antiquity is vouched for also by Thucydides, who (II 15, 4) mentions as one of the four most ancient sanctuaries of primitive Athens lying immediately outside the Acropolis τὸ Πύθιον. This Pythium must be the cave with its adjacent temenos.

This Pythium is yet again and still more clearly identified as the cave in the northwest face of the Acropolis rock by Strabo and by Philostratus. The geographer, speaking of a place called Harma in Boeotia, warns us against confusing it with another Harma, an Attic village near Phyle on the slopes of Mount Parnes. It was in connection with the Attic Harma, he says,[1] that the proverb "when the lightning flashes across Harma"[2] arose; for certain augurs of Apollo's, called "Pythiasts," who took their observations by the altar of Zeus Astrapaeus in (upon) the wall between the Pythium and the Olympieum, watched for the lightning, looking toward Harma. And when they saw a flash across Harma, they sent their sacrifice to the Pythian god at Delphi. This Pythium must be the cave-temple, not the temple by the Ilissus; for neither Harma nor any part of the region about Harma could have been observed from that quarter. The Acropolis blocks the view in that direction completely. The wall from which the Pythiasts connected with this Pythium watched was probably a relic of the old Pelargicum, and the altar of Zeus of the Lightning's Flash was just inside it. Philostratus[3] is still more direct in his location of the Pythium near the entrance to the Acropolis. In a description of the great festival he speaks of the Panathenaic ship, which, he says, "started from the Ceramicus, sailed up to the Eleusinium, and, having made a circuit of it, passed the Pelargicum, and was carried on to the Pythium, where it was anchored." And there "near the Acropolis" Pausanias saw a Panathenaic ship.[4]

It is now no easy matter to clamber up the steep northwest face of the Acropolis to the cave of Apollo. It was probably still less easy, certainly no more so, in ancient times. For that reason the caves were comparatively little visited. And so Creusa can well call it "deserted" or "lonesome" (Eur. Ion 1494–1496):

| | |
|---|---|
| ἀνὰ δ' ἄντρον ἔρημον . . . | and up in that lonesome cave |
| . . . . . . | . . . . . . |
| . . . ἐκβάλλει | she cast thee forth |

Everything tallies with our identification of the Cave of Apollo with the ancient Pythium of the northwest Acropolis slope.

The cave of Pan is close to that of Apollo; the cave of Apollo is close to the Clepsydra. So short, indeed, is the distance between these three points of interest mentioned by Pausanias about the north-west corner of the Acropolis, that the Scholiast to Aristophanes's Lysistrate 911 could properly locate the spring of Clepsydra by the sanctuary of Pan:

| | |
|---|---|
| πλησίον δὲ τοῦ Πανείου | and near to the sanctuary of Pan |
| ἡ Κλεψύδρα ἦν ἡ κρήνη | was the spring of Clepsydra |

For the scene in the Lysistrate text, Clepsydra is most conveniently located close by the cave of Pan and the entrance to the Acropolis. Myrrhine has come out of the citadel for

---

[1] IX 11 (p. 404): ἐντεῦθεν δὲ ἡ παροιμία τὴν ἀρχὴν ἔσχεν ἡ λέγουσα «ὁπόταν δι' Ἅρματος ἀστράψῃ,» ἀστραπὴν τινα σημειουμένων κατὰ χρησμὸν τῶν λεγομένων Πυθιαστῶν, βλεπόντων ὡς ἐπὶ τὸ Ἅρμα καὶ τότε πεμπόντων τὴν θυσίαν εἰς Δελφοὺς ὅταν ἀστράψαντα ἴδωσιν· ἐτήρουν δ'... ἀπὸ τῆς ἐσχάρας τοῦ ἀστραπαίου Διὸς ἔστι δι' αὕτη ἐν τῷ τείχει μεταξὺ τοῦ Πυθίου καὶ τοῦ Ὀλυμπίου.

[2] Our proverb of "the lightning striking" a politician has its counterpart in ancient Greek life, with a happy parody on the sacred phrase (Inc. Inc. Frag. 49 K.):

$$\text{ὅταν ἀστράψῃ διὰ Πυκνός}$$

[3] Vit. Soph. II 1, 5: ἐκ Κεραμεικοῦ ἄρασαν ... ἀφεῖναι ἐπὶ τὸ Ἐλευσίνιον καὶ περιβαλοῦσαν αὐτὸ παραμεῖψαι τὸ Πελαργικόν, κομιζομένην τε παρὰ τὸ Πύθιον ἐλθεῖν οἱ νῦν ὥρμασται.

[4] I 29, 1.

a brief visit with her husband and child.   Cinesias begs for a meeting in private (Ar. Lys. 910–913):

| | |
|---|---|
| ΜΥ. ποῦ γὰρ ἄν τις καί, τάλαν, | MY. And where, pray, you mischief, could one |
| δράσειε τοῦθ’; ΚΙ. ὅπου; τὸ τοῦ Πανὸς | do that?  CI. Where?  Pan's place would be all |
| χαλόν. | right. |
| ΜΥ. καὶ πῶς ἔθ’ ἁγνὴ δῆτ’ ἂν ἔλθοιμ’ ἐς πόλιν; | MY. And how could I go back purified into the city [i.e. the Acropolis]? |
| ΚΙ. κάλλιστα δήπου, λουσαμένη τῇ Κλεψύδρᾳ | CI. Easiest thing in the world: you could wash in the Clepsydra |

The Clepsydra spring is, of course, the well-known spring to which we descend by the long staircase (69 steps), ancient in part, in the angle between the Agrippa pedestal and the north wing of the Propylaea; since the removal of the modern bastion of Odysseus Androutsos (who built his wall to enclose the spring[1] just as "Agrolas and Hyperbius"[2] in the early days included the Clepsydra within the walls of the Pelargicum in order to insure the unfailing supply of water as an essential part of their great nine-gated fortification[3]) we may more conveniently from outside the Acropolis walls enter the little Byzantine chapel of the Holy Apostles built over the spring, thirty feet below.   It is largely due to the dramatic poets that we can with so thorough certainty identify Clepsydra: from the passage already quoted from Aristophanes's Lysistrate (910–913), we see that the spring was outside the Acropolis proper; from the Scholiast on the passage we learn further that it was close to the grotto of Pan.   Its name, says the Scholiast, was originally Empedo; but, according to Hesychius,[4] it was called Clepsydra ("hiding water") because, though it sometimes overflowed, it also sometimes ran very low.   Hesychius adds that the water of its overflow ran underground to Phalerum.   Mr. Frazer[5] cites also the quotation by the Scholiast on Aristophanes's Birds 1964 from Ister's History, that "like the Nile and the Spring at Delos, the water of the Clepsydra rose when the etesian winds began to blow and sank when they ceased; and he says that a blood-stained cup, which had fallen into the spring, reappeared in the bay of Phalerum twenty furlongs off.   The Scholiast adds that the spring was said to be bottomless and that its water was brackish."   It is now and probably was, normally, at least, clear and sweet, and it is said never to fail even at the height of the dry season.

To return to the cave of Pan.   We have already seen that one of the grottos by the northwest corner of the Acropolis was consecrated to Pan.   Lucian also in two passages confirms the location that we have accepted.   In the Bis Accusatus, Hermes and Justice have dropped down from heaven upon the Acropolis of Athens; Pan, a stranger to Dike, approaches, and Hermes introduces him as the unexpected helper of the Athenians at Marathon, who since that time (Bis Acc. 9)

| | |
|---|---|
| τὸ ὑπὸ τῇ 'Ακροπόλει σπήλαιον | has received the concession of yonder cave |
| τοῦτο ἀπολαβόμενος οἰκεῖ μικρὸν | below the Acropolis[6] and lives there, just a little |
| ὑπὲρ τοῦ Πελαργικοῦ | above the Pelargicum |

The outermost ring of that nine-gated fortress, as we have seen,[7] abutted against the Acropolis wall just to the east of Pan's grotto.   Lucian is, therefore, perfectly accurate in placing the Paneum just a little above the (outer) Pelargicum.

The passages cited above from Euripides's Ion have led us to identify in the two grottos about the northwest corner of the Acropolis the cave-sanctuaries of Apollo and Pan.   We have also, on the strength of Euripides's testimony, identified the cave of Apollo as the scene of Apollo's rape of Creusa and the exposure of her child.   But there is another passage in the Ion that points to the cave of Pan as that scene (ll. 492–507):

---

[1] In the second year of the Greek Revolution (1822).

[2] Pliny, N. H. VII 194, thus names the mythical architects of the Pelargicum (see pp. 252 ff.).

[3] The outermost rings of the Pelargicum no longer protected the spring in the first century of our era; for Aristion, besieged in the Acropolis by the armies of Sulla, was forced to surrender for want of water.   He had no access to Clepsydra, and the cisterns of the citadel failed him.

[4] *s. v.* Κλεψύδρα.

[5] *Paus.* I 28, 4 (Vol. II, p. 359).

[6] In Deor. Dial. (22, 3) Lucian makes Pan boast of his prowess at Marathon and tell his father how he received as the first prize of valor τὸ ὑπὸ τῇ 'Ακροπόλει σπήλαιον.   And Hdt. also locates the cave of Pan "below the Acropolis" (VI 105): 'Αθηναῖοι . . . ἱδρύσαντο ὑπὸ τῇ 'Ακροπόλι ἱρόν.

[7] Cp. also the author's *Hist. of the Akr.*, pp. 487–489 (A. J. A. VIII) (1893) and Pickard, *Dionysus* ἐν Λίμναις, *Papers of the American School*, 1891, pp. 130 ff.

| | |
|---|---|
| ὦ Πανὸς θακήματα καὶ | oh ye haunts of Pan and thou |
| παραυλίζουσα πέτρα | cliff that risest near by |
| μυχώδεσι Μακραῖς, | Macrae filled with caves, |
| ἵνα χορούς στείβουσι ποδοῖν | where the maidens three to Agraulos born |
| ᾽Αγραύλου κόραι τρίγονοι | tread with their feet the dance o'er |
| στάδια χλοερὰ πρὸ Παλλάδος | the grassy lawns before Pallas's |
| ναῶν, συρίγγων | shrines, moving in songs to the |
| ὑπ᾽ αἰόλας ἰαχᾶς | accompaniment of |
| ὕμνων, ὅτ᾽ ἀναλίας | pipes, when thou, oh |
| συρίζεις, ὦ Πάν, | Pan, pipest at thy |
| τοῖσι σοῖς ἐν ἄντροις, | sunless grottos. There |
| ἵνα τεχοῦσα τις | a maiden, hapless child, having |
| παρθένος, ὦ μελέα, βρέφος | borne a babe to Phoebus |
| Φοίβῳ, πτανοῖς ἐξώρισε θοίναν | and cast it forth for a feast to birds |
| θηρσί τε φοινίαν δαῖτα | and a gory banquet for beasts of prey |

We have again the cave of Pan and the rock-wall of Macrae rising about it and a hint at the cave of Agraulos still farther to the east. But the most striking thing in this passage is the consistent use of the plural—θακήματα "haunts" and ἄντροις "grottos" of Pan. Had he, then, more than one grotto, more than one spot about Macrae that he haunted? And was it in one of them that Apollo came upon Creusa and in one of them that she exposed her child?

If we examine the topography more carefully, we find about twenty-five feet to the east of the cave that we have assigned to Apollo a great tri-partite fissure in the Acropolis rock, a higher, rather shallow chamber, from which lead off two lower, deeper ones. Lolling,[1] after careful examination of this fissure and the neighboring topography, came to the conclusion that this must be the sanctuary of Apollo. The order in which Pausanias names "Clepsydra, cave of Apollo, cave of Pan" is alone quite conclusive against Lolling's clever arguments. Much more likely is it that this long fissure extending up into the citadel and artificially closed above is the "hole" communicating with the "cottage of Pan" that Lysistrate caught one of her man-mad women picking open to escape from the Acropolis (Ar. Lys. 720–721):

| | |
|---|---|
| τὴν μέν γε πρώτην διαλέγουσαν τὴν ὁπὴν | the first one I caught picking open |
| κατέλαβον ᾗ τοῦ Πανός ἐστι ταὔλιον | the hole where Pan's grotto is |

Obviously, from this, the temenos of Pan's shrine was one of considerable extent, including even more than the fissure in the rock, which was the most important part of Pan's sacred demesnes. Granting this, then Euripides's plurals—Πανὸς θακήματα "haunts of Pan," and ἀναλίοις . . . τοῖς σοῖς . . . ἄντροις "thy sunless grottos" and στάδια χλοερά "grassy lawns," and his ἄδυτα καὶ βωμοί (Ion 938) "shrines and altars"—take on a definite and natural meaning. And if Pan's temenos (ἱρόν Hdt.) extended to the west as well as to the east of the cave, Euripides's ἵνα τεχοῦσα . . . βρέφος . . . ἐξώρισε "having borne a child, cast it forth" is in complete harmony with his other passages in which the cave of Apollo is the scene of Ion's exposure; for ἵνα is inexact and may mean "in which neighborhood." Euripides only *seems* to transfer the scene from Apollo's cave to Pan's, just as in lines 936–938 he locates the former by the latter as more familiar to his audience. There is no more confusion of locality in this case than there is when he makes Creusa call the scene of her crime "the caves of Cecrops" (Ion 1398–1400):

| | |
|---|---|
| ὁρῶ γὰρ ἄγγος οὐξέθηκ᾽ ἐγώ ποτέ | for I see the cradle in which once I set thee forth, |
| σέ γ᾽, ὦ τέκνον μοι, βρέφος ὄντα νήπιον, | my child, while thou wert yet an infant babe, |
| Κέκροπος ἐς ἄντρα καὶ Μακρᾶς πετρηρεφεῖς | at Cecrops's caves and Macrae roofed with cliffs |

As features of the Acropolis, all the caves and chasms about the rock were "Cecrops's caves."

We find, therefore, that the deepest, most secluded, of the several caves at the northwest corner of the Acropolis was a shrine of Pan, very popular in the worship of the Athenians, that it was a temenos of considerable extent with grassy lawns, that it was not merely a σπήλαιον (Lucian) "cave" or ἄντρον "grotto," but that it was a ἱρόν (Herodotus) "sanctuary" or "sanctuaries" (ἄδυτα), and that it contained altars for offerings of sacrifice. In the

[1] *Göttinger Nachrichten* 1873, p. 498 ff.

excavations conducted on this site by the Greek Archaeological Society in 1896 and 1897 only one altar was brought to light: this is the large, rock-hewn altar at the northwest corner of Apollo's cave.

Still further to the east, and directly below the Erechtheum, is the cave of Aglauros but vaguely suggested in the name Agraulos incidentally introduced in line 496 of Euripides's Ion (see pages 185–186).

The limestone mountains and hills of Greece were full of caves which the simple minds of the early inhabitants of the land assigned to Pan or to Nymphs or to Graces or to various combinations of deities. Euripides alone seems to allude to such a sacred grotto of the Nymphs and of Pan on the slopes of Cithaeron in Boeotia. When his fatal madness begins to take possession of Pentheus, he fancies himself endued with such titanic strength that he might upon his shoulders raise the glens of Mount Cithaeron and with his hands tear up the lofty mountain heights; but Dionysus interposes the pious injunction (Eur. Bacch. 951–952):

| | |
|---|---|
| μὴ σύ γε τὰ Νυμφῶν διολέσῃς ἱδρύματα | nay, destroy thou not the shrines of the Nymphs |
| καὶ Πανὸς ἕδρας, ἔνθ' ἔχει συρίγματα | and haunts of Pan, where his pipings ring |

It is only natural that the wild slopes of Cithaeron with its wooded dells and many rich upland pastures should have been an abode of Pan and that he should have been honored there with altar and shrine. But this is our only evidence. The nearest sanctuary of Pan in Pausanias's list is the Corycian Grotto[1] up high on Mount Parnassus; and, no strange coincidence, the Nymphs share this sanctuary also with the shepherds' god.

We can, however, with the help of Pausanias and Plutarch, locate the "shrines of the Nymphs" not far from Plataea, and thus the location of Pan's sanctuary also becomes fairly clear and definite.

### 28. Sanctuaries of the Nymphs

#### a. *On Mount Cithaeron*

Pan and the Nymphs are often closely associated. And, like the shepherd god, the Nymphs also had many altars and shrines in Greece. Pausanias cites not a few of them— in Attica,[2] Boeotia,[3] Phocis,[4] Elis,[5] Laconia.[6] One of the two Boeotian places named by Pausanias as consecrated to the Nymphs was on Mount Cithaeron, fifteen stadia from the altar of Hera upon the summit of the mountain, and, judging by the context, not far from Plataea. The periegete describes the place in the following words (IX 3, 9):

| | |
|---|---|
| ὑπὸ δὲ τῆς κορυφῆς ἐφ' ᾗ τὸν βω- | and below the summit, on which they erect their |
| μὸν ποιοῦνται, πέντε που μάλιστα | altar, you will find, when you have |
| καὶ δέκα ὑποκαταβάντι σταδίους | descended approximately fifteen stadia, a cave |
| Νυμφῶν ἐστιν ἄντρον Κιθαιρωνίδων, | of the Nymphs of Cithaeron, |
| Σφραγίδιον μὲν ὀνομαζόμενον, | called Sphragidium; and tra- |
| μαντεύεσθαι δὲ τὰς Νύμφας τὸ | dition has it that from of old the |
| ἀρχαῖον αὐτόθι ἔχει λόγος | Nymphs give oracles here |

This must surely be the sanctuary of the Nymphs to which Euripides alludes (Bacch. 951–952) in the passage quoted above. Pentheus is starting from Thebes under the guidance of Dionysus to spy upon the Bacchanals. They are celebrating their orgies amid the upland glades and pastures of the mountain on the side directly facing Thebes, that is, below the northwest peak of the mountain and above Plataea. Though both give but scanty information, Pausanias and Euripides are in perfect accord.

A little further light is thrown on the topography by Plutarch (Arist. XI 4):

| | |
|---|---|
| τὸ τῶν Σφραγιτίδων νυμφῶν ἄντρον ἐν | the cave of the Sphragitidian nymphs is |
| μιᾷ κορυφῇ τοῦ Κιθαιρῶνός ἐστιν, εἰς δυσ- | on one of the peaks of Cithaeron facing |
| μὰς ἡλίου θερινὰς τετραμμένον, ἐν ᾧ καὶ | the summer sunsets [northwest]; and in it, |
| μαντεῖον ἦν πρότερον, ὥς φασι, καὶ πολ- | they say, there was in former days an oracle, |
| λοὶ κατείχοντο τῶν ἐπιχωρίων | and many of the natives were possessed . . . |

[1] Paus. X 32, 7.
[2] I 31, 4; 34, 3.
[3] IX 3, 9; 24, 4.
[4] X 32, 7.
[5] V 5, 11; 14, 10; 15, 3; 6; VI 22, 7.
[6] III 10, 7.

Combining the evidence of the three authorities, then, we have a cave sacred to the Nymphs of Cithaeron, surnamed "the Sphragitidian," about half way up the northwest slope of the mountain. This shrine had also been a seat of oracles. And facing the cave with the Nymphs, or closely connected with their worship there, we find also Pan.

Caves there are also, and in abundance, on the slopes of Cithaeron. Leake was tempted to identify with this Sphragitidian cave the grotto just above Plataea. But that one is too low down upon the mountain. We must look for one higher up.[1]

### b. *At Phyle*

One of the most charming spots in Attica and one of the most interesting historically is Phyle on the heights of Mount Parnes, with its magnificent fifth century fortifications and its associations with Pisistratus and Thrasybulus and liberty, with its mountain crags and canyons and the entrancing evening views of Athens, Hymettus, the Attic plain, and the Saronic Gulf with the island of Aegina and the coasts of the Peloponnesus. As one climbs the approach to Phyle from the Attic side, one comes to the meeting of two wild canyons— the western one leads up to the fort and across the mountain to Thebes; the eastern one leads to the monastery of Our Lady of the Canyons and on to the head-waters of the stream. Far up the gorge there is in the face of the precipitous eastern side a cave with a narrow mouth about which are some cuttings that once held votive offerings, and under them may still be seen the time-worn inscriptions of the donors. They remind one irresistibly of the cuttings about the cave of Pan on the northwest face of the Acropolis, and one of them names Pan, who is the recognized leader of the Nymphs. In the interior, which is dark, have been found quantities of potsherds, broken lamps, and other vases.

The cave itself and all its archaeological remains point to the definite conclusion that here we have another sanctuary of Pan and the Nymphs and that this is the Nymphaeum named by Menander (Δύσκ., Frag. 127 K.) (it is possibly Pan himself that speaks the prolog):

| | |
|---|---|
| τῆς 'Αττικῆς νομίζετ' εἶναι τὸν τόπον<br>Φυλήν, τὸ Νυμφαῖον δ' ὅθεν προέρχομαι<br><br>Φυλασίων | the scene you may recognize as Phyle in Attica,<br>and the place from which I am come is the Nymphaeum<br>of Phyle |

This is the only reference in literature to the Nymphaeum of Phyle, but we are told that the Phylesians offered sacrifices to Pan.[2] This cave, therefore, may well be another sanctuary common to Pan and the Nymphs.

### 29. The Temples of the Muses at the Foot of Mount Helicon

Opposite Ascra, the birthplace of Hesiod, among the many springs at the base of Helicon was the Vale of the Muses. The worship of the Muses on Mount Helicon was first instituted by the Aloidae, Otus and Ephialtes, the giant sons of Poseidon and Iphimedia, the reputed founders of Ascra.[3] The Aloidae knew of only three Muses—Melete, Mneme, and Aoede;[4] the nine familiar to us were imported to Thespiae by Pierus of Macedon. Here first the nine Pierides become known.

In the account given by Pausanias, Otus and Ephialtes are said to have offered sacrifice to the Muses in the Vale of Mount Helicon. The sons of Aloeus are given no credit for having built a temple or temples. Neither does Pausanias mention any temple there. There is a grove (IX 29, 5); there are springs (IX 29, 1; 5); there are statues (IX 30, 1); from Pausanias alone it would be natural to conclude that the sanctuary of the Muses was a sacred grove with altars and statues, but without any building. Temples to the Muses are not common. In Sparta, just beside the sanctuary of Athena of the House of Bronze, there was a sanctuary of the Muses (Paus. III. 17, 5); but whether it contained a temple building or not we are not told. Statues in honor of the Muses are frequently met with— at Tegea, for example (Paus. VIII 47, 3); and the fine series in the Vatican is familiar to all. But the only temple of the Muses specifically mentioned by Pausanias is the little one in the city of Thespiae (IX 27, 5):

[1] See Frazer, *Paus.* V, p. 20.
[2] Aelian, Ep. Rus. 15.
[3] Paus. IX 29, 1.
[4] Paus. IX 29, 2.

| | |
|---|---|
| τῆς ἀγορᾶς οὐ | not far from the market-place |
| πόρρω Νίκη τε χαλκοῦ | there is a Nike of bronze |
| καὶ ναὸς Μουσῶν ἐστιν οὐ | and a temple of the Muses—not a |
| μέγας· ἀγάλματα δὲ ἐν αὐτῷ | large one; and in it are small |
| μικρὰ λίθου πεποιημένα | statues of marble |

The Thespians were, above all other cities of Greece, devoted to the worship of the Muses. They had a temple within their city; they had charge of the great festival of the Muses on Helicon; the priest of the Muses in the Vale was one of their own citizens and responsible to them.

In the Vale itself topographers and archaeologists have sought for nine temples of the nine Muses. From my own note-book I take the following words of description of my visit to the site in the summer of 1886: We drank of the sparkling water of Aganippe and went down to the grove of the Muses. The grove itself is but slightly preserved—there being only a few live-oaks about each of the chapels[1] clustered there. These churches are built for the most part of ancient building stones among which were the inscriptions which Mr. Stamatakes[2] carried to Thespiae for safe keeping. These leave no doubt that here was the Muses' grove and here their altars and their temples.

And in the first year of M. Jamot's explorations on the site, the Journal of Hellenic Studies reports as follows: "In the Valley of the Muses, near Thespiae, a theatre and several small temples have come to light; one of these seems to be the temple of the Muses."[3]

One temple would seem, indeed, to be ample for all the Muses together. But Euripides speaks apparently of a plurality of buildings (H. F. 789–792):

| | |
|---|---|
| ὦ | oh tree-clad cliff |
| Πυθίου δενδρῶτι πέτρα | of the Pythian and halls |
| Μουσῶν θ' Ἑλικωνιάδων δώματα, | of the Muses of Helicon, |
| ἥξετ'[4] . . . | come . . . |

But does Euripides mean necessarily separate temples, one for each Muse? Or is he merely echoing the Homeric ἔσπετε νῦν μοι, Μοῦσαι, Ὀλύμπια δώματ' ἔχουσαι[5] ("Tell now, I pray, ye Muses, that have your dwellings in Olympus")? And does δώματα mean simply a dwelling, with its various appurtenances?

To contribute to the solution of the problems, the French School in Athens instituted excavations on the site in 1888 under the direction of M. Paul Jamot and continued until 1890.

The excavations of M. Jamot brought to light but one temple. The various churches built within the sacred grove would point, as suggested above, to a number of shrines. But the evidence of the French excavations is all against a plurality of temples of the Muses and in favor of one common temple. For they had also, as we know from epigraphic evidence,[6] one priest in common, a ἱερεὺς τῶν Μουσῶν.[7] The ἱερὸν τῶν Μουσῶν of the inscriptions[8] may refer not to the temple but to the sanctuary in general. The temple brought to light occupies exactly the site of the ruined chapel of Ἁγία Τριάδα, now entirely cleared away. It measures 12.50 x 6.50 M. It was a simple Ionic amphiprostylos tetrastylos—four Ionic columns at each end, no columns on the sides. It had, accordingly, the general appearance of the Nike temple on the Acropolis of Athens but was somewhat wider and considerably longer. In Roman times it was rebuilt and widened, so that the base formed a square 12.50 M. on each side. It had neither pronaos nor opisthodome, and, strangely enough, the entrance was on the west side.

The question as to the number of temples, therefore, seems definitely answered: the Muses of Helicon had one common temple and one priest in common.

[1] Ἁγία Τριάδα, Ἅγιος Κωνσταντῖνος, Ἁγία Αἰκατερίνη, Ἁγία Παρασκευή, Ἅγιος Λουκᾶς
[2] See his report in Πρακτικά, 1882, p. 66.
[3] J. H. S. X (1889), p. 273.
[4] Dind. reads κλήξετ' ("call"); Wilamowitz reads ἠχεῖτ' ("ring").
[5] B 484; Λ 218; Ξ 508; Π 112, etc. Cp. also Hes. Theog. 36–43.
[6] B. C. H. XIX (1895), pp. 314 ff.
[7] Inscription 1, line 2, column 1 of the long inscription, l. c.; Inscription 6, line 2; Inscription 8, lines 3–4; Inscription 10, line 3; etc.
[8] Inscription 1, lines 13–14, column 2.

Facing the entrance at the west, M. Jamot found also a great Ionic colonnade, 100 meters long. To the general regret, no detailed account of the excavations or of the architectural discoveries has yet been published, though eighteen years have elapsed since their completion.

Within the sanctuary stood statues of the Muses—a group by Cephisodotus, and further on, as Pausanias proceeds, another group of the nine; of this latter group, three were from the hand of Cephisodotus, three by Strongylion, and three by Olympiosthenes. There, too, were Apollo and Hermes contending for the lyre; two statues of Dionysus, the one by Lysippus and the other a transcendent masterpiece of Myron's; and portraits of some of the famous poets of the olden times.[1]

The excavations conducted by M. Jamot brought to light considerable remains also of a very large pedestal, on which statues of the Muses originally stood. There are also other inscribed bases of statues[2] erected here to the Muses; but all of them are of later date than the artists named by Pausanias, though earlier than the visit of the periegete to the Vale of the Muses on Helicon.

Here, too, in the Vale of the Muses were celebrated every four years the Musea, games in honor of the Muses—ἀγῶνες στεφανῖται ἰσοπύθιοι—contests in music and poetry like the original Pythia at Delphi,[3] flourishing most from the third century B. C. until the third century of our era. And there on the first slopes of Helicon above the sacred grove of the Muses, M. Jamot cleared up the small theatre, already known from the investigations of M. Stamatakes. It was apparently built primarily for these contests and adapted to their needs, though by the middle of the first century B. C. this theatre witnessed also dramatic contests—tragedy, comedy, and satyr-play.[4]

## 30. OTHER TEMPLES AND SHRINES

Many other temples and shrines are referred to by the poets, of which they tell us practically nothing and of which we have no information from other sources. Some of them may have been great temples in their day; some of them may have been nothing more than the wayside shrines of modern Tyrol and Italy.

### a. Meadow Shrines

Such unpretentious little shrines the Greeks had in abundance. They were attached not to highways but usually to open meadows. They rarely receive mention in the prose writers of antiquity. But the poets occasionally make mention of them. They are not the subject of elaborate description but appear only by way of allusion, and what is said of them fails to make even the faintest contribution to the history of art. The principal factor of interest is the existence itself of such ναΐσκοι, "little shrines."

Allusion to such a meadow shrine we have, for instance, in Euripides's Phoenissae (24–25):

| | |
|---|---|
| λειμῶν' ἐς Ἥρας καὶ Κιθαιρῶνος λέπας | he gave the babe to herdsmen to expose on |
| δίδωσι βουκόλοισιν ἐκθεῖναι βρέφος | Hera's Mead upon Cithaeron's range |

Just where upon Cithaeron's range this meadow was we are not told. But as Laius's supreme purpose was to make sure of having the babe's life surely ended, we may be safe in assuming that the meadow was well up in the mountains, where the wild beasts would not fail to find him promptly.

Down in the pleasant lowlands, on the other hand, was the meadow-shrine of Artemis at Aulis (Eur. I. A. 1462–1463):

| | |
|---|---|
| πατρὸς δ' ὀπαδῶν τῶν δέ τίς με πεμπέτω | let one of my father's attendants here escort me |
| Ἀρτέμιδος εἰς λειμῶν', ὅπου σφαγήσομαι | to Artemis's Mead, where I shall be sacrificed |

[1] Paus. IX 30, 1–2.

[2] B. C. H. XXVI (1902), pp. 128–160; 291–321; cf. also B. C. H. XIV (1890), pp. 546–551; XV (1891), pp. 381–403; XVIII (1894), pp. 201–215; XIX (1895), pp. 321–385.

[3] A full account of the games and the inscriptions pertaining to them are given by Jamot, B. C. H. XIX (1895), pp. 321–385.

[4] B. C. H. XIX (1895), p. 363.

The "Meadow" demesnes of the goddess were apparently extensive, like the Crisaean plain when it was all consecrated to Apollo, and it included also some timber-land. Both Sophocles and Euripides speak of "the goddess's grove" (Eur. I. A. 1543–1544):

| | |
|---|---|
| ἐπεὶ γὰρ ἱκόμεσθα τῆς Διὸς κόρης | for when we came to the grove and flowery |
| Ἀρτέμιδος ἄλσος λειμακάς τ' ἀνθεσφόρους | meads of Zeus's daughter Artemis |

(Soph. El. 566–568):

| | |
|---|---|
| πατήρ ποθ' οὑμός, ὡς ἐγὼ κλύω, θεᾶς | my father, as I am told, was one day rambling through |
| παίζων κατ' ἄλσος ἐξεκίνησεν ποδοῖν | the goddess's grove and startled with his footsteps a |
| στικτὸν κεράστην ἔλαφον | hornèd, dappled deer |

The sanctity of the "Meadow" and the "Grove" made them inviolable, and they were rich in flora and fauna, all sacred to Zeus's daughter. It was a sort of sacred park (Eur. Hip. 1137-1138):

| | |
|---|---|
| ἀστέφανοι δὲ κόρας ἀνάπαυλαι | but ungarlanded the bowers of Leto's |
| Λατοῦς βαθεῖαν ἀνὰ χλόαν | daughter in the meadow deep |

These sacred meadows had also their shrines and altars. It was at the altar of Artemis in her meadow at Aulis that Iphigenia was to be sacrificed, and the altar stood before her shrine (Eur. I. A. 1480–1481):

| | |
|---|---|
| ἑλίσσετ' ἀμφὶ ναὸν ἀμφὶ βωμὸν | wind about shrine and wind about |
| τὰν ἄνασσαν Ἄρτεμιν | altar, in honor of Artemis Queen |

and both were in the grove (Eur. I. A. 1548):

| | |
|---|---|
| ἐπὶ σφαγὰς στείχουσαν εἰς ἄλσος κόρην | the maiden moving into the grove to her sacrifice |

As Iphigenia proceeds to the altar for her sacrifice,[1] she enters the sacred grove. Altar and shrine were so close together that Achilles could say (Eur. I. A. 1426):

| | |
|---|---|
| ἐλθὼν τάδ' ὅπλα θήσομαι βωμοῦ πέλας | I will go and lay these arms beside the altar |

and follow it up in line 1431 with

| | |
|---|---|
| ἐλθὼν δὲ σὺν ὅπλοις τοῖσδε πρὸς ναὸν θεᾶς | I will go with these arms to the goddess's shrine |

The altar was for offerings not merely of fruits and flowers, but also sometimes of blood. In the Tauric Iphigenia (26–27), Iphigenia speaks of the altar at Aulis at which she was offered up as an altar of burnt sacrifice:

| | |
|---|---|
| ἐλθοῦσα δ' Αὐλίδ' ἡ τάλαιν' ὑπὲρ πυρᾶς | I went to Aulis, unhappy that I was, and, seized and |
| μεταρσία ληφθεῖσ' ἐκαινόμην ξίφει | lifted up above the altar, I saw the knife about to strike |

And there at the fire-altar of Artemis, Clytaemnestra was convinced that she saw the sacrifice consummated (Eur. El. 1022–1023):

| | |
|---|---|
| ἐνθ' ὑπερτείνας πυρᾶς | there he drew Iphigenia's snowy throat |
| λευκὴν διῆμησ' Ἰφιγόνης παρηΐδα | over the altar and shore it through |

In Homer, too, there were at Aulis "sacred altars" and the "spring" "beneath a beautiful plane-tree, whence flowed sparkling water"[2]—a suggestion of meadow, grove, and altars; but no temple is mentioned; the grove was the temple.

The sacred demesnes of Artemis at Aulis—meadow, grove, shrine, altar[3]—lay across the little bay from Chalcis (Eur. I. A. 1492–1493):

| | |
|---|---|
| συνεπαείδετ' Ἄρτεμιν | join in the song to Artemis |
| Χαλκίδος ἀντίπορον | across the straits from Chalcis |

[1] Cf. Eur. I. A. 1555–1556: πρὸς βωμὸν θεᾶς
ἄγοντας.
I. T. 359–360.

[2] B 305–307: ἡμεῖς δ' ἀμφὶ περὶ κρήνην ἱεροὺς κατὰ βωμοὺς
ἔρδομεν ἀθανάτοισι τεληέσσας ἑκατόμβας,
καλῇ ὑπὸ πλατανίστῳ, ὅθεν ῥέεν ἀγλαὸν ὕδωρ.

[3] The temple is mentioned only in the passages cited above; the altar comes in for repeated mention. Besides the passages quoted above, the altar is named also in Eur. I. A. 1444; 1514; 1568; 1589; 1593; 1595.

Such a meadow with its little shrine and altar had all the sanctity of a great temple and its rich temenos (Eur. Hip. 73–81):

| | |
|---|---|
| σοὶ τόνδε πλεκτὸν στέφανον ἐξ ἀκηράτου | for thee, our Lady, this woven garland from a mead |
| λειμῶνος, ὦ δέσποινα, κοσμήσας φέρω, | undefiled I have twined and bring it thee; there |
| ἔνθ' οὔτε ποιμὴν ἀξιοῖ φέρβειν βοτὰ | shepherd dares not feed his flock; there no |
| οὔτ' ἦλθέ πω σίδηρος, ἔνθ' ἀκήρατον | steel ever came; but only the bee in spring- |
| μέλισσα λειμῶν' ἠρινὸν διέρχεται· | time moves across the mead undefiled; |
| Αἰδὼς δὲ ποταμίαισι κηπεύει δρόσοις. | and Reverence aye fresheneth it with river dews. |
| ὅσοις διδακτὸν μηδέν, ἀλλ' ἐν τῇ φύσει | Only those who have self-control in |
| τὸ σωφρονεῖν εἴληχεν εἰς τὰ πάνθ' ὁμῶς, | all things alike—purity inborn, not taught— |
| τούτοις δρέπεσθαι, τοῖς κακοῖσι δ' οὐ θέμις | have a right to gather flowers there; the impure have none |

Thus we see that, though it was herdsmen that in the Phoenissae carried the baby Oedipus to Hera's Mead upon Cithaeron, the meadow in which they were to expose him was a place apart from their pastures. Such a meadow was not to be used for pasturing flocks or herds; it could not be mowed for hay; only the pure of heart and of hand might enter there, and they came to gather garlands for the honor of the divinity whose place it was. In the light of such religious sanctity, we realize the more fully the enormity of Agamemnon's sin, when, rambling through the grove of Artemis at Aulis, he started up a fawn sacred to the goddess and sacrilegiously killed it, and then added to his crime with an offensive boast (Soph. El. 566–569):

| | |
|---|---|
| πατὴρ ποθ' οὑμός, ὡς ἐγὼ κλύω, θεᾶς | my father, as I am told, was one day rambling through |
| παίζων κατ' ἄλσος ἐξεκίνησεν ποδοῖν | the goddess's grove and startled with his foot-steps a |
| στικτὸν κεράστην ἔλαφον, οὗ κατὰ σφαγὰς | hornèd, dappled deer; he shot it and chanced to |
| ἐκκομπάσας ἔπος τι τυγχάνει βαλών | let fall some boastful word about it |

In the number of otherwise unknown and for all that we learn from the drama quite unknown temples are mentioned some more pretentious sanctuaries, some which date so far back into dim antiquity that the poets knew and could know even less than we do about them, and some perhaps that never existed at all.

### b. The Serangeum at the Piraeus

At the Munychia hill in the Piraeus was a heroüm of Serangus, of whom nothing is known except that he gave his name to or received his name from the caves and water-eaten rocks (σήραγγες) that frame in the tiny bay that thrusts itself back into the shore-line between the little harbors of Zea and Munychia, below the place where stood the Asclepieum of the Piraeus. It is named in Aristophanes's "Farmers" (Frag. 122 K.): Σηράγγιον.[1] All that we really know of it is that it was a place in the Piraeus; that it was founded by Serangus; that there was a heroüm in it;[2] that there was a bathing establishment with the same name.[3] The baths have been discovered—a large, mosaic-floored room in the form of a cross, with three apses, a circular dressing room with eighteen "lockers," a forty-foot gallery with a southern exposure facing directly upon the sea.[4] Of the heroüm we know nothing; we might be more fortunate if we had the context of Aristophanes's "Farmers."

### c. A Temple at Sidon

Phrynichus (Phoenissae, Frag. 9 and 10 N.) mentions a "temple of Sidon":

| | |
|---|---|
| Σιδώνιον ἄστυ λιποῦσαι | leaving the city of Sidon |
| καὶ δροσερὰν Ἄραδον | and the waters of Aradus |
| . . . . . . . . . . . . . | . . . . . . . . . . . . . |
| καὶ Σιδῶνος προλιπόντα ναόν | and leaving the temple of Sidon |

[1] Harpocration: χωρίον τι τοῦ Πειραιῶς οὕτως ἐκαλεῖτο. μνημονεύει δ' αὐτοῦ καὶ Ἀρ. Γεωργοῖς
[2] Photius 509–510: Σηράγγειον· τόπος τοῦ Πειραιῶς, κτισθεὶς ὑπὸ Σηράγγου, καὶ ἡρῷον ἐν αὐτῷ.
[3] Hesychius: Σηράγγιον· βαλανεῖον, ἐν ᾧ οἱ κακοῦργοι ἐκρύπτοντο.
Cf. Is. VI 33: τὸ ἐν Σηραγγείῳ βαλανεῖον.
[4] Δραγατσῆς, Πρακτικά 1896, 16; A. J. A. I (1897), p. 350.

The ancient metropolis of Phoenicia is known to us chiefly for its early preëminence in manufactures and commerce and for the luxurious life of its inhabitants. We know that its religion was an "abomination" in the eyes of Israel. Its chief gods were, of course, Baal and Astarte. Phrynichus's "temple of Sidon" may well have been the temple of one of these divinities, but we do not know. Neither have we from any other source, literary or monumental, any information about the architecture of the temples or the "high places" or "groves" of these Phoenician gods.

### d. *A Fides Temple in Athens*

One of the oldest and most revered deities of the Roman city was the Goddess of Good Faith. Numa built her a temple adjoining the temple of Jupiter on the Capitoline hill. There international agreements were sealed; and there the senate often met.

The Italian mind was ever open to the acceptance of gods that were purely abstract ideas like Faith and Honor. Not so the Greek. And yet Plautus in "The Pot of Gold," which of course was based, however loosely, on some play of the Middle Comedy, places the temple of Fides in the midst of the scene of his play, which is laid in Athens (Pl. Aul. Act III 6—IV 2, ll. 582–622; 667–668):

> Nunc hoc mihi factum est optumum ut te [the pot of gold] auferam
> aulam in Fidei fanum; ibi abstrudam probe.
> Fides, novisti me et ego te. . . . . . . .
>
> . . . . .
> ibo ad te, fretus tua, Fides, fiducia.
>
> . . . . .
> tu modo cave quoiquam indicassis aurum meum esse istic, Fides:
> non metuo ne quisquam veniat, ita probe in latebris situmst.
> edepol ne illic pulcram praedam agat; . . . . . . . . .
>
> . . . . . . . . .
> . . . verum id te quaeso ut prohibessis, Fides.
> . . . vide, Fides, etiam atque etiam nunc, salvam ut aulam abs te auferam:
> tuae fide concredidi aurum, in tuo loco et fano est situm.
>
> . . . . . . . . .
> se aulam onustam auri abstrusisse hic intus in fano Fide.
>
> . . . . . . . . . .
> . . . . . . sed si reppero, o Fides,
> mulsi congialem plenam faciam tibi fideliam
>
> . . . . . . . . . .
> Fide censebam maxumam multo fidem
> esse

We do not know of any temple in Athens with which Plautus could have identified the Fides temple of his play. It seems so genuinely Roman and so thoroughly un-Greek, that we are forced to the conclusion that this is one of the passages of Plautus in which the setting of his Greek original was completely abandoned and everything made strictly Roman. Whatever the divinity may have been in the Greek play, Fides was eminently the most appropriate divinity for the scene in which Euclio entrusts the precious pot to the divine keeping.

### e. *Temples at Troy*

It is safe to assume that Artemis, or a goddess whom the Greeks identified with Artemis, had a temple at Troy; at all events, Euripides assumes such a sanctuary there (Eur. Hec. 935–936):

σεμνὰν προσίζουσ'  |  and though I threw myself at the feet
οὐκ ἤνυσ' Ἄρτεμιν ἁ τλάμων  |  of Artemis revered, nought did it avail me

The poet does not venture to describe this Artemisium; he may have thought of it as a stately temple or simply as a modest shrine with its statue of Artemis or merely an altar with its image.

Apollo, who with Poseidon built the walls and towers of Ilium, must have had a great temple there. But the tragic poets knew no more of it than we do. Cassandra, his priestess, sings of her service at Apollo's shrine but she tells us nothing of it beyond its mere existence (Eur. Tro. 308; 310):

| | |
|---|---|
| σέβω, φλέγω | I offer worship, I illuminate |
| . . . . . . . . | . . . . . . . . |
| λαμπάσι τόδ ἱερὸν | with torches this shrine |

(*ibid.* 329–330):

| | |
|---|---|
| κατὰ σὸν ἐν δάφναις | at thy lordly dwelling amid the laurels |
| ἀνάκτορον θυηπολῶ | I have tended the sacrifice |

Here seems to be an echo of the temple of Apollo at Delphi, with its grove of laurel trees.[1]

The great temple of Apollo at Troy must have been on the acropolis. But there was at least one other sanctuary of Apollo at or near Troy. One of the most famous centres of Apollo worship in Asia was the oracular shrine of Apollo at Thymbra. It was near this temple that Achilles received his mortal wound at the hand of Paris.[2] The site of the temple is usually placed in the valley of the Thymbrius, a small stream that empties into the Scamander a few miles south of Troy.[3] But the fame of the shrine in the Thymbrius valley spread far and wide, and Thymbrian became a standing epithet of the mantic Apollo, just as Pythian did, and for the same reason. Thus Aeneas (Virg. Aen. III 85) at Apollo's oracle at Delos addresses the god as "Thymbraee"; and the chorus in Euripides's Rhesus (224–225) addresses him as

| | |
|---|---|
| Θυμβραῖε καὶ Δάλιε καὶ Λυκίας | Apollo Thymbraean and Delian and |
| ναὸν ἐμβατεύων, Ἄπολλον | haunting the shrine of Lycia |

Close by Troy town there was also a shrine of Apollo surnamed Thymbraean. Near it bivouacked the Lycians and the gallant Mysians in the Trojan War.[4] Dolon gives this information to Odysseus and Diomedes as they were preparing their *coup de main* on the sleeping Trojans and their allies. This Thymbra was close under the walls of Troy and not some miles away to the south. Euripides unequivocally places the Thymbraean altar "close to the city" (Eur. Rh. 507–509):

| | |
|---|---|
| ἀεὶ δ' ἐν λόχοις εὑρίσκεται | and aye in ambush is he found |
| Θυμβραῖον ἀμφὶ βωμὸν ἄστεος πέλας | lurking about the Thymbraean altar |
| θάσσων | near the city |

In the light of the topography of the Dolonia and the probable scene of the wounding of Achilles and the explicit statement of the Rhesus, we must assume a shrine of the Thymbraean Apollo near the city of Troy, between the Pergama and the Grecian camp or the sea. It was in all probability in the valley of the Simois, not far from its confluence with the Scamander; and so important was this shrine of the Thymbraean Apollo that it gave its name to the Simois and it still survives in Dumbrek-Tchai (the modern name of the Simois) and Dumbrek-Köi (the chief village on the stream). Dumbrek is most obviously a survival of Δύμβρις, which, Eustathius[5] informs us, was a parallel form to Θύμβρις.

Poseidon, the partner of Apollo in the building of Troy, must also have been a most popular divinity of the Trojan people and would most naturally have had a temple there. The poets have nothing to say of it. As speaker of the prolog of the Troades, the sea-god refers to his altars but not to any temple of his at Ilium (Eur. Tro. 25):

| | |
|---|---|
| λείπω τὸ κλεινὸν Ἴλιον βωμούς τ' ἐμούς | I am leaving the glorious Ilium and mine altars |

The altars suggest but do not necessarily imply a temple.

[1] See pp. 83–84.

[2] Eustath. ad K 430: λέγει δὲ ὁ αὐτὸς καὶ ποταμὸν αὐτόθι Θύμβριν, ἀφ' οὗ Ἀπόλλωνος Θυμβραίου ἱερόν, ἐν ᾧ ἐτοξεύθη Ἀχιλλεύς. Serv. ad Virg. Ae. III 85: Thymbraeus Apollo dicitur a loco Troiae, id est agro vicino, pleno thymbra, quae satureia dicitur. Et bene Deli positus Thymbraeum appellat quem in Troia adsueverat colere in agro, in quo eius et nemus et templum, ubi a Paride Achilles occisus est . . . ergo Thymbraeus, ut Delius; nam numina a locis frequenter nomen accipiunt.

[3] Strabo XIII, p. 598.

[4] K 430: πρὸς Θύμβρης δ' ἔλαχον Λύκιοι Μυσοί τ' ἀγέρωχοι.

[5] ad K 430.

In the Iliad no temple plays a larger rôle than that of Athena on the summit of the acropolis of Troy. We should naturally expect the tragedies that deal with the Trojan story to have something to say of it. But the temple that Andromache knew, the temple to which Hecabe went bearing gifts,[1] the temple that once housed the fateful Palladium and witnessed the rape of Cassandra,[2] was gone; and the sixth century temple on the old site had little interest for poet or people in fifth century Athens. Euripides makes occasional reference to it (Hec. 1008–1010):

| | |
|---|---|
| ΕΚ. οἶσθ' οὖν 'Αθάνας 'Ιλίας ἵνα στέγαι; | HEC. Knowst thou, then, where stand Ilian Athena's roofs? |
| ΠΟ. ἐνταῦθ' ὁ χρυσός ἐστι; σημεῖον δὲ τί; | POL. There? Is the gold there? and what to mark the spot? |
| ΕΚ. μέλαινα πέτρα γῆς ὑπερτίλλουσ' ἄνω. | HEC. A black stone projecting above the ground. |

What the "black stone projecting above the ground" was we cannot guess. Perhaps it is only a part of the Trojan queen's scheme to excite the avaricious curiosity of the Thracian king. At any rate, we learn nothing at all about Ilian Athena's shrine.

Once also Euripides alludes to the rape of the Palladium from the temple (Rh. 501–502):

| | |
|---|---|
| ὃς εἰς 'Αθάνας σηκὸν ἔννυχος μολὼν | who came by night to Athena's shrine and |
| κλέψας ἄγαλμα ναῦς ἐπ' 'Αργείων φέρει | stole the statue and carried it to the Argives' ships |

but again the poet tells us nothing of the temple itself nor of its precious image. But in the Trojan Women Euripides does give us one or two small details of the Trojan temple of Athena, as he thought of it (Eur. Tro. 539–541):

| | |
|---|---|
| εἰς ἕδρανα | unto the stone-built shrine of the goddess |
| λάϊνα δάπεδά τε φόνια πατρίδι | Pallas and the pavements now stained with our |
| Παλλάδος θέσαν θεᾶς | country's blood they brought and set it |

True to the style of building that we know in the excavated sixth city at Hissarlik, the temple was built of stone, not of sun-dried brick; and the sacred precinct was paved, as in the Roman Troy.

Euripides assumes also a temple of Zeus at Troy (Tro. 1060–1064):

| | |
|---|---|
| οὕτω δὴ τὸν ἐν 'Ιλίῳ | and thus, even thus, thy temple |
| ναὸν καὶ θυόεντα βω- | in Ilium and thy altar of incense |
| μὸν προύδωκας 'Αχαίοις, | thou hast betrayed to the Achaeans, |
| ὦ Ζεῦ | oh Zeus |

It was to the Greek poet a matter of course that a great city like Troy should have its temples and altars in honor of the greatest of all the gods that Hellas knew.

### f. *Ammon Temples in Egypt*

In the same way, Euripides assumes Ammon worship and Ammon shrines for Egypt (Alc. 116–119):

| | |
|---|---|
| εἴτ' ἐπὶ τὰς ἀνύδρους | or to the waterless |
| 'Αμμωνίδας ἕδρας | seats of Ammon, |
| δυστάνου παραλῦσαι | to set free the un- |
| ψυχάν | happy one's soul |

(El. 734–736):

| | |
|---|---|
| ξηραί τ' 'Αμμωνίδες ἕδραι | and Ammon's parched seats |
| φθίνουσ' ἀπειρόδροσοι, | waste away with no portion of dew |
| καλλίστων ὄμβρων Διόθεν στερεῖσαι | but deprived of fairest showers from Zeus |

In neither passage is there contained anything but a hint that in a rainless land Ammon had his dwellings. Ammon worship filled the Nile valley; but Euripides, if he knew aught

---

[1] Z 86 ff.; 269 ff.; 297 ff.
[2] Eur. Tro. 69–70: ΑΘ. οὐκ οἶσθ' ὑβρισθεῖσάν με καὶ ναοὺς ἐμούς;
　　　　　　ΠΟ. οἶδ', ἡνίκ' Αἴας εἶλκε Κασάνδραν βίᾳ.
Cf. also *ibid.* 85–86.

of it, has nothing to tell us. Neither has Aristophanes in the one line in which he mentions Ammon.[1]

### g. *The Achilleum of Leuce*

The worship of Achilles seems to have spread in many directions from his heroüm a Sigeum—to Elis, Thessaly, Delphi, Epirus, and many other parts of the ancient world. By far the most famous centre of Achilles-worship was the little island of Leuce in the Black Sea, just off the mouth of the Danube. The sanctuary there had its temple and its cultus image of the hero. To these Euripides seems to refer (Andr. 1260–1262):

| | |
|---|---|
| τὸν φίλτατον σοὶ παῖδ' ἐμοί τ' Ἀχιλλέα | and Achilles, son most dear to thee and to me, |
| ὄψει δόμους ναίοντα νησιωτικοὺς | thou shalt see dwelling in an island home— |
| Λευκὴν κατ' ἀκτὴν ἐντὸς Εὐξείνου πόρου | Leuce, opposite the mainland in the Euxine Sea |

Besides the temple, the sacred precinct of the Nereid's son contained the needful accessories for the continuance of the activities that had occupied him in his mortal life—exercise in the use of arms of war and athletics. A sanctuary of the "fleet-footed Achilles" would have been quite incomplete without a stadium. That a stadium was not wanting at Leuce seems clear from Euripides's Iphigenia in Tauris (435–438):

| | |
|---|---|
| τὰν πολυόρνιθον ἐπ' αἶαν, | to the land of many birds, |
| λευκὰν ἀκτάν, Ἀχιλῆος | the White Strand, Achilles's |
| δρόμους καλλισταδίους | courses in stadium splendid, |
| ἄξεινον κατὰ πόντον | along the inhospitable sea |

The "White Strand" is of course the isle of Leuce; the Axine Sea is the Euxine Sea; the splendid stadium was in Euripides's day doubtless a well-known reality. For Leuce, standing out before the entrance to the Danube, was a very important landmark for the Greek mariner carrying the commerce of Greece into the far northeast in exchange for lumber and grain and other provisions. And from very early times Greek colonists had taken possession there, and the later inhabitants of the narrow strip of land, toward the northwest of the Danube Delta, the Δρόμος Ἀχίλλειος proper, called themselves Achillodromites.[2]

The level stretch where the race-course was is named in an unidentified tragic fragment (Inc. Inc. Frag. 202 N.):

| | |
|---|---|
| Ἀχίλλειον πλάκα | Achilles's level ground |

and possibly also in the ἀχιλλείων of Sophocles's Scythians (Frag. 507 N., *q. v.*).

---

[1] Av. 716; see p. 87.

[2] For the full discussion of the cultus of the deified Achilles and the seats of his worship see Fleischer in Roscher's *Myth. Lex.* I Sp. 56–66.

# V. DWELLINGS

## *Mycenaean Palace and Historical House*

The dramatic poets give many details of temples that we have found helpful in restoring to our minds some of the famous buildings of classical Greece. Often, too, the scene of a play is laid not before a temple but before the palace of a king or by a peasant's cot. May we look for similar light to be thrown upon profane architecture, palaces of the rich and powerful and homes of common people?

The bare words οἶκος, δόμος, δόμοι, δῶμα, δώματα, δωμάτιον, μέλαθρον, μέλαθρα, στέγη, στέγαι, aedes, aedicula, are of too common occurrence to call for citation or comment; Lucius Pomponius Bonomiensis gives a list of types of profane buildings that may be quite as Hellenic as it sounds Latin, but he gives nothing but names (Fab. Atel., Cretula vel Pet. 37–38 R.²):

balnea<br>forus macellus fana portus porticus

No passage will be discussed or cited unless some epithet or detail is added that will help our understanding of ancient architecture, heroic or scenic.[1]

The problem here is obviously a very difficult one. For the tragic poets do not hesitate to attribute to the palaces of their heroic times architectural features that may belong peculiarly to the dwelling houses of fifth century Athens. And the comic poets in dealing with the architecture of their own day use terms that have so wide a range of meaning that it is sometimes wholly impossible to interpret them. Neither can we confidently rely upon the scholiasts and lexicographers for help; for chronological difficulties through them are often only multiplied. Still the poets themselves do throw considerable light on the problems of both the Mycenaean palace and the classical residence.

Various Mycenaean palaces, the remains of which we now know in reality, figure in the tragedies. Prominent among them are the Palace of the Atridae at Mycenae (Ae. Ag., Cho.; Soph. El.; Eur. Or., El., I. A., I. T., H. F.), the Erechtheid palace at Athens (Ae. Eum. 854–856; Eur. Ion 234–235; 1293),[2] the Labdacid palace at Thebes (Ae. Sep.; Soph. O. T., Ant.; Eur. Ph.),[3] and the Protean palace at Pharos (Eur. Hel.).

To us the general plan of the heroic palaces of prehomeric days has become familiar in the realities that we know at Tiryns, Mycenae, Arne, Cnossus, Phaestus, Ἁγία Τριάδα,

---

[1] Often we have added to the words for "house" or "palace" epithets that only adorn; they tell us nothing of the architecture (e.g. Ae. Cho. 343):

| μελάθροις ἐν βασιλείοις | in the royal halls |

The same phrase occurs again in line 1065. Compare Eur. Hel. 144:

| ἦλθον τούσδε βασιλείους δόμους | I have come to these royal halls |

It is the palace of Proteus (Theoclymenus) in Egypt. As the court of the ruler, it is, of course, a royal palace. Later in the play the same palace is βασίλειοι δόμοι and δώματα (459–460):

| ΜΕ. τίς ἥδε χώρα; τοῦ δὲ βασίλειοι δόμοι; | ME. What land is this? Whose royal halls? |
| ΓΡ. Πρωτεὺς τάδ' οἰκεῖ δώματ', Αἴγυπτος δὲ | GR. Proteus dwells in these apartments; Egypt the land |

and again (781):

| θανεῖ πρὸς ἀνδρὸς οὗ τάδ' ἔστι δώματα | thou shalt die by the hand of the man whose halls these are |

Similar is Aeschylus's Agamemnon 957:

| εἶμ' ἐς δόμων μέλαθρα | I will enter the halls of my palace |

Sometimes the palace of Agamemnon at Mycenae is a high-sounding phrase like μέλαθρα βασίλεια (Ae. Cho. 343); sometimes it is a simple οἶκος (Ae. Ag. 961); sometimes it is a δόμος (Ae. Ag. 962); or δόμοι (Ae. Ag. 964). Even an epithet like εὐδαίμων (Eur. El. 1289) adds nothing for our purpose:

| χώρει πρὸς οἶκον Κεκροπίας εὐδαίμονα | go to Cecropia's dwelling blest |

The palace of Cecrops on the citadel of Athens is now, even in its scanty ruins, a familiar feature of the Acropolis, and it was in Mycenaean days wealthy and powerful. But in this passage Cecropia's dwelling is simply Athens, the blest.

[2] For a detailed study of the remains of "the goodly house of Erechtheus," wall by wall and almost stone by stone, see Wiegand, *die Archaische Poros-Architektur der Akropolis zu Athen* and Holland, *Erechtheum Papers II, A. J. A.* XXVIII (1924); also Cavvadias und Kawerau, *Ausgrabung der Akropolis.*

[3] For a detailed account of the remains of this palace see Κεραμόπουλλος, Ἀρχ. Δελτ. III (1917), pp. 2, 4, 77, 95, 125, 127–138.

Troy. We can but wonder how much the tragic poets knew about Mycenaean and Minoan architecture. They knew the Cyclopean walls of Athens, Mycenae, Tiryns, at least, and probably other walls of the same epoch. They could not see, as we may, the palaces at Troy, but they trusted their Homer and echo his "polished stones."

In the same way they knew about the palace of Agamemnon on the citadel of Mycenae. The whole castle had been sunk in ruins and laid under a curse by the Dorian invasion. But its fame had lived. The poets and story-tellers had passed it on; and, drawing from some of them, Seneca has given us a picture of the palace that is fairly full (Thy. 641–665):

> In arce summa Pelopia pars est domus
> conversa ad Austros, cuius extremum latus
> aequale monti crescit atque urbem premit
> et contumacem regibus populum suis
> habet sub ictu. fulget hic turbae capax
> immane tectum, cuius auratas trabes
> variis columnae nobiles maculis ferunt.
> post ista volgo nota quae populi colunt,
> in multa dives spatia discedit domus.
>
> Arcana in imo regio secessu iacet,
> alta vetustum valle compescens nemus,
> penetrale regni nulla qua laetus solet
> praebere ramos arbos aut ferro coli,
> sed taxus et cupressus et nigra ilice
> obscura nutat silva, quam supra eminens
> despectat alte quercus et vincit nemus.
> hinc auspicari regna Tantalidae solent,
> hinc petere lassis rebus ac dubiis opem.
>
> Affixa inhaerent dona, vocales tubae
> fractique currus spolia Myrtoi maris,
> victaeque falsis axibus pendent rotae,
> et omne gentis facinus, hoc Phrygius loco
> fixus tiaras Pelopis, hic praeda hostium
> et de triumpho picta barbarico chlamys.
> fons stat sub umbra tristis. . . .

What Seneca's source was we do not know; but following his description we can see the magnificent Pelopian house, in its retired nook of Argos, rising with its spacious halls, terrace above terrace, to the summit of the acropolis of Mycenae; we can see its great roof, with its copings, its splendid columns, its gilded beams and cornices, its groves, its fountain of Perseia, its pomp and power. Seneca's word painting is in striking harmony with what we can reconstruct from the Mycenae that we know to-day.

Even on the flat Delta of Egypt the palace of Proteus is a mighty fortress, a house of royal wealth and magnificence (Eur. Hel. 68–70):

| | |
|---|---|
| τίς τῶνδ' ἐρυμνῶν δωμάτων ἔχει κράτος; | who sways the power in these castle halls? |
| Πλούτου γὰρ οἶκος ἄξιος προσεικάσαι | For it merits the conjecture that 'tis Plutus's hall— |
| βασίλειά τ' ἀμφιβλήματ' εὔθριγκοί θ' ἕδραι | a palace with its princely walls and goodly cornices |

Such is the splendor of the Protean palace occupied by Theoclymenus and Helen, that Teucer, coming from Salamis and familiar with the "goodly house of Erechtheus," likens this Egyptian castle to the dwelling of the god of wealth himself—walls of fortification, with towers for its defense, and with architectural decorations to match.

The lordly palace of Priam and his sons upon the citadel of Troy was builded in reality of "polished stones,"[1] and so also we find it in the tragedy (Eur. Or. 1388–1389):

| | |
|---|---|
| ξεστῶν περγάμων 'Απολλωνίων ἐρινύν | avenging spirit of Apollo's polished Pergama |

[1] Z 244; 248.

THE CITADEL OF MYCENAE

The recurrence of the epithet "polished" is striking. And further to suggest the magnificence of the Trojan palaces, Euripides ascribes them, as well as the walls, to Apollo's architecture.[1]

From the polish of Homer's palace at Troy the same high quality of finish has been passed on to other cities of the heroic age. Thus, at Thebes, whole streets become polished (Eur. H. F. 781–783):

| | |
|---|---|
| Ἴσμην' ὦ στεφανηφόρει, | crown thyself with garlands, Ismenus; |
| ξεσταί θ' ἑπταπύλου πόλεως | and leap into dancing, ye polished |
| ἀναχορήσατ' ἀγυιαί | streets of the seven-gated city. |

We have here, in Thebes, to think of a succession of dwellings, all of polished stone, along the streets, just as at Troy, with its detached palaces of the sons and daughters of Priam, one might with propriety have spoken of the "polished streets" of Ilium also.

Among these dwellings along this "polished street" of Thebes were the palaces of Cadmus and of Amphion, who built the city and its walls. Sophocles recognizes the presence of both these ancient palaces (Ant. 1155):

| | |
|---|---|
| Κάδμου πάροικοι καὶ δόμων 'Αμφίονος | ye neighbors of Cadmus and of Amphion's palace |

Aeschylus introduced the palace of Amphion in a passage in his Niobe (Frag. 160 N.[2]), which Aristophanes parodies and adds a temple of Zeus—signifying, perhaps, that the temple of Zeus on the Cadmea of Thebes was related to the palace of Amphion there in much the same way as the temple of Athena on the Acropolis of Athens was related to the "goodly house of Erechtheus" [3] (Ar. Av. 1246–1248):

| | |
|---|---|
| ἆρ' οἶσθ' ὅτι Ζεὺς εἴ με λυπήσει πέρα, | say—do you know that if Zeus goes on bothering me, |
| μέλαθρα μὲν αὐτοῦ καὶ δόμους 'Αμφίονος | I'll burn to ashes, with fire-carrying eagles, |
| καταιθαλώσω πυρφόροισιν ἀετοῖς | his own roof and the palace of Amphion |

We have still another "polished street" at Argos; for the same interpretation may be placed upon the fragment from the Bellerophon of Euripides (Frag. 305 N.):

| | |
|---|---|
| καὶ ξεστὸν ὄχθον Δαναϊδῶν ἑδρασμάτων | and the polished hillside with the seats of the Danaids . . . |
| στὰς ἐν μέσοισιν εἶπε κηρύκων < ὕπο > | standing in the midst he spake by the voice of heralds |

At Argos, too, it seems, there was a great palace, or line of palaces, along the slope of the Larissa hill, and these also were builded of polished stones so notable that the hill itself could be called "polished."

The site that may possibly here be alluded to remained identified in the traditions of the people until late times. This is clearly hinted at in the scholium to Euripides's Orestes 872 (II, p. 225, 5):

| | |
|---|---|
| δεικνύουσι καὶ νῦν ἔτι ὑπεράνω τοῦ | they point out even unto this day above the |
| καλουμένου πρωνὸς χῶμα παντελῶς | so-called foreland a pile of utter ruins |
| οὗ συμβαίνει τοὺς 'Αργείους δικάζειν. | where, it happens, the Argives hold court. |
| τάχα δ' ἂν τούτου καὶ ἐν Βελλεροφόν- | It may be this also that he has in mind |
| τῃ μνημονεύει εἰπὼν καὶ ξεστὸν κ.τ.λ. | when he says in the Bellerophon: "And the polished, etc." |

It is, of course, possible that ἑδράσματα may mean "the everlasting abiding place," the tombs, of the daughters of Danaus. The assembly place of the Argives on the ruins of the tomb, if such be meant, recalls vividly the theatre built upon the ruins of the "tomb of Clytaemnestra"[4] at Mycenae.

Before the palace at Tiryns is the large, general court, entered through the great propylaea on the eastern side. This is the standard arrangement in the ground plan of a prehomeric palace. The palace at Thebes also had its general court (αὐλή), and this had its doorway leading into the public street. Thus, in the opening scene of the Antigone of Sophocles,

---

[1] Cp. also Eur. Andr. 1009–1018.
[2] The latter half of the three lines quoted below from Aristophanes's Birds.
[3] See p. 45.
[4] Better known as Mrs. Schliemann's Treasury. See pp. 235 ff.

Antigone, who has heard among the people the rumor of the king's intentions, has sent for her sister to come out of doors into the public highway to hear alone the news (18–19):

| σ' ἐκτὸς αὐλείων πυλῶν<br>τοῦδ' οὕνεκ' ἐξέπεμπον | and for that reason I sent for thee to<br>come outside the courtyard gates |

Just inside the greater propylaea at Tiryns, to the right as one enters the great outer court, are two rooms that are usually called "the gate-keepers' lodge." And such they in all probability are. The gate-keepers might be men or they might be maid-servants, and some of them had to be on duty by relays night and day. The chorus in the Troades look with sad hearts forward to the time when they will have to be performing such service in the palaces of their conquerors (Eur. Tro. 194):

| τὰν παρὰ προθύροις φυλακὰν κατέχουσ' | keeping watch at the front doors |

The πρόθυρα stand for the principal entrance to the palace, especially where there is but one court, instead of two as at Tiryns.

Crossing diagonally the great outer court of the palace at Tiryns, one passes through the lesser propylaea into the court of the men's megaron. On the south side of this latter court, on the axis of the great hall, there is what is generally recognized to be a place of sacrifice—a sacrificial pit, if not an altar, sacred to Zeus Herceius (Soph. Ant. 486–487):

| ἀλλ' εἴτ' ἀδελφῆς εἴθ' ὁμαιμονεστέρα<br><br>τοῦ παντὸς ἡμῖν Ζηνὸς Ἑρκείου κυρεῖ | nay, if she chance to be my sister's child, or closer<br>of kin<br>than anyone who worships at the altar of our<br>Zeus Herceius |

(Eur. Tro. 16–17):

| πρὸς δὲ κρηπίδων βάθροις<br>πέπτωκε Πρίαμος Ζηνὸς Ἑρκείου θανών | and on the altar-steps of<br>Zeus Herceius Priam has fallen and lies dead |

This altar of Zeus Herceius was an altar of burnt sacrifice, even as the sacrificial pit in the court at Tiryns had to do with burnt sacrifice. That comes out clearly in a later passage in the Troades where Hecabe uses for it the word that has to do with fire (482–483):

| τοῖσδε δ' εἶδον ὄμμασιν<br>αὐτὴ κατασφαγέντ' ἐφ' ἑρκείῳ πυρᾷ | but with these eyes of mine I saw him<br>slaughtered at the altar of the court |

The very name she uses implies that this "altar of the court" is the fire-altar of Zeus Herceius.

In the orchestra of the Greek theatre was always an altar. While in reality that altar belonged to Dionysus, it might in the presentation of plays have been for the occasion the altar of the deity most nearly concerned. In the Cyclops, the altar must have been the altar of Dionysus; and by it must have stood a statue of the same god. Both come in for explicit mention (345–346):

| τῷ κατ' αὔλιον θεῷ<br>ἵν' ἀμφὶ βωμὸν στάντες εὐωχεῖτέ με | in order that, standing about the altar<br>of the courtyard god, ye may make me good cheer |

The orchestra in this satyr-play represents the court before Polyphemus's cave; the altar in the centre of the orchestra is, of course, the altar of the god of the enclosure—in this instance, Dionysus himself; and the statue is also Dionysus. In the Andromache of Euripides it would be the altar of Thetis; in the Helen, the altar of Proteus; in the Ion, the great altar of Phoebus. In the Hercules Furens of Euripides it would be the altar of Zeus (48):

| βωμὸν καθίζω τόνδε σωτῆρος Διός | I sit here at the altar of Savior Zeus |

This would naturally be the altar of Zeus Herceius, but the epithet of Zeus is, this time, not Herceius but Soter.[1] The only building represented on the proscenium in this play is the palace of Heracles. Megara and the rest whose death is imminent are in the palace court; and the altar of Zeus Soter occupies the place of sacrifice at this temple, as it does also in the men's court of the palace at Tiryns. In the Oedipus Tyrannus of Sophocles the altar

[1] In line 922 it is the "hearth of Zeus," without any epithet: ἱερὰ μὲν ἦν πάροιθεν ἐσχάρας Διός, and in line 927 simple βωμοῦ. Cf. also 521–522; 984; 1145.

before the palace of Oedipus is probably the altar of Zeus Herceius, though we are not expressly told so (15–16):

| | |
|---|---|
| προσήμεθα | we sit |
| βωμοῖσι τοῖς σοῖς | at thine altars |

The plural βωμοῖσι probably means no more than *altaria*—one altar with its steps and altar block.

The altar of the palace court would naturally be the altar of Zeus Herceius. This would not, however, preclude the possibility of various other altars in or about the house. We find, for example, at the palace of Mycenae an altar at which Aegisthus is preparing a sacrifice to the Nymphs and at which he himself is slain by the hand of Orestes (Eur. El. 785–786; 792; 803–804):

| | |
|---|---|
| τυγχάνω δὲ βουθυτῶν | it happens I am sacrificing |
| Νύμφαις[1] | to the Nymphs[1] |
| . . . . . . . | . . . . . . . |
| ὡς ἀμφὶ βωμὸν στῶσι | that they may stand about the altar |
| . . . . . . . | . . . . . . . |
| λαβὼν προχύτας.... | he took the meal and |
| ἔβαλλε βωμούς | cast it on the altar |

Even the private house of fifth century Athens had its altar to Zeus Herceius; such religious customs are tenacious in human society. And so we find in at least one comic scene, which may, if we may judge by the title of the play, be mock-heroic, the altar dedicated to the Zeus of the home-enclosure (Ar. Δάν., Frag. 245 K.):

| | |
|---|---|
| μαρτύρομαι δὲ Ζηνὸς Ἑρκείου χύτρας | and I call to witness Zeus Herceius's pots |
| μεθ’ ὧν ὁ βωμὸς οὗτος ἱδρύθη ποτέ | with which this altar once was consecrated |

We have in this couplet not only the altar of Zeus Herceius, but we have also a suggestion of the rites observed in the dedication of such an altar: when they came to dedicate or consecrate altars or statues to a god, they boiled pulse and made of this the first offering, apportioning to the object of the dedication thank-offerings of the first meal. The pots in which the pulse was cooked went with the offering, of course.[2] In the more pretentious houses of the wealthy the altar of Zeus stood in the court; in the simpler homes of the poor it was by the hearth or identical with the hearth.

When Heracles comes upon the scene and cries (Eur. H. F. 523)

| | |
|---|---|
| ὦ χαῖρε, μέλαθρον πρόπυλά θ’ ἑστίας ἐμῆς | all hail, my hall and portals of my hearth |

has the poet in mind a propylaea building like that at Tiryns? Or does πρόπυλα signify nothing more than "front door"? The limitations of the proscenium of the theatre would naturally lead us to answer the first question in the negative and the latter in the affirmative. But the stage properties easily permitted a pillared front to the stage palace.

Very much the same phrase occurs in Sophocles's Electra 1374–1375:

| | |
|---|---|
| πατρῷα προσκύσανθ’ ἕδη | when we have done obeisance to the images of our |
| θεῶν, ὅσοιπερ πρόπυλα ναίουσιν τάδε | fathers' gods that dwell here at the portal |

Orestes with Pylades is just on the point of entering the palace at Mycenae. In the propylaea forming the entrance to his ancestral halls stood images of the gods of his native land. Was this entrance a propylon, like the greater and lesser propylaea at Tiryns and the propylon in City II at Troy, or was it simply a doorway in the pillared front of the proscenium? We must leave the question unanswered in this case also, as in the former. In all probability the poet means no more by πρόπυλα in either of these passages than is meant by πρόθυρα in Euripides's Hypsipyle (Frag. 1 II 15–18, Ox. Pap. VI, p. 35):

| | |
|---|---|
| τί σὺ παρὰ προθύροις, φίλα; | what dost thou at the vestibule, dear? |
| πότερα δώματος εἰσόδους | Art thou sweeping the entrance to the |
| σαίρεις ἢ δρόσον ἐπὶ πέδῳ | palace or sprinkling drops |
| βάλλεις | upon the floor |

[1] Cf. also line 805.

[2] Schol. Ar. Pax 923 and Pl. 1198: ὁπότε μέλλοιεν βωμοὺς καθιδρύειν ἢ ἀγάλματα θεοῦ, ἕψοντες ὄσπρια ἀπήρχοντο τούτων, τοῖς ἐφιδρυμένοις χαριστήρια ἀπονέμοντες τῆς πρώτης διαίτης.

The vestibule—the "place before the door"—is obviously the paved and covered portico of the palace of the king at Nemea.

At all events, the royal palace had its great portal with its double gates. Often the propylon at Tiryns or that at Troy (City II) is called to mind, with its gateway and the great stone threshold in the midst (Ae. Cho. 571):

εἰ δ' οὖν ἀμείψω βαλὸν ἑρκείων πυλῶν | but if I cross the threshold of the court-yard gates

We have a clearly outlined picture of the gateway, the threshold, the enclosed court before the megaron of the king beyond. Aeschylus even shows us the prothyron at Agamemnon's palace (Cho. 965–966):

τάχα δὲ παντελὴς χρόνος ἀμείψεται
πρόθυρα δωμάτων

| and soon all-accomplishing Time will pass
the front doors of the palace

He lets us see its doors, which open from the propylaea upon the palace court, and hear the stranger knocking at the doors (Cho. 653):

θύρας ἄκουσον ἑρκείας κτύπον | harken to the knocking at the courtyard doors

The same doors are also called gates (l. 732):

ποῖ δὲ πατεῖς, Κίλισσα, δωμάτων πύλας; | whither bound, Cilissa, dost thou pass the palace gates?

The "doors" might be the entrance to the megaron; but "gates" must be the great double doors of the propylaeum; they are *par excellence* the gates of the palace. The big front door is also called a portal (θυρών) (Soph. El. 328):

πρὸς θυρῶνος ἐξόδοις | at the exit of the portal

The context makes it clear that this portal was the great gateway in the palace propylaea opening upon the street. In the Oedipus Tyrannus 1241–1242 the "portal" is the great double door opening from the court into the interior of the house.[1]

A simpler arrangement would, of course, be a doorway with flanking doorposts.[2] And this too we have (Soph. El. 1331–1332):

ἀλλ' εἰ σταθμοῖσι τοῖσδε μὴ 'κύρουν ἐγὼ
πάλαι φυλάσσων

| but had I not chanced to be keeping watch
by these doorposts all this while

Here is not necessarily a pillared portico. Still less is it a pillared portico in the Mad Hercules of Seneca (1004–1005):

huc eat et illuc valva deiecto obice
ruantque[3] postes

The bar is to be thrown down, the double doors swung one this way and one that, and the doorposts overturned. The front of the palace of Amphitryon is a very modest one.

But there are more pretentious ones. And in the poets and in the reality at some Mycenaean centres, we have both the round columns and the simpler front assured, with entablature above them, according to strict Doric regulations. The palace of Pentheus at Thebes is a fair example of the palace with pillared front (Eur. Bacch. 591–592):

ἴδετε λάϊνα κίοσιν ἔμβολα
διάδρομα τάδε

| see yonder the marble beams upon
the pillars starting asunder

In this palace we see columns along the front of the building, and architrave blocks of stone resting upon them. Between the pillars of such a façade was the great doorway or gateway of the palace; and upon them rested the entablature—triglyphon and frieze. The stately

---

[1] See p. 207.

[2] In the theatre, such doorposts were, of course, of stone. Aristophanes leaves little doubt on this point (Ach. 449 = Inc. Inc. Frag. 44 N.): ἄπελθε λαΐνων σταθμῶν | depart from my doorposts of stone. Euripides is the speaker and the doorway represented is that of his own home; but the words have a highly tragic flavor and are probably a parody upon a line of some tragedy of Euripides himself. In the original setting the doorposts may have belonged to a temple or a palace; and part of the fun of the parody might possibly have been found in the fact that the doorposts of Euripides's own house were of wood.

[3] Ruantque is the conjectural reading of Peiper and Richter for rumpatque of the MSS.

portal and the encircling frieze of Proteus's palace are specifically mentioned in Euripides's Helen (430–432):

| | |
|---|---|
| ἰδὼν δὲ δῶμα περιφερὲς θριγκοῖς τόδε | and since I caught sight of this palace with its encircling frieze |
| πύλας τε σεμνὰς ἀνδρὸς ὀλβίου τινὸς προσῆλθον | and splendid gateway of some man of wealth, I have approached |

The stately portal and the encircling frieze were both in plain sight from the tomb at which the speaker stood before the gates.

The place of the heroic propylaea is taken in historical times sometimes by a reduced propylaeum, consisting of two columns in antis, with the street-door set back in the wall flanked by two antae. Such house-fronts we still have from the good period in Delos. They correspond exactly to the specifications presented by the poet of the Old Comedy in the fifth century (Crat. Διον., Frag. 42 K.):

| | |
|---|---|
| παραστάδας καὶ πρόθυρα βούλει ποικίλα | you wish for decorated portico and antae |

πρόθυρα and προπύλαια seem to be synonymous. And Cratinus's character demands an elaborate front door. Sometimes, on the other hand, instead of such a propylum, we may have a portico or gallery running not only across the front of the building but also around the sides. Xenophon was familiar with such architectural devices, and he has Cyrus build galleries on the different stories of the huge movable towers he used in the great battle.[1] Aristophanes also has some woman in his Old Age standing on the gallery of her apartment (Γῆρας, Frag. 133 K.):

| | |
|---|---|
| ἐπὶ τοῦ περιδρόμου στᾶσα τῆς συνοικίας | she stood upon the gallery of her apartment |

Pollux in citing the line remarks (IX 39):

| | |
|---|---|
| καὶ τὸ πλῆθος τῶν οἰκοδομημάτων οἰκίαι καὶ συνοικίαι καὶ οἰκίας | and in the case of most structures there are dwellings and apartments and attached to the dwelling |
| περίδρομος, ὡς ἐν τῷ Γήρᾳ 'Αρ. | a gallery, as Aristophanes has it in his Old Age |

According to the poets, the heroic palace had also its Doric triglyphon above the architrave (Eur. Or. 1369–1371):

| | |
|---|---|
| πέφευγα | I have 'scaped |
| . . . . . . . . | . . . . . . . . |
| κέδρωτα παστάδων ὑπὲρ τέραμνα | over the cedar beams of the chamber |
| Δωρικάς τε τριγλύφους | and through the Doric triglyphs |

The Phrygian slave, terror-stricken at the vengeance of Orestes and Pylades within the palace and unable to pass the doors, has climbed over the architrave beams and dropped into the presence of the astounded chorus.[2]

The palace of Pentheus, too, is thought of as adorned with a triglyphon; for to the triglyphs Agave proposes to have her son's head nailed (Eur. Bacch. 1212–1215; see above pages 115 and 117).

So important are these "beams" that τέραμνα is often used by synecdoche for the building itself (Eur. Hip. 536–537):

| | |
|---|---|
| ἐπὶ Πυθίοις τεράμνοις | at the Pythian roof-tree |
| βούταν φόνον Ἑλλὰς αἶ' ἀέξει | Hellas-land pours out the blood of bulls |

By the Πύθια τέραμνα the poet means, of course, the temple of Apollo at Delphi. Again (Eur. Alc. 456–457):

| | |
|---|---|
| δυναίμαν δέ σε πέμψαι | would that I could convey thee |
| φάος ἐξ 'Αίδα τεράμνων | from Hades's roof-tree to the light of day |

And once more (Eur. Tro. 1296):

| | |
|---|---|
| Περγάμων τε πυρὶ καταίθεται τέραμνα | and the roof-trees of Pergama are burning down with fire |

---

[1] Xen. Cyr. VI 1, 53.
[2] See above, p. 113.

As upon the lordly temple of Apollo at Delphi the capitals of columns, the cornices, triglyphs, and architrave were adorned by its wealthy patrons with inlaid gold, so the palaces of the lords of such castles as Mycenae "rich in gold" might be expected to receive similar costly decoration.  And so we find in the Agamemnon abodes fairly glittering with gold[1] (Ae. Ag. 776):

τὰ χρυσόπαστα ἔδεθλα[1] | the gold-bespangled abodes

Mycenae "rich in gold" made use of her precious metal everywhere—inside and outside the palace and the tombs, for personal adornment, for architectural embellishment, for household furnishings—wealth of gold everywhere.  "Rich in gold" was a standing epithet of the city; the interior of the king's palace called for similar epithets (for example, Ae. Cho. 800–802):

οἵ τ' ἔσω δωμάτων | and ye that within the palace
πλουτογαθῆ μυχὸν ἐνίζετε, | dwell in the chamber that rejoiceth in wealth—
κλῦτε, σύμφρονες θεοί | hearken, ye gods in purpose one

In the same way, the Thracian king, whose realm was proverbial for its riches of gold, might speak of the palaces of rich gold to which he was accustomed (Eur. Rh. 439):

οὐδ' ἐν ζαχρύσοις δώμασιν κοιμώμενος | nor sleeping in palaces of precious gold

And Helen, in similar vein, refers to the palace of Troy, equally proverbial for its wealth, as

πολυχρύσους δόμους | halls of much gold (Eur. Hel. 928)

Agamemnon's, we see, was only one of many such lordly castles of enormous wealth.  In the palace of his brother Menelaus at Sparta, rivaling the splendors of the palace of Zeus himself, amazement filled the soul of Telemachus "as he looked upon the glitter of bronze and silver and gold and electrum and ivory throughout the echoing halls."[2]  Some of this may have been outside adornment of the palace; some was also interior decoration about the walls and columns of the great hall.

Euripides in the Aulid Iphigenia implies that decoration in ivory also was general in the ancient palaces of Hellas (I. A. 581–583):

ἅ σ' Ἑλλάδα πέμπει | who sent thee to Hellas to stand
τῶν ἐλεφαντοδέτων πάροι- | in the presence of halls bedight with
θεν δόμων[3] | ivory

Both gold and ivory richly adorned the palace of King Priam (Enn. Fab. 169):[4]

o Priami domu' . . . caelatis lacuatis, auro, ebore instructam regifice

Such extravagance of splendor is reminiscent of the orient, whence came the grandsire of Agamemnon, king of men.  We are, therefore, not surprised to find in Aeschylus's own times the palace of Darius agleam with decorations of inlaid gold (Ae. Pers. 159–160):

ταῦτα δὴ λιποῦσ'ἱκάνω χρυσεοστόλμους δόμους | yea, thus am I come, leaving the palace bedight
 | with gold,
καὶ τὸ Δαρείου τε κάμὸν εὐνατήριον | the bridal bower of Darius and myself

The joys and luxuries of the settled, peaceful state of Cloud-cuckoo-town include also a gold-bespangled palace of the heroic type; and at the festive conclusion of the Birds, Pisthetaerus comes in royal splendor to ascend the throne.  His arrival is announced by the messenger in mock-tragic tone (Ar. Av. 1709–1710):

προσέρχεται γὰρ οἷος οὔτε παμφαὴς | for he draws nigh his gold-bespangled palace as
ἀστὴρ ἰδεῖν ἔλαμψε χρυσαυγεῖ δόμῳ | never a glittering star gleamed upon the sight

Even in classical times the private dwelling, though wanting in the splendor of the princely palace of the heroic age, might have its triglyphon and other Doric ornamentation (Diph. Παράσ. 61, 1–4 K.):

---

[1] If the commonly accepted conjecture of Auratus is correct; the MSS. read ἐσθλά.
[2] δ 71–75.
[3] There is no occasion to alter δόμων to θρόνων with Hermann, who could see no possible sense in an ἐλεφαντοδέτος δόμος.  A column inlaid with ivory would naturally be ἐλεφαντόδετος; and to a series of such columns might well be applied the phrase ἐλεφαντόδετος δόμος.
[4] Cf. Bacchyl. 27, 8 and Cic. Paradox. I 3, 13, both quoted on p. 59.

ὅταν με καλέσῃ πλούσιος δεῖπνον ποιῶν,

ού κατανοῶ τὰ τρίγλυφ' οὐδὲ τὰς στέγας,
οὐδὲ δοκιμάζω τοὺς Κορινθίους κάδους,
ἀτενὲς δὲ τηρῶ τοῦ μαγείρου τὸν καπνόν

when a rich man invites me to a dinner he is giving,
I do not notice his triglyphs or his roof;
I do not calculate upon the casks from Corinth;
but I do note carefully the smoke from his kitchen

The triglyphs and the entablature of the mansion do not necessarily mean to the parasite, who speaks, that there is luxurious living in the home thus adorned; he seems to imply that only the well-to-do would have a house of such pretensions and that the humbler homes would have no Doric triglyphs. But the important thing in his hungry eyes is the evidence of good living afforded by the kitchen.

For the sort of Doric palace that we have been studying, with columns in antis, architrave, guttae, and triglyphon, we have striking monumental corroboration in the famous Amphiaraus vase from Caere now in Berlin.[1] Upon it we have two such palace buildings. The one at the left is that of Amphiaraus at Argos. The vase is high archaic. We have, therefore, in the buildings it represents, the conception of an early sixth (or possibly late seventh) century vase-painter of what a palace of the heroic age ought to look like and of what a well-to-do dwelling of his own day probably did look like. The picture does not include anything above the triglyphon. The whole composition tallies, even to the minutest details, with Pausanias's description of the corresponding scene on the Cypselus chest;[2] and as the names appearing beside the various figures in the scene are written in Corinthian letters, it is safe to say that we have in the vase a copy, more or less close, of a portion of the chest of Cypselus. The chest of Cypselus, accordingly, had just such a Doric palace as the palace of Amphiaraus on the vase.

Above the triglyphon we look naturally to find a cornice or frieze on our palace front. And there we have already found it (Eur. Hel. 430–432)[3] and we may possibly find it again in Euripides's Helen 69–70.[4]

There is a cornice also about the edge of the roof, and it is this upper cornice that must be meant when cornice and roof are named together (Eur. El. 1150–1151):

ἰάχησε δὲ στέγα λάϊνοί
τε θριγκοὶ δόμων

then shrieked the palace's roof
and cornices of stone

The same cornice, or the raking cornice above the gable of a temple, gave rise to the figurative use of θριγκός as the capstone or crown or limit. So Hecabe, speaking of her loss of husband, children, youth, health, happiness, and home, and looking forward to her declining days in slavery, cries (Eur. Tro. 489–490):

τὸ λοίσθιον δέ, θριγκὸς ἀθλίων κακῶν,
δούλη γυνὴ γραῦς 'Ελλάδ' εἰσαφίξομαι

and last, the crown of my unhappiness and woe,
I shall go to Hellas, an aged woman and a slave

We find also the verb θριγκόω in the same figurative sense (Eur. H. F. 1280):

παιδοκτονήσας δῶμα θριγκῶσαι κακοῖς

to slay my children and put upon my home its
crown of woes

So Aeschylus in the Agamemnon (1283):

κάτεισιν, ἄτας τάσδε θριγκώσων φίλοις

he shall come back to put upon his loved ones
the crown of all these woes

In the passage just quoted from Euripides's Electra the cornice is of stone, befitting the palace of the king of men. The material, however, is not a point to be emphasized; for in the Orestes that same palace of Agamemnon, in keeping with what we know of Mycenaean architecture, has a superstructure of inflammable material (Eur. Or. 1618–1620):

ἀλλ' εἶ', ὕφαπτε δώματ', 'Ηλέκτρα, τάδε.
σύ τ', ὦ φίλων μοι τῶν ἐμῶν σαφέστατε,
Πυλάδη, κάταιθε γεῖσα τειχέων τάδε

what ho! Electra, set fire to the palace yonder;
and thou, Pylades, truest of my friends to me,
kindle to flames the eaves of yonder walls

[1] Reproduced in Baum. *Denkm.* I, p. 67, Fig. 69.
[2] Paus. V 17, 4.
[3] Quoted on p. 203.
[4] See p. 198.

The distinction between θριγχός and γεῖσον is not great: the γεῖσον is the projecting portion of the roof; the θριγχός, the plain or decorated face of the γεῖσον.[1] Even the most technical words, we see, find place in these descriptions.

Again, when, in her dream, Iphigenia sees the ruin of her father's halls, the cornice is one of the architectural members that come prominently to view (Eur. I. T. 47–52):

| | |
|---|---|
| κἄξω στᾶσα θριγχὸν εἰσιδεῖν | without I stood and saw the palace's cornice |
| δόμων πίτνοντα, πᾶν δ᾽ ἐρείψιμον στέγος | falling and all the entablature from the |
| βεβλημένον πρὸς οὖδας ἐξ ἄκρων σταθμῶν. | summits of the pillars crashing in ruins |
| μόνος δ᾽ ἐλείφθη στῦλος, ὡς ἔδοξέ μοι, | to the ground.  One column alone, meseemed, was left |
| δόμων πατρῴων, ἐκ δ᾽ ἐπικράνων κόμας | from my father's halls, and from its capital |
| ξανθὰς καθεῖναι . . . | flowed golden locks . . . |

Here we have round columns, with shaft and capital, and entablature, with cornice and roof.  In the Agamemnon of Aeschylus we find again the round column,[2] supporting a roof that was high (897–898):

| | |
|---|---|
| σωτῆρα ναὸς πρότονον, ὑψηλῆς στέγης | saving forestay of the ship, the high roof's |
| στῦλον ποδήρη | firm-footed column |

However metaphorical the phrasing of this passage, the scene is laid in front of Agamemnon's palace, and the king is himself the column that supports his home.  A still further grouping of details of the palace at Mycenae we have in the Orestes of Euripides (1567–1572):

| | |
|---|---|
| οὗτος σύ, κλήθρων τῶνδε μὴ ψαύσῃς χερί, | thou there! lay not thy hand upon those bolts— |
| Μενέλαον εἶπον, ὃς πεπύργωσαι θράσει· | thou, Menelaus, fortified with insolence; touch them, and |
| ἢ τῷδε θριγχῷ κρᾶτα συνθραύσω σέθεν, | I tear off the coping, wrought of builders, old, |
| ῥήξας παλαιὰ γεῖσα, τεκτόνων πόνον. | and with this cornice crush thy head.  The bars |
| μοχλοῖς δ᾽ ἄραρε κλῆθρα, σῆς βοηδρόμου | are fastened tight with bolts and will shut out thy res- |
| σπουδῆς ἅ σ᾽ εἴρξει, μὴ δόμων εἴσω περᾶν | cuing haste and keep thee from forcing thy way into the palace |

In all these passages, except, perhaps, the second one (p. 205), the frieze is a part of the entablature of the building.  The cornice with which Orestes threatens to crush his uncle's head is most naturally a cornice of stone.  In the Electra we are told in so many words that the cornice of the palace at Mycenae was made of stone.[3]  The θριγχὸς κυάνοιο of Alcinous's palace[4] may or may not have decorated the γεῖσον or any other part of the entablature of the Scherian royal residence.  The cyanus frieze of Tiryns, we are now all pretty thoroughly agreed, upon the basis of the most recent investigations, was not set up high upon the building but rested upon the floor of the anteroom to the men's megaron.  It may well have adorned the base of a bench or succession of stone seats like those of Phaestus with their alabaster frieze.  The red breccia friezes from Mycenae with a similar design in half rosettes may have served a like purpose.

In Euripides's Helen (69–70)[5]

| | |
|---|---|
| Πλούτου γὰρ οἶκος ἄξιος προσεικάσαι | for it merits the conjecture that 'tis Plutus's hall |
| βασίλειά τ᾽ ἀμφιβλήματ᾽ εὔθριγχοί θ᾽ ἕδραι | —a palace with princely walls and seats with goodly cornices |

the εὔθριγχοι ἕδραι may quite as literally be rendered by "seats with goodly frieze."  I am very much inclined to believe that this is the correct meaning and that Euripides is talking about just such seats as those at Phaestus and Tiryns;[6] the "goodly frieze" in that case is,

---

[1] The decorative effect of the γεῖσον is vividly suggested when Aristophanes calls the fringe about the border of a mantle γεῖσα: Et. Mag. 229, 40: Γεισίποδες· παρὰ τὸ εἶναι βάσεις τῶν θεμελίων. καὶ γεισῶσαι καὶ γείωσις τὸ τῆς γῆς ἔκθεμα. Ἀριστοφάνης δὲ καὶ τὰς ὤας τοῦ ἱματίου γεῖσα εἶπε (Frag. 762 K.).

[2] Cf. also I. T. 57: στῦλος γὰρ οἴκων παῖδές εἰσιν ἄρσενες.

[3] Eur. El. 1150–1151, quoted on p. 205.

[4] η 87.

[5] Quoted on p. 198, where a slightly different rendering is given.

[6] Euripides seems to have similar seats in mind in the Medea, where the elders sit about the fountain of Pirene (68–69):

πεσσοὺς προσελθών, ἔνθα δὴ παλαίτατοι
θάσσουσι, σεμνὸν ἀμφὶ Πειρήνης ὕδωρ.

of course, the frieze that ornaments the base of the bench. In the two certain examples from the Minoan age the material is of alabaster, more or less richly carved and decorated. The epithet "with goodly frieze" as applied to the benches at the palace of Pharos would find its fitting explanation in the reality that we know.

The roof of Mycenaean palace and of historical Greek dwelling house is mentioned in the drama so often (μέλαθρον, στέγη, τέγος, etc.) and can be so thoroughly taken for granted, that we need enter upon no discussion of the passages in which the mere mention of a roof occurs. As in Homer,[1] so in the tragedy the imposing splendor of the great palace of Mycenaean days may be suggested with the epithet "high-roofed" (Eur. H. F. 107):

| | |
|---|---|
| ὑψόροφα μέλαθρα | high-roofed palace |

It may be interesting to note that in the Clouds of Aristophanes the roof of Socrates's Phrontisterium is flat and that Strepsiades proposes to get into the "think-shop," just as the four friends of the paralytic gained access to the Master in Mark II 4, by climbing up with a ladder and making a hole through the roof—only Strepsiades means to bring the house down upon the heads of the philosophers (Ar. Nub. 1486–1488):

| | |
|---|---|
| κλίμακα λαβὼν ἔξελθε καὶ σμινύην φέρων, | go get a ladder and bring a mattock |
| κἄπειτ' ἀναβὰς ἐπὶ τὸ φροντιστήριον | and then climb up upon the think-shop |
| τὸ τέγος κατάσκαπτ' | and dig up the roof |

Returning to the front of our Mycenaean palace, we pass across the court with its altar to Zeus Herceius, approach the vestibule, and stand before the great front door. It receives a different appellation from that of the interior doors of the house (Soph. O. T. 1241–1242):

| | |
|---|---|
| παρῆλθ' ἔσω θυρῶνος | he passed within the portal |

The great portal is θυρών; the interior doors are πύλαι (Soph. O. T. 1244–1245):

| | |
|---|---|
| πύλας δ', ὅπως εἰσῆλθ', ἐπιρράξας ἔσω | and when he had passed in, he slammed the doors to |
| καλεῖ . . . | and called, within, . . . |

In the classical house the front door is the αὔλειος (or αὔλεία or αὔλιος or αὐλία) θύρα, so called because in the Greek house, unlike the Roman or the Graeco-Roman, as we know it at Pompeii, the street door opened immediately into the αὐλή or peristyle[2] (Ar. Pax. 981–982):

| | |
|---|---|
| παρακλίνασαι τῆς αὐλείας παρακύπτουσιν | they open the front door a bit and peep out surreptitiously |

This becomes still clearer from the home-economic law laid down in Menander (Inc. Frag. 546, 1–3 K.):

| | |
|---|---|
| τοὺς τῆς γαμετῆς ὅρους ὑπερβαίνεις, γύναι, | wife, you are passing a married woman's bounds— |
| τὴν αὐλίαν· πέρας γὰρ αὔλειος θύρα | the front door; for the front door of her |
| ἐλευθέρᾳ γυναικὶ νενόμισται οἰκίας | house has been fixed as the limit for a free woman |

But the ordinary house of the fifth or fourth century had more than one door. When Lysias is telling about his escape from Damnippus, when held up at the latter's house, he explains that the house was ἀμφίθυρος—it had both a front door and a back door. And while the plunderers were keeping watch at the front door (ἐπὶ τῇ αὐλείῳ θύρᾳ), he started to make his escape, and there were three doors through which he had to pass, and all three happened to be open. That is, there were two doors between him and the back door or "garden gate" (κηπαία θύρα), for each house normally had its bit of garden[3] (Pl. Mos. 1046–1047):

> ostium quod in angiportost horti, patefeci fores,
> eaque eduxi omnem legionem, et maris et feminas

In the passage cited above[4] from Euripides's Orestes (1567–1572) various other details of palace architecture are introduced. Among others we find emphasis laid upon the means

---

[1] Γ 423; Ω 192; β 337; ε 42.
[2] See Vitruv. VI 7. Harpocr.: αὔλειος· ἡ ἀπὸ τῆς ὁδοῦ πρώτη θύρα τῆς οἰκίας. Eust. ad X 66, p. 1257. Cf. also Ar. Δαν., Frag. 255 K.
[3] Cf. Ter. Ad. 908.
[4] P. 206.

of fastening the doors. Bolts and bars for fastening the doors against intrusion are often brought into play. All doors would seem to have been provided with locks and bolts and bars, whether it be the great, massive gates of the propylaea of the fortress-palace or the front doors of the megaron or the doors of the inner apartments or the outbuildings of the castle (Eur. Or. 1127):

| | |
|---|---|
| ἐκκλῄσομεν σφᾶς ἄλλον ἄλλοσε στέγης | we will lock them up—one in one part of the palace, another in another[1] |

Theoclymenus, in haste to leave his palace in pursuit of the fugitive Helen and Menelaus, calls to unbar the gates—the great front doorway leading from the court of his palace to the street (Eur. Hel. 1180):[2]

| | |
|---|---|
| ὠή, χαλᾶτε κλῇθρα | what ho! undo the bars |

we can even fairly hear the clank of the bolts as the great doors are unbarred (*ibid*. 859–860):

| | |
|---|---|
| κτυπεῖ δόμος<br>κλῄθρων λυθέντων | the palace echoes<br>as the bolts are shot back |

In tragic style and with language that applies only to the prehistoric palace as represented on the tragic scene, the old dicast in Aristophanes's Wasps cries (1482; 1484):

| | |
|---|---|
| τίς ἐπ' αὐλείοισι θύραις θάσσει; | who hath his seat at the courtyard gates? |
| . . . . . . . . | . . . . . . . . |
| κλῇθρα χαλάσθω τάδε | Be these bolts undone. |

We find both bars and bolts in Euripides's Andromache (950–951):

| | |
|---|---|
| πρὸς τάδ' εὖ φυλάσσετε<br>κλῄθροισι καὶ μοχλοῖσι δωμάτων πύλας | therefore guard ye well with<br>bolts and bars the doors of your halls |

These particular bolts and bars were not for the purpose of keeping out thieves or assassins, but (quite as expedient, according to the philosophy of Euripides) to keep women from getting together and gossiping, to the wreck and ruin of society!

As in the Odyssey, at the slaying of the suitors, the women's apartments could be effectively shut off from the men's megaron, so in the tragedy also the Mycenaean palace is so arranged that communication with the women's quarters may be easily barred by lock and bolt and key. We have it again in Aeschylus's Choephori (878–879):

| | |
|---|---|
| γυναικείους πύλας<br>μοχλοῖς χαλᾶτε | open the bars<br>of the women's doors |

In the classical period, as in the heroic age, the women dwelt apart in their own private quarters in the home.[3] These were, as we have seen, in the interior portion of the house. Its retirement is suggested by the poets' word for the gynaeceum, μυχός, μυχοί. Antigone complains bitterly of the curtailment of her liberties in being shut in, like an Athenian woman, but quite unlike a Mycenaean princess or a Spartan girl (Ae. Cho. 446):

| | |
|---|---|
| μυχῷ δ' ἄφερκτος πολυσινοῦς κυνὸς δίκαν | shut up in the inner recesses of the place, like a vicious cur |

At the beginning of the same play the Chorus emphasizes with the same strong word the complete retirement of the women's apartments (Ae. Cho. 35–36):

| | |
|---|---|
| μυχόθεν ἔλακε περὶ φόβῳ,<br>γυναικείοισιν ἐν δώμασιν βαρὺς πίτνων | uttered a cry from within in terror,<br>heavily falling upon the women's apartments |

They were far away from the great front door and the courtyard of the palace, in order that the women folk might not be exposed to the casual view of men or strangers and at the same time that they might not too readily see men and strangers. In the Antigone of Sophocles, Eurydice commits suicide in her own apartments; the messenger tells the story

[1] The similar passage from the Orestes (1448–1450), which is in reality a picture of fifth century conditions, is discussed below, p. 220.

[2] Cf. Ion, Λαέρ., Frag. 14 N. From this we have the frequent use of the words in the figurative sense of placing a lock upon the lips or tongue (Soph. Inc. Frag. 849 N.; Μάν., Frag. 360 N.; Ae. Inc. Frag. 316 N.

[3] Cf. Eur. Med. 1143: στέγας γυναικῶν σὺν τέκνοις ἅμ' ἑσπόμην.

of her self-inflicted death; the eccyclema rolls up making, as it were, a transverse section of the inner rooms; and the messenger remarks (Soph. Ant. 1293):

| | |
|---|---|
| ὁρᾶν πάρεστιν· οὐ γὰρ ἐν μυχοῖς ἔτι | thou mayst see; for she is no longer in the interior recesses of the house |

The young girls of the family had their rooms in the best protected part of the women's quarters (Eur. I. A. 738):

| | |
|---|---|
| ὀχυροῖσι παρθενῶσι φρουροῦνται καλῶς | they are well protected in maiden-bowers secure |

Thus Agamemnon may confidently speak of his royal daughters' apartments in the Pelopid palace of Mycenae. And in them, as the most secure part of the castle, was deposited for safe keeping the ancient spear of Pelops (Eur. I. T. 823; 826):

| | |
|---|---|
| Πέλοπος παλαιὰν ἐν δόμοις λόγχην πατρός, | and in our father's palace, Pelops's ancient spear |
| . . . . . . . . . | . . . . . . . |
| ἐν παρθενῶσι[1] τοῖς σοῖς κεκρυμμένην | safe hidden in thy maiden-bowers[1] |

In the Homeric poems the women's apartments are always in the upper story (ὑπερῷον) of the house. At Tiryns and at Troy, if our identification of the rooms is correct, it was not so. They are on the ground floor but thoroughly segregated from the men's quarters. And so we often have the women's apartments on the ground floor in the tragedy. When Jocasta, in her passionate despair, rushes through the big front door of the palace into her bridal chamber, and Oedipus bursts into the same room, and the attendants see him cut down the queen's body and plunge the brooch-pins into his eyes (Soph. O. T. 1241–1270) —those events are not taking place in any upper story of the palace.

In the same way, houses varied in classical times. Some were houses of one story, some of more than one, as will be made clear when we have passed through the house and up the stairs to the upper rooms.[2]

All ancient doors, whether those of royal palaces or temples or bourgeois homes, were secured in the same general manner with bolts and bars. The bolts were of strong, hard wood, or, more commonly, of bronze (Eur. I. T. 99):

| | |
|---|---|
| ἢ χαλκότευκτα κλῆθρα λύσαντες μοχλοῖς | or springing the bronze-forged bolts with crowbars |

They were let into sockets in lintel and threshold (Soph. O. T. 1261–1262):

| | |
|---|---|
| πύλαις διπλαῖς ἐνήλατ' ἐκ δὲ πυθμένων | he leaped against the double doors; and from their sockets |
| ἔκλινε κοῖλα κλῆθρα | he forced the bolts and left them hollow |

Such bars and bolts were fastened with locks that could be opened with a turn of the hand on the inside, with a turn of a key from the outside. When Oedipus in his frenzy stands before the doors of the queen's apartments, he has no key; so he calls to those within to throw back the bolts (Soph. O. T. 1287):

| | |
|---|---|
| βοᾷ ἀνοίγειν κλῆθρα | he calls to throw back the bolts |

And when after his blinding he is about to leave the boudoir of the dead queen, the messenger says (Soph. O. T. 1294–1295):

| | |
|---|---|
| κλῆθρα γὰρ πυλῶν τάδε | for the bolts of the doors yonder |
| διοίγεται | are being drawn |

When Oedipus passed in and slammed the doors to, they seem to have barred and locked themselves automatically. But such locks may also be manipulated either way by hand (Eur. Or. 1551):

| | |
|---|---|
| οὐκέτ' ἂν φθάνοιτε κλῆθρα συμπεραίνοντες μοχλοῖς | make haste and bar and bolt the doors |

---

[1] παρθενῶνες is used again of Iphigenia's rooms in Agamemnon's palace (Eur. I. A. 1175) and of Antigone's maiden-bower [Eur. Ph. 89–90 (see p. 227, where the passage is quoted); 194; 1275].

[2] See below, pp. 227 ff.

The doors seem always to have been secured, perhaps automatically, as people went in and out through them.  Amphitryon and Megara, with the three children of Heracles, appear at the altar in the court of the palace at Thebes at the opening of the Hercules Furens.  They had come from the palace.  Lycus held the keys, and they could not pass within until he and his attendants unbarred the doors (Eur. H. F. 330; 332):

| | |
|---|---|
| ΜΕ. δόμους ἀνοίξας· νῦν γὰρ ἐχκεχλήμεθα | ME.  Open the doors; for now we have been locked out |
| ΛΥ. οἴγειν κλῆθρα προσπόλοις λέγω | LY.  I bid my attendants open the bolts[1] |

So, too, in Sophocles's Antigone (1186–1187), in a scene in which only friends of the court occupy the space before the palace, the queen, starting forth from the palace to bear offerings to Athena's temple, explains her presence with these words:

| | |
|---|---|
| καὶ τυγχάνω τε κλῆθρ' ἀνασπαστοῦ πύλης | and, as it happens, too, I loosed the bolts of the door and |
| χαλῶσα | drew it open |

The normal condition of a house-door was to have the lock set—even as in a modern city apartment.  And thus Menelaus in wrath accuses his royal brother of sitting behind his bolted doors, inaccessible to friends and subjects (Eur. I. A. 345):

| | |
|---|---|
| ἔσω τε κλῇθρων σπάνιος | behind bolts and rarely seen[2] |

The fastening by these bars and bolts afforded security against ordinary force (Eur. Med. 1314–1317):

| | |
|---|---|
| Ι. χαλᾶτε κλῇδας ὡς τάχιστα, πρόσπολοι, | J.  Shoot back the bolts with all speed, servants mine; |
| ἐκλύεθ' ἁρμούς, ὡς ἴδω διπλοῦν κακόν | loose the fastenings, that I may see my two-fold woe |
| Μ. τί τάσδε κινεῖς κ'ἀναμοχλεύεις πύλας; | M.  Why dost thou shake those doors and try to pry them open? |

The chorus has tried to break in the door at line 1276 and failed.  Before Jason can force an entrance, Medea appears.  Orestes considers the barred doors of the palace at Mycenae adequate defence against any assault that Menelaus can make against that castle, however much he may threaten to smash his uncle's head with the coping stones from above if Menelaus dare but touch the locks (Eur. Or. 1567; 1571–1572):

| | |
|---|---|
| οὗτος σύ, κλῄθρων τῶνδε μὴ ψαύσῃς χερί | ho there! lay not thy hand on yonder bolts |
| μοχλοῖς δ' ἄραρε κλῇθρα σῆς βοηδρόμου | the bars are fitted tight with bolts, and they will prevent thy |
| σπουδῆς ἅ σ' εἴρξει, μὴ δόμων εἴσω περᾶν | rescuing haste and keep thee from forcing thy way into the halls |

Menelaus can no more force the bars and bolts of the palace at Mycenae in the Orestes than Jason could those of the royal palace at Corinth.[3]

In the Hercules Furens Heracles, with all his strength, pulls down the house in ruins, when he in his madness breaks in the doors in the interior of his own palace.[4]  The security afforded by the bars and bolts is suggested again in Euripides's Erechtheus (Frag. 362, 19–20 N.):

| | |
|---|---|
| τοὺς δὲ πρὸς χάριν σὺν ἡδονῇ<br>τῇ σῇ πονηροὺς κλῇθρον εἰργέτω στέγης | but the bad who incline to favor and to please—<br>let a bolt bar such from thy roof |

and still again (Eur. Or. 1366–1367):

| | |
|---|---|
| ἀλλὰ κτυπεῖ γὰρ κλῇθρα βασιλικῶν δόμων<br>σιγήσατ' . . . . . . | but hush! for there is a clanking of the bolts of the royal halls |

[1] Cf. also Eur. Hip. 578: σὺ παρὰ κλῆθρα.
[2] Cf. l. 340: καὶ θύρας ἔχων ἀκλήστους τῷ θέλοντι δημοτῶν.
[3] In the same way the ordinary dwelling of classical times could be most effectively closed (Pl. Cur. 16): ostium occlusissimum.
[4] Eur. H. F. 999–1000; see p. 218.  Cf. also Sen. H. F. 1004–1005, quoted on p. 202.

The "bars and bolts" were from the outside opened and shut with keys. In the chapter on the Tauric Artemisium we saw Iphigenia frequently in the capacity of the keeper of the keys of the temple. So the royal palace doors, with their bolts and bars, were fitted with keys. Hecabe sees herself a warder of the royal doors of her future master in the land of Hellas (Eur. Tro. 492–493):

| | |
|---|---|
| τούτοις με προσθήσουσιν, ἢ θυρῶν λάτριν<br>κλῇδας φυλάσσειν | to such tasks will they set me, or as<br>portress to keep the door-keys |

When the key was applied, the bars and bolts yielded, releasing the door above and below (and in the centre?) (Eur. H. F. 1029–1030):

| | |
|---|---|
| ἴδεσθε, διάνδιχα κλῇθρα<br>κλίνεται ὑψιπύλων δόμων | lo! the bolts of the high-portaled<br>halls yield this way and that |

From the inside, of course, no key was needed; the bolts and bars were easily shot open or shut with the hand (Eur. Hip. 808–809):

| | |
|---|---|
| χαλᾶτε κλῇθρα, πρόσπολοι, πυλωμάτων,<br><br>ἐκλύεθ' ἁρμούς, ὡς ἴδω πικρὰν θέαν | shoot back the bolts of the doors, attendants<br>mine;<br>loose the bars, that I may see the bitter sight |

These citations refer to the main door of the palace, though πύλωμα would naturally be a great gate, like a city gate. But not only here, but also in Euripides's Helen (789–790) πύλωμα is a palace door:

| | |
|---|---|
| ΕΛ. ποίοις ἐπιστὰς βαρβάροις πυλώμασιν; | HEL. At which barbarian doors didst take thy<br>station? |
| ΜΕ. τοῖσδ' ἔνθεν ὥσπερ πτωχὸς ἐξηλαυνόμην. | MEN. At yonder doors, whence they tried to<br>drive me like a beggar. |

And this passage, with its deictic τοῖσδ', shows that the πύλωμα is before the speaker's eyes and must, therefore, refer to the great portal of the palace, at which even a beggar might knock to ask for alms.

For additional security the doors might be not only locked but, when locked, have the locks sealed. We find such sealing of the locks in that apartment of the palace of Zeus which served as the magazine for his thunderbolts (Ae. Eum. 827–828):

| | |
|---|---|
| καὶ κλῇδας οἶδα δώματος μόνη θεῶν<br>ἐν ᾧ κεραυνός ἐστιν ἐσφραγισμένος | and I alone of gods know the keys of the chamber<br>in which the thunder is sealed up |

The door was locked, and the owner set his seal upon the lock, so that it could not be tampered with without the fact's at once being betrayed. We have the same procedure at the tomb-treasuries of the Mycenaean epoch. In Euripides's lost tragedy, Phaethon (Frag. 781, 8–10 N.), Clymene, proposing to bury the body of her son, says:

| | |
|---|---|
| κρύψω δέ νιν<br>ξεστοῖσι θαλάμοις, ἔνθ' ἐμῷ κεῖται πόσει<br>χρυσός· μόνη δὲ κλῇθρ' ἐγὼ σφραγίζομαι | and I will lay him away in<br>polished chambers where my husband's gold is<br>stored; and I alone seal up the locks |

Fourfold protection could thus be secured: bars, bolts, locks, seals set upon the locks.

The system of bars and bolts, locks and keys, that we find in the palaces of the heroic age is not greatly changed in the bourgeois homes of fifth century Athens. The comic poets have many allusions to the means of securing the houses of their own day, and it may be that in many instances the tragic poets are transferring conditions of their own times to the times represented in their plays. Most features of the devices for securing the doors were doubtless common to both ages. The doors are locked from the outside with a key (κλειδίον, Ar. Αἰολ., Frag. 16 K.) (Ar. Lys. 1072):

| | |
|---|---|
| ἡ θύρα κεκλείσεται | you'll find the door locked |

(Apollod. Car. Διάβ., Frag. 6 K.):[1]

| | |
|---|---|
| καὶ κλῇεθ' ἡ θύρα μοχλοῖς· ἀλλ' οὐδὲ εἷς<br>τέκτων ὀχυρὰν οὕτως ἐποίησεν θύραν,<br>δι' ἧς γαλῆ καὶ μοιχὸς οὐκ εἰσέρχεται | and the door is locked and barred; but never a<br>builder made a door so strong but that<br>a weasel or a lover can get in |

[1] Cf. Ar. Λημ., Frag. 369 K.

The obvious implication is that such locking and barring is very effective—except against lovers. The bars may be thrown back with a key from the outside, with the hand from the inside (Ar. Inc. Frag. 654 K.):

| | |
|---|---|
| τὴν θύραν ἀναζυγώσας | unbarring the door |

Even the sealing of the doors is a familiar procedure in comedy as in tragedy. In the Thesmophoriazusae one of the women complains bitterly of the treatment of her sex as a result of the misogynistic teachings of Euripides. And one of the worst things that Euripides has taught is the exclusion—the forcible exclusion—of women from public activities by locking them up in their own apartments at home (Ar. Thes. 414–416):

| | |
|---|---|
| εἶτα διὰ τοῦτον ταῖς γυναικωνίτισιν | and then, he is to blame for their putting bars on the doors |
| σφραγίδας ἐπιβάλλουσιν ἤδη καὶ μοχλοὺς | of the women's apartments and seals on the locks, |
| τηροῦντες ἡμᾶς . . . . . . | as they do now, to keep us in . . . |

And even at home the women are grossly maltreated by their husbands' placing under lock and key and seal the dainties with which they love to indulge themselves and to which they heretofore have had ready and rightful access (*ibid.* 420–428):

| | |
|---|---|
| ἄλφιτον, ἔλαιον, οἶνον, οὐδὲ ταῦτ' ἔτι<br>ἔξεστιν. οἱ γὰρ ἄνδρες ἤδη κλῃδία | cakes, oil, wine—we can't have any of them<br>any more. For the men now-a-days carry the keys |
| αὐτοὶ φοροῦσι κρυπτὰ κακοηθέστατα,<br>Λακωνίκ' ἄττα, τρεῖς ἔχοντα γομφίους.<br>καὶ τοῦ μὲν οὖν ἦν ἀλλ' ὑποῖξαι τὴν θύραν | in their own pockets—most atrocious things—<br>of Spartan model—with triple wards.<br>It used to be possible for us to get the door open without getting caught at it |
| ποιησαμέναισι δακτύλιον τριοβόλου.<br>νῦν δ' οὗτος αὐτοὺς ᾠκότριψ Εὐριπίδης<br>ἐδίδαξε θριπήδεστ' ἔχειν σφραγίδια<br>ἐξαψαμένους | —by having a simple seal-ring made for a nickel.<br>But now this clown Euripides has<br>taught them to keep attached to their persons<br>their poor seals, all worm-eaten |

Woman to woman might be much more trustful and generous. When Selenium, in the Casket Comedy, is going away, she turns over to Gymnasium her bunch of keys and gives her carte blanche to help herself to anything she wants (Pl. Cis. 111):

accipias clavis; si quid opus tibi erit prompto, promito

The particular part of the house in question here is, of course, the pantry or storeroom, the *promptaria cella* of Plautus's Amphitryon (156).

The mistress of the home is the logical holder of the keys (κλῃδοῦχος γυνή, Inc. Inc. Frag. 222 N.); but for one reason and another she was often deprived of her natural rights. Circumstances, as we have seen, may alter cases; and the lord of the house may assume the custody of all the keys. He may even let the household keys pass into the hands of others than his wife (Men. Ψευδ., Frag. 519 K.):

| | |
|---|---|
| νῦν δ' εἰς γυναικονῖτιν εἰσιόνθ' ὅταν | but now, when I see a parasite going into the women's quarters |
| ἴδω παράσιτον, τὸν δὲ Δία τὸν κτήσιον<br>ἔχοντα τὸ ταμιεῖον οὐ κεκλεισμένον<br>ἀλλ' εἰστρέχοντα πορνίδια | and Zeus the guardian of our property<br>leaving the store-room not locked,<br>but little hussies running in |

But the complaint just quoted from the Thesmophoriazusae tells the whole story—bars with locks and keys, intricate devices imported from Laconia, hard to pick or fit with a duplicate key, and sealed with the seal of the lord of the home.[1] Ordinary keys were often counterfeited, and seals could be forged (Plat. Μέτ., Frag. 77 K.):

σημεῖα παρασημεῖα, κλεῖν παρακλείδιον

But the Laconian locks were different; they were the Yale locks of antiquity. Plautus has preserved from Philemon another allusion to the confidence people had in the security they afforded (Most. 404–405):

clavem mi harunc aedium Laconicam<br>iam iube efferri intus: hasce ego aedis occludam hinc foris

[1] Cf. also Ar. Lys. 1199 (see Vol. II, Chap. X 4, k).

Evidently the Laconian lock, with its intricate wards, was a kind of padlock which was attached only to the outside of a door and could not be touched or manipulated from within.[1] Tranio locks the lovers in quite as effectively as he locks Theopropides out. Suidas's comment tells the same story:

| | |
|---|---|
| Λακωνικαὶ κλεῖδες..... ἔξωθεν<br>περικλείεται μοχλοῦ παρατιθεμένου<br>ἤ τινος τοιούτου ὥστε τοῖς ἔνδον<br>μὴ εἶναι ἀνοῖξαι | Laconian keys: the locking is done<br>from the outside by throwing a bar<br>or something of that sort, so that those inside<br>cannot open it |

When the door is thus secured the possessor of the key carries it away with him (Men. Μισ., Frag. 343 K.):[2]

| | |
|---|---|
| Λακωνικὴ<br>κλείς ἐστιν ὡς ἔοικέ μοι περιοιστέα | I must, as it seems,<br>carry a Laconian key around with me |

And any one thus locked in is imprisoned until the door is unlocked from the outside. So also Lysias tells the story of the wife of Euphiletus, who "got up and went away and secured the door, pretending it was a joke. She turned the key, and he was her prisoner. Next day she came back and unlocked the door."[3]

Euripides apparently loved to dwell upon the need of coercion for women and the lock, key, and seal method of keeping them out of mischief. But, in spite of the testimony of the women in the Thesmophoriazusae, Euripides does not always recommend such measures (Frag. Inc. 1063 N.):

| | |
|---|---|
| οὔποτ' ἄνδρα χρὴ σοφὸν<br>λίαν φυλάσσειν ἄλοχον ἐν μυχοῖς δόμων· | a wise man should never keep<br>too close a guard upon his spouse inside the home; |
| . . . . . . .<br>τό τ' ἄρσεν ἀεὶ τοῦ κεκρυμμένου λίχνον. | . . . . . . .<br>men are always curious about what is out of sight. |
| ὅστις δὲ μοχλοῖς καὶ διὰ σφραγισμάτων<br>σῴζει δάμαρτα, δρᾶν τι δὴ δοκῶν σοφὸν<br>μάταιός ἐστι καὶ φρονῶν οὐδὲν φρονεῖ | Whoso keeps his wife with locks and seals<br>may think he is doing something wise but<br>he deceives himself and for all his wisdom is not wise; |
| . . . . . . .<br>ἀνήρ τ' ἀχρεῖος χἠ γυνὴ διοίχεται | . . . . . . .<br>the man is unprofited, and his wife slips out |

The bars and bolts and locks and seals for keeping women safe at home are introduced. But we must note that Euripides is not the first to introduce such a motive. Aeschylus has it long before. The lord of lords put away his thunderbolts and secured them under lock and key and seal, that no member of the Olympian household might, in too great zeal for some cause, meddle with them. Athenian gentlemen treated their wives and the treasures of their larders in similar fashion and carried keys and seals securely about their persons.

The Latin comic poets reflect the Greek method of securing the outside doors of the house, which may, of course, at the same time be the Roman method (Pl. Cis. 649):

occludite aedis pessulis, repagulis

The plural "bars and bolts" is used because there were necessarily two—the horizontal bar and the upright bolt. In the Aulularia (103–104) Plautus specifies their duality:

occlude sis
fores ambobus pessulis

Or there may have been separate bolts for each of the doors; for the doorway is regularly constructed with double doors (Pl. Cap. 831):

aperite hasce ambas fores

The light springing of the bolts at a turn of the hand on the mechanism inside the door is well brought out in Phaedromus's song to the bolts of his sweetheart's door in Plautus's Curculio (147–157):

[1] Cf. Lambinus ad Pl. Most. 444 (Delph. Ed. Varior. Clas. IV p. 1966).
[2] With unreproducible puns, Aristophon Πειρ., Frag. 7 K.
[3] Lys. 92, 42.

Pessuli, heus pessuli, vos saluto lubens,

. . . .

fite causa mea ludii barbari,
sussilite, obsecro, et mittite istanc foras,

. . . .

hoc vide ut dormiunt pessuli pessumi
nec mea gratia commovent se ocius.

. . . . . . . .

. . . . . . . sentio sonitum
tandem edepol mihi morigeri pessuli fiunt

The "bars and bolts" are generally plural; but Terence sometimes has the singular (Eun. 603):

pessulum ostio obdo

(Heaut. 278):

anus foribus obdit pessulum[1]

The passages quoted thus far, dealing with locks and keys, all have to do with securing against intrusion from the outside. It is only rarely that the need should present itself for locking some one up inside a house. Yet this situation does arise: when Oedipus, blinded by his own guilt-maddened hand, laboring under the curse of an offended god, persisted in staying on in Thebes and threatening the stability of the State, his sons deemed it necessary to resort to rigorous measures to save their father from the violence of the people and to prevent the ex-king from interfering with their policies. Accordingly he was imprisoned securely in the palace behind bars and bolts (Eur. Ph. 64):

κλήθροις ἔκρυψαν πατέρ' | they kept their father out of sight behind the bars

In the Wasps of Aristophanes, Philocleon has to be kept away from the courts; his son and his servants shut him up in his house and bar and fasten the doors from the outside so that the old man cannot pass (Ar. Vesp. 112–113):

τοῦτον οὖν φυλάττομεν | so we are keeping him
μοχλοῖσιν ἐνδήσαντες, ὡς ἂν μὴ 'ξίη | locked in with bars, to keep him from getting out

The doors are securely locked from the outside; Philocleon cannot pass (*ibid.* 334–335):

τίς γάρ ἐσθ' ὁ ταῦτα σ' εἴργων | who is it that thus shuts you in
κἀποκλῄων τὰς θύρας; | and locks the doors against you?

How the locking in is effected is explained when Bdelycleon and Xanthias have the job completed (Ar. Vesp. 198–202):

ἔνδον κέκραχθι τῆς θύρας κεκλημένης. | holler away in there, now that the door is locked.
ὤθει σὺ πολλοὺς τῶν λίθων πρὸς τὴν θύραν, | Here, you; push up a pile of stones against the door;
καὶ τὴν βάλανον ἔμβαλλε πάλιν ἐς τὸν μοχλόν, | put the peg back into the bar;
καὶ τῇ δοκῷ προσθεὶς τὸν ὅλμον τὸν μέγαν | be quick and roll up the big trough and
ἀνύσας τι προσκύλισον | set it against the beam

The pile of stones and the trough have nothing to do with architecture; but we are interested in the "beam," the "bar," and the "peg." The "beam" is obviously an improvised upright stanchion, like the upright member of the interior fastening of a door; the "bar" is the horizontal piece drawn across the door and thrust into a hole in the door-jamb; and the "peg" runs through a hole in the bar and into the jamb, like a staple, and the whole thing is then absolutely secured with a padlock (Ar. Vesp. 152–155):

ὅδε τὴν θύραν ὠθεῖ· πίεζέ νυν σφόδρα | there, he is shoving against the door; push, now, with all your might
εὖ κἀνδρικῶς· κἀγὼ γὰρ ἐνταῦθ' ἔρχομαι· | and main. Hold the fort, for I'll be there in a minute.
καὶ τῆς κατακλῇδος ἐπιμέλου, καὶ τοῦ μοχλοῦ | and be careful about the lock, and look out for the
φύλατθ' ὅπως μὴ τὴν βάλανον ἐκτρώξεται | bar, that he may not gnaw off the pin

The pin holds the bar; the lock secures the whole.

[1] Cf. Pl. Cas. 891; Truc. 351.

Under ordinary circumstances there was no need of the padlock; the peg was security enough.[1]  So important was this peg, that "pegging" the door came to mean "locking securely."  So we have it in Aristophanes's Ecclesiazusae (361; 369–370):

| | |
|---|---|
| νῦν μὲν γὰρ οὗτος βεβαλάνωκε τὴν θύραν | for now that fellow has "pegged" the door |
| . . . . . . . . . | . . . . . . . |
| . . . . . . μή με περιίδῃς | . . . . . . do not look on and let me |
| διαρραγέντα μηδὲ βεβαλανωμένον | burst or stay "pegged in" |

This fastening, too, was on the outside of the door, and Blepyrus was securely locked in. On the outside also were the bar and peg in the scene of the Danaids (Ar. Δαν., Frag. 251 K.):

| | |
|---|---|
| οὐδεὶς βεβαλάνωκε τὴν θύραν | no one has "pegged" the door |

But these devices were on the inside of the city gates of Cloud-cuckoo-town (Ar. Av. 1158–1159):

| | |
|---|---|
| καὶ νῦν ἅπαντ' ἐκεῖνα πεπύλωται πύλαις | and now all those walls are provided with gates; |
| καὶ βεβαλάνωται | and they are barred and "pegged" |

We have seen[2] that the temples of Greece had great double valves of bronze, swung on hinges of bronze; and we have called attention to the grating noise that such doors would necessarily make as they rolled open or shut.  The doors of private houses, though usually and probably always of wood, swung on hinges of bronze or iron[3] and, unless properly lubricated, they would also creak.[2]  The creaking of the door announced the entrance of a new person on the scene and allusions to it in both the Old and the New Comedy, as well as in the tragedy, are very numerous (Eur. H. F. 77–78):

| | |
|---|---|
| θαυμάζων δ' ὅταν | and wondering every one would start |
| πύλαι ψοφῶσι, πᾶς ἀνίστησιν πόδα | up whenever the doors creaked |

(Eur. Ion 515–516):

| | |
|---|---|
| ὡς ἐπ' ἐξόδοισιν ὄντος τῶν δ' ἀκούομεν πυλῶν | we hear a noise, as if he were at the exit of the doors |
| δοῦπον, ἐξιόντα τ' ἤδη δεσπότην ὁρᾶν πάρα | yonder, and now we may see our master coming forth |

(Enn. Andr. Ae. 2, 25 R.[2]):

saeptum altisono cardine templum

(Sen. Med. 177):

sed cuius ictu regius cardo strepit?

(Gracch. Pel. et Atab. 1, 2, 30):

sonat impulso regia cardo[4]

. . . . .

o grata cardo regium egressum indicans

(Pacuv. Dul. 1, 92, 12):

quidnam autem hoc soniti est, quod strident fores[5]

(Att. Clyt. 1, 139, 1 R.[3]):

sed valvae resonunt regiae[6]

(Ar. Ran. 603–604):

| | |
|---|---|
| ὡς ἀκούω | when I hear the |
| τῆς θύρας καὶ δὴ ψόφον | creaking of the door |

[1] It could be removed with a βαλανάγρα — a hook made on purpose for unfastening the bar that was merely pegged.

[2] P. 64.

[3] Pl. Amph. 1026; paene effregisti, fatue, foribus cardines; cf. Pl. As. 384–391; Arist. de Aud. 802 b, 41: καὶ τοῦ χαλκοῦ καὶ τοῦ σιδήρου.

[4] Cf. Virg. Aen. I 449; VI 573–574; Hor. Sat. II 6, 111–112.

[5] Cf. Sen. Oed. 995; Pl. Cur. 156–158.

[6] Cf. Att. Neopt. 1, 196, 6 R.[3]; Pac. I. 102, 15 R.[3]

(Men. Sam. 365; 467):[1]

| | |
|---|---|
| ἡ θύρα πάλιν ψοφεῖ | the door is creaking again |
| . . . . . . . . | . . . . . . . |
| ἐψόφηκε προιὼν τὴν θύραν | he made the door creak as he came forth |

(Pl. Mil. 1377):

sonitum fecerunt fores[2]

(Pl. Am. 496):

crepuit foris[3]

(Pl. Bac. 234):

sed foris concrepuit nostra[4]

(Pl. Bac. 833):

forem hanc pauxillum aperi; placide, ne crepa[5]

It was the perfectly natural thing for a door to creak upon its hinges. To prevent the creaking, the hinge had to be lubricated. Instead of using oil, the ancients seem to have applied water as a lubricant for hinges to keep them from creaking and betraying an illicit exit (Ar. Thes. 487–488):

| | |
|---|---|
| ἐγὼ δὲ καταχέασα τοῦ στροφέως ὕδωρ | but I poured a little water on the hinge |
| ἐξῆλθον ὡς τὸν μοιχόν | and slipped out to my lover |

It is quite possible that Plautus had this very passage in mind and elaborated it considerably in the Curculio; or it may have been a commonplace of the New Comedy that he found elaborated ready to his hand; at any rate, he thought it amusing also to a second century Roman audience to have a lady put water on the hinges of her door, so that she could slip out unheard and unobserved to a rendezvous with her sweetheart (Pl. Cur. 158–161):

> LE.  Placide egredere et sonitum prohibe forium et crepitum cardinum,
>         ne quod hic agimus erus percipiat fieri, mea Planesium.
>         mane, suffundam aquolam.  PAL.  Viden ut anus tremula medicinam facit?
>         eapse merum condidicit bibere, foribus dat aquam quam bibant

In the scene before Phaedromus had lubricated the same hinges with wine (Pl. Cur. 20–22; 93–94):

> Bellissimum hercle vidi et taciturnissimum,
> numquam ullum verbum muttit. cum aperitur tacet;
> cum illa noctu clanculum ad me exit, tacet.
>
> . . . . . . . . . . .
> viden ut aperiuntur aedes festivissumae?
> num muttit cardo? est lepidus.

The head of squill (or of sea-urchin[6]) that Danaus (?) would have buried (?) by the hinge of his courtyard door would seem to have had some magic power for warding off evil spirits rather than lubricating the rusty joints (Ar. Δαν., Frag. 255 K.):

| | |
|---|---|
| πρὸς τὸν στροφέα τῆς αὐλείας σχίνου[6] | to bury a head of squill by the hinge |
| κεφαλὴν κατορύττειν | of the front door |

Pythagoras was acquainted with the superstition of hanging a bunch of squills above the threshold to keep out evil (Plin. N. H. XX 101): Pythagoras scillam in limine quoque ianuae suspensam malorum introitum pellere tradit. Burying it beside the doorway might have had the same potency. Perhaps the vegetable took the place of the "Hermes of the Hinges" ('Ερμῆς Στροφαῖος; Ar. Pl. 1153–1156; see Vol. II, Chap. IV, 2 e).

Let us return again to the Mycenaean palace. Beside the doors or before the doors we find at the palace of Nestor in Pylus "seats whereon Nestor sat with his sons."[7]  Dr. Schlie-

---

[1] Cf. Men. Epitr. 659–660; Per. 196; 885; Inc. Frag. 860–861.

[2] Cf. Pl. Trin. 1123.

[3] Cf. Pl. Aul. 665; Bac. 1057; Cas. 163; 874; Cur. 486; Poen. 741; Ps. 129–130; Ter. Ad. 264; etc.

[4] Cf. Pl. Bac. 610; Cas. 936; Men. 348; 523; Mil. 154; 271; 329; 411; Mos. 506; 1062; Pers. 404; Poen. 609–610; Ter. And. 682; Eun. 1029; Hec. 521; etc.

[5] Cf. Pl. Bac. 798; Cas. 434; 779; 813; 872; etc.

[6] The MSS. read ἐχίνου; but what the head of a sea-urchin might be, the zoologists have not made out; so Meineke's correction to σχίνου is generally accepted.

[7] ἷξον δ' ἐς Πυλίων ἀνδρῶν ἄγυρίν τε καὶ ἕδρας,
    ἔνθ' ἄρα Νέστωρ ἧστο σὺν υἱάσιν  .  .  .  (γ 31–32).

mann thought he found the counterpart of this description in reality in the great circle about the shaft graves at Mycenae. Adler saw those seats in the two seat-like objects upon which the plinth rests that supports the paws of the lions at the lion-gate of Mycenae. They do look like seats—seats for the king and queen, guarded by the king of beasts. The general form of the base of these seats is suggestive of the half-rosette ornamentation of the "cyanus frieze" of Tiryns, which, as we have seen,[1] may have ornamented the base of a bench or row of seats in the anteroom of the men's megaron at Tiryns. A bench, or row of seats, also of decorated alabaster, we have *in situ* in the vestibule of the southern wing of the palace of Phaestus and in the throne-room of the palace at Cnossus. So also there were seats for the royal personages in front of the palace at Pylus, according to Homer, and there were seats for royalty in front of the palace at Mycenae, according to Aeschylus (Ag. 518–521):

| | |
|---|---|
| ἰὼ μέλαθρα βασιλέων, φίλαι στέγαι, | all hail, oh palace of my kings, dear home, |
| σεμνοί τε θᾶκοι, δαίμονές τ' ἀνθήλιοι, | and oh ye seats august and gods that front the sun, |
| εὖ που πάλαι, φαιδροῖσι τοισίδ' ὄμμασι | if ever before, with cheering glances *now* after long |
| δέξασθε κόσμῳ βασιλέα πολλῷ χρόνῳ | lapse of time duly receive your king |

As the herald enters and stands before the royal palace, the first thing that he sees and addresses, after the palace itself, is the seats of the royal house. Whether they looked like the "seats" upon the lion-gate or the seats at Phaestus or elsewhere in the actual Minoan world, whether they were a circular bench after the style of the enclosing wall of the shaft-graves, whether they were a long, straight bench, or whether they were something entirely different from any of these things we are not told and can only surmise. But there were seats—very important features of the palace of Agamemnon—and they were "august seats," and they were to have a part in the reception of their returning king. The palace of Proteus also had its seats: see the discussion, pages 206–207.

Before the palace stood also statues of the gods; these may be an anachronism transferred by Aeschylus from his familiar Hermae and his Apollo Agyieus of the later period to the times and conditions of the heroic age.[2]

Passing through the outer entrance we find, between the main entrance and the megaron of the palaces at Troy, Mycenae, and Tiryns, a vestibule with parastades—substantial pilasters of stone—finishing off the walls of sundried brick and flanking the openings for the doorways. True to the reality, as we know it, the dramatic poets also speak of vestibules in the royal palaces of their scenes (Soph. El. 1433):

| | |
|---|---|
| βᾶτε κατ' ἀντιθύρων | make for the vestibule |

and sometimes the vestibules have parastades (Eur. Ph. 415):[3]

| | |
|---|---|
| νὺξ ἦν, 'Αδράστου δ' ἦλθον εἰς παραστάδας | 'twas night, and I came to Adrastus's pillared vestibule |

In nearly the same sense Euripides seems to use ἀμφίπυλον, "a room with a door on either side," "an anteroom" (Med. 134–135):

| | |
|---|---|
| ἐπ' ἀμφιπύλου γὰρ ἔσω μελάθρου γόον ἔκλυον | for at the gate I heard a voice of weeping within the palace |

The literal meaning of the word suggests at once the anteroom between the vestibule and the men's megaron at Tiryns.

The doors leading from the vestibule to the megaron might be paneled doors (Eur. Or. 1221):

| | |
|---|---|
| σανίδα παίσασ' | knock on the panel |

Even the threshold (naturally of stone) in the door of the private house is casually mentioned by the comic poets (Frag. Sup. 570 c, K.):

| | |
|---|---|
| κέχρουκας τὸν βατῆρα τῆς θύρας | you have trodden the threshold of the door |

(Amips. Inc. Frag. 26 K.):

| | |
|---|---|
| ἐπ' αὐτὸν ἥκεις τὸν βατῆρα τῆς θύρας | to the very threshold of the door you are come |

[1] P. 206.
[2] For a discussion of the "gods that front the sun" see Vol. II, Chap. VIII.
[3] See pp. 76–77.

Passing through the doors to the interior of the palace, we find in the great hall, as at the palace of Alcinous,[1] at Mycenae, and at Tiryns, the hearth with pillars about it to support the roof. Again, true to the reality and to Homeric tradition, the tragic poets represent their royal halls adorned with interior columns[2] (Eur. H. F. 973–1038):

| | |
|---|---|
| ὁ δ' ὑπὸ κίονος σκιὰν | one boy crouched in the shadow of a column; |
| ἄλλος δὲ βωμὸν ὄρνις ὡς ἔπτηξ' ὕπο | another, like a bird, behind the altar. |
| . . . . . . . | . . . . . . . |
| ὁ δ' ἐξελίσσων παῖδα κίονος κύκλῳ | but he, chasing the lad around about the column |
| τόρευμα δεινὸν ποδός, ἐναντίον σταθεὶς | in hideous turning course, stopped face to face with him |
| βάλλει πρὸς ἧπαρ· ὕπτιος δὲ λαΐνους | and shot him to the heart; the boy fell backward and |
| ὀρθοστάτας ἔδευσεν ἐκπνέων βίον | bedewed the column's shaft of stone with blood, breathing out his life. |
| . . . . . . . | . . . . . . . |
| ἄλλῳ δ' ἐπεῖχε τόξ', ὃς ἀμφὶ βωμίαν | For the second then he drew his bow, who crouched at the |
| ἔπτηξε κρηπῖδ' ὡς λεληθέναι δοκῶν. | altar's base in hope to be unseen. |
| ἀλλὰ φθάνει νιν ἡ τάλαιν' εἴσω δόμων | But the poor mother caught up her child before the blow could fall |
| μήτηρ ὑπεκλαβοῦσα καὶ κλῄει πύλας. | and with him 'scaped into a chamber and bolted fast the door. |
| ὁ δ' ὡς ἐπ' αὐτοῖς Κυκλωπίοισιν ὢν | But he, as if he were before the Cyclopean walls themselves, |
| σκάπτει μοχλεύει θύρετρα, κἀκβαλὼν σταθμὰ | dug down, pried open the doors, and crashing the doorposts from their place |
| δάμαρτα καὶ παῖδ' ἐνὶ κατέστρωσεν βέλει. | he with one bolt laid low wife and child. |
| . . . . . . . | . . . . . . . |
| πίτνει δ' ἐς πέδον, πρὸς κίονα | And he fell upon the floor, striking his |
| νῶτον πατάξας, ὃς πεσήμασι στέγης | back against a column that, burst in twain by |
| διχορραγὴς ἔκειτο κρηπίδων ἔπι· | the roof's fall, lay there upon the stylobate. |
| ἡμεῖς δ' ἐλευθεροῦντες ἐκ δρασμῶν πόδα | And we released our feet from panic flight and, |
| σὺν τῷ γέροντι δεσμὰ σειραίων βρόχων | with the old man's help, we bound him with knots |
| ἀνήπτομεν πρὸς κίον' . . . | of twisted rope to a column. . . . |
| . . . . . . . | . . . . . . . |
| περὶ δὲ δεσμὰ καὶ πολύβροχ' ἁμμάτων | and about him these knots and manifold fastenings of |
| ἐρείσμαθ' Ἡράκλειον | rope hold Heracles bound |
| ἀμφὶ δέμας τάδε λαΐνοις | to the marble columns |
| ἀνημμένα κίοσιν οἴκων | of the palace |

In this vivid description of messenger and chorus we see the interior hall of a house, with at least one adjoining chamber communicating with it by means of a door provided with a lock and flanked by doorposts. The central space of the hall is apparently lower than the border, and upon the edge of this raised border as a stylobate runs a colonnade. The hero in his mad might had pulled down the house, and there upon the border lay the broken shaft of a column of stone.

In the Homeric palace we find also attached to one of the columns of the great hall a rack to receive the spears of the lord of the manor or his guests. So, for example, at the palace of Odysseus in Ithaca, at one of the great columns nearest to the vestibule was the receptacle for the spears (α 126–129):

| | |
|---|---|
| οἱ δ' ὅτε δή ῥ' ἔντοσθεν ἔσαν δόμου ὑψηλοῖο, | and when they were now within the lofty palace, |
| ἔγχος μέν ῥ' ἔστησε φέρων πρὸς κίονα μακρὴν | he carried her spear to a tall column and set it |
| δουροδόκης ἔντοσθεν εὐξόου, ἔνθα περ' ἄλλα | in the well-polished spear-rack, in which stood |
| ἔγχε' Ὀδυσσῆος ταλασίφρονος ἵστατο πολλά | many others—the spears of the stout-hearted Odysseus |

[1] ζ 307; θ 66; and elsewhere.
[2] Such an interior column seems to be meant in Euripides's Antiope (Frag. 203 N.):
ἔνδον δὲ θαλάμοις βουκόλον. . . .
κομῶντα κισσῷ στῦλον εὐίου θεοῦ.

An allusion to a similar arrangement we have in a chorus in Euripides's Hecuba (920):

| | |
|---|---|
| ξυστὸν δ' ἐπὶ πασσάλῳ | and his spear upon its peg |

We seem here to hark back to the wooden columns with which we are familiar in the Mycenaean palaces at Tiryns, Mycenae, and elsewhere. Into such a column of wood pegs were often fastened, and upon such pegs might be suspended arms,[1] musical instruments,[2] and so forth. The spear-rack of α 128 was something more elaborate than a mere peg. We can imagine it as a piece of furniture constructed around the shaft of the column, a receptacle below for the butt end of the lance and a series of pegs above to support the different spears that it might contain. Such would be the natural interpretation of the peg for holding the spear in the Trojan palace of Euripides's Hecuba 920.

The pillars at Troy, Mycenae, and Tiryns were wooden columns on slightly raised bases of stone. The columns in the palace of Heracles here described are columns of marble. That is stated once in line 979; the poet takes pains to emphasize it again (H. F. 1096–1097):

| | |
|---|---|
| πρὸς ἡμιθραύστῳ λαΐνῳ τυκίσματι | I sit here bound to this hewn stone that now is cleft in |
| ἧμαι | twain |

When we think of the vast complex of rooms in the palace of Tiryns or in that of Cnossus or on the citadel of Troy, we begin to comprehend the privacy of the guest rooms of the palace of Admetus, where Heracles could carouse and sing without interfering with the funeral of Alcestis and be in no danger of being disturbed in his feasting by the weeping and wailing attending the obsequies of the queen (Eur. Alc. 543; 546–550):

| | |
|---|---|
| χωρὶς ξενῶνές εἰσιν οἵ σ' ἐσάξομεν. | private are the guest rooms where we will entertain thee. |
| · · · · · · · · · · | · · · · · · · · · · |
| ἡγοῦ σὺ τῷδε δωμάτων ἐξωπίους | Sirrah, lead thou the way and open for him the guest rooms |
| ξενῶνας οἴξας, τοῖς τ' ἐφεστῶσιν φράσον | well removed from the palace halls. Bid those in charge |
| σίτων παρεῖναι πλῆθος· ἐν δὲ κλῄσατε | set plenteous food before him. Close fast the doors |
| θύρας μεσαύλους· οὐ πρέπει θοινωμένους | leading to the mid-court. It is not meet that guests |
| κλύειν στεναγμῶν οὐδὲ λυπεῖσθαι ξένους | while banqueting should hear sounds of mourning and be disturbed |

Admetus's guest rooms are completely separated, as at Tiryns, from either the men's or the women's megaron. ἐξώπιος means literally "out of sight of," but the literal meaning need not be insisted upon here any more than in Euripides's Medea 624 or Suppliants 1038. It means simply "well away from." The Thessalian palace's guest rooms were connected by hallways with the main court. The doors leading thither were by Admetus's orders to be closed. With such precautions, at Pherae, as at Tiryns, no sound from the main hall could possibly have reached the ears of Heracles; nor could even the stentorian tones of Heracles have reached the halls of mourning.

The rooms in the interior of this palace were far removed from the main hall, and the arrangement corresponds with what we know of the Mycenaean palace. But in another passage, as in the passage from the Hercules Furens discussed a little farther back, we have again an inner chamber connected with the atrium by a well-fastened door with flanking posts (Eur. Or. 1475–1476):

| | |
|---|---|
| ἰαχᾷ δόμων θύρετρα καὶ σταθμοὺς | with a shout, we crashed down with levers |
| μοχλοῖσιν ἐκβαλόντες, ἔνθ' ἐμίμνομεν | doorposts and door of the chamber in which we bode |

[1] Pandarus, for example, took down his curved bow from such a peg (E 209–210), though Homer does not state specifically that the peg was fastened to a column; and Penelope takes down from a peg in her inner chamber the bow of Iphitus (φ 53–54).

[2] A peg upon a column was the appointed place for the harp of the blind bard Demodocus (θ 67, 105, etc.).

The ceiling of the inner chamber is one of open work with beams exposed and free (Eur. Hip. 417–418):

| | |
|---|---|
| οὐδὲ σκότον φρίσσουσι τὸν ξυνεργάτην | and they tremble not in fear of the darkness, their accomplice, |
| τέραμνά τ' οἴκων μή ποτε φθογγὴν ἀφῇ | nor of the beams of the hall, lest they utter a voice |

This arrangement of the architectural members affords a convenient gibbet to the suicide (Eur. Ph. 333):

| | |
|---|---|
| ὑπὲρ τέραμνά τ' ἀγχόνας | to the noose cast over the beams |

(Eur. Hip. 768–770):

| | |
|---|---|
| τεράμνων | she will fasten the noose |
| ἀπὸ νυμφιδίων κρεμαστὸν | suspended from the beams of her bridal |
| ἄψεται ἀμφὶ βρόχον | chamber |

Interiors were, of course, not presented to the physical eyes of the audience, except when emergency called for the use of the eccyclema. The poet makes no effort with his description to translate his hearers to heroic times and conditions; he is obviously describing the better type of dwelling of his own day, not so very different from the houses that we know at Delos and at Pompeii. A most obvious anachronism we have in Euripides's Orestes (1448–1450):

| | |
|---|---|
| ἔκλησε δ' ἄλλον ἄλλοσ' ἐν στέγαις· | one he locked up in one part of the hall, another in another; |
| τοὺς μὲν ἐν σταθμοῖσιν ἱππικοῖσι, | some he prisoned in the horses' stalls,[1] |
| τοὺς δ' ἐν ἐξέδραισι, τοὺς δ' ἐκεῖσ' ἐκεῖθεν | some in the sitting-rooms, some here, some there |

The horse-stable of the classical home was next the street, on the opposite side of the *fauces* (θυρωρεῖον) from the gate-keeper's lodge; the ἐξέδρα was an open room provided with seats and adjoining the peristyle; both are strictly classical and unknown to the ante-classical palace. But Euripides, speaking of what his audience cannot see but knows from every-day experience, puts them into his Mycenaean palace. Note, too, that the servants are thus imprisoned and made, with the help of locks and keys, inaccessible to their mistress.

The centre of the men's megaron in the palace of Mycenaean times was occupied by the hearth. In the poets also it is there. It is not visible to the spectators, but it plays its part (for example, Eur. H. F. 715):

| | |
|---|---|
| ἱκέτιν πρὸς ἀγνοῖς ἑστίας θάσσειν βάθροις | she sits a suppliant at the hearth's holy step |

The hearth is, as always in antiquity, a holy place. By it gods as well as men gathered in intimate relations to the home; Zeus himself had a natural place there (Soph. Aj. 492):

| | |
|---|---|
| καί σ' ἀντιάζω πρός τ' ἐφεστίου Διός | I appeal to thee in the name of Zeus of thy hearth |

Nor was Zeus the only god of the hearth; all gods of good will belonged there (Ae. Cho. 800–802):

| | |
|---|---|
| οἵ τ' ἔσω δωμάτων | and ye that within the palace |
| πλουτογαθῆ μυχὸν ἐνίζετε, | dwell in the chamber that rejoiceth in wealth— |
| κλῦτε, σύμφρονες θεοί | hearken, ye gods in purpose one |

They dwelt there, as Athena dwelt in the "goodly house of Erechtheus" and had there her hearth (Ae. Eum. 439–441):

| | |
|---|---|
| βρέτας τόδε | keeping this image |
| ἧσαι φυλάσσων ἑστίας ἐμᾶς πέλας | thou sittest by my hearth, |
| σεμνὸς προσίκτωρ | a suppliant revered |

The hearth was the shrine of the gods who graced the home with their presence, and thither Agamemnon on his return from Troy hastens first to greet them (Ae. Ag. 851–852):

---

[1] The stable, standing "hard by" (πέλας) the palace of Pentheus, also is utilized as a prison for no less a captive than Dionysus himself (Eur. Bac. 509–510).

νῦν δ' ἐς μέλαθρα καὶ δόμους ἐφεστίους[1]

ἐλθὼν θεοῖσι πρῶτα δεξιώσομαι

| | |
|---|---|
| νῦν δ' ἐς μέλαθρα καὶ δόμους ἐφεστίους[1] | and now will I go into the palace and the halls, and by |
| ἐλθὼν θεοῖσι πρῶτα δεξιώσομαι | the hearth will I give greeting to the gods |

And there at the hearth, in the central living room of the home, libations were wont to be poured to the gods of the fireside (Soph. El. 269–270):

| | |
|---|---|
| παρεστίους σπένδοντα λοιβὰς ἔνθ' ἐκεῖνον ἀπώλεσεν | pouring libations by the fireside where she murdered him |

Here we have together the bloodless and the bloody sacrifice. It was probably bloodless sacrifices that Clytaemnestra offered at the hearth to the Erinyes (Ae. Eum. 108–109):

| | |
|---|---|
| καὶ νυκτίσεμνα δεῖπν' ἐπ' ἐσχάρᾳ πυρὸς | and at the blazing hearth I offered dread banquets of |
| ἔθυον, ὥραν οὐδενὸς κοινὴν θεῶν | the night, an hour not shared with you by any of the gods |

But not always were the sacrifices by the home's hearth bloodless offerings; even burnt sacrifice of victims slain was sometimes offered there (Ae. Ag. 1056–1057):

| | |
|---|---|
| τὰ μὲν γὰρ ἑστίας μεσομφάλου ἕστηκεν ἤδη μῆλα πρὸς σφαγὰς πυρός | for they stand by the mid-navel hearth —the sheep ready for the sacrifice of fire |

The "mid-navel hearth" is, of course, the hearth in the innermost part of the royal palace, the hearth in the central living room of the home. Such bloody sacrifices are assumed a little further on in the same tragedy as a matter of course (1309–1310):

| | |
|---|---|
| ΚΑ. φόνον δόμοι πνέουσιν αἱματοσταγῆ. | CA. There comes from the halls a breath of slaughter dripping with blood. |
| ΧΟ. καὶ πῶς; τόδ' ὄζει θυμάτων ἐφεστίων | CHO. To be sure. This scent comes from sacrifices at the hearth |

Under their keeping was the prince's throne and sceptre; and to the hearth the spirit of Agamemnon came, in the queen's dream, and fixed the symbol of his royal power (Soph. El. 419–420):

| | |
|---|---|
| τόνδ' ἐφέστιον πῆξαι λαβόντα σκῆπτρον | he took the sceptre and planted it by the hearth |

Like any other holy place, the hearth, the family altar, might be defiled and would have to be purified with cleansing rites. The altar of Zeus before the palace of Pelasgus might be defiled by the presence of the suppliant daughters of Danaus; if it should be, formal purification would have to follow (Ae. Sup. 365–372):

| | |
|---|---|
| ΒΑ. οὔτοι κάθησθε δωμάτων ἐφέστιοι ἐμῶν· τὸ κοινὸν δ' εἰ μιαίνεται πόλις, | K. It is not at the hearth of my halls that ye suppliant sit; and if the State in common be defiled, |
| ξυνῇ μελέσθω λαὸς ἐκπονεῖν ἄκη. | be it the people's common task to work the cure. |
| ΧΟ. σύ τοι πόλις... | CHO. Thou art the State . . . |
| κρατύνεις βωμὸν ἑστίας χθονός | Thou art lord of the country's altar-hearth |

The hearth is here called unequivocally "the altar." The royal hearth of a Mycenaean prince was an altar of the State.

The hearth of the palace of Mycenae had been defiled almost beyond all hope of cleansing, and yet the Chorus of the Choephori ventures to hope that "all-accomplishing Time" may bring the needed purification (Ae. Cho. 965–968):

| | |
|---|---|
| τάχα δὲ παντελὴς χρόνος ἀμείψεται πρόθυρα δωμάτων, ὅταν ἀφ' ἑστίας μῦσος πᾶν ἐλύσῃ[2] καθαρμοῖσιν ἀτᾶν ἐλατηρίοις | and soon all-accomplishing Time will pass the palace doors, when from the hearth He has cleansed away all the pollution with cleansings that will banish the woes |

[1] I suspect that for ἐφεστίους we should read ἐφεστίοις. The translation then would run: "I will go . . . into the halls and first of all give greeting to the gods of my fireside."

[2] I have not hesitated to adopt Sidgwick's χλύσῃ for the MSS. ἐλάσῃ(-ει), which could easily have crept into the text from ἐλατηρίοις below it.

As the family altar and the holiest spot in the house, the central hearth was the place of refuge for the suppliant and there he might sit secure. The suppliant priests thus sit at the altars of Oedipus (Soph. O. T. 32):

| | |
|---|---|
| ἐζόμεσθ' ἐφέστιοι | we sit as suppliants at thy hearth |

The natural place for the suppliant to sit was upon the raised border (βάθρα) that ran about the altar and confined the ashes. Such a border we have in Euripides (H. F. 715[1]) and its counterpart in reality we have in the men's megaron of Agamemnon's palace at Mycenae. The plural, βάθρα, also finds its explanation in the Pelopid palace: it rises in three steps from floor to inner edge.

As of the hearth, the altar of the home, so also βάθρα may be used of altar steps (Soph. O. T. 142–143):

| | |
|---|---|
| βάθρων | from the altar steps |
| ἵστασθε | arise |

It is usually plural also in the case of an altar. We have it in the singular in Sophocles's Ajax, when the hero, on the point of falling on his sword, thinks of home and native land (860):

| | |
|---|---|
| ὦ πατρῷον ἑστίας βάθρον | oh step of my father's hearth |

By this phrase Ajax means simply "my home."[2]

The smoke from the fire went up and out through a kind of clerestory. But the dwelling of classical times had some sort of chimney, at least for the kitchen. The chimney and the kitchen seem to go together in the comedy (Alex. Παν., Frag. 173, 13–14 K.):

| | |
|---|---|
| Α. ὀπτάνιόν ἐστιν; Β. ἔστι. Α. καὶ κάπνην ἔχει; | A. Is there a kitchen? B. Yes. A. And has it a chimney? |
| Β. δηλονότι. Α. μή μοι δῆλον· ἀλλ' ἔχει κάπνην; | B. Looks like it. A. Cut out your looks; tell me, has it a chimney? |

κάπνη and καπνοδόκη seem to have been used interchangeably for "chimney."[3]

The parasite in Diphilus's Παράσιτος sagely remarks that when a rich man invites him to dinner, he isn't impressed by the triglyphs or other architecture of the palatial home, but, he says (Frag. 61, 4 K.):

| | |
|---|---|
| ἀτενὲς δὲ τηρῶ τοῦ μαγείρου τὸν καπνόν | but I do have a keen eye for the smoke coming out of the kitchen |

In another play of the same poet one of the men climbs up on the housetop and gets a real thrill (Diph. Χρυσ., Frag. 84 K.):

| | |
|---|---|
| διακύψας ὁρῶ | I peeped down through the open tile |
| διὰ τῆς ὀπαίας κεραμίδος καλὴν σφόδρα | and saw the prettiest . . . |

[1] Quoted on p. 220.

[2] The use of the word βάθρον, or more commonly in the plural βάθρα, is not confined to the steps about a hearth. Coming from the root of βαίνω, it means literally "that on which anything steps" or "stands." Thus we have seen it used of the steps in a stairway (Soph. O. C. 1591), of the rounds of a ladder (Eur. Ph. 1179), of the foundations of temples (Ae. Pers. 812), of the foundations of cities (Eur. Sup. 1198; H. F. 944), of the high-set throne of Justice (Soph. Ant. 854–855), and, by a transfer of meaning, of the foundations of prosperity (Eur. Tro. 47).

A further step in the development, and βάθρα is no longer that on which one *steps* but that on which one *sits*—a bench, a seat (Soph. O. C. 101; Phryn. Com. Ἐφ., Frag. 3, 5 K.).

The word is used in a figurative sense of the rising strand, as the "step" of the island, the home of Ajax (Soph. Aj. 134–135):

| | |
|---|---|
| Τελαμώνιε παῖ, τῆς ἀμφιρύτου | son of Telamon, who holdest the |
| Σαλαμῖνος ἔχων βάθρον ἀγχιάλου | step of sea-girt Salamis's strand |

A very similar usage is found in Sophocles's Philoctetes, 1000:

| | |
|---|---|
| γῆς τόδ' αἰπεινὸν βάθρον | the rugged step of this land |

In these last two passages cited the word approaches the meaning of "land." It passes entirely over into metaphor in Euripides's Cyclops, 352:

| | |
|---|---|
| ἀφῖγμαι κἀπὶ κινδύνου βάθρα | I have arrived at danger's stepping-off place |

[3] Eup. Βάπτ., Frag. 88 K. (κάπνη); Δῆμ., Frag. 133 K. (καπνοδόκη) (Pollux VII 123): κάπνην δὲ καὶ καπνοδόκην Εὔπολις τὸ μὲν εἴρηκεν ἐν Βάπταις, τὸ δὲ ἐν Δήμοις. In the Tyrannis of Pherecrates (Frag. 141 K.) some god, explaining how the gods got rid of the appearance of sitting as beggars at the altars, says that Zeus made a "great chimney" (καπνοδόκην μεγάλην, meaning the brazen vault of heaven) to carry the savor of the sacrifice directly up to them.

Photius explains:

ὀπαία κεραμίς· ἡ τὴν κάπνην ἔχουσα | open tile: that which comprises the chimney

And Meineke (*ad loc.*): dicit tegulam qua operiebatur fumarium.

As this fellow climbed up on the roof to peep down into the kitchen at the pretty cook, so, in the Wasps of Aristophanes, Philocleon, locked up a prisoner in his own house, tries to make his escape by way of the chimney. He has gone into the kitchen and is crawling up the chimney, when his son, on guard on the roof, discovers his father's attempt to break jail (Ar. Vesp. 139–148):

ΒΔ. ὁ γὰρ πατὴρ ἐς τὸν ἰπνὸν εἰσελήλυθεν
καὶ μυσπολεῖ τι καταδεδυκώς· ἀλλ᾽ ἄθρει,

κατὰ τῆς πυέλου τὸ τρῆμ᾽ ὅπως μὴ ᾽κδύσεται·

σὺ δὲ τῇ θύρᾳ πρόσκεισο. ΞΑ. ταῦτ᾽ ὦ δέσποτα.

ΒΔ. ἄναξ Πόσειδον, τί ποτ᾽ ἄρ᾽ ἡ κάπνη ψοφεῖ;

οὗτος, τίς εἶ σύ; ΦΙ. καπνὸς ἔγωγ᾽ ἐξέρχομαι.

. . . . . . .
ΒΔ. . . . ποῦ ᾽σθ᾽ ἡ τηλία;
δύου πάλιν· φέρ᾽ ἐπαναθῶ σοι καὶ ξύλον

BD. For my father has gone into the kitchen; he has crept in and is poking about like a mouse. But look
out that he doesn't slip out through the exhaust of the kitchen sink!
And you brace yourself against the door! XA. All right, master.
BD. Lord Poseidon! What in the world is that racket in the chimney?
Say, you, who are you? PH. Me? I'm smoke coming out.

. . . . . . .
BD. . . . Where is the chimney-board?
Get down in again. There, let me put a log on you, too

In these lines we have a more complete picture of an ancient Greek kitchen than we find anywhere else. ἰπνός usually means "furnace," or "fire-place." But as the fire-place was so essential a feature of a kitchen, the word came to be used for the "kitchen" itself, as it doubtless does here, though it has been variously interpreted.[1] πύελος I have rendered by "kitchen-sink." The first meaning of the word is "trough"; then it means a "bath-tub"; then, "any trough or tub-shaped vessel." Liddell and Scott translate it here with "kitchen-boiler," and Hickie follows the dictionary; Graves, Merry, and Droysen render the word with "bath." But the kitchen was not a bathroom! And Philocleon could hardly have hoped to get out of doors by crawling into "the hole of the kitchen-boiler"! But the piece of kitchen furnishing that surely did have an opening, and a fairly large one, into the outer world was the kitchen-sink; and "a sink" is very close indeed to the first meaning of the word.

The kitchen also had a door. The front door was locked and barred and bolted and barricaded with stones; the kitchen door, which may also have been visible to the spectators, had been neglected in the general blockade; so Xanthias is ordered to brace himself against it to prevent the old man's making a break for liberty through it. Accordingly, his only hope is to climb up through the chimney. The Scholiast says it was σωληνοειδές τι, "a tube-like construction"—a very modern sort of chimney. The chimney (at least on the stage) was not high. The noise of his crawling up catches the attention of Bdelycleon, and as Philocleon pokes his head out of the top of the chimney, his son arrests him, forces him down the flue, claps a big board over the top, and weights it down with an extra log. The τηλία was, in the usual usage of the word, a big kneading-board. It might evidently mean also a wide board made on purpose to cover the chimney of a house, when there was no fire below, to keep out bats and swifts and other undesirable visitors.

Our word for kitchen (ἰπνός), it must be added, is most troublesome. In Aristophanes's Wasps (837) it is with unanimity explained as kitchen:

ὁ κύων παράξας ἐς τὸν ἰπνὸν ὑφαρπάσας
τροφαλίδα τυροῦ Σικελικὴν κατεδήδοκεν

the dog darted past into the kitchen, stole a fresh Sicilian cheese and bolted it

[1] L. and S., "an oven or furnace . . . especially for heating water for the bath"; Merry, " 'into the furnace,' probably used for heating the bath"; Droysen, "in die Fuerung"; Hickie, "into the furnace." The Scholiast says μαγειρεῖον, and he is certainly right; all interpreters agree that ἰπνός is the kitchen in line 837; and it must be so here also.

In the earlier passage from the Wasps it is, to me, quite as surely the kitchen; and it occurs again in the Birds, where, in spite of wide divergence of opinion, I am convinced that it is the kitchen (Ar. Av. 435–437):

ἄγε δὴ σὺ καὶ σὺ τὴν πανοπλίαν μὲν πάλιν | go, you and you, and take this panoply back
ταύτην λαβόντε κρεμάσατον τυχἀγαθῇ | into the kitchen and hang it up beside the
ἐς τὸν ἰπνὸν εἴσω, πλησίον τοὐπιστάτου | pot-rack—and heaven bless the deed

This interpretation seems simple enough: the warlike gear is to be taken into the kitchen and hung up alongside of the kitchen hardware, the kindred pots and kettles and pans and knives and forks and so on. But ἰπνός may have its first meaning and be "the fire-place," and τοὐπιστάτου may be the genitive not of ἐπίστατον, "the lazy back," the iron bar or crane on which pots and kettles are hung, but of ἐπιστάτης, "the supervisor," that is, the clay image of Hephaestus, the god who presides over the fire-place.[1] Taking τοὐπιστάτου apparently in the sense of "a tripod or a hook for supporting pots over the fire," Merry translates ἐς τὸν ἰπνὸν "in the chimney." Droysen renders:

> "Auf, du und du! nun nehmet euer Waffenthum,
> Und hängt in Gottes Namen Alles wiederum
> Am heilgen Herd auf in den Tellerschrank."

Hickie translates: "hang up this panoply again . . . . in the chimney-corner within, near the tripod."[2] Others make ἐπιστάτης the cauldron for heating water over such a tripod. But again I believe that Scholiast right who says that the ἐπίστατον (or ἐπιστάτης) is

ξύλον κόρακας ἔχον ἐξ οὗ κρεμῶσι | a wooden bar with hooks, on which
τὰ μαγειρικὰ ἐργαλεῖα | the kitchen utensils are hung

and in accordance with this scholium I have translated.

Although in these passages ἰπνός is clearly the kitchen, in a fragment of Antiphanes it is quite as clearly a bake-oven ('Ομφ., Frag. 176, 3–4 K.):

ὁρῶν μὲν ἄρτους τούσδε λευκοσωμάτους | seeing these loaves of white bread
ἰπνὸν κατέχοντας | filling the oven

What the word means in Aristophanes's Plutus (815), in the passage where all the utensils of the house, by the magic of the god of wealth, are transmuted into precious material, it is impossible to say with certainty:

ὁ δ' ἰπνὸς γέγον' ἡμῖν ἐξαπίνης ἐλεφάντινος

Is it our "kitchen" or our "chimney" or our "oven" or our "toilet-room" or our "lantern" that has suddenly "become ivory"? The word may have any of these meanings. In Aristophanes's Peace (841) ἰπνός is a lantern; in a fragment of his Cocalus (Frag. 353 K.) ἰπνός is a dunghill or privy.[3] The derivative ἰπνίτης in a fragment of Timocles may be "something from the kitchen" or "something from the fire-place" (Ψευδ., Frag. 33 K.):

καταμαθὼν δὲ κειμένην | finding set before me a
θερμὴν σκάφην θερμῶν ἰπνιτῶν ἤσθιον | hot bowl of hot things from the kitchen, I began
 | to eat

'Ιπνός seems to be a perfectly good word for kitchen, but it is not the first and most natural meaning of the word. The natural and usual word for that important room in the house is ὀπτάνιον "the place where things are roasted or cooked." From it the chimney rose, as we saw in the fragment of Alexis quoted on page 222. Tidiness was a virtue in the kitchen in classical days as it is now (Ar. Pax. 891):

τουτὶ δ' ὅρα τοὐπτάνιον ἡμῖν ὡς καλόν | see how fine our kitchen here is

(Heges. 'Αδ., Frag. 1, 18–19 K.):

ἂν δὲ δὴ λάβω | but if I obtain
τὰ δέοντα καὶ τοὐπτάνιον ἁρμόσωμ' ἅπαξ | what I need and once get the kitchen in order

---

[1] The ἰπνολέβης in Luc. Lexiph. 8 is certainly the fire-place cauldron for heating water: ὁ μέντοι ἰπνολέβης ὑπερπαφλάζων ἐς κεφαλὴν ἡμῖν ἐπέτρεπε τοὺς ἄνθρακας.

[2] So Bentley and others. See Roger's note Ar. Av. 437 and his additional note on the Sigeian inscriptions, pp. 238–239.

[3] Hesych: ἰπνός· 'Αριστοφάνης δὲ ἐν Κωκάλῳ καὶ τὸν κοπρῶνα οὕτως εἶπεν. Pollux V 91: τὸν δὲ κοπρῶνα καὶ ἰπνὸν 'Αριστοφάνης καλεῖ.

Untidiness seems to call for censure (Philemon Παρ., Frag. 61, 1 K.):

| | |
|---|---|
| περὶ τοὐπτάνιον οὐ γίνεθ' ἡ σκευωρία | we do not have the tidiness about the kitchen |

An essential part of the kitchen furnishings was the stove or oven, variously called a κρίβανος (Ar. Γηρυτ., Frag. 155 K.) or a κάμινος (Inc. Inc. Frag. 633 K.).

It goes without saying that in the kitchen may be found all sorts of dishes and good things to eat, and the comedy does not fail to dwell on that feature of the home (Alciphron 3, 53, 1; Kock 'Αδέσπ. 1558–1560):

| | |
|---|---|
| εἰσέφρησα εἰς τοὐπτάνιον· ἔπειτα | I let myself into the kitchen; and then |
| εὑρὼν λοπάδα εὖ μάλα κεχαρυκευμένην | I found a dish fixed up with delicious sauce |
| κἀλεκτρύον' ὀπτὸν χύτραν τε μεμβράδας | and roast capon and a bowl with anchovies |
| ἔχουσαν καὶ ἀφύας Μεγαρικὰς ἐξήρπασα | and Megarian sardines—and I swiped them |

Similarly Aristophanes (Eq. 1033–1034):

| | |
|---|---|
| ἐσφοιτῶν τ' ἐς τοὐπτάνιον λήσει σε κυνηδὸν | and he'll sneak in unobserved into your kitchen like a dog |
| νύκτωρ τὰς λοπάδας καὶ τὰς νήσους διαλείχων | at night and lick your dishes clean—and your islands |

Damoxenus (Σύντρ. 2, ll. 44, 45, 49 K.):

| | |
|---|---|
| οὐ τὸ διανίζειν λοπάδας οὐδ' ὄζειν καπνοῦ. | not to wash up dishes nor to smell smoke. |
| ἐγὼ γὰρ εἰς τοὐπτάνιον οὐκ εἰσέρχομαι. | For I don't go into the kitchen—not I. |
| Β. ἁρμονικὸς εἶ μάγειρος. Α. ἐπίτεινον τὸ πῦρ | B. You're a proper chef. A. Stir up the fire |

As is seems, the ancient chimneys did not always draw well!

Apparently not all kitchens were properly covered in; they were sometimes open-air cooking-places. Smoke would be particularly troublesome in the latter kind. So the caterer whose services are being sought in the fragment of Alexis quoted on page 222 makes the special point of asking not only if there is a kitchen, but if it has a chimney. On receiving an affirmative answer to this last question he ejaculates (Παν., Frag. 173, 15 K.):

| | |
|---|---|
| κακόν, εἰ τύφουσαν | the devil to pay, if it smokes! |

Another caterer in Menander's Girl from Samos makes condition after condition for his services, and among others (78–79):

| | |
|---|---|
| εἰ κέραμός ἐστ' ἔνδοθεν | if you have enough dishes at your |
| ὑμῖν ἱκανός, εἰ τοὐπτάνιον κατάστεγον | house; if your kitchen is covered in |

And in a fragment of Sosipater still another chef is laying down the laws of architecture from his point of view and dealing with such an open-air kitchen (Καταψ., Frag. 1, 39–43 K.):[1]

| | |
|---|---|
| τοὐπτάνιον ὀρθῶς καταβαλέσθ' καὶ τὸ φῶς | the kitchen he must construct properly, secure as much |
| λαβεῖν ὅσον δεῖ καὶ τὸ πνεῦμ' ἰδεῖν πόθεν | light as is necessary, and see what direction the |
| ἔστιν, μεγάλην χρείαν τιν' εἰς τὸ πρᾶγμ' ἔχει. | wind comes from—these points are essential. |
| ὁ καπνὸς φερόμενος δεῦρο κἀκεῖ διαφορὰν | Whether the smoke is carried this way or that usually makes |
| εἴωθε τοῖς ὄψοισιν ἐμποιεῖν τινα | a big difference with the viands |

The passage quoted on page 204 from the Parasite of Diphilus (Frag. 61, 1–4 K.) suggests another interesting feature of the ancient kitchen: it is not the architectural beauty of the rich man's home to which he is invited nor the number of his wine-casks that appeals to him:

| | |
|---|---|
| ἀτενὲς δὲ τηρῶ τοῦ μαγείρου τὸν καπνὸν | but I do note carefully the smoke rising from his kitchen |

The amount of smoke issuing from the kitchen chimney is to the parasite an index of the number of viands preparing in the kitchen. As with the modern Greek range, there were as many fires as there were different things to cook.

[1] Cf. also Nicom. Εἰλ., Frag. 1, 25–28 K.

Somewhere in or adjacent to the kitchen or dining room was the cupboard—the κυλικεῖον, "the place where the cups were kept."[1] What the classical Greek cupboard looked like we are not told; but it may be imagined very like its modern descendant. Instead of glass doors, it may have had only a curtain across its front to keep out dust and dirt (Ar. Γεωρ., Frag. 104 K.):

| | |
|---|---|
| ὥσπερ κυλικείου τουθόνιον προσπέπταται | she had a veil drawn over her front—like a cupboard's |

To the wanderer returned from the wars in foreign lands the cupboard was the symbol of home and friends and good cheer, dearer than all the rights of citizenship that he voluntarily forfeited. One such exclaims (Cratinus minor Χείρων, Frag. 9 K.):

| | |
|---|---|
| πολλοστῷ δ' ἔτει | and after many a year I |
| ἐκ τῶν πολεμίων οἴκαδ' ἥκων, ξυγγενεῖς | have come home from the enemy land; I have with |
| καὶ φράτερας καὶ δημότας εὑρὼν μόλις, | difficulty found my clansmen and demesmen; |
| εἰς τὸ κυλικεῖον ἐνεγράφην· Ζεὺς ἔστι μοι | I have enrolled my name in the cupboard; that is my Zeus |
| ἑρκεῖος, ἔστι φράτριος, τὰ τέλη τελῶ | Herceius, Zeus Phratrius; there I pay tribute |

The invention of this precious piece of furniture is ascribed to some one (Dionysus?) in Eubulus's Harpgirl (Ψαλ., Frag. 118 K.):

| | |
|---|---|
| τὰ κυλικεῖα δὲ | and cupboards |
| ἐξεῦρεν ἡμῖν | he invented for us |

The object of the invention was the protection of the fragile earthenware. But even in such a shelter, the cups were not always safe (Eub. Λαχ., Frag. 62 K.):

| | |
|---|---|
| ὡσπερεὶ σπονδὴν διδοὺς | as if offering a libation |
| ἐν τῷ κυλικείῳ συντέτριφεν τὰ ποτήρια | he has smashed the cups in the cupboard |

The sanctity of the cupboard was presided over not by Dionysus, as one would naturally expect, but, at all events in the tavern, by Hermes, the god of traffic. And by the cupboard, therefore, would be placed a statue of the god of commerce polished as bright as the cups under his protecting care (Eub. Σεμ. ἢ Διόν., Frag. 96 K.):

| | |
|---|---|
| Ἑρμῆς ὁ Μαίας λίθινος, ὃν προσεύγμασιν | Hermes the son of Maia, whom polished |
| ἐν τῷ κυλικείῳ λαμπρὸν ἐκτετριμμένον | bright at the cupboard with vows . . . |

But in the home the presiding deity is more appropriately "Zeus, the guardian of the property" (Ζεὺς Κτήσιος), as we have seen him looking after the pantry, in the fragment of Menander (Ψευδ., Frag. 519 K.),[2] or more specifically "Zeus, the guardian of the cupboard" (Ἐπικυλίκειος Ζεύς), as he is called in an unidentified comic fragment (Inc. Inc. Frag. 861 K.).

The cupboard may have held any possible assortment or combination of pitchers and bowls and cups and vases and dishes, the subject of our chapter on Vases (Vol III, Chap. XIII).

In the palace of Odysseus the apartments of Penelope were in the upper story. Indeed, all the palaces of Homer's heroes had an upper story;[3] the palace at Tiryns apparently had such an upper story, that at Cnossus had at least a second and a third, with stairways still in part preserved. In the dramatists also we find an upper story in the royal palaces and sometimes in humbler homes.

The stairways leading from one story to another were built of wood,[4] stone, or concrete. The steps were sometimes reinforced with metal, as in our public buildings, to prolong the life of the steps (Soph. O. C. 1590–1591):

| | |
|---|---|
| ἐπεὶ δ' ἀφῖκτο τὸν καταρράκτην ὁδὸν | and when he came to the sheer threshold, |
| χαλκοῖς βάθροισι γῆθεν ἐρριζωμένον | with treads of bronze firmly let into the earth |

[1] Athenaeus comments (XI 460 d-e): εἴρηται δὲ οὕτως (κυλικεῖον) ἡ τῶν ποτηρίων σκευοθήκη. Cf. also Anaxandr. Μελ., Frag. 29 K.

[2] Quoted on p. 212.

[3] Β 514; Π 184; α 362; ο 517; τ 594; etc.

[4] Eur. Ph. 100; see p. 27.

This is, to be sure, not a palace, but a sanctuary of the "Dread Goddesses." Still the light it throws upon stairway construction is strong and clear. These steps, by which one went deeper down into the entrance to the lower world at Colonus, were cut out of the live rock; they were reinforced with bronze treads "rooted" into the stone of Colonus hill.[1]

The roof of the Greek house also is not only at the present time but also in the classical period and in the Homeric days a convenient part of the dwelling, affording a comfortable place to sleep out in the cool open air. The roof was flat and as extensive as the ground-plan of the apartments it covered. Elpenor, in the Odyssey, slept upon the roof of Circe's palace.[2] So in the opening lines of the Agamemnon we find the watchman just awakened from sleep upon the roof of the palace at Mycenae (Ae. Ag. 2–4):

| | |
|---|---|
| φρουρᾶς ἐτείας μῆκος, ἣν κοιμώμενος | through this long year of watching, while I, crouching |
| στέγαις 'Ατρειδῶν ἄγκαθεν, κυνὸς δίκην, | like a watch-dog upon the Atridae's roof, |
| ἄστρων κάτοιδα νυκτέρων ὁμήγυριν | have come to know the company of the stars of night |

In the same tragedy the ghosts of the murdered children of Thyestes appear to the supernatural vision of Cassandra seated upon the roof of the same palace at Mycenae, as if the roof had been the scene of the hideous banquet at which their flesh had been served to their father (Ae. Ag. 1217–1222):

| | |
|---|---|
| ὁρᾶτε τούσδε τοὺς δόμοις ἐφημένους | see ye yon children sitting upon the house-top, |
| νέους, ὀνείρων προσφερεῖς μορφώμασι; | in fashion, like to phantom forms of dreams? |
| παῖδες θανόντες, ὡσπερεὶ πρὸς τῶν φίλων, | Children they seem, by their own loved ones slain, |
| χεῖρας κρεῶν πλήθοντες οἰκείας βορᾶς | their hands full of the viands of their own flesh, |
| σὺν ἐντέροις τε σπλάγχν', ἐποίκιστον γέμος, | entrails and vitals I see them hold—the rueful cheer |
| πρέπουσ' ἔχοντες, ὧν πατὴρ ἐγεύσατο | on which their father fed |

The ghosts of the children had risen before Cassandra's prophetic gaze a little while before; it is not said in the earlier passage that they were seated upon the roof; but they had the same gruesome suggestions of the awful Thyestes banquet (1096–1097):

| | |
|---|---|
| κλαιόμενα τάδε βρέφη σφαγάς, | yonder are babes bewailing their own murder |
| ὀπτάς τε σάρκας πρὸς πατρὸς βεβρωμένας | and roasted flesh on which their father fed |

So in the Wasps, Bdelycleon sleeps on the roof of the house, whether for greater comfort or to be on hand if his father should try to escape by way of the roof (Ar. Vesp. 67–68):[3]

| | |
|---|---|
| ἔστιν γὰρ ἡμῖν δεσπότης ἐκεινοσὶ | now, that is our master sleeping up |
| ἄνω καθεύδων, ὁ μέγας οὑπὶ τοῦ τέγους | there—the big fellow on the roof |

The spacious, airy roof may, therefore, afford not only most comfortable night-quarters and spacious banquet halls, but it also commands the most extensive view. That was the principal reason why the watchman was posted there in the Agamemnon. And so the old paedagogus at the beginning of the Phoenissae takes Antigone to the roof to view her brother's hostile army (Eur. Ph. 89–105):

| | |
|---|---|
| ΠΑΙ. ἐπεί σε μήτηρ παρθενῶνας ἐκλιπεῖν | PAE. Now that thy mother hath consented to thy leaving thy |
| μεθῆκε μελάθρων ἐς διῆρες ἔσχατον | maiden-bower and mounting to the palace-roof |
| στράτευμ' ἰδεῖν 'Αργεῖον . . . . | to view the Argive host. . . . |
| . . . . . . . . | . . . . . . . . |
| κέδρου παλαιὰν κλίμακ' ἔκπερα ποδί· | mount with thy foot the ancient cedar stair; |
| σκόπει δὲ πεδία καὶ παρ' 'Ισμηνοῦ ῥοὰς | look out upon the plains and along Ismenus's brooks |
| Δίρκης τε νᾶμα, πολεμίων στράτευμ' ὅσον. | and Dirce's stream and see what a host of foes. |
| ΑΝΤ. ὄρεγέ νυν, ὄρεγε γεραιὰν νέᾳ | ANT. Lend me thine hand, thine aged hand, to me |
| χεῖρ' ἀπὸ κλιμάκων ποδὸς | that am young and help my footsteps up the |
| ἴχνος ἐπαντέλλων | stair |

[1] For the fuller discussion see pages 149–150.
[2] x 554–560; λ 62–65.
[3] Cp. also Ar. Nub. 1502: οὗτος, τί ποιεῖς ἐτεόν, οὑπὶ τοῦ τέγους;

Mercury, in Plautus's Amphitryo, which seems to be based upon a Greek satyr-play, takes his place upon the roof of the Theban palace for the double purpose: first, to have a commanding view of Amphitryon's approach; and second, to have a post of vantage for giving the king a ducking and finally driving him away (1000–1001):

> illuc susum escendero: inde optume aspellam virum
> de supero, cum huc accesserit; faciam ut sit madidus sobrius

(1008):

> susum ascendam in tectum, ut illum hinc prohibeam

As in Homer, so in the passage from the Phoenissae, the roof is accessible from the interior of the house by means of a stairway—in this instance, a stairway of wood, not of stone. We may note further that Euripides specifies the kind of wood of which the stairway is constructed: it is cedar.

To the housetop Orestes and Pylades flee with Hermione at the approach of Menelaus in the closing scene of Euripides's Orestes (1574–1575):

| δόμων ἐπ' ἄκρων τούσδε πυργηρουμένους | and upon the housetop yonder men entowered |
| ξίφος δ' ἐμῆς θυγατρὸς ἐπίφρουρον δέρῃ | and the sword laid to my daughter's throat! |

They are standing by the parapet that encloses the space upon the roof and are in plain sight to those approaching below. And there Orestes threatens to tear off the cornice and with the stone to dash out his uncle's brains if he show fight.[1]

The housetop is not what Homer gives us to understand by ὑπερῷον; the ὑπερῷα are upper apartments of a palace; the διῆρες ἔσχατον is the flat roof with its enclosing balustrade. Its technical name is γεισιπόδισμα—strictly, the "projecting beams supporting the eaves."[2] But the three words, διῆρες, διστεγία ("second story"), and ὑπερῷον are synonymous, and even Pollux who gives us the accurate technical definition gets them confused (IV 19):

| ἡ δὲ διστεγία ποτὲ μὲν ἐν οἴκῳ | but the second story sometimes in a royal |
| βασιλείῳ διῆρες δωμάτιον, οἷον | palace is an upper chamber, as, for example, |
| ἀφ' οὗ ἐν Φοινίσσαις ἡ Ἀντιγόνη | that from which in the Phoenissae Antigone |
| βλέπει τὸν στρατόν | views the host |

But most obviously Antigone has left her "maiden-bower" in the upper story of the palace and ascends to the διῆρες ἔσχατον, the "roof-garden," and from there sees both east (toward Ismenus's brooks) and west (toward Dirce's stream) and north (toward the Proetidian Gate).

This flat roof was the prevailing type of roof construction in the private houses of fifth and early fourth century Athens.[3] Upon such a roof the women danced and sang the Adonis-dirge at the festival of Adonia, when the ill-fated expedition was setting out for Sicily (Ar. Lys. 389):

| ὅ τ' Ἀδωνιασμὸς οὗτος οὑπὶ τῶν τεγῶν | and that Adonis-dirge upon the roofs |

(ibid. 392–396):

| ἡ γυνὴ δ' ὀρχουμένη | but the woman dancing |
| «αἰαῖ Ἄδωνιν», φησίν . . . . | cried "Woe, woe for Adonis" . . . . |
| . . . . ἡ γυνὴ 'πὶ τοῦ τέγους. . . . | . . . and the woman on the roof |
| «κόπτεσθ' Ἄδωνιν,» φησίν . . . | cried "Weep and wail for Adonis" |

From such a roof also the women would view processions passing through the streets (Ar. Ach. 262):

| σὺ δ', ὦ γύναι, θεῶ μ' ἀπὸ τοῦ τέγους | and you, wife, may look at me from the roof |

We find the διῆρες ὑπερῷον also in the comedy, and it still retains its meaning as an upper story (Plato Ποιητής, Frag. 112 K.):

| ὁρᾶτε τὸ διῆρες ὑπερῷον[4] | see the upper story[4] |

---

[1] Cp. pages 206–207.

[2] Pollux I 81: αἱ δὲ προσβολαὶ τῶν ὑπερῴων οἰκημάτων, αἱ ὑπὲρ τοὺς κάτω τοίχους προύχουσαι, γεισιποδίσματα· καὶ τὰ φέροντα αὐτὰς ξύλα γεισίποδες.

[3] Cp. pp. 30 ff.

[4] Hesychius adds but little with his definition: διῆρες· ὑπερῷον. ἡ κλῖμαξ. It is accessible by a stairway, of course.

Aristophanes takes the upper story of the well-to-do houses of his day as a matter of course. The pretty lady looks out of the window of her chamber in an upper story and invites the young man in (Ar. Ec. 698–699):

| | |
|---|---|
| φήσει τις ἄνωθ' ἐξ ὑπερῴου, | some one will say from the upper story above, |
| καὶ καλλίστη καὶ λευκοτάτη | the most beautiful and fair |

At line 961 the girl is asked to come down stairs (καταδραμοῦσα) and open the door. In the Thesmophoriazusae the woman goes down (καταβαίνω[1]) from her chamber and meets her lover at the door (ll. 482 ff.). The bed-chamber of the lady of the house was, apparently, always on an upper floor. In the house of Chremylus one of the upper stories was, it would seem, an attic and used primarily as a storeroom (Ar. Pl. 811):

| | |
|---|---|
| τὸ δ' ὑπερῷον ἰσχάδων [γέμει] | and the upper story is packed with dried figs |

The ordinary houses of fifth century Athens would seem to have had such an attic store-room (Ar. Ran. 565–566):

| | |
|---|---|
| νὼ δὲ δεισάσα γέ που | and we two in terror, you remember, |
| ἐπὶ τὴν κατήλιφ' εὐθὺς ἀνεπηδήσαμεν | scampered pell-mell up to the loft |

There may be some doubt as to just what the κατήλιφ was; but it certainly was not a "shelf or ledge running along the back of the cook-shop, and formed by the upper surface either of a cross-beam or of a partition not reaching the ceiling," as Mr. Rogers in his note on the passage interprets. Plathane and her sister would never have jumped up on a perch like that to get away from a mad Heracles raging about with a drawn sword. The ancient commentators seem to have had as much trouble in explaining the word as modern scholars have. To Hesychius κατήλιφ was the "space along the wall," Homer's μεσόδμη, or a "roof-beam."[2] Photius, Pollux, and Suidas agree. But neither roof-beam nor μεσόδμη could have afforded any sort of security for the terrified women in their flight before the hero in his pretended madness. A loft could have done so; we may even imagine that they scrambled up a ladder into the loft and pulled the ladder up after them. Then Heracles could have raved about as long as he would and have "gone off in a whirl taking the mattresses with him." Such would seem to be also the "better interpretation of others," suggested by Hesychius.[2]

At all events, all are agreed that the κατήλιφ was a place for storing provisions, like the ὑπερῷον in the house of Chremylus in the Plutus. Lucian may have had this passage in mind when he wrote (Lexiph. 8):

| | |
|---|---|
| ὁ μέν τις ἐπὶ τὴν κατήλιφα | and one scrambled up into |
| ἀναρριχησάμενος, ἐπιφόρη- | the loft and went hunting for |
| μα ἐζήτει | something for dessert |

The "scrambling up" suggests again the ladder; and the "something for dessert" recalls the store-room for provisions; and Lucian is certainly using words that affect the Old Comedy.

The women's apartments, we may assume, had no windows opening upon the outer world.[3] The Minoan palaces in Crete, we may be sure from the tablets of Cnossus, had windows in each story of the men's apartments. The tragic poets never mention windows in the Mycenaean palaces taken as the scenes of their plays. But Aristophanes offers abundant evidence of the presence of windows in the buildings that figure in his comedies. Temples, like the Erechtheum, had windows—beautiful windows; the homes of Athenian bourgeois also had windows. The windows of Philocleon's house were among the first openings that his son had to stop up to keep the old man away from the law courts (Ar. Vesp. 126–128):

| | |
|---|---|
| ὁ δ' ἐξεδίδρασκε διά τε τῶν ὑδορροῶν | but he would make his escape through the rain-pipes |
| καὶ τῶν ὀπῶν. ἡμεῖς δ' ὅσ' ἦν τετρημένα | and the windows. So all the openings there were |
| ἐνεβύσαμεν ῥακίοισι | we stuffed up with rags |

[1] Cp. also Ar. Vesp. 347.

[2] κατήλιφ· μεσόδμη, μεσότοιχον, δόκος ἡ ὑπένερθε βαστάζουσα τὸν ὄροφον· οἱ δὲ ἰκρίωμα τὸ ἐν τῷ οἴκῳ, ὃ καὶ βέλτιον.

[3] The Young Man in the Ecclesiazusae makes love to the Girl at the upstairs window (884–976), and the Chorus in the Thesmophoriazusae includes in the list of feminine peccadillos "peeping out of the window" (797), but in neither case, is it at all likely that the window is in the women's apartments.

Though ἀντηρίς may mean a "window," the ἀντηρίς from which a woman is bidden to hang herself in the doubtful fragment of Eupolis (455 K.) need not be a window in her apartments nor even a window at all; ἀντηρίς also means a "beam," and that is the more likely interpretation of the word.

And through the window only could he hear the voices of his fellow-heliasts in the street below rousing his passion for their company (*ibid.* 317–319):

φίλοι, τήκομαι μὲν
πάλαι διὰ τῆς ὀπῆς
ὑμῶν ὑπακούων

friends, I have this long time
been fretting to death at hearing
you only through the window

These openings were high; otherwise Philocleon could have seen his friends through them; they were stuffed so tight full of rags that not even a midge could get through them (vs. 352); yet he could hear through them (vss. 318–319) and be heard through them (vs. 350):

ἔστιν ὀπὴ δῆθ' ἥν τιν' ἂν ἔνδοθεν οἷός τ' εἴης
διαλέξαι[1]
εἶτ' ἐκδῦναι ῥάκεσιν κρυφθείς, ὥσπερ πολύμητις
'Οδυσσεύς;

is there a window through which you could hold
converse from within[1]
and then slip out through it covered with rags
like Odysseus of many devices

Philocleon could hear through the windows; he could be heard; he could not see through and could not get through, because his son had effectively stuffed them full of rags or nailed them up. Moreover, the window had been barred[2] or screened with strong net work—perhaps wire screens. The whole court (like our modern porches) had been so securely screened as to hold the old man in; he could not simply tear a hole through them; he might gnaw a hole through, but his teeth are too poor (Ar. Vesp. 131–132):

ἡμεῖς δὲ τὴν αὐλὴν ἅπασαν δικτύοις
καταπετάσαντες ἐν κύκλῳ φυλάττομεν

and we have screened in all the
court all 'round and keep him in

(164):

διατρώξομαι τοίνυν τὸ δίκτυον

well then, I'll gnaw through the screen

In the same way the windows of the upper story had been strongly screened[2] (Ar. Vesp. 368–371):

ΦΙ. διατραγεῖν τοίνυν κράτιστόν ἐστί μοι
τὸ δίκτυον.
ἡ δέ μοι Δίκτυννα συγγνώμην ἔχοι τοῦ
δικτύου.
ΧΟ. ταῦτα μὲν πρὸς ἀνδρός ἐστ' ἄγοντος
ἐς σωτηρίαν. . . .
ΦΙ. διατέτρωκται τοῦτό γ' . . . . . .

PHI.  Well then, the best thing for me to do is
to gnaw through the net.
And may our Lady of the Nets forgive me for the
net.
CHO.  That's the talk for a man who is working
his way to safety. . . .
PHI.  This one, at least, is gnawed through. . . .

In a scanty fragment Aristophanes has a similar situation (Αἰολ., Frag. 11 K.):

καὶ δι' ὀπῆς κἀπὶ τέγους

and through a window and on the roof

Gravert (comparing Xenarchus IV 11, 12) concludes that the context would give us a woman as determined to get out of the house and join her lover as Philocleon was to get out and join his fellow-heliasts.

In all these passages where ὀπή is used, it may well be, as I have argued above,[3] that we have to deal with the open metope between two triglyph blocks of a Doric front. But at all events, the open metope was, after all, a kind of window. However, we are not left to ὀπή alone for our knowledge of the windows in the houses of fifth century Athens. We know what the window opening on the east portico of the Erechtheum looked like; and we have a word for window that leaves no ambiguity as to its meaning. When Philocleon has succeeded in "gnawing" through the screen on the window, the Chorus exhorts him (Ar. Vesp. 379–380):

ἀλλ' ἐξάψας διὰ τῆς θυρίδος τὸ καλῷδιον
εἶτα καθίμα
δήσας σαυτόν

but fasten the rope through the window and
then
tie it round yourself and let yourself down

[1] The reading of Dindorf, ex glossis Hesych.
[2] Windows were commonly barred or latticed (Pl. Mil. 379–380):
nam certo neque solarium apud nos neque hortus ullus
neque fenestra nisi clatrata
[3] Pages 116–117.

This time the word is θυρίς which means just what we mean by "window." And it is the same thing that a moment ago was ὀπή. And it is still high—so high that to reach the ground from it Philocleon must use a rope to let himself down; and he is afraid, even then, that the rope may break or slip and that he may break his neck in the attempt to get down, or that (worse still, perhaps) his persecutors may catch him in the act and haul him back up through the window into confinement again (381–382; 385–386):

| | |
|---|---|
| ἄγε νῦν, ἢν αἰσθομένω τούτω ζητητόν μ' ἐσχαλαμᾶσθαι | pray, now, if those two fellows see me and try to fish me up |
| χἀνασπαστὸν ποιεῖν εἴσω, τί ποιήσετε; | and haul me back in, what will you do? |
| . . . . . . . . | . . . . . . . . |
| ἤν τι πάθω 'γώ, | if anything happens to me, |
| ἀνελόντες καὶ κατακλαύσαντες θεῖναί μ' ὑπὸ τοῖσι δρυφάκτοις | gather me up and weep over me and bury me under the bar |

He still hesitates at the lofty window. The fun of the situation was intensified by the realities in the theatre, where the window-ledge could have been barely eight or ten feet above the street. The humor is helped on by the Chorus's eager encouragement (387–388):

| | |
|---|---|
| οὐδὲν πείσει· μηδὲν δείσῃς. ἀλλ', ὦ βέλτιστε, καθίει | you won't get hurt; don't be scared; but, dear sir, let your- |
| σαυτὸν θαρρῶν κἀπευξάμενος τοῖσι πατρῴοισι θεοῖσι | self down and don't be afraid but offer up a prayer to your father's gods |

And Philocleon, with wildly ejaculated prayers, lets himself down, down, down—eight or ten feet—to the ground. But before he reaches the ground, Bdelycleon discovers him in the act (396–397):

| | |
|---|---|
| καθιμᾷ | he is letting himself down |
| αὑτὸν δήσας | by a rope |

and calls his two servants to help save the day. One of them runs to haul the fugitive back through the window (397):

| | |
|---|---|
| οὐ μὴ καταβήσει | you shall not go down |

Bdelycleon orders the other to run up below him and beat him back up the rope into the window again (398–399):

| | |
|---|---|
| ἀνάβαιν' ἀνύσας κατὰ τὴν ἑτέραν καὶ ταῖσι φυλλάσι παῖε, | run up, quick! on the other side [1] and beat him with the branches, |
| ἤν πως πρύμνην ἀνακρούσηται πληγεὶς ταῖς εἰρεσιώναις | and see if haply he will back astern when beaten with the boughs |

With much ado he is apparently hauled back through the window to prison again.

θυρίς "window" occurs again in the parabasis of the Thesmophoriazusae. The Chorus discusses woman as the alleged mischief and cause of all mischief in the world, and yet she is the world's desire (Ar. Thes. 797):

| | |
|---|---|
| κἂν ἐκ θυρίδος παρακύπτωμεν, ζητεῖ τὸ κακὸν τεθεᾶσθαι | and if we peep through a window,[2] every one strives to catch a glimpse of "the mischief" |

Windows, therefore, we have, looking out upon the street, as well as into the court, in both classical dwellings and Minoan palaces.

The general plan of the private house of the period of the New Comedy is drawn for us with considerable detail by Plautus in the Mostellaria—vestibule, pillars, colonnades, rooms, baths, women's quarters, promenades, almost everything (755 ff.):

> TR.  Gynaeceum aedificare volt hic in suis,
> et balineas et ambulacrum et porticum
>
> . . . . . .
>
> ad eam rem facere volt novom gynaeceum.
> nam sibi laudavisse hasce ait architectonem

[1] These words are often taken to mean "at the other window"—as if Philocleon were coming down from a second story window and Sosias were to beat him back by striking him from a first story window. That is, of course, a possible, but not a necessary interpretation. Droysen, less happily, renders: Du hinauf! schnell, schnell! an das Fenster da links! und schlag' auf ihn los mit den Ruthen!

[2] So the young girl in the Ecclesiazusae peeps out of her window and sings to her lover (930 ff.).

(817 ff.):

TR.   Viden vestibulum ante aedis hoc et ambulacrum quoiusmodi?
TH.   Luculentum edepol profecto.   TR. Age specta postes, quoiusmodi,
      quanta firmitate facti et quanta crassitudine.
TH.   Non videor vidisse postis pulcriores.   SI. Pol mihi
      eo pretio empti fuerant olim

. . . . .

      tris minas pro istis duobus praeter vecturam dedi

(843):

      circumduce hasce aedis et conclavia

The colonnade with its promenade ran round the atrium, with which we are familiar from the Graeco-Roman house of Pompeii and Delos, with its adjoining chambers.   And the roof above these, sloping from its several directions toward the atrium, made the impluvium, which also is variously mentioned in the comedy (Pl. Mil. 288):

      forte fortuna per impluvium huc despexi in proxumum

Sceledrus, scampering over the roof of the house hunting for the stray monkey, had the finest kind of opportunity for peeping into the impluvium and the chambers beyond the colonnade opposite to him.[1]

Beyond the atrium of the more pretentious houses was the peristyle with its garden or gardens (Pl. Mil. 341):

      neque solarium neque hortum nisi per impluvium

(*ibid*. 379–380):

      nam certo neque solarium apud nos neque hortus ullus
      neque fenestra nisi clatrata

In this particular house in Ephesus there was no sun-parlor (attached to the peristyle), and no garden (within the peristyle), and therefore no back or side gate to afford communication between it and the next door neighbor's house; the only way of access, save by the street doors, was through the impluvium.   Even the windows were barred.

Down through the impluvium of Amphitryon's palace rolled the two serpents sent to devour the infant Hercules (Pl. Am. 1108):

      devolant angues iubati deorsum in impluvium duo

These passages all have to do with dwellings of the period of the New Comedy.   But even in fifth century Athens the homes of the very wealthy had their colonnaded atria and, perhaps, their colonnaded peristyles.   Strepsiades in the Clouds of Aristophanes speaks of the columns of his millionaire brother-in-law's house as the very type and symbol of his wealth (Ar. Nub. 815):

ἀλλ' ἔσθ' ἐλθὼν τοὺς Μεγακλέους κίονας      | well, go and eat up Megacles's columns

In the atrium of Nicobulus's house also were columns; these might upon occasion serve other purposes than that of supporting the roof of the impluvium (Pl. Bac. 822–823):

      abducite hunc
      intro atque adstringite ad columnam fortiter

The great Mycenaean palace all under one roof, like those at Tiryns and Cnossus, had no close neighbors with whom to share a party wall.   Even the detached dwellings of Homeric Troy are not built up against one another.   But in classical times, houses in the city, where building sites were more expensive, were built close together, and two frequently had one party wall in common.[2]   Thus in the Miles Gloriosus, the Captain has chanced to secure a lodging for his sweetheart Philocomasium that is immediately next door to the home of her lover's friend and host, and there is a party wall between them[3] (Pl. Mi., Arg. I 6):

      geminis communem . . . parietem in aedibus

[1] Cf. Pl. Mil. 159; 173; 553.  From the wide-spreading opening of the impluvium, the ladies of the period represented by the original of Plautus's Epidicus called their crinolines "skylight skirts" (224–225):
      EP. Impluviatam, ut istaec faciunt vestimentis nomina.
      PE. Ut in impluvium induta fuerit?
[2] Cf. Thuc. II 3, 3; Is. 60, 17.
[3] So in Menander's Phasma there was a party wall between the homes of two neighbors (Donatus ad. Ter. Eun. 9).

and Palaestrio, the confidential slave, bores a hole through the wall so that the lovers may meet clandestinely (Pl. Mi. 142–143):

> in eo conclavid ego perfodi parietem,
> qua commeatus clam esset hinc huc mulieri

These two houses also had a continuous roof, which plays an important part in Act II of the Miles.

The Mycenaean palace, furthermore, is provided with clothes-presses, closets, like the palaces of the Iliad. In the Iliad (Z 288–289) Hecabe, in order to bring forth the appeasing gift for Athena, "went down [from the ὑπερῷον (?)] into a fragrant chamber, where she had robes all richly wrought, the handiwork of Sidonian women." The clothes-press is a chamber; it is fragrant. We are not told of what it was redolent, but it may well have been of cedar wood which was used as a means of preserving. We are the safer in making this assumption in view of the definite statement in Ω 191–192, where Priam, to bring forth in his turn appeasing gifts for Achilles, "went down into a fragrant chamber, of cedar wood, high-roofed, that contained many pieces of finery." Apparently, this is the same chamber as that to which Hecabe in Z went to fetch the peplus for Athena; for there were quantities of feminine apparel there,[1] and from it Priam brought out for Achilles dozens of pieces of women's apparel. We have then in the Homeric palace at Troy a great closet paneled with cedar wood. And such a one, too, we have at the palace of Admetus in Pherae. For, in preparing for her own obsequies, Alcestis brought out from such a store-room the raiment and the jewels, to deck herself for her burial (Eur. Alc. 160–161):

| | |
|---|---|
| ἐκ δ’ ἐλοῦσα κεδρίνων δόμων | and from rooms of cedar wood she took |
| ἐσθῆτα κόσμον τ’ εὐπρεπῶς ἠσκήσατο | raiment and ornaments and decked herself becomingly |

This palace also had its store-chamber paneled with cedar wood to guard its contents against moths and decay.

As Hecabe and Priam went down into the store-rooms of the Trojan palace, we may assume that these were in the deeper recesses of the house. And so they are also at Mycenae, as we may safely infer from Aeschylus's use of μυχόθεν (Ag. 96):

| | |
|---|---|
| πελάνῳ μυχόθεν βασιλείῳ | massy drops from the royal store within |

The oil here referred to was kept in a closet in the inner recesses of the palace. Such closets were sometimes so far in the innermost recesses of the house that they were absolutely dark. A dark closet of that kind, admitting not a ray of light, Dejanira seems to have had in her home at Trachis (Soph. Tr. 685–686):

| | |
|---|---|
| τὸ φάρμακον τοῦτ’ ἄπυρον ἀκτῖνός τ’ ἀεὶ | this drug [he bade me] store away in the innermost |
| θερμῆς ἄθικτον ἐν μυχοῖς σώζειν | part of the house, where no firelight or warm ray of sun could reach it. |

And in such a closet she preserved it against that fatal day.

By those "dwelling-places of cedar" in the Alcestis some interpreters are inclined to understand cedar chests. If that interpretation be correct, we would naturally associate with them in our minds such boxes as the famous cedar chest of Cypselus at Olympia, with its elaborate wealth of sculptured decoration.[2] Large chests of that sort are mentioned in tragedy but once; they play a more frequent part in the comedy. They are 1) clothes-chests (Soph. Tr. 691–692):

| | |
|---|---|
| κάθηκα συμπτύξασ’ ἀλαμπὲς ἡλίου | I folded up the gift and laid it away safe |
| κοίλῳ ζυγάστρῳ δῶρον | from the sunlight, in the depths of a chest |

(Pl. Men. 691):

> [pallam] in loculos compingite

(*ibid.* 803):

> at ille suppilat mihi . . . pallas ex arcis

---

[1] Z 289–295.
[2] Paus. V 17, 5– 19, 10;  Cp. Overbeck, *Gr. Pl.*⁴, I pp. 64 ff.;  Frazer, *Paus.* III pp. 600–620, and the literature there cited.

2) chests for the safe-keeping of gold plate (Pl. Amph. 420):

> [patera aurea] est in cistula[1]

(Ter. Eun. 754):

> [cistella cum crepundiis] in risco [sita est]

3) money chests (Pl. Aul. 823):[2]

> LYC. . . . .
> ubi id est aurum?
> L. S.   In arca apud me

It will be noted that these large chests are called variously arca, loculus, riscus,[3] cistula, and even cistella.   But such a chest might be large enough for a grown person to hide in (like the chest of Cypselus in the Heraeum) or under (Pl. Cas. 664):

> omnes sub arcis, sub lectis latentes

The maker of wooden chests was called in Latin an arcularius (Pl. Aul. 518).

Not unlike such a chest of cedar were the cedar coffins occasionally mentioned in both the tragedy (Eur. Alc. 365; Or. 1053; Tro. 1141) and the comedy (Ar. Lys. 600; Vesp. 1365). That even these coffins for the dead might be decorated with works of art is suggested by the phrase in the passage cited from the Orestes (1053):

> καὶ μνῆμα δέξαιθ' ἕν, κέδρου τεχνάσματα      |   and one tomb receive, cedarn craft of art

When the wrathful matron in Plautus's Asinaria calls her false husband carnufex, capuli decus (892), she obviously is not thinking of any sort of decoration for his coffin save that which should be provided by the old man's dead body.

We have no description of any decoration upon such a coffin as that suggested in the Orestes; but Pausanias's description of the Chest of Cypselus and the magnificent sarcophagi in Constantinople suggest what Euripides may have had in mind.

[1] Cf. also Pl. Amph. 773; 783; 792.
[2] Cf. also 830; Bac. 943.
[3] Cf. also Antiph. Κυб., Frag. 130 K.:
> ῥίσκος ἦν ὃν εἶπεν

AGAMEMNON'S TOMB AT MYCENAE

# VI. MYCENAEAN TOMBS

With the Mycenaean palace we may include also the Mycenaean tomb. The tomb of Proteus is the central feature of the scene of Euripides's Helen,[1] before the eyes of the spectators throughout the play. It is located just outside the palace gates (1165–1168):

| | |
|---|---|
| ὦ χαῖρε πατρὸς μνῆμ'· ἐπ' ἐξόδοισι γὰρ | all hail, my father's tomb. For at the gates did I |
| ἔθαψα, Πρωτεῦ, σ' ἔνεκ' ἐμῆς προσρήσεως· | bury thee, Proteus, to receive my greeting thus; |
| ἀεὶ δὲ ἐξιών τε κεἰσιὼν δόμους | and ever, as I leave or enter my home, lo, |
| Θεοκλύμενος παῖς ὅδε προσεννέπει, πάτερ | thy son, Theoclymenus, father, pays his respects to thee |

It is built of stone (961–962):

| | |
|---|---|
| λέξω τάδ' ἀμφὶ μνῆμα σοῦ πατρὸς πεσών· | this will I utter upon my knees beside thy father's tomb: |
| ὦ γέρον, ὃς οἰκεῖς τόνδε λάϊνον τάφον | oh Sire, who dwellest in this tomb of stone |

Sophocles states the same simple fact in regard to Antigone's tomb (Ant. 1204–1205):[2]

| | |
|---|---|
| πρὸς λιθόστρωτον κόρης | we went up and proceeded to enter the |
| νυμφεῖον ῞Αιδου κοῖλον εἰσεβαίνομεν | maiden's hollow stone-built bridal-chamber of death |

Other passages bring before us the heaping up of the earthen mound above the kernel of heavy masonry (Eur. I. T. 702):[3]

| | |
|---|---|
| τύμβον τε χῶσον κἄπιθες μνημεῖά μοι | and heap up a tomb for me and place upon it memorials of me |

In this one line we find expressed the whole spirit of the Greek gravestone, from the days of Homer to the late classical period. Elpenor's ghost begs Odysseus to heap up for him a barrow on the shore of the gray sea and to set up upon it an oar, wherewith he used to row when he was alive with his comrades.[4] And so the beautiful Attic sepulchral reliefs of the fifth and fourth centuries are memorials, in the truest sense, of the departed, characteristic of them as they were wont to appear in their daily life among their friends.

Still again, we have the finished product of the heaping up of the tomb (Eur. Hec. 220–221):

| | |
|---|---|
| παῖδα τὴν Πολυξένην | to slay thy child Polyxena |
| σφάξαι πρὸς ὀρθὸν χῶμ' 'Αχιλλείου τάφου | at the grave-mound height of Achilles's tomb |

Euripides may well have been familiar with the traditional tomb of Achilles at Sigeum, so familiar to all travelers who have sailed into the Hellespont. And Seneca also was familiar with the great conical mound of earth, with its core of Mycenaean masonry, rising conspicuously close by the ancient shore-line of the Hellespont and the steeply sloping hill of Rhoeteum, where reposed the bones and ashes of the great Achilles (Sen. Tro. 1120–1124; 1148–1150):[5]

> idem ille populus aliud ad facinus redit
> tumulumque Achillis. cuius extremum latus
> Rhoetea leni verberant fluctu vada;
> adversa cingit campus et clivo levi
> erecta medium vallis includens locum.
>
> . . .
>
> ut primum ardui
> sublime montis tetigit atque alte edito
> iuvenis paterni vertice in busti stetit

[1] It finds direct mention many times: for example, 64, 315, 324, 466, 528, 544, 551, 556, 797, 842, 962, 981, 984, 986, 1009, 1084, 1086, 1165–1168, 1178, 1203, 1228. Ar. Thes. (885–886) quotes Eur. Hel. 466.
[2] Cf. Eur. El. 327–328: ἐνθρώσκει τάφῳ
　　πέτροις τε λεύει μνῆμα λάϊνον πατρός.
[3] Eur. Ion 388; Or. 116; 402; 1585; Ar. Ran. 1172.
[4] λ 71–78; μ 14–15.
[5] Cf. also lines 180; 196; 361; 940; 1164.

With these passages a monument of the type of the so-called Tomb of Agamemnon or Treasury of Atreus at Mycenae begins to assume shape before our mental vision. It becomes still more real when we read (Eur. Alc. 835–836):

| | |
|---|---|
| ὀρθὴν παρ' οἶμον, ἢ 'πὶ Λάρισσαν φέρει, | beside the road that leads straight toward Larissa |
| τύμβον κατόψει ξεστὸν ἐκ προαστίου | thou shalt come in sight of a polished tomb just outside the town |

Mycenae, especially the Tomb of Clytaemnestra ("Mrs. Schliemann's Tomb") with its perfectly polished walls, is recalled still more vividly with these two lines: the great tomb built of polished stone, just outside the fortress walls, close beside the direct road that leads toward Larissa, which is also the Mycenaean name of the citadel of Argos. The poets apply the epithet "polished" to such structures as if it were characteristic of them. Euripides employs it also of the tomb of Proteus in Egypt (Hel. 986):

| | |
|---|---|
| νεκρὼ δύ' ἐξῆς τῷδ' ἐπὶ ξεστῷ τάφῳ | corpses twain together on this polished tomb |

And over there at Argos was another Mycenaean tomb. We may have an allusion to the grave of the unhappy daughters of Danaus, also built of that same polished masonry, in the Bellerophon of Euripides (Frag. 305 N.):

| | |
|---|---|
| καὶ ξεστὸν ὄχθον Δαναϊδῶν ἐδρασμάτων | and the polished slope of the Danaids' resting-place . . . |
| στὰς ἐν μέσοισιν εἶπε κηρύκων <ὕπο>[1] | standing in the midst he spake by the voice of heralds |

With this "polished slope," if, indeed, we are dealing with a tomb and not a palace,[2] the beehive construction begins to assume form; with ὄχθον the poet draws a picture of the lofty vault, covered over with débris and overgrown. One such possible tomb has been discovered at Argos; and one such at least must have been known to Euripides; for even his Scholiast knew of it.[2]

On the southeast slope of the northeast spur[3] of the hill of Larissa there has been found what appears to have been a beehive tomb of the Mycenaean period. It has a δρόμος sixty-five feet long leading to a circular chamber in the depths of the hill. The walls of this δρόμος, however, are not polished but roughly hewn stones. And in another respect they are unlike the more famous tombs of Mycenae; the walls are not vertical but approach each other like the upper courses of the so-called Tirynthian arch. In this feature they resemble closely the many tombs cut into the solid hillside at Mycenae, without any veneering of carefully cut stone.

This subterranean structure may be identified with one of the monuments "starred" by Pausanias among the notable sights of Argos (II 23, 7):

| | |
|---|---|
| ἄλλα δέ ἐστιν Ἀργείοις θέας ἄξια· | Argos has other things worth seeing: there used to be |
| κατάγεων οἰκοδόμημα, ἐπ' αὐτῷ δὲ | an underground building and over it a |
| ἦν ὁ χαλκοῦς θάλαμος, ὃν Ἀκρίσιός | chamber of bronze that Acrisius once had |
| ποτε ἐπὶ φρουρᾷ τῆς θυγατρὸς ἐποίησε· | made in which to keep his daughter. |
| Περίλαος δὲ καθεῖλεν αὐτὸν τυραννήσας. | But when Perilaus became king, he had it destroyed. . . . |
| . . . . Κρησίου δὲ ὕστερον ὠνομάσθη, | It later received the name of Cretan, |
| διότι Ἀριάδνην ἀποθανοῦσαν ἔθαψαν ἐνταῦθα | because, when Ariadne died, they buried her in it |

If it is to be identified with the vault of Danae's imprisonment, it may or may not be identical with the monument of the daughters of Danaus mentioned by Euripides in the Bellerophon.[4] There are, of course, no traces left of the bronze plates or, rather, bronze rosettes that gave it its epithets as *turris aënea*[5] or χαλκοῦς θάλαμος. But at Argos must have been such a tomb with the bronze upon its walls; we have palpable evidence of such decoration on the walls of the principal chamber of the so-called Treasury of Atreus at Mycenae. We have a

[1] Supplied by Cobet.
[2] See p. 199 above.
[3] Probably to be identified with Pausanias's "Diras" (II 24, 1).
[4] Quoted above.
[5] Hor. Car. III 16, 1.

similarly elaborate and rich system of decoration also at Argos, attested both by Pausanias, in the passage just quoted, by Horace, in his *turris aënea*,[1] and by the general tradition, and also by Sophocles (Ant. 944–947):

| | |
|---|---|
| ἔτλα καὶ Δανάας οὐράνιον φῶς | and Danae in her beauty was made to exchange the |
| ἀλλάξαι δέμας ἐν χαλκοδέτοις αὐλαῖς· | light of heaven for a bronze-covered lodge; and |
| κρυπτομένα δ' ἐν τυμβήρει θαλάμῳ κατεζεύχθη | buried in a tomblike chamber she was securely imprisoned |

In a similar way, the tomb in which Antigone was immured, is called a chamber—a bridal chamber—in Sophocles's Antigone (1206–1207):

| | |
|---|---|
| ὀρθίων κωκυμάτων | one of us heard loud shrieks |
| κλύει τις ἀκτέριστον ἀμφὶ παστάδα | coming from the direction of the unhallowed chamber |

Thus far, then, we have from our tragic poets a fairly clear picture corresponding absolutely with the great vaulted beehive tombs of Mycenae and Orchomenus, great mounds with polished walls of masonry, with and without the adorning pieces of bronze upon the smoothly finished courses of stone.

The lofty, spacious, vaulted chamber of the beehive tomb is suggested again in Antigone's pathetic apostrophe to her burial place (*ibid.* 891–893):

| | |
|---|---|
| ὦ τύμβος, νυμφεῖον, ὦ κατασκαφῆς | oh tomb, my bridal chamber, oh vaulted |
| οἴκησις ἀείφρουρος, οἷ πορεύομαι | home forever guarding me, to which |
| πρὸς τοὺς ἐμαυτῆς | I go to join mine own |

The same form is suggested once more where Antigone says (Soph. Ant. 848–849):

| | |
|---|---|
| πρὸς ἔργμα τυμβόχυστον ἔρχομαι | to the moundlike prison of my |
| τάφου ποταινίου | strange tomb I go |

and a little further on Creon mentions the grave (885–886) as

| | |
|---|---|
| κατηρεφεῖ | her vaulted |
| τύμβῳ προσπτύξαντες | tomb enclosing her |

Such tombs must necessarily be underground. And a standing epithet might be κατῶρυξ[2] (for example, Soph. Ant. 1100–1101):

| | |
|---|---|
| ἐλθὼν κόρην μὲν ἐκ κατώρυχος στέγης ἄνες | go, set the maiden free from her subterranean dwelling |

Being underground, they must have also a practical means of approach. In the reality, at Mycenaean sites, we have the familiar δρόμος, the long passage-way, cutting the hillock or mound down to the level of the threshold of the door of the tomb. The vaulted chamber was secured both by locking its own great doors and also by closing up the outer entrance to the δρόμος. Did we not have the reality, we should not easily comprehend the poets' allusions to this feature of the Mycenaean tomb; but, with the marvelous "treasuries" of Mycenae, both the poets and the tombs are better understood (Ant. 1215–1217; 1220–1221):

| | |
|---|---|
| παραστάντες τάφῳ | take your places by the grave and |
| ἀθρήσαυ, ἁρμὸν χώματος λιθοσπαδῆ | look; make your way into the stone-drawn fitting |
| δύντες πρὸς αὐτὸ στόμιον . . . . . . . . | —clear up to the very mouth of the vault |
| . . . . . . . . . | . . . . . . . . . |
| ἠθροῦμεν. ἐν δὲ λοισθίῳ τυμβεύματι | We looked; and in the innermost part of the tomb-chamber |
| τὴν μὲν κρεμαστὴν αὐχένος κατείδομεν | we beheld her hanged by the neck |

In the light of what we know, particularly at Mycenae, we can fairly see Creon's attendants come up to the entrance to the δρόμος, work their way through the opening that Haemon had made by pulling out some of the stones in the masonry that had been laid to block that entrance and locked and sealed up when Antigone had been immured within, penetrating

---

[1] Car. III 16, 1.
[2] Cp. also Soph. Ant. 774, discussed pp. 238–239.

to the doorway (αὐτὸ στόμιον) of the beehive, peering through the dim interior into the tomb-chamber, and seeing the terrible climax of Antigone's tragic life within. For thus, surely, the Sophoclean passage is to be interpreted. The tomb-chamber (τύμβευμα) is the first suggestion in the passages thus far cited of more than one chamber in the Mycenaean tomb. The Treasury of Atreus is our positive proof of the existence of such an arrangement. And the correctness of our interpretation of the passage in the Antigone is further established by a passage from Euripides's Phaethon (Frag. 781, 8–10 N.):

| | |
|---|---|
| 　　　　　κρύψω δέ νιν | and I will lay him away in |
| ξεστοῖσι θαλάμοις, ἔνθ' ἐμῷ κεῖται πόσει | polished chambers where my husband's gold is |
| χρυσός· μόνη δὲ κλῆθρ' ἐγὼ σφραγίζομαι | stored; and I alone seal up the locks |

In this one passage, in the very fewest words, we have the tomb built in smoothly surfaced masonry, with its plural (equivalent to dual?) chambers, its seal upon the locks upon the doors. And, striking corroboration of the double names of "Treasury" and "Tomb," the tomb is also the place where the prince's treasures of gold are stored. The beehive tombs were treasure-houses and doubtless once contained treasures of gold richer even than the finds in the shaft-graves of Mycenae suggest.

In all probability honors were paid to the dead in those pre-Hellenic times, even as in classical times. This we may assume; the tragic poet assumed it, too (Eur. Hel. 546–547):

| | |
|---|---|
| σὲ τὴν ὄρεγμα δεινὸν ἡμιλλημένην | thou that with fearful effort strugglest on to the steps and |
| τύμβου 'πὶ κρηπῖδ' ἐμπύρους τ' ὀρθοστάτας | upright block of the altar of burnt sacrifice |

At the tomb of Proteus, at which Helen has taken refuge, is an altar of the regulation type, with steps and raised block, on which sacrifice was offered to the spirit of the dead. A like arrangement we may safely assume for every Mycenaean tomb. In the opening scene of Sophocles's Electra, Orestes is to go to his father's tomb and pour libations and crown it with the glory of severed hair (51–53); and there upon the summit (not at an altar) of the mound Chrysothemis later discovers her brother's offerings to their long-buried father (894–896; 901–902):[1]

| | |
|---|---|
| ὁρῶ κολώνης ἐξ ἄκρας νεορρύτους | I saw streams of milk that had newly flowed from |
| πηγὰς γάλακτος καὶ περιστεφῆ κύκλῳ | the top of the mound and our father's grave crowned |
| πάντων ὅσ' ἔστιν ἀνθέων θήκην πατρός | about with wreaths of all the flowers we have |
| .　.　.　.　.　.　.　.　.　.　. | .　.　.　.　.　.　.　.　.　.　. |
| .　.　. ἐσχάτης δ' ὁρῶ | . . . and at the side of the tomb I saw |
| πυρᾶς νεώρη βόστρυχον τετμημένον | a lock of hair newly shorn |

It may be, however, that Sophocles is here guilty of an anachronism and that his words are more readily applicable to a grave of the fifth century type. But the poets more than once speak of offerings made upon the top of the high-heaped barrows of Homeric heroes. Thus Polyxena was sacrificed upon the height of the mound, while the host of the Achaeans stood "before the tomb" (Eur. Hec. 521–524):

| | |
|---|---|
| παρῆν μὲν ὄχλος πᾶς Ἀχαϊκοῦ στρατοῦ | and all the host of the Achaean army was there |
| πλήρης πρὸ τύμβου σῆς κόρης ἐπὶ σφαγάς· | in full numbers before the tomb to witness the sacrifice of thy daughter; |
| λαβὼν δ' Ἀχιλλέως παῖς Πολυξένην χερὸς | then Achilles's son took Polyxena by the hand |
| ἔστησ' ἐπ' ἄκρου χώματος | and placed her upon the height of the mound |

The beehive tombs of Mycenae are, most of them, like the tomb of Alcestis and the tomb of Proteus in Euripides, close beside the principal road leading to the feudal castle. But some of those at Mycenae are across the hill on the western slope far out of sight from any part of the palace. In like manner Creon threatens to put Antigone out of the way, burying her alive in a vault far removed, where no human footfall ever comes (Soph. Ant. 773–774):

| | |
|---|---|
| ἄγων ἔρημος ἔνθ' ἂν ᾖ βροτῶν στίβος | I will take thee away to a place where no human foot-step ever |
| κρύψω πετρώδει ζῶσαν ἐν κατώρυχι | comes and bury thee alive in a rock-cut vault |

[1] Cf. Eur. El. 90–92; 324–325; 511–515; Or. 124–125; 1187; 1321–1322.

And yet, as a matter of fact, this part of the threat was not carried out.  Creon, in the heat of his first wrath against his niece, is determined to make the punishment of her crime as horrible as possible, putting her to death in the presence of her lover, and including her innocent sister also in the vengeance for the violated law.  These latter extremes are omitted.  And the site finally selected for her living entombment was, while far away, yet in sight from the Theban palace (Soph. Ant. 1108–1110):

| | |
|---|---|
| ἴτ᾿, ἴτ᾿, ὀπάονες,<br>οἵ τ᾿ ὄντες οἵ τ᾿ ἀπόντες, ἀξίνας χεροῖν<br><br>ὁρμᾶσθ᾿ ἑλόντες εἰς ἐπόψιον τόπον | go, attendants, go,<br>both ye that are here and ye that are not; take pick-axes<br>in your hands and hurry to yon spot far seen |

## 1. The Niobideum at Thebes

Near the Proetidian gate of Thebes, between the modern suburb of Ἅγιοι Θεόδωροι and the Cadmea, stood a group of tombs (Paus. IX 16, 7):

| | |
|---|---|
| Σεμέλης μνῆμά ἐστιν....<br>Θηβαίοις δὲ ἐνταῦθα καὶ τὰ<br>μνήματα πεποίηται τῶν<br>Ἀμφίονος παίδων, χωρὶς<br>μὲν τῶν ἀρσένων, ἰδίᾳ δὲ<br>ταῖς παρθένοις | there is Semele's tomb. . . .<br>And here also the Thebans had<br>constructed the tombs of Am-<br>phion's children, the sons in<br>one place and the daughters in<br>a place by themselves |

A hundred yards away were the remains of the funeral pyres on which the bodies of the unhappy Niobids were burned (Paus. IX 17, 2):

| | |
|---|---|
| ἀπέχει δὲ ἡ πυρὰ τῶν Ἀμφίονος<br>παίδων ἥμισυ σταδίου μάλιστα<br>ἀπὸ τῶν τάφων· μένει δὲ ἡ<br>τέφρα καὶ ἐς τόδε ἔτι ἀπὸ<br>τῆς πυρᾶς | the funeral pyre of Amphion's<br>children is at most half a stadium<br>from their tombs; and the ashes<br>from the pyre are left unto<br>this day |

It is the group of tombs near the Proetidian gate that Euripides recalls in the opening scene of the Phoenissae, where the old paedagogus points out to Antigone the different heroes of the hostile army (159–160):

| | |
|---|---|
| ἐκεῖνος[1] ἑπτὰ παρθένων τάφου πέλας<br>Νιόβης Ἀδράστῳ πλησίον παραστατεῖ | there he [1] is, standing beside Adrastus,<br>near the tomb of Niobe's seven daughters |

Euripides confirms apparently the statement of Pausanias that the girls had a tomb separate from that of the boys.

Near the banks of the Ismenus, just outside the northeast gate of the city, stood seven structures of stone with no firmer foundation than the soil on which they were erected.  These, according to the history of Thebes by Armenidas (F. H. G. III 329), marked the site of the funeral pyres of either the seven heroes or the seven children [sons] of Niobe.  Inasmuch as only four of the seven heroes found burial at Thebes,[2] the decision would seem to be easy in favor of the Niobids.  And yet the Theban Pindar more than once speaks of seven pyres as if they were the ones on which the corpses of the seven heroes were burned at Thebes (Ol. 6, 15):

| | |
|---|---|
| ἑπτὰ δ᾿ ἔπειτα πυρᾶν νεκρῶν τελεσθεισᾶν<br>　　　　　　　　　Ταλαϊονίδας<br>εἶπεν ἐν Θήβαις | and when the full tale of the seven pyres of the<br>dead had been made up, Talaus's son<br>spake at Thebes |

(Nem. 9, 24):

| | |
|---|---|
| ἑπτὰ γὰρ δαίσαντο πυραὶ νεογυίους φῶτας | for seven pyres feasted on the men with limbs of<br>youth |

[1] Polynices.

[2] The whole plot of the Suppliants of Euripides turns upon the burial of the bodies of the Argive dead. The sole survivor of the seven, Adrastus, is one of the persons of the drama; the corpses of five are brought in for burial (861; 872; 881; 889; 901); Amphiaraus had been swallowed up by the earth, Adrastus is living, but *seven* are finally buried (1207)!

The fact that, according to another tradition, the children of Niobe were slain on the slopes of Mount Cithaeron affords not the slightest argument against their having been buried by the gates of their royal city. As the Proetidian Gate in question was the northeast gate of the Cadmea, the tombs of Niobe's children must have been somewhere on the eastern slope of the Cadmean hill below the Amphium, or in the western face of the hills known to-day as τὰ Καστέλλια; and there on the higher hill, at a considerable distance apart, Keramopoullos[1] excavated two Mycenaean tombs, and two only, with dromos and burial chamber, though there are probably more there, and still more on Ismenus hill and in the face of the hills to the south of Thebes.[2] Both the Mycenaean tombs in the face of the Castellia would have been visible from the roof of the royal palace on the summit of the Cadmea.

The Scholiast, commenting on the Euripidean passage, quotes Aristodemus, a Theban historian (F. H. G. III 309), only to contradict his assertion that there was no Niobid tomb whatever at Thebes, ὅπερ ἐστὶν ἀληθές. It is impossible to reconcile this direct contradiction with the testimony of Aristodemus. With the corroborative statements of so many credible witnesses, we must accept the Scholiast's decisive "but there is"; and Hellanicus, too, obtains his hebdomad of Niobids from the seven pyres at Thebes.

The Niobe of Aeschylus, if it were preserved to us, would probably add nothing to our knowledge of the topography of Thebes, for the scene of the Aeschylean drama seems to have been laid not at Thebes but in Lydia (Frags. 157–159 N.). Sophocles, on the other hand, if he is the poet to whom Aristotle alludes (Poet. 18), might throw light upon the question if we had his Niobe; but less than two lines are preserved from it.

The vase painter who designed the representation of the tomb of the Niobids upon the beautiful Ruvo amphora[3] in the Museo Nazionale in Naples made no pretensions, of course, at reproducing the actually existing monument at Thebes. The vase-painting was made to tell its own story—inspired, perhaps, by Aeschylus's Niobe: the centre is occupied by an Ionic, gabled roof borne by four delicate columns resting upon a base adorned with rich arabesques; the sorrowing queen stands between the columns; in attitude of sympathy Antiope (?) appears at one side sitting, Tantalus at the other side standing; attendants wait on either side and below; above appear five divinities—Leto with Apollo and Artemis, Zeus with Hermes.

## 2. The Zetheum at Thebes

Only a little distance from the Niobideum was the tomb of Zethus and Amphion. Pausanias passes immediately from the pyre of Amphion's children to this monument (IX 17, 4–7):

| | |
|---|---|
| Ζήθῳ δὲ μνῆμα καὶ Ἀμφίονι ἐν κοινῷ γῆς χῶμά ἐστιν οὐ μέγα. | Zethus and Amphion have a tomb in common—a mound of earth not large. |
| . . . . . . . | . . . . . . . |
| τοὺς δὲ παρὰ τὸ Ἀμφίονος μνῆμα λίθους, οἳ κάτωθεν ὑποβέβληνται, μήτε ἄλλως εἰργασμένοι πρὸς τὸ ἀκριβέστατον, ἐκείνας εἶναί φασι τὰς πέτρας αἳ τῇ ᾠδῇ τοῦ Ἀμφίονος ἠκολούθησαν | As for the stones at Amphion's tomb (those which are laid at the base and are not wrought with any particular finish)—these, they say, are the very rocks that followed Amphion's singing |

Ulrichs[4] and Fabricius[5] locate the tomb of Amphion upon the hillock just below the Cadmea, between the modern town and the railway station of Thebes.[6] On that hillock we may look for the Amphium, the sanctuary of Amphion inside the city, mentioned by

---

[1] Ἀρχ. Δελτ. III (1917) pp. 108–109. On p. 395 he suggests that the two hills themselves are the monuments of the two sons of Oedipus.

[2] Keramopoullos opened no less than twenty-eight late Minoan tombs on the sides of Κολωνάκι hill alone, just south of the modern city.

[3] Published in Roscher, Myth. Lex., s. v. Niobe, Sp. 407–408.

[4] Reisen und Forschungen, II p. 17.

[5] Theben, pp. 19 and 31.

[6] And there the investigations of Keramopoullos have more exactly established the Amphium—γῆς χῶμα οὐ μέγα, an artificially raised mound upon a greyish stratum, which in turn lies upon the conglomerate mass that forms the body of the hill. And below the Amphium, thus bringing it clearly within the walls of the Cadmea, he found remains of the Cyclopean walls of the citadel (Ἀρχ. Δελτ. III [1917] pp. 385–387).

Xenophon[1] and Plutarch[2] and Arrian.[3] But the tragic poets forbid our confusing the Amphium inside the city with the tomb of Zethus and Amphion outside the walls. Euripides, in the same scene in which the tomb of the Niobids is pointed out to Antigone, passes on to another figure in the marshalling hosts before the city (Ph. 145–146):

| | |
|---|---|
| τίς δ' οὗτος ἀμφὶ μνῆμα τὸ Ζήθου περᾷ<br>καταββόστρυχος; | who is yon hero with the curling locks<br>passing by Zethus's tomb? |

Accordingly, the tomb of Zethus (and Amphion) is not very far from the Proetidian Gate of the ancient city. Indeed, the Scholiast on this passage says explicitly:

| | |
|---|---|
| κοινὸς μὲν ἀμφοῖν ὁ τάφος, Ζήθου<br>καὶ 'Αμφίονος, συλληπτικῶς δὲ εἶπεν.<br>τινὲς δέ φασι τὸν 'Αμφίονα πρὸς<br>ταῖς Προιτίσι.... | a common tomb of both, Zethus<br>and Amphion; he uses the word collectively.<br>Some, however, say that Amphion [was<br>buried] by the Proetidian . . . |

Again we have the double tradition—a tomb at the Proetidian Gate; another consecrated place somewhere else.

With the help of Aeschylus we may locate the spot outside the city a little more accurately (Sep. 526–529):

| | |
|---|---|
| τὸν πέμπτον αὖ λέγω<br>Παρθενοπαῖον 'Αρκάδ', 'Αταλάντης γόνον,<br>πέμπταισι προσταχθέντα βορραίας πύλαις<br>τύμβον κατ' αὐτὸν Διογενοῦς 'Αμφίονος | and now I name the fifth,<br>Parthenopaeus of Arcadia, Atalanta's child,<br>assigned to the fifth—the northern gate—<br>right at the tomb of Amphion, Zeus's son |

By the "northern" gate Aeschylus cannot mean the Proetidian Gate. He must mean the Crenaean; for he has already placed the first named of his seven heroes, Tydeus, at the Proetidian Gate (Sep. 377–379):

| | |
|---|---|
| Τυδεὺς μὲν ἤδη πρὸς Πύλαισι Προιτίσιν<br>βρέμει, πόρον δ' 'Ισμηνὸν οὐκ ἐᾷ περᾶν<br>ὁ μάντις | even now Tydeus is thundering before the<br>  Proetidian<br>Gate; but the seer forbids his crossing Ismenus's<br>stream |

The Proetidian Gate known to Aeschylus is obviously at the northeast corner of the city, not far from the stream of Ismenus: Tydeus may thunder at the gate but he may not cross the stream, not because it is inside the Mycenaean city wall, for, as we shall see, it is not; but the seer had some deeper reason for forbidding such a movement. The Argive army has come from Teumessus,[4] to the east of Thebes; the Proetidian is the first gate they would approach from that side.

At all events, it is clear from the agreement between the two poets that they were conscientiously accurate in dealing with the features of familiar topography; and by their help we not only distinguish between the Amphium of the inner city and the tomb of the hero brothers outside the walls, but we also locate the common tomb of Zethus and Amphion on the north side of the city outside the Proetidian Gate of Thebes, and nearer to the Crenaean Gate than to the Proetidian.

In the famous passage in Euripides's Suppliants 650 ff., describing the battle between the Athenians under Theseus and the Thebans, Euripides has intentionally transported us away from the topography of his own day, with the wide circuit of walls of the classical city, to the Cadmean fortress of the days in which his scene is set. The messenger from Thebes has come to the suppliant women at Eleusis; he recites how he had climbed a high tower by the Electran Gate, looked over across the intervening valley, and seen the army of Theseus ranged in three divisions against the town: Theseus with the centre occupied the hill of Ismenus; the left stretched from the Ismenium round the southern side of the citadel toward the spring of Ares, flanked by the cavalry; the right wing held the line of hills running

[1] Hel. V 4, 8.
[2] de Gen. Soc. 4.
[3] An. I 8, 6.
[4] Eur. Ph. 1098–1100.

from the Ismenium to the north and on that flank were drawn up the chariots on the comparatively level ground northeast of the modern town, below the memorial of Amphion:[1]

| | |
|---|---|
| ἀμφὶ δ' Ἠλέκτρας πύλας<br>ἔστην θεατής, πύργον εὐαυγῆ[2] λαβών. | and at the Electran gate I took<br>my stand upon a commanding tower to view the scene. |
| ὁρῶ δὲ φῦλα τρία τριῶν στρατευμάτων·<br>τευχεσφόρον μὲν λαὸν ἐκτείνοντ' ἄνω<br>Ἰσμήνιον πρὸς ὄχθον, ὡς μὲν ἦν λόγος,[3]<br>αὐτόν τ' ἄνακτα, παῖδα κλεινὸν Αἰγέως<br>καὶ τοὺς ξὺν αὐτῷ· δεξιὸν τεταγμένους | And I saw the three tribes and divisions three:<br>a host in armor clad extending upward<br>to Ismenus' hill (so men said[3]),<br>and the king himself, Aegeus's famous son,<br>and those with him; on the right wing were drawn up |
| κέρας παλαιοὺς Κεκροπίας οἰκήτορας·<br>λαιὸν[4] δὲ Πάραλον, ἐστολισμένον δορί. | the folk of Cecrops's ancient land;<br>and on the left were the seaboard men equipped with spears; |
| κρήνην παρ' αὐτὴν δ' Ἄρεος ἱππότην ὄχλον | and by the spring of Ares were drawn up the troops of horsemen, |
| πρὸς κρασπέδοισι στρατοπέδου τεταγμένον<br>ἴσους ἀριθμόν· ἁρμάτων δ' ὀχήματα<br>ἔνερθε σεμνῶν μνημάτων Ἀμφίονος | like in number, on the fringes of the<br>host; the lines of chariots were drawn up<br>below Amphion's hallowed monument |

We have here various interesting points in Theban topography: (1) The Gate Electrae,[5] which was in ancient times the southern entrance to the town. It is at this gate also that Pentheus naturally orders the gathering of his troops to march against the Bacchanals who were celebrating their orgies on the slopes of Mount Cithaeron directly to the south of Thebes (Eur. Bac. 780–781):

| | |
|---|---|
| στεῖχ' ἐπ' Ἠλέκτρας ἰὼν<br>πύλας | go, proceed to the Electran<br>Gate |

From a high tower at the southeast corner of the Cadmea, a little to the east of the present gate, the messenger could easily have seen all that he describes. The Messenger in the Phoenissae stresses the nearness of the walls to the field of combat and the ease with which the beleaguered folk within the citadel could know what took place below (Eur. Ph. 1356–1358):

| | |
|---|---|
| τὰ μὲν πρὸ πύργων εὐτυχήματα χθονὸς<br>οἶσθ'· οὐ μακρὰν γὰρ τειχέων περιπτυχαί,<br>ὥστ' οὐχ ἅπαντά σ' εἰδέναι τὰ δρώμενα | our land's successes before the towers thou<br>knowest, for the encircling walls are not so far<br>but that thou knowest everything that goes on |

(2) The hill of Ismenus southeast of the town, where in recent years the foundations of the temple of Ismenian Apollo[6] have been brought to light close by the church of St. Luke; (3) The spring of Ares, by which apparently Euripides understood the now generally accepted spring of Παραπόρτι at the south-west foot of the Cadmea, and not the rival claimant for the name in the gardens of the brothers Δελδιναχιώτης; for the armies of Theseus were assaulting a fortress and facing an army arrayed upon and before the walls it was to defend; (4) Amphion's monument, by which Euripides meant not the tomb of Zethus and Amphion in the plain between the Proetidian and Crenaean gates but the Amphium upon the hillock between the Cadmea and the plains to the north. Nowhere about Cadmean Thebes, save "below Amphion's hallowed monument," could the force of chariots have manoeuvred effectively at all.

The identification of the springs calls for further comment. There has been confusion, early and late. Pausanias certainly found in the Δελδιναχιώτης spring, which irrigates the

---

[1] Wilamowitz-Möllendorff and Way transpose the lines of this passage in the most arbitrary fashion, each to suit his own preconceived idea of what Theban topography ought to be; and the former's idea seems to have been to draw up the chariot force in the deep gulley by the Παραπόρτι spring where they could scarcely have moved in single file in a line parallel to the hostile walls!

[2] εὐαυγῆ: Hemst., for εὐαγῆ.

[3] That is, "such," they said, "was its name." For what the messenger is describing he brings ἐξ αὐτοψίας.

[4] λαιὸν: Markland, for αὐτόν.

[5] The historicity of the Electran Gate in later as well as in earlier times is attested by Pausanias IX 8, 7; Pind. (Isthm. 3, 79); Pherecydes (Anton. Liber. 33); Schol. T 99; Hellanicus, Schol. Ap. Rh. I 916; Schol. Eur. Ph. 7; 1129.

[6] See pp. 173–174; cf. also Paus. IX 10, 2–4.

THE ΔΕΛΒΙΝΑΚΙΩΤΗΣ SPRING AT THEBES

extensive vegetable gardens south of Thebes (or, perhaps, in the Κεφαλάρι spring) the "Spring of Ares" and in the cave beside it the "dragon's cave." He says (IX 10, 5):

| | |
|---|---|
| ἀνωτέρω δὲ τοῦ Ἰσμηνίου τὴν κρήνην ἴδοις | up beyond the Ismenium one may see the spring |
| ἂν ἥντινα Ἄρεώς φασιν ἱερὰν εἶναι καὶ | that they say is sacred to Ares, and they add that |
| δράκοντα ὑπὸ τοῦ Ἄρεως ἐπιτετάχθαι φύλακα | a dragon was set there by Ares at the source |
| τῇ πηγῇ | to guard it |

Evidently each spring and each cave had in ancient as in modern Thebes its partisans supporting its claims to the lawful title of being the genuine "Ares Spring" and "Dragon's Cave"; Pausanias chose the southeast spring, Euripides the southwest. Again in the Phoenissae (931–933) Euripides unequivocally points to the southwest cave as the dragon's cave, and the spring beside it would be the spring of Ares:

| | |
|---|---|
| δεῖ τόνδε θαλάμοις, οὗ δράκων ὁ γηγενὴς | he must, slain, pour as an oblation his red blood |
| ἐγένετο Δίρκης ναμάτων ἐπίσκοπος, | before the den wherein the earth-born dragon was |
| σφαγέντα φόνιον αἷμα γῇ δοῦναι χοάς | made a watcher over Dirce's streams |

The dragon obviously has his abode where he can watch over Dirce's streams. A topographer could hardly be more exact in his description of a place. The most conspicuous features of the landscape, as one faces the Cadmea from the west even to-day, are the great spring, with its eight mouths, at the base of the rock and the spacious cave beside and above it in the face of the Cadmea and Dirce's slender stream into which the spring discharges its crystal water but a few yards away. Euripides, with many passages, makes it perfectly clear that his Ares Spring and the Dragon's Cave are on the Dirce side of the citadel. We have it almost as clearly again (Ph. 645–648; 657–661):

| | |
|---|---|
| καλλιπόταμος ὕδατος ἵνα τε | and where the fair-rippling flood |
| νοτὶς ἐπέρχεται ῥυτᾶς | of water from Dirce's stream |
| Δίρκας χλοηφόρους | spreads over the grain- |
| καὶ βαθυσπόρους γύας | bearing meadows deep in corn |
| . . . . . . . . . . | |
| ἔνθα φόνιος ἦν δράκων | there lay the murderous dragon |
| Ἄρεος, ὠμόφρων φύλαξ | of Ares, a savage warder, |
| νάματ' ἔνυδρα καὶ ῥέεθρα | watching with far-ranging glance |
| χλοερὰ δεργμάτων κόραισι | of his eyes over the water- |
| πολυπλάνοις ἐπισκοπῶν | filled streams and rills |

Again the dragon and Dirce are brought together.

But the young Menoeceus, accepting his appointed fate, is a little more exact in his interpretation of the prophet's topography (Eur. Ph. 1009–1011):

| | |
|---|---|
| ἀλλ' εἶμι καὶ στὰς ἐξ ἐπάλξεων ἄκρων | well, go I will; and I will take my stand upon the bat- |
| σφάξας ἐμαυτὸν σηκὸν ἐς μελαμβαθῆ | tlements' height and spill my blood into the dragon's dark, |
| δράκοντος, ἔνθ' ὁ μάντις ἐξεγήσατο | deep cave, even where the seer declared |

Menoeceus proposes, standing upon the battlements of Thebes, to cut his throat, and let his blood fall into the dragon's cave. And Creon later rescues his son's dead body from the dragon's cliffs (1315–1316):

| | |
|---|---|
| ὃν ἄρτι κρημνῶν ἐκ δρακοντείων ἑλὼν | and I have rescued his self-slain body from the dragon's |
| αὐτοσφαγῆ | cliffs |

There are no cliffs anywhere near the Δελθιναχιώτης spring; but there is a very real precipice on the southwest side of Cadmea immediately above and about the spring and the cave there; and Dirce's streams flow by only a few yards from the cave. Moreover, Menoeceus could not have fallen dead from the tower into a chasm half a mile (or a mile, if Κεφαλάρι is the right fountain) beyond the city walls, and as far away from Dirce's streams which the water of the Δελθιναχιώτης fountain is long in reaching. And it was certainly a tower from which the young prince in his self-immolation plunged to the dragon's cave (1090–1091):

| | |
|---|---|
| Κρέοντος παῖς ὁ γῆς ὑπερθανὼν | Creon's son, who for his country died, |
| πύργων ἐπ' ἄκρων στάς | took his stand upon the towers' height |

And there, near the spring and the cave, just outside the Neïstan Gate, even in Roman times stood the tomb or monument (μνῆμα) of the heroic youth.[1]

In the Antiope Euripides left no possible vestige of doubt that his "Spring of Ares" was the Παραπόρτι spring at the foot of the southwest hill of the Cadmea (Fragment first published in Hermathena 1891, page 47; republished in Hermes XXVI [1891] page 242). Toward the end of the play Hermes (apparently *deus ex machina*) says to Lycus:

| | |
|---|---|
| ὅταν δὲ θάψῃς ἄλοχον εἰς πυρὰν βαλὼν | and when thou doest burial of thy wife, when thou hast collected |
| σαρκῶν ἀθροίσας τῆς ταλαιπόρου φύσιν | the remains of her poor body and laid them on |
| ὀστᾶ πυρώσας Ἄρεος εἰς χρήνην βαλεῖν, | the pyre, burn her bones and cast the ashes into Ares Spring, |
| ὡς ἂν τὸ Δίρχης ὄνομ' ἐπώνυμον λάβῃ | that the outflow from the spring may be called by Dirce's[2] |
| χρήνης ἀπορρούς, ὃς δίεισιν ἄστεως | name, as it passes through the city and forever |
| πεδία τὰ Θήβης ὕδασιν ἐξάρδων ἀεὶ | with its water irrigates Thebe's plains |

There can be no doubt that this Ares spring is the Παραπόρτι spring and not the Δελβινακιώτης spring; the latter does not find its way to the Dircaean stream until it has passed far beyond the Cadmea and even the modern railway line and almost reached the city limits of classical Thebes; the other gushes out hard by the southern city limits, drops almost directly into the Dircaean stream, and mingling with the stream passes clear through the later city and irrigates the gardens of Πυρί and the plains beyond.

### 3. Semele's Tomb at Thebes

Another famous tomb at Thebes was that of Semele, the mother of Bacchus. Her monument seems to have stood on the Cadmea near the palace of the ancient kings. Pausanias makes no mention of the tomb itself; but Euripides introduces it along with the still smouldering ruins of her home (Bac. 5–12):

| | |
|---|---|
| πάρειμι Δίρχης νάματ' Ἰσμηνοῦ θ' ὕδωρ. | I am come to Dirce's streams and Ismenus's waters. |
| ὁρῶ δὲ μητρὸς μνῆμα τῆς κεραυνίας | I see my thunder-blasted mother's tomb here |
| τόδ' ἐγγὺς οἴκων καὶ δόμων ἐρείπια | near the palace and the ruins of her home |
| τυφόμενα Δίου πυρὸς ἔτι ζῶσαν φλόγα, | smouldering with the still living flame of Zeus— |
| ἀθάνατον Ἥρας μητέρ' εἰς ἐμὴν ὕβριν. | Hera's undying outrage upon my mother. |
| αἰνῶ δὲ Κάδμον, ἄβατον ὃς πέδον τόδε | Cadmus I approve who set apart this inviolable |
| τίθησι, θυγατρὸς σηκόν· ἀμπέλου δέ νιν | spot, his daughter's consecrated ground. With the vine's |
| πέριξ ἐγὼ 'κάλυψα βοτρυώδει χλόη | clustering green have I covered it round |

In spite of the supernatural fire, smouldering during all the time that Semele's unborn babe was coming to maturity in the thigh of Zeus and growing to manhood and traveling all over the world bringing civilization as he went, the tomb of Semele must have been a very real and familiar landmark in Thebes. The details described by her son must also be true to life: the sacred enclosure overgrown with vines, the consecrated ground where none might tread.

The principal features of these facts are, moreover, substantially corroborated by Pausanias (IX 12, 3–4):

---

[1] Paus. IX 25, 1.

[2] This is not the fountain but the river Dirce. Pausanias and Pindar know only the river Dirce, but no Dirce Spring; but the tragic poets know both: Ae. Sep. 273; 307; Soph. Ant. 104; Eur. Bac. 519; H. F. 573; 784; I. T. 401; Ph. 101; 131; 238; 643; 645; 730; 825; 932.

THE ΠΑΡΑΠΟΡΤΙ SPRING, WITH THE DRAGON'S CAVE AND THE DIRCAEAN STREAM
AT THEBES

φασὶ δὲ οἱ Θηβαῖοι, καθότι τῆς ἀκρο-
πόλεως ἀγορά σφισιν ἐφ' ἡμῶν πεποίηται, Κάδμου τὸ ἀρχαῖον οἰκίαν
εἶναι· θαλάμων δὲ ἀποφαίνουσι τοῦ
μὲν 'Αρμονίας ἐρείπια καὶ ὃν Σεμέλης φασὶν εἶναι· τοῦτον δὲ καὶ
εἰς ἡμᾶς ἔτι ἄβατον φυλάσσουσιν
ἀνθρώποις...... λέγεται δὲ καὶ
τόδε, ὡς ὁμοῦ τῷ κεραυνῷ βληθέντι ἐς
τὸν Σεμέλης θάλαμον πέσοι ξύλον....

now the Thebans say that where the agora
upon the acropolis is builded in our day
the palace of Cadmus stood of old;
and they point out the ruins of two chambers—
the one, Harmonia's, and that which they say
is Semele's; even to our day they suffer
no man to set foot within this latter.
. . . This story is also told
that along with the thunderbolt that was hurled
into Semele's chamber a log of wood fell etc.

This sacred, inviolable spot was associated with the death of Semele in the lightning's rush. Her "tomb" was obviously in close proximity to where the palace chamber had been. The "log" was probably one of the wooden columns of the megaron.

The close proximity of the monument to the palace of the king is emphasized again in Euripides when Dionysus with earthquake and fire wrecks the home of Pentheus, and still the never-dying fire from the thunderbolt that consumed Semele is burning (Eur. Bac. 596–599):

ἄ, ἄ,
πῦρ οὐ λεύσσεις οὐδ' αὐγάζει
Σεμέλας ἱερὸν ἀμφὶ τάφον, ἄν
ποτε κεραυνόβολος ἔλιπε φλόγα
Δίου βροντᾶς;

ha! dost thou not see the fire
about Semele's sacred tomb or mark
well the flame that, thunderblasted, once she
left from the crash of Zeus?

In spite of the fact that Euripides repeatedly calls this famous landmark a "tomb" (τάφος, μνῆμα), it was not the place in which Semele's mortal remains were buried. Graves must always lie outside the city. And so, in a far later day, Pausanias finds just outside the Cadmea, near the theatre and the temple of Dionysus, along the road leading from the Proetidian Gate in the direction of Chalcis, the tomb of Semele and her statue.[1] It is to this monument, and not the inviolate site where she was stricken by the lightning of Zeus, that Hyginus refers when he says the Cadmean walls extended usque ad Semelae bustum.[2]

The inviolate site in the heart of the Cadmea, preserved from the Mycenaean days until well into the Christian Era, was the destroyed palace of Cadmus, left as a sacred memorial of the awful visitation of Zeus. To protect its inviolability, it must have been securely fenced in. And there, almost in the centre of the Theban acropolis, Keramopoullos[3] found the remains of an early Mycenaean palace that had been destroyed in an awful conflagration and never rebuilt. The later palace of the kings of Thebes was built upon another site. Here, in his time, Pausanias saw only a statue and an altar of Dionysus;[4] but here had been, half a millennium earlier, according to the inscriptions on the parastades of the Theban Treasury at Delphi,[5] an "asylum" in the sanctuary of "the Cadmean Dionysus"; it would appear, therefore, that in classical times there was a temple of Dionysus on the site of his first birth and that the inviolate enclosure of his mother's chamber was included in the sacred precincts of the god.

### 4. Tombs of the Children of Heracles

The palace of Amphitryon, the home of his heroic foster-son at Thebes, stood just outside the Electran Gate of the Cadmean city. There in the times of Pausanias the ruins of the house of Amphitryon and Alcmene were pointed out. As it was outside the city walls, the family tomb[6] could be on the premises, like the tombs before the villas on the Appian Way. And there Pausanias found the monument to the children of Heracles and Megara slain by

[1] IX 16, 6–7: τὸ ἕτερον τῶν ἀγαλμάτων... Σεμέλης.... καὶ Σεμέλης μνῆμά ἐστιν.
[2] Fab. 9.
[3] 'Αρχ. Δελτ. III (1917), pp. 338–346.
[4] IX 12, 4.
[5] *Fouilles de Delphes*, III p. 80; C. I. G. VII 2447.
[6] There was Amphitryon's famous tomb: Pind. Nem. 4, 20; Pyth. 9, 81–82.

their mad father's hand.[1]   Euripides also seems to make definite allusion to the children's tomb (H. F. 1360):

δὸς τούσδε τύμβῳ                              | consign them to the tomb

(1390–1391):

ἔλθετ' εἰς τάφον                              |        go to my children's tomb
παίδων, ἄπαντας δ' ἐνὶ λόγῳ πενθήσατε    | and with one word mourn for all

[1] Paus. IX 11, 2. Cf. Pind. Isth. 3, 61–64.

TIRYNS

With so many scenes laid at the palaces of princes of the Mycenaean age, with the locality of the plays suggested by a reproduction of the Lion Gate or the Castalian Fount or a Cyclopean fortress-wall, and with the Greek imagination picturing to itself as the play proceeded the familiar Pelargicum of the Athenian Acropolis, the citadel of Mycenae, or Tiryns, or Argos, we may expect to find the poet's words also dealing occasionally with architecture of that kind. And we shall find that "Cyclopean" masonry plays no small part in his architectural settings.

We look to the Argolid as the centre of Mycenaean culture in Greece proper. There the poets have taught us to look, and there the spade has most revealed. But before the day of archaeological discovery, the walls of Tiryns and Mycenae, never completely demolished nor covered with débris but open to view in the fifth century B. C. and even better preserved then than at the present day, stood as types of the Mycenaean fortress of the heroic age. Thus in Euripides's Troades (1087–1088) Hecabe anticipates her sad voyage

| | |
|---|---|
| ἱππόβοτον Ἄργος, ἵνα τείχεα | to horse-grazing Argos, where Cyclopean |
| λάϊνα Κυκλώπι' οὐράνια νέμονται | walls of stone soar to heaven |

Euripides had seen those stone wonders, Tiryns and Mycenae, and so had many another Athenian who witnessed the production of the Daughters of Troy. Even now the walls of Tiryns stand twenty-five feet above the plain, with a thickness of sixteen to fifty-seven feet. The older walls at Mycenae are quite like them, varying in thickness to-day from ten to twenty-three feet and in height from thirteen to thirty-five feet. Originally both walls were much higher. No wonder that Euripides could say they "soar to heaven," as he does in the passage just quoted and again in the Electra (1156–1159):

| | |
|---|---|
| ἅ πόσιν | who with the sharp-whetted weapon |
| χρόνιον ἱκόμενον εἰς οἴκους | in her own hand slew her lord |
| Κυκλώπειά τ' οὐράνια τείχε' ὀ- | as he came home to the Cyclopean |
| ξυθήκτῳ βέλει κατέκταν' αὐτόχειρ | walls that soar to heaven |

The picture that the visitor to-day obtains as he approaches Tiryns from the west or east is of a huge tower, with a flat level top, thrusting itself up out of the plain. Evidently Sophocles caught that same picture (Tr. 270; 271; 273):

| | |
|---|---|
| ὡς ἵκετ' αὖθις Ἴφιτος Τιρυνθίαν | when Iphitus came back to the hill |
| πρὸς κλιτύν...... | of Tiryns, he [Heracles] hurled him |
| ....ἀπ' ἄκρας ἧκε πυργώδους πλακός | [Iphitus] from the summit of the towering plateau |

And not only did those walls soar to heaven but they were built of blocks of enormous size. The visitor to Mycenae and Tiryns to-day marvels at their size and wonders by what science of engineering they were ever raised to their position. Euripides speaks of such single stones as making a wagon-load (Ph. 1156–1158):

| | |
|---|---|
| ἀλλ' ἔσχε μαργῶντ' αὐτὸν ἐναλίου θεοῦ | but Periclymenus, the seagod's son, checked his frenzy, |
| Περικλύμενος παῖς λᾶαν ἐμβαλὼν κάρᾳ | hurling down upon his head a wain-load |
| ἀμαξοπληθῆ, γεῖσ' ἐπάλξεων ἄπο | stone, a piece of cornice from the battlements |

We learn also from this passage what we never could have learned from the remains of Mycenaean walls in Greece that even the great Cyclopean fortress-walls were finished off with a cornice (γεῖσα) at the top; and the cornice-blocks were of the same huge proportions as the rest of the wall, for the piece of cornice that Periclymenus hurled down would alone have made a wagon load.[1]

[1] The Sicilian Cyclops handles even vaster blocks than these. When Polyphemus closed up his cave-dwelling for the night (ι 240–242),

| | |
|---|---|
| ἐπέθηκε θυρεὸν μέγαν ὑψόσ' ἀείρας | he lifted high and set in place the great doorstone |
| ὄβριμον· οὐκ ἂν τόν γε δύω καὶ εἴκοσ' ἄμαξαι | —a huge one; not even two and twenty strong, four-wheeled |
| ἐσθλαὶ τετράκυκλοι ἀπ' οὔδεος ὀχλίσσειαν | wagons could have heaved it from the threshold |

The walls of Tiryns built of those huge blocks, six to ten feet long by three or four feet in the other dimensions, blocks that Pausanias[1] says a span of mules could not move, with great towers flanking the entrance and massive gate locked with Titanic bars, seem to us impregnable. And yet these mighty fortresses fell, and with them fell the Mycenaean civilization. The fortifications of Mycenae are scarcely less formidable than those of Tiryns, and the walls of Troy more mighty still. And Agamemnon, marshalling at Aulis the hosts of Greece for the conquest of Troy, expresses the hopelessness of his defending himself behind the walls of Mycenae against the angered Greeks (Eur. I. A. 533–535):

| | |
|---|---|
| κἄν πρὸς Ἄργος ἐκφύγω, | and if I make my escape to Argos |
| ἐλθόντες αὐτοῖς τείχεσιν Κυκλωπίοις | they will come and annihilate us, |
| ξυναρπάσουσι...... | in spite of all our Cyclopean walls . . . |

Only a Heracles could think of going and storming them single-handed (Eur. H. F. 943–946):

| | |
|---|---|
| πρὸς τὰς Μυκήνας εἶμι· λάζυσθαι χρεὼν | to Mycenae I go! Bars and picks must |
| μοχλοὺς δικέλλας θ', ὡς τὰ Κυκλώπων βάθρα | I take along to shatter with the curvèd |
| φοίνικι κανόνι καὶ τύκοις ἡρμοσμένα | steel the city, its Cyclopes' foundations fitted with the |
| στρεπτῷ σιδήρῳ συντριαινώσω πόλιν | red chalk-line and mason's picks |

The thought is echoed again in Seneca (H. F. 1001–1003):

maius mihi
bellum Mycenis restat ut Cyclopia
eversa manibus saxa nostris concidant

With pick-axes he would undermine the foundations of the walls; with levers he would pry the tremendous blocks from their place and bring the whole superstructure crashing down. And so, in his madness, he operates against his own palace walls (Eur. H. F. 998–1000):

| | |
|---|---|
| ὁ δ' ὡς ἐπ' αὐτοῖς δὴ Κυκλωπίοισιν ὤν | but he, as if he were before the Cyclopean walls themselves, |
| σκάπτει μοχλεύει θύρετρα κἀκβαλὼν σταθμὰ | digs under, pries open the doors, and crashing down the doorposts |
| δάμαρτα....κατέστρωσεν | from their place he laid low his wife |

So markedly characteristic of Mycenae were its giant walls that "Cyclopean" became an epithet of the city (Eur. I. A. 265–267):

| | |
|---|---|
| ἐκ Μυκήνας δὲ τὰς Κυκλωπίας | and Atreus's son from Cyclopean |
| παῖς Ἀτρέως ἔπεμπε ναυβάτας | Mycenae sent marshalled hosts |
| ναῶν ἑκατὸν ἠθροισμένους | upon a hundred ships |

(Eur. H. F. 15–16):

| | |
|---|---|
| Ἀργεῖα τείχη καὶ Κυκλωπίαν πόλιν | he yearned to dwell in Argive walls |
| ὠρέξατ' οἰκεῖν | and the Cyclopean town |

(Eur. Or. 965):

| | |
|---|---|
| ἰαχείτω δὲ γᾶ Κυκλωπία | let the Cyclopean land cry aloud |

(Soph. Heracl., Frag. 207 N.):

| | |
|---|---|
| Κυκλώπιον τροχόν | Cyclopean ring |

(Eur. I. T. 845–846):

| | |
|---|---|
| ὦ Κυκλωπίδες ἑστίαι, ὦ πατρίς, | oh Cyclopean hearths, my native land, |
| Μυκήνα φίλα. | beloved Mycenae |

This constantly recurring epithet Κυκλώπιος "Cyclopean" in Euripides means that the poet accepted the popular tradition that the walls of Mycenae and Tiryns were built by the Cyclopes. Indeed, he does not hesitate to give us direct statements of the fact. (Eur I. A. 152):

| | |
|---|---|
| ἐπὶ Κυκλώπων ἱεὶς θυμέλας | speeding them back to the Cyclopes' towers |

[1] II 25, 8.

and still more unequivocally (1500–1501):

χαλεῖς πόλισμα Περσέως,
Κυκλωπίων πόνον χερῶν;

| dost thou call on Perseus's city,
| the labor of Cyclopes' hands?

We may perhaps go even further and say that it is Euripides who made the epithet "Cyclopean" a part of the vocabulary of art; for over against the many times that we find the term in his tragedies, we find it but the one time in Sophocles and once in an unidentified fragment (which *may* be Euripides), and nowhere else in all the dramatic poets. The unidentified fragment is ('Αδέσπ. 269 N.):

Τιρύνθιον πλίνθευμα, Κυκλώπιον ἔδος

| Tirynthian masonry, Cyclopean abode

Hesychius, who cites the passage, comments briefly (4, p. 159):

Τιρύνθιον πλίνθευμα· ἀντὶ τοῦ τεῖχος.
ὑπὸ δὲ Κυκλώπων κατεσκεύαστο

| Tirynthian masonry: for "wall."
| It was built by Cyclopes

and (2, p. 550):

Κυκλώπιον ἔδος· ἐπειδὴ Κύκλωπες
ἐτείχισαν τὰς Μυκήνας

| Cyclopean abode: for Cyclopes
| built the walls of Mycenae

The tradition was generally accepted that the "Cyclopean walls" of Tiryns and Mycenae were built by the Cyclopes.

Who these Cyclopes were the poets do not deign to tell us. They simply accepted them as the builders of those great walls, just as they also accepted the story of their importation by Perseus (or Proetus) from Lycia (or Thrace[1]) for the building of the walls. The story is given in its simplest form by Apollodorus (II 2, 1)[2]:

'Ακρίσιος Προῖτον "Αργους ἐξελαύνει. ὁ
δὲ ἧκεν εἰς Λυκίαν πρὸς 'Ιοβάτην
. . . . καὶ γαμεῖ τὴν τούτου θυγατέρα . . . .
κατάγει δὲ αὐτὸν ὁ κηδεστὴς μετὰ
στρατοῦ Λυκίων καὶ καταλαμβάνει
Τίρυνθα, ταύτην αὐτῷ Κυκλώπων
τειχισάντων

| Acrisius expelled Proetus from Argos.
| He then went to Iobates in Lycia . . .
| and married the latter's daughter . . .
| His father-in-law then with the help of an
| army of Lycians restored him and took possession
| of Tiryns, for the Cyclopes had built the
| walls for him

Pausanias adopts the current tradition (II 16, 5):

λείπεται δὲ ὅμως ἔτι καὶ ἄλλα τοῦ περιβόλου
καὶ ἡ πύλη. λέοντες δὲ ἐφεστήκασιν
αὐτῇ. Κυκλώπων δὲ καὶ ταῦτα
ἔργα εἶναι λέγουσιν, οἳ Προίτῳ τὸ τεῖχος
ἐποίησαν τὸ ἐν Τίρυνθι

| in spite of the destruction there are still left
| the gate and other parts of the circuit-wall; lions
| stand above the gate; these walls also are
| said to be the work of the Cyclopes who
| built the wall at Tiryns for Proetus

and (VII 25, 6):

Μυκηναίοις γὰρ τὸ μὲν τεῖχος ἁλῶναι
κατὰ τὸ ἰσχυρὸν οὐκ ἐδύνατο ὑπὸ
'Αργείων, ἐτετείχιστο γὰρ κατὰ
ταὐτὰ τῷ ἐν Τίρυνθι ὑπὸ τῶν
Κυκλώπων καλουμένων

| for the wall of Mycenae, on
| account of its strength, could not be stormed by
| the Argives, for it had been built in
| the same fashion as that at Tiryns by
| the so-called Cyclopes

and (II 25, 8):

τὸ δὴ τεῖχος, ὃ δὴ μόνον τῶν ἐρειπίων
λείπεται, Κυκλώπων μέν ἐστιν ἔργον,
πεποίηται δὲ ἀργῶν λίθων, μέγεθος
ἔχων ἕκαστος λίθος ὡς ἀπ' αὐτῶν μήδ' ἂν ἀρχὴν κινηθῆναι τὸν
μικρότατον ὑπὸ ζεύγους ἡμιόνων

| now the wall—and that is all that is left of the
| ruins [of Tiryns]—is the work of the Cyclopes;
| it is built of undressed stones, and
| each stone is so huge that even the smallest one
| of them could not be budged an inch
| by a span of mules

We need not stop to moderate Pausanias's extravagant exaggeration. Suffice it to say, however, that the success in overcoming the technical difficulties in constructing such walls as those of Mycenae and Tiryns was no less astounding to the ancients than to us, and they

---

[1] Schol. Eur. Or. 965: Κύκλωπες· Θρακικὸν ἔθνος ἀπὸ Κύκλωπος βασιλέως.
[2] Strabo (VIII p. 372 a) tells the same story, apparently drawing from the same source.

naturally ascribed the work to superhuman agencies; these imported Lycian Cyclopes were no mere men (Sen. Thy. 407–408):

| | |
|---|---|
| cerno Cyclopum sacras<br>turres labore maius humano decus | I behold the Cyclopes' sacred towers,<br>a glory of superhuman labor |

The most famous fortress of Cyclopean masonry was that of Ilium. But the ruins of those walls and towers had been long since hidden from view by the new structures of cities VII and VIII, and the Greek authors of classical and subsequent times had no opportunity to see them as they saw the famous Mycenaean castles, fairly well preserved, on the mainland of Greece. But the fame of the mighty walls of Troy had not passed into oblivion; tradition was still strong and vivid.[1] And it was no mere Cyclopes but the gods themselves, Apollo and Poseidon, that built those walls (Eur. Andr. 1009–1017):

| | |
|---|---|
| ὦ Φοῖβε πυργώσας<br>τὸν ἐν ᾽Ιλίῳ εὐτειχῆ πάγον,<br>καὶ πόντιε κυανέαις<br>ἵπποις διφρεύων ἅλιον πέλαγος,<br><br>τίνος εἵνεκ᾽ ἄτιμον ὀργά-<br>ναν χέρα τεκτοσύνας ᾽Ε-<br>νυαλίῳ δοριμήστορι προσθέντες τάλαιναν<br>τάλαιναν μεθεῖτε Τροίαν; | oh Phoebus, that entoweredst<br>the well-walled hill at Ilium,<br>and thou god of the ocean that drivest thy car<br>with steeds of the deep blue sea over the briny<br>   depths,<br>for what cause did ye set the handiwork<br>of your builder's art in scorn<br>and give over unhappy Troy—unhappy—<br>a prey to Enyalius the waster with spears? |

Again and again Phoebus and Poseidon are named as the builders of those glorious towers (Eur. Tro. 4–6):

| | |
|---|---|
| ἐξ οὗ γὰρ ἀμφὶ τήνδε Τρωικὴν χθόνα<br>Φοῖβός τε κἀγὼ λαΐνους πύργους πέριξ<br>ὀρθοῖσιν ἔθεμεν κανόσιν | for ever since about this land of Troy<br>Phoebus and I these towers of stone did<br>set with straight-edge and plummet |

(Soph. Ποιμ., Frag. 465 N.):

| | |
|---|---|
| τειχέων καὶ δὴ τοὺς Ποσειδείους<br>....θριγκοὺς ἀποσεισαμένη | and shaking off the cornices of the<br>walls Poseidon built |

Plautus, in a passage full of allusions to the Trojan story, refers to the rearing of the walls of Ilium "by hand divine" (Bac. 926):

Priami patriam Pergamum divina moenitum manu

Sometimes the building of the walls of Troy is ascribed to Apollo alone (Eur. Tro. 1173–1175):

| | |
|---|---|
| δύστηνε, κρατὸς ὥς σ᾽ ἔκειρεν ἀθλίως | unhappy child, how unhappily from thy head<br>   thine |
| τείχη πατρῷα Λοξίου πυργώματα | ancestral walls, the towers upreared by Loxias,<br>   have |
| ὃν πόλλ᾽ ἐκήπευσεν ἡ τεκοῦσα βόστρυχον | shorn the curls thy mother oft hath tended |

(ibid. 813):

| | |
|---|---|
| κανόνων δὲ τυκίσματα Φοίβου | and the plummet-true masonry of Phoebus |

[1] Dörpfeld's excavations have opened up on the southeast side of the citadel alone three great towers; tradition knew of only one remaining after the destruction of the city by the Argive hosts under Agamemnon (Sen. Tro. 622):

e turre, lapsis sola quae muris manet

(ibid. 1068–1076):

est una magna turris e Troia super,<br>
adsueta Priamo, cuius e fastigio<br>
smmisque pinnis arbiter belli sedens<br>
regebat acies. turre in hac blando sinu<br>
fovens nepotem, cum metu versos gravi<br>
Danaos fugaret Hector et ferro et face,<br>
paterna puero bella monstrabat senex.<br>
haec nota quondam turris et muri decus,<br>
nunc sola cautes . . .

Cf. also lines 368–369; 1091–1092; 1110–1112; 1118

EAST WALL OF TROY VI

(After Dörpfeld)

(Eur. Hel. 1510–1511):

| οὐκ ἐλθοῦσά ποτ' Ἰλίου <br> Φοιβείους ἐπὶ πύργους | for thou didst never go to <br> Phoebus's towers at Ilium |

(Eur. Rh. 226–232):

| Ἄπολλον . . . . . . <br><br> ὦ παγκρατές, ὦ Τροίας <br> τείχη παλαιὰ δείμας | Apollo. . . . thou <br><br> almighty one, thou that builtest <br> Troy's ancient walls |

Rarely do we meet with references to walls outside the Hellenic world. One such is the very brief allusion by Bacchus, who traveled the whole world over, to the walls of Bactria (Eur. Bac. 15):

| Βάκτριά τε τείχη | and walls of Bactria |

Not a word of description or characterization is given—only the simple fact that in Bactria walls of defense might have been found in the Mycenaean age.

The work of the gods was not in unhewn stone, like that of the Cyclopes at Tiryns,[1] but of carefully dressed masonry. Homer had sung the praise of the apartments of the royal palace with their polished masonry[2] and Euripides has an echo of the same careful workmanship that we see in the towers of Troy even to this day (Tro. 45–46):

| ἀλλ', ὦ ποτ' εὐτυχοῦσα, χαῖρέ μοι, πόλις <br> ξεστόν γε πύργωμ' | but, oh my city, prosperous once, and <br> polished towers, farewell |

Perhaps Euripides is only echoing the ξεστοῖο λίθοιο of Homer; perhaps also, forasmuch as Homer's "polished stones" have to do only with the royal palace, Euripides is reflecting a tradition of the splendid masonry of the walls and towers of Troy, which after three thousand years of ruin show the care with which the individual stones were worked and polished and the striving after aesthetic effect with which the walls as a whole were finished and beautified. It seems to him to be no mere jingle of well-sounding words when he says (Eur. I. T. 12–13):

| τὸν καλλίνικον στέφανον Ἰλίου θέλων <br> λαβεῖν Ἀχαιούς | and willed that the Achaeans should <br> capture Ilium's crown with glorious victory |

The circlet of walls and towers about the Pergama of Troy was a worthy diadem about the head of that fair city.

The great gates at the entrances to such fortresses as we know at Tiryns, Mycenae, and Troy must have been proportionately no less massive than the walls and towers to the interior of which they gave admission. Evidence still at hand at Tiryns and Mycenae goes to prove that the mighty doors themselves were constructed of heavy oak that could not easily be battered down and that they were covered on the outside with metal that they might not be burned by an attacking enemy. Across the inside of the gateway with its double doors (Mycenae, Tiryns) was thrown a huge bar nearly eight inches in diameter, as the holes into which this bar was shot home still show.

Such, in a word, is the reality with which we are familiar. No further light is thrown upon it by the poets; but corroboration of our understanding is furnished by such a passage as Euripides's Phoenissae 114–116:

| ἆρα πύλαι κλήθροις χαλκόδετά τ' ἔμβολα <br> λαϊνέοισιν Ἀμφίονος ὀργάνοις <br><br> τείχεος ἥρμοσται | pray, are the gates, with bronze-covered panels, <br> close-fastened with bars shot into the stone <br> casings <br> of Amphion's walls? |

The χαλκόδετα ἔμβολα "bronze-covered panels" are not, as the Scholiast explains, drawbridges, raised and lowered with a windlass in times of war and left down to serve only as bridges in times of peace, when the great gates swinging on their hinges would afford ample security; neither are they the fastening bars of the gates, as Liddell and Scott interpret;

[1] See Paus. II 25, 8 (quoted on p. 249 above).
[2] Z 244: πεντήκοντ' ἔνεσαν θάλαμοι ξεστοῖο λίθοιο.
  Z 248: δώδεκ' ἔσαν τέγεοι θάλαμοι ξεστοῖο λίθοιο.

the bars are already denoted, and properly, with κλήθροις; the big bar needed no binding of bronze. An ἔμβολον is "something thrown" or "placed in" or "upon" something; it might possibly mean a bolt or bar; but in Euripides's Bacchae 591 ἔμβολα are architrave blocks;[1] and here they are the panels of the oaken doors. These needed and these had their covering of bronze, and the poet clearly confirms our architectural theories in regard to the construction of the doors. πύλαι χαλκόδετά τ' ἔμβολα is hendiadys for "gates with bronze-covered panels."

ὀργάνοις also has been found difficult of interpretation. Liddell and Scott make it here equivalent to ἔργοις—the finished product of the work, so that ὀργάνοις τείχεος is nothing more or less than "wall." And this is the usual interpretation of the words. But again Euripides is more technical in his choice of words: ὄργανον is primarily an "instrument"; in its second meaning, it is "material"; here it is "the stone casing of the doorway"—with the fittings above and below and on either side carefully sawn, as we see them at Mycenae and Tiryns, to receive the great doors when they are closed and barred.

The Mycenaean gateways in actual existence and the words of the poet are in perfect agreement: great gateways with sawn recesses in the casings to receive the doors; massive doors of oak covered on the outside with bronze; huge bars for securing them within.

### 1. The Acropolis of Athens—Pelargicum and Propylaea

In the southern part of the precincts of ancient Athens there once rose up from the plain a rugged, chasm-torn rock—the last spur but one of the chain of hills that runs from Pentelicus to the southern coast of Attica. Its highest point was but 156.2 metres above the level of the sea, and less than 100 metres higher than the plain on which it stood. On the west side only did it offer a comparatively easy ascent. Everywhere else it fell precipitously to the plain with declivities more or less inacessible. Of all the many hills that lay in and around Athens this was the only one with much of a surface on its summit, presenting as it did an area of 270 by 135 metres. Thus in its entire formation this rock seemed by nature designed for a fastness, and this destiny it fulfilled in becoming the most glorious fortress the world has ever seen—the Acropolis of Athens.

It is, as it always has been, the most prominent feature of the landscape, the centre of attraction to which the eye ever turns, wherever one may stand in the plain or on the hills about Athens. And when it became also the centre of political and of religious interest, especially when crowned with the peerless creations of the Periclean age, with Parthenon, Erechtheum, Nike-temple, Propylaea in their pristine splendor, gleaming out in the glorious sunshine of Attica, its effect must have been overpowering. With the natural self-control and moderation of the Athenian temper, we are surprised not that they so rarely gave expression to their feelings and impressions of the magnificence of their wonderful Acropolis, but that any one ever ventured to attempt to give expression to that for which words—even Greek words—were so inadequate. And when, as rarely happens, an Athenian poet does unseal his lips to speak of the glories of his city, it is with that self-control and self-restraint which make us feel that for him to have said more would have been to detract from the transcendent beauty and dignity of Athena's sacred rock.[2] An unidentified comic fragment ('Αδέσπ. 428 K.) suggests the position of the Acropolis rock conspicuous from every direction, gleaming out from every point of view in the unutterable beauty that covered it with the most perfect creations of man's hand since the world began:

| 'Ακρόπολις | the Acropolis |
| πόρρωθεν ἀστράπτουσ' ἀπὸ πάσης εἰσόδου | gleaming from far, from every approach |

[1] See p. 202.

[2] πέτραν.... Παλλάδος (Eur. Hip. 30); λαῶν... σκόπελον ὃν ναίουσ' ἐμόν (Eur. Ion 1578); τὰν ἐπ' ἐμοῖς σκοπέλοισι θεάν Eur. Ion 871). The stronghold could at the same time be a great sanctuary (Dem. F. L. 272, p. 428): ὅλης οὔσης ἱερᾶς τῆς 'Ακροπόλεως.

It can hardly be called extravagant when the Chorus exclaims in Aristophanes's Knights (1329):

ὦ ταὶ λιπαραὶ καὶ ἰοστέφανοι καὶ ἀριζήλωτοι 'Αθῆναι    |    oh bright and envied Athens of the violet crown

or when Eupolis calls it the most beautiful city of all that Cleon looks upon (Χρ. Γέν., Frag. 290, 1 K.):

ὦ καλλίστη πόλι πασῶν ὅσας Κλέων ἐφορᾷ

and the city best beloved of Heaven (Inc. Frag. 307 K.):

πόλιν γε θεοφιλεστάτην
οἰκοῦσιν ἀφθονεστάτην τε χρήμασιν

Aristophanes, too, almost allows himself on one occasion, in a lyric passage, to say what was in his heart about the wonder of the Acropolis; but he checks himself with genuine Hellenic restraint (Lys. 480–483):

| | |
|---|---|
| ὅτι βουλόμεναί ποτε τὴν | what in the world they meant |
| Κραναὰν κατέλαβον, | by seizing the Rocky Height, |
| ἐφ' ὅ τι μεγαλόπετρον, ἄβατον Ἀκρόπολιν, | and to what end they had taken the great rock of the Acropolis, |
| ἱερὸν τέμενος | the sacred enclosure inviolate |

These poets are speaking, of course, of the Acropolis as they knew it after the dedication of the Parthenon and the Erechtheum and the completion (as far as it ever was completed) of the Mnesiclean Propylaea. But the Acropolis was not always exclusively a "sacred enclosure, inviolate." The top of the hill was not always the smooth plateau that we now find it, but originally, as the excavations completed in the middle nineties prove, everywhere a jagged, uneven, rocky surface, rough and rent with many fissures.

Partly by hewing away the jags of rock and partly by filling up the chasms with stones and earth, the earliest inhabitants of Attica created on this uneven hilltop a number of smaller plateaus for their dwellings and sanctuaries. In a condition of society where universal warfare continually prevails, as we find it, according to Thucydides,[1] at the dawn of Greek history, the first settlements are necessarily made with a view to every possible advantage afforded by natural protection. They sought, not the highest hill, but the one that offered the broadest surface on its summit and had the steepest sides. Accordingly, we should look to the Acropolis for the earliest inhabitants of the land. And here, in truth, they were; and the first settlement on the sacred rock of Athens dates back, as relics of the Stone Age found upon the Acropolis unquestionably prove, to an inconceivably remote period.[2] We learn further from Thucydides[3] and the common use of the word πόλις (city) elsewhere[4]—especially in Attic inscriptions[5] that the citadel originally was "the city," since by this word in its limited sense the Acropolis itself is officially designated. And before there was a "lower city," there was no occasion for the word Ἀκρόπολις to distinguish an "upper" from a "lower town."

To Aristophanes also the Acropolis was still "the City"—πόλις (Nub. 69):

| | |
|---|---|
| ὅταν σὺ μέγας ἄρμ' ἐλαύνῃς πρὸς πόλιν | when you grow up and drive your chariot to the City |

Phidippides's mother is dreaming of the day when her boy, an ἀποβάτης, will, as a victor in the games, drive his chariot and prancing horses in the Panathenaic procession up to the entrance of the Acropolis; hence πρὸς πόλιν—the line of the procession from the Dipylum Gate in the direction of the Acropolis.

Still more matter-of-fact is Cleon's remark in the Knights (267–268):

| | |
|---|---|
| δίκαιον ἐν πόλει | it is right to set up in |
| ἱστάναι μνημεῖον ὑμῶν ἐστιν ἀνδρείας χάριν | the City a monument to your valor |

where "in the City" means "upon the Acropolis," just as (ll. 1092–1093) "out from the City" means "out from the Acropolis":

| | |
|---|---|
| καὶ μοὐδόκει ἡ θεὸς αὐτὴ | and methought the goddess herself |
| ἐκ πόλεως ἐλθεῖν καὶ γλαῦξ αὐτῇ ἐπικαθῆσθαι | came out from the City and an owl rested upon her |

[1] I 2.

[2] Köhler, *Hermes*, VI p. 105.

[3] II 15, 3–4: τὸ δὲ πρὸ τούτου (i.e. the time of Theseus) ἡ Ἀκρόπολις ἡ νῦν οὖσα πόλις ἦν.... τεκμήριον δέ· τὰ γὰρ ἱερὰ ἐν αὐτῇ τῇ Ἀκροπόλει καὶ ἄλλων θεῶν ἐστι [καὶ τὸ τῆς Ἀθηνᾶς]... καλεῖται δὲ διὰ τὴν παλαιὰν ταύτην κατοίκησιν καὶ ἡ Ἀκρόπολις μέχρι τοῦδε ἔτι ὑπὸ τῶν Ἀθηναίων πόλις "But before the time of Theseus, what is now called the Acropolis was the city: and a proof of it is that we find on the Acropolis itself the sanctuaries not only of Athena, but of other gods as well . . . And unto this day on account of its being anciently inhabited the Athenians still call the Acropolis "Polis" ("The City")." So the island in the Seine is still *la Cité* of Paris, and the oldest part of London is "The City."

[4] Cf. Paus. I 26, 6: ἐν τῇ νῦν Ἀκροπόλει, τότε δὲ ὀνομαζομένη πόλει.

[5] E. g. C.I.A. I 32 B, 4 and 10; 58, 11; II 11, 26; 20, 2; 42, 7; 45, 5; 85, 13; etc. After the middle of the first century B.C. this use of πόλις in inscriptions ceases.

while in Aristophanes's Thesmophoriazusae (317–319) Athena, as indweller of the "city," is the goddess whose shrine is the Acropolis:

| | |
|---|---|
| καὶ σὺ παγκρατὴς κόρα | and thou all-mighty maiden, |
| γλαυκῶπι χρυσόλογχε, πόλιν | of the flashing eyes and lance of gold, thou that |
| οἰκοῦσα περιμάχητον, ἐλθὲ δεῦρο | dwellest in a city fit prize of battle, hither come |

Even clearer is the expression in Aristophanes's Lysistrate 265–266:

| | |
|---|---|
| τὰ προπύλαια πακτοῦν;[1] | close fast the Propylaea?[1] |
| ἀλλ' ὡς τάχιστα πρὸς πόλιν σπεύσωμεν | But let us haste with all speed to the City |

The chorus of elders urge their way *toward* "the city," with its gateway, the Propylaea. They presently arrive at the saddle between the Areopagus and the Acropolis, where they stop to catch their breath before beginning the taxing drive up the last, the steepest stretch to the "city" (Ar. Lys. 286–290):

| | |
|---|---|
| ἀλλ' αὐτὸ γάρ μοι τῆς ὁδοῦ | but wait. For all I have left of the journey |
| λοιπόν ἐστι χωρίον | up to the City is this short |
| τὸ πρὸς πόλιν, τὸ σιμὸν οἷ σπουδὴν ἔχω· | stretch—the steep incline, up which I must drive; |
| χὤπως ποτ' ἐξαμπρεύσομεν | and that we may pull through |
| τοῦτ' ἄνευ κανθηλίου. . . . | this without an ass's help. . . . |

And then the final rush with their fagots to the "city" (Ar. Lys. 302–304):

| | |
|---|---|
| σπεῦδε πρόσθεν ἐς πόλιν | hurry on to the City |
| καὶ βοήθει τῇ θεῷ· | and come to the rescue of the goddess; |
| ἢ πότ' αὐτῇ μᾶλλον ἢ νῦν ἀρήξομεν; | or when shall we aid her rather than now? |

It is the call of the semi-chorus as the conservative old citizens hasten to force the Acropolis citadel and rescue it from Lysistrate and the women who have seized the fortress from which to carry on the militants' fight for peace. And in the parley that follows the first phase of the conflict, the Deputy demands an explanation of their seizure of the Acropolis (Ar. Lys. 486–487):

| | |
|---|---|
| τοῦτ' ἐπιθυμῶ νὴ τὸν Δία πρῶτα πυθέσθαι | the first thing I want to know, by Zeus, is |
| ὅ τι βουλόμεναι τὴν πόλιν ἡμῶν ἀπεκλῄσατε | what you meant by locking up our City with the |
|            τοῖσι μοχλοῖσι | bars |

One of the most timid of Lysistrate's Amazons is so frightened by the Erichthonius serpent of the Erechtheum that she cannot sleep up there "in the city" (Ar. Lys. 758–759):[2]

| | |
|---|---|
| ἀλλ' οὐ δύναμαι 'γωγ' οὐδὲ κοιμᾶσθ' ἐν πόλει | why, I can't even sleep in the City, |
| ἐξ οὗ τὴν ὄφιν εἶδον τὸν οἰκουρόν ποτε | since I once saw that snake which keeps the house [3] |

Another pretends that her time of confinement is at hand and that the sacred, inviolable precincts of the Acropolis are in immediate danger of being defiled by her imminent delivery (Ar. Lys. 753–754):

| | |
|---|---|
| μ' εἰ καταλάβοι | if my confinement should |
| ὁ τόκος ἐν πόλει | overtake me in the City |

And at the end of the play, to celebrate the end of warfare and the reconciliation of all Greece, Lysistrate proposes to give the peacemakers a banquet on the Acropolis (1182–1184):

| | |
|---|---|
| νῦν οὖν ὅπως ἁγνεύσετε, | now then purify yourselves, |
| ὅπως ἂν αἱ γυναῖκες ὑμᾶς ἐν πόλει | so that we women may entertain |
| ξενίσωμεν | you in the City |

[1] Pollux cites, apparently from an unidentified fragment of Aristophanes (608 D.), as parallel to this passage, καὶ πάλιν «ἐπιπακτοῦν τὰς θύρας.» Whether "the doors" are the gates of the Propylaea or of some other building is a matter of the merest conjecture.

[2] Still other instances of "city" in the sense of the Acropolis are Ar. Lys. 245; 912; Eup. Μαρ. (Frag. 183 K.); Men. Sam. 113:

ὦ πόλισμα Κεκροπίας χθονός

[3] As Rogers remarks (a. l.) "Lysistrate's young friend should have been flattered at obtaining an actual sight of the serpent, which apparently nobody else in historic times had ever been privileged to see." "It was the warder of the Temple itself (ὁ φύλαξ τοῦ ναοῦ, Scholiast); ὁ φύλαξ τῆς Πολιάδος, Heysch. s. v. οἰκουρὸς Eust. ad α 357), and also generally, the Warder of the Acr. (ὁ φύλαξ τῆς Ἀκροπόλιος, Hdt. VIII 41; Hesych.)."

Even at the time of the production of the Lysistrate, we see from these numerous passages, the Acropolis was in the popular speech of Athens "the City."

On the north side of the Acropolis about the Erechtheum are plainly to be seen the heavy foundation walls of a great royal palace. A number of apartments stretching one after the other from east to west may be distinguished, but just how far toward the south and west this palace extended cannot be determined, as the foundation walls in those directions were even in antiquity too far demolished. But as far as the outlines can be made out, the building that stood here corresponded exactly in material, in construction, and in general arrangement with the similar royal residences in Tiryns, Mycenae, and Ilium; and by analogy with these we may very justly infer that in Athens also a large part of the citadel was once taken up by the palace of the ruling prince.

Behind the palace, that is at its northeast corner, a narrow stairway leads from the royal house down through a cleft in the rock artificially widened to receive it, under the present wall of the Acropolis and almost straight toward the quarter called κῆποι "the gardens"; this little rear gateway may also, like the similar ones in Mycenae and Tiryns, have served for fetching water in time of need. It was, of course, entirely covered up in the fifth century by the building of the north wall of the Acropolis—the so-called wall of Themistocles. This little stairway, hewn in part out of the live rock, is scarcely at all different in its general plan and style of construction from that in Tiryns. The ancient palace on the Athenian Acropolis had, like the royal palaces at Tiryns and Mycenae, besides the main entrance in the west, a second approach from the side directly opposite. This second approach was, in each and every case, a narrow flight of steps, built in a half-hidden, secluded corner and in a steep place, accessible to pedestrians only.

Furthermore, in the great court, which we find west of the Erechtheum near the spot where that primeval, crooked, gnarled, old olive tree of Athena stood, was the altar of Zeus Herceius[1]—the hearth and centre of the state—at which the king, as the head of his tribe and father of the whole people, was wont to sacrifice. In the houses, the foundations of which we observe west of the Erechtheum, we may perhaps recognize the habitations of the king's retainers, who must have dwelt in the closest proximity to their prince's palace. The altar of Zeus Polieus, too, erected by the first king, Cecrops, must have stood close by. Athena also had a sanctury within the palace.[2]

The 'Ερεχθῆος πυκινὸς δόμος "the goodly house of Erechtheus" is, as the Homeric use of the words must signify, not the old Hecatompedon (the old temple between the Erechtheum and the Parthenon), nor yet necessarily the common temple of Athena and Erechtheus, but the Erechtheid palace, and by implication that part of the Erechtheid palace occupied by the shrine of Athena. For, in the first place, δόμος in Homer never means "temple" unless accompanied by the adjective ἱερός "sacred"; and in the second place, πυκινὸς δόμος "goodly house" is Homer's standing epithet for royal palaces.[3] But it is obvious that Athena came to Athens and entered the "goodly house of Erechtheus" for no other reason than that she had a sanctuary located within its gates and forming a part of it.[4]

Homer is obviously well acquainted with the royal palace of the Erechtheids on the Acropolis. So also are the tragic poets; it is entirely possible that its ruins may have been conspicuously visible in the days of Aeschylus and Euripides, though it may, of course, have been but a memory of the more ancient days that Aeschylus recalls in the Eumenides (854–856):

| καὶ σὺ τιμίαν | and thou [the Eumenides] shalt occupy a |
| ἕδραν ἔχουσα πρὸς δόμοις 'Ερεχθέως | seat of honor before Erechtheus's halls |
| τεύξει........ | and receive. . . . |

In "Erechtheus's halls" we recognize the most ancient dwelling upon the Acropolis, before the gates of which lay the Areopagus with the cave set apart by Athena for the abiding-place of the Dread Goddesses.

In the Ion of Euripides, Creusa, the daughter of Erechtheus, refers to her father's palace in Athens without defining its location (1293):

| κἀπίμπρης γ' 'Ερεχθέως δόμους | and wast for setting fire to Erechtheus's halls |

---

[1] Philoch., *ap.* Dion. Hal. 13 (Frag. 146).
[2] For the temple of Athena attached to the Erechtheid palace see pp. 44–45.
[3] Cf. also ζ 134; K 267; etc.
[4] See pp. 44–45.

but the chorus of Creusa's handmaids, in an earlier passage of the same play, speaks of the Erechtheid palace in very much the same vein as Homer in the passage cited above (234–235):

| | |
|---|---|
| Παλλάδος ἔνοικα τρόφιμα μέλαθρα | my sovereigns' halls indwelt of Pallas |
| τῶν ἐμῶν τυράννων | are the home that nurtured me |

Here again we have the great complex of the palace upon the Acropolis, with its plurality of halls, and somewhere within its walls the sanctuary of the city's tutelary divinity, even Pallas Athena.

From the earliest times down at least to the middle of the second century of our era the Athenian Acropolis never entirely surrendered its character as a fortress. The rock was chosen for the first settlement because, as we have seen, it could be easily fortified. The Mycenaean city was a feudal castle fronted with its nine-gated series of concentric walls; in the walls built about it by Cimon and Themistocles the defensory idea was not the least prominent; with the erection of the Mnesiclean Propylaea the fortress was in no wise weakened; its strength as a fort was thoroughly demonstrated in Sulla's siege in 86 B. C.; and the architectural connection between the great Roman stairway and the bastions flanking the Porte Beulé makes it clear that under the Roman empire the Acropolis was still a mighty fortress. The fortificatory nature of the Acropolis walls in the long history of the citadel is thoroughly discussed by the present writer in the *American Journal of Archaeology* VIII (1893) pages 473 ff. Not a little of the evidence for the establishment of the facts is furnished by the dramatic poets.

It is not without significance that the Latin writers, even as early as Terence, take the Acropolis of their Greek originals over into Latin as *Arx* (Ter. Hec. 431–433):

> PAM. In arcem transcurso opus est. PAR. Quoi homini? PAM. Tibi.
> PAR. In arcem? quid eo? PAM. Callidemidem . . . . conveni.

So also *ibid.* 800–801:

> frustra ubi totum desedi diem,
> . . . . dum expecto in arce Callidemidem.

The word is found in a fragment probably considerably older than Terence [Inc. Inc. Fab. (CLIII) 259 R.[3]]:

> in arce Athenis statio mea nunc <mihi> placet.

The arx is the Acropolis; and an arx is a citadel—an elevated, strong place of defense. Down to the time of Themistocles the city of Athens possessed no other walls of defense than those about the Acropolis. Those fortifications dated from the Mycenaean Age and were called the Pelargicum.[1] The dramatic poets have contributed not a little to our knowledge of the structure and the history of the mighty nine-gated fort. Aeschylus alludes to its great towers, such as we know at Mycenae and Tiryns and Troy, and the occasion when the Amazons invaded Attica in the time of Theseus and from the hill of Ares laid siege to the Acropolis itself (Eum. 685–688):

| | |
|---|---|
| πάγον δ' Ἄρειον τόνδ' Ἀμαζόνων ἕδραν | this hill of Ares, where the Amazons took their stand and pitched |
| σκηνάς θ' ὅτ' ἦλθον Θησέως κατὰ φθόνον | their tents, what time in despite of Theseus they came |
| στρατηλατῆσαι, καὶ πτόλιν νεόπτολιν | marshalling their hosts and reared then the lofty |
| τήνδ' ὑψίπυργον ἀντεπύργωσαν τότε | towers of this new city against the old |

The vast system of fortifications about the Acropolis, the Pelargicum, was still unimpaired in its strength in the days of the last tyrants.[2] To the impregnability of the Pelargicum in the days of the tyrants, when Hippias had taken refuge behind its walls, Aristophanes makes direct reference in the Lysistrate (274–275; 281–282):

| | |
|---|---|
| ἐπεὶ οὐδὲ Κλεομένης, ὃς αὐτὴν κατέσχε πρῶτος, | for not even Cleomenes, who was the first man to gain possession of it, |
| ἀπῆλθεν ἀψάλακτος. . . . | came off unscathed. . . . |
| οὕτως ἐπολιόρκησ' ἐγὼ τὸν ἄνδρ' ἐκεῖνον ὠμῶς | So furiously did I lay siege to that man, |
| ἐφ' ἑπτακαίδεχ' ἀσπίδας πρὸς ταῖς πύλαις καθεύδων | as I slept—seventeen shields deep—before the gates |

---

[1] For the author's full discussion of this gigantic piece of military engineering see A. J. A. VIII (1893) pp. 481 ff.

[2] Ar. Lys. 1150–1155, whereon the Scholiast remarks that the fortifications were τὸ τεῖχος τὸ Πελαργικόν.

WEST FRONT OF THE ACROPOLIS

The patriots were unable to storm the Acropolis and dislodge the tyrants. They called in the Spartan king Cleomenes to their aid; and he it was that managed to secure the capitulation of the citadel and to send Hippias away into exile.

Neither Amazons nor liberators were able to capture the citadel with its tremendous walls. Neither, a generation after the tyrants' fall, was the overwhelming host of the Persians under Mardonius strong enough to take it.[1] The Persians secured an entrance only by climbing up κατὰ τὸ ἱρὸν τῆς Κέκροπος θυγατρὸς Ἀγλαύρου "by the sanctuary of Aglauros, the daughter of Cecrops," which was ὄπισθεν τῶν πυλέων "behind," that is, "beyond," "outside the gates" (for Herodotus is speaking from the point of view of the Persians); and of course the Athenians always had free communication between the Acropolis and the Aglaurium through this same cleft in the rock. But certainly this passage-way was not open to the general public—hence the surprise of the Athenians that the Persians should come up that way—and it should be remembered in passing that the stone staircase in this cleft as at present existing was not built until after the Persian wars.

Even when the new Propylaea was built, it was fitted into the system of the Pelargicum fort. This we see from the way in which the southwest wing of the Mnesiclean Propylaea is worked into that uppermost circuit of the Pelargicum which still stands three metres high and six metres thick at that point. And when Mnesicles built his great gateway, that "Pelasgic" wall was still standing to a height of ten metres or more. For we observe that the southeast corner of the southwest wing of the Propylaea is beveled vertically from base-stone to cornice so as to fit up squarely against this wall, and this fact proves beyond a peradventure that this upper wall of the Pelargicum was still standing when the Propylaea was built and was still higher than the roof of the southwest hall (30 feet). Otherwise such a bevel corner would have been worse than senseless. And it further proves that even Mnesicles and his associates still recognized the necessity of preserving the old fortifications for their original purpose; otherwise enough of that old wall would have been removed to make way for the new gateway, and there would have been no occasion thus to mar the corner of the southwest wing. And the condition of this upper wall at that time shows how well preserved the remains must have been, not only of the upper circuit, but of the lower walls as well; for the upper wall, which in the last quarter of the fifth century they took so much pains to conserve, would have been practically useless without the lower walls.

In the Birds Aristophanes transfers the Pelargicum, as he does so many other features of Athens, bodily into Cloud-cuckoo-town (832–836):

τίς δαὶ καθέξει τῆς πόλεως τὸ Πελαργικόν;

ΧΟ. ὄρνις ἀφ' ἡμῶν τοῦ γένους τοῦ Περσικοῦ,
ὅσπερ λέγεται δεινότατος εἶναι πανταχοῦ

Ἄρεως νεοττός. ΕΥ. ὦ νεοττὲ δέσποτα,
ὡς ὁ θεὸς ἐπιτήδειος οἰκεῖν ἐπὶ πετρῶν

who, pray, will stand guard over the Pelargicum of "the City"?

CHO. One of us—a bird of the Persian breed— one that is called the most redoubtable everywhere

—Ares's chick. EU. Master Chick, how well suited to bide on the Rock!

"The City" is again the Acropolis, of course, as is also "the Rock." In 414 B. C., the year in which Aristophanes brought out the Birds, the Pelargicum was still a reality and a mighty military defense. The "Chick of Ares" is the cock, foredoomed, from the day when he failed as sentry at the loves of Ares and Aphrodite,[2] to serve forever as a sentinel with helm and crest and with his shrill clarion to announce the coming of Hyperion Helius,[3] and he is called a "Persian bird" with perhaps an allusion to the only foreigner that had ever gained possession of the fortress. Some lines later in the same play Aristophanes again makes allusion to the Pelargicum in an appeal to the god of the sea (Ar. Av. 869):

ὦ Σουνιέρακε, χαῖρ' ἄναξ Πελαργικέ

thou Hawk of Sunium, all hail, oh Lord Pelargicus (of storkland)

for Poseidon had a sanctuary within the engirdling nine-gated walls.

The great gate-building of Mnesicles had been for twenty years practically completed, when (in 412–411) Aristophanes brought out the Lysistrate. So impregnable a fortress is the Acropolis in these fateful years of the Peloponnesian War, and so thoroughly unified

[1] Hdt. VIII 52–53.
[2] θ 266–366.
[3] Luc. Gal. 3.

with the old system of the fortifications is the Propylaea, that the little band of women under Lysistrate's leadership could seize the citadel, close and bar the outer gates of the old Pelargicum, and hold the place against all comers. The men of Athens could no more storm the Acropolis with its women defenders than the Persian armies two generations earlier could force its lines, with the handful of priests and old men behind the nine-gated ramparts. Lysistrate had her campaign thoroughly planned (Ar. Lys. 175–179):

| | |
|---|---|
| ἀλλ' ἔστι καὶ τοῦτ' εὖ παρεσκευασμένον· | yes, but proper provision has been made for that, too: |
| καταλήψομεν γὰρ τὴν Ἀκρόπολιν τήμερον. | we are going to seize the Acropolis to-day. |
| ταῖς πρεσβυτάταις γὰρ προστέτακται τοῦτο δρᾶν, | The elderesses have been instructed to effect this coup: |
| ἕως ἂν ἡμεῖς ταῦτα συντιθώμεθα, | while we are settling these matter, they, |
| θύειν δοκούσαις καταλαβεῖν τὴν Ἀκρόπολιν | under pretense of offering sacrifice, are to seize the Acropolis |

The strategy succeeds; the women seize the fort; the shout of initial victory descends into the lower city (Ar. Lys. 240–242; 245–246):

| | |
|---|---|
| ΛΑ. τίς ὠλολυγά; ΛΥ. τοῦτ' ἐκεῖν' οὑγὼ 'λεγον· | What means this alarum? LY. This is what I was telling you about: |
| αἱ γὰρ γυναῖκες τὴν Ἀκρόπολιν τῆς θεοῦ ἤδη κατειλήφασιν...... | the women have already seized the Acropolis of the goddess. . . . |
| ἡμεῖς δὲ ταῖς ἄλλαισι ταῖσιν ἐν πόλει ξυνεμβάλωμεν εἰσιοῦσαι τοὺς μοχλούς | And we will go in and join the rest of the women in "the City" and throw the bars in place |

Lysistrate, we observe, speaks of "*the* bars." Evidently the means employed by the women for securing the entrance to the Acropolis were no suddenly improvised bars, but the regular old apparatus for locking the ancient gates familiar to every Athenian. Accordingly, when the Deputy, the Probulus, demands an explanation of the situation, he also refers very naturally to "the bars" (Ar. Lys. 486–487):

| | |
|---|---|
| τοῦτ' ἐπιθυμῶ νὴ τὸν Δία πρῶτα πυθέσθαι, ὅ τι βουλόμεναι τὴν πόλιν ἡμῶν ἀπεκλήσατε τοῖσι μοχλοῖσιν | the first thing I want to know, by Zeus, is what you meant by locking up our City with the bars |

The bars have been shot into place; the Acropolis is securely in the hands of the women (Ar. Lys. 423):

| | |
|---|---|
| ὑπὸ τῶν γυναικῶν ἀποκέκλεισμαι τῶν πυλῶν | I have been shut out of the gates by the women |

But the war partizans determine to dislodge them (Ar. Lys. 259–260; 262–270):

| | |
|---|---|
| τίς ἄν ποτ' ἤλπισ' . . . . ἀκοῦσαι γυναῖκας ἃς ἐβόσκομεν | who would ever have thought to hear that women whom we had supported |
| . . . . . . . . . | . . . . . . . |
| κατὰ μὲν ἅγιον ἔχειν βρέτας, | would take the holy image |
| κατὰ δ' Ἀκρόπολιν ἐμὰν λαβεῖν, | and seize my Acropolis |
| μοχλοῖς δὲ καὶ κλήθροισιν | and with bars and bolts |
| τὰ προπύλαια πακτοῦν; | fast close the outer gates? |
| ἀλλ' ὡς τάχιστα πρὸς πόλιν σπεύσωμεν, ὦ Φιλοῦργε, | but let us hasten with all speed to the City, Philurgus, |
| ὅπως ἂν αὐτὰς ἐν κύκλῳ θέντες τὰ πρέμνα ταυτί, | that we may lay these logs around about them |
| ὅσαι τὸ πρᾶγμα τοῦτ' ἐνεστήσαντο καὶ μετῆλθον | and for all those who have started this proposition and put it into effect |
| μίαν πυρὰν νήσαντες ἐμπρήσομεν αὐτόχειρες πάσας | rear one great funeral pile and with our own hands burn them all up together |

The men propose to burn[1] the "wooden walls" just as the Persians had burned the wooden palisades erected on the walls of the Pelargicum nearly eighty years before. And the women, safe behind the same defenses and the barred and bolted gates of the Pelargicum, could defy all the assaults of the militarist men as confidently as the defenders of "the city" looked down upon Mardonius and his Medes and Persians (Ar. Lys. 247–251):

[1] The burning operation is a long one, extending from line 249 to line 387. It is at its height during the two long choruses, lines 289–318 and 319–352.

ΚΑ. οὐκοῦν ἐφ' ἡμᾶς ξυμβοηθήσειν οἴει

τοὺς ἄνδρας εὐθύς; ΛΥ. ὀλίγον ἐμοὶ μέλει.
οὐ γὰρ τοσαύτας οὔτ' ἀπειλὰς οὔτε πῦρ
ἥξουσ' ἔχοντες ὥστ' ἀνοῖξαι τὰς πύλας
ταύτας

CA. Don't you suppose the men will at once make
an assault upon us? LY. Little do I care.
For they will not come with threats or fire
enough to get these gates
open

The chorus, the conservative citizens of Athens, come up to the gates with their two sticks of cord-wood apiece, throw their fuel down against the gates, and set the pile of inflammable material on fire. The gates were great, heavy portals of oak covered with bronze, it would seem—like the gates at Mycenae and Tiryns. But the pile of fuel that the chorus carried up and set on fire against the jambs of the doors would soon reduce the stone to lime and make it possible to pry the doors from their hinges with the crowbars that the men carried with them[1] and thus open the way into the citadel, if the fire were allowed to burn but a little while. The conflagration is started (Ar. Lys. 307–311):

τὼ μὲν ξύλω θείμεσθα πρῶτον αὐτοῦ,
τῆς ἀμπέλου δ' ἐς τὴν χύτραν τὸν φανὸν
           ἐγκαθέντες
ἅψαντες εἶτ' ἐς τὴν θύραν κριηδὸν ἐμπέσοιμεν;
κἂν μὴ καλούντων τοὺς μοχλοὺς χαλῶσιν αἱ
           γυναῖκες,
ἐμπιμπράναι χρὴ τὰς θύρας καὶ τῷ καπνῷ
           πιέζειν

the sticks of wood we first place here;
should we thrust the grapevine torch into the pot of coals,
kindle the blaze, and then buck the gate?
And if the women do not loose the bars at our demand,
we must burn down the doors and smother them in the smoke

The flames and smoke roll up and threaten destruction to gates and defenders (*ibid.* 321–324):

λιγνὺν δοκῶ μοι καθορᾶν τὸν καπνόν,
ὥσπερ πυρὸς καομένου·......
πέτου, πέτου, Νικοδίκη,
πρὶν ἐμπεπρῆσθαι Καλύκην
τε καὶ Κρίτυλλαν

it seems to me I see lurid flames and smoke
as from a blazing conflagration; . . .
fly, fly, Nicodice,
before Calyce and Critylla
are burned to death

But the women run to the rescue with their water-pitchers—a volunteer fire-department—and extinguish the flames. The task was much simpler with the properties of the comic theatre than it would have been at the Acropolis gateway itself. The imitation Acropolis was barely ten or twelve feet above the orchestra; the gateway of the Pelargicum formed the main entrance in the centre of the proscenium; the Clepsydra Spring may well have been represented on one of the πίνακες to the left; it was, therefore, a very simple matter for the women to run with their pitchers and carry water to extinguish the flames only a few feet away (Ar. Lys. 327–334; 347–349):

νῦν δὴ γὰρ ἐμπλησαμένη τὴν ὑδρίαν κνεφαία
μόγις ἀπὸ κρήνης ὑπ' ὄχλου καὶ θορύβου καὶ
           παταγοῦ χυτρείου,

δούλησιν ὠστιζομένη
στιγματίαις θ' ἁρπαλέως
ἀραμένη, ταῖσιν ἐμαῖς
δημότισιν καιομέναις
φέρουσ' ὕδωρ βοηθῶ

. . . . . .
. . . ἤν τις ἐκεί-
νας ὑποπίμπρησιν ἀνὴρ
φέρειν ὕδωρ μεθ' ἡμῶν

for now that I have filled my pitcher at dawn
at the spring, with no end of trouble
because of the jam and confusion and clatter of jugs,

jostling with servant girls
and knaves, I have caught up my
pitcher in haste and am running to
rescue my fellow citizenesses
who are in danger of burning to death

. . . . . .
. . . if any man try to
burn them out, help us
carry water to save them

It is quite possible that the Enneacrunus Fountain rather than the Clepsydra was represented on one of the πίνακες. The Clepsydra was right at the very doors of the Propylaea, but the Enneacrunus was at the western foot of the Acropolis, and it would not be forcing the stage properties over much to have the main scene of the action in the Agora with the Acropolis rising directly up above it. The crowd of women thronging to the fountain to

[1] Cp. p. 260 below.

fetch their water in the early morning, the jam of servant girls and slaves and knaves, the clatter of jars, and the hustle and bustle are far more characteristic of the Enneacrunus than of the Clepsydra; for the Clepsydra was never a general source of supply for household needs but only for emergencies inside the citadel. The Clepsydra, moreover, was inside the Acropolis walls, and the women of the chorus are always on the outside.

This second possibility becomes practical certainty, when we grasp the point of Aristophanes's allusion a little further on in line 378. The main body of the feminists have barricaded the Acropolis; the chorus of old men have climbed up the steep ascent and now have entered the scene from one side, while the chorus of women have entered from the other side; they are both just below the Propylaea and the Nike-bastion.[1] By just what route the chorus of women have arrived in the orchestra, we are not told. No matter. They make it perfectly clear that they came up from the Enneacrunus, and probably by the festal street; for they came from a spring that every morning was crowded with girls who came to draw their day's supply of water, and that was situated conveniently to the entrance to the Acropolis,[2] and they bring their pitchers full for the drenching of the old men (Lys. 377–378):

| | |
|---|---|
| ΧΟ. ΓΥ... λουτρόν γ' ἐγὼ παρέξω. | CHO. WO. . . . I'll provide a bath for you. |
| ΧΟ. ΓΕ. ἐμοὶ σὺ λουτρόν, ὦ σαπρά; | CHO. MEN. You a bath for me, you rotten thing! |
| ΧΟ. ΓΥ. καὶ ταῦτα νυμφικόν γε. | CHO. WO. Ay; and a bride-bath, at that. |

The Scholiast on the passage explains this as a jest at the old age of the men of the chorus. But there is more than that in the women's joke: the old men are to get a bath, and it will be the most solemn and significant kind of bath, a bath with hallowed water. For, as we have just seen, it was from the Enneacrunus that the water was always carried for the bath of the bride.[3]

But the women trusted in the strength of their position; and the men, too, realized the strength of the bars that fastened the gates—there was no bursting of them nor passing through, unless the women saw fit to unbar the doors, without burning the whole thing down, as set forth above (Ar. Lys. 310–311):

| | |
|---|---|
| κἂν μὴ καλούντων τοὺς μοχλοὺς<br>    χαλῶσιν αἱ γυναῖκες<br>ἐμπιμπράναι χρὴ τὰς θύρας καὶ<br>    τῷ καπνῷ πιέζειν | unless the women, on our demand, shall draw the bars,<br>we shall have to burn down the gates and smother them with the smoke |

And so, when the Probulus arrives from the Committee of Ten and finds himself locked out, he proposes to force the gates with crowbars; and Lysistrate, fearful of the success of his plans, comes out for a parley with him (Ar. Lys. 423–425; 428–432):

| | |
|---|---|
| ΠΡ. ὑπὸ τῶν γυναικῶν ἀποκέκλεισμαι τῶν<br>        πυλῶν<br>ἀλλ' οὐδὲν ἔργον ἑστάναι. φέρε τοὺς<br>        μοχλούς,<br>ὅπως ἂν αὐτὰς τῆς ὕβρεως ἐγὼ σχέθω | PR. The women have locked the gates in my face!<br>Well; there's no use standing here; bring the crowbars,<br>and I'll put a stop to their impudence |
| . . . . . . . . . .<br>οὐχ ὑποβαλόντες τοὺς μοχλοὺς ὑπὸ τὰς πύλας<br>ἐντεῦθεν ἐκμοχλεύσετ'; ἐνθενδὶ δ' ἐγὼ<br>ξυνεκμοχλεύσω. ΛΥ. μηδὲν ἐκμοχλεύετε·<br>ἐξέρχομαι γὰρ αὐτομάτη. τί δεῖ μοχλῶν;<br><br>οὐ γὰρ μοχλῶν δεῖ μᾶλλον ἢ νοῦ καὶ φρενῶν | . . . . . . . . . .<br>Drive those crowbars under the gates<br>and pry them loose. Here, I'll<br>help pry. LY. Don't pry any more!<br>I'll come out of my own accord. What's the use of crowbars?<br>You don't need crows, but brains and common sense! |

The poets, accordingly, while they do not give us any details of the architecture or plans or changes of plans[4] of the Propylaea, do make it clear that the building of the Mnesiclean gateway did not do away with the fortificatory nature of the Acropolis, even in the days of

[1] See below, p. 261.
[2] See pp. 127 ff.
[3] Thuc. II 15, 3–4, quoted on p. 130.
[4] See Dörpfeld, Ath. Mitt. X, pp. 38 ff. and 131 ff.

its dazzling splendors of art, and they throw some light also upon the historical development of the upper citadel.[1]

When the Lysistrate was produced (411 B. C.), not only was the Propylaea as nearly completed as it ever was, but the new temple of Athena Nike also crowned the bastion above the winding approach to the citadel. If the Parthenon in its new splendor and glory called forth so little in the way of recognition at the hands of contemporary poets, as we have seen, what may we expect for the little temple of Athena Nike before the Propylaea? In just one passage do we find a possible allusion to the temple: in the Lysistrate of Aristophanes, the Chorus of Elders, climbing up the approach to the locked and bolted gates of the citadel with their fagots and tinder-boxes to "smoke" the women out, appeal, as they reach the gates, to "sovereign Nike," indweller of the temple above them, to lend them her aid and grant them to set up a trophy over the women and their unpardonable presumption (Ar. Lys. 316–318):

| | |
|---|---|
| τὴν λαμπάδ' ἡμμένην ὅπως πρόφρων ἐμοὶ προσοίσεις. | I pray you, apply the lighted torch with might and main. |
| δέσποινα Νίκη, ξυγγενοῦ, τῶν τ' ἐν πόλει γυναικῶν | Be with us, Sovereign Victory, and grant that we may |
| τοῦ νῦν παρεστῶτος θράσους θέσθαι τρόπαιον ἡμᾶς | set up a trophy over the women in the Acropolis for their present presumption |

Aristophanes makes no contribution to our knowledge of the temple of Athena Nike. He does not even mention the temple directly. The allusion to it is so remote that we are forced to interpret the passage by our knowledge of the topography. The presence of the temple in the scene—in all probability represented on one of the πίνακες of the proscenium—suggests to the chorus, already at the very gates of the Propylaea, with the Nike temple directly beside or behind or above them, that Nike is on their side and will help them if properly invoked.

The Parthenon, as we have seen, is barely mentioned by name and but little is said of it by the dramatic poets; the Propylaea is mentioned just once (Ar. Eq. 1326):

| | |
|---|---|
| ἀνοιγνυμένων ψόφος ἤδη τῶν Προπυλαίων | right now there is a noise as the Propylaea opens |

—the great doors swing round on their wheels and hinges of bronze and grate and creak as they roll; the Nike temple is probably once alluded to; the Erechtheum is not even recognized, though one of the miraculous "signs," Athena's olive tree, fares better at the poets' hands. Phidias set it in the centre of the western pediment of the Parthenon, and Euripides sings its praises in no less than three passages. In one the olive is made an identifying epithet of the Acropolis hill, the rock where the nightingale sings (Ion 1478–1480; 1482):

| | |
|---|---|
| ΚΡ. ἴστω Γοργοφόνα—ΙΩΝ. τί τοῦτ' ἔλεξας; | CR. The Gorgon-slayer be witness—ION. What meanest thou by that? |
| ΚΡ. ἃ σκοπέλοις ἐπ' ἐμοῖς τὸν ἐλαιοφυῆ πάγον θάσσει | CR.—Who hath her seat upon my rock, the hill where the olive groweth |
| . . . . . . . . | . . . . . . . . |
| παρ' ἀηδόνιον πέτραν | by the rock where the nightingale sings |

In four lines Euripides briefly sums up the story told in Herodotus[2] of the miraculous tree whose leaf could not wither, whose life even the Persian fires could not destroy (Ion 1433–1436):

| | |
|---|---|
| στέφανον ἐλαίας ἀμφέθηκά σοι τότε, ἣν πρῶτ' Ἀθάνα σκόπελον ἐξηνέγκατο, ὅς, εἴπερ ἔστιν, οὔποτ' ἐκλείπει χλόην, θάλλει δ' ἐλαίας ἐξ ἀκηράτου γεγώς | a wreath I then hung about thee from the olive which Athena first brought to her high rock. If that is there, it hath never lost its green but flourisheth still, for it comes from the olive that never suffered harm |

[1] There is a curious fragment of Phoenicides (Μισ., Frag. 2 K.), in which προπύλαια (if the reading is correct) seems to be some sort of food:

| | |
|---|---|
| Α. μύρτων λέγουσι καὶ μέλιτος ἐγκώμια καὶ τῶν προπυλαίων καὶ τέταρτον ἰσχάδων· τούτων ἐγευσάμην καταπλεύσας εὐθέως — Β. καὶ τῶν προπυλαίων; Α. οὐδὲν ἦν τούτων | A. They speak the praises of myrtle-berries and honey and the propylaea and, fourth, dried figs; these I tasted, the moment I landed— B. And the propylaea? A. Not one of these viands would |
| πρὸς ἀτταγῆνα συμβαλεῖν τῶν βρωμάτων | for a moment compare with grouse |

[2] VIII 55

And once more, with pious admiration of the wonders of divine creation, the poet soars on the wings of praise of the sacred olive tree (Eur. Tro. 796–801):

| | |
|---|---|
| νάσου περικύμονος.... | the wave-girt isle . . . |
| τὰς ἐπικεκλιμένας ὄχθοις ἱεροῖς, ἵν' ἐλαίας | that lieth over against the sacred slopes, where Athena |
| πρῶτον ἔδειξε κλάδον γλαυκᾶς 'Αθάνα, | first produced the grey-green olive branch, for |
| οὐράνιον στέφανον λιπαραῖσί τε κόσμον 'Αθήναις | Athens the bright a heavenly crown and ornament |

It is from an unidentified fragment of Aristophanes that we learn that the miraculously created olive was small and gnarled (664 D.):

| | |
|---|---|
| πάγκυφος ἐλαία | the gnarled olive tree |

on which Hesychius remarks:[1]

| | |
|---|---|
| ἀστὴ ἐλαία· ἡ ἐν 'Ακροπόλει ἡ καλουμένη πάγκυφος διὰ χθαμαλότητα | the city olive: the one on the Acropolis called "the gnarled" because of its squattiness |

## 2. Seven-gated Thebes

The discussion of the various problems of Theban topography in the preceding chapter (V c) makes it almost impossible to avoid the vext question of the topography of the gates of Thebes also. Aeschylus paints with hasty stroke the splendid system of fortifications with its gates, its towers, its battlements and breastworks (Sep. 30–34):[2]

| | |
|---|---|
| ἀλλ' ἔς τ' ἀπάλξεις καὶ πύλας πυργωμάτων | but to the battlements and gates of the towered walls |
| ὁρμᾶσθε πάντες, σοῦσθε σὺν παντευχίᾳ, πληροῦτε θωρακεῖα, κἀπὶ σέλμασιν | hasten, all; speed you in full panoply of war; man the breastworks; take your stand upon the bridges |
| πύργων στάθητε, καὶ πυλῶν ἐπ' ἐξόδοις μίμνοντες εὐθαρσεῖτε | of the towers and at the exits of the gates; hold fast and have no fear |

Because of their rearing themselves by the miracle-working power of a son of Zeus[3] the walls were holy (Eur. Hip. 555–556):

| | |
|---|---|
| ὦ Θήβας ἱερὸν τεῖχος | oh Thebe's hallowed wall |

Pausanias gives the interesting note (IX 8, 4):

| | |
|---|---|
| Θηβαίοις δὲ ἐν τῷ περιβόλῳ τοῦ ἀρχαίου τείχους ἑπτὰ ἀριθμὸν ἦσαν πύλαι, μένουσι δὲ καὶ εἰς ἡμᾶς ἔτι | in the circuit wall of ancient Thebes there were gates seven in number, and they remain even unto our day |

The Thebes of Cadmus, of Amphion, of Oedipus and Eteocles was seven-gated. So say Homer[4] and all the tragic poets with one accord;[5] even the comedy has it once (Anaxandr. Πρωτ., Frag. 41, 21 K.[6]); and so, says Pausanias, was the Thebes of his own day. For the Thebes of the Macedonians and of the Romans was, like the Thebes of Oedipus and Creon, confined to the space enclosed by the acropolis walls of the Cadmea. The city of Epaminondas was something quite different. Before the end of the sixth century Thebes had expanded far beyond the Cadmean hill—westward, northward, and especially eastward. The expansion had demanded new lines of defense and the great wall of stone and brick was built, the lines of which we can trace by the foundations of heavy masonry, almost without

---

[1] Cf. also Pollux IX 17.

[2] Cf. also Ae. Sep. 549; 823. In the Phoenissae 1098 and 1176 Euripides gives the walls the epic appellation of πέργαμα ὄρθια and πέργαμα ἄκρα.

[3] Eur. Ph. 115–116:'Αμφίονος.... τείχεος; 823–824; Eur. Antiope (see p. 264); Hyps. Frag. 1 II 30–33, Ox. Pap. VI p. 35:

τὸ τᾶς κιθάρας ἔρυμα
τᾶς 'Αμφίονος ἔργον χερός

[4] Δ 406; λ 263.

[5] E. g., Ae. Sep. 165; 282–284; Soph. Ant. 101; 119; 141; Inc. Frag. 705N.; Eur. Bac. 919; H. F. 28; 543; 782; Ph. 79; 287; 739; 748–749; 974; 1058; 1078; 1094; Sup. 401; 1221; Sen. H. F. 1292.

[6] Θήβας τὰς ἑπταπύλους.

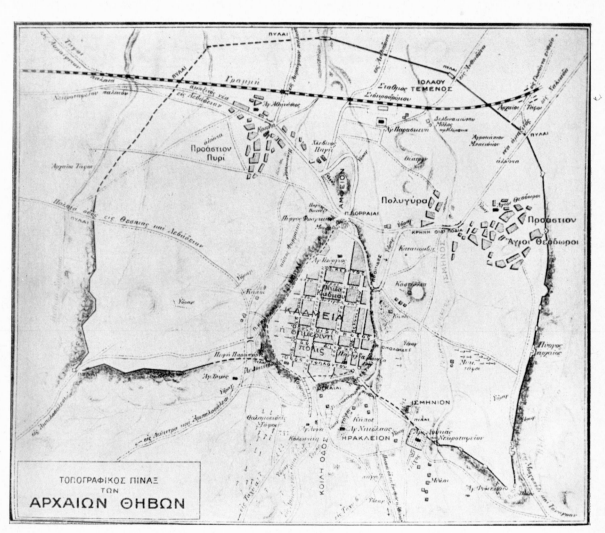

PLAN OF THEBES

(After Κερχμότουλλος)

interruption, from the Ismenium to the top of the round hill to the southeast, and from thence northward beyond the modern suburb of Ἅγιοι Θεόδωροι; enough remains to enable us to follow the course of the late sixth or early fifth century walls north of the railway line and along the higher range of hills west of the Cadmea, beyond the stream of Dirce. Of the wall on the southern side but slight traces have been found; it must have crossed the two valleys in a line not far south of the Cadmea proper. This circuit wall is commonly called the wall of Cassander. But the city that Cassander desired to help and protect needed no such circuit wall. Alexander had in 336 absolutely destroyed Thebes; not a single building, save the house of Pindar, had been left standing; the inhabitants had been put to the sword or sold into slavery; the real estate had been assigned to other towns or apportioned to Macedonian proprietors.[1]

Accordingly, when Cassander proposed to restore the city for the pitifully small remnant of the scattered people that could be recalled from the dispersion, the Cadmea was ample room indeed; and Cassander's restoration was confined to the Cadmea.[2] And never again from Cassander's day till now did Thebes outgrow the limits of the old acropolis. It was not the city of Epaminondas that Pausanias[3] and Strabo visited, but the Thebes of Cassander, Demetrius Poliorcetes, and Sulla.

Pausanias is perfectly explicit on this point: he says that the lower city was entirely desolate and destroyed, except the sanctuaries, and that the people lived only upon the acropolis.[4] And in telling of the most memorable war of the heroic age he states that the battle between Adrastus and the Thebans was fought at the Ismenian sanctuary (inside the sixth and fifth century walls), that the Thebans were defeated in the fight, and that, when turned to rout, they fled for safety inside the wall (the fortifications of the Cadmea).[5] The western wall of the lower city was about as far to the west of the Cadmea as its eastern wall is east of it.

The city of Amphion and Eteocles was bounded by the stream of Ismenus on the east and that of Dirce on the west. So much seems to be perfectly clear from Euripides's Phoenissae (101–102):

| | |
|---|---|
| σκόπει δὲ πεδία καὶ παρ' Ἰσμηνοῦ ῥοὰς | look out upon the plains and along Ismenus's brooks |
| Δίρκης τε νᾶμα, πολεμίων στράτευμ' ὅσον | and Dirce's stream and see how great a host of foes |

Antigone and the paedagogus have climbed to the palace roof on the heights of the Cadmea to view the Argive army; that army has approached Thebes from the northeast and is now spread along the plains to the north of Cadmea and extends its wings up the valleys of the two streams. They are "along Ismenus's brooks and Dirce's streams" and yet outside the city walls. They must be thought of as occupying the space between the Ismenus and the later east wall, on the one side, and between Dirce and the later west wall, on the other side. Thus Dirce and Ismenus, at the remotest, would become the western and eastern city limits of Mycenaean Thebes; but both lie outside that city. Antigone and the old paedagogus see Tydeus crossing the Dircaean stream before ever the battle begins,[6] and Eteocles presents as an argument in favor of his impetuous plan for a surprise attack upon the foe the suggestion that Dirce's deep ford would hamper the enemy's retreat (Eur. Ph. 730):

| | |
|---|---|
| βαθύς γέ τοι Διρκαῖος ἀναχωρεῖν πόρος | deep, thou knowest, is Dirce's ford for a retreat |

—not that the water was dangerously deep; it never was, except after a veritable cloud-burst; but the bed was deep-cut and still is. But the main point is that the Argive lines occupied ground between the Dircaean stream and the Cadmean wall. It is also clear that

---

[1] See Arr. An. I 9; Diod. XVII 12; Aelian XIII 7; Strabo IX 2, 5.

[2] Pausanias's words (IX 7, 4) Θηβαίοις δὲ ἐπὶ μὲν Κασσάνδρου πᾶς ὁ ἀρχαῖος περίβολος ἀνῳκίσθη have reference only to the peribolos-wall of the Cadmea; the word ἀρχαῖος in Pausanias must mean just that.

[3] IX 7, 1.

[4] IX 7, 6: καί σφισιν μὲν ἡ μὲν κάτω πόλις πᾶσα ἔρημος ἦν ἐπ' ἐμοῦ πλὴν τὰ ἱερά, τὴν δὲ ἀκρόπολιν οἰκοῦσι Θήβας καὶ οὐ Καδμείαν καλουμένην.

[5] Paus. IX 9, 2: γενομένης δὲ πρὸς Ἰσμηνίῳ μάχης ἐκρατήθησαν οἱ Θηβαῖοι τῇ συμβολῇ, καὶ ὡς ἐτράποντο, καταφεύγουσιν ἐς τὸ τεῖχος.

[6] Eur. Ph. 131: τόνδ' ἐξαμείβοντ' οὐχ ὁρᾷς Δίρκης ὕδωρ; All that they are represented as seeing is easily possible from the highest point of the Cadmea, where the palace stood. In Aeschylus's Seven the Chorus both sees and hears only too much for their comfort (e.g., 81 ff.; 89 ff.; 100; 103; 114 ff.; 122; 151; 153 ff.; 203 ff.; 239; 245).

the Argive camp that Eteocles rashly (as it seems to Creon) proposes to storm is not between Dirce and the main part of the Cadmea; there would be no room for it there, and the Argives would have been in very serious danger from the Thebans on the walls above them, if they had attempted to secure a position there. Euripides, if he is thinking in terms of topography at all (and I am convinced that he is), has in mind the more open ground farther to the north, in the neighborhood of Πυρί; for when his other propositions are, one after another, rejected by Creon, Eteocles proposes at last to charge *down* upon them with "the horse," that is, with the war-chariots. Down the steep, partly precipitous, western side of the Cadmea a charge of chariots would have been utterly unthinkable. Besides, Creon opposes, the Argives have their position strengthened with their chariots round about (Eur. Ph. 732–733):

| | |
|---|---|
| ET. τί δ', εἰ καθιππεύσαιμεν Ἀργείων στρατόν; | ET. What if we should charge with our horse down upon the army of the Argives? |
| ΚΡ. κἀκεῖ πέφρακται λαὸς ἅρμασιν πέριξ. | CR. There, too, the host is fenced about with chariots. |

There could have been no "fencing about" with chariots between the walls and the upper reaches of the Dircaean stream or even the hills beyond the Dircaean stream to the west.

As Euripides leaves no doubt as to his view of the location of Creon's city east of the stream of Dirce, he just as clearly locates it west of the waters of Ismenus (Sup. 383–384):

| | |
|---|---|
| ἐλθὼν δ' ὑπέρ τ' Ἀσωπὸν Ἰσμηνοῦ θ' ὕδωρ | go back across the Asopus and the waters of Ismenus |
| σεμνῷ τυράννῳ φράζε Καδμείων τάδε | and bear this message to the august king of the Cadmeans |

Theseus speaks the words at the altar of Demeter at Eleusis. The messenger returning to Thebes would cross the divide and pass the Asopus and the Ismenus before he reached the home of the king of the Cadmeans.

The Ismenus is outside the city to the east; Dirce is outside the city to the west. This narrower compass of the Cadmean wall is in perfect harmony also with the description of the position of Theseus's army in the passage from Euripides's Suppliants (650 ff.) discussed above[1] and is still more emphatically confirmed by the fragment from the end of the Antiope, in which Hermes (as *deus ex machina*) instructs his brethren, Amphion and Zethus, as to the building of the walls (*Hermathena* 1891; *Hermes* 1891, p. 242):

| | |
|---|---|
| ὑμεῖς δ' ἐπειδὰν ὅσιος ᾖ Κάδμου πόλις, | and ye, lads, when Cadmus's city is purified, |
| χωρεῖτε, παῖδες, ἄστυ δ' Ἰσμηνὸν πάρα | go and along Ismenus provide with towered gates |
| ἑπτάστομον πύλαισιν ἐξαρτύετε | the city of the seven openings |

The location of Amphion's castle-city on the hill between the two streams is still more explicitly specified, corrupt as the text may be, in Euripides's Phoenissae (823–827):

| | |
|---|---|
| φόρμιγγί τε τείχεα Θήβας | and to the notes of the harp the walls of Thebes |
| τᾶς Ἀμφιονίας τε λύρας ὕπο πύργος ἀνέστα | and the towers arose, under the spell of Amphion's lyre, |
| διδύμων ποταμῶν πόρον ἀμφὶ μέσον | in the space between the rivers twain— |
| Δίρκας, χλοεροτρόφον ἃ πεδίον | of Dirce, which, running parallel with Ismenus, |
| πρόπαρ Ἰσμηνοῦ καταδεύει | watereth the plain putting forth fresh green |

The picture is complete: Amphion's city is a castle with seven great gates on the Cadmean hill between the streams of Dirce and Ismenus, even as the earlier "city" of Athens was the castle upon the Acropolis, with its nine gates, between the streams of Ilissus and Cephissus.

These conclusions are further verified by the topography, as we find it to-day: the Cadmea was, as we have repeatedly observed, a Mycenaean castle fortified with Cyclopean walls; in the face of the immediately adjacent hills to the east and south are Mycenaean tombs.[2] After the analogy of Mycenae, these burial places must have been just beyond the city limits. As usual, the poets and the facts are in perfect accord.

Three of the seven gates we can locate with a fair degree of certainty. The Electran gate is the one by which travelers from Plataea entered the city (Paus. IX. 8, 7):

[1] Pp. 241, 242.
[2] Κεραμόπουλλος, Ἀρχ. Δελτ. III (1917) pp. 25–33; 80–98; 100–209.

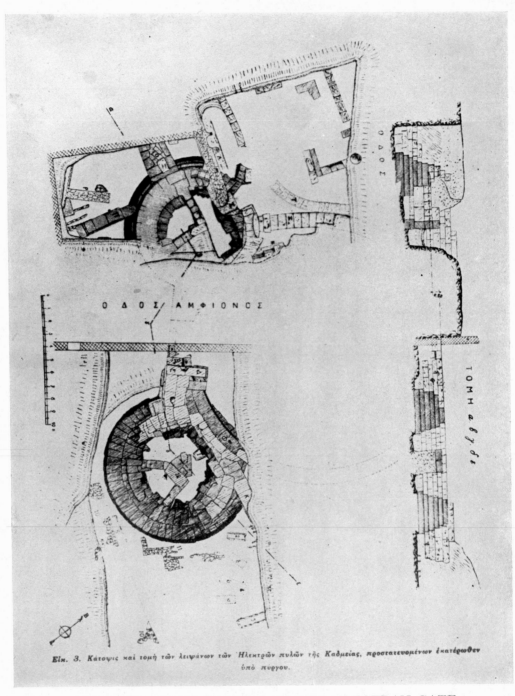

Εἰκ. 3. Κάτοψις καὶ τομὴ τῶν λειψάνων τῶν Ἠλεκτρῶν πυλῶν τῆς Καδμείας, προστατευομένων ἑκατέρωθεν ὑπὸ πύργου.

PLAN AND CROSS-SECTION OF THE ELECTRAN GATE
(After Κεραμόπουλλος)

ἐρχομένῳ δὲ ἐκ Πλαταίας ἔσοδος | as you come from Plataea, the entrance
ἐς τὰς Θήβας κατὰ πύλας ἐστὶν | to Thebes is by the Gate
Ἠλέκτρας | Electrae

Pausanias had come from Plataea by way of Potniae, the modern village of Ταχό; this was also the main road to Eleusis and Athens, leaving Thebes by the valley between the hill of Ismenian Apollo and Κολωνάκι, the next line of hills to the west.

On most maps of Thebes the present day entrance is labeled the "Electran Gate," obviously because the great highway from Eleusis and Athens enters the town at that point. But that modern carriage road was not built until 1851–1861; before that date the only modern route from Eleusis and Athens led through the valley below and entered Thebes at the southeast corner of the Cadmea. The principal entrance to the town continued, therefore, unchanged from the days when the walls and towers rose at the strains of Amphion's lyre to the time when the royal highway was opened in 1861. For even in the days when Thebes stood at its highest glory, surrounded by its wide circuit of classical walls in the fifth and fourth centuries, the principal gate of the lower city corresponded exactly with this old Electran Gate and was only a few yards distant from it.[1]

And there, on that corner of the Cadmean wall, where Amphion Street leads out from modern Thebes to the cemetery and the trail to Athens, Keramopoullos instituted excavations in 1908–1910 and found evidence of a great gateway dating from the Mycenaean period and rebuilt at various times down through the centuries. The principal existing remains from classical times present the appearance of a great dipylon gate with four round towers, two flanking the outer and two the inner gateway, with a large circular court between them, the whole reminding one forcibly of the Arcadian Gate at Messene, which, we recall, was built by Epaminondas at the time of Thebes' greatest power and prosperity. The Thebans would seem to have fortified their new city in the Peloponnesus after the model of their ancient capital on the Cadmean hill.

In that quarter Euripides also locates the Gate Electrae; for at the Electran Gate Pentheus orders the marshalling of his forces for their march against the Bacchanals who were celebrating their orgies on Mount Cithaeron directly to the south of Thebes (Eur. Bac. 780–781):

στεῖχ' ἐπ' Ἠλέκτρας ἰὼν | go; proceed to the Electran
πύλας | Gate

The Proetidian Gate opened upon the highway from Thebes to Chalcis (Paus. IX 18, 1):

ἐκ Θηβῶν δὲ ὁδὸς ἐς Χαλκίδα | from Thebes a road to Chalcis
κατὰ πύλας ταύτας ἐστὶ τὰς | starts here at the Gate
Προιτίδας | Proetidian

And there before the gate was the tomb of Melanippus, where, according to Aeschylus, he fought and slew Tydeus and was himself slain by Amphiaraus. The road to Chalcis leads to the northeast; accordingly, we must place the Proetidian Gate at the northeast corner of the city, on the ridge between the Cadmea and Ἅγιοι Θεόδωροι, as we have already shown.[2]

The location of the Neïstan Gate is not so certain; its name appears also in the form of Neïtan, which seems to be derived from νήϊτος "lowest." If the Hypsistan Gate is true to its name and is to be sought on the height of the southwest ridge of the Cadmea, then the Neïtan, true to its name, ought to be found at the lowest point touched by the city walls, low down at the end of the Dircaean gully. But Pausanias tells us that the Neïstan Gate opens into the road to the sanctuary of Themis and of the Cabirian Demeter and of the Cabiri,[3] and so on to Thespiae. The two Cabirian sanctuaries we now know,[4] and they are straight west from the Cadmea. Furthermore, Pausanias passes the gate before he crosses the Dircaean stream, and he finds close beside the gate the monument of Menoeceus, Creon's son, near the spot where the youth slew himself over the Dragon's cave,[5] and the scene of the fatal duel between Eteocles and Polynices. We conclude, therefore, with practical certainty that the Neïstan Gate was a gate of the Cadmean city and not a gate in the fifth century

---

[1] Arr. An. I 7, 9; 8, 5. Cf. also Eur. Sup. 651 (quoted on p. 242).
[2] Pp. 241, 242.
[3] Paus. IX 25, 4: κατὰ δὲ τὴν ὁδὸν ἀπὸ τῶν πυλῶν τῶν Νηϊστῶν τὸ μὲν Θέμιδός ἐστιν ἱερόν.... καὶ Δήμητρος Καβειρίας καὶ... τῶν Καβείρων τὸ ἱερόν...
[4] See pp. 132–135.
[5] See Paus. IX 25, 1, and pp. 242–247.

wall.  After Pausanias has passed the Gate Neïstan and crossed Dirce (he seems to be so eager to make it clear that he has really crossed the stream, that he reiterates his assertion that he has crossed it),[1] he is still inside the classical city and comes to the house of Pindar, the temple of Dindymene, and various other points of interest.  Pindar's house was not in the Cadmea but in the newer city; the Neïstan Gate was not in the fifth century wall but in the walls of the Cadmean city and close by the Paraporti Spring.  It may well, therefore, have been the "lowest gate"—a postern gate, low down like the postern gate of Tiryns— and have afforded convenient access for the ancient Cadmeans to their most copious spring.

It is, of course, quite within the range of possibilities that there was a Neïstan Gate also in the later outer circuit wall, corresponding to the Neïstan Gate of the old Cadmean city; but *the* Neïstan Gate was a Cadmean city gate, low down toward the Dircaean stream but above its right bank.

Of these three gates alone of the seven we can fix the location with reasonable certainty. For their exact topographical relations, and for the possible location of the others Pausanias helps but little.  Aeschylus and Euripides help us much more.  Furthermore, Euripides (Ph. 1100 ff.) has the Argive host advance against the town from Teumessus,[2] which lay a few miles northeast from Thebes; and when they approach near the city, they divide for the assault upon the gates.  He names the famous seven heroes in order: Parthenopaeus, Amphiaraus, Hippomedon, Tydeus, Polynices, Capaneus, Adrastus.  But why he chose that order is beyond the hope of successful conjecture.  One's first guess would be that he is following the order adopted for his heroes, because he had already determined to follow a topographic order in the list of gates.  His gates are, in the order named: Neïstan, Proetidian, Ogygian, Homoloïdian, Crenaean, Electran, and "the seventh" (Hypsistan?).  But that is anything but topographic order.  The first named gate, the Neïstan, is apparently far removed from the second named gate, the Proetidian, which was certainly the nearest one to the approaching Argive army.  But Euripides may, with that wide separation, wish to have us see the gallant, impetuous, young Parthenopaeus dash half way round the fortress to attack the Neïstan Gate, while the staid old prophet advances cautiously against the nearest gate.

The Ogygian Gate we have already assigned, in a general way, to the south side of the city, near the sanctuary of Athena Onca.[3]  But just where may we look for the Gate Ogygian or Oncaean?  Not merely its location but even its very existence has been questioned.[4] But scepticism as to the reality of a gate by that name at Thebes seems ill-placed.  Euripides (Ph. 1113) knew a gate Ogygian; Pausanias includes it in the list of the seven (IX 8, 5) and declares "Ogygian" to be the oldest name of all, derived from the autochthonous king Ogygus (IX 5, 1); Apollodorus (III 6, 6) and Statius (Theb. VIII 353; X 495; 921; XI 665) also include the Ogygian in their lists of the seven gates.  Following Pausanias, we found Athena Onca somewhat to the west of the Heracleum,[5] which, in turn, was somewhat to the west of Apollo of the Embers.  As Athena Onca is "close neighbor" to the Ogygian gate, the gate would be the first or second one west of the Electran Gate, possibly on the site of the present entrance to the city from the south.

The Crenaean, Homoloïdian, and Hypsistan Gates cannot be located with any degree of absolute certainty.  Pausanias states definitely that the Hypsistan had its name from the temple of Zeus Hypsistus, but he does not tell us where that temple was.  It is only assumption, if we place it upon the high hill at the southwest corner of the modern city.  If Hypsistan has to do with ὕψιστος, that gate ought to be at the highest point in the circuit wall, as the Neïstan (or, as the more correct form of the name seems to be, Neïtan, νήιτος) ought to be at the lowest point.  Keramopoullos[6] also has located it there, on the highest elevation on the south side of the city, and identified it with the "Oncaean" Gate which, following Pausanias[7] and the Scholiast to Aeschylus's Septem (486), I have made identical with the Ogygian.[8]

---

[1] Paus. IX 25, 3:Διαβάντων δὲ ποταμὸν καλούμενον ἀπὸ τῆς Λύκου Δίρκην... διαβᾶσιν οὖν τὴν Δίρκην οἰκίας τε ἐρείπια τῆς Πινδάρου καὶ μητρὸς Δινδυμήνης ἱερὸν κ.τ.λ.

[2] Ph. 1098–1100; see p. 241.

[3] See pp. 175–176.

[4] Frazer, *Paus.* Vol. V, p. 48.

[5] See above, p. 176.

[6] Ἀρχ. Δελτ. III (1917) pp. 336–337; 466–467; 473–475.

[7] IX 8, 5.

[8] The Ogygian Keramopoullos identifies with Aeschylus's "Northern" Gate.

SOUTH TOWER OF THE ELECTRAN GATE

(After Κερμμόπουλλος)

The Crenaean Gate stood, it is commonly assumed, at the point where the Dircaean stream left the city. But is that assumption fully warranted? We may very seriously question its generally accepted assignment to the north-central side of the city. The word seems to have to do with χρήνη, and we should look for a spring or springs in its neighborhood. The Scholiast on Euripides's Phoenissae 1123 hazards the conjecture ἴσως τῇ Δίρχη παρέχειντο καὶ ἀπὸ ταύτης ὠνομάσθησαν "perhaps it was close by Dirce and got its name from that." And Statius apparently assumes the same topographical condition and has Menoeceus take his stand beside the "Dircaean Gate" to slay himself, an offering for his city; and we know from Euripides that in his vicarious sacrifice his blood fell into the Ares Spring that flows into the Dircaean stream hard by the Ogygian or Oncaean Gate. Apollodorus, however, has all three names in his list: Crenaean, Ogygian, and Oncaean. The last two are probably one and the same. Is it conceivable that he made three gates out of one? Furthermore, there are many springs about modern Thebes: the Παραπόρτι, the Δελδιναχιώτης, the Βρανέζι, the Oedipodea, the "Dircaean Springs" a couple of miles south of Thebes, and others more. The waters of all these flow together in the north central part of the classical city, and near the confluence Fabricius has placed his Crenaean Gate. That may answer for the Crenaean Gate of the classical fortifications, but the city of Oedipus and Eteocles could never have extended so far from the Cadmea into the plain. The Crenaean Gate of Mycenaean times must have been in the walls of the Cadmea and may be the gate at the northwest curve of the Cadmea, above the spring Βρανέζι.[1]

To resume, then, the Electran Gate is, we may be sure, the southeastern; the Proetidian, the northeastern; the Neïstan, a postern-gate, low down near the Παραπόρτι Spring; the Ogygian (*alias* Oncaean), diagonally across the city from the Proetidian and just west of the Electran. For the other three we must resort to little better than guesswork and assign them to suit our own individual ideas of convenience about the circuit wall of Cadmea. The Crenaean must be toward the northern side;[2] the Hypsistan would seem to have been somewhere on the southwest; the Homoloïdian must have been between the Electran and the Proetidian—somewhere on the east.

Euripides's order of heroes and gates is (Ph. 1104–1134):

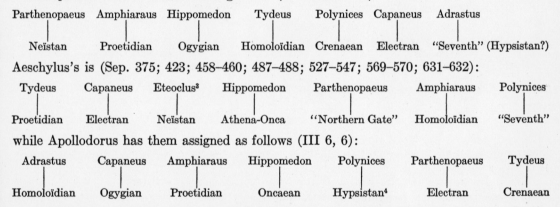

| Parthenopaeus | Amphiaraus | Hippomedon | Tydeus | Polynices | Capaneus | Adrastus |
|---|---|---|---|---|---|---|
| Neïstan | Proetidian | Ogygian | Homoloïdian | Crenaean | Electran | "Seventh" (Hypsistan?) |

Aeschylus's is (Sep. 375; 423; 458–460; 487–488; 527–547; 569–570; 631–632):

| Tydeus | Capaneus | Eteoclus[3] | Hippomedon | Parthenopaeus | Amphiaraus | Polynices |
|---|---|---|---|---|---|---|
| Proetidian | Electran | Neïstan | Athena-Onca | "Northern Gate" | Homoloïdian | "Seventh" |

while Apollodorus has them assigned as follows (III 6, 6):

| Adrastus | Capaneus | Amphiaraus | Hippomedon | Polynices | Parthenopaeus | Tydeus |
|---|---|---|---|---|---|---|
| Homoloïdian | Ogygian | Proetidian | Oncaean | Hypsistan[4] | Electran | Crenaean |

Apollodorus must have had a good source, but we do not know whence he drew. In the source or sources from which Apollodorus was compiling we should probably find the same gate named variously Oncaean and Ogygian. That this gate had the double appellation is clear from the scholium to Aeschylus's Septem 486:

Ὄγκας Ἀθηνᾶς· τὰς Ὠγυγίας πύλας λέγει | Onca Athena: he means the Ogygian Gate

As a consequence of his making two gates out of what was one and the same, Apollodorus was forced to leave out of his list one of the best attested of the time-honored seven, and the Neïstan was sacrificed. But whatever the source from which Apollodorus drew, it is

[1] See pp. 241–242.
[2] See p. 241.
[3] Both Aeschylus and Sophocles (O. C. 1313 sqq.) name Eteoclus in place of Adrastus, who, in the tradition they followed, is leader of the expedition but not one of the seven heroes; for he came back alive.
[4] None of the Greek poets use this name. Statius has it in his list in the Thebaid (VIII 353–357); Pausanias also has it in his list (IX 8, 4–7), which is identical with that of Euripides, save that Euripides has "the seventh" instead of "Hypsistan."

clear that there was no fixed traditional assignment or that no importance was attached by the poets to such tradition. In these three alone we have almost complete confusion. The gates are assigned:[1]

| | | | | |
|---|---|---|---|---|
| *Neïstan* | Eteoclus (Ae. Sep. 460) Parthenopaeus (Eur. Ph. 1104–1106) Not named in Apollodorus [2] | *Homoloïdian* | Amphiaraus (Ae. Sep. 570) Tydeus (Eur. Ph. 1119–1120) Adrastus (Ap.[2]) |
| *Ogygian* | Not named in Aeschylus Hippomedon (Eur. Ph. 1113) Capaneus (Ap.[2]) | *Electran* | Capaneus (Ae. Sep. 423) Capaneus (Eur. Ph. 1129) Parthenopaeus (Ap.[2]) |
| *Crenaean* | Not named in Aeschylus Polynices (Eur. Ph. 1123) Tydeus (Ap.[2]) | *Athena Onca* | Hippomedon (Ae. Sep. 486) Hippomedon (Ap.[2]) |
| *Hypsistan* | Not named in Aeschylus Not named in Euripides Polynices (Ap.[2]) | *Northern* | Parthenopaeus (Ae. Sep. 527) |
| *Proetidian* | Tydeus (Ae. Sep. 377) Amphiaraus (Eur. Ph. 1109–1111) Amphiaraus (Ap.[2]) | *Seventh* | Polynices (Ae. Sep. 631[3]) Adrastus (Eur. Ph. 1134) |

Or, arranging them by the Argive heroes we get the corresponding confusion:

| | | | | |
|---|---|---|---|---|
| *Adrastus* | Not named in Aeschylus "The Seventh" (Eur. Ph. 1134–1138, Homoloïdian (Ap.) | *Amphiaraus* | Homoloïdian (Ae. Sep. 570) Proetidian (Eur. Ph. 1109–1112) Proetidian (Ap.) |
| *Eteoclus* | Neïstan (Ae. Sep. 460) Not named in Euripides Not named in Apollodorus | *Capaneus* | Electran (Ae. Sep. 423) Electran (Eur. Ph. 1129–1132) Ogygian (Ap.) |
| *Parthenopaeus* | "Northern Gate" (Ae. Sep. 527) Neïstan (Eur. Ph. 1100–1104) Electran (Ap.) | *Hippomedon* | Athena Onca (Ae. Sep. 486) Ogygian (Eur. Ph. 1113–1118) Oncaean (Ap.) |
| *Tydeus* | Proetidian (Ae. Sep. 377) Homoloïdian (Eur. Ph. 1119–1122) Crenaean (Ap.) | *Polynices* | "Seventh" (Ae. Sep. 631[4]) Crenaean (Eur. Ph. 1123–1127) Hypsistan (Ap.) |

The possibilities of variation are large; these three authors have in the rarest instances happened to coincide.

Aeschylus apparently has arranged the order of his heroes with the two most terrible pairs of warriors at the beginning and the end respectively, and with the tragic climax of Polynices at the last. There is a slight variation in the names of the heroes; there is a larger discrepancy in the names and in the assignment of the gates: Aeschylus does not specifically name the Ogygian, Crenaean, or Hypsistan Gate; in place of them we have a gate near the sanctuary of "Athena Onca,"[5] the "northern gate," and, like Euripides, "the Seventh." The "northern gate" is almost certainly the Crenaean; in the case of the other two, no decision can be made. The order of Aeschylus's gates is as far from the topographical as Euripides's, and no conclusions can be drawn. It is interesting to note that in one instance and one only Aeschylus and Euripides have the same Argive hero at the same gate—the

[1] Aeschylus gives the Theban defenders of the gates: *Neïstan*, Megareus against Eteoclus (474); *Proetidian*, Melanippus against Tydeus (414); *Homoloïdian*, Lasthenes against Amphiaraus (620); *Electran*, Polyphontes against Capaneus (448); *Oncaean*, Hyperbius against Hippomedon (504); *Northern*, Actor against Parthenopaeus (555); *Seventh*, Eteocles against Polynices (672).

[2] The entire list is given in III 6, 6.

[3] It may be that in Aeschylus "Seventh" is used as nomen proprium: cf. ll. 714; 800.

[4] Cf. also 800–802.

[5] See pp. 175–176.

EAST TOWER OF THE ELECTRAN GATE

(After Κεραμόπουλλος)

Electran. And though Euripides assigns Polynices and Eteocles to the Crenaean Gate, the fatal duel between the brothers is fought before the Electran (Ph. 1570).[1]

The seven gates were flanked by seven towers.[2] If we attempt to visualize them, we naturally think of the great towers guarding the gateways at Mycenae and Tiryns and Troy. So at Mycenaean Thebes the approaches to the gates were defended by great towers (Eur. Ph. 1058):

| | |
|---|---|
| τὰ δ' ἑπτάπυργα κλῇθρα γᾶς | our country's seven-towered bars |

(*ibid.* 1090–1091):

| | |
|---|---|
| Κρέοντος παῖς | Creon's son . . . took his stand |
| πύργων ἐπ' ἄκρων στὰς | upon the towers' height |

All seven gates had bars and bolts to secure them; that is implied in the verse just quoted: They are specifically mentioned in connection with the Proetidian Gate (Ae. Sep. 395–396):

| | |
|---|---|
| τίς Προίτου πυλῶν | who is competent to open the bars |
| κλῇθρων λυθέντων προστατεῖν φερέγγυος; | of Proetus's Gate and stand in defense of it? |

The bar was drawn across the gate, when closed, and shot into strong sockets in the great stone jambs, as we see them still at Tiryns and Mycenae (Eur. Ph. 114–116):

| | |
|---|---|
| ἆρα πύλαι κλῇθροις χαλκόδετ' ἔμβολά τε | pray, are the gates, with bronze-covered panels, |
| λαϊνέοισιν 'Αμφίονος ὀργάνοις | close-fastened with bars shot into the stone-casings |
| τείχεος ἥρμοσται; | of Amphion's walls? |

About the summit of the walls ran a coping or cornice to finish them off (Eur. Ph. 1180):

| | |
|---|---|
| ἤδη δ' ὑπερβαίνοντα γεῖσα τειχέων | and as he was just gaining the coping of the walls |

Capaneus is scaling the walls of the city; the point chosen by him for his attack may have been a tower by the gate assigned to him, or it may have been some weaker place in the circuit wall. At all events, walls and towers alike would seem to have been finished off with a cornice, both for looks and for defensory purposes.

In an article on *Die Sieben Thore Thebens* in *Hermes* XXVI (1891) pp. 191–242, worked out with all that famous scholar's acumen and brilliance, von Wilamowitz-Möllendorff attempts to prove that "seven-gated" Thebes is all a myth as far as the seven gates are concerned. They were a poetic invention from Homer to Pindar and the tragic poets and Pausanias. He waives aside Pausanias's μένουσι δὲ καὶ εἰς ἡμᾶς ἔτι "and they are still there to our own day" as credulity to poetic tradition; for the periegete, he says, uses only three of the seven gates for his topographical purposes! Granting that the Attic tragic poets, presenting in fifth century Athens plays that deal with eleventh or twelfth century Thebes, might have played fast and loose with a "seven-gated" fortification about their rival neighbor city, though its general topography and its walls and towers were perfectly familiar to a large portion of the audience, what kind of folly must he attribute to Pindar, whose favorite epithet of his own native town is "seven-gated"![3] Even the "Boeotian Swine," his fellow-townsmen, would have laughed him out of court or run him out of town for singing forever of their city with its three gates as "seven-gated."

As final proof (*die Hauptsache*) that Thebes never had more then three gates Wilamowitz-Möllendorff states that modern Thebes has only three entrances. At least he found only three! There may be only three entrances for carriages. But if Wilamowitz-Möllendorff will go again to Thebes and try once more, he may be led into or out of the Cadmea by four more entrances at least as easy of ascent or descent as the postern way at Tiryns or at Mycenae or at Mycenaean Athens. He cites these pre-Homeric castles as further proof of the adherence of the Mycenaean princes to the principle of having as few openings as possible in the castle walls. Ergo, Thebes also could have had not more than three. But Mycenaean Troy had not yet been discovered, when Wilamowitz-Möllendorff wrote, with

---

[1] Cf. Paus. IX 9, 2 and p. 263 footnote 5. In IX 25, 1–2, Pausanias definitely assigns the scene of the duel between the brothers to the space before the Neïstan Gate, on the west side of the Cadmea.

[2] Eur. Antiope; Ph. 823–827; see p. 264.

[3] Used eight times in the Epinicians alone: Pyth. 3, 90; 8, 39; 9, 80; 11, 11; Isth. 1, 66; 7 (8), 15 b; Ne. 4, 19; 9, 18; Frag. 104, 63–64.

its three gates in less than one third of the circuit of the citadel, and we are all pretty well agreed that not one of these three is the Scaean Gate or the Dardanian Gate. Of course both City II and City VI at Troy had too many gates, and some of them were walled up in the course of time. But there are the gates. So, too, the Mycenaean Acropolis of Athens had three entrances: the nine-gated Pelargicum, and two on the north. The castle of Gla in Lake Copais—not a city at all, but only a strongly fortified palace—had four. And to me it is more than a striking coincidence that there are to-day just seven entrances to Thebes, the successor of the ancient Cadmea.

As surely as there was a war of the Seven against Thebes—yea, far more surely and better attested—there was a wall of fortification about that city, broken by its seven gates. Our witnesses are numerous and they are reliable—Homer, Pindar, Aeschylus, Sophocles, Euripides, Apollodorus, Pherecydes, Aristodemus, Pausanias, and the Romans.

Of the walls of Mycenaean Thebes only the fewest stones remain: there are a few remains, huge blocks like those of which the walls of Tiryns are constructed, uncovered near the Proetidian gate at the northeast corner of the Cadmea, less considerable fragments at the northeast corner of the Frankish tower, and a more considerable fragment of a great Mycenaean wall four metres thick on the western slope of the citadel at the end of Proetus Street.

a. The Areopagus Court; b. The Heliastic Courts; c. The Stoas—the Royal Stoa, the Stoa Basileus, the Stoa of the Flour-merchants, the Poecile Stoa; d. The Odeum and the Orchestra; e. The Stadium; f. The Arsenal in Athens.

## 1. The Areopagus Court

One of the most fascinating problems and at the same time one of the least clear points of interest in the city of Athens is the Areopagus. It figures large in the Eumenides of Aeschylus;[1] but Aeschylus may take it for granted that his audience knew every inch of the ground, and he tells us next to nothing. He gives its name and explains the etymology (Eum. 685; 689–690):

| | |
|---|---|
| πάγον δ' Ἄρειον τόνδ', Ἀμαζόνων ἕδραν | and the hill of Ares here, where the Amazons took their stand |
| Ἄρει δ' ἔθυον, ἔνθεν ἔστ' ἐπώνυμος πέτρα πάγος τ' Ἄρειος | and they sacrificed to Ares, whence the rock bears the name of Hill of Ares |

He speaks of it as a "council-room" or "place of council" (Eum. 570):

| | |
|---|---|
| πληρουμένου γὰρ τοῦδε βουλευτηρίου | while the council-room here is filling |

The word βουλευτήριον ordinarily means a chamber, a building, but it does not necessarily mean anything more than a place where councilmen meet. Aeschylus uses the same word for the Areopagus court again (Eum. 683–684):

| | |
|---|---|
| ἔσται δὲ καὶ τὸ λοιπὸν Αἰγέως στρατῷ ἀεὶ δικαστῶν τοῦτο βουλευτήριον | and this shall be for Aegeus's folk henceforth forever the council-room of the judges |

and again (ibid. 704–706):

| | |
|---|---|
| κερδῶν ἄθικτον τοῦτο βουλευτήριον, αἰδοῖον, ὀξύθυμον, εὐδόντων ὕπερ ἐγρηγορὸς φρούρημα γῆς καθίσταμαι | this I establish a council-room incorruptible, quick to wrath, a guardian of the land ever vigilant for those who sleep |

The epithets in this last passage make it clear that it is here the judges of the Areopagus court, not their council-chamber or their place of meeting, that is meant by βουλευτήριον.

The court was convened by the blasts of a trumpet (Ae. Eum. 567–569):

| | |
|---|---|
| ἥ τ' οὖν διάτορος αἰθέρος Τυρσηνικὴ σάλπιγξ, βροτείου πνεύματος πληρουμένη, ὑπέρτονον γήρυμα φαινέτω στρατῷ | let the Tuscan trumpet, piercing the sky, be filled with the breath of a man and attune its haughty clangor to the people's ear |

The summit of the hill is bare rock, artificially leveled, with cuttings for altars or benches (?). The spade is incapable of helping here. We must depend upon our literary sources, and they are strangely silent.

Besides the story of Ares's trial for the slaying of Halirrhothius,[2] Euripides contributes one brief passage of topographical interest (I. T. 961–964):

| | |
|---|---|
| ὡς δ' εἰς Ἄρειον ὄχθον ἧκον, ἐς δίκην τ' ἔστην, ἐγὼ μὲν θάτερον λαβὼν βάθρον, τὸ δ' ἄλλο πρέσβειρ' ἥπερ ἦν Ἐρινύων· εἰπὼν δ' ἀκούσας θ' αἵματος μητρὸς πέρι .... | and when I came to Ares' Hill and faced my trial, I took the one platform, and she who was the eldest of the Erinyes the other. Then having heard and spoken on the charge of mother's bloodshed . . . |

[1] Cp. also Eur. I. T. 1469–1472.

[2] Eur. El. 1258–1269: ἔστιν δ' Ἄρεώς τις ὄχθος, οὗ πρῶτον θεοὶ
ἕζοντ' ἐπὶ ψήφοισιν αἵματος πέρι,
Ἁλιρρόθιον ὅτ' ἔκταν' ὠμόφρων Ἄρης,
μῆνιν θυγατρὸς ἀνοσίων νυμφευμάτων,
πόντου κρέοντος παῖδ', ἵν' εὐσεβεστάτη
ψῆφος βεβαία τ' ἐστὶν † ἔκ γε τοῦ θεοῖς.
..................
νικᾶν ἴσαις ψήφοισι τὸν φεύγοντ' ἀεί

We are not told of any building there; there is no trace upon the rock of the existence of any building at any time. It is true, Vitruvius does mention[1] as still standing in his day upon the Areopagus an ancient building roofed with clay. What it was we do not know. It was not the courthouse of the Areopagus Court; for that tribunal held its sessions under the open sky.[2] Other building there was none; but there were the two platforms. Perhaps two of the cuttings still to be seen may have carried the bases of the two βάθρα that Euripides knew.

All that Pausanias tells us (I 28, 5) he could have taken, paraphrased directly from Euripides, stories and all, with slight additions:

καθὸ καὶ ὁ Ἄρειος πάγος. ἔστι δὲ
Ἄρειος πάγος καλούμενος, ὅτι
πρῶτος Ἄρης ἐνταῦθα ἐκρίθη. . . .
κριθῆναι δὲ καὶ ὕστερον Ὀρέστην
λέγουσιν ἐπὶ τῷ φόνῳ τῆς μητρός·
καὶ βωμός ἐστιν Ἀθηνᾶς Ἀρείας,
ὃν ἀνέθηκεν ἀποφυγὼν τὴν δίκην.
τοὺς δὲ ἀργοὺς λίθους, ἐφ' ὧν

ἐστᾶσιν ὅσοι δίκας ὑπέχουσι καὶ οἱ
διώκοντες, τὸν μὲν Ὕβρεως τὸν δὲ
Ἀναιδείας αὐτῶν ὀνομάζουσι.

and then the Areopagus. Now, it is called Areopagus because Ares was the first to be tried there. . . . And they say that later Orestes also was tried for the murder of his mother. There is also an altar to Athena Areia, which he dedicated for that he was acquitted. As for the two unfinished stones upon which defendants and prosecutors take their stand, the people call them respectively "the stone of Injury" and "the stone of Ruthlessness."

His account adds to Euripides's only the altar of Athena Areia and gives the names of the two stones.

Frazer comments upon them as follows:[3] "Theophrastus (cited by Zenobius, IV 36) says that there were altars of Injury and Ruthlessness at Athens; he probably refers to these stones, which may have been altar-shaped blocks. According to Cicero (de Legg. II 11, 28) the Athenians, after expiating the Cylonian massacre, erected a shrine of Contumely and Impudence, by which Cicero means the altars or stones of Injury and Ruthlessness. Xenophon alludes to the stone of Ruthlessness when he says (Symp. VIII 35) that the Lacedaemonians esteemed Ruth (αἰδώς, i.e. 'pity,' 'reverence') a goddess but not Ruthlessness (ἀναιδεία). Euripides refers to the two stones when he makes Orestes say (I. T. 961 sqq.) that on coming to the Areopagus to be tried he occupied one pedestal or seat (βάθρον), while the eldest of the Furies (his accusers) took the other. On a cameo[4] and a vase-painting which represent the acquittal of Orestes, the accused is seen with his right foot planted on a rough stone, probably the stone of Injury (Daremberg and Saglio, Dict. des Antiqq., I p. 398 sq., figs. 491 and 493). Some have fancied they could identify the two stones with two blocks standing on the platform on the top of the hill. Wordsworth says: 'Immediately above the steps, on the level of the hill, is a bench of stone excavated in the limestone rock, forming three sides of a quadrangle, like a triclinium: it faces south: on its east and west side is a raised block; the former may perhaps have been the tribunal, the latter the rude stones which Pausanias saw here' (Athens and Attica, p. 62).

"Perhaps the two stones were used to swear on, the accuser and accused standing on them as they took their oaths. We have seen (note on I 3, 1) that in the Royal Colonnade at Athens there was a stone which was used for a like purpose. The custom of swearing on a stone is not uncommon among primitive peoples."

Upon the famous Corsini silver bowl,[5] which gives us in a fine relief a copy of a composition of Zopyrus, a contemporary of Pompey, representing the acquittal of Orestes, we find one of the Erinyes (?) sitting upon an unwrought stone. The unfinished surface of the hill is suggested by the rough stone against which she sets her right foot; and the open-air court-room is reproduced in the two pillars set to mark the entrance to the judicial space. The unwrought stone upon which the Erinys sits is inside the space in which stand the official voting urns upon the sacred table, and Athena is just in the act of dropping into one of them the deciding ballot. As the stone seat of the accuser is wholly unwrought, no name

---

[1] II 1, 5.
[2] Pollux, VIII 118. They avoided the heat of the sun by sitting at night (Luc. Hermot. 64; de domo 18).
[3] Paus. II, p. 364.
[4] In St. Petersburg. Reproduced also in Roscher, Myth. Lex. III, 1 Sp. 991.
[5] Reproduced in Roscher, Myth. Lex. III 1, Sp. 987–988; Baum., Denkm. II, p. 1119 (Fig. 1316); see also the literature there quoted.

appears upon it. But an example of a named and inscribed stone upon which witnesses were required to stand when giving their testimony we have in the well known Darius vase in Naples.[1] Before the Great King stands the exiled Spartan king Damaratus (?) upon a round plinth painted in light yellow and inscribed with the word ΠΕΡΣΑΙ. And from Aelian (Var. Hist. XII 62) we learn that if any one ventured to bring before the Persian king any deep secret or doubtful information, he took his stand upon a plinth of gold to present his testimony before the king.

The significance of the name inscribed is suggestive of the tremendous power of the Persian State. The contrast between the golden bar of Persia and the unwrought stones of Athens is also significant. In both cases we have as a "witness box" a basis bearing a meaningful name.

## 2. The Heliastic Courts

Besides the Court of the Areopagus, there were in Athens ordinary civil courts of justice, known as the Heliastic Courts. There were a number of them—just how many we do not know. These had regular court-house buildings, though, when Solon created the institution, they probably sat under the open sky.[2]

Pausanias[3] gives the names of several of the civil courts—the Parabystum, in an obscure part of the city;[4] the Trigonum, so named from its shape; the Batrachium and the Phoenicium, so called from their colors; the Palladium; the Delphinium; the Prytaneum; Phreattys; and, the largest and most commodius of all, the Heliaea.[5] But they were all conducted by the select bodies of Heliasts.

All the old courts under the open sky (except the Heliaea) seem to have been succeeded by new court-houses.[6] Indeed, "the New" seems to have been a name for one of them (Ar. Vesp. 120):

ἐδίκαζεν εἰς τὸ Καινὸν ἐμπεσὼν  |  he plunged into the New and went to pleading a case

Some of the names assigned by Pausanias are not found elsewhere—Batrachium and Phoenicium, for example; but the Palladium, as well as the Heliaea, plays a part in the comedies of Aristophanes. We know from Pausanias[7] and Aristotle[8] that the especial business of the court of the Palladium was to try cases of involuntary homicide, conspiracy (to kill), and the slaying of a slave, a resident alien, or a foreigner. It was called "Palladium," according to Pausanias,[9] from an incident in the return of the Greek heroes from Troy, when the Argives under Diomedes stopped off at Athens, and Demophon, the son of Theseus, carried off the famous image of Pallas. In the struggle that ensued an Athenian was accidentally knocked down and trampled to death by Demophon's horse. A court was instituted on the spot for the trial of Demophon on a charge of homicide. And there (at Phalerum) the

[1] Reproduced in Baum., Denkm. I, Tafel VI (between pp. 416 and 417).

[2] The weight of authority is on the side of the derivation of Ἡλιαία from ἥλιος; but many also derive the name from ἀλίζεσθαι. Both etymologies are ancient: Schol. Dem. XXV 21: ἡ Ἡλιαία λέγεται αὐτὸς ὁ τόπος τοῦ μεγάλου δικαστηρίου καὶ τὸ ἄθροισμα τῶν ἐκεῖσε δικαζόντων. Ἡλιαία δὲ ἐκλήθη ὁ τόπος παρὰ τὸ ἐκεῖσε ἀλίζεσθαι καὶ συναθροίζεσθαι τὸ πλῆθος τῶν δικαστῶν.... τινὲς δὲ λέγουσιν ἐκ τοῦ ὕπαιθρον εἶναι τὸν τόπον καὶ τὸν ἥλιον ἐκεῖ ἔνδον προσβάλλειν. Cf. Schol. Ar. Vesp. 88: ἀπὸ τοῦ μεγίστου δικαστηρίου τῆς ἡλιαίας, ὅπερ οὕτω καλεῖται διὰ τὸ ἐν ὑπαίθρῳ εἶναι καὶ ἡλίῳ βάλλεσθαι. Cf. also the play upon the words: Ar. Vesp. 772 ἡλιάσει πρὸς ἥλιον, and Ar. Av. 109–110: ΕΠ. μῶν ἡλιαστά; ΕΥ. μάλλὰ θατέρου τρόπου,
        ἀπηλιαστά.

[3] I 28, 8.

[4] It may have stood in the market-place (Ant. V 10), and Pausanias's "obscure place" may be an attempt at etymologizing. See Frazer, Paus. II, p. 368.

[5] Aristophanes also calls the Heliaea by name but tells us nothing of it, except perhaps the crowd that thronged the place (Eq. 897–898):
        κἄπειτ' ἐν Ἡλιαίᾳ
        βδέοντες ἀποκτείνειαν οἱ δικασταί.

[6] Antiphon (V 11) implies that while certain courts [we might name the Areopagus, Palladium, Phreatto, Delphinium, Prytaneum] were held under the open sky, the heliastic courts were under roofs: ἔπειτα δέ, ὃ πάντας οἶμαι ὑμᾶς ἐπίστασθαι, ἅπαντα τὰ δικαστήρια ἐν ὑπαίθρῳ δικάζοι τὰς δίκας τοῦ φόνου.... ὁ διώκων τὴν δίκην τοῦ φόνου ἵνα μὴ ὁμωρόφιος γίγνηται τῷ αὐθέντῃ.

[7] I 28, 8: ὁπόσα δὲ ἐπὶ τοῖς φονεῦσίν ἐστιν, ἄλλα καὶ ἐπὶ Παλλαδίῳ καλοῦσι, καὶ τοῖς ἀποκτείνασιν ἀκουσίως κρίσις καθέστηκε.

[8] Const. Ath. 57.

[9] I 28, 9. According to the more common version of the story, it was Agamemnon, not Diomedes, that landed in Attica with the Palladium, and it was a pitched battle in which some Argives were killed that caused the trial for homicide.

Palladium was set up. And from it the name was given to the court for the trial of involuntary homicides. To this central fact Aristophanes also bears witness in a fragment of an unidentified play (Frag. 585 K.):

| | |
|---|---|
| ἄκων κτενῶ σε, τέκνον· ὁ δ' ἀπεκρίνατο, | "I shall kill you accidentally, my child"; and he answered: |
| ἐπὶ Παλλαδίῳ τἄρ', ὦ πάτερ, δώσεις δίκην | "Then, father, you will pay the penalty at the order of the Palladium" |

Aristophanes gives us many details of the arrangements of a Heliastic Court. The courtroom was entered through a latticed door or gate in a latticed fence. So important was the rôle played by this latticed gate that the law-court fanatic, Philocleon, cannot conceive of litigation without that most essential feature (Ar. Vesp. 829–833):

| | |
|---|---|
| ΦΙ. ἐπίσχες οὗτος· ὡς ὀλίγου μ' ἀπώλεσας. | PH. Hold on there! You've pretty nearly done me up! |
| ἄνευ δρυφράκτου τὴν δίκην μέλλεις καλεῖν, | You mean to open court without a lattice? |
| ὃ πρῶτον ἡμῖν τῶν ἱερῶν ἐφαίνετο; | We thought that the first step in the rites. |
| ΒΔ. μὰ τὸν Δί' οὐ πάρεστιν. ΦΙ. ἀλλ' ἐγὼ δραμὼν | BD. By Zeus! we haven't any. PH. Well, I'll run |
| αὐτὸς κομιοῦμαι τό γε παραυτίκ' ἔνδοθεν | in and bring one out in a minute myself |

That Philocleon can so suddenly improvise a portable lattice suggests the fact that the fence or gate to the heliastic courts could not have been a very heavy or substantial architectural piece. And when he re-enters with his "bar," Bdelycleon asks in surprise (844):

| | |
|---|---|
| τουτὶ τί ἐστι; | what in the world is that thing? |

and his father answers:

| | |
|---|---|
| χοιροκομεῖον 'Εστίας | Hestia's pigsty |

"Hestia's pigsty" is the little crate of withes in which the little pigs consecrated to the hearth-goddess were kept on the premises—perhaps at the very hearth itself. This lattice fence Philocleon could easily pick up and carry out before the house. The use of a pigsty for the courtroom may contain an additional element of satire on the Athenian jury!

The word for "lattice" in the passage above (l. 830) is singular in form; it is usually plural, but the meaning is the same.[1] The plural may contain some connotation of the number of slats used in the construction of the door itself, or in the latticed fence that enclosed the whole space set aside for the jury. The Senate house (Βουλή) had the same sort of fence and lattice door for the admission of the members to the "floor." The law courts, being held for the most part under the open sky, were enclosed only within this latticed fence. It was capable of being locked up, though perhaps none too securely, when court was not in session (Ar. Eq. 1317):

| | |
|---|---|
| τὰ δικαστήρια συγκλείειν, οἷς ἡ πόλις ἥδε γέγηθεν | to lock up the law courts in which the city finds its joy |

The lattice work was not only weak in construction, but it was low enough for a man to jump over. When the Prytanies hear from the Sausage-Seller the announcement of a great catch of herring and the dirt-cheap price of the fish, they refuse to wait to listen to peace-talk and in their eagerness to get to the fish-market they jump over the lattices, right and left (Ar. Eq. 675):

| | |
|---|---|
| εἶθ' ὑπερεπήδων τοὺς δρυφάκτους πανταχῆ | they then went jumping over the lattices in every direction |

The word πανταχῆ "on every side, right and left" implies beyond a doubt that the δρύφακτοι were a latticed fence enclosing the space reserved for the Prytanies, if not for the whole body of the Senate. So at the law courts there was the latticed fence inside which the judges sat. And under this fence the arch-pleader expresses his desire to be buried, when death should cut him off from the pleasures of the courts (Ar. Vesp. 385–386):

---

[1] In Arist. Const. Ath. (50, 2) δρύφακτος is apparently a fence; the writer lists among the duties of the ἀστυνόμοι that of seeing to it that people do not encroach upon the public streets with their buildings and fences; καὶ τὰς ὁδοὺς κωλύουσι κατοικοδομεῖν, καὶ δρυφάκτους ὑπὲρ τῶν ὁδῶν ὑπερτείνειν.

| | |
|---|---|
| ἢν τι πάθω 'γώ,... | if anything happens to me, . . . |
| ἀνελόντες καὶ κατακλαύσαντες θεῖναί μ' ὑπὸ | carry me out and mourn over me and lay |
| τοῖσι δρυφάκτοις | me under the lattices |

And there at the lattice men with cases awaited their summons before the judges (Ar. Vesp. 552–553):

| | |
|---|---|
| ὃν πρῶτα μὲν ἕρποντ' ἐξ εὐνῆς τηροῦσ' ἐπὶ | and at the lattices they wait for him as |
| τοῖς δρυφάκτοις | he comes leisurely from his couch— |
| ἄνδρες μεγάλοι καὶ τετραπήχεις | those big, six-foot fellows |

In this latticed fence there is a latticed gate through which passed the Heliasts, or, in the case of the Bule, the Senators. The little gate itself might be called δρύφακτος,[1] but in a narrower and more technical sense it is a κιγκλίς. The two things belong intimately together but they are not identical. This we know from the unequivocal statements of Pollux (VIII 17):

| | |
|---|---|
| τῶν δὲ τοῦ δικαστηρίου μερῶν ἐστι | of the arrangements of the court we have |
| καὶ κιγκλὶς καὶ δρύφακτος | the lattice gate and the lattice fence |

For the identification of κιγκλίς as the wicket gate we have also the exact definition of Pollux (VIII 124):

| | |
|---|---|
| αἱ μὲν οὖν τῶν δικαστηρίων θύραι | so the doors of the court rooms |
| κιγκλίδες ἐκαλοῦντο, ἃς 'Ρωμαῖοι, | were called "lattices"; the Romans |
| καγκελλωτὰς λέγουσιν | call them *cancelli* ("lattices," "bars") |

and Salmasius explains carefully (Hist. Aug. p. 483): Latini tamen cancellos non tantum fores τοῦ δικαστηρίου, sed etiam omne consaeptum appellant.[2]

The Thesmothetae had charge of the wicket, and during business hours one of them stood by the gate to admit authorized jurymen and to exclude such as had no right to enter. The gate was closed at the opening of the court and after that no one was supposed to get through (Ar. Vesp. 775):

| | |
|---|---|
| οὐδείς σ' ἀποκλήσει θεσμοθέτης τῇ κιγκλίδι | no officer shall shut you out by closing the bar |

The "bar" is the gate through which those who had a right to attend the session of the court were permitted to pass. It is the classical counterpart to the Temple Bar of London. It is interesting to note that in fifth century Athens we find "the bar" used in almost every sense in which we have it to-day.[3] So, Philocleon appears "at the bar," meaning "in court" (Ar. Vesp. 124):

| | |
|---|---|
| ὁ δ' ἀνεφάνη κνεφαῖος ἐπὶ τῇ κιγκλίδι | and before daylight he appeared again at the bar |

(Ar. Διαιτ., Frag. 210 K.):

| | |
|---|---|
| ὁ δ' ἡλιαστὴς εἷρπε πρὸς τὴν κιγκλίδα | and the heliast marched to the bar |

That the "bar" (κιγκλίς) is the door to the court room is attested also by Harpocration commenting on this fragment:

| | |
|---|---|
| κιγκλίς· αἱ τῶν δικαστηρίων | bar: the doors of the court- |
| θύραι κιγκλίδες ἐκαλοῦντο | rooms were called bars |

That they were made of lattice work, or pickets, seems clear also from another line in the Wasps (Ar. Vesp. 349):

| | |
|---|---|
| οὕτω κιττῶ διὰ τῶν σανίδων μετὰ χοιρίνης | I itch so to get through the pickets and |
| περιελθεῖν | go round with my ballot in hand |

So the Scholiast interprets it when he says that διὰ τῶν σανίδων means

| | |
|---|---|
| διὰ τῶν δρυφάκτων, ἵνα λέγῃ ἐπιθυμῶ | through the lattices, meaning: I |
| ἐν τὸ δικαστηρίῳ ἐλθεῖν | wish to go to the court-house |

---

[1] Schol. Ar. Vesp. 830: δρύφακτος· τὸ παρατεινόμενον ξύλον τοῖς δικασταῖς.

[2] We find in late authorities (Et. Mag. p. 289, 5; Hesychius, s. v. δρύφακτοι; Bekker, An. Gr. I p. 271, 33) the same confusion between δρύφακτοι and κιγκλίς.

[3] Schol. Ar. Vesp. 124: [κιγκλίδι] ἀντὶ τοῦ ἐν τῷ δικαστηρίῳ.... κιγκλὶς γὰρ ἡ θύρα τοῦ δικαστηρίου.

But in line 848 σανίδες are something entirely different:

| | |
|---|---|
| φέρε νυν, ἐνέγκω τὰς σανίδας καὶ τὰς γραφὰς | come now, let me bring the [bulletin] boards and the indictments |

The old man has just lugged in the paling-fence for the judge's enclosure; everything seems to be ready for the opening of the court proceedings; but more of the court paraphernalia must be improvised, and Bdelycleon proposes to bring in the bulletin boards containing the announcements of the cases to be tried in the particular court. Hesychius seems to have this passage in mind when he defines

| | |
|---|---|
| σανίδες· τὸ λεύκωμα ὅπου αἱ δίκαι λέγονται | boards: the whitened [board] on which the cases are told |

Mr. Merry would have the same meaning for σανίδες in both passages. In the former (l. 349), he sees Philocleon going about from bulletin board to bulletin board sizing up the various cases and making up his mind in advance as to the disposition he will make of the voting-shell in his hand. Wachsmuth[1] sees in the "boards" a tribune—a temporary platform built of planks on which the presiding judge of the court had his seat. That is not nearly so satisfactory. It is possible that when Bdelycleon says ἐνέγκω τὰς σανίδας he means "let me carry the lattice"; and his taking the "pigsty" out of his father's hands provokes the impatient protest that follows from the old man. But Bdelycleon is making game of the new law court by insisting on bringing in every possible detail, and there are more to follow. I, for my part, do not see why we cannot have σανίδες used in different senses in the two different passages far apart.

Another word for the bulletin board is πινάκιον; there can be no doubt as to its meaning as used by Aristophanes in the Birds (450):

| | |
|---|---|
| σκοπεῖν δ' ὅτι ἂν προγράφωμεν ἐν τοῖς πινακίοις | and watch for what we post on the bulletin boards |

The πινάκιον "bulletin board" is constructed of σανίδες "boards."

That the lattice work construction of fence and gate was not very strong is clear from the passage in the Knights of Aristophanes, where the Sausage-seller at a meeting of the Senate gives the door a violent shove with his hip and forces it from its place (640–641):

| | |
|---|---|
| τῷ πρωκτῷ θενὼν τὴν κιγκλίδ' ἐξήραξα | I gave the bar a shove with my hip and forced an entrance |

While the "bar" itself was of no great strength, it was apparently swung from a substantial post. I have no other guess as to the identification of the "pillar" or "post" against which Philocleon leans and sleeps through the long night waiting for the court to open at daybreak (Ar. Vesp. 105):

| | |
|---|---|
| ὥσπερ λεπὰς προσεχόμενος τῷ κίονι | sticks to the post like a limpet |

The post must be very close to the wicket gate, for Philocleon must be the first to gain admission and secure a front seat (ll. 89–90; see below). Mr. Merry, commenting on the line, suggests that it may have been the pillar on which court bulletins were posted. Possibly; but it seems to me more in keeping with the spirit of the old pleader to have him leaning asleep against the gatepost, where he had taken his stand so as to slip into the court the minute the gate opened in the early morning.

In the immediate proximity of the courtroom, an almost indispensable adjunct of it, was the heroum of the guardian of the courts, the hero Lycus.[2] It seemed to Philocleon so essential a feature of the atmosphere of the court that he demanded it at the court set up for him at home (Ar. Vesp. 818–823):

| | |
|---|---|
| ΦΙ. ἓν ἀντιποθῶ, τὰ δ' ἄλλ' ἀρέσκει μοι. ΒΔ. τὸ τί; | PH. One thing more I miss; I am pleased with all the rest. BD. And what's that? |
| ΦΙ. θήρῷον εἴ πως ἐκκομίσαις τὸ τοῦ Λύκου. | PH. If you could somehow manage to bring on the heroum of Lycus. |

---

[1] *Stadt Athen* II, p. 369, footnote 4; p. 371, footnote 5.
[2] Pollux (VIII 121) says that Lycus was patron of that particular court which bore his name ἐπὶ Λύκῳ.

ΒΔ. πάρεστι τουτί, χαὐτὸς ἄναξ οὑτοσί.

ΦΙ. ὦ δέσποθ' ἥρως, ὡς χαλεπῶς ἄρ' ἦσθ'
           ἰδεῖν.

ΒΔ. οἱόσπερ ἡμῖν φαίνεται Κλεώνυμος.

ΦΙ. οὔκουν ἔχει γ' οὐδ' αὐτὸς ἥρως ὢν ὅπλα.

BD. Here it is; and here is the sovereign one himself.

PH. Oh hero lord, how austere thou wert to look upon!

BD. He does look austere—just like Cleonymus.

PH. And so he hasn't any armor on, hero though he is.

Beginning with Eratosthenes,[1] we hear of this Lycus as a hero in wolf's form.[2] The name, of course, led commentators into inevitable temptation, and the wolf was the symbol of the guilty suppliant at the shrine of Lycus. But the passage just cited leaves no shadow of doubt that the hero of the law courts had human features: he is addressed as "hero" and as "sovereign"; at Philocleon's private court, he is caricatured to look like Cleonymus; and, like that notorious coward who threw away his arms and ran, the statue at the court house had no armor on.

The shrine stood within sight and hearing of the bar (Ar. Vesp. 389–394):

ὦ Λύκε δέσποτα, γείτων ἥρως· σὺ γὰρ οἷσπερ
          ἐγὼ κεχάρησαι
τοῖς δακρύοισιν τῶν φευγόντων ἀεὶ καὶ τοῖς
          ὀλοφυρμοῖς·
ᾤκησας γοῦν ἐπίτηδες ἰὼν ἐνταῦθ' ἵνα ταῦτ'
          ἀκροῷο,

κἀβουλήθης μόνος ἡρώων παρὰ τὸν κλάοντα
          καθῆσθαι.
ἐλέησον καὶ σῶσον νυνὶ τὸν σαυτοῦ πλησιόχορον·

κοὐ μή ποτε παρὰ τὰς κάννας οὐρήσω μηδ'
          ἀποπαρδῶ

oh Lord Lycus, hero, neighbor, thou ever hast joy in the same things as I—
the tears of the accused and their piteous cries;

therefore hast thou come hither and taken up thy dwelling, that thou mayst hear these things,

and thou, alone of heroes, hast wished to have thy seat beside the one who weeps.
So have mercy upon me now and save thy neighbor;

and never will I defile thy pickets. . . .

The heroum of Lycus, with his statue, was within easy hearing distance of the bench and the prisoner's bar; it was fenced in with some sort of latticed fence; it was not inside the courtroom, but just beyond the gates—a convenient place for the dirty ancestor of the dirty modern citizen of the Mediterranean lands, with no reverence for things ancient or things sacred, or the laws of sanitation, to defile.

Inside the courtroom the principal furnishings consisted of the benches for the jurymen. And they were *benches* in the literal sense—benches made of wood (Ar. Vesp. 89–90):

καὶ στένει
εἰ μὴ 'πὶ τοῦ πρώτου καθίζηται ξύλου

and he is grieved
if he does not get a seat on the front bench

The assemblymen in the ecclesia had the same sort of seats for their comfort in the performance of their duties as statesmen (Ar. Ach. 24–25):

διωστιοῦνται πῶς δοκεῖς
ἐλθόντες ἀλλήλοισι περὶ πρώτου ξύλου

how they push and shove one another,
when they do come, to get seats on the front bench

And yet at least some of the seats seem to have been of stone, either carved chairs or cut in the rock (Ar. Eq. 783–785):

ἐπὶ ταῖσι πέτραις οὐ φροντίζει σκληρῶς σε
          καθήμενον οὕτως,
οὐχ ὥσπερ ἐγὼ ῥαψάμενός σοι τουτί φέρω.
          ἀλλ' ἐπαναίρου,
κᾆτα καθίζου μαλακῶς

he doesn't care if he does see you sitting thus upon the hard stones—
not like me who bring you this cushion that I have stitched. But raise yourself up
and then you will have a comfortable seat

Each assemblyman and, of course, each heliastic judge also, like the spectators in the theatre, might bring with him his own cushion to alleviate the discomfort of the bare wooden benches or bare rock.[3] The ordinary cushions in the dicasteries were the familiar rush mats (ψιάθια[4]).

---

[1] Quoted by Harpocr. s. v. δεκάζων.

[2] So the Paroemiographers and Lexicographers; and so Droysen, van Leuwen, and others (on Ar. Vesp. 389).

[3] Cp. Theophr. Char. II (κόλαξ): τοῦ παιδὸς ἐν τῷ θεάτρῳ τὸ προσκεφάλαιον αὐτὸς ὑποστρῶσαι.

[4] Hesych. ψιάθια· τὰ ἐν τοῖς δικαστηρίοις ἐπὶ τῶν καθεδρῶν ἐπιστορνύμενα. Cf. Pollux VIII 133.

In the dicasteries the judges' bench was the Bema,[1] probably of wood. In her sweeping reforms of Athenian public life Praxagora is going to turn it into a sort of butler's table for the mixing bowls and water pitchers (Ar. Ec. 676–678):

| | |
|---|---|
| ΠΡ. τὰ δικαστήρια καὶ τὰς στοιὰς ἀνδρῶνας<br>πάντα ποιήσω.<br>ΒΛ. τὸ δὲ βῆμα τί σοι χρήσιμον ἔσται;<br>ΠΡ. τοὺς κρατῆρας καθήσω<br>καὶ τὰς ὑδρίας | PR.  The courtrooms and the porticoes I will<br>turn into dining-halls—all of them.<br>BL.  And what use will you make of the Bema?<br>PR.  I'll use it to set the mixing bowls<br>and the water pitchers on |

Praxagora is going to have her mixing bowls and her water pitchers at the side of the judges' bench instead of the usual urns to which the men citizens of Athens were accustomed.[2] For by the presiding judges' bench stood the two voting-urns into which the jurymen dropped their ballots (Phryn. Μοῦσαι, Frag. 32 K.):

| | |
|---|---|
| ἰδού, δέχου τὴν ψῆφον· ὁ καδίσκος δέ σοι<br>ὁ μὲν ἀπολύων οὗτος, ὁ δ' ἀπολλὺς ὁδί | there; take your ballot.  And this is your<br>urn for acquittal; and this one here for conviction[3] |

In this fragment the clerk of the court is instructing a green juryman how to deposit his vote.

Usually the voting-urn in the ecclesia and in the dicasteries was called, as here,[4] καδίσκος, or κάδος.[5]  Often, too, it is called κημός from the funnel-shaped hopper down through which the ballots dropped into the voting-urn (Ar. Vesp. 99):

| | |
|---|---|
| «κημὸς καλός» [6] | "pretty ballot-box" [6] |

Once the voting-urn is called a box (Ar. Vesp. 674):

| | |
|---|---|
| ἐκ κηθαρίου λαγαρυζόμενον καὶ τραγαλίζοντα<br>μηδέν | getting a poor living from the ballot-box and<br>having nothing to eat |

Before the Bema, the judges' bench, stood a marble-top table upon which the ballots were turned out of the voting-urn and counted (Ar. Vesp. 332–333):

| | |
|---|---|
| δῆτα λίθον με ποίησον ἐφ' οὗ<br>τὰς χοιρίνας ἀριθμοῦσιν | I pray thee turn me to stone—the stone on which<br>they count the ballots |

(Ar. Ach. 683–684):

| | |
|---|---|
| τονθυρίζοντες δὲ γήρᾳ τῷ λίθῳ παρέσταμεν<br><br>οὐχ ὁρῶντες εἰ μὴ τῆς δίκης τὴν ἠλύγην | and stammering with age we take our stand by<br>the stone,<br>with an eye to nothing except the dark intricacies<br>of the case |

Somewhere in the court stood, or hung, the clepsydra, the water-clock which regulated the time that might be occupied by counsel in their speeches for the prosecution and the defense before the jury.[7]  The clepsydra was an essential article of the courtroom furnishings. So characteristic of the courtroom was it that its name, clepsydra, may be used figuratively for the dicastery itself (Ar. Av. 1694–1696):

[1] The Bema of the dicasteries was probably similar in form to the Bema of the Pnyx.  The latter is a great, square platform hewn out of the live rock of the Pnyx hill.  It is for that reason sometimes referred to as "the rock" (e. g., Ar. Eq. 956): λᾶρος κεχηνὼς ἐπὶ πέτρας δημηγορῶν.  For the Bema of the courts see Dem. XLVIII 31; Aesch. III 207; Plat. Inc. Frag. 185 K.

[2] Cf. Dem. XIX (de falsa Leg.) 311 [441]: Men. Dub. Frag. 1121 K.):
ὁρῶ τιν' ἐπὶ τοῦ βήματος καθεδούμενον

[3] Cp. the riddle in Eub. Σφιγγ. (Frag. 107, 23–26 K.):
ἔστιν ἄγαλμα βεβηκὸς ἄνω, τὰ δὲ κάτω κεχηνός,
εἰς πόδας ἐκ κεφαλῆς τετρημένον, ὀξὺ διαπρό,
ἀνθρώπους τίκτον κατὰ τὴν πυγὴν ἕν' ἕκαστον·
ὧν οἱ μὲν μοίρας ἔλαχον βίου, οἱ δὲ πλανῶνται......

[4] So also Ar. Vesp. 853; 854.

[5] It is often dual, as there were always two of them (Ar. Av. 1032; 1053):
οὐκ ἀποίσεις τὼ κάδω;
ἐγὼ δὲ σοῦ γε τὼ κάδω διασκεδῶ.

See also Vol. III Alphabetical List, *s. v.* κάδος, καδίσκος.

[6] Cf. also Ar. Vesp. 754; 1339; Eq. 1150.

[7] Cf. Dem. in Steph. 10; 58.

ἔστι δ' ἐν Φαναῖσι πρὸς τῇ | there is in the land of Phanae by the
Κλεψύδρᾳ πανοῦργον ἐγγλωττογαστόρων | Clepsydra a nation of scoundrels
γένος | who fill their bellies with their tongues

(Ar. Vesp. 93):

ὁ νοῦς πέτεται τὴν νύκτα περὶ τὴν κλεψύδραν | his wits flit about the clepsydra all night long

(Ar. Ach. 693):

γέροντ' ἀπολέσαι πολιὸν ἄνδρα περὶ κλεψύδραν | to ruin a grey-haired old man about the clepsydra

In all three passages the necessary piece of furnishing for a courtroom is used for the court-room itself. One step farther, and the clepsydra may be used metaphorically for the judicial decisions that are handed down in its presence (Eub. 'Ολ6., Frag. 74 K., quoted in full below, pp. 285–286). So essential to the courtroom is the clepsydra, that Bdelycleon insists upon improvising such a clock even for his father's make-believe court (Ar. Vesp. 856–859):

ΒΔ. ......πάντα γὰρ πάρεστι νῷν | BD. ......there, now we have everything
ὅσων δεόμεθα, πλήν γε δὴ τῆς κλεψύδρας. | that we need, except, to be sure, the clepsydra.
ΦΙ. ἡδὶ δὲ δὴ τίς ἐστιν; οὐχὶ κλεψύδρα; | PH. But what pray is this here? Isn't it a clepsydra?
ΒΔ. εὖ γ' ἐκπορίζεις αὐτὰ κἀπιχωρίως | BD. Good! you make clever provision for everything

With ἡδὶ Philocleon points to the pot that his son has hung upon a peg beside his bench for his convenience.[1] The coarse humor of the situation lies in the substitution of that homely vessel for the (probably) elegant timepiece that adorned the wall of an Athenian courtroom. In picturing to ourselves the appearance of a courthouse clepsydra, we must not imagine a great piece of mechanism on anything like the scale of the water-clock in the Tower of the Winds—the Horologium of Andronicus Cyrrhestes. The Scholiast on Aristophanes's Acharnians (694) describes the simple timepiece of the dicasteries:

ἀγγεῖόν ἐστιν ἔχον μικροτάτην | it is a vessel with a very small
ὀπὴν περὶ τὸν πυθμένα, ὅπερ | opening at the bottom, which is
ἐν τῷ δικαστηρίῳ μεστὸν ὕδατος | filled with water and set up in
ἐτίθετο, πρὸς ὃ ἔλεγον οἱ | the courthouse; the speakers time
ῥήτορες | their speeches by it

It was obviously a device something like the modern hourglass, only operating with water instead of with sand. A vessel (an ἀγγεῖον, according to the Scholiast just quoted; an amphora, according to Sextus Empiricus[2]) with a small aperture at the bottom and holding one to eleven amphorae, according to the importance of the case, was filled and set up over another vessel and when the allowance of water was run out, the orator's speech must end.[3]

In the 'Υποβαλλόμεναι of Epinicus one of the characters has, by a humorous turn, to drink "by the clock." In the squirting of the wine from the little end of the horn there may also be a suggestion of the water dropping from the upper vessel of the clepsydra into the lower (Epin., Frag. 2, 1–3 K.):

τῶν ῥυτῶν τὰ μέγιστα τῶν ὄντων τρία | three of the biggest horns there are I
πίνειν δεήσει τήμερον πρὸς κλεψύδραν | shall have to drink to-day by the clock,
κρουνιζόμενον | catching the jet as it squirts

The appliance got its name from the way in which the water escaped, as it were, by stealth through the tiny aperture in the container. The container was, as described by Aristotle[4] and as implied by Aristophanes,[5] a globe-shaped vessel flattened at the top[6] and provided

---

[1] Ll. 807–808: ἀμὶς μέν, ἣν οὐρητιάσῃς αὐτηὶ
  παρά σοι κρεμήσετ' ἐγγὺς ἐπὶ τοῦ παττάλου.

[2] adv. Math. V 24, p. 732 Bekk.: ἀμφορέα τετρημένον πληρώσαντες ὕδατος εἴασαν ῥεῖν εἰς τι ἕτερον ὑποκείμενον ἀγγεῖον. So Apuleius, Met. III: vasculum in vicem coli graciliter fistulatam.

[3] In the Roman law courts clepsydrae were used that normally ran out in half an hour. In exceptional cases, the time might be extended. From this limitation came the proverbial ἄλλως ἀναλίσκεις ὕδωρ (Inc. Inc. Frag. 655 K.) applied to one who uses many words to no purpose.

[4] Prob. XVI 8.

[5] Improvising his mock clepsydra out of an ἀμίς (Vesp. 807–808; 857–858).

[6] Because of this peculiar shape it was sometimes called κώδεια or κωδία ("poppy-fruit").

with a funnel-like neck through which the water was poured in. By inserting a cork in this neck the clock could be stopped at will. This was always done during the reading of laws, decrees, and other documents by the clerk of court. A special officer of the court was placed in charge[1] to manage the clock.

Whether the courtroom clocks stood or hung is not perfectly clear. Philocleon's improvised clepsydra evidently hung upon a peg near his bench. But Lydus makes the definite statement that the upper vessel was supported by a tripod (On the Roman Magistrates, II 16):

| | |
|---|---|
| ὁ τρίπους ἐν μέσῳ τοῦ ἀκροατηρίου, | the tripod in the middle of the auditorium, |
| ἐξηρτημένου κατὰ μέσον τοῦ κανθάρου, | with the bowl suspended in its midst, |
| καὶ κρατὴρ παρακείμενος· δι' οὗ ποτε | and the crater standing by; and the bowl |
| πληρούμενος ὁ κάνθαρος ὕδατος τοσοῦτον | filled with water from it allowed so much |
| ἐδίδου καιρὸν τῷ τῆς δίκης τέρματι, | time for the duration of the trial |
| ἐφ' ὅσον διά τινος γνώμονος τοῦ ἐνόντος | until the water that was in it trickled |
| αὐτῷ ὕδατος διηθουμένου ὁ κύαθος | through the clock and the cup was |
| ἀπηλλάττετο | changed |

The only thing that is a distinct contribution here is the tripod; upon it Lydus has a "cantharus," instead of an "amphora" or a "vessel," while at the end of the passage his "cantharus" dwindles down to a "cyathus." But the arrangement is still perfectly clear that the clepsydra consists of a tripod with a vessel filled with water above through the bottom of which the water in it "trickles" down into another vessel below.

But the clepsydra of the courts was not the only timepiece that we know from the ancient drama. Though the consideration of the general question of clocks has nothing to do with the courthouses of classical times, the discussion of the clepsydra naturally prompts that of the larger problem.

The next stage of development from the clock that stood on a tripod or hung on a wall would be a portable timepiece. And such were not wanting in antiquity. Vitruvius's contemporaries had their *viatoria pensilia* (ὡρολόγια), which we might translate, without undue violence, as "watches." And long before the time of Vitruvius such "watches" were not unknown in Greece. We have one reference to a kind of pocket "watch" in the New Comedy (Baton, 'Ανδροφ., Frag. 2, 12–14 K.):

| | |
|---|---|
| ἔπειθ' ἔωθεν περιάγεις τὴν λήκυθον, | and then from early morning you carry around your oil-pot |
| καταμανθάνων τοὔλαιον, ὥστε περιφέρειν | and carefully observe the oil, so that people shall think |
| ὡρολόγιον δόξεις τι, οὐχὶ λήκυθον | you are carrying a "watch" and not an oil-pot |

The manner in which Baton's character with his oil-pot could make people think he was carrying a chronometer may at first be puzzling. Winckelmann thought the portable watch of antiquity to be simply a small hourglass, made of transparent glass. But the clepsydra was not a clock that told the hours of the day but an instrument for measuring a definite period of time. The timepiece alluded to in Baton's comedy was an instrument that would tell the time of day. The invention of such a clock was ascribed to Plato.[2] Its mechanism is made clear by Galen's description, as interpreted by Marquardt:[3] The body of the clock was made of glass or other transparent material; into it the water (or oil) flowed in a tiny but steady, uniform stream. The height at which the fluid stood was the measure of time; careful experimentation fixed the markings on the dial. The dial was drawn on the face of the transparent container. Had the ancients divided their day into astronomical hours, as we do, there would have been no difficulty in arranging the dial of their clock; they could simply have drawn twelve horizontal rings about the clock with the proper intervals, and the timepiece would have been complete. But with the ancients every day of the year was twelve hours long, and every night twelve hours. That method of dividing the day complicated things. So they drew upon the face of their clock four vertical lines dividing the surface of the container into four approximately equal parts. The first line represented the summer solstice; the second, the autumnal equinox; the third, the winter solstice; and the

[1] ὁ ἐφ' ὕδωρ.
[2] Ath. IV 174 c.
[3] *Privatl. d. Römer*, pp. 773 ff.

fourth the vernal equinox. On these four vertical lines they marked off the twelve hours of the day: on the second and fourth the distances between the horizontal marks would be the same; those on the third would be much closer, and those on the first much farther apart. If they had stopped there, the clock would have given accurate time for only four days in the year—a sort of sublimated standard time. But by the simple device of drawing several sloping lines about the body of the vessel, running through the corresponding hours of the day marked on the four verticals, they had the approximate hour for any day in any season of the year. A further development produced a clock with twelve vertical lines, instead of four, one for each month, and the twelve hours of the day marked on each of the twelve vertical lines.

Baton's portable "watch" was an oil-flask; as people observed the height of the water in the water-clock, so he diligently observed the oil in his instrument; his man may have been trying to run a great bluff with his make-believe watch; but the jest would have no point at all, if such watches had not been familiar to the Greeks of the fourth century.[1] These articles of luxury may have been made of glass; for we know that the ancient Greeks had glass lecythi.[2]

Any kind of timepiece, whether clepsydra or sundial or water-clock or oil-watch, was called a *solarium* by the Romans. Apropos of the "oil-watch" in Baton's fragment Meineke quotes Vitruvius (IX 8, 1): ὡρολόγιον est viatorium pensile. ac solarii Herculanensis summa est cum ampulla olearia similitudo.

The kind of timepiece that we usually first think of as ancient is the sundial, with its twelve-hour day set off upon its face. The invention of that device came from the East, from Babylon.[3] The first one, so far as we know, to be set up in Athens was placed upon the Pnyx Hill by the famous astronomer Meton in the year 433 B. C.[4] Another was erected in the Market-place—on the Colonus Agoraeus (Ar. Av. 997–998):

| | |
|---|---|
| ὅστις εἴμ' ἐγώ; Μέτων, | Who am I?  Meton, |
| ὃν οἶδεν Ἑλλὰς χὠ Κολωνός | whom Hellas knows and Colonus |

Colonus, we may infer, knew him, because the populace that daily thronged the Agora were forever observing the time of day by the great scientist's sundial; and all Hellas knew him, because that same sort of horologium was by this time becoming common and soon became universal throughout the Hellenic world [Pl. Boeotia I (Gell. III 3, 5) (Leo, Plaut. II p. 527)[5]]:

> ut illum di perdant, primus qui horas repperit
> quique adeo primus statuit hic solarium;[6]
> qui mihi comminuit misero articulatim diem.
>
> . . . . . . . . .
>
> itaque adeo iam oppletum oppidum est solariis.

The speaker of these lines protests against the dial's showing of the dinner hour; he has a far more accurate timepiece in his vest:

> nam < unum > me puero venter erat solarium,[6]
> multo omnium istorum optimum et verissimum.

The town that was chock full of sundials was probably not Rome, as the lines are usually interpreted, but the town of Plautus's Greek original, most probably Athens; and the most interesting information that they could give seems to have been to tell the hour for dinner or for the bath. So Aristophanes, Ecclesiazusae 651–652:

| | |
|---|---|
| σοὶ δὲ μελήσει | and it will be your lookout, |
| ὅταν ᾖ δεκάπουν τὸ στοιχεῖον, λιπαρῷ χωρεῖν | when the shadow is ten feet long, to slick up and |
| ἐπὶ δεῖπνον | go to dinner |

[1] Such mechanisms excited the wonder and admiration of Cicero (de Nat. Deor. II 38): An cum machinatione quadam moveri aliquid videmus, ut sphaeram, ut horas, ut alia permulta, non dubitamus, quin illa opera sint rationis.

[2] Cf. Ath. VI 47 (p. 245): τοῦ δὲ Χαιρεφῶντος γυμνοῦ ἔν τινι δείπνῳ διαναστάντος, ὦ Χαιρεφῶν, εἶπεν, ὥσπερ τὰς ληκύθους ὁρῶ σε μέχρι πόσου μεστὸς εἶ –  Compare also the epigram of Hedylus quoted by Ath. XI 71 (p. 486): κεῖται πορφυρέης λέσβιον ἐξ ὑέλου.

[3] Hdt. II 109: πόλον μὲν γὰρ καὶ γνώμονα καὶ τὰ δυώδεκα μέρεα τῆς ἡμέρης παρὰ Βαβυλωνίων ἔμαθον οἱ Ἕλληνες.  But, according to Diogenes Laertius (II 1), the inventor was Anaximander, and the first one set up in Greece was the public clock of Sparta.

[4] Schol. Ar. Av. 997: ἐν τῇ νῦν οὔσῃ ἐκκλησίᾳ, πρὸς τῷ τείχει τῷ ἐν τῇ Πνυκί.  Cp. also pp. 32 ff.

[5] Ascribed to Aquilius, Ribbeck, Frag. I (p. 33³).

[6] The solarium of Pl. Mil. 341 and 379 is not a sundial but a sun-parlor.

The longest shadow cast by the finger of the dial was "twelve feet"—at sunrise and at sunset (Men. Ὀργή, Frag. 364, 2–5 K.[1]):

| | |
|---|---|
| κληθείς ποτε | once invited |
| εἰς ἑστίασιν δωδεκάποδος, ὄρθριος | to a banquet at the twelve-foot mark, he saw the shadow |
| πρὸς τὴν σελήνην ἔτρεχε τὴν σκιὰν ἰδών | cast by the moon before dawn and ran |
| ὡς ὑστερίζων, καὶ παρῆν ἅμ' ἡμέρᾳ | for fear he'd be late, and was on hand at daybreak! |

The length of the shadow is not to be taken too literally; for it must necessarily vary with the varying position of the sun from summer solstice to winter solstice. The lines marking the twelve hours of daylight came to have fixed names, disregarding the varying length of the hours with the varying length of the days. Eubulus once, in comic exaggeration of the elongated stature of one Philocrates, has the shadows on a dial for him double the standard length (Eub. Inc. Frag. 119, 5–12):

| | |
|---|---|
| ὅν φασί ποτε κληθέντ' ἐπὶ δεῖπνον πρὸς φίλου τινὸς | he was once invited to dinner, they say, by a friend; |
| εἰπόντος αὐτῷ τοῦ φίλου, ὁπηνίκ' ἄν εἴκοσι ποδῶν μετροῦντι τὸ στοιχεῖον ᾖ, | his friend told him to come at the hour when, as he observed the dial, the shadow was twenty feet long; |
| ἥκειν, ἔωθεν αὐτὸν εὐθὺς ἡλίου μετρεῖν ἀνέχοντος, μακροτέρας δ' οὔσης ἔτι πλεῖν ἢ δυοῖν ποδοῖν παρεῖναι τῆς σκιᾶς ἔπειτα φάναι, μικρὸν ὀψιαίτερον δι' ἀσχολίαν ἥκειν, παρόνθ' ἅμ' ἡμέρᾳ | so he observed it early in the morning, as soon as the sun was up, and came when the shadow was longer still by more than two feet; and then he apologized for being a little late— he had been detained—though he was on hand at daybreak! |

The many ancient sundials that have come down to us—in Athens, Rome, Pompeii, Herculaneum, Puteoli, Ravenna, and many other places[2]—are all constructed on the same general plan: the dial is slightly concave;[3] at the upper edge (the 90° point) is set the hand; radiating from this central point, the lines marking the hours are incised (sometimes inlaid with metal) and usually intersected with two or three arcs of circles of different radius, according to the varying length of the days. At right angles to the perpendicular line marking the hour of noon a horizontal line is sometimes drawn from east to west; when the shadow of the hand (the γνώμων[4]) falls upon a given point of intersection (an upper in mid-winter, a lower in mid-summer, and a middle one in spring and autumn), it marks sharply the hour of the day.

Aristophanes has one clear allusion to the sundial (Γηρυτ., Frag. 163 K.):[5]

| | |
|---|---|
| πόλος τόδ' ἐστί; εἶτα πόστην ἥλιος τέτραπται; | this is a dial? Then to what o'clock does the sun point? |

What it was that was called a dial we cannot begin to guess; but the dial (πόλος) was a very familiar object in fifth century Athens.

Somewhere, too, about the courtroom provision may have been made for a cashier's desk for the payment of the dicast's fee or for the delivery of the voucher authorizing the payment of the fee elsewhere; for every juryman was entitled to his fee (Ar. Nub. 863):

| | |
|---|---|
| ὃν πρῶτον ἔλαβον ὀβολὸν[6] ἡλιαστικόν | the first heliastic obol[6] I received |

The token authorizing the juryman's admission to the space within the latticed fence was obtained daily at the place of allotment—the cleroterium. This place was near the

---

[1] Cp. Schol. ad loc.: ἡ τοῦ ἡλίου σκιὰ ὅταν ᾖ δέκα πηχῶν. θέλει οὖν εἰπεῖν, ὅτε γίνεται ὄψε. Ἄλλως· τὸ παλαιὸν καλοῦντες ἐπὶ δεῖπνον καὶ καλούμενοι παρεσημαίνοντο τὴν σκιὰν καὶ οὕτως οἱ μὲν ἔμενον τοὺς κληθέντας, οἱ δὲ ἀπήεσαν ἐπὶ τὰς ἑστιάσεις οὐδέπω τηρήσεως οὔσης ἑτέρας, ἐφ' ἧς οἷόν τε ἦν τεκμήρασθαι εἰς πόσας ὥρας προσήκει. Cf. also Philem. Ὑποβ., Frag. 83 K.

[2] See Marquardt, *Privatl. d. Römer*, VII pp. 766 ff.

[3] From its concave surface it was likened to a dish and called λεκανίς (Pollux VI 110).

[4] Suidas: γνώμων· τὸ ἐν τοῖς ἡλιοτροπίοις πηγνύμενον, ὅπερ ἐφεῦρεν Ἀναξίμανδρος καὶ ἔστησεν ἐπὶ τῶν σκιοθήρων.

[5] On this Pollux remarks (IX 46): τὸ δὲ καλούμενον ὡρολόγιον ἢ που πόλον ἄν τις εἴποι.

[6] Not that the juryman's fee was a single obol; for we know from the definite statement of Aristotle (Const. Ath. 27; 62) that the remuneration fixed by Pericles for that distinguished service was three obols: τὰ δικ[αστήρια] τρεῖς ὀβολούς. But the pay may have varied from one to three obols, as the Scholiast, commenting on Ar. Vesp. 684, says: τοὺς τρεῖς ὀβολούς· τὸν φόρον λέγει, ἀφ' ὧν ἐδίδοτο τὸ τριώβολον, τοῦτο δὲ ἄλλοτε ἄλλως ἐδίδοτο, τῶν δημηγορῶν τὰ πλήθη κολακευόντων, ὥς φησιν Ἀριστοτέλης ἐν Πολιτείαις.

Agora. In it stood two urns presided over by the Thesmothetae.[1] Each of the six thousand heliasts drew a lot from each urn: the one assigned him to his jury section; the other assigned him his court-house, designated by letter (A′–K′, that is, the number of his court). Armed with these two tokens he presented himself at the place allotted, according to the letter on his ticket[2] (Ar. Pl. 277–278):

| | |
|---|---|
| ἐν τῇ σορῷ νυνὶ λαχὸν τὸ γράμμα σου δικάζειν, | you have your letter assigning you to jury-duty— in your coffin; |
| σὺ δ’ οὐ βαδίζεις; ὁ δὲ Χάρων τὸ ξύμβολον δίδωσιν | why don’t you go? Charon is ready to hand you your ticket |

("Charon" looks like an obvious anagram for archon.) The word Cleroterium is used by Aristophanes for the place where the allotment was made (Γῆρας, Frag. 146 K.): κληρωτήριον. But Pollux, who preserves this brief item of information, adds that while Aristophanes seems to use the word of the *place*, it may also be applied to the *urns*, from which the lots were drawn.[3] It is clear from this comment of Pollux that in the *Old Age* of Aristophanes the Cleroterium is a place. That the word is often so used is set beyond dispute by Aristotle[4] and Phrynichus.[5] But that the cleroteria may also be, as Pollux says, the urns used in connection with the allotments is perfectly clear from another passage of Aristophanes (Ec. 681–686):[6]

| | |
|---|---|
| ΒΛ. τὰ δὲ κληρωτήρια ποῖ τρέψεις; ΠΡ. εἰς τὴν ἀγορὰν καταθήσω· | BL. But what disposition will you make of the cleroteria? PR. I’ll set them down in the market-place, |
| κᾆτα στήσασα παρ’ Ἁρμοδίῳ κληρώσω πάντας ἕως ἂν | and then I’ll set them up beside Harmodius and assign lots to all, until |
| εἰδὼς ὁ λαχὼν ἀπίῃ χαίρων ἐν ὁποίῳ γράμματι δειπνεῖ· | everybody gets his lot and knows under what letter he is to eat and goes his way rejoicing; |
| καὶ κηρύξει τοὺς ἐκ τοῦ βῆτ’ ἐπὶ τὴν στοιὰν ἀκολουθεῖν | and the herald will call all those with a Beta to follow to the Royal |
| τὴν βασίλειον δειπνήσοντας· τὸ δὲ θῆτ’ ἐς τὴν παρὰ ταύτην, | Stoa to eat; those with a Theta, to the stoa adjoining; |
| τοὺς δ’ ἐκ τοῦ κάππ’ ἐς τὴν στοιὰν χωρεῖν τὴν ἀλφιτόπωλιν | those with Kappa, to pass on to the Stoa of the Flour Market |

Blepyrus’s question and Praxagora’s answer both show clearly that the cleroteria of this passage are articles that a woman can handle; they are the urns used in assigning the lots. But as courts will be superfluous under the reforms of the women-controlled state, the tickets drawn from the urns will henceforth assign the holders not to jury duty but to a seat at the public dining halls, each to that hall marked with the letter corresponding to the one he draws. The numbers in this parody are the same as in the real court procedure, A′–K′. The reason why Praxagora singles out Beta, Theta, and Kappa for particular mention is not apparent.

All these data from the comedy are confirmed by Aristotle (Const. Ath. 63):

| | |
|---|---|
| τὰ δὲ δικαστήρια κληροῦσιν οἱ θ′ | the nine archons assign jurymen to the courts by lot, |
| ἄρχοντες κατὰ φυλάς, ὁ δὲ γραμματεὺς | each archon looking after his own tribe, while the secretary |
| τῶν θεσμοθετῶν τῆς δεκάτης φυλῆς. | of the Thesmothetae looks after the tenth tribe. |

[1] Arist. Const. Ath. 59: οἱ δὲ θεσμοθέται πρῶτον μὲν τοῦ προγράψαι τὰ δικαστήριά εἰσι κύριοι τίσιν ἡμέραις δεῖ δικάζειν, [ἔπε]ιτα] ποῦ δοῦναι ταῖς ἀρχαῖς· καθότι γὰρ ἂν οὗτοι δῶσιν, κατὰ τοῦτο χρῶνται.

[2] The same sort of ticket was handed to the ecclesiast as he went to the Assembly; on his leaving the ecclesia he presented the ticket and received his three obols (Ar. Ec. 296–298):

ὅπως δὲ τὸ ξύμβολον
λαβόντες ἔπειτα πλή-
σιοι καθεδούμεθ’

[3] Pollux X 61: εἰ γὰρ καὶ ἐπὶ τούτου τοῦ τόπου ἔοικεν εἰρῆσθαι τοὔνομα ἐν τῷ Γήρᾳ Ἀριστοφάνους, ἀλλὰ καὶ ἐπὶ τοῦ ἀγγείου ἐναρμόσειεν.

[4] Const. Ath. 63, quoted below.

[5] Bekker, Anecd. Gr. I p. 47, 15: κληρωτήρια ἔνθα κληροῦνται οἱ δικασταί.

[6] Rogers, following Poste (in *C. R.* VII and X), interprets these κληρωτήρια also as voting booths, like those used in our elections. He thinks that for her Utopia Praxagora will take these portable booths to the Agora and set them there for dinner allotments to the people. The urn is much more reasonable as set forth in the text above.

εἴσοδοι δέ εἰσιν εἰς τὰ δικαστήρια
δέκα, μία τῇ φυλῇ ἑκάστῃ, καὶ
κληρωτήρια εἴκοσι, δύο τῆς φυλῆς
ἑκάστης, καὶ κιβώτια ἑκατόν,
δέκα τῇ φυλῇ ἑκάστῃ, καὶ ἕτερα
κιβώτια δέκα, οἷς ἐμβάλλεται τῶν
λαχόντων δικαστῶν τὰ πινάκια· καὶ
ὑδρίαι δύο καὶ βακτηρίαι παρατίθενται
κατὰ τὴν εἴσοδον ἑκάστην
ὅσοι περ οἱ δικασταί, καὶ βάλανοι
εἰς τὴν ὑδρίαν ἐμβάλλονται ἴσαι
ταῖς βακτηρίαις, γέγραπται δὲ
ἐν ταῖς βαλάνοις τὰ στοιχεῖα
ἀπὸ τοῦ ἑνδεκάτου, τοῦ λ, ὅσαπερ
ἐὰν μέλλῃ τὰ δικαστήρια πληρω-
θήσεσθαι................
ἔχει δ' ἕκαστος δικαστὴς πινάκιον
πύξινον, ἐπιγεγραμμένον τὸ
ὄνομα τὸ ἑαυτοῦ πατρόθεν καὶ
τοῦ δήμου καὶ γράμμα ἓν τῶν
στοιχείων μέχρι τοῦ κ· νενέμην-
ται γὰρ κατὰ φυλὰς δέκα μέρη
οἱ δικασταί, παραπλησίως ἴσοι
ἐν ἑκάστῳ τῷ γράμματι. ἐπειδὰν

δὲ ὁ θεσμοθέτης ἐπικληρώσῃ
τὰ γράμματα ἃ δεῖ προσπαρα-
γίνεσθαι τοῖς δικαστηρίοις, ἐπέ-
θηκε φέρων ὁ ὑπηρέτης ἐφ' ἕκαστον
δικαστήριον τὸ γράμμα τὸ λαχόν

There are ten entrances to the courtrooms, one for each tribe; there are twenty cleroteria, two for each tribe; and one hundred boxes, ten for each tribe; and ten more boxes, in which are placed the tickets of jurymen selected by lot. Two urns also are placed there beside each entrance and as many staves as there are jurymen; and as many acorns are dropped into the urn as there are staves; and upon the acorns are written letters, beginning with the eleventh, and including as many as there are courts to be filled. . . . . . . . . . . . Each juryman has a ticket of boxwood, on which is inscribed his own name and his father's and that of his deme and one of the letters from A to K. The whole panel of jurymen is divided into ten divisions according to tribes; and under each letter sits a jury of approximately the same number. And when the Thesmothete has assigned by lot the letters that are to be attached to the several courtrooms, the clerk of court takes the several letters allotted and posts them on the several courtrooms.

The red tape of the Athenian law courts, it seems, was not less complicated than our own. Many items in Aristotle's statement baffle our understanding: does he mean, for instance, that each of the various courthouses had ten entrances—ten κιγκλίδες—one for each tribe? Perhaps such a convenience was very desirable to expedite getting those immense juries in their places without delay and without confusion. At all events, the question that most immediately concerns us here—the matter of the cleroteria—receives considerable light. There were twenty places of allotment near the Agora—two for each tribe. There were in all one hundred "boxes," or urns, in which the lots were placed—ten for each tribe. This multiplication of boxes was surely for the purpose of expediting the business of securing the various juries with the greatest possible rapidity. Apparently each tribe had for its convenience five pairs of urns—one of each pair holding the tickets assigning the dicast to his jury section; the other, assigning him to his court room. The tickets in them corresponded to the number of jurymen required on the given day; the tickets in the one box were labeled with the letter (A' – K', that is, the number) of that one of the ten sections into which the whole body of heliasts was divided; the tickets in the other bore the letter of the court room—continuing from Λ on down the alphabet as far as might be required by the business of the day. Thus, for example, if a juror drew B from one urn and M from the other, he knew that he was to sit with jury B in court room M. The clerk of the court, as suggested in the closing lines of the Constitution of Athens, had, probably during the drawing of the lots, hung up a big B, the letter of the jury, upon court room M; and so on with the rest.

The "ten more boxes in which are placed the tickets of the jurymen selected by lot" seem to be the boxes in which are placed those tickets carried by the several jurymen, each bearing the juryman's name, his father's name, and the name of his deme. It was upon the presentation of this ticket, together with the voucher (σύμβολον) handed to him as he entered the court room, that he received at the end of the day's session the three obols of pay to which he was by law entitled for his services. The tickets were deposited in the ten boxes.

The "acorns"[1] were not the fruit of the oak tree, but the tickets, gland-shaped, on

[1] They are also called σφηνίσκοι "little wedges." The thick end of the "little wedge" may have been rounded off like an acorn.

which were inscribed the letters from Λ on to designate the court rooms; the "staves" were not wands or walking-sticks, but elongated tickets on which were inscribed the letters from A to K to designate the jury-sections.

Still another precaution against general confusion and blundering jurymen getting into the wrong place was provided by a simple color-scheme. Each court had its own peculiar color; that is the significance of such names of individual courts as Βατραχιοῦν "frog-green," Φοινικιοῦν "scarlet"; and the "staves" were painted to correspond with the color of the court room to which it assigned the bearer. Staves and court room, therefore, both had not only corresponding letters but identical colors.

The Scholiast on Aristophanes's Plutus 277[1] gives a like explanation of the ticket (γράμμα):

| | |
|---|---|
| ἕκαστον τούτων [τῶν δικαστηρίων] | each of these [courts] |
| εἶχεν ἔν τι τῶν στοιχείων εἰδικὸν | had one of the letters for its own particular |
| ὄνομα· οἷον ἦν τι τῶν δικαστηρίων | name: for example, one of the courts |
| λεγόμενον ἄλφα, ὁμοίως | was called Alpha; likewise, |
| ἄλλο βῆτα, ἄλλο γάμμα καὶ | another, Beta; another, Gamma; and |
| ἐξῆς τὸ δ' καὶ τὸ ε' καὶ οὕτως | then Delta and Epsilon, and so |
| ἕως τοῦ κ'. δέκα γὰρ ἦν τὰ | on to Kappa; for there were in |
| δικαστήρια τὰ πάντα ἐν | all ten courts at Athens. |
| Ἀθήναις. καὶ πρὸ θυρῶν δὲ ἑκάστου | And in front of the doors of each |
| δικαστηρίου ἐγέγραπτο πυρρῷ | court there was painted with red |
| βάμματι τὸ στοιχεῖον, ᾧτινι | paint that letter by which that |
| τὸ δικαστήριον ὠνομάζετο. ὅσοι | court was named. And as |
| δὲ δικασταὶ ἦσαν ἐν Ἀθήναις, | many dicasts as there were at Athens, |
| ἕκαστος καθ' ἕκαστον δικαστήριον | each one, according to each several court, |
| εἶχε δέλτον, τουτέστι πινάκιον | had a tablet, that is, a ticket |
| ἐν ᾧ ἐγγεγραμμένον ἦν τὸ ὄνομα | on which was inscribed his name |
| αὐτοῦ καὶ τοῦ δικαστηρίου. εἶχε | and the name of his court. And he had |
| δὲ καὶ ῥάβδον ἅμα τῷ πινακίῳ | also a staff in addition to his ticket, |
| καὶ ἐν αὐτῇ δὲ τῇ ῥάβδῳ ἦν | and on that staff also was |
| τὸ ὄνομα τοῦ δικαστηρίου ἐγ- | inscribed the name of the |
| γεγραμμένον. ὅτε οὖν συνέβαινε | court. So, when the time |
| καιρὸς τοῦ δικάζειν, ἤρχοντο | came for holding court, all the |
| πάντες οἱ δικασταὶ εἰς τὴν ἀγορὰν | dicasts came to the Agora |
| κἀκεῖ κλήρους ἔβαλλον, | and there they drew lots; |
| καὶ ὅστις ἂν ἐκληροῦτο κλῆρον | and the man who drew a lot |
| ἔχοντα τὸ α' ἀπήρχετο εἰς τὸ | bearing an Alpha went to |
| α' δικαστήριον ὁμοίως εἰς | court room Alpha; and so also |
| τὸ β' καὶ τὰ ἐφεξῆς. καὶ πρῶτον | with Beta, et cetera. The first |
| μὲν ἐδείκνυε τῷ κήρυκι | thing he had to do was to show to the |
| τοῦ δικαστηρίου τὸν κλῆρον | crier of the court the allotment |
| τοῦ στοιχείου· ὁ δὲ κῆρυξ | letter, and the crier then |
| λοιπὸν ἐδίδου αὐτῷ τὸ πινάκιον | gave him his ticket |
| αὐτοῦ καὶ τὴν ῥάβδον, | and his staff. And then, |
| εἶτα οὕτως ἐδίκαζεν | thus provided, he was impaneled |

Not everything in this scholium is perfectly accurate. For example, it is stated that "in all there were ten courts at Athens." There may have been ten or more than ten, according to whether we include the courts having jurisdiction in cases of capital crimes or not. The Scholiast probably means by "ten" the jury sections, not the court rooms, which is a perfectly proper use of δικαστήρια. But in general the account given in the scholium is in complete harmony with the account given by Aristotle and with the allusions in the texts of the poets.

As the clepsydra, as we saw above, could be used figuratively for the court room or the court itself, so the Cleroteria also came to be used metaphorically for court decisions. In a fragment of the Olbia of Eubulus one character is telling another of all the fine things that one can buy in the market-place of Athens; every time he stops to catch his breath, his companion throws in, with bitter irony, such other purchasable items as—"advocates"—"witnesses"—"verdicts"—"judicial decisions" (Frag. 74 K.):

[1] The line is quoted on p. 283.

| | |
|---|---|
| Α. ἐν τῷ γὰρ αὐτῷ πάνθ' ὁμοῦ πωλήσεται ἐν ταῖς 'Αθήναις· σῦκα — Β. κλητῆρες | A. For in that same place you can buy anything at Athens: figs, B. advocates |
| Α. βότρυς, γογγυλίδες, ἄπιοι, μῆλα —Β. μάρτυρες Α. ῥόδα, μέσπιλα, χόρια, σχαδόνες, ἐρέβινθοι — Β. δίκαι | A. grapes, turnips, pears, apples,—B. witnesses A. roses, medlars, haggis, honey, peas,—B. verdicts |
| Α. πυός, πυριάτη, μύρτα — Β. κληρωτήρια | A. beestings, pudding, myrtle-berries,—B. cleroteria |
| Α. ὑάκινθος, ἄρνες — Β. κλεψύδραι, νόμοι, γραφαί | A. hyacinths, mutton,—B. clepsydras, laws, indictments |

Thus, we see, our poets (with the help of the scholia upon their lines) have contributed much to clear up the age-long disputes that have raged about the court rooms of Athens and the red tape and paraphernalia for the conduct of civil cases.

## 3 The Stoas

The law courts and the stoas were, for the most part, in the general neighborhood of the market-place. The market-place in course of time became practically surrounded with colonnades, in the shelter of which most of the business of ancient Athens, both public and private, was transacted. Here, too, was the natural gathering ground of "all the Athenians and strangers which were there" who "spent their time in nothing else, but either to tell or to hear some new thing."[1] The stoas took the place not only of the modern public reading-room, with its array of daily newspapers and magazines for the dissemination of the news of the day, domestic and foreign, for the discussion of problems of economics, finance, and politics, but also of the modern public lecture hall and university class room. A suggestion of all these varied interests of public and private business and of social and intellectual activity we have in a fragment of Philemon ('Εφ., Frag. 28, 1–3 K.):

| | |
|---|---|
| οὐ τοῖς πλέουσι τὴν θάλατταν γίνεται | those who sail the sea, Laches, are not the only ones |
| μόνοισι χειμών, ὡς ἔοικεν, ἀλλὰ καὶ τοῖς περιπατοῦσί που, Λάχης, ἐν τῇ στοᾷ | it seems, that storms o'ertake, but also those who walk about in the stoa |

A fragment of Dioxippus, so badly mutilated and corrupt as to be quite unintelligible, still points to the stoa as a part of the market-system ('Ιστ., Frag. 3 K.):

| | |
|---|---|
| τὴν στοὰν διεξέπαιον 'Αμφικλῆς μήτρας δύο | . . . they rushed through the stoa, and Amphicles, pointing at two paunches |
| κρεμαμένας δείξας, ἐκεῖνον πέμπε, φῄς, ἐὰν ἴδῃς | hanging there, said, "Send me that fellow, if you see him" |

The centre of the public administration of the city was the Royal Stoa, in which the King Archon had his office. This is the first building that Pausanias describes after he enters the Agora (I 3, 1):

| | |
|---|---|
| πρώτη δέ ἐστιν ἐν δεξιᾷ καλουμένη στοὰ βασίλειος | the first building on the right is the so-called Royal Stoa |
| . . . . . . . . . | . . . . . . . . . |
| ταύτης ἔπεστι τῷ κεράμῳ τῆς στοᾶς ἀγάλματα ὀπτῆς γῆς, ἀφιεὶς Θησεὺς ἐς θάλασ- σαν Σκίρωνα καὶ φέρουσα 'Ημέρα Κέφαλον | upon the roof of it there are figures in terra cot- ta—Theseus, hurling Sciron into the sea, and Day car- rying off Cephalus |

As Pausanias entered the city by the Dipylum Gate, and as the Theseum stood directly above it, we should expect to find the Royal Stoa at the northeastern foot of the Market Hill; and granting the now generally accepted identification of the so-called Theseum with Pausanias's Temple of Hephaestus, the Royal Stoa stood not far from the foundations that Dörpfeld[2] found deep down directly east of the Theseum; for the temple of Hephaestus

---

[1] Acts XVII 21.
[2] Ath. Mitt. XXI (1896) pp. 107–109.

stood above the Ceramicus and the Royal Stoa (Paus. I 14, 6):

| | |
|---|---|
| ὑπὲρ δὲ τὸν Κεραμεικὸν καὶ | and above the Ceramicus and |
| στοὰν τὴν καλουμένην βασίλειον | the so-called Royal Stoa |
| ναός ἐστιν Ἡφαίστου | is the temple of Hephaestus |

The remains at first claimed by Dörpfeld as the foundations of the Royal Stoa are too scanty to help much in the reconstruction of the building. The terra cotta sculptures named by Pausanias may have been acroteria. The subjects of them are strongly suggestive of acroteria compositions. If the building was orientated north and south, as we should naturally expect, such acroteria would hardly have caught the periegete's attention as he came into the market-place; if the building was orientated east and west, the western gable with its acroterium would have been conspicuous, and Pausanias, seeing it, would very properly have added a word about the eastern one, especially if they were archaic; and we may assume, not only from the material and the subjects of the sculptures but also from the character of the remains of the foundations, that they were. The foundations reveal a public building, containing a large[1] hall with a fairly deep portico or vestibule on the east of it, and seem to show an east and west orientation.[2]

The Royal Stoa served not only as the official headquarters of the King Archon during his term of office[3] but also sometimes as a court room for the trial of cases of impiety.[4] The building discovered by Dörpfeld and at once accepted as the Stoa Basileüs would have been too small for the session of the court of the Areopagus. Either the Pseudo-Demosthenes[4] was all wrong in assigning such trials to the Royal Stoa, or the building the foundations of which we have is not the Royal Stoa. It may be, as Judeich suggests,[5] the Stoa of Zeus Eleutherius which stood alongside the Royal Stoa,[6] in which case we must seek the latter a little farther north, or it may be what is left of some other one of the many stoas that encircled the Agora.

The dramatic poets occasionally make mention of the public porticoes, sometimes in a general way and sometimes specifically. In the Ecclesiazusae of Aristophanes, Praxagora, in the sweeping reforms contemplated under the feminist administration of Athens, proposes to turn stoas, law courts, and all the waste places of man's mismanagement to good use as mess rooms for the men (Ar. Ec. 676):

| | |
|---|---|
| τὰ δικαστήρια καὶ τὰς στοιὰς ἀνδρῶνας πάντα | the court rooms and stoas—I will |
| ποιήσω | make them all into mess rooms for men |

One certain group of men is to be assigned to the Royal Stoa, another group to the Porch of the Flour-merchants (*ibid.* 684–686):[7]

| | |
|---|---|
| καὶ κηρύξει τοὺς ἐκ τοῦ βῆτ' ἐπὶ τὴν στοιὰν | and the herald will summon those under Beta to |
| ἀκολουθεῖν | follow to the |
| τὴν βασίλειον[8] δειπνήσοντας· τὸ δὲ θῆτ' ἐς | Royal Stoa to dine; those under Theta to the one |
| τὴν παρὰ ταύτην· | next thereto; |
| τοὺς δ' ἐκ τοῦ κάππ' ἐς τὴν στοιὰν χωρεῖν | and those under Kappa to pass to the Flour- |
| τὴν ἀλφιτόπωλιν | merchants' Stoa |

We have here apparently in these three lines three important porches of the Agora named in their topographical succession: the Royal Stoa at the northwest corner of the Market-place; the one next to it is, of course, the Stoa of Zeus Eleutherius, closely adjoining the Royal Stoa on the south; and then the Stoa of the Flour-merchants, which may be the long building at the southern limit of Dörpfeld's excavations. But the Stoa of the Flour-merchants is generally located near the docks at the Piraeus.[9] The Piraeus would be a very appropriate

---

[1] About 15 M. square.

[2] The excavations soon to be inaugurated by the American School will, it is hoped, bring to light the real Royal Stoa and also settle definitely the long debated question of the real indweller of the "Theseum."

[3] Paus. I 3, 1.

[4] (Pseudo-) Dem. XXV 22–23.

[5] *Topogr. v. Ath.*, pp. 296–298, and footnote 5.

[6] Harpocr. (Suid.): βασίλειος στοά· δύο εἰσὶ στοαὶ παρ' ἀλλήλας, ἥ τε τοῦ Ἐλευθερίου Διὸς καὶ ἡ βασίλειος.

[7] The significance of the letters is discussed above, pp. 282 ff.

[8] Our classical authors always call the Royal Stoa ἡ στοὰ ἡ βασίλειος or ἡ τοῦ βασιλέως στοά. But its official name seems to have been ἡ στοὰ ἡ βασίλεια (C. I. A. I 61, 5; Arist. Frag. 346; Harpocr. *s. v.* κύρβεις).

[9] Schol. Ar. Ach. 548: τῆς λεγομένης Ἀλφιτοπώλιδος, ἣν ᾠκοδόμησε Περικλῆς, ὅπου καὶ σῖτος ἀπέκειτο τῆς πόλεως. This may be the same as that which Pausanias calls the Long Stoa (I 1, 3): τῆς στοᾶς τῆς μακρᾶς, ἔνθα καθέστηκεν ἀγορὰ τοῖς ἐπὶ θαλάσσῃ. Cf. also Dem. in Phorm. 42, p. 918.

place for a grain or flour storehouse; but there must have been a flour-market in the city also; and in Praxagora's ideal state, the Kappa men of the city were not going to be obliged to hike down to the Piraeus docks for their meals! The way in which Aristophanes puts his Royal Stoa and Flour-merchants' Stoa together must indicate that they belong together.

Such a stoa as that of the Flour-merchants is the kind that would seem to have been common for the general wholesale and retail business of Athens, public and private stores. In the Acharnians of Aristophanes (539 ff.) Dicaeopolis draws a picture of the preparations for war—army, navy, funds, ordnance, supplies, and "roaring colonnade" (στοᾶς στεναχούσης l. 548). The colonnade is the depot for the stores, and it "roars" because of the business that it has to do in getting ready for the great war.

Even in the fifth century the "stoa" might be used, without any thought of a colonnade, of the storerooms of a private home (Ar. Ec. 14–15):

| | |
|---|---|
| στοάς τε χαρποῦ Βαχχίου τε νάματος<br>πλήρεις ὑποιγνύσαισι συμπαραστατεῖς | and when we open secretly the store-rooms filled with food and the juice of Bacchus thou standest by us |

The Painted Porch (Στοὰ Ποιχίλη) also is mentioned by name once, and once by clear allusion, in the drama. The stoas were favorite lounging places of the Athenians; and there Zeno and Cleanthes and later philosophasters found men to talk to and to instruct, as Socrates had done before (Theog. Φάσ. ἢ Φιλάργ., Frag. 1, 1–2 K.):[1]

| | |
|---|---|
| ἄνθρωπ', ἀπολεῖς με· τῶν γὰρ ἐκ τῆς Ποιχίλης | man, you'll be the death of me; for you are so stuffed full of |
| στοᾶς λογαρίων ἀναπεπλησμένος νοσεῖς | the phrases from the Painted Stoa that it makes you sick |

Of all the stoas of Athens, the Poecile is the most familiar to us. And yet we do not know where it stood nor what it looked like nor who built it. We know it was in the Agora;[2] and from Pausanias's description of the Market-place, we may be sure that the Painted Porch was not far from the Royal Stoa and the temple of Hephaestus (the "Theseum") and the temple of Aphrodite Urania;[3] but in what direction it stood from any one of these we do not know. From the manner of its mural decoration, we infer that it was in form like the Lesche of the Cnidians at Delphi, a hollow square but with the southern side open. Thus arranged, it was an ideal lounging place for the leisure class and for the *conversazioni* of the philosophers; and in the fragment just quoted from Theognis, we see that the Painted Portico is the very type of such ready-made lecture halls.

The architect's name is unknown; but from the fact that before the famous paintings were added it was called the "Pisianactean Stoa,"[4] we learn that the man originally responsible for its erection was Pisianax, the Alcmaeonid, a brother-in-law of the great Cimon.

The fame of the Poecile Stoa rested chiefly upon the wonderful paintings with which Polygnotus of Thasos, assisted by Micon and Panaenus, covered its walls: 1) The Greeks after the capture of Troy; 2) a battle between the Athenians and the Amazons; 3) the battle of Marathon; and 4) (mentioned by Pausanias alone) the battle of Oenoe. The first was the work of Polygnotus himself;[5] the second was by Micon;[6] the third, by Micon and Panaenus working together.[7]

The discussion of the paintings must be reserved for the chapter on Painting, in Volume III.

In the Stoa Poecile were hung, as memorials of glorious victories in war, some bronze shields taken at Scione and at Pylus (Paus. I 15, 4):

[1] Cf. Luc. Jup. Trag. 16; Icarom. 34; Dial. Meretr. X 1; Pisc. 13.
[2] Aesch. III 186.
[3] Paus. I 14–15.
[4] Plut. Cim. 4: ἐν τῇ Πεισιανακτείῳ τότε καλουμένη, Ποιχίλη δὲ νῦν στοᾷ; D. L. VII 5: ἐν τῇ Ποιχίλη στοᾷ τῇ καὶ Πεισιανακτείῳ καλουμένη ἀπὸ δὲ τῆς γραφῆς τῆς Πολυγνώτου Ποιχίλη; Schol. Dem. XX 112: ἡ δὲ Πεισιανακτὶς ἀπὸ Πεισιάναχτος τοῦ κτίσαντος; Schol. Aesch. III 186; Cramer, Anecd. Gr. IV p. 21; Isidor. Orig. VIII 6: porticus fuit Athenis, quam Pisianactiam appellabant, in qua picta erant gesta sapientium atque virorum fortium historia.
[5] Plut. Cim. 4.
[6] Ar. Lys. 678–679; schol. a. l.; Arr. An. VII 13, 5.
[7] Aelian de An. Nat. VII 38; Arr. An. VII 13, 5; Sop. I 8; Paus. V 11, 6.

ἐνταῦθα ἀσπίδες κεῖνται χαλκαῖ,
καὶ ταῖς μέν ἐστιν ἐπίγραμμα
ἀπὸ Σκιωναίων καὶ τῶν ἐπικούρων

εἶναι, τὰς δὲ ἐπαληλιμμένας πίσσῃ μὴ σφᾶς
ὅ τε χρόνος λυμήνηται
καὶ ὁ ἰός, Λακεδαιμονίων
εἶναι λέγεται τῶν ἁλόντων
ἐν τῇ Σφακτηρίᾳ νήσῳ

here are placed bronze shields;
upon one part of them is an inscription, to
the effect that they were taken from the
    Scionaeans and their allies; the rest,
smeared with pitch to prevent their
being corroded by time and rust,
are said to have been taken from the
Spartans captured on the
island of Sphacteria

Scione revolted from Athens in 423 B. C.   In 421 it was taken by the Athenians and destroyed.[1]  The victory at Sphacteria and Pylus in 425 B. C. seemed at the time to the Athenians to be the turning point assuring them of complete victory in a short time.  Though time soon proved them to have been misled by the immediate advantage, Pylus was always a name to conjure with in Athens, and the shields, including that of the gallant Brasidas, were always among the proudest war monuments of Athens.[2]  Aristophanes makes Cleon, the self-created hero of Sphacteria, boast of these glorious trophies (Eq. 845–846):

ἀπαξάπαντας τοὺς ἐμοὺς ἐχθροὺς ἐπιστομίζειν,
ἕως ἂν ᾖ τῶν ἀσπίδων τῶν ἐκ Πύλου τι λοιπόν

to put a gag on every one of my enemies,
as long as there is anything left of the shields
    from Pylus

When such shields were dedicated, they were ordinarily stripped of their handles, in order, it seems, to allow them to fit squarely against the walls; for the Sausage-seller retorts (Eq. 847–849):

ἐπίσχες ἐν ταῖς ἀσπίσιν· λαβὴν γὰρ ἐνδέδωκας.

οὐ γάρ σ' ἐχρῆν, εἴπερ φιλεῖς τὸν δῆμον,
                                    ἐκ προνοίας
ταύτας ἐᾶν αὐτοῖσι πόρπαξιν ἀνατεθῆναι

stop right there with your shields; for you have
    given me a handle!
If you really love Demus, you ought not pur-
    posely
to have let them be dedicated, handles and all

As if, by removing the leather handles and using them on new shields of Athenian manufacture, the military authorities would spoil the tanner's chances for selling the government so many new handles from his own leather establishment.

The Stoa of Zeus also is mentioned once and only once in the drama (Men. Ψοφ., Frag. 526 K.):

ἐπίσημον οὖν τὴν ἀσπίδ' εἰς τὴν τοῦ Διὸς
στοὰν ἀνέθηκαν

so they put an inscription on the shield
and set it up in the Stoa of Zeus

What particular shield this was we do not know.  There is not enough of Menander's play left even to guess at its plot.  So much only is obvious: not only the Poecile but also the other porticoes about the Athenian Agora, including the Stoa of Zeus Eleutherius, had been turned to a greater or less extent into national museums.  The shield here referred to must have been a conspicuous trophy, and the inscription mentioned would have told of the occasion on which it was won.

## 4. The Odeum and the Orchestra

One of the most famous buildings of Periclean Athens was the Odeum or "Music Hall" built under the superintendence of the peerless statesman for the musical contests of the Panathenaic games.[3]  Many ancient writers mention this splendid building; Plutarch gives us the most information (Per. XIII 4–6):

τὸ δ' Ὠιδεῖον, τῇ μὲν ἐντὸς
διαθέσει πολύεδρον καὶ πο-
λύστολον,[4] τῇ δ' ἐρέψει
περικλινὲς καὶ κάταντες ἐκ μιᾶς

the Odeum, arranged inside
with many seats and many columns,[4] with its roof constructed
in the form of a cone sloping

[1] Thuc. IV 120; 131; V 32.
[2] Dio Chrysos. Or. II, Vol. I p. 27 (Dind.); cf. Thuc. IV 12; 38; Diod. XII 62; Plut. de Gl. Ath. 7.
[3] Strabo IX 396; Plut. Per. XIII 6; Suid. and Phot., s.v. ᾠδεῖον.
[4] Cf. Vitruv. V 9; Theophr. Char. 3.

χορυφῆς πεποιημένον, εἰ-
κόνα λέγουσι γενέσθαι καὶ
μίμημα τῆς βασιλέως σκηνῆς¹,
ἐπιστατοῦντος καὶ τούτῳ Πε-
ρικλέους. διὸ καὶ πάλιν Κρατῖνος
ἐν Θρήτταις παίζει πρὸς αὐτόν

(Crat. Θρῆτ., Frag. 71 K.):

ὁ σχοινοκέφαλος Ζεὺς ὅδε προσέρχεται
Περικλῆς, τῴδεῖον ἐπὶ τοῦ κρανίου
ἔχων, ἐπειδὴ τοῦστρακον² παροίχεται

from a single peak, was built,
a reproduction and imitation, they
say, of the King's Tent,[1]
under the superintendence of Pericles.
And so Cratinus in his Thracian Women makes fun of him again:

here comes the squill-head Zeus,
Pericles, with the Odeum on his dome—
for the potsherd [2] has had its day

The walls, with the many tiers of seats resting against them, and the many columns of the interior were, of course, of stone—probably Pentelic Marble. The timbers of the conical roof, which the comic poet with bitter sarcasm compares with the peculiar shape of the statesman's cranium, were the masts and spars of the captured Persian ships; the roof itself was doubtless covered with marble tiles. It was one of the finest creations of the Periclean age and famed as the most beautiful concert hall in the world.[3]

The Odeum of Pericles was erected just above the Dionysiac theatre on the southeast slope of the Acropolis during the same years in which the Parthenon was building. It was burned on the order of Aristion during the siege of Sulla (86 B. C.). A new one was erected on the site.[4] The spade has begun to reveal something of it; the excavations conducted by Soteriades immediately adjoining the cavea of the Dionysiac Theatre on the east have already brought to light a great, square, covered, theatre-shaped building very much after the manner of the Thersilion in connection with the theatre of Megalopolis and of the square building, the so-called "Buleuterium" adjoining the theatre at Messene.

Notwithstanding the magnificence that we may assume for the great music hall built by Pericles at the southeast corner of the Acropolis, east of the Dionysiac Theatre, when the ancient writers speak simply of "The Odeum," they mean the older concert hall of the ancient Market-place, at the northwest base of the Areopagus, or the northeast base of the Hill of the Nymphs, adjoining the ancient Agora.

Pausanias, in his circuit of the Agora, which he enters from the Ceramicus, takes up in turn the Royal Stoa, the Stoa of Zeus Eleutherius, the Metroüm, the Buleuterium, the Tholus, a long array of statues of Egyptians and Eponymous Heroes, and, finally, the Tyrannicides,[5] which brings him to the doors of the Odeum. The next object of interest he comes to is the Enneacrunus, not far away (I 8, 6):

Τοῦ θεάτρου δὲ ὃ καλοῦσιν Ὠιδεῖον
ἀνδριάντες πρὸ τῆς ἐσόδου βασιλέ-
ων εἰσὶν Αἰγυπτίων

Before the entrance of the theatre that they
call the Odeum are statues of
the Egyptian Kings

(I 14, 1):

ἐς δὲ τὸ Ἀθήνησιν ἐσελθοῦσιν
Ὠιδεῖον ἄλλα τε καὶ Διόνυσος
κεῖται θέας ἄξιος. πλησίον δέ
ἐστι κρήνη, καλοῦσι δὲ αὐτὴν
Ἐννεάκρουνον

as one enters the Odeum at Athens,
there is to be found, among other things,
also a Dionysus worth looking at. And
near by is a fountain; they call it
Enneacrunus

We know the position of the Tyrannicides at the market-place; we know the location of the Enneacrunus between the southwest spur of the Areopagus and the Pnyx. Obviously, therefore, this music hall is not the Odeum of Pericles at the southeast foot of the Acropolis, but the older Odeum of the Agora.

Pausanias calls the Odeum a "theatre," just as we also sometimes call the Odeum of Herodes Atticus a theatre. The Scholiast on Aristophanes's Wasps 1109 is a little more guarded and calls it "theatre-like":

¹ So also Paus. I 20, 4.
² See Vol. III, Alphabetical List, *s.v.* ὄστρακον.
³ Pseudo-Dicearch. (F.H.G. I p. 254).
⁴ Paus. I 20, 4.
⁵ Paus. I 8, 5.

ἔστι τόπος θεατροειδὴς ἐν ᾧ
εἰώθασι τὰ ποιήματα ἀπαγγέλλειν
πρὶν τῆς εἰς τὸ θέατρον ἀπαγγελίας

it is a theatre-like place, in which
they used to present poems
before the presentation in the theatre

What the Scholiast seems to be trying to say is that the Odeum was a theatre-like place in which the dramas were rehearsed before their formal presentation in the great theatre.[1] The Scholiast to Aeschines III 67 states the same fact in words that cannot be misunderstood:

ἐγίγνοντο πρὸ τῶν μεγάλων
Διονυσίων ἡμέραις ὀλίγαις
ἔμπροσθεν ἐν τῷ ᾿Ωιδείῳ
καλουμένῳ τῶν τραγῳδῶν
ἀγὼν καὶ ἐπίδειξις ὧν
μέλλουσιν δραμάτων ἀγω-
νίζεσθαι ἐν τῷ θεάτρῳ

a few days before the great
Dionysia there took place
in the so-called Odeum a
competition and exhibition by
the dramatic poets of
the dramas with which they
proposed to compete in the theatre

Not only the rehearsals took place in the Odeum; the final presentation also seems to have occurred in the theatre facing northward across the Agora and the Ceramicus. Aristophanes's Clouds must have been played in a theatre that faced north (323–327):

ΣΩ. βλέπε νυν δευρὶ πρὸς τὴν Πάρνηθ᾿·
            ἤδη γὰρ ὁρῶ κατιούσας
ἡσυχῇ αὐτάς. ΣΤ. φέρε, ποῦ; δεῖξον. ΣΩ.
            χωροῦσ᾿ αὗται πάνυ πολλαὶ
διὰ τῶν κοίλων καὶ τῶν δασέων, αὗται
            πλάγιαι. ΣΤ. τί τὸ χρῆμα;

ὡς οὐ καθορῶ. ΣΩ. παρὰ τὴν εἴσοδον. ΣΤ.
            ἤδη νυνὶ μόλις οὕτως.
ΣΩ. νῦν γέ τοι ἤδη καθορᾷς αὐτάς, εἰ
            μὴ λημιᾷς κολοκύνταις.

SO. Look over that way toward Parnes; for now
    I see them coming
softly down. ST. Tell me, where? Show me.
    SO. There they come in great numbers
winding their way through the hollows and
    thickets and trailing off yonder. ST. What's
    the matter?
I don't see them. SO. Along the entrance-way.
    ST. Ay, now I can just see them a bit.
SO. Yes; now you must see them, unless you are
    worse than high-gravel blind.

When these lines were spoken in the theatre, Parnes must have been in sight, both for the speakers and for the audience. No one, neither actor nor spectator, could see Parnes from the Dionysiac Theatre. If the presentation had been there, the poet would naturally have used Hymettus rather than Parnes for the source of his clouds.

In some sort of close connection with the Odeum stood the Orchestra—"the semicircle of the theatre in the Agora,"[2] "a spot affording a fine view for celebrations."[3] Here, too, it was that the dramatic contests took place before the permanent theatre was built. The orchestra was the original dancing-centre for the chorus ( Inc. Inc. Frag. 54 K.):

εἰς τὴν ὀρχήστραν· ἔτι γὰρ τὴν θέαν ᾤκειτ᾿
            ἐκεῖ

into the orchestra; for you still held the show
there

And on the slopes of the Hill of the Nymphs, in the early days, the temporary wooden seats were erected.[4]

Though closely connected in place and sometimes united in function, the Orchestra and the Odeum are nevertheless separate architectural units, and either one may be turned to some use without the other. Thus we see their juxtaposition but separate identity in Andocides[5] as he presents the information lodged by Dioclides against the mutilators of the Hermae. Dioclides starts through the city to go to Laurium; when he reaches the entrance to the temple of Dionysus, he sees in the light of the full moon a large number of men "coming down from the Odeum into the Orchestra." The Odeum is obviously the *cavea*

[1] In this older Odeum song recitals also used to be given before the great theatre and the Odeum of Pericles were built (Hesych. ᾠδεῖον· τόπος ἐν ᾧ πρὶν τὸ θέατρον κατασκευασθῆναι οἱ ῥαψῳδοὶ καὶ οἱ κιθαρῳδοὶ ἠγωνίζοντο.)
[2] Phot. 351, 16: πρῶτον ἐκλήθη ἐν τῇ ἀγορᾷ, εἶτα καὶ τοῦ θεάτρου τὸ κάτω ἡμικύκλιον, οὗ καὶ οἱ χοροὶ ᾖδον καὶ ὠρχοῦντο.
[3] Timaeus Lex.:᾿Ορχήστρα᾿ ..... τόπος ἐπιφανὴς εἰς πανήγυριν, ἔνθα ῾Αρμοδίου καὶ ᾿Αριστογείτονος εἰκόνες.
[4] Ar. Thes. 395–396: εἰσιόντες ἀπὸ τῶν ἰκρίων
            ὑποβλέπουσ᾿ ἡμᾶς
Phot. (Eust. ad γ 350, p. 1472, 4): ἴκρια· τὰ ἐν ἀγορᾷ, ἀφ᾿ ὧν ἐθεῶντο τοὺς Διονυσιακοὺς ἀγῶνας πρὶν κατασκευασθῆναι τὸ ἐν Διονύσου θέατρον. Cf. Suid. s.v. Αἰσχύλος and s. v. Πρατίνας.
[5] I 38.

upon the slopes of the hill; the Orchestra is the great level space at its base. As he catches sight of these men, Dioclides slips into the shadow of a pillar of the gateway and through the clear light of the Attic full moon he observes the men in the orchestra closely and recognizes the faces of most of them.

This passage of Andocides is usually taken to refer to the Odeum of Pericles and to the orchestra of the great Dionysiac Theatre.[1] I cannot persuade myself that that interpretation is correct and that it is the Dionysiac Theatre or the Odeum of Pericles that Dioclides is talking about in his testimony against the mutilators of the Hermae. It is from the "propylaeum" of Dionysus that he sees the men descend from the Odeum into the orchestra; that is, from a gateway in the temenos wall of the sanctuary of Dionysus. The only gateway in that wall of which we have any definite knowledge is the gateway by which Pausanias enters the sanctuary from the Street of the Tripods and by which again he leaves it in order to visit the Odeum of Pericles.[2] If that was the "propylaeum" by which Dioclides halted, he would have been within arm's length of the marauders as they came down from the Odeum into the orchestra of the Dionysiac Theatre; if such had been the fact, it must have been brought out in his testimony. Furthermore we must ask how and why Dioclides came to be away up there on the hillside of the Acropolis when he was hurrying away toward Laurium. And if he stopped by a "propylaeum" in the south peribolus wall, no matter where we locate such a gateway, he could not possibly have seen—much less recognized—people coming down from the Odeum into the orchestra.

The difficulty with "the column" and "the pillar on which is the general of bronze" is the same, no matter where we put Dioclides in the shadow.

The temple of Dionysus at whose gateway Dioclides halted must surely be the temple of Dionysus-in-the-Marshes. That lies directly beside a great highway, by which he would naturally be pursuing his journey toward Laurium. And standing in the shadow of the gateway to that temple and looking down the ancient street corresponding to the modern Street of the Apostle Paul, Dioclides would have looked straight into the Odeum and the Orchestra and in that wonderful Attic moonlight which misled Dioclides himself into thinking that it was day, it was entirely possible for him to recognize familiar figures.[3]

The audience room of the Odeum and the Orchestra were used not only for concerts and dramatic exhibitions but, like the great theatre when rebuilt by Lycurgus, for all sorts of assemblies. Among other things, they were sometimes turned to military uses. For example, when Thrasybulus was threatening the security of their rule, the Thirty Tyrants "called into the Odeum the hoplites and the cavalry-men of their new levy. . . . And the members of the Spartan garrison also were in one half of the Odeum under arms. . . . And the cavalry kept watch in the Odeum, with their horses and their shields."[4] The Orchestra seems here to be included with the music hall under the one name "Odeum"; and to accommodate so many troops—horses, arms, and all—the site must have been a very spacious one.

The Odeum was used also as a court of law (Ar. Vesp. 1109):

οἱ δ' ἐν Ὠιδείῳ δικάζουσ' | and some are trying cases in the Odeum

The dicasteries sitting in the Odeum tried cases of alimony; so we are informed by Pollux (VIII 33):[5]

τὰς ἐπὶ σίτῳ δίκας ἐν τῷ | in the Odeum they tried the cases
Ὠιδείῳ ἐδίκαζον· σῖτος δέ | for alimony; now alimony
ἐστιν αἱ ὀφειλόμεναι τροφαί | means support that is due

There, too, state provisions were sometimes stored.[6]

---

[1] So Jebb, *Selections from the Attic Orators*, a. l.; Grote, *Hist. Gr.*, Part II Ch. LVIII (Vol. VI p. 35, Murray); Dörpfeld-Reisch, *Griech. Theater*, pp. 11; 32.

[2] Paus. I 20, 2–4.

[3] Andoc. I 38: ψευσθεὶς τῆς ὥρας βαδίζειν· εἶναι δὲ πανσέληνον. ἐπεὶ δὲ παρὰ τὸ προπύλαιον τοῦ Διονύσου ἦν, ὁρᾶν ἀνθρώπους πολλοὺς ἀπὸ τοῦ Ὠιδείου καταβαίνοντας εἰς τὴν ὀρχήστραν. . . . ὁρῶν δὲ αὐτῶν πρὸς τὴν σελήνην τὰ πρόσωπα τῶν πλείστων γιγνώσκειν.

[4] Xen. Hel. II 4, 9: εἰ τὸ Ὠιδεῖον παρεκάλεσαν τοὺς ἐν τῷ καταλόγῳ ὁπλίτας καὶ τοὺς ἄλλους ἱππέας. . . . 10. οἱ δὲ Λακωνικοὶ φρουροὶ ἐν τῷ ἡμίσει τοῦ Ὠιδείου ἐξωπλισμένοι ἦσαν. . . . 24. ἐξεκάθευδον δὲ καὶ οἱ ἱππεῖς ἐν τῷ Ὠιδείῳ τούς τε ἵππους καὶ τὰς ἀσπίδας ἔχοντες. . . .

[5] Cf. Dem. c. Neaer. 52: λαχόντος δὲ τοῦ Στεφάνου αὐτῷ δίκην σίτου εἰς Ὠιδεῖον, κατὰ τὸν νόμον ὃς κελεύει, ἐὰν ἀποπέμπῃ τὴν γυναῖκα, ἀποδιδόναι τὴν προῖκα, ἐὰν δὲ μή, ἐπ' ἐννέ' ὀβολοῖς τοκοφορεῖν, καὶ σίτου εἰς Ὠιδεῖον εἶναι δικάσασθαι ὑπὲρ τῆς γυναικὸς τῷ κυρίῳ. . . . 54. καὶ λαχόντος αὐτῷ Στεφάνου εἰς Ὠιδεῖον σίτου διαλύσασθαι πρὸς αὐτόν. . . .

[6] Dem. c. Phorm. 37: ἐν ᾧ ὑμῶν οἱ μὲν ἐν τῷ ἄστει οἰκοῦντες διεμαρτυροῦντο τὰ ἄλφιτα ἐν τῷ Ὠιδείῳ. . . .

Like the stoas about the Agora, so also the Odeum served as a lounging-place for the leisure classes (σχολή) and a convenient centre for the philosophers' lectures.[1] The last lecture of the great Stoic Chrysippus was delivered to his pupils at the Odeum.[2] There must have been colonnades at the entrances in the back part of the *cavea*, as we still see them in the great theatre at Taormina; and here the philosophers and their pupils were wont to resort. Of this we have abundant evidence in the words of the comic poet Alexis ('Aσωτ., Frag. 25, 1–3 K.):

| | |
|---|---|
| τί ταῦτα ληρεῖς, φληναφῶν ἄνω κάτω | what do you mean by this nonsense—yapping up and down |
| Λύκειον, 'Ακαδήμειαν, 'Ωιδείου πύλας, λήρους σοφιστῶν; οὐδὲ ἕν τούτων καλόν | the Lyceum, the Academy, the Odeum doors—sophists' nonsense? Not one of these things is right |

The Odeum, by the early part of the fourth century, came to need repairs[3] and in Roman times may have had to be substantially restored or, perhaps, entirely rebuilt; for it seems to have been this Odeum that later bore the name of Agrippeum (Philostr. Vit. Soph. II 5, 4):

| | |
|---|---|
| τὸ ἐν Κεραμεικῷ θέατρον ὃ δὴ ἐπωνόμασται 'Αγριππεῖον | the theatre in the Ceramicus, which has received the appellation of Agrippeum |

And in Roman times it still continued to be used as a school building by the philosophers.

The erection of the Odeum dates back into the sixth century B. C. Who the builder was we do not know. But we may be perfectly sure that it was not the orator Lycurgus, to whom Hyperides seems to ascribe it ('Υπὲρ τῶν Λυκούργου Παίδων 118):

| | |
|---|---|
| ᾠκοδόμησε δὲ τὸ θέατρον, τὸ ᾠδεῖον, τὰ νεώρια, τριήρεις ἐποιήσατο, λιμένας | he erected the Theatre, the Odeum, the Arsenal; he had triremes built and harbors |

The two especial monuments that stood in Athens to the glory of Lycurgus were the Theatre and the Stadium. The Stadium is not mentioned in this list, which, Hyperides says, every one would mention as he passed the great orator's tomb; we know, furthermore, from what we have just seen, that Lycurgus could have had nothing to do with the building of the Odeum. It has, therefore, been suggested that for ᾠδεῖον we read στάδιον;[4] with that change every difficulty is removed. If the text is sound and the reading ᾠδεῖον is correct, then we can at best suppose that Lycurgus did some extensive repairing on a building that was well-nigh two hundred years old in his day.

## 5. The Assembly Hall on the Pnyx

The hill rising west by southwest of the Acropolis, directly south of the Areopagus, between the Hill of the Nymphs and the Hill of the Muses, is the Pnyx. On the northern slopes of this hill in very early days the Athenians constructed their public assembly hall— a great auditorium, the "floor of the house" supported by a massive, semicircular, or rather hemielliptical, supporting wall with a chord (east-west) of one hundred and twenty meters and an axis (north-south) of seventy meters, a platform for the speakers (the Bema), an altar of sacrifice, and a bench for the presiding officers.

The heavy supporting wall, built of huge, well-finished blocks of carefully joined polygonal masonry, still stands to about one-third its original height, so that in the olden times the floor sloped gently down to the Bema. The chord of the semicircle is a wall, now about thirteen feet high, cut perpendicularly in the face of the rock on the summit of the hill. This wall is not perfectly straight but in the middle makes an angle of a little less than one hundred and eighty degrees. At this angle is left, projecting from the live rock, a great cube, rising above a three-fold base like an altar. These steps afforded a platform for the

---

[1] Plut. de Exil. 14: ἐπὶ τοὺς σοφοὺς ἐλθὲ καὶ τὰς σοφὰς 'Αθήνησι σχολὰς καὶ διατριβάς· ἀναπέμπασαι τὰς ἐν Λυκείῳ, τὰς ἐν 'Ακαδημείᾳ, τὴν στοάν, τὸ Παλλάδιον, τὸ 'Ωιδεῖον....

[2] D. L. VII 184: τοῦτον ἐν τῷ 'Ωιδείῳ σχολάζοντά φησιν "Ερμιππος ἐπὶ θυσίαν ὑπὸ τῶν μαθητῶν κληθῆναι....

[3] We have a mutilated account of the cost of such repairs in an inscription published by Foucart, B. C. H. X (1886), p. 452.

[4] Wachsmuth, *Stadt Athen*, I, p. 602 note 1.

speakers, accessible by means of the three steps that rise on all three sides, also cut out of the live rock. At the back of the cube on either side and against the rock-cut wall is a flight of six more steps leading to the top of the cube and the terrace above.

On this upper terrace are cuttings that are identified as the seats of the Prytanes, the presiding officers of the popular assembly. For it was in this place of meeting, on the Pnyx, that the Athenian demus met to transact the public business until Lycurgus remodeled the Dionysiac Theatre. And even after the rebuilding of the theatre, the Pnyx was not entirely abandoned.

The great cube with its wide platform is 9.67 meters wide on the side facing the auditorium, 5.6 meters deep on the west, 6.37 meters deep on the east side; it is three meters high. The speaker would have a rostrum thirty-two feet wide and seven feet three inches deep, which would be abundant space for action even for a Demosthenes. An orator of really violent action could run about upon the Bema (Eup. Πολ., Frag. 207, 3 K.):

ἀναβὰς γὰρ ἐπὶ τὸ βῆμ' ὑλακτεῖ περιτρέχων    |    for he mounts the Bema and runs about and barks

We should naturally expect the poets of the Old Comedy, with all their participation in the political problems and personalities of their day, to have considerable to say about the Pnyx and the assemblies held there in the fifth and early fourth centuries, and we are not wholly disappointed. The scene of the Ecclesiazusae throughout is laid in the Assembly Hall on the Pnyx; the Knights also deals with an assembly on the Pnyx. The first act of the Acharnians is a major assembly (χυρία ἐκκλησία) on the Pnyx. We get the whole procedure (travestied, of course) but we get amazingly little about the topography or the building. And yet we have something (Ar. Ach. 19–26):

| | |
|---|---|
| οὔσης χυρίας ἐκκλησίας | when we have a major assembly and |
| ἑωθινῆς ἔρημος ἡ Πνὺξ αὑτηί· | it's early morning, and here's the Pnyx empty. |
| οἱ δ' ἐν ἀγορᾷ λαλοῦσι, χάνω χαὶ χάτω | But the people are in the Agora chattering, and dodging, |
| τὸ σχοινίον φεύγουσι τὸ μεμιλτωμένον. | this way and that, the vermilioned rope. |
| οὐδ' οἱ Πρυτάνεις ἥχουσιν, ἀλλ' ἀωρίαν | Even the Prytanes haven't come. They'll come, but |
| ἥχοντες, εἶτα ὠστιοῦνται πῶς δοκεῖς | they'll be late; and then, when they do come, you can't im- |
| ἐλθόντες ἀλλήλοισι περὶ πρώτου ξύλου | agine how they'll push and shove to get a front bench, |
| ἀθρόοι χαταρρέοντες | as they all pour in together |

Dicaeopolis, obedient to the law, has gone to the Pnyx at dawn. The great body of citizens, like our average American good citizen, is doing business in the market-place instead of going to the polls. To enforce attendance, Athens had a statutory provision requiring the officers of the law to close up all approaches to the Agora except that leading to the Pnyx and then, beginning at the farther end, with a rope dripping with vermilion[1] drag the market-square for slackers. Any one caught in town with vermilion on his clothes was fined. When the sovereign citizens do come, they will be enthusiastic and they will all try to get front seats. And with these words Aristophanes does give us some light on the building. As the theatre down to his time had no permanent seats of stone, so the Pnyx auditorium had no seats of stone but only temporary wooden benches.

But the Prytanes did have stone seats—they are still there above the Bema (Ar. Eq. 313):

ἀπὸ τῶν πετρῶν ἄνωθεν τοὺς φόρους θυννο-       |    from the stones above watching the revenues,
                                    σχοπῶν       |    like a tunny-fisher

The Ecclesiazusae, though in this play the Pnyx is mentioned several times,[2] tells us nothing about it.

The comic poets help us to identify the Bema with the platform cut from the living rock of the Pnyx hill (Ar. Eq. 956):

λάρος κεχηνὼς ἐπὶ πέτρας δημηγορῶν       |    a gull with open mouth, standing on a rock and
                                         |    addressing the people

[1] Cf. also Ar. Ec. 378; Plat. Inc. Frag. 214 K.
[2] E. g. Ar. Ec. 243–244; 281–284; 384; Eq. 164–165; 751.

The rock is the Bema; the people are sitting in popular assembly; the gull is Cleon.  In this passage the Bema is πέτρα; in the Ecclesiazusae and the Peace it is λίθος (Ar. Pax 680):

| | |
|---|---|
| ὅστις κρατεῖ νῦν τοῦ λίθου τοῦ ’ν τῇ Πυκνὶ | who now is lord of the stone on the Pnyx |

(Ar. Ec. 86–87):

| | |
|---|---|
| δεῖ σε καταλαβεῖν ἕδρας | you are to take your seats |
| ὑπὸ τῷ λίθῳ τῶν Πρυτάνεων κατάντικρυ | below the stone, facing the Prytanes |

Here we have the front seats of the auditorium down below the Bema and facing directly the presiding officers' bench.

And at the altar, which is part of the Bema, the orators took oath that they would support the constitution and strive for the good of the people (Inc. Inc. Frag. 667 K.):

| | |
|---|---|
| λιθωμόται δημηγόροι | speakers who have taken oath upon the stone |

Even the great wall is mentioned by Aristophanes (Ec. 496–499):

| | |
|---|---|
| ἀλλ’ εἶα δεῦρ’ ἐπὶ σκιᾶς | but here—come hither |
| ἐλθοῦσα πρὸς τὸ τειχίον | to the wall and in its shadow |
| . . . . . . . . | . . . . . . . . |
| πάλιν μετασκεύαζε σαυτήν | change your dress again |

The wall rose high enough to afford a sort of foyer about the back of the auditorium, in which the women ecclesiasts could put off their men's clothing in comparative retirement and don their own again.  It was on the back wall of the Assembly Hall, in a place where the sun's light fell freely and where all could see, that Meton, the famous astronomer, erected the first public sun-dial in Athens.[1]

### 6. The Stadium

Although the Stadium of Athens plays so important a part in the great festival of Athens with its Panathenaic games, no dramatic poet, nor any other authority earlier than the late fourth century, ever refers directly to it.  It was only after Lycurgus secured for the city the hollow between Ardettus and the next hill to the northeast and leveled off the site and created the permanent Stadium, that it became an object worth mentioning.

When, therefore, the dramatists allude to a stadium, it is only in the most general way and without reference to any particular stadium.  Very little light, accordingly, may we expect from them on the athletic grounds.

Euripides twice refers to the length of the single course of the stadium (El. 883–884):

| | |
|---|---|
| οὐκ ἀχρεῖον ἔκπλεθρον δραμὼν | having run no useless course |
| ἀγῶν’ | of six plethra |

(Med. 1181–1182):

| | |
|---|---|
| ἤδη δ’ ἂν ἕλκων κῶλον ἐκπλέθρου δρόμου | and now a fast sprinter, at a rapid stride, would |
| ταχὺς βαδιστὴς τερμόνων ἀνθήπτετο | have been reaching the goal of a six-plethra course |

"Six plethra" are, of course, one stadium.

In these two passages the poet refers to the race through the single length of the stadium—the two hundred yard dash.  Sometimes we find reference to the four hundred yard dash —the race up the stadium and back to the starting-point (Ae. Ag. 344):

| | |
|---|---|
| κάμψαι διαύλου θάτερον κῶλον πάλιν | to swing about the second lap of the double course |

(Soph. El. 690–691):

| | |
|---|---|
| ὅσων γὰρ εἰσεκήρυξαν βραβῆς | for of all the races through the double course for which |
| δρόμων διαύλων ἆθλ’ ἅπερ νομίζεται | the judges proclaimed the customary prizes |

(Eur. El. 824–825):

| | |
|---|---|
| θᾶσσον δὲ βύρσαν ἐξέδειρεν ἢ δρομεὺς | and flayed off the hide more quickly than a runner |
| δισσοὺς διαύλους ἱππίους διήνυσεν | finishes the two-fold lap of the horses' double course |

[1] Schol. Ar. Av. 997.

So in a figurative sense (Eur. H. F. 660–662):

| | |
|---|---|
| κατθανόντες τ’ | and after death, returned |
| εἰς αὐγὰς πάλιν ἁλίου | again to the light of the sun, |
| δισσοὺς ἂν ἔβαν διαύλους | they should run a double course |

(*ibid.* 1101–1102):

| | |
|---|---|
| οὔπω κατῆλθον αὖθις εἰς Ἅιδου πάλιν, | I have not gone down again to Hades, have I, and |
| Εὐρυσθέως δίαυλον ἐξ Ἅιδου μολών; | run once more from Hades Eurystheus's double course |

(Alexis Τραυμ., Frag. 235 K.):

| | |
|---|---|
| τὸν γὰρ ὕστατον | for running now the last lap of the |
| τρέχων δίαυλον τοῦ βίου ζῆν βούλομαι | double course of life, I wish to live |

The word "stadium" does not occur in the drama in the sense of a building or scene for athletic contests. Aristophanes uses it several times as a measure of distance (Nub. 430):

| | |
|---|---|
| ἑκατὸν σταδίοισιν ἄριστον | best by a hundred miles |

(Ran. 91):

| | |
|---|---|
| Εὐριπίδου πλεῖν ἢ σταδίῳ λαλίστερα | in long-windedness they have Euripides skinned a mile |

(Av. 6):

| | |
|---|---|
| ὁδοῦ περιελθεῖν στάδια πλεῖν ἢ χίλια | tramp around more than one hundred miles |

(Antiph. Ἐφ., Frag. 100, 2–3):

| | |
|---|---|
| στάδια ἑκατὸν | I assure you I'd rather walk one hundred |
| ἐλθεῖν που δὴ κρεῖττον ἢ πλεῦσαι πλέθρον | miles than sail one hundred feet |

In the Ion of Euripides stadia are "grassy lawns" (497).

The only details of the stadium that the poets give us are the starting-point and the goal-posts. Athletes in the foot-race and horses in the hippodrome were assigned their places by lot behind the "marks." The "marks" of the ancient stadium are preserved for us at Epidaurus, at Olympia, and at Delphi. They consist of a line of marble slabs with grooves for toes (and for fingers?), extending across the entire width of the race-course and divided by marble posts into spaces (twenty at Olympia) of four feet each for the runners. Upon these grooves the athletes took their places, even as our runners "get on their marks" (Eur. Med. 1245): ἔρπε πρὸς βαλβῖδα which, if it were comedy and not the height of a tragic situation, we should not hesitate to translate with "get on your marks." In the Acharnians of Aristophanes, Dicaeopolis uses the "marks" metaphorically for the starting-point of his supreme endeavor and says (483):

| | |
|---|---|
| γραμμὴ δ’ αὑτηί | here is the scratch |

Against these posts was stretched a rope (ὕσπληξ) across the course; at a signal given by a blast upon a trumpet, the rope was dropped, and the racers leaped into the course.[1] Though in figurative speech, we see the rope dropped and the race begin, in three passages of Aristophanes (Eq. 1159):

| | |
|---|---|
| ἄφες ἀπὸ βαλβίδων ἐμέ τε καὶ τουτονί | release me and him from the barriers |

(Vesp. 548–549):

| | |
|---|---|
| καὶ μὴν εὐθὺς γ’ ἀπὸ βαλβίδων περὶ τῆς ἀρχῆς ἀποδείξω | jumping right from the marks, I'll prove in regard to |
| τῆς ἡμετέρας ὡς.... | our sovereignty that.... |

(Lys. 1000–1001):

| | |
|---|---|
| γυναῖκες ἅπερ ἀπὸ μιᾶς ὑσπλαγίδος | the women drove away the men |
| ἀπήλαον τὼς ἄνδρας | as if at the dropping of the rope |

[1] Hor. Sat. I 1, 114: cum carceribus missos rapit ungula currus;
Virg. Geor. I 512: cum carceribus sese effuderе quadrigae.

As the rope dropped, the athletes, who had been crouching low waiting for the signal, sprang forward, with head thrown back, and dashed away on the race (Eur. H. F. 867):

| | |
|---|---|
| χαὶ δὴ τινάσσει κρᾶτα βαλβίδων ἄπο | lo! he tosses his head [as he leaps] from the barriers |

Both starting-place and goal are mentioned together by the Paedagogus in his account of the athletic prowess of Orestes in Sophocles's Electra (686):

| | |
|---|---|
| ἰσώσας τῇ ἀφέσει τὰ τέρματα | he made the goal equal with the starting place |

that is, Orestes ran so like lightning that he annihilated all the space between the marks of the starting-place and the goal-posts at the end, even as Arias the son of Menecles did, according to the epigram of Antipater of Sidon[1] (39):

| | |
|---|---|
| ἢ γὰρ ἐφ' ὑσπλήγων ἢ τέρματος εἶδέ τις ἄκρου | now on his marks one saw him set, that splendid, young athlete |
| ἠΐθεον, μέσσῳ δ' οὔποτ' ἐνὶ σταδίῳ | now at the goal was he seen; ne'er in the midst of the course |

The starting-place and the goal-posts had precisely the same arrangement of marble slabs, grooves, and posts, as we see them at Olympia and Epidaurus. We may assume the same plan for practically all classical Greek stadia.

### 7. The Arsenal[2] of Athens

Imperial Athens, like imperial Cnossus in an earlier, and imperial England in a later age, rested confidently in the security afforded by her fleet which ruled the seas. For her warships Athens made wonderful provision in the arsenal at the easily defended harbors of Zea and Munychia. To the Athenian, the arsenal ranked with the Parthenon among the glories of his proud city (Com. Frag., 'Αδέσπ. 340 K.):

| | |
|---|---|
| δέσποιν' ἀπασῶν, πότνι' 'Αθηναίων πόλι, | mistress of the world, august city of Athens, |
| ὡς πάγκαλόν σου φαίνεται τὸ νεώριον , | how perfectly beautiful seems thy arsenal, |
| ὡς καλὸς ὁ Παρθενών, καλὸς δ' ὁ Πειραιεύς. | how beautiful the Parthenon, and how beautiful the Piraeus! |
| ἄλση δὲ τίς πω τοιάδ' ἔσχ' ἄλλη πόλις; | What other city ever had such parks? |
| καὶ τοὐρανοῦ γ', ὥς φασιν, ἐστὶν ἐν καλῷ[3] | It stands, as they say, in the beauty of heaven![3] |

It was the last of the magnificent buildings erected by Athens in the days of her independence.

Modern philistinism is prone to measure the splendor of public buildings by their cost; it may not be uninteresting to note that the arsenal, without the storerooms, cost the state not less than one thousand talents[4]—three times as much as the magnificent temple of Apollo at Delphi, built by the Alcmaeonidae. When the Spartans, at the close of the Peloponnesian War, caused all the military and naval equipment of Athens to be destroyed, the Thirty Tyrants pulled the ship-houses down and sold them as building material for three talents.[5] And when they were being rebuilt, an annual tax of ten talents was levied to provide a sinking fund for the building operation.[6] And the arsenal, with all the things

[1] We have no records of the time in which the ancient Greek athletes ran the sprints or the long distance races. They did not compete to break records but to beat the other fellow, especially the fellow from another town. But Antipater's epigram and Sophocles's line suggest that those athletes did some sprinting. Lucian adapts the same idea to the speed with which the god of wealth can travel (Tim. 20): ἅμα γοῦν ἔπεσεν ἡ ὕσπληξ, κἀγὼ ἤδη ἀνακηρύττομαι νενικηκώς, ὑπερπηδήσας τὸ στάδιον, οὐδὲ ἰδόντων ἐνίοτε τῶν θεατῶν. When wealth comes in our direction, he creeps so slowly that we may be old, old men before he gets to us; but when he gets ready to leave us, "hardly does the rope fall, and he is at once proclaimed winner in the race, speeding across the stadium so fast that the spectators can't even see him."

[2] The "Arsenal" includes both the ship-sheds (νεώρια) and the storerooms for equipment (the σκευοθήκη of Philon) (Bekker, Anecd. 282, 1: τὰ νεώρια δὲ τῶν ὅλων περιβολή).

[3] In strikingly similar vein Demosthenes gives vent to the national pride in the architectural glories of Athens (c. Androt. XXII 76, p. 617): ἀφ' ὧν κτήματ' ἀθάνατ' αὐτῷ περίεστι, τὰ μὲν τῶν ἔργων ἡ μνήμη, τὰ δὲ τῶν ἀναθημάτων τῶν ἐπ' ἐκείνοις σταθέντων τὸ κάλλος, Προπύλαια ταῦθ', ὁ Παρθενών, στοαί, νεώσοικοι......

[4] Isoc. VII (Areop.) 66.

[5] Isoc. VII (Areop.) 66; Lys. XII (c. Erat.) 99.

[6] This extended over the years 347–6 to 323–2 (C.I.A. II No. 270). The credit for the rebuilding is due in large measure to the orator Lycurgus.

that Athens held most precious, was in the keeping of Basilea, the sovereign power of Zeus[1] (Ar. Av. 1537–1541):

ΠΕ. τίς ἐστιν ἡ Βασίλεια; ΠΡ. καλλίστη κόρη,

ἥπερ ταμιεύει τὸν κεραυνὸν τοῦ Διὸς
καὶ τἄλλ' ἀπαξάπαντα, τὴν εὐβουλίαν,
τὴν εὐνομίαν, τὴν σωφροσύνην, τὰ νεώρια,
τὴν λοιδορίαν, τὸν κωλαγρέτην, τὰ τριώβολα

PI. Who is Basilea? PR. A most beautiful maiden,
who has charge of Zeus's thunderbolt
and all the rest of the things—good counsel,
good government, sanity, arsenals,
freedom of speech, pay-clerks, three-obols

In the former passage the word for "arsenal" is singular (νεώριον); in the latter it is plural (νεώρια). The poets, following usage both popular and official,[2] would make no more distinction between the singular and the plural than they do between δόμος and δόμοι; both these words mean "house," but the plural apparently divides the house into its various apartments. So also νεώριον may refer to the whole great naval plant; νεώρια may suggest the various departments—Zea, Munychia, Cantharus, and all the rest that together made up the arsenal[3] (Schol. Ar. Ach. 920):

νεώριον καλεῖται ὁ τόπος ὁ περι-
έχων τὰ πλοῖα ἡνίκ' ἂν ἑλκυσθῶσιν

"arsenal" is the name of the place containing the ships when they are docked

It is an Athenian in the Casina of Plautus that uses what was to him a very natural metaphor of hauling a ship back into her berth, meaning getting things back into proper shape (557):

ibo, intro, ut subducam navim rursus in pulvinaria

The excavations conducted at Zea and Munychia by the Greek Archaeological Society in 1885 brought to light considerable remains of the old ship-sheds—the lower courses of the sloping[4] ways in which the galleys were drawn up and drydocked and the foundations of the low walls carrying the colonnades that separated the slips each from the other and supported the gabled roof over each pair of berths; for the ancient ships needed protection against the weather.[5] In the time of Lycurgus there were three hundred and seventy-two ship-houses—one hundred and ninety-six at Zea, eighty-two at Munychia, and ninety-four at Cantharus.[6] These would ordinarily accommodate all the vessels that needed to be under shelter. The fleet comprised somewhat more than that number, though it probably never greatly exceeded four hundred war galleys. The total strength of the Athenian navy at the outbreak of the Peloponnesian War was about three hundred ships.[7] It might happen that more ships than there was room for needed to be docked at the same time. In that case the extra galleys were simply beached and protected behind some sort of temporary fortifications. Of this we have direct testimony from the drama (Crat. Πυτ., Frag. 197 K.):

οὐ δύναται πάντα ποιοῦσαι νεωσοίκων λαχεῖν

οὐδὲ κάννης

in spite of every effort, they cannot obtain berths,
not even a mat

Of the great naval docking system, about fifty berths can still be identified at Zea and Munychia harbors. "The flat beach all round the basin of Zea was enclosed by a wall of ashlar masonry, which ran round the harbor in the form of a regular polygon with somewhat obtuse angles, at a distance of about 50 to 60 feet from the water's edge. This formed the back wall of all the ship-sheds, which extended at right angles to it and parallel to each other down to the water. The average breadth of each ship-shed or berth was about 6.50

---

[1] Humanly speaking, the management of the arsenal and all the department of the navy was vested in a board of ten elected annually—one from each tribe—and known as οἱ τῶν νεωρίων ἐπιμεληταί or οἱ τῶν νεωρίων ἄρχοντες, presided over by a ταμίας εἰς τὰ νεώρια. See Boeckh, *Staatsh.* I, pp. 48 ff.; Wachsmuth, *Stadt Athen*, II, pp. 54 ff.

[2] C. I. A. II 811, Col. b, ll. 1 ff.: ἀπελάβομεν σκεύη ξύλινα ἐν νεωρίοις· ἐν νεωρίῳ παρελάβομεν κτλ. C. I. A. II 809, Col. b, ll. 48 ff.: ἀπελάβομεν σκεύη ξύλινα ἐν νεωρίοις· ἐν νεωρίοις παρελάβομεν.... ἐν νεωρίῳ παρέδομεν κτλ.

[3] Zea and Munychia are not contiguous by any means, though both of them lie at the east base of Munychia Hill. Cantharus, on the other hand, is widely separated from the other two, lying clear across not only the town but also the harbor of Piraeus.

[4] Modern ways usually have a slope of 1:12; most of those at Zea have a slope of 1:18, or 3° 10' 48".

[5] So considerable are the remains that from them Dörpfeld could reconstruct the whole system with unquestionable accuracy. See Πρακτικά for 1885 (the written report by Δραγάτσης, the drawings by Dörpfeld).

[6] C. I. A. II No. 807, col. c; No. 808, col. d; No. 811, col. c.

[7] Xen. An. VII 1, 27. So Strabo (IX 395) says four hundred; but Pliny (N. H. VII 125), with more than ordinary exaggeration, says a thousand.

THE ZEA HARBOR

metres. The sheds were separated from each other by rows of unfluted columns of Piraeic limestone, the foundations of which, bedded on the shelving rocky beach, descend in steps to the edge of the water, and are continued under the water at the same angle for some distance. These columns supported the roofs, which were probably wooden, for no remains of a stone roof have been found. Between these partition-rows of columns the rock has been hollowed out and smoothed, so that it forms an inclined plane descending gradually, like the rows of columns, to the water and continued under the surface of the water for some distance. Each of these inclined planes, cut in the rock and bounded on either side by a row of columns, was the floor of a ship-shed. In the middle of each of these floors is built a stone pier, about 10 feet wide and a yard or so high; in some places the native rock, hewn out at the sides, has been left standing in the centre so as to form a pier of similar dimensions. These piers, whether built or consisting of the native rock, slope gently into the water; and on them the ancient ships were hauled up and down. A groove for the ship's keel was probably cut down the middle of each pier. Remains of these piers may still be seen all round the harbour of Zea running out under the clear water.

"Similar constructions, including pieces of the back-wall running round the harbour and of the stone piers extending into the water, are also to be seen in the harbour of Munychia, where, however, the breadth of the ship-sheds (6.25 metres) seems to have been somewhat less than that of the ship-sheds in Zea. At Munychia a stone with a groove for the ship's keel has been found; also three stones to which ropes seem to have been fastened for the purpose of hauling up the ships to their berths. In the great harbour the ship-sheds were situated in the bay which forms the southern extremity of the harbour, to the right of the entrance; for here the stone piers on which the ships were hauled up could still be seen in the first half of the nineteenth century."[1]

Not the least magnificent part of the arsenal system was the building for the ships' stores, sails, oars, ropes, etc.—the σκευοθήκη. We have in official accounts of the building[2] very full and definite information in regard to the Skeuotheke as rebuilt in the fourth century, after the destruction of the Periclean building by the Spartans at the end of the Peloponnesian War. This was the arsenal storehouse erected by Philon of Eleusis—a huge building 400 feet long by 50 feet wide (inside measurements), divided into three aisles by two rows of fifty-three Ionic columns of Piraeus limestone, each 8.88 M. high by 0.81 M in diameter at the base. The central aisle afforded an open passage-way communicating with the store-rooms, which were constructed in two stories, in the colonnade on either side.

What the Periclean Skeuotheke, the place of which was taken by the Philonian, was like we do not know; but that such an arsenal supply-building or buildings existed we may be sure not only from a priori evidence, but we also have direct testimony in a passage in Aristophanes's Acharnians. In case of a declaration of war, the poet says (544–554):

| | |
|---|---|
| ἂν εὐθέως καθήλκετε<br>τριακοσίας ναῦς, ἢν δ' ἂν ἡ πόλις πλέα<br>θορύβου στρατιωτῶν, περὶ τριηράρχου βοῆς, | you would be forthwith launching<br>300 ships; the city would be full of<br>the tramp of soldiers' feet and cries about the<br>  trierarch; |
| μισθοῦ διδομένου, Παλλαδίων χρυσουμένων,<br>στοᾶς στεναχούσης σιτίων μετρουμένων,<br>ἀσκῶν, τροπωτήρων, κάδους ὠνουμένων, | of payment of wages, gilding Palladia,<br>of roaring colonnades and measuring out rations,<br>of wine-skins, oarlocks, buying casks, |
| . . . . . . . . . . | . . . . . . . . . . |
| τὸ νεώριον δ' αὖ κοπέων πλατουμένων,<br>τύλων ψοφούντων, θαλαμιῶν τροπουμένων.<br>αὐλῶν, κελευστῶν, τιγλάρων, συριγμάτων | and the arsenal, too, would be full of shaping oars,<br>hammering pegs, and adjusting oars;<br>of flutes, boatswains, pipes, whistles |

---

[1] The substance of Wachsmuth, *Stadt Athen*, II pp. 66 ff., as given by Frazer, *Paus.* II pp. 16–17; see the literature there cited. For the σκευοθήκη of Philon, see Frazer, *Paus.* II pp. 18–20; Dörpfeld, *die Skeuothek des Philon, Ath. Mitt.* VIII (1883), pp. 147 ff.

[2] C. I. A. II No. 270; No. 793 (357–356 B. C.); No. 795 (353–352 B. C.); No. 807 (326–325 B. C.). These deal with the earlier stages of the Skeuotheke. In April, 1882, was found an inscription (C. I. A. II No. 1054) which gives detailed specifications of the whole building program. It is fully discussed by Foucart, *Bull. de Cor. Hel.* VI pp. 540–555; Fabricius, *Hermes* XVII pp. 551–594; and by Keil, *Hermes* XIX pp. 149 ff. Cp. also Dörpfeld, *Ath. Mitt.* VIII (1883) pp. 147–164; Wachsmuth, *Stadt Athen* II pp. 80 ff. "The directions [the specifications for the building given in the inscriptions] are so full, clear, and precise that we now know Philo's arsenal from roof to foundation better than any other building of ancient Greece, though not a stone of it has been found." Frazer, *l. c.*

All these items from the ordnance department may have to do with the arsenal and its stores; the last three lines, with their oars and pegs and whistles, certainly do.

We have another reference to the arsenal in a fragment of Aeschylus (Ψυχαγ., Frag. 274 N.):

| | |
|---|---|
| καὶ σκευοθηκῶν ναυτικῶν τ' ἐρειπίων | and arsenals and naval wreckage |

For the defense of the station from the land side there must have been a strong encircling wall. We have a hint that such a defensory wall about the arsenal was a matter of course, when Euripides transfers the Athenian peribolus wall to the city of Theoclymenus in Egypt (Hel. 1530):

| | |
|---|---|
| ὡς δ' ἤλθομεν σῶν περίβολον νεωρίων | and when we came to the wall that encircles thy arsenal |

As one great entrance admits to the extensive Arsenal of modern Venice, so the colossal plant at Zea had its great propylaeum opening upon the arsenal from the market-place[1]— σκευοθήκη first and ship-houses following. No less care needed to be taken in antiquity than in modern times to defend an arsenal against acts of espionage and sabotage. We all remember the daring but unsuccessful attempt of Cnemus and Brasidas, in the winter of 430–429 B. C., to burn the Athenian arsenal.[2] The raid of the Spartan admirals rudely awakened Athens from her false dream of security and made her absolutely panicky in regard to her arsenal. A few years later, at the presentation of the Acharnians, Aristophanes can still make merry over the wild fears of the people on that score (918–922):

| | |
|---|---|
| (θρυαλλίδα) | a Boeotian might ram |
| ἐνθεὶς ἂν ἐς τίφην ἀνὴρ Βοιώτιος | into the funnel of a reed a lighted |
| ἄψας ἂν ἐσπέμψειεν ἐς τὸ νεώριον | wick and shoot it into the ar- |
| δι' ὑδρορρόας | senal through a water main |

The ridiculous supposition, intended by the poet to be the height of nonsense, that an enemy could insert fire into a reed,[3] like Prometheus, and then start it on a voyage through the city water mains to the arsenal at the Piraeus, and so destroy the key to Athens' safety, does not really concern us here. What is of present interest is the fact that the arsenal contained so much inflammable material,[4] that it could be so carefully safeguarded, and that it was supplied with good water through the city waterworks.[5]

[1] C. I. A. II 1054, l. 4: ἀπὸ τοῦ προπυλαίου τοῦ ἐξ ἀγορᾶς.

[2] Thuc. II 93.

[3] The Scholiast on the passage, failing to get the full absurdity of the proposition, interprets τίφην as ζῶον κανθαρωδές ("a beetle-like creature"), in order to find a play upon the name of the harbor Cantharus and so have the fire thrust into the Cantharus to destroy the arsenal.

[4] Alciphron I 32; Pollux IX 156; cp. Wachsmuth, *Stadt Athen*, II p. 60, footnote 1.

[5] ὑδρορρόα in this passage apparently calls for the interpretation that I have given. In Ar. Ach. 1186 τοιαῦτα λέξας εἰς ὑδρορρόαν πεσὼν it is probably an open "sewer" into which Lamachus falls.

THE THEATRE OF EPIDAURUS

# IX. STAGE ARCHITECTURE

In all of the foregoing discussion of architecture described or suggested by the dramatic poets, our effort has been to get a vision of the actual, historical building to which reference is made. The Athenian in the audience in the theatre at the presentation of a tragedy or comedy had his thoughts turned by the poet's words to the famous temples, which he had seen with his own eyes or the wonders of which he had heard by others told; and his mental picture of them, when the scene of action was laid in their presence, was assisted by the theatrical devices and the stage properties, introduced for that purpose—the scene, the proscenium, the periacti, the parascenia, etc.—"the whole visible apparatus of the theatre."[1]

Thus, in the case of the temple of Apollo at Delphi, when Ion appears and pronounces the words (Eur. Ion 137–140):

| | |
|---|---|
| τὸν βόσκοντα γὰρ εὐλογῶ, | for I extol him that feedeth me |
| τὸ δ' ὠφέλιμον ἐμοὶ πατέρος | and the name of "father" I give |
| ὄνομα λέγω, | to the sustaining hand of |
| Φοίβου τοῦ κατὰ ναὸν | Phoebus, whose temple this is |

there, forming the centre of the proscenium, is a Doric temple to which Ion directs attention; the spectator sees a small Doric façade, with columns and door;[2] with gilded cornices;[3] with a pediment filled with the likeness of the famous groups;[4] with roof[5] crowned with its acroteria.[6] When Hermes in the prolog says (Ion 38–39):

| | |
|---|---|
| τὸν παῖδα κρηπίδων ἔπι | upon this temple's steps |
| τίθημι ναοῦ τοῦδ' | the babe I lay |

a suggestion of the reality is there before him and before the assembled Athenians in the theatre. And when the chorus of Creusa's handmaids enters and the one section cries (Ion 190–192):

| | |
|---|---|
| ἰδοὺ τάνδ', ἄθρησον, | look here! See; the son of |
| Λερναῖον ὕδραν ἐναίρει | Zeus is slaying the Lernaean |
| .......... ὁ Διὸς παῖς | hydra |

and another section answers (*ibid.* 193–195):

| | |
|---|---|
| ἀθρῶ. καὶ πέλας ἄλλος αὐ- | I see. And by him is another |
| τοῦ πανὸν πυρίφλεκτον αἴ- | lifting a blazing torch of |
| ρει τις | fire |

the audience follows the description of what was reproduced after the reality at Delphi upon the entablature of the proscenium before their eyes. And so on through all the sculptures described by the chorus, at least a suggestion of the Delphic reality was before chorus and audience. Not less clearly does this fact come out, though no details are given, in the fragment of Euripides's Hypsipyle (764 N.):

| | |
|---|---|
| ἰδοὺ πρὸς αἰθέρ' ἐξαμίλλησαι κόρας | look! Turn thine eyes toward heaven and |
| γραπτούς <κ' ἐν αἰετῖ> οἷσι πρόσβλεψον τύπους | see the painted figures in the gables |

The unaided imagination of the Greek might have sufficed, but the evidence is conclusive that imagination was assisted by realities.

The original "stage-building," the "scene" of the fifth and early fourth century, was a "booth" σκηνή constructed of wood and canvas; its original purpose was to provide a place in which the performers could dress for their parts and await the cue for their entrances. For this purpose the "booth" could have been small. As the theatre developed, the booth grew in importance and significance and became also a part of the scene and carried the scenery.

[1] Flickinger, *The Greek Theater and its Drama*, p. XII.
[2] See pp. 50–54; 58.
[3] See pp. 59–60; Ion 172–173; 156–157.
[4] See pp. 52–58.
[5] See p. 51; Ion 89–90.
[6] See pp. 51–52.

We should hardly expect the word for this booth or scene to occur in the drama. But the comic poets, as we shall find, do not hesitate to allude to the machinery of their art with most unblushing frankness. And so once Aristophanes does mention "the scenes" in our sense of "the stage" and its appurtenances (Pax 729–731):

| | |
|---|---|
| τάδε τὰ σκεύη παραδόντες<br>τοῖς ἀκολούθοις δῶμεν σῴζειν, ὡς εἰώθασι μά-<br>λιστα<br>περὶ τὰς σκηνὰς πλεῖστοι κλέπται κυπτάζειν<br>καὶ κακοποιεῖν | let us turn over these traps to the<br>attendants and give them charge of them, for<br>there are a lot of thieves<br>usually hanging about the scenes to do some<br>mischief |

In Sophocles's Ajax and Euripides's Hecuba the scene before the eyes of the spectators was made up of real tents—such booths as the Greek heroes had for their dwellings during the siege of Troy. It is, therefore, not primarily in any technical sense that the word is used in those plays (Soph. Aj. 3–4):

| | |
|---|---|
| ἐπὶ σκηναῖς σε ναυτικαῖς ὁρῶ<br>Αἴαντος | by the tents of Ajax's fleet<br>I see thee |

(*ibid.* 753–754):

| | |
|---|---|
| εἶρξαι......<br>Αἴανθ' ὑπὸ σκηναῖσι | to keep . . .<br>Ajax within the tents |

(*ibid.* 795–796):

| | |
|---|---|
| ἐκεῖνον εἴργειν......<br>σκηνῆς ὕπαυλον | to keep him . . .<br>within the shelter of the tent |

(Eur. Hec. 53–54):

| | |
|---|---|
| περᾷ γὰρ ἥδ' ὑπὸ σκηνῆς πόδα<br>Ἀγαμέμνονος | for she is setting forth her foot<br>from Agamemnon's tent |

(*ibid.* 733):

| | |
|---|---|
| τίν' ἄνδρα τόνδ' ἐπὶ σκηναῖς ὁρῶ | who is the man I see here at the tents |

(Soph. Aj. 579–580):

| | |
|---|---|
| μηδ' ἐπισκήνους γόους<br>δάκρυε | shed no tears nor make lament<br>here at the tents |

The "scene" in the Peace of Aristophanes is the house of Trygaeus.[1] In the earlier periods of the drama, there were, of course, when two or three houses played their parts in the tragedy or comedy, two or three booths erected in front of the spectators beyond the orchestra. In the Hecuba there are at least two tents—that of Agamemnon and that of Hecuba and the Trojan women. These two or three booths gradually united, architecturally, and thus the playhouse was easily evolved—a σκηνή in the technical sense, "a stage building."

The next step in the evolution of the stage is easy, and the booth, the "scene," becomes the background of the action, the decorative setting of the play. At this stage of theatrical development the use of a painted scene was easily and naturally introduced, and we have such extended scenes as those required in the Persians and Suppliants of Aeschylus or the Oedipus at Colonus of Sophocles. And so in the Roman Comedy *scaena* is the setting of the play represented by the decorative background of the stage[2] (Pl. Cap. 60):

foris illic extra scaenam fient proelia
(Pl. Ps. 2): fabula in scaenam venit
(*ibid.* 568): qui in scaenam provenit
(Poen. 20): neu sessum ducat, dum histrio in scaena siet

[1] Cf. Isidorus XVIII 43: dicta autem scaena Graeca appellatione eo, quod in speciem domus erat instructa. For a full discussion of ἡ σκηνή and the ancient "stage" see Dörpfeld-Reisch, *d. griech. Theater*, pp. 283–365; Dörpfeld, *die griech. Bühne*, Ath. Mitt. XXVIII (1903); Flickinger, *The Greek Theater and its Drama*, passim (Index, s. v. σκηνή).

[2] Out of this particular stage in the development of the meaning of the words, σκηνή and *scaena* came to be used for "landscape painting," just as we use "scene" in English also.

Before this background on the slightly elevated platform (*pulpitum*) of no great depth the actors performed their parts. Plautus alludes to the diminished needs of his kind of drama (Truc. 1):

> perparvam partem postulat Plautus loci

And though the Roman stage seems so very different from the Greek orchestra and proscenium background, there is nevertheless but little difference in reality: the half of the orchestra next to the audience has been lowered about three feet; the other half is still the place for the actors, for there is no longer any chorus; and there before the proscenium colonnade the scene takes place, and the columns belong to the houses as of old (Pl. As. 425):

> iussin columnis deiici operas araneorum?

As the idea of a decorative background became more and more generally accepted, the playhouse became more and more unified and conventional and extended approximately the length of the diameter of the orchestra across the space beyond the dancing–floor. As a decorative "front of the scene" or a decorative background "in front of the scene" it was, in either conception, a *proscenium*.

In the earlier period of the drama the proscenium was constructed, like the booths of the primitive days, of wood and canvas, the form and size varying according to the exigencies of each performance. The commonest form was the colonnade, with columns of wood and intercolumniations of canvas painted to suit the scene.[1] The next stage of development is the proscenium colonnade, with columns of stone and painted panels in the intercolumniations not used for doors or entrances. The invention of the proscenium, as well as of the painted panels and the exostra, is ascribed to Sophocles or Aeschylus.[2]

However ancient the proscenium as a part of the theatre, the word προσκήνιον does not occur in any Greek dramatic poet. It does not occur in Greek at all until comparatively late. But it is used by Plautus occasionally, and usually in the Greek sense of "the background of the action" (Truc. 10–11):

> Athenis tracto ita ut hoc est proscaenium,
> tantisper dum transigimus hanc comoediam

(Poen. 57):

> locus argumento suos sibist proscaenium

(*ibid*. 17–18):

> scortum exoletum ne quod in proscaenio
> sedeat. . . . .

Once *proscaenium* seems to be used by synecdoche for the whole theatre or the stage alone (Amph. 91–92):

> etiam, histriones anno cum in proscaenio hic
> Iovem invocarunt, venit, auxilio is fuit

Through the doorways in this proscenium, the decorative background of the play, actors might enter the scene of action from the scene-building, the outgrowth of the one-time booth or booths of the primitive days of the drama. Such entrances could be used only by those characters of the play whose residence or place of occupation was represented in the buildings occupying the proscenium or who had in the course of the play entered one of those buildings from the orchestra. Characters entering the scene from elsewhere would of course come in through one or the other of the parodoi.

Abutting the proscenium at either end (or the scene, where a proscenium is wanting), and projecting out into the parodoi where these open upon the orchestra, we find in many of the still existing Greek theatres the parascenia. This word also is not to be found in the Greek drama; it makes its first appearance in Demosthenes;[3] but the "rooms beside the scenes" were a familiar architectural element in theatre construction long before Demosthenes was born. It may be that they owe their origin to the primitive booths that were

[1] Proscenium and πίνακες "panels" are vouched for in the inscription upon the architrave of the first or second century (B. C.) theatre at the Amphiaraeum near Oropus. At least four such panels, with the proscenium, we find vouched for in an inscription containing an official account of work on the theatre of Delos in the year 282 B. C.: Ἡρακλείδῃ εἰς τὸ προσκήνιον γράψαντι πίνακες δύο . . . . . . Ἀντιδότῳ τοῦ προσκηνίου γράψαντι πίνακες δύο. See *B. C. H.* XVIII p. 162. One form of flattery of Demetrius Poliorcetes found expression in the exhibition of his portrait on the proscenium at Athens (Athen. XII 536 a): γενομένων δὲ τῶν Δημητρίων Ἀθήνησιν ἐγράφετο ἐπὶ τοῦ προσκηνίου ἐπὶ τῆς Οἰκουμένης ὀχούμενος.

[2] Cramer, *Anecd. Paris.* I 19, quoted by Reisch, *op. cit.* p. 294.

[3] in Mid. 17.

originally erected off to one side of the scene, comparatively out of sight, and later, when the proscenium became a unit, moved up and made to serve as an artistic frame finishing off the proscenium at either end. They then further served as an extension of the proscenium, with their own entrances and their own scenic decoration. Projecting, as they do, beyond the line of the proscenium, they might often serve also to keep out of sight, until the proper psychological moment arrived, a person of the drama approaching from the outside through one of the parodoi, or to conceal a person who must speedily disappear from the sight of the rest of the players and of the audience and the direction of whose departure would not permit him to disappear behind the scenes.

When the proscenium is elevated with a second story, the parascenia also must have a second story.

When the proscenium has a complete second story, it has, of course, a roof above that. Upon this roof a god may appear; with that, we have, to all intents and purposes, a third story to our stage buildings. Such a third story is indispensable in such scenes as that in which Orestes and Pylades and Hermione are already upon the roof of the palace at Mycenae, and Apollo, with Helen, appears above their heads.[1] An upper story was certainly provided in the stone theatre of Delos in the early third century[2] and can safely be assumed for others.[3]

Another feature of the theatre building, essential for any classical performance but unmentioned in any piece of ancient drama, is the parodos. But its unfailing presence in every ancient theatre and its mention in various Greek authors from Aristotle to Plutarch and Athenaeus leave no room for dispute as to the nature and function of the parodoi.[4] Through them the chorus usually and the other actors often make their entrance to the scene of action—the orchestra and the space between the orchestra and the proscenium.

Far more important than the stage-building in the historical development of the drama and in the presentation of a tragedy or comedy in classical times is the orchestra. The movements of the primitive dithyrambic choruses demanded a place for their songs and dances—an orchestra. About the orchestra the spectators gathered. As the festival became more elaborate and more splendid and the crowds became greater, the dance-floor had to be selected in a spot where there was a level space at the base of a gently rising slope on which the crowds could take their places and all see and hear what was going on in the orchestra. When classical drama had so far developed that a permanent theatre was required, the old dancing-floor took on its fixed form in the circular space between the rising tiers of seats for the spectators and the scene-building. The orchestra is the almost exclusive scene of action in the classical Greek drama. But in spite of its supreme importance in the dramatic art of classical times, not once does the word occur in the extant drama.

An essential feature of the orchestra, apparently, was the thymele (derived from θύειν "to sacrifice"), "the place of sacrifice," "the altar." There might be various altars connected with the temples or houses represented in the proscenium of any given play; but the thymele was the permanent altar in the centre of the orchestra of the permanent theatre, a survival of the days of the dithyrambic chorus when the orchestra was the whole theatre and the altar in its centre was the place of sacrifice to the god of the festival; and here sacrifice continued always to be paid to him at the opening of the dramatic contests. Thymele is occasionally used even by the dramatic poets in the original sense of "the place of sacrifice" (Pratinas, in a Hyporcheme, Frag. 1 B, Ath. XIV 617 C, 1–2):

| | |
|---|---|
| τίς ὁ θόρυβος ὅδε; τί τάδε τὰ χορεύματα; | what means this confusion? What mean these |
| τίς ὕβρις ἔμολεν ἐπὶ | choral dances? What disrespect |
| Διονυσιάδα πολυπάταγα θυμέλαν; | has come to the much trodden place of sacrifice of Dionysus? |

And Alciphron puts into Menander's mouth (II 3, p. 240 Bergler):

---

[1] Eur. Or. 1567–1636.

[2] These two-storied parascenia are fully vouched for in the inscription containing the official accounts of the repairs upon the Delian theatre in 274 B. C.; it speaks not only of αἱ ἐπάνω σκηναί but also of τὰ παρασκήνια τὰ ἐπάνω καὶ τὰ ὑποκάτω. The same inscription mentions also the painted panels in the parascenia: πίνακες τῶν παρασκηνίων.

[3] Gram. de Com. p. XX, 28 Dübner (quoted by Reisch, op. cit. p. 271): ἐν ἐαρινῷ καιρῷ πολυτελέσι δαπάναις κατεσκευάζετο ἡ σκηνὴ τριωρόφοις οἰκοδομήμασι, πεποικιλμένη παραπετάσμασι καὶ ὀθόναις λευκαῖς καὶ μελαίναις...... εἰς τύπον θαλάσσης ταρτάρου ᾅδου.... γῆς οὐρανοῦ ἀνακτόρων καὶ πάντων ἁπλῶς.

[4] See Dörpfeld-Reisch, d. griech. Theater, pp. 280–281.

δραματουργεῖν τι καινὸν ταῖς ἐτησίαις θυμέλαις | to bring out some new play at the annual places of sacrifice

On this altar's steps stood the flute-player who accompanied the lyrical parts of the plays; on its steps also an actor might take his place when it was desirable for him to speak his part from a slight elevation in the midst of the chorus in the orchestra. The broad, spacious, lower step of the altar was called "the Bema," just as "the step" on which the orator in the assembly stood was called "the Bema." This Bema was the nearest approach we have to a raised stage in the early Greek theatre, and it was in fact a necessity in the days when there was no raising of the seats about the dancing-floor. To provide sufficient space for more elaborate action, the altar step might receive a considerable extension; it was then called the "table" (τράπεζα or ἐλεός).[1] A raised platform in the middle of the orchestra was a necessity if the actors in the primitive drama was to be seen and heard by more than a few in a great crowd of spectators standing or sitting on the comparatively level ground about the chorus. Aristophanes introduces the "table" literally and employs it for an elevation from which the Sausage-seller may see the whole Athenian empire. The Sausage-seller approaches, unseen by the spectators, in the pursuit of his business. While still far out in the parodos, he is hailed by Demus to enter and become the savior of the State (Ar. Eq. 149):

ἀνάβαινε σωτὴρ τῇ πόλει καὶ νῷν φανείς | come up here, for you have arisen to be the savior of the State and us

The Sausage-seller answers from away down the parodos (150):

τί ἔστι; τί με καλεῖτε | what's up? What are you calling me for?

He ascends the sloping parodos to the scene, with his butcher's table and sausage-stuff; but Nicias and Demus are determined to make a statesman of him (Ar. Eq. 152; 155):

ἴθι δὴ κάθελ' αὐτοῦ τοὐλεόν | come now, make him put down his table
. . . . . . . .
ἄγε δὴ σὺ κατάθου πρῶτα τὰ σκεύη χαμαί | come, you, come, first put your traps down

He is at last persuaded to put down his sausage-seller's table and all that went with it; he has pointed out to him the power he is to have in local government; but that is not all (Ar. Eq. 169–170):

ἀλλ' ἐπανάβηθι κἀπὶ τοὐλεὸν τοδὶ | but get up on this table here
καὶ κάτιδε τὰς νήσους ἁπάσας ἐν κύκλῳ | and take a view of all the islands round about

Therewith he mounts the table and sees all the empire of Athens and the glories thereof— a very natural reversion to the old days when the ἐλεός was a real part of the theatrical machinery.

The adjective θυμελικός derived from θυμέλη is used for the most part of musical performances that are not dramatic (Isid. Origg. XVIII 47): thymelici autem erant musici scenici, qui in organis et lyris et citharis praecinebant et dicti thymelici, quod olim in orchestra stantes cantabant supra pulpitum, quod thymele vocabatur. And so with the Greek grammarians, thymelic contests are contrasted with dramatic contests (Inc. Inc. Frag. 57 K.):[2]

θυμελικὰν ἴθι μάκαρ φιλοφρόνως εἰς ἔριν | come, blest, with heart full of devotion, to the thymelic contest

but in late Greek writers thymele comes to be identical with the stage.[3]

With this hasty review of the essential parts of the Greek theatre architecturally, let us return to the study of the theatre building in the light of the ancient dramas that have come down to us.

[1] Pollux IV 123: ὀρχήστρα...... ἐν ᾗ καὶ ἡ θυμέλη, εἴτε βῆμά τι οὖσα, εἴτε βωμός.... ἐλεὸς δὲ ἦν τράπεζα ἀρχαία, ἐφ' ἧν πρὸ Θέσπιδος εἴς τις ἀναβὰς τοῖς χορευταῖς ἀπεκρίνατο. Et. Mag. θυμέλη· ἡ τοῦ θεάτρου μέχρι νῦν ἀπὸ τῆς τραπέζης ὠνόμασται παρὰ τὸ ἐπ' αὐτῆς τὰ θύη μερίζεσθαι, τουτέστι τὰ θυόμενα ἱερεῖα. τράπεζα δ' ἦν, ἐφ' ἧς ἑστῶτες ἐν τοῖς ἀγροῖς ᾖδον, μήπω τάξιν λαβούσης τραγῳδίας.

[2] Meineke claims this fragment for some unknown comic poet, possibly Phrynicus; Kock also vindicates the comic claim; but Bergk has included it among his unidentified lyric bards (Frag. Adesp. 107).

[3] Cp. Dörpfeld-Reisch, *d. griech. Theater*, pp. 279–280.

The proscenium, as we have seen, may be made to represent any sort of building required by the play. It may be and often is a palace or a temple. In the proscenium the doors of the building are represented realistically; they open and shut; they sometimes are, in the fiction, bolted and barred;[1] even the keys are upon occasion produced.[2] And when the central door of the proscenium at the production of the Ion swings open, there in the dim background beyond the door stands a likeness of the primitive wooden statue in the Delphic shrine; so, too, in the Iphigenia among the Tauri, the image, which plays so important a rôle is necessarily seen within the temple, when the doors are opened, as well as in the arms of Iphigenia when she carries the statue out from the temple to the sea.

Sometimes the proscenium is made to represent a peripteral temple, as in the case of the temple of Apollo at Delphi; sometimes it is a *templum in antis*, as in the case of the Tauric Artemisium.[3] In one play we have above the columns and the architrave a triglyphon with sculptured or painted metopes; in the presentation of the Iphigenia among the Tauri[4] and the Orestes[5] of Euripides there are no metope blocks at all but openings between the triglyphs (μετόπαι, in the literal sense) through which actors under stress of need may make surreptitiously their exit or their entrance: Orestes and Pylades propose to steal their way into the Artemisium by climbing up to the frieze and letting themselves down inside the temple; the Phrygian slave scrambles over the architrave, through the metope opening, and drops to the scene below.

But the Tauric Iphigenia and the Orestes are not the only plays in which Euripides employs the device of having an actor leave the scene in some such extraordinary manner. In the Suppliants we have an example of exceptional realism in Euripides's stage properties: the centre of the scene represents the temple of Demeter at Eleusis. True to nature as we still see it at Eleusis, it is in Euripides's scene overhung by the rocks of the cliff out of which the temple structure is, in part, hewn. Beyond the temple the pyres of the dead heroes of the ill-fated expedition against Thebes are erected. The chorus of mournful widows look out through the parodos and break into hopeless weeping for their dead. But Evadne, sister of the slain Eteoclus and widow of the lightning-blasted Capaneus, by some means mounts to the roof of the temple and to the crag of rock above it and leaps off, eluding the possibility of hindrance or rescue at the hands of her father or her friends, down upon the blazing pyre of Capaneus. Her husband's pyre must have been in the same place close by the common pyre of the other heroes; and the ashes of all of them are later borne upon the scene in urns in the hands of their sons. It is altogether erroneous to suppose, as has generally been done, that the blazing pyre of Capaneus was actually present upon the scene in the theatre and that Evadne literally threw herself from the rock towering above the temple roof into the flames, to be consumed with her husband in the fire. Such action would have been preposterous to the Greek audience and altogether in violation of the laws of Greek tragedy, if not physically impossible. We must think of the pyre of Capaneus outside—in imaginary view of the chorus gazing down the parodos—and his urn must accompany those of his fellow-chieftains and be borne in at the end by his son. The entire passage in question is contained in lines 980–1182. The most important verses for our consideration are 980–989:

καὶ μὴν θαλάμας τάσδ' ἐσορῶ δὴ
Καπανέως ἤδη τύμβον θ' ἱερὸν
μελάθρων τ' ἐκτὸς
Θησέως ἀναθήματα νεκροῖς
κλεινὴν τ' ἄλοχον τοῦ καταφθιμένου
τοῦδε κεραυνῷ πέλας Εὐάδνην

τίποτ' αἰθερίαν ἔστηκε πέτραν,

ἢ τῶνδε δόμων ὑπερακρίζει,
τήνδ' ἐμβαίνουσα κέλευθον;

Io! now I look upon yon cells
and Capaneus's holy tomb and,
without the halls,
Theseus's offerings to the dead,
and Evadne, the famèd spouse of yonder man
who lies blasted by the thunderbolt.

What meaneth the stand she hath taken upon
   the towering rock
that overhangs this building, and why
hath she trodden this path?

[1] See above, pp. 107–108.
[2] See above, p. 107.
[3] See above, pp. 106; 113.
[4] See above, pp. 110; 114.
[5] See above, p. 113.

With these words the chorus has caught sight of the pyres, Evadne has managed to reach the temple roof and climb upon the towering cliff in the direction of the pyre of Capaneus, and she now begins her dying song—an ode expressing the oneness of her lot with his, in death as in life. As I understand it, Evadne has perched herself upon the towering rock above the parascenium, and the pyre of Capaneus is conceived as beyond the bounds of the doorway of the parodos (1009–1011) (the chorus to Evadne):

| | |
|---|---|
| καὶ μὴν ὁρᾷς τήνδ' ἧς ἐφέστηκας πέλας | lo! thou seest yonder the pyre above which thou hast |
| πυράν.... ἔνθ' ἔνεστι σὸς πόσις...... | taken thy stand hard by, and on which rests thy husband .... |

And Evadne continues her monody (1012–1024):

| | |
|---|---|
| ὁρῶ δὴ τελευτάν, | even here where I have taken my stand |
| ἵν' ἔστηκα· τύχα δέ μοι | I see the end; fortune favors |
| ξυνάπτει ποδός· ἀλλὰ τᾶς | my course; but for my good name's |
| εὐκλείας χάριν ἔνθεν ὁρ- | sake I will throw myself |
| μάσω τᾶσδ' ἀπὸ πέτρας | hence from this rock, |
| πηδήσασα πυρὸς ἔσω | leaping into the fire .... |
| . . . . . . . . | . . . . . . . . |
| χρῶτα χρωτὶ πέλας θεμένα | And side by side with thee |
| Περσεφονείας ἥξω θαλάμους, | will I enter Persephone's chambers, |
| σὲ τὸν θανόντ' οὔποτ' ἐμᾷ | and never shall my soul forsake thee |
| προδοῦσα ψυχᾷ κατὰ γᾶς | beneath the earth, now thou art dead |

Hereupon enters Evadne's father, Iphis. He fails to see his daughter standing high up upon the towering rock. She calls his attention to her lofty position (1045–1047):

| | |
|---|---|
| ἥδ' ἐγὼ πέτρας ἔπι | here, father, upon the cliff, aloft, in my woe, I am lightly perched, like a bird, |
| ὄρνις τις ὡσεὶ Καπανέως ὑπὲρ πυρᾶς | above the pyre of Capaneus |
| δύστηνον αἰώρημα κουφίζω, πάτερ | |

And then, in an extended stichomythy, she reveals to him her fateful purpose (1065–1071):

| | |
|---|---|
| E. ᾄσσω θανόντος Καπανέως τήνδ' εἰς πυράν | E. I plunge to yon pyre of my dead Capaneus |
| I. ἀλλ' οὐδέ τοί σοι πείσομαι δρώσῃ τάδε. | I. But I will not suffer thee to do it. |
| E. ὅμοιον· οὐ γὰρ μὴ κίχῃς μ' ἑλὼν χερί, | E. Suffer or not, 'tis all one; for thou canst not reach me with thy hand; |
| καὶ δὴ παρεῖται σῶμα, σοὶ μὲν οὐ φίλον, | lo! my body takes its plunge—no joy to thee |
| ἡμῖν δὲ καὶ τῷ συμπυρουμένῳ πόσει | but to me and to him with me consumed |

With that Evadne hurls herself off the rocks into the fire; that is, she drops down behind the upper parascenium wall[1] that framed in the theologeum and is gone; she has disappeared from the view of the spectators; and the chorus and Iphis look toward the blazing pyre beyond, into which she has apparently cast herself, and pour forth their sad laments, in the course of which enters the procession, in which are the "After-born" bearing the urns with the ashes of the dead heroes.

Thus, too, Medea with her dragon-drawn chariot appears at once to view upon the palace roof of Creon (Eur. Med. 1317).[2] The great door in the back wall of the upper story of the scene-building has opened, or the curtain before the opening has been drawn; unseen she has ascended with her car by means of some sort of inclined plane, similar to the one by which Evadne in the Suppliants makes her spectacular exit;[3] and there upon the roof of the proscenium she suddenly appears before the astonished eyes of Jason. So also Athena makes her spectacular entrance in the Ion (1549), suddenly appearing in her chariot above the

[1] Such an arrangement of a parapet or balustrade above the parascenium, or even of upper parascenia, is fully vouched for in an inscription concerning the Delian Theatre in 274 B. C. See *B. C. H.* 1894, p. 161. Moreover, the proscenium colonnade of the theatre of Priene as actually existing to-day is finished off above with such a balustrade or parapet.

[2] So the Scholiast a. l.: ἄνω ἐπὶ ὕψους ἑστῶσα ταῦτα λέγει, and on 1320: ἐπὶ ὕψους γὰρ παραφαίνεται ἡ Μήδεια, ὀχουμένη δρακοντίνοις ἅρμασι καὶ βαστάζουσα τοὺς παῖδας. Cf. Hypoth.: ἐφ' ἅρματος δρακόντων πτερωτῶν, ὃ παρ' Ἡλίου ἔλαβεν, ἔποχος γενομένη ἀποδιδράσκει εἰς Ἀθήνας.

[3] We have remains of such ramps or inclined planes leading up to the roof of the proscenium at the theatre of Epidaurus and of Sicyon.

heads of Creusa and her son; and so enter miraculously, above the heads of the other dramatis personae, Lyssa and Iris in the Hercules Furens. In the theatre of Eretria the excavators from our American School found in the second story of the stage-building two marble thresholds, with cuttings upon their upper surface made most obviously to carry the wheels of a chariot. From these two existing thresholds with chariot tracks we may assume a similar arrangement for all Greek theatres; for the sudden apparition of a divinity with horses and chariot is, relatively speaking, not uncommon.

As Orestes and Pylades propose to climb up with a ladder to make their way through the metopes into the temple in Tauria, so Agave, in the Bacchae of Euripides (1212–1215) orders an attendant to get a ladder and climb up and nail "this lion's head" to the triglyph blocks.[1]

As the Tauric temple with its triglyph frieze was represented in the theatre, so also the palace of Pentheus was represented upon the proscenium; the columns were there with the architrave resting upon them (Eur. Bac. 591–592):

| | |
|---|---|
| ἴδετε λάϊνα κίοσιν ἔμβολα | see yonder the marble beams upon the |
| διάδρομα τάδε | pillars starting asunder |

The columns were there, as the deictic τάδε "yonder" proves; and with ἴδετε "see" the chorus calls the attention of the audience, as well as of its own members, to their bodily presence. The scenery doubtless shows no starting of the blocks nor the crashing of the palace in ruins either here or in the Hercules Furens 905. That is left to the imagination of the spectators.

Above the triglyphon we have seen cornices and flat roofs, on the palaces; on the temples (Delphi and Tauria), gilded cornices, sculptured gables and acroteria, and sloping roofs. All these are easily adapted to representation upon the proscenium of the Greek theatre as it has been reconstructed for us by Professor Dörpfeld.

Monuments to the dead may also find adequate representation upon the proscenium. Beside the ancient palace on the Cadmea of Thebes stood the monument of Semele. With the columns across the front of the proscenium and the openings between, such realistic representations were entirely feasible. And so, when Dionysus enters at the opening of the Bacchae of Euripides and says (6–8)

| | |
|---|---|
| ὁρῶ δὲ μητρὸς μνῆμα τῆς κεραυνίας | I see my thunder-blasted mother's tomb |
| τόδ' ἐγγὺς οἴκων καὶ δόμων ἐρείπια | here near the palace and the ruins of her home |
| τυφόμενα Δίου πυρὸς ἔτι ζῶσαν φλόγα | smouldering with the still living flame of Zeus |

there was the monument, with pillars and funereal decoration, and miraculous smoke was still rising from the ancient ruins.[2]

Whatever the scene of the action of the play—whether temple or palace or cottage or tented camp—the constant[3] use of the demonstrative ὅδε "here," "yonder," implies a gesture toward the structure represented in the proscenium with its pillars and doors, and, upon painted panels (πίνακες) between the pillars, sculptures, and so forth. Plutarch speaks of paintings and statues as perfectly familiar features of the proscenium of the theatre of his own and of far more ancient days.[4] We have the panels (πίνακες) vouched for also in inscriptions of Delos and of Oropus dealing with the construction or repair of the scene-building and the proscenium of those theatres.[5] There is no escaping, even if we would, the constant use of painted scenes in the classical Greek theatre.

One such painted πίναξ "panel" seems clearly to be before the spectators at the opening of the Bacchae of Euripides (5–12):

| | |
|---|---|
| πάρειμι Δίρκης νάματ' Ἰσμηνοῦ θ' ὕδωρ | I am come to Dirce's streams and Ismenus's waters. |
| ὁρῶ δὲ μητρὸς μνῆμα τῆς κεραυνίας | I see my thunder-blasted mother's tomb here |
| τόδ' ἐγγὺς οἴκων καὶ δόμων ἐρείπια | near the palace and the ruins of her home |
| τυφόμενα Δίου πυρὸς ἔτι ζῶσαν φλόγα, | smouldering with the still living flame of Zeus— |
| ἀθάνατον Ἥρας μητέρ' εἰς ἐμὴν ὕβριν. | Hera's undying outrage upon my mother. |

[1] See above pp. 115 f.
[2] See above pp. 244–245.
[3] Cf. Eur. Andr. 24; 35; 44; 115; 380; Ion 510.
[4] Lyc. 6.
[5] See footnote 1, p. 303; see also Haigh, *Attic Theatre*,[3] pp. 379 ff.; Flickinger, *The Gk. Theater and its Drama*, pp. 101, 109.

αἰνῶ δὲ Κάδμον, ἄβατον ὅς πέδον τόδε
τίθησι, θυγατρὸς σηκόν· ἀμπέλου δέ νιν

πέριξ ἐγὼ ’χάλυψα βοτρυώδει χλόη

| | Cadmus I approve who set apart this inviolable spot, his daughter's consecrated ground. With the vine's clustering green have I covered it 'round |

The scene of the play was thus identified for the people gathering in the theatre, even before the entrance of Dionysus and the spoken words of his prolog. One panel of the proscenium may well have had a picture of the Theban Cadmea with the Ismenium and the Ismenus valley painted upon it; another may well have had the Cadmea with the Dircaean streams below its western cliffs; a third would have had a picture of Semele's tomb in its inviolable enclosure and the palace smouldering in its ruins, with flickering flames and smoke still rising to tell the tale of Zeus's terrible visitation.

The use of the intercolumniations of the proscenium, after the addition of this decorative background in front of the scene-building, is easily comprehended. The proscenium took the place of the booths that had represented temple or palace in the temporary structures of the "scene" in the days of the great poets themselves. The central opening was regularly the principal entrance for those actors who lived or had their being in the building behind it; it was the door of the palace at Mycenae in the Agamemnon of Aeschylus or in the Electra of Sophocles; it was the door of the temple of Apollo at Delphi in the Eumenides of Aeschylus or in the Ion of Euripides; it was the entrance to the cave in the Cyclops of Euripides; it was the front door of Lysistrate's house in the comedy of Aristophanes. In many plays there was no other entrance save the central one. In others there were three. For example, in the Oedipus Rex, we probably have the palace of the king in the middle, and that of Creon on the one side, while the third door may have formed the entrance to the women's apartments of the royal palace or to the residence of Tiresias. In Terence's Phormio we certainly have three—the houses of Demipho, Chremes, and Dorio. Three also are required in Aristophanes's Ecclesiazusae—the house of Praxagora and Blepyrus, that of Chremes, and that of the citizen who calls out and lines up his chattels for delivery to the State for the common good. So in the Lysistrate the central space was occupied by the gateway into the Acropolis; the houses of Lysistrate and Calonice stood on either side. In the Autolycus of Eupolis we have three entrances, three dwellings, expressly pointed out to us (Frag. 42 K.):

οἰκοῦσι δ’ ἐνθάδ’ ἐν τρισὶ καλιδίοις,
οἴκημ’ ἔχων ἔκαστος

| | and they live here in three cabins having each his own residence |

Two houses suffice for the Clouds of Aristophanes, that of Socrates and that of Strepsiades; one only is required for the Knights or the Plutus; two occupy the proscenium in the Andria and Adelphi of Terence;[1] while for the earliest extant plays of Aeschylus, the Persians, Suppliants, and the Seven against Thebes, no door at all is needed. When those tragedies were brought out by Aeschylus himself, the theatre was still in that primitive stage in which there was no proscenium, no decorative background, nor even any playhouse beyond the modest booth set up not far from the orchestra to serve as a greenroom for the performers. For the Suppliants, the scene is simply the orchestra—a sacred enclosure with its altar in the midst thereof. For the Seven, the scene is likewise simply the orchestra—an open space, perhaps a square upon the acropolis of Thebes, adorned with images of the gods[2] (Ae. Sep. 240–241):

τάνδ’ ἐς ἀκρόπτολιν,
τίμιον ἕδος, ἱκόμαν

| | here to the acropolis, high-honored seat, am I come |

Thither rush the terror-stricken Theban women, and thither at the end of the play Antigone and Ismene bring the corpses of their brothers to lie in state. For the Persians, the scene is the orchestra, with some sort of proscenium in the background representing the grave of

[1] The proscenium was conventionally broken by three entrances, (Pollux IV 124): τριῶν δὲ κατὰ τὴν σκηνὴν θυρῶν ἡ μέση μὲν βασίλειον ἢ σπήλαιον ἢ οἶκος ἔνδοξος ἢ πᾶν τοῦ πρωταγωνιστοῦ τοῦ δράματος, ἡ δὲ δεξιὰ τοῦ δευτεραγωνιστοῦντος καταγώγιον, ἡ δὲ ἀριστερὰ τὸ εὐτελέστατον ἔχει πρόσωπον ἢ ἱερὸν ἐξηρημιωμένον, ἢ ἄοικός ἐστιν. (Vitruv. V 6, 8): tragicae (scenae) deformantur columnis et fastigiis et signis reliquisque regalibus rebus, comicae autem aedificiorum privatorum et maenianorum habent speciem prospectusque fenestris dispositos imitatione communium aedificiorum rationis, satyricae vero ornantur arboribus speluncis reliquisque agrestibus rebus in topiarii speciem deformatis. . . . Ipsae autem scenae suas habent rationes explicatas ita, uti mediae valvae ornatus habeant aulae regiae, dextra ac sinistra hospitalia.

[2] See Vol. II, Chap. VIII.

Darius[1] and, perhaps, the senate house in which the Persian elders were accustomed to hold their sessions (Ae. Pers. 138–140):

| | |
|---|---|
| ἀλλ' ἄγε, Πέρσαι, | so come, ye Persians, let us |
| τόδ' ἐνεζόμενοι στέγος ἀρχαῖον | take our seats in yonder ancient hall |

When the Persians was produced, a proscenium must have been prepared with at least enough to suggest the tomb of Darius and the senate house, to which the chorus proposes to retire for their deliberations but which is never called into requisition.[2] In all three plays the exits and the entrances are all made through the improvised parodoi.

The remains of the stone theatre of Delos reveal clearly the adaptability of the stage arrangements for either one, two, or three doors. The space is so distributed that the central intercolumniation was constructed as a permanent double door, the principal entrance; and that, with the two intercolumniations on either side, provided the space necessary for the most important building, occupying the centre of the scene. The adjoining houses on either side could then each occupy three intercolumniations, with a doorway in the middle one of each group of three. The three houses thus claim eleven of the intercolumniations of the proscenium. Usually there must be a passageway between the central house and each of the neighboring houses.[3] This makes a total of thirteen intercolumniations, or fourteen columns, in the proscenium colonnade, exactly the number that we find at the theatre of Delos, of Epidaurus, of Eretria, of Assos, and of the Piraeus. Similar is the arrangement at Athens and at Priene also.

There were other possible entrances through the parascenia and through the great parodoi, all of which were often used.

When the play called for less than three entrances, the extra intercolumniations were fitted with painted panels or drop curtains, such as we find briefly described by Pollux.[4] They may have been made of canvas stretched on frames, as was usual in the earlier days, or they may have been panels of wood, as they seem regularly to have been in the permanent theatre of stone. In either case, they ran into place between the columns and fitted snugly in grooves in the sides of the columns and were held fast in place by a bar. The grooves and the hole for the bar or bars we may still see unto this day upon the columns and in the floor in the theatres of Delos and Epidaurus and Megalopolis and Messene. The grooves of two adjacent columns, or half-columns, function very much as does the rim of a modern picture frame; indeed, the grooved half-columns look very like a modern picture moulding and had very much the same general effect. Even more pronounced than those of Delos are the grooved half-columns of the proscenium of the theatre at the Amphiaraeum near Oropus, while at Epidaurus and at Megalopolis the device is similar.

Whether of canvas or of wood, the πίναξ "panel" bore a painted representation of a mountain[5] or the sea[6] or a grove[7] or a river[8] or a cave[9] or something characteristic of the place in which the scene was laid, according to the requirements of each particular play. We would naturally think of the Lion Gate painted on one such panel as part of the stage-setting of the Electra of Sophocles, the Argive Heraeum on another, the Lycaean Agora of the wolf-slaying god on a third, the grove of Io on a fourth. Such a proscenium is vividly suggested in the opening lines of the prolog (1–10):

| | |
|---|---|
| Ὦ τοῦ στρατηγήσαντος ἐν Τροίᾳ ποτὲ | Son of Agamemnon, who once led our hosts |
| Ἀγαμέμνονος παῖ, νῦν ἐκεῖν' ἔξεστί σοι | at Troy, now canst thou look in presence |
| παρόντι λεύσσειν ὧν πρόθυμος ἦσθ' ἀεί. | upon those scenes which thou wast ever eager to behold: |

[1] Hypothesis: ἡ σκηνὴ τοῦ δράματος παρὰ τῷ τάφῳ Δαρείου. Cf. vs. 518 ff.; 597 ff.; 850.

[2] Wilamowitz, die Bühne des Aischylos, Hermes XXI (1886) pp. 607–608, argues that there was no back-scene at all for the representation of the Persians; that all was left free for the imagination of the audience; and yet he must have on the scene the grave of Darius and seats for the elders.

[3] The alleyway (angiportus) is a frequent feature of the scenes of Plautus and Terence. Sometimes in place of the neighbors' houses, the buildings adjacent to the central or principal house are stables or workshops or something of that sort (Pl. Trin. 194; 1085; 1174; Most. 1046).

[4] Pollux IV 131: καταβλήματα δὲ ὑφάσματα ἢ πίνακες ἦσαν ἔχοντες γραφὰς τῇ χρείᾳ τῶν δραμάτων προσφόρους· κατεβάλλετο δ' ἐπὶ τὰς περιάκτους ὄρος δεικνύντα ἢ θάλατταν ἢ ποταμὸν ἢ ἄλλο τι τοιοῦτον.

[5] E.g., Ae. P. V.

[6] E.g., Eur. Andromeda; Pl. Rudens.

[7] E.g., Soph. O. C.; Ajax.

[8] E.g., Eur. Rh.; Hel.; Tro.

[9] E.g., Eur. Cy.; Soph. Phil.; Ar. Av.

τὸ γὰρ παλαιὸν ῎Αργος οὑπόθεις τόδε,

τῆς οἰστροπλῆγος ἄλσος ᾽Ινάχου κόρης·

αὕτη δ᾽, ᾽Ορέστα, τοῦ λυχοχτόνου θεοῦ
ἀγορὰ Λύχειος· οὑξ ἀριστερᾶς δ᾽ ὅδε
῝Ηρας ὁ χλεινὸς ναός· οἶ δ᾽ ἱχάνομεν,
φάσχειν Μυχήνας τὰς πολυχρύσους ὁρᾶν

Yonder is the ancient Argos, for which thou didst
yearn,
the grove of the vext wanderer, Inachus's
daughter;
and there, Orestes, is the wolf-slaying god's
Lycean Agora; yonder, to the left, is
Hera's famous shrine; and where we stand,
deem that thou seest Mycenae rich in gold

With the words, the Paedagogus may have pointed out each scene upon the several inter-columniations of the proscenium.

Similar would have been the stage-decoration for the presentation of the Agamemnon of Aeschylus. At the production of the Ion of Euripides, the centre of the scene represented the oracular temple of Delphi; one neighboring panel may have borne a representation of the Castalian Fountain; another the Plistus valley; and another the Treasury or the Lesche of the Athenians. Mount Cithaeron, in the distance, would seem to be a necessary feature of the landscape of the Bacchae; the seashore, of the Hippolytus; the Hellespont, of the Troades; the Nile with the Pyramids, of the Helen.

When more than one entrance was needed, a panel was removed, and the intercolumniation was made into a door, as in the Ecclesiazusae and in the Oedipus the King, for which, as we have seen, there may have been need of three houses and three entrances in the proscenium. The doorways of the scene-building back of the proscenium had little to do with the production of a play, save as they contributed to the convenience of the actors. In huge theatres, therefore, like those of Athens, Epidaurus, Ephesus, there are three such doors leading from the σχηνή into the proscenium; in a few small theatres, like those of the Amphiaraeum and Pleuron, the architects provided but one door. Even as large a theatre as that of Delos has but one such door.

The discussion of painted panels, slid into place between columns of stone, can apply strictly only to the Hellenistic or Roman period when we have theatres built of stone, with permanent scene-buildings also built of stone. And yet the same principle of stage-setting and stage decoration holds good for the more or less flimsy temporary wooden structures of the days of Aeschylus and Sophocles. The Hellenistic theatre, which we know so well from the many ruins left to us in the Greek world, differed in its arrangements from the classical theatre at no essential point.[1] This must be necessarily so; for when Lycurgus rebuilt the Dionysiac theatre in Athens in stone, and other theatres in Greece were built on the same plan, they were surely building with the thought and purpose of producing the old fifth century dramas in the new theatres in the same way as that in which they had originally been presented. Proscenium colonnade, scene-building, circular orchestra, with all their stage devices, are practically identical in form and function, though not in material, in both the Hellenistic theatre and the older Greek type. In the earlier period the temples and palaces and tombs were temporary structures erected in wood and canvas across the space occupied by the later proscenium.

We have for the earlier period of the drama abundant evidence, both literary and monumental, for the erection of such accessories in the space beyond the orchestra, just as in actual life the Athenians built porticoes and other accessories against the front of their houses and thus encroached upon the public streets.[2] Such a portico is still to be seen in Graeco-Roman Delos.[3] For the tragedy, we have in the beautiful red-figured Medea Vase in Munich, obviously an illustration of a scene from the theatre, just such a portico with six Ionic columns, three in front and three in back, and gable roof built against the stage-building and functioning as a proscenium, and representing the interior of the royal palace of Corinth. The vase-painter has taken the liberty of reproducing two different scenes at the same time, the one narrated—Creusa in the palace, in her death agonies in the presence of her father, with the queen, the nurse, the paedogogus, and others running to her rescue; the other—Medea slaying her children, Jason rushing in to save them, and the Fury with torches and

---

[1] Dörpfeld, *die griechische Bühne, Ath. Mitt.* XXVIII (1903), pp. 383 ff.

[2] This custom is attested even in sixth century Athens; Arist. Oec. II p. 1347 (Bekker): ῾Ιππίας ὁ ᾽Αθηναῖος τὰ ὑπερέχοντα τῶν ὑπερῴων εἰς τὰς δημοσίους ὁδοὺς καὶ τοὺς ἀναβαθμοὺς καὶ τὰ προφθάγματα καὶ τὰς θύρας τὰς ἀνοιγομένας ἔξω ἐπάλησεν. Cf. Bekker, *Charicles*, II pp. 132 f.; Dörpfeld-Reisch, *d. griech. Theater*, pp. 196–197; 200; 208 ff.

[3] Guhl and Koner, Figs. 92 and 93.

dragon-drawn car waiting to convey the Colchian to Athens.[1]  The pillared vestibule was drawn by the vase-painter merely to suggest, not to reproduce with accuracy, the stage-building of the theatre with its added portico for the palace of Creon.  In the Mostellaria of Plautus such a projecting portico before a house is described in considerable detail (817–819):

> TR. Viden vestibulum ante aedis hoc et ambulacrum quoiusmodi?
> TH. Luculentum edepol profecto.  TR. Age specta postes, quoiusmodi,
> quanta firmitate facti et quanta crassitudine.

Such a pillared vestibule need be only a shallow porch with no more than two columns with antae.  It may sometimes be deeper and more richly constructed.

Such a vestibule afforded a convenient place for one person's overhearing a conversation not intended for his ears or witnessing an action not meant for his eyes (Pl. Aul. 666):

> tantisper huc ago ad ianuam concessero

and with these words Strobilus slips into the recess of the doorway to spy upon Euclio and see what he is going to do with his pot of gold.  Thus, too, Eutychus in the Mercator (477) stops in the vestibule of his home and overhears all Charinus's tale of woe:

> omnia ego istaec auscultavi ab ostio, omnem rem scio

In Aristophanes's Wasps, the house of Bdelycleon had such a vestibule; the old man's address to his Apollo of the Ways leaves no possibility of doubt (875):

| | |
|---|---|
| ὦ δέσποτ' ἄναξ, γεῖτον 'Αγυιεῦ τοὐμοῦ<br>προθύρου προπύλαιε | oh sovereign Lord of the Ways, my neighbor, and<br>guardian of the vestibule of my door |

It may have been in this vestibule that Sosias and Xanthias in the opening scene of the Wasps, and Strepsiades and Phidippides in the Clouds, and Orestes in Euripides's tragedy that bears his name, are sleeping as these plays open.  The vestibule afforded popular sleeping quarters from the days of Homer[2] on.  In the permanent theatre of stone, there would have been no need of such an accessory; the scene could have been arranged perfectly by means of an easily removable curtain in one of the intercolumniations of the proscenium. (See below, pp. 325–326.)

When Aeschylus brought out the Choephori in 458 B. C., he had his scene so arranged that the palace of Mycenae stood in the centre.  To one side, with as large an interval as practicable between, he had so constructed the tomb of Agamemnon that it might seem to be beyond the palace gates.  In the later permanent theatre, the tomb would have occupied one of the painted panels remote as possible from the centre; the proscenium step would have afforded Electra a place to sit or kneel; the adjoining intercolumniations would have been open, so that she could stand in sight of the audience but out of sight of her brother.

In the days of the temporary structure, as well as in the later period, the painter helped out the builder with his art.  Sophocles was, we are told on good authority,[3] the inventor of scene-painting; and he introduced this important innovation while Aeschylus was still bringing out plays at Athens.  Indeed, Vitruvius, in the passage just cited, informs us that the famous painter Agatharchus painted a scene decoration for Aeschylus himself.[4]  We can thus date as early as the year 458 B. C., perhaps as early as 468, the employment of painted panels introduced upon the temporary proscenium, with its pillars or posts of wood, in some way analogous to their insertion in the intercolumniations of the later stone-built theatre.

In the permanent theatre of the next generation these panels were easily run into place and out of place, as the stage property-men prepared the proscenium for each drama.  For the ancient theatre of Greece also had its property-men, employing people to act in the capacity of stage-hands, scene-shifters, makers and managers of stage properties, just as our modern theatres must do.  An anonymous comic fragment refers to these stagers as

---

[1] The vase is reproduced in Baum., *Denkm.* II p. 903, Fig. 980; Roscher, *Myth. Lex.*, II² Sp. 2509–2510; Flickinger, *The Gk. Theater and its Drama*, p. 237, Fig. 73.  Cf. Dörpfeld-Reisch, *d. griech. Theater*, pp. 306 ff., where this and various other vases with illustrations from the stage are discussed.

[2] γ 399; δ 297; 302.

[3] Arist. Poet. 4 (p. 1449 a 18); Vitruv. de Arch. VII, praef. 11; cf. Dörpfeld-Reisch, *d. griech. Theater*, pp. 200 ff.

[4] See p. 314 below, with footnote 3.

σκηνοποιοί.[1] Among other tasks that must have fallen to these stage property-men, besides the "making of scenes," must have been such as turning the periacti[2] for a change of scene; arranging the πίνακες "panels" in advance of each performance, filling in the various intercolumniations of the proscenium according to the demands of the play to be presented, and shifting them according to the exigencies of the action as it developed; working the eccyclema, the crane, Charon's stair-case, the theologeum, and all the other accessories essential to the successful presentation of a tragedy or comedy.

Besides the anonymous comic fragment just quoted, Aristophanes more than once introduces the stage-hand. As Trygaeus in the Peace is being hoisted to heaven by means of the crane, the rope apparently begins to twist, he grows dizzy and nauseated and cries out to the stage property-man to be careful and avert the threatening disaster (Ar. Pax 174–176):

| | |
|---|---|
| ὦ μηχανοποιέ, πρόσεχε τὸν νοῦν ὡς ἐμέ· | say, you property-man, have a little thought for me; |
| ἤδη στρέφει τι πνεῦμα περὶ τὸν ὀμφαλόν, | the wind is already whizzing about my navel, |
| κεἰ μὴ φυλάξει, χορτάσω τὸν κάνθαρον | and if you don't watch out, I'll be feeding the beetle |

In a fragment of the Daedalus, the comic poet refers to the danger attending the manipulation of the crane and the responsibility laid upon the property-man (Ar. Frag. 188 K.):

| | |
|---|---|
| ὁ μηχανοποιός, ὁπότε βούλει τὸν τροχὸν | the property-man—when you want him to hoist |
| ἱμᾶν ἀνεκάς, λέγε, χαῖρε φέγγος ἡλίου | the wheel clear to the top, say, "Hello, sunshine" |

It was not only the periacti of the later theatre that could be turned to change a scene suddenly. A panel-picture in an intercolumniation of the proscenium could also be slid out of place and another panel slid after it into its place, effecting in a moment a partial or a complete change of scene. The extreme illustration would, of course, be the shifting of the scene of the Eumenides of Aeschylus at once from Delphi to Athens. The panels (πίνακες) that had but now represented Delphi—its temple, Athenian treasury or Lesche, Phaedriades, Castalia, Plistus, or some other prominent features of Delphian topography— are suddenly shifted, and in their place we see the Areopagus, with its court and Cave of the Furies, the Cimonian Propylaea, the old Athena temple, and perhaps some other characteristic feature of the Athens of the early fifth century.

Similarly, in the Knights of Aristophanes, one panel rolls back and another glides into its place, and by that simple operation the gates of the Athenian Propylaea open and reveal to the eyes of spectators and chorus the glories of the inner Acropolis reproduced before them. Agoracritus gives the word (Ar. Eq. 1326):

| | |
|---|---|
| ὄψεσθε δέ· καὶ γὰρ ἀνοιγνυμένων ψόφος ἤδη τῶν προπυλαίων | you shall see. Hark, even now there is a noise of the Propylaea opening |

The panel representing the Propylaea makes way for a representation of the inner Acropolis, and Agoracritus cries (1327–1328):

| | |
|---|---|
| ἀλλ' ὀλολύξατε φαινομέναισιν ταῖς ἀρχαίαισιν Ἀθήναις | now shout for joy at the appearing of our ancient Athens, |
| καὶ θαυμασταῖς καὶ πολυύμνοις, ἵν' ὁ κλεινὸς Δῆμος ἐνοικεῖ | the wonderful, the praisèd in song, wherein our renownèd Demus dwells |

And the chorus, filled with wonder and pride, as they look upon the painted scene, give utterance to the famous line (1329):

| | |
|---|---|
| ὦ ταὶ λιπαραὶ καὶ ἰοστέφανοι καὶ ἀριζήλωτοι Ἀθάναι | oh bright and enviable Athens, city of the violet crown |

---

[1] Inc. Inc. Frag. 98 K.: σκηνοποιούς. To which Pollux adds (VII 189): σκηνικοὺς οἱ παλαιοὶ ὠνόμασαν. (C) τοὺς μηχανοποιοὺς ἡ παλαιὰ κωμῳδία ὠνόμαζεν.

[2] For the periacti see Dörpfeld-Reisch, *d. griech. Theater*, p. 126; Holwerda, Παρασκήνια, Πάροδοι, Περίακτοι, *Ath. Mitt.* XXIII (1898), pp. 382 ff.

And in the midst of the citadel sits enthroned in imperial power once more the Demus of Athens (1330 ff.).[1]

The effect of this change of scenery must have been startling in its beauty and dignity. The best painters of Athens must have been drawn into the service of the drama to paint panels that would be worthy of the best art of fifth century Athens. We are expressly told by Vitruvius that Agatharchus, one of the most famous painters of the fifth century in Athens,[2] executed a "scene" for Aeschylus and actually wrote a book on the subject of scene decoration.[3] Vitruvius would lead us to believe that such decoration went farther in the way of detail than the faint suggestions of landscape with which the vase-painters have familiarized us—a single tree suggesting a forest; a dolphin, the sea; a column or two, a house; and so on.

Just as the best graphic talent of Athens was called into requisition for the decoration of the panels, so, too, no mean architectural and plastic ability was required for the other features of the proscenium. Though the temples and palaces, when introduced into scenes of the tragedy with their elaborate architectural details and sculptures and other ornamentation, were but greatly reduced, practically miniature counterparts of the reality they were meant to represent, the representation must satisfy the requirements of the artistic taste of the Athenian public. Such art must have been expensive, but Athens was famous for loving the beautiful and securing it "with cheapness."

We are accustomed to think of the scenic decoration of the Athenian theatre as leaving as much to the imagination of the spectators as we usually assume for the stage of Shakespeare. Shakespeare may have had much more in the way of stage properties than is commonly assumed; obviously the "stage" of Aeschylus and Aristophanes had far more in the way of architecture, painting, and sculpture for "stage-effect" than we have hitherto been led to accept.

A third instance of sudden shifting of the scene, perhaps even more striking than those of the Eumenides and the Knights, is found in the Ajax of Sophocles. The scene is laid upon the seashore near Ajax's tent, the door of which forms the central entrance from the stage building to the orchestra. One panel, or more, doubtless, even in the old proscenium of wood and canvas, represented the shore of the Hellespont; another (perhaps it required more than one), the more distant "baths and meadows by the beach."[4] At line 815 that panel or couple of panels or a curtain is suddenly withdrawn revealing Ajax standing alone in a glade[5] by the strand of the sea. Evidently there were pictures behind pictures here. The hero falls upon his sword into the glade—that is, behind the trees and bushes painted on the panel of the next intercolumniation of the proscenium; and there his body is found by Tecmessa and the chorus a little later on.[6]

Closely akin to such a change of scenery as that in the Ajax just mentioned are those scenes in which the spectators are permitted to look behind the scenes and see what is occurring or what has occurred inside a palace or a temple. In an earlier passage of the same play, Tecmessa has described[7] to the chorus the deeds of Ajax in his madness—the slaughter of

---

[1] The noise attending the opening of the gates of the Propylaea in the Knights and the painted scene representing the Acropolis would fit one of the periacti quite as well as a panel. And the periacti may have been invented early enough in the last quarter of the fifth century for use in the production of the Knights. Moreover, the periacti, triangular prisms with pictures on each face, or two-faced slabs that turned on a column as a pivot, stood in front of the doors of the parascenia; and as they turned upon their pivots they must have made noise enough for the situation under discussion (Pollux IV 126; 131): παρ' ἑκάτερα δὲ τῶν δύο θυρῶν τῶν περὶ τὴν μέσην ἄλλαι δύο εἶεν ἄν, μία ἑκατέρωθεν, πρὸς ἃς αἱ περίακτοι συμπεπήγασιν, ἡ μὲν δεξιὰ τὰ ἔξω πόλεως δηλοῦσα, ἡ δ' ἑτέρα τὰ ἐκ πόλεως, μάλιστα τὰ ἐκ λιμένος... εἰ δ' ἐπιστρεφεῖεν αἱ περίακτοι, ἡ δεξιὰ μὲν ἀμείβει τὸ πᾶν, ἀμφότεραι δὲ χώραν ὑπαλλάττουσιν.... κατεβλήματα δὲ ὑφάσματα ἢ πίνακες ἦσαν ἔχοντες γραφὰς τῇ χρείᾳ τῶν δραμάτων προσφόρους· κατεβάλλετο δ' ἐπὶ τὰς περιάκτους ὄρος δεικνύντα ἢ θάλατταν ἢ ποταμὸν ἢ ἄλλο τι τοιοῦτον. See also Holwerda, Παρασκήνια, Πάροδοι, Περίακτοι, *Ath. Mitt.* XXIII (1898).

[2] Agatharchus flourished about 430–425 B.C.

[3] Vitruv. VII praef. 11: Primum Agatharchus Athenis Aeschylo docente tragoediam scaenam fecit et de ea commentarium reliquit. See Dörpfeld-Reisch, *d. griech. Theater*, pp. 200 f.

[4] Soph. Aj. 654–655: ἀλλ' εἶμι πρός τε λουτρὰ καὶ παρακτίους λειμῶνας....

[5] πάραυλος νάπους (l. 892).

[6] For this change of scene in the Ajax, Reisch assumes a provisional tent erected between the orchestra and the "playhouse." On either side of the tent were side-buildings, after the manner of parascenia, and these were closed in with trees and bushes to form the "glade." At the change of scene from before the tent to the scene of Ajax's suicide, the tent itself was removed—perhaps by drawing apart the canvas of the front wall of the tent—thus making of the proscenium one continuous forest glade. See Dörpfeld-Reisch, *d. griech. Theater*, p. 212.

[7] Soph. Aj. 284–330.

the cattle and the sheep—and the hero, now half come to himself, sitting "a wreck amid the wreck of carcasses" and bemoaning his state. When the chorus have heard the story and the hero's lamentations, they cry (344–345):

| | |
|---|---|
| ἀλλ' ἀνοίγετε. | open; quick! |
| τάχ' ἄν τιν' αἰδῶ κἀπ' ἐμοὶ βλέψας λάβοι | Haply he may have some regard for me, when he sees me |

Tecmessa opens the tent; that is, she draws aside, or seems to draw aside, a curtain covering one or more intercolumniations of the proscenium and reveals to chorus and to audience the demented Ajax brooding over the work of his mad hands (346–347):

| | |
|---|---|
| ἰδού, διοίγω· προσβλέπειν δ' ἔξεστί σοι | lo! I open. And thou mayst look upon |
| τὰ τοῦδε πράγη, καὐτὸς ὡς ἔχων κυρεῖ | his deeds and his own plight |

The chorus, standing close up to the proscenium, see it all—Ajax and the slaughtered beasts. The audience see enough—Ajax sitting close beside the open doorway and a suggestion of the butchery. As the open doors of a great temple like the Parthenon or the temple of Zeus at Olympia admitted light sufficient for the adequate illumination of the vast interior, so in the bright sunshine of Attica the opening of one or more intercolumniations of the proscenium would afford satisfactory seeing to the spectators in the theatre, except, perhaps, for those who sat farthest around on the wings.

It is not the central intercolumniation, we must observe—not the doorway of Ajax's tent—that is opened. That seems clear from the fact that, though Ajax calls at line 340 for Eurysaces, he does not see the boy until the attendant brings him through the doorway, out into the open, and into the presence of his father (541–545) still sitting as he was when the scene was opened. When the father's love for his babe has found expression, he bids an attendant, perhaps Tecmessa herself, close the place (579–581):

| | |
|---|---|
| δῶμα πάκτου, μηδ' ἐπισκήνους γόους | shut up the place, and do not weep |
| δάκρυε· κάρτα τοι φιλοίκτιστον γυνή. | and wail here at the tent. In sooth, a woman is a thing the loves to make lament. |
| πύκαζε θᾶσσον | Quick, close it up |

Here he addresses one person, as if that person were responsible for carrying out his bidding, but nothing is done, and (line 593) he gives the plural order:

| | |
|---|---|
| οὐ ξυνέρξεσθ' ὡς τάχος | close ye it up; make haste |

The replacing of the panels required the work of more than one attendant; this seems to establish our suggestion that more than one panel had been rolled back.

A very similar procedure takes place in Euripides's Hecuba, in the scene in which the murdered sons of Polymestor are exhibited inside the tent. The Trojan queen has drained the cup of revenge to the very dregs; she has put out the eyes of her enemy and slain his children, and comes forth and says (1049; 1051):

| | |
|---|---|
| ὄψει νιν αὐτίχ' . . . . | thou shalt see him presently. . . . |
| . . . . . . . . . . | . . . . . . . . |
| παίδων τε δισσῶν σώμαθ' | and the bodies of his children twain |

The blinded Thracian king gropes his way through the tent door, the curtains of which are drawn apart to let him pass and at the same time to bring to view the bodies of the children laid out just inside the opened tent. And when Agamemnon enters a few moments later, among his first questions is (1116–1117):

| | |
|---|---|
| τίς . . . | and who . . . |
| παῖδάς τε τούσδ' ἔκτεινεν; | murdered these children here? |

Agamemnon sees the little bodies plainly, as does the chorus; the spectators also see them.

The Scholiast commenting on line 346 of the Ajax says that Ajax and the slaughtered herds and flocks were brought into view by means of the "eccyclema."[1] Just what was the eccyclema? Ἐκκύκλημα is defined by Liddell and Scott as follows: "*a theatrical machine,*

---

[1] ἐνταῦθα ἐκκύκλημά τι γίνεται, ἵνα φανῇ ἐν μέσοις ὁ Αἴας ποιμνίοις . . . . δείκνυται δὲ ξιφήρης ἠκατωμένος μεταξὺ τῶν ποιμνίων καθήμενος.

which served the purpose of drawing back the scenes, and disclosing the interior to the spectators. It was commonly used to exhibit murders *after* perpetration, as in Aeschylus's Agamemnon, 1372, Clytaemnestra is discovered standing over the bodies of her husband and Cassandra . . . . and by this means Aristophanes exhibits Euripides and Agatho in their studies (Ach. 408; Thes. 96). The way in which it worked is uncertain: some think it was the same with the ἐξώστρα, a sort of platform on wheels, which was pushed through the great doors in the back-scene; others, that it was a contrivance to roll off or draw aside the back-scene itself; v. Müller, Eumenides §28, and against him *Herm. Opusc.* 6. 2. p. 165— both appealing to Pollux 4. 128."

The disputed passage from Pollux IV 128 reads:

| | |
|---|---|
| τὸ μὲν ἐκκύκλημα ἐπὶ ξύλων | the eccyclema is a high platform upon |
| ὑψηλὸν βάθρον, ᾧ ἐπίκειται θρόνος· | a wooden frame, and on it stands a chair. |
| δείκνυσι δὲ τὰ ὑπὸ σκηνὴν ἐν | It reveals the secret things committed |
| ταῖς οἰκίαις ἀπόρρητα πραχθέντα· | in the houses, behind the scenes. |
| καὶ τὸ ῥῆμα τοῦ ἔργου καλεῖται | The verb, corresponding to the action, is |
| ἐκκυκλεῖν· ἐφ' οὗ δὲ εἰσάγεται | "to wheel out." When the "out-wheeling machine" is |
| τὸ ἐκκύκλημα, εἰσκύκλημα ὀνομάζεται· | taken in, it is called "in-wheeling." |
| καὶ χρὴ τοῦτο νοεῖσθαι | We must assume this contrivance |
| καθ' ἑκάστην θύραν, οἰονεὶ καθ' | for each entrance, just as for |
| ἑκάστην οἰκίαν | each house |

The passage from Pollux confuses two distinct stage devices, as Reisch long ago recognized:[1] the first sentence most obviously has reference to some definite, specific scene, such as that in Euripides's Hippolytus, where Phaedra, heart-sick and body-sick, is brought upon the scene from out the palace upon her bed (170–171; 178–180):

| | |
|---|---|
| ΧΟ. ἀλλ' ἥδε τροφὸς γεραιὰ πρὸ θυρῶν | CHO.  But here comes the old nurse, bringing her |
| τήνδε κομίζουσ' ἔξω μελάθρων· | out of doors from out the halls |
| . . . . . . | . . . . . . |
| ΤΡ. τόδε σοι φέγγος λαμπρόν, ὅδ' αἰθήρ· | NU.  Lo here the bright light, here the open sky. |
| ἔξω δὲ δόμων ἤδη νοσερᾶς | And out of doors is now the couch |
| δέμνια κοίτης | of thy sick-bed |

The queen has been too sick even to lift her head or to realize that she has passed from the palace to the sunshine out of doors. She has not walked out supported by her nurse. She has been "rolled out." So says the Scholiast, commenting on line 172: "The poet employs the eccyclema."[2] This is precisely the kind of eccyclema that Pollux had in mind when he defined the device as a "platform upon a wooden frame, with a chair standing upon it." Behind the scenes Phaedra's couch had been placed upon this four-wheeled platform, and as she lay in her stupor, she was "rolled out" upon it, attended by her nurse (κομίζουσ'), through the palace doors into the orchestra.

Exactly the same type of eccyclema figures in the Thesmophoriazusae of Aristophanes. Euripides needs a woman to represent him at the Thesmophoria. The most effeminate man in the world is the man to help him supply his need. He decides to call upon the tragic poet Agathon and bids summon him forth. Presently the delicate, dandified Agathon is made to enter from his own luxurious chambers. But so delicate and effeminate he is, that he does not walk forth into the orchestra but is "rolled out" reclining in effeminate robes upon his luxurious couch. Euripides's companion, Mnesilochus, is not looking for any such apparition and asks wonderingly (Ar. Thes. 96):

| | |
|---|---|
| καὶ ποῦ ποτ' ἐστίν; | and where in the world is he? |

and Euripides answers (*ibid.*):

| | |
|---|---|
| οὗτος ἐκκυκλούμενος | why, there, rolling out |

His couch rests upon the platform on wheels or is provided with casters of its own, and out it rolls with Agathon and all sorts of articles of effeminate refinement about him. He con-

[1] Dörpfeld-Reisch, *d. griech. Theater*, p. 235.
[2] τῷ ἐκκυκλήματι χρώμενος.

tinues throughout the scene to recline there and sing his soft and effeminate lyrics, contributing from time to time to the transformation of Mnesilochus into a woman. And at the end of the scene Agathon, still sunk in the cushions of his downy couch, bids an attendant roll him back into his apartment (265):

εἴσω τις ὡς τάχιστ' μ' ἐσκυκλησάτω | some one, please, roll me in at once

The "out-wheeling machine" becomes, as Pollux says it should, an "in-wheeling machine." This platform, rolling on wheels and carrying a couch or a "throne" or even heavier freight, is identical with the ἐξώστρα "the push-machine" mentioned by Pollux (IV 127; 129). There is no warrant for constructing, out of Pollux's words, as some scholars have done, a small stage on wheels or rollers, that represented the interior of a house and was pushed through the central door of the proscenium to serve as a temporary stage for the interior scene, and then pushed back again. The Scholiast on Aristophanes's Thesmophoriazusae 277 shared the same misconception, and, as the stage direction in the manuscripts shows, a shifting of scene was assumed at that point:

(ὀλολύζουσι. τὸ ἱερὸν ὠθεῖται) | (Shouting. The temple is pushed forward)

The assumption was that here the proscenium opens and a large temple, the Thesmophorium of Athens, is pushed forward into the centre of the scene. But if ὠθεῖται "is pushed" means anything in the way of stage machinery, it means that a panel, making manifest the scene before the Thesmophorium on the Pnyx, was at this point slid into place in the proscenium. It cannot possibly mean that the interior of a great temple with a chorus of twenty-four, and others besides, was wheeled through the comparatively narrow door of the proscenium of any Greek theatre, early or late, to effect a change of scene.

In one of Euripides's lost tragedies, the Meleager, the same sort of eccyclema as in the Hippolytus was employed for the hero's death scene. We have the scene reproduced for us upon a fine amphora from Armentum in the Museo Nazionale in Naples.[1] The fateful billet of wood has been thrown into the fire; Meleager's life has been slipping away upon his deathbed within the palace; but for his last interview with his brother and sister, Tydeus and Dejanira, and his friends Peleus and Theseus, his couch, luxuriously adorned, has been placed upon the wheeled platform and rolled out between the columns of the proscenium; and there, before our eyes, we see the young man sinking fainting, supported by one of his young friends, back into his pillows. At the end of the scene, the platform with the dying, or perhaps dead, Meleager is rolled back into the house.

We have, then, from our ancient sources, two clearly defined theatrical devices for revealing to the chorus and the spectators events that are taking place, or have taken place, within doors: 1) by the removal of panels in the proscenium colonnade; 2) by rolling in the eccyclema or exostra—a platform provided with wheels or casters and capable of carrying a throne or couch or even larger burden. There is, apparently, a third sort of eccyclema, as this device is understood by the Scholiast on Aristophanes's Acharnians 408:

ἐκκύκλημα δὲ λέγεται μηχάνημα | the eccyclema, as it is called, is a piece of
ξύλινον τροχοὺς ἔχον, ὅπερ περι- | wooden machinery with wheels; as this was
στρεφόμενον τὰ δοκοῦντα ἔνδον ὡς | turned about, it revealed to the people outside (I
ἐν οἰκίᾳ πράττεσθαι καὶ τοῖς ἔξω | mean the spectators) the things that were supposed
| posed
ἐδείκνυε, λέγω δὲ τοῖς θεαταῖς | to be taking place inside the house

The same idea is expressed by the Scholiast on Clement of Alexandria (Protrept. ed. Klotz IV 97):

σκεῦός τι ὑπότροχον ἐκτὸς τῆς | a device on wheels, outside the
σκηνῆς, οὗ στρεφομένου ἐδόκει | scene; as it turns, it produces the effect of
| bringing
τὰ εἴσω τοῖς ἔξω φανερὰ γίνεσθαι | things inside into the view of people on the outside

Out of such statements some modern commentators have reconstructed under the name eccyclema "a piece of apparatus by which the outer wall, which stood on wheels or rollers,

---

[1] Published in the *Arch. Ztg.* 1867, Taf. 220; *Bull. Arch. Nap.* VIII, Tav. VI.

was turned round as on a pivot, not only disclosing, but also bringing out with itself a part of, the interior of the house."[1]

How one who entertains such a theory imagines the wall of the temple of Delphi "turned round on a pivot" at the first presentation of the Eumenides, with its temporary proscenium, passes all understanding. With the permanent proscenium with its colonnade of stone, such a pivotal operation would be comprehensible only on the supposition that one of the panels in the intercolumniations of the proscenium was slid out of place, or perhaps better, that two of the panels swung round upon a column as on a pivot, instead of being slid entirely out of place, as I have set forth above.

But all that the sources say is that "something turned on wheels or rollers" and so afforded the spectators a sight of what was supposed to be taking place inside. The fact is, the Scholiasts are rather loose in their use of the term eccyclema; almost any piece of stage machinery may be "a sort of eccyclema" (ἐκκύκλημά τι). Thus, as we have seen, the opening of a panel in the proscenium colonnade for the chorus and the audience to see Ajax amid the havoc of his cattle is, to the Scholiast, "a kind of eccyclema"; and thus even the crane that swung a god or hero out into lofty space above the actors is termed "a kind of eccyclema."[2] And the verbs, "roll out" and "roll in," are also used of the appearance of the *deus ex machina*, without any possible thought of any type of eccyclema that we have been considering. (Luc. Philops. 29):

| | |
|---|---|
| θεὸν ἀπὸ | and methought that a god was |
| μηχανῆς ἐπεισκυκληθῆναί | rolled in here with |
| μοι τοῦτον ᾤμην ὑπὸ τῆς | a machine in the hands of |
| Τύχης | Fortune |

If any theatrical machine was in Lucian's mind, it was the crane, and not the eccyclema. He uses the same metaphor again (Deor. Concil. 9):

| | |
|---|---|
| ἀλλ' ὁ "Αττις γε..... καὶ ὁ Σαβάζιος | but Attis . . . and Sabazius—whence |
| πόθεν ἡμῖν ἐπεισεκύκλησαν οὗτοι | were these rolled in on us?[3] |

Hesychius actually defines ἐκκυκλεῖ· ἐκκαλύπτει roll out: reveal. Both "roll out" and "roll in" are used, even in fifth century drama, without any direct reference to the stage machinery; for example, Bdelycleon in the Wasps, complaining that the demagogs only make game of the gullible people says (Ar. Vesp. 699):

| | |
|---|---|
| ὑπὸ τῶν ἀεὶ δημιζόντων οὐκ οἶδ' ὅποι ἐγκεκύκλησαι[4] | the demagogs of the day roll you in—I don't know where |

(*ibid.* 1475):

| | |
|---|---|
| δαίμων τις εἰσκεκύκληκεν εἰς τὴν οἰκίαν | some divinity has rolled into our house |

With an apparent allusion to the eccyclema and its employment in tragedy and probably quoting literally a line from Euripides's Bellerophon, Aristophanes makes the Paphlagonian, who cannot be thought of as standing on an eccyclema but only as having reached, with the loss of all he held dear, the bounds of life and therefore ready to be rolled in like Meleager (Ar. Eq. 1249):

| | |
|---|---|
| κυλίνδετ' εἴσω τόνδε τὸν δυσδαίμονα | roll this unhappy man within |

Which variety of eccyclema we have to deal with in Aristophanes's Acharnians, in the scene in which Dicaeopolis comes to Euripides's house to borrow the beggar's disguise, is by no means clear. Dicaeopolis stands before the poet's house and calls him; Euripides answers from within that he hasn't time to see him; Dicaeopolis pleads (408–414):

| | |
|---|---|
| ΔΙ. ἀλλ' ἐκκυκλήθητ'. ΕΥ. ἀλλ' ἀδύνατον. ΔΙ. ἀλλ' ὅμως. | DI. Well, roll out. EU. Can't be done. DI. Nay, please do. |
| ΕΥ. ἀλλ' ἐκκυκλήσομαι· καταβαίνειν δ' οὐ σχολή. | EU. Well, I will roll out; but I haven't time to descend. |

[1] Rogers, Ar. Ach., p. XXXIX.
[2] Bekk. Anecd. I 208: μηχανή ἐστι.... ἐκκυκλήματός τι εἶδος ἀπὸ συνθήκης πρὸς ὃ φέρεται ὁ <ὑποκριτὴς> εἰς τὴν σκηνὴν δείξεως χάριν θεοῦ ἢ ἄλλου τινὸς ἥρωος.
[3] Add Philostr. V Apoll. VI 11, p. 245: φιλοσοφίας.... ἣν ἐς τὸ πρόσφορον Ἰνδοὶ στείλαντες ἐφ' ὑψηλῆς καὶ θείας μηχανῆς ἐκκυκλοῦσιν.
[4] Blaydes reads εἰσκεκύκλησαι.

ΔΙ. Εὐριπίδη, ΕΥ. τί λέλαχας; ΔΙ. ἀναβάδην
            ποιεῖς,
ἐξὸν καταβάδην· οὐκ ἐτὸς χωλοὺς ποιεῖς.

| DI. Euripides—EU. What speakest thou? DI.
| You make poetry up there, when
| you might down here; no wonder you make
| cripples.

. . . . . . . . . .

ἀλλ' ἀντιβολῶ πρὸς τῶν γονάτων σ', Εὐριπίδη,

But I implore you by your knees, Euripides,

The difficulties attending the question how and where Euripides "rolls out" are many. The words καταβαίνειν "descend," and ἀναβάδην "up there" over against καταβάδην "down here" have prompted most interpreters, beginning with the ancient Scholiast, to the theory that Euripides has been at work in an upstairs room; that when he "rolls out," the front wall of his upper story opens, revealing Euripides in his study with rags and crutches and pitiful masks and all the rest of the trumpery of his tragic art about him. But when Dicaeopolis implores him "by his knees," it would be reasonable to suppose that he clasps his knees. And while, at verses 432–434, Euripides orders a servant to hand his troublesome visitor the rags of Telephus, at 449 it is evidently Euripides himself that hands him the beggar's staff that he required; and at 465 it is again Euripides himself who hands him the little pitcher for which he begs; he would hardly toss it down to him from the second story. Furthermore, as Reisch has shown,[1] ἀναβάδην, which I have translated with "up there," does not necessarily mean "up aloft"; it may just as well mean here, as it regularly means in the case of a person reclining, "with one's feet upon the couch."[2] The opposite term, καταβάδην, could then only mean "with your feet upon the floor." And that is nonsense. It may be that by the withdrawal of a curtain across part of the theologeum, Euripides was brought into view in his upstairs study, for we certainly may have upstairs rooms sometimes. In the Peace the upstairs apartments belong to the gods, to be sure, as we should expect them to; and when Trygaeus is landed on the heights of the heavenly Olympus (on the roof of the theologeum), he beholds the residence of Zeus (Ar. Pax 177–178):

ἀτὰρ ἐγγὺς εἶναι τῶν θεῶν ἐμοὶ δοκῶ,
καὶ δὴ καθορῶ τὴν οἰκίαν τοῦ Διὸς

| it looks to me as if I were near the gods;
| surely that's the residence of Zeus that I see

On the other hand, it may be, in the scene from the Acharnians, that an eccyclema, a platform on wheels, rolled Euripides out upon his study couch to a position between the "stone pillars" of his house (449). How he was "rolled in" at the end of the scene, we are left to guess. At verse 472, Dicaeopolis leaves the scene, only to hurry back a moment later, in distraction at having forgotten the one thing most essential and pleading for a bunch of chevril (475–478). Euripides, who probably disappeared from sight at 471, is furious at the fling at his mother's trade and gives the tragic order heard from within (479):

ἀνὴρ ὑβρίζει· κλεῖε πηκτὰ δωμάτων | the man is insolent; bar fast the halls

This also sounds as if Euripides had passed out and in through the street door of his home.

At the same time, the possibility remains open that with Euripides's words "Well, I will be rolled out," a panel in the proscenium was rolled out of place revealing the interior of his study on the ground floor, and that Euripides remained there reclining in his room throughout the scene; and with his order to "bar fast the halls," the panel was slid into its place again and firmly secured. For, as cannot be too often emphasized, ἐκκυκλήθητ' "roll out" (vs. 408) need mean no more, as the Scholiast says, than φανερὸς γενοῦ "let yourself be seen," and ἐκκυκλήσομαι (409) would then mean "I will let myself be seen," and he adds "but I won't leave my couch." And that is exactly what the Scholiast on Euripides's Medea 96 means when he says:

τάδε λέγει Μήδεια ἔσω οὖσα
οὐδέπω ἐκκεκυκλημένη

| Medea speaks these lines within, for
| she has not yet been rolled out

There is no manner of stage device employed for bringing Medea out upon the scene; she calmly walks out through the open doors.

We can reject as impractical, if not as altogether impossible, the theory of the opening of temple walls or palace walls as the eccyclema that reveals events occurring behind the scenes. We can also reject with even less hesitation the theory of huge stages rolled in on wheels, suddenly substituting an interior scene for the scene presented by the proscenium. Such

---

[1] Dörpfeld-Reisch, *d. griech. Theater*, pp. 238–239.
[2] And so the Scholiast understood it (on l. 398): ἀναβάδην· ἄνω τοὺς πόδας ἔχων ἐπὶ ὑψηλοῦ τόπου καθήμενος.

a device is as unnatural for the early theatre as it is impossible for the permanent theatre. Yet such a piece of machinery has been accepted by many even for the first scene in Aeschylus's Eumenides. At the opening of the play the Pythian prophetess comes out and speaks her introductory prolog. She goes back into the temple (vs. 33) and comes out with her tale of the horrible creatures that she has found snoring in the sanctuary, with breathings deadly pouring forth blood and fire (vs. 53).

Exit the Pythia. Enter Apollo, with Hermes, giving Orestes directions as to his future course of action to escape the Furies of his mother. Hermes takes charge of the fugitive and leads him away toward Athens. The ghost of Clytaemnestra then appears rousing the sleeping Furies to the pursuit (94–116). They groan and mutter in their sleep, as she spurs them on, until, as she vanishes, one or two of them start up and rouse the rest (140–142).

The Scholiast remarks:

| | |
|---|---|
| καὶ δευτέρα δὲ γίνεται φαντασία· | and here begins a second scene: |
| στραφέντα γὰρ μηχανήματα ἔν- | machines turned round make |
| δηλα ποιεῖ τὰ κατὰ τὸ μαντεῖον | visible how things are on |
| ὡς ἔχει | the (in)side of the oracle |

And out of this scholars have actually reconstructed, with the fancied help of the already quoted passage from Pollux, a huge platform on wheels, rolled in at this point as a substitute for the front of the temple, and carrying out from the scene-structure and down its step (vs. 632) the whole interior of the temple, with its omphalus (39–40), its temple statues (55), Orestes, Apollo, Hermes, twelve or fifteen Furies, and the "thrones" ranged about on which these latter were sitting asleep (46–47). Even with our modern electrical and hydraulic machinery, such a performance would be next to impossible. And granting that this lumbering vehicle, with all that freight, could be rolled out of the scene-building (which in 458 B. C. did not exist!) through the proscenium with its temple façade, what kind of effect would it have had on the artistic feelings of those fifth century Athenians for those weird sisters to be rolled out of the dim interior of the great Delphic temple and go on sleeping and snoring for some time in the garish light of the Attic sunshine! And where would that huge platform have found a proper resting place without encroaching unduly on the orchestra, even if it could thus have been rolled (from nowhere, into an orchestra that dropped off sheer six feet into the temenos of Dionysus below) out and down the proscenium step! Surely children would not have died or women miscarried, as we are told[1] they did, at the sudden apparition of such Furies! And when the temple was thus turned inside out, where was the priestess, who had already gone in, and how did Apollo go back into such a temple at his own exit?

We may in this case safely ignore the scholium. When the priestess comes forth from the temple, the great double doors are left ajar; they remain open throughout the scene, and the curiosity of the audience is awakened and their imagination stirred to the highest pitch as they peer into the recesses of the temple and get vague impressions of the horrors within, and their excitement grows at each step in the dramatic development:

Apollo appears with Hermes at the open door and from the temple portals delivers his directions to Orestes, who is still within the sanctuary (64–84). Orestes comes out, makes answer to his divine patron and protector (85–87), and disappears down the left parodos with Hermes (93). Hereupon rises the ghost of Clytaemnestra and rebukes and admonishes the sleeping Furies (94–139).[2] Their groans and mutterings are heard from the interior of

---

[1] Vit. Ae. (p. 380 Kirchhoff).

[2] How she rose is a question that we cannot answer with any degree of assurance. That she did not come up by "Charon's Staircase" (Pollux IV 132) when the play was first brought out in Athens, seems quite certain. There is an underground passage with a stair-way leading up into the orchestra at Eretria, at Sicyon, and at Magnesia in Asia, which, in those theatres, may well be Charon's staircase; but there seems to be no such arrangement in the theatre of Lycurgus in Athens, and there almost certainly was no such provision in the temporary theatre of the fifth century. The ghost of Darius, in the Persae of Aeschylus, does not come up through an aperture in the ground; his mausoleum was represented on one of the painted panels of the scene; and when the moment for his appearing arrived, the panel opened, and Darius stood forth in the door of his tomb and held converse with the queen and the chorus (Ae. Pers. 681 ff.) and then vanished into the tomb, and the panel closed again.

Similar must have been the egress of Sisyphus from the underworld, in Aeschylus's satyr play named for him. But in the case of the ghost of Clytaemnestra in the Eumenides the probabilities are that she did not appear visibly to mortal eyes at all. She says she appears only "as a dream" or "in a dream" to recall the Furies to action (116): ὄναρ γὰρ ὑμᾶς νῦν Κλυταιμνήστρα καλῶ.

It would seem, therefore, that the ghost of the murdered queen stood out of sight of all mortals, just within the temple doors, and that only her voice was heard by the audience.

the temple (116–130); then, first one and then another awakes, and through the wide open doorway these may be dimly descried moving about and waking the others (140–142), until with their wild

| | |
|---|---|
| ἰού, ἰού, πόπαξ | Yah! Yah! Horrors! |

those awful fiends bound with all their hideous make-up into the orchestra and scare the women and children, literally, into fits (143). Apollo's order (179–180)

| | |
|---|---|
| ἔξω, κελεύω, τῶνδε δωμάτων τάχος χωρεῖτ', ἀπαλλάσσεσθε μαντικῶν μυχῶν | avaunt! Go with all speed, I bid you, from these halls, and get you from the mantic shrines |

delivered after the first choral ode, the parados, is given to the entire chorus in the orchestra and must have reference, not to the interior of the temple, for they were already out of that, but to the sacred enclosure.

There is no real eccyclema here—neither traveling stage nor opening walls—nothing, beyond the wheels on which the great doors rolled open at the first appearance of the Pythia (line 1); and through those open doors the audience saw all that they were meant to see of what took place inside the Delphic temple when the Eumenides of Aeschylus was given.

Our eccyclema, then, becomes either the platform carrying a couch or a throne, as in the Hippolytus and the Meleager and the Thesmophoriazusae, or simply a panel running on casters and rolled back, with the column on one side acting as a pivot, or slid entirely out of the way. Into the one category or the other all cases of the employment of the eccyclema will be found easily to fit.

The type of eccyclema most commonly employed in the tragedy is that which presents to the chorus and the audience the bodies of persons of the drama slain behind the scenes. The earliest instance of its use of which we know is in the Oresteian Trilogy of Aeschylus. The king and Cassandra have been murdered; the front of the scene opens; the spectators and the chorus behold the guilty queen triumphantly exulting over the corpses of those she has hated (Ae. Ag. 1379; 1404; 1440; 1539–1540):

| | |
|---|---|
| ΚΛ. ἔστηκα δ' ἔνθ' ἔπαισ' – ἐπ' ἐξειργασμένοις. | CL.  Here stand I where I struck the blow—over deeds accomplished. |
| . . . οὗτός ἐστιν Ἀγαμέμνων . . . | . . . This is Agamemnon. . . . |
| ἥ τ' αἰχμάλωτος ἥδε καὶ τερασκόπος. . . . | and this his captive prophetess. . . . |
| ΧΟ. πρὶν τόνδ' ἐπιδεῖν ἀργυροτοίχου δροίτας κατέχοντα χαμεύναν | CHO. . . . ere that I beheld him the tenant of a silver-walled bath for his lowly bier |

We see directly into the bathroom of the palace of Mycenae.[1] In the tub in which he has been slaughtered lies Agamemnon's body entangled in the fatal net; beside him lies the murdered daughter of Priam; and over them, by the doorway, towers the triumphant queen exulting in her deed of vengeance.

What has happened at the hands of the μηχανοποιοί "the property-men"? Has the scene-building parted wide and let a new stage representing the bathroom roll out? Or has the scene-building parted and revealed another scene behind it? Or have the stagehands rolled back or slid away a panel or two of the temporary scene, or, when the play was reproduced a century later, of the proscenium colonnade, and permitted us thus to look into the interior of the palace? The last explanation is the simplest—even for the early theatre with its scene of wood and canvas—and by far the most natural.

Almost the same incident is repeated, with dramatic power, at the climax of the second tragedy of the trilogy. Orestes and Pylades have passed into the palace and wrought retributive justice upon the queen and her paramour. A panel (or two) rolls back and there before our eyes stand, on either side, in imposing tableau, Orestes and Pylades over the bodies of Clytaemnestra and Aegisthus, on the very spot where they had murdered the king some ten years before (Ae. Cho. 973–974):

| | |
|---|---|
| ἴδεσθε χώρας τὴν διπλῆν τυραννίδα πατροκτόνους τε δωμάτων πορθήτορας | behold the country's two-fold royalty, my father's slayers and the destroyers of his home |

[1] The bathrooms at Tiryns and Cnossus are located well toward the front of those palaces. So there is nothing unnatural or improbable in the chorus's looking from the court (the orchestra) directly into the bathroom.

In the scene in the Agamemnon we assumed that Clytaemnestra stood by the opening in the scene-building as she boldly vaunted her deed before the chorus. In this scene in the Choephori we know that Orestes stands just inside, or perhaps just outside, the opening; for, as he has exhibited to the chorus the net in which his father had been snared, he appeals to Helius to look upon his mother's hideous crime. He must be standing where the Sun-god can look directly upon him.

The corresponding scene in the Electra of Sophocles shows the same sort of eccyclema in operation. After Orestes and Pylades have "given their despatch" to the queen, they have come out, but, warned by the chorus of the approach of Aegisthus, they "make for the vestibule" (1433) and pass again into the room where lies the body of the queen, covered with a winding sheet, so that her corpse may be mistaken by Aegisthus for that of Orestes. Aegisthus enters, falls into the trap set for him, and hastens to let all his subjects see that any hope of Orestes's removing him from power is vain (1458–1459):

| | |
|---|---|
| σιγᾶν ἄνωγα χἀναδεικνύναι πύλας<br>πᾶσιν Μυκηναίοισιν Ἀργείοις θ' ὁρᾶν | I bid keep silence and open wide the gates<br>for all Mycenae and Argos to see |

He says, we observe, "open wide the gates." The thought suggests itself again at once that one of the panels of the scene-building contained a picture of the gate of Mycenae, the famous lion gate; for "the gates" are not the palace doors through which Orestes and Pylades had passed. At this command from Aegisthus, the lion gate rolls back, and there Aegisthus and the audience behold the queen lying in state, Orestes and Pylades standing on either side of her body. Orestes probably has stepped outside the colonnade when he orders Aegisthus to pass in that he also may die on the selfsame spot where he had slain the king of men (1491; 1493):

| | |
|---|---|
| ΟΡ. χωροῖς ἂν εἴσω σὺν τάχει. . . . | OR. Pass in—at once. . . . |
| AI. τί δ' ἐς δόμους ἄγεις με. . . . | AE. Why lead me into the house. . . . |

The Choephori of Aeschylus, the Electra of Sophocles, and the Electra of Euripides must all have the same dénouement. The same sort of stage machinery might be assumed for all three. Sophocles and Aeschylus do both present the effective tableau with Orestes and Pylades standing at the opened gates of the palace building over the bodies of the slain. But in Euripides, as we should expect, there is a change. Orestes and Pylades, after their deed of vengeance upon the guilt-stained queen and her consort, rush out upon the scene through the palace doors; the doors are left wide open behind them, and Orestes cries (Eur. El. 1177–1179):

| | |
|---|---|
| ἰὼ Γᾶ καὶ Ζεῦ πανδερκέτα<br>βροτῶν, ἴδετε τάδ' ἔργα φόνια<br>μυσαρά, δίγονα σώματ' ἐν<br>χθονὶ κείμενα | oh earth and Zeus "whose all-beholding eye is<br>over men,"[1] behold these deeds of murder<br>hideous, corpses twain stretched<br>upon the ground |

Earth and Zeus behold them. Spectators have a more or less unimpeded view of them. The chorus standing closer about the palace door look in and see them with their ghastly wounds and break into lamentations (1186):

| | |
|---|---|
| ἰὼ τύχας, τᾶς σᾶς τύχας, μᾶτερ τεκοῦσ' | alas for the lot, for thy lot, oh mother that bare<br>him |

Orestes and Electra stand, presumably, on either side the open door as Orestes bids his sister (1227–1228):

| | |
|---|---|
| λαβοῦ, κάλυπτε μέλεα ματέρος πέπλοις<br>καὶ καθάρμοσον σφαγάς | take and cover with vestments our mother's body<br>and close her wounds |

Most readers' feelings will revolt, I think, at the idea of having Orestes's attendants follow on his heels carrying out the bodies of the slain immediately after him as he rushes out into the orchestra.[2] It is much more reasonable to assume that the dummies representing the bodies of Clytaemnestra and Aegisthus have, in the interval, been placed at the doorway and are visible to the chorus and the audience as soon as the doors open to let the murderers out.

[1] From Way's translation.
[2] See Reisch, *op. cit.*, p. 242.

We have only to recall the various instances in which the eccyclema is employed, to find how readily they adapt themselves to a scene or proscenium colonnade with its movable panels. Like those we have just seen, the tableau at the close of Sophocles's Antigone is presented by the opening of a panel. Creon, just returned from the tomb in which Antigone and his son have taken their lives, is informed of his queen's suicide also. The cumulation of woe is beyond his belief, and the messenger, assuring him that he may have the evidence of his own eyes, says (1293):

| | |
|---|---|
| ὁρᾶν πάρεστιν· οὐ γὰρ ἐν μυχοῖς ἔτι | thou mayst see; for she is no longer hidden within |

At these words a panel is rolled back, and we see into the women's apartments—the queen's body lying upon a bier just inside the opening left by the removal of the panel.

Exactly the same procedure in Euripides's Hippolytus permits Theseus and the chorus and the audience to look upon the body of Phaedra, whose suicide has just been announced by the servant's cries heard from within. Instead of bursting into the palace through the doors, Theseus bids (808–810):

| | |
|---|---|
| χαλᾶτε κλῆθρα, πρόσπολοι, πυλωμάτων, | shoot back the bolts of the gates, attendants mine; |
| ἐχλύεθ' ἁρμούς, ὡς ἴδω πικρὰν θέαν | loose the bars, that I may see the bitter sight |
| γυναικός, ἥ με κατθανοῦσ' ἀπώλεσεν | of my wife, who dying hath undone me |

One of the panels on this occasion would have represented the gates of the Mycenaean fortress at Troezen. At this command from Theseus, his attendants go through the motion of unbolting and unbarring the gate—not the front door of the palace; the panel rolls back, revealing the interior of the women's apartments; the dead queen lies just within; and at sight of her body the chorus, standing close by, breaks out into the lamentation beginning (811):

| | |
|---|---|
| ἰὼ ἰὼ τάλαινα μελέων κακῶν | alas! alas! unhappy for thy grievous woes |

The same process of bringing to view the interior of a palace we find in the Mad Heracles of Euripides. A messenger has reported the hero's going mad, slaying his wife and children, tearing down the columns of the hall, wrecking the palace, and finally, through the intervention of Athena, being bound to a shattered, fallen pillar (922–1015). The chorus sings a brief ode in point and closes with (1029–1030):

| | |
|---|---|
| ἴδεσθε, διάνδιχα κλῆθρα | lo! the bolts of the high-portaled |
| κλίνεται ὑψιπύλων δόμων | halls yield this way and that |

This, again, is not the main doorway of the house. The messenger had come and gone through that and nothing had been seen of the tragedy within. Again it is a panel, or two panels, with a representation of a second gateway to the palace, opening into the great megaron. This time the bolts are unfastened from within; by whom, we are not told; but the panel rolls away; and with the chorus we look through the opening and see, close by the door, the broken column and Heracles securely bound down to it, and the corpses of his murdered wife and children by him. Over against the sleeping hero stands the aged Amphitryon bowed with unutterable grief. This wonderfully dramatic tableau lasts only for the moment that it takes the chorus to sing eight short lines of lament, and Amphitryon steps through the opening to take his part in the action (1031–1041):

| | |
|---|---|
| ἰώ μοι· | oh woe is me! |
| ἴδεσθε τάδε τέκνα πρὸ πατρὸς | See here the children laid low before |
| ἄθλια κείμενα δυστάνου, | their unhappy father—poor things!— |
| εὔδοντος ὕπνον δεινὸν ἐκ παίδων φόνου. | while he sleeps in slumber unnatural after the murder of his babes. |
| περὶ δὲ δεσμὰ καὶ πολύβροχ' ἁμμάτων | And about him these knots and manifold fastenings |
| ἐρείσμαθ' Ἡράκλειον | of ropes hold Heracles bound |
| ἀμφὶ δέμας τάδε λαΐνοις | to the marble columns |
| ἀνημμένα κίοσιν οἴκων. | of the palace. |
| ὁ δ'ὥς τις ὄρνις ἄπτερον καταστένων | And like a bird mourning over its |
| ὠδῖνα τέκνων, πρέσβυς ὑστέρῳ ποδὶ | unfledged brood, now comes this way |
| πικρὰν διώκων ἤλυσιν πάρεσθ' ὅδε | the old man pursuing with halting step a bitter path |

This eccyclema is no platform on wheels, still less a secondary stage rolled out from the playhouse, but a panel sliding away, or two panels turned about on pivot hinges and opening two intercolumniations in the proscenium and thus making visible the interior of the palace of old Thebes.

In the Clouds of Aristophanes it is the central door in the proscenium that performs the act of the eccyclema and reveals to spectators and actors outside what is going on within (Ar. Nub. 183–184):

| | |
|---|---|
| ἀλλ᾽ ἄνοιγε τὴν θύραν. | please open the door. |
| ὦ Ἡράκλεις, ταυτὶ ποδαπὰ θηρία; | Oh Heracles! what kind of creatures are these? |

On this passage the Scholiast remarks:

| | |
|---|---|
| ὁρᾷ δὲ ὡς φιλοσόφους κομῶντας | the eccyclema turns and he sees the |
| στραφέντος τοῦ ἐκκυκλήματος | students of philosophy at their humbuggery |

The theory that the eccyclema turns a house inside out, impracticable with a proscenium of wood and canvas, impossible with a proscenium of stone, still crops out in certain quarters. We find even in Rogers's splendid edition of Aristophanes this note on line 183: "In answer to this appeal not the door only, but the whole house opens. . . . By means of the Eccyclema . . . . the entire front of the house is wheeled round, bringing out and exposing to the view of the audience the inner court of the Phrontisterium. . . ." One is tempted to return to Mr. Rogers the compliment he pays another theory in regard to the eccyclema, and say a "grotesque idea"! Pollux tells us, in the passage quoted at the beginning of this discussion,[1] that each and every door—that is, each and every possible opening in the proscenium—was provided with an eccyclema, a contrivance running on casters or wheels. The central door also had its wheels. And so, in this scene in the Clouds, when Strepsiades begs to have the door opened, the door opens and the audience can see enough to suggest the schoolroom with its students of philosophy in their absurd postures investigating, while Strepsiades, standing close by the door, is represented as seeing a great deal more than the spectators can see.

To resume, then, the eccyclema, as we find it employed in Greek drama, is, with rare exceptions, simply the arrangement of panels in the intercolumniations of the proscenium colonnade, so constructed and provided with casters that any of them may be swung upon their columns as a pivot, or rolled entirely out of place, thus opening the proscenium sufficiently to afford a satisfactory view of what is going on or has been going on behind the scenes. In the rare exceptions, "eccyclema" may be used of the small platforms on wheels that rolled the beds of the sick or dying or studious or indolent out through the doors upon the scene. To a people used, as the Greeks were, to living most of the time and doing almost everything out of doors, there was nothing incongruous in that.

Larger paintings than the panels in the intercolumniations were sometimes required. In the days of the earlier, primitive theatre, Proteus's grave, for example, in Euripides's Helen, may have filled a considerable portion of the space occupied by the proscenium in the later theatre; but at the same time, the tomb may have been no more than a panel picture located near the parodos farthest from the door that led to the women's quarters of the palace and having the adjoining spaces about it open. It may have been located upon one of the parascenia. Helen may have taken refuge at such a painted tomb (lines 1 ff.); and Menelaus may easily have kept himself out of sight behind a tomb thus arranged.

But for the Oedipus at Colonus of Sophocles, the poet must have required an extensive painting of grove and thicket. The crag from which, in the Prometheus of Aeschylus, Io proposes to hurl herself and so be free from all her toils[2] is obviously built up adjoining the rock on which Prometheus is fettered, even as the parascenium adjoined the proscenium of the permanent theatre.

For such purposes such an arrangement as we find in the *scaena ductilis* in the later period at Megalopolis and elsewhere would have been admirably adapted. This large movable scene, containing a picture of the groves of Colonus could have been rolled into place for the Oedipus at Colonus and as easily rolled out again for the next tragedy of the day.

[1] See p. 316.
[2] Ae. P. V. 747–750.

And these larger paintings were not confined to the space belonging to the lower proscenium. In Euripides's Suppliants the proscenium represented at least the façade of the great temple of the mysteries at Eleusis. The back-ground of the second story of the stage-building must have contained a painting of the crags that rose behind the temple. We may assume also a great painting of the walls and ramparts of Troy, and the conflagration in which Priam's city went down, as forming the background of the theologeum at the production of Euripides's Troades.

Another stage device for bringing about a change of scene we find in the two periacti—triangular prisms, or two-faced, double panels, which turned on pivots in front of the doors of the parascenia. The panels rolled into their places between the columns of the proscenium on casters;[1] or, as suggested above on the strength of the testimony of Pollux,[2] in the place of the πίναξ there may have been a sort of drop curtain. Some such device, corresponding to our modern drop curtain, seems to be demanded in various plays. The Clouds of Aristophanes opens at dawn with Strepsiades and Phidippides lying in their beds where they have been sleeping all through the night just past. Would an Athenian audience have tolerated the sight of those two worthies walking in through the parodos or through the doors of the scene-building and taking their places in their beds before the proscenium, and one of them beginning to snore as if he had been snoring all night and the other acting as if he had only just shaken off his sleep? Far more probably the old man and his son were already ensconced in their beds behind the colonnade of the proscenium before the play began; and at the signal for the opening of the play, a πίναξ (whether framed panel or painted curtain) was drawn aside, suddenly revealing to the audience the father and his precious son in their beds, and the action began.

So at the beginning of Euripides's Orestes, the hero of the play has been already lying for five days[3] upon his sick-bed. When in the action did he take to his bed? It is, to me at least, unthinkable that the artist Euripides should have planned to have the bed-ridden Orestes calmly walk in and lie down on his bed before the doors of the Argive palace, asleep, and then have Electra come in and tell her story, explaining that it is now the sixth day that he has been lying thus. Again, the probability amounts almost to certainty that the scene opens with the drawing of a curtain or a panel which reveals Orestes upon his couch and Electra standing solicitously at his bedside.

The opening of Euripides's Helen also assumes that the heroine has been sitting for some time at the grave of Proteus, whither she has long since taken refuge to escape being forced into marriage with the king. The suppliant priests have been kneeling at the palace altar for a long time before the king comes forth in the Oedipus Tyrannus. In the Mad Heracles, the first scene opens with Amphitryon, Megara, and the children of Heracles sitting at the steps of the altar of Zeus Herceius; and so at the opening of Euripides's Andromache we find the heroine sitting at the altar of Thetis. Similar situations are presented in the opening scenes of Euripides's Suppliants, Troades, and Andromeda, and in Aeschylus's Prometheus Unbound. For all these plays a curtain—the necessary precursor of the curtain that we know in the Roman comic theatre—seems indispensable. The projecting parascenia afforded most convenient and substantial supports to which to attach the ropes for the manipulation of a curtain that would cover the entire proscenium.

We need sometimes, it seems quite certain, a movable curtain for the openings in the proscenium below; the same need is apparent for the sudden appearance and disappearance of gods above the roof of the proscenium. Reisch assumes such a curtain before the doorway or doorways of the upper story of the playhouse, and from behind the curtain a god could suddenly stand forth and behind it as suddenly disappear. Such a curtain in the theologeum was apparently called into requisition in connection with the manipulation of the crane by means of which gods and disembodied spirits were swung out and poised in the air. The curtain not only concealed the machinery of the crane but it might also on occasion help out the illusion of the supernatural apparition's having thus been poised for a considerable space of time. Thus, for example, the ghost of the unhappy Polydorus has been hovering

---

[1] Schol. Ar. Ach. 407.
[2] Quoted p. 314.
[3] Vs. 39.

above the tent in which his mother bides, flitting about the place for some days before the play opens (Eur. Hec. 30–32):

| | |
|---|---|
| νῦν δ' ὑπὲρ μητρὸς φίλης | and now above my dear mother |
| Ἑκάβης ἀΐσσω, σῶμ' ἐρημώσας ἐμόν, | Hecabe I flit, my body left behind; |
| τριταῖον ἤδη φέγγος αἰωρούμενος | the third bright day I hover here |

While the last spectators have been drifting into the theatre, the stage hands have swung the ghost of Priam's murdered son up into the air by means of the crane behind a drop curtain; at the very first words of the prolog, the curtain drops, and there is the spirit of the boy hovering in the air above the tent; he is not suddenly swung out from the background, just arriving from the gates of gloom; he has already been hovering thus, lo! these two or three days.

The crane (γέρανος or simply ἡ μηχανή) was another device that Euripides, in particular, was fond of employing for sudden supernatural effects. By means of this contrivance a god or a disembodied spirit could be swung out through the central door of the second story of the stage-building and made to fly or to float in the vacant air above the heads of the mortals in the orchestra below; and by proper manipulation of the crane the divinity could be made to alight safely upon the theologeum, the roof of the proscenium, or deliver his message swung high up in the vacant air.[1]

Euripides's too frequent recourse to the machine made it a joke with Aristophanes, and the comic poet not only swings Socrates, by means of the crane, out into transcendental air above the heads of his disciples so high and so far away that it requires an extraordinarily loud shout to reach him (Ar. Nub. 218; 220; 225–229):

| | |
|---|---|
| ΣΤ. φέρε τίς γὰρ οὗτος οὑπὶ τῆς κρεμάθρας ἀνήρ; | ST. Say, who's that man in the basket? |
| . . . . . . . . . | . . . . . . . . . |
| ἴθ' οὗτος ἀναβόησον αὐτόν μοι μέγα. | come, you sir, please holler to him—loud! |
| ΣΩ. ἀεροβατῶ καὶ περιφρονῶ τὸν ἥλιον. | SO. I tread on air, and my thoughts traverse beyond the sun. |
| ΣΤ. ἔπειτ' ἀπὸ ταρροῦ τοὺς θεοὺς ὑπερφρονεῖς, | ST. So then, from your basket you look down on the gods, |
| ἀλλ' οὐκ ἀπὸ τῆς γῆς εἴπερ; ΣΩ. οὐ γὰρ ἄν ποτε | and not from the earth, eh? SO. Yea, verily; for I |
| ἐξεῦρον ὀρθῶς τὰ μετέωρα πράγματα, | should never have succeeded in finding heavenly things in their reality |
| εἰ μὴ κρεμάσας τὸ νόημα | except by suspending thought |

but he actually reverses the Euripidean process and, in the Peace, swings Trygaeus on the wings of his giant beetle up to the doors of Zeus (Pax 149–181). Not that Aristophanes was the first poet to think of translating a mortal to the skies; doubtless the thought of Trygaeus's flying to heaven on his tumble-bug is a bit of rollicking horseplay, a parody inspired by the hero's flying to heaven on the back of Pegasus in Euripides's Bellerophon. The Scholiast on Aristophanes's Acharnians 80 calls the crane that carried Trygaeus to heaven a "hoisting machine" (ἐώρημα, that is αἰώρημα), and Suidas says (s. v. ἐώρημα):

| | |
|---|---|
| ἐν αὐτῇ κατῆγον | by means of it they brought down |
| τοὺς θεοὺς καὶ τοὺς ἐν | the gods and those who talked |
| ἀέρι λαλοῦντας | from mid-air |

As Reisch remarks, Suidas is drawing from the same source as Pollux (IV 131):

| | |
|---|---|
| ἀώρας δ' ἂν εἴποις τοὺς κάλους, | hoists one might call those ropes which are |
| οἳ κατήρτηνται ἐξ ὕψους ἀνέχειν | attached to a point up high to hold aloft |
| τοὺς ἐπὶ τοῦ ἀέρος φέρεσθαι | heroes or gods who are supposed |
| δοκοῦντας ἥρως ἢ θεούς | to be wafted through the air |

Antiphanes also makes merry over the tragic poets' fondness for the "machine" as a trick of their trade (Ποι., Frag. 191, 13–16 K.):[2]

---

[1] See the full discussion in Dörpfeld-Reisch, *d. griech. Theater*, pp. 227 ff., especially, pp. 230–234, and the literature there cited.

[2] Cf. also Men. Θεοφ., Frag. 227 = Κερκ., Frag. 278 K.: ἀπὸ μηχανῆς θεὸς ἐμ.(ἐπι)φανής

ἔπειθ' ὅταν μηδὲν δύνωντ' εἰπεῖν ἔτι,
κομιδῇ δ' ἀπειρήκωσιν ἐν τοῖς δράμασιν,
αἴρουσιν ὥσπερ δάκτυλον τὴν μηχανήν,

καὶ τοῖς θεωμένοισιν ἀποχρώντως ἔχει

then, when they haven't anything more to say
and have quite petered out in their action,
they lift up a machine as readily as they'd lift a
  finger,
and the spectators are perfectly satisfied

The theatrical crane was constructed like the ordinary modern crane. The cables mentioned by Suidas ran through a pulley on the end of the arm of the crane (Ar. Δαιδ., Frag. 188 K.):

ὁ μηχανοποιός· ὁπότε βούλει τὸν τροχὸν
ἱμᾶν ἀνεκὰς, λέγε, χαῖρε φέγγος ἡλίου

the operator:—When you want the pulley
to run you aloft, say: "Goodbye to the light of
  the sun"[1]

To the end of the cable running through the pulley was attached a hook which gripped the actor's girdles or special harness, or the ropes or handles of the platform or other support for god or hero appearing as *deus ex machina*, mounted upon a horse,[2] or a chariot[3] or simply poised in mid-air.[4]

The entire machine was manipulated by a property-man unseen (Bekker, Anecd. I 232):

ἐν τῇ σκηνῇ ἅρπαξ,[5] κατε-
σκευασμένος ὑπὸ τοῦ μηχανο-
ποιοῦ, ἐξ οὗ ὁ ἐσκευασμένος
(κρεμάμενος) ὑποκριτὴς τραγῳδεῖ

in the theatre they have a grip,[5]
constructed by the property-
man; suspended by this the
tragic actor performs his part

The crane, with all the necessary machinery for its manipulation, as well as its operator were, in the tragedy, hidden from the eyes of the spectators by some sort of screen erected on the forward part of the second story of the stage-building and usually above the left hand parascenium.[6] In the comedy, when this machinery was employed for paratragoedic effect, the whole apparatus, with its operator, may have been in plain sight before the proscenium. At all events its presence is so thoroughly taken for granted that Aristophanes has Trygaeus, as he is being hoisted up to heaven, call to the operator to be careful and not let the ropes spin him about and make him seasick.[7]

The operation of such a machine could not have been very pleasant to the actor whose rôle required his use of it. Trygaeus cries out against its discomfort. In a fragment of Alexis's "Cauldron," a victim of the profiteering of the fishmongers is loud in his approval of a proposed law of Aristonicus in accordance with which the fishdealers shall be required to surrender their comfortable seats at their counters and henceforth transact business

---

[1] Perhaps this exclamation ought to be translated "Hello, Sunlight!" See p. 313.

[2] Reisch, *op. cit.*, assumes that the Dioscuri at the end of Euripides's Electra, sweep through the air upon their horses (1234; 1349) and appear above the palace roof before Orestes and Electra and the chorus. It may have been so; but there is nothing in the text of Euripides to indicate it; they may have been sufficiently characterized by their egg-shaped hats, as they sometimes are upon the Greek vases and reliefs, without the presence of their steeds. In the Bellerophon of Euripides, however, there can be do doubt that the hero soars upward mounted upon the wingèd Pegasus.

[3] So Athena appears upon her chariot above the Delphic temple to undo the knot of Euripides's Ion (1549; 1550; 1570):

ἔα· τίς οἴκων θυοδόκων ὑπερτελὴς
ἀντήλιον πρόσωπον ἐκφαίνει θεῶν;
...............................
ἐφ' οἷσιν ἔζευξ' ἅρματ'........

And so the chorus of Oceanids in Ae. P. V. seem to ride into the mountain heights of Caucasus and dismount for their work in the orchestra, while Oceanus himself is conveyed to the scene upon some sort of wingèd hippocampus (279–287).

[4] At the end of Eur. I. T., Athena appears, apparently without her car; there is no mention of chariot or horses, and Athena proposes to accompany Orestes and Iphigenia on their boat, which she could much more conveniently do when unencumbered by horses and chariot.

[5] The grip, here called ἅρπαξ, is called ἀγκυρίς "hook" or κράδη "the quivering spray at the end of a branch" by Zenobius, Mill. III 156 (Plut. Prov. 116), and Hesych. (s. v. κράδη); cf. Schol. Ar. Pax 727; Pollux IV 128. The whole crane is devised for "gripping" and hoisting. (Pollux IV 130): ἡ δὲ γέρανος μηχάνημά ἐστι ἐκ μετεώρου καταφερόμενον ἐφ' ἁρπαγῇ σώματος, ᾧκέχρηται Ἠὼς ἁρπάζουσα τὸ σῶμα τοῦ Μέμνονος.

[6] See Eur. I. T. 1446; Hel. 1662; Ar. Pax 164–165. Cf. Pollux IV 128: ἡ μηχανή...... κεῖται κατὰ τὴν ἀριστερὰν πάροδον, ὑπὲρ τὴν σκηνὴν τὸ ὕψος. Cf. Schol. Luc. Philops. VII, p. 537 (Lehmann), quoted by Reisch *l. c.*, p. 233.

[7] Ar. Pax 174–176 (quoted on p. 313).

hanging in the air—with the *double entendre*, of course, that the profiteers deserve nothing less than hanging (Alex. Λέϐης, Frag. 126, 14–19 K.):

| | |
|---|---|
| νυνί τε χαινὸν εἰσφέρει νόμον τινὰ χρυσοῦν, τὸ μὴ πωλεῖν καθημένους ἔτι τοὺς ἰχθυοπώλας, διὰ τέλους δ' ἑστηχότας· | and now he is introducing a new law —solid gold!—that fishmongers shall no longer sit down to do their selling but henceforth stand up. |
| εἶτ' εἰς νέωτά φησι γράψειν κρεμαμένους, | Next year, he says, he will introduce a bill requiring them to do business hanging; |
| καὶ θᾶττον ἀποπέμψουσι τοὺς ὠνουμένους, | and then they will let their customers off with more despatch |
| ἀπὸ μηχανῆς πωλοῦντες ὥσπερ οἱ θεοί | when they do their selling from a machine, like the gods |

Obvious traces of the crane are before us in the theatre at Eretria and at the Amphiaraeum.

The word "theatre" itself occurs but a few times in all extant Greek drama; and generally it is used not of the building but of the audience assembled to witness the plays (Ar. Eq. 1318):[1]

| | |
|---|---|
| ἐπὶ χαιναῖσιν δ'εὐτυχίαισιν παιωνίζειν τὸ θέατρον | and for the theatre to shout praises for their new good fortune |

(Ar. Eq. 233):

| | |
|---|---|
| τὸ γὰρ θέατρον δεξιόν | for the theatre-crowd is clever |

The coryphaeus in the parabasis regularly "comes before" the "theatre" (Ar. Pax 735):[2]

| | |
|---|---|
| πρὸς τὸ θέατρον παραϐάς | stepping out before the theatre-crowd |

(Metagenes Φιλοθ., Frag. 14 K.):

| | |
|---|---|
| κατ' ἐπεισόδιον μεταβάλλω τὸν λόγον, ὡς ἂν χαιναῖσι παροψίσι καὶ πολλαῖς εὐωχήσω τὸ θέατρον | by way of interlude I'll change the story, so as to feast the theatre with a great number of new side-dishes |

This is the first and most literal meaning of the word; from that it came to be transferred to the place where the "sight-seers" sat, whether to "see" a Dionysiac festival or any other sort of spectacle. From the importance and magnificence of the space occupied by the audience in the great stone playhouses of Greece, the word "theatre" soon came to be used of the whole building.

The dramatic poets, as has been noted, rarely speak of the theatre-building. Such theatres as those of Pergamon and Syracuse and Epidaurus excite our wonder and admiration for their fine architecture, with their beautiful proportions and lines and splendid acoustic properties, and their enormous seating capacity. The former qualities our dramatic poets seem to take as a matter of course; but one comic poet was sufficiently impressed by the size of some of the classical theatres to give expression to the wonder of it (Inc. Inc. Frag. 349 K.):[3]

| | |
|---|---|
| εἰς τὰς πανηγύρεις ἀπιὼν τοσοῦτον πλῆθος ἀνθρώπων ὁρᾷ (χαὶ) θέατρα μυρίανδρα συμπληρούμενα καὶ τοὺς ἀγωνιστάς | off to the festivals you go and such a mob of people you see, (and) theatres accommodating tens of thousands filled, and the contestants |

Once a woman's complaint about the poor seats assigned to women in the theatre is voiced (Alex. Γυν., Frag. 41 K.):

| | |
|---|---|
| ἐνταῦθα περὶ τὴν ἐσχάτην δεῖ χερχίδα ὑμᾶς καθεζούσας θεωρεῖν ὡς ξένας | there you have to take seats in the outermost wedge, like foreigners, to see the show |

It is interesting to note that Alexis uses the technical word χερχίς "wedge" for the divisions of the theatre made by the flights of steps running up and down through the audience room like radii from the orchestra.

---

[1] θεάτης and θεάτρια "spectator at the theatre" are common (Ar. Nub. 575; Σχ. Κατ., Frag. 472 K.: συνθεάτρια; Inc. Inc. Frag. 92 K.).
[2] Cf. Ar. Ach. 629; Eq. 508.
[3] Cf. Inc. Inc. Frag. 1198 K.: χρεμψιθέατρον.

When we think of the part that the great theatre of Dionysus in Athens played in the life of the people and especially in the careers of the Attic comic poets, it is surprising that we find that wonderful building mentioned but once, and then only casually, as a part of the topography about the Asclepieum (Inc. Inc. Frag. 104, 15 K.):

τὴν ἀκρόπολιν, τὸ θέατρον | the acropolis, the theatre

Beginning with line 12 and continuing to the end (line 18) the fragment is hopelessly mutilated and corrupt; but it is clear that some one has been miraculously and wonderfully healed at the Asclepieum[1] and locates the sanitarium in some way with reference to the Acropolis and the Theatre.

Plautus turns θέατρον in this sense into Latin, and very naturally, with cavea. Cavea is strictly the "audience room of the theatre," as is θέατρον. But in the Truculentus (931) cavea is "the theatre":

venitne in mentem tibi quod verbum in cavea dixit histrio

[1] See pp. 164 ff.